CAMBRIDGE LATIN AMERICAN STUDIES

EDITORS
DAVID JOSLIN TIMOTHY KING
CLIFFORD T. SMITH JOHN STREET

14

A GUIDE TO THE
HISTORICAL GEOGRAPHY
OF NEW SPAIN

THE SERIES

A GUIDE TO THE
HISTORICAL GEOGRAPHY
OF NEW SPAIN

by

PETER GERHARD

CAMBRIDGE · AT THE UNIVERSITY PRESS
1972

Published by the Syndics of the Cambridge University Press
Bentley House, 200 Euston Road, London NW1 2DB
American Branch: 32 East 57th Street, New York, N.Y.10022

Library of Congress Catalogue Card Number: 72–163058

ISBN: 0 521 08073 8

Printed in Great Britain
at the University Printing House, Cambridge
(Brooke Crutchley, University Printer)

Contents

(v)

Contents

Maps

These maps and the regional maps in the main texts were drawn by Reginald Piggott

Text figure and tables

(vii)

Preface

This guide, which it is hoped will be of use to those interested in various aspects of Mexico's past, is essentially an outline intended to simplify the study of Mexican historical geography during the period when the Old and New World races and cultures came together. It provides a regional listing of contemporary source material descriptive of central and southern Mexico throughout the three centuries of Spanish rule, and a synthesis of certain data gleaned from these documents.

The present work is confined geographically to the *gobierno* of Nueva España, the area which from 1535 to 1787 was ruled by the viceroy in the capacity of *gobernador*. This includes the country south to the isthmus of Tehuantepec, the Gulf coast north to the Pánuco river, and the Pacific side as far as Puerto de la Navidad, with extensions northward to San Luis Potosí and almost to Guadalajara. In fields other than administrative the viceroyalty exceeded these limits, but we are concerned here with New Spain in its narrowest sense. It is hoped to continue this approach in a later publication dealing with Yucatán and Nueva Galicia and other gobiernos, until all of what is now Mexico will have been treated in the same fashion.

Attention will be focused on the *alcaldías mayores*, the civil jurisdictions into which New Spain was divided before the introduction of the intendancy system in 1786–7. Under each of these 129 minor administrative units there will be a brief mention of physical features and climate, an attempted reconstruction of the native political geography at the moment of first Spanish contact, and a discussion of *encomiendas*, colonial political history, ecclesiastical division, population and settlements, and sources. Certain general remarks on each of the topics covered will follow this preface.

The scholar who has concentrated on a particular region of those considered here will, no doubt, have gone far beyond these notes. Some areas that have been exhaustively studied elsewhere receive only brief attention in these chapters. My purpose is to cast a pale, uniform light on the whole changing map of Mexico, from Conquest to Independence, and to show how it can be better illumined.

I am indebted and grateful to those who have shared their wisdom and encouraged the present work. Special thanks are due to Woodrow Borah, Donald Brand, Luis Castañeda Guzmán, Howard Cline, Adèle Kibre, John Lynch, Francisco Miranda, the late José Miranda, J. Benedict Warren, and Robert West. The directors and staffs of the Archivo Arquiepiscopal (Mexico), the Archivo General de Indias, the Archivo General de la Nación (Mexico), the Archivo General de Simancas, the Archivo Histórico del Departamento Agrario (Mexico), the Archivo Histórico de Hacienda (Mexico), the Archivo Histórico Nacional (Madrid), the Bancroft Library at the University of California (Berkeley), the Hispanic Society of New York, the Library of Congress, the Museo Nacional de Antropología e Historia (Mexico), the National Libraries of France, Mexico, and Spain, the Ayer Collection of Newberry Library (Chicago), the New York Public Library, the Real Academia de Historia (Madrid), the Real Biblioteca de San Lorenzo del Escorial, the library of the Sociedad Mexicana de Geografía y Estadística, and the Latin American Collection of the University of Texas Library were most helpful. Funds for research were provided by grants from the Hispanic Foundation and the John Simon Guggenheim Memorial Foundation.

P.G.

Tepoztlán,
May, 1971

INTRODUCTION

New Spain in 1519

The physical features and climates of the region we are concerned with have changed little between 1519 and the present time. Central and southern Mexico when the Spaniards came was a land crowded with farmers whose ancestors had been exploiting their environment in much the same lands were acquired by vast, Spanish-owned haciendas. Areas long cultivated became pastures for immense herds of cattle. Sheep and goats further denuded the barren hillsides, while old maize fields and previously untilled lands were planted to wheat and sugar cane. Terraces were

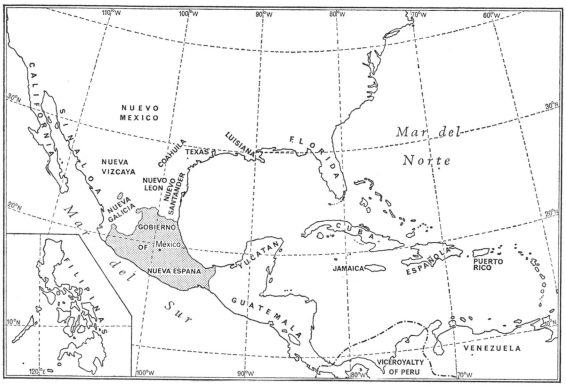

MAP I. Greater New Spain

way for millennia. The population, at least in some regions, had increased to a point where ecological strain was evident (the rural density was generally far greater than it is today). Soils were exhausted from overuse, forests had been destroyed, severe erosion had created badlands (cf. Cook, 1949b; Cook and Borah, 1968). After the Conquest, the population pressure was relieved but the process of exploitation continued, with differences. As native communities declined and even disappeared, many of the old communal less used for agriculture, and some alluvial soils were worked for the first time, with wooden plows. Forests near cities and mining camps disappeared entirely, canyons cut deeper into the plateaus. Many of the lake-filled volcanic basins dried up, some artificially drained, others through natural desiccation. Volcanoes became dormant while others were born. Rivers changed course and extended their deltas. A full record of these and other alterations in the natural landscape would require much field study, and they will

MAP 2. Central Mexico in 1519

only be summarily treated in the paragraphs below.

In most of this region the Spaniards found long-established native political structures, military-theocratic in nature, supported economically by agriculture and, in some cases, by the exaction of tribute in slaves, labor, and kind. The smallest political unit was the clan or group of families living in one place (Náhuatl, *calpulli*; plural, *calpultin*). The male heads of these families met to consider local disputes and problems and to choose a representative in the tribal council, which was thus composed of prominent members or elders from a number of calpultin. The council in turn, according to ancient custom, chose a ruler (Náhuatl, *tlatoani*; plural, *tlatoque*). In a more sophisticated state, the tribal elders had become a hereditary nobility who selected the tlatoani from eligible members of a ruling family; the latter could be forced from power by the council and replaced by another family in unusual circumstances. The ruler, once elected, might be dominated by the council or he might govern more or less autocratically and even name his successor. Normally he functioned as a supreme religious, military, and political leader, although in some cases these attributes were shared by two or more persons.

There were varying degrees of independence among these native states, and considerable difference in size and importance. Often a state consisted of a group of calpultin within a very small area, or even part of a single, complex settlement, with its own ruler, nobility, commoners, and slaves. Not infrequently, adjoining states would have related dynasties, either through marriage or because a ruler had divided his realm among his heirs. While boundaries between states were carefully drawn in most cases, occasionally there would be an unoccupied zone separating neighboring communities (Gibson, 1964, pp. 23-4; Motolinia, p. 207). A few states through warfare and intimidation had become more powerful than their neighbors and wielded

4

a military and economic (and sometimes political) hegemony over them, a situation to which the term 'empire' might be applied. Thus the largest empire, the famed Triple Alliance of the Mexica, Tepaneca, and Acolhuaque, controlled much of the area through garrisons and tribute collection and had a supreme Mexica military-religious leader (*hueytlatoani*). Within this complex were countless quite autonomous states with their own tlatoque, together with others ruled by military governors (*cuauhtlatoque, tlacatecameh*) and tribute collectors (*calpixque*) imposed by a tlatoani of a dominant state or by the hueytlatoani himself.

Rivals of the Triple Alliance, Michoacán and Tototépec (on the Pacific coast), and perhaps Metztitlan, were smaller empires in the same sense. Other areas, among them Coatzacualco, the Huaxteca, Mixteca, Zapoteca, Tlapaneca, and Tlaxcallan, seem to have been composed of numerous small states loosely united through dynastic ties or in military federations but generally without a dominant leader. Elsewhere, the political map of Mexico in 1519 was divided into fragments, each little kingdom often surrounded by hostile neighbors.

In some areas there were people on a relatively primitive cultural level with simpler social and political institutions. Such seem to have been the Chontal and the Huave of Oaxaca, and certain tribes in Guerrero who were looked down upon, dominated, and exploited by their neighbors. The Otomí in parts of the central plateau often occupied an inferior status within a Náhuatl community. Some of these groups were vestiges of an earlier population while others seem to have been more recent immigrants, retaining their languages and customs as sub-strata of society. The wild Chichimecs in the arid plains and mountains of the north, hunters and gatherers, were logically considered barbarians by the Mexica, the Tarascans, the Huaxtecans, and other sedentary peoples who alternately defended their frontiers from these marauders, enslaved them, and occasionally civilized them. It is in the successive waves of Chichimec migration and the contact between these nomads and their farmer neighbors to the south that one may trace the

pattern of Mesoamerican cultural history from *c.* 5000 B.C. (cf. Kirchhoff, 1948; MacNeish, 1964).

Information about the political situation in 1519 is derived from many sources (cf. Gerhard, 1970). For the Triple Alliance or Aztec empire, we have the well-known *Matrícula de Tributos*, analysed by Barlow (1949), other pre-Columbian conquest and tribute lists (Anonymous, 1897; ENE, XIV, pp. 118–22; Kelly and Palerm, pp. 264–317; Motolinia, pp. 353–6; Ramírez, 1885; Scholes and Adams, 1957), and various accounts of the Spanish Conquest. For the Tarascan area, there is the *Relación de...Michoacán*, together with fragments of the first inspection report made by Spaniards (Warren, 1963a). The *relaciones geográficas* of 1579–85 (*see below*), in which native informants were questioned regarding political institutions and alliances several generations earlier, should be used with caution. The prime sources are early *encomienda* lists and sixteenth-century reports in general, as the Spaniards usually recognized native dynasties and retained local political boundaries.

TABLE A. *Known language groups*

UTO AZTECAN			
Nahuan			
Cazcan	Coixca	Nahua	Sayultecan
Coca	Guachichil	Náhuatl	Zacatecan
OTOMANGUEAN			
Otopamian			
Jonaz	Matlatzincan	Ocuiltecan	Pame
Matlame	Mazahuan	Otomí	
Chinantecan			
Zapotecan			
Chatino		Zapotecan	
Mixtecan			
Amuzgan		Mixtecan	
Cuicatecan		Trique	
Popolocan			
Chocho		Mazatecan	
Ixcatecan		Popolocan	
MAYAN			
Mayan			
Huaxtecan			
Mixe–Zoquean			
Mixe	Popolucan	Zoquean	
Totonacan			
Tepehuan		Totonacan	
HOKALTECAN			
Chontal of Oaxaca		Tamaulipecan	Tlapanecan
HUAVE			
TARASCAN			

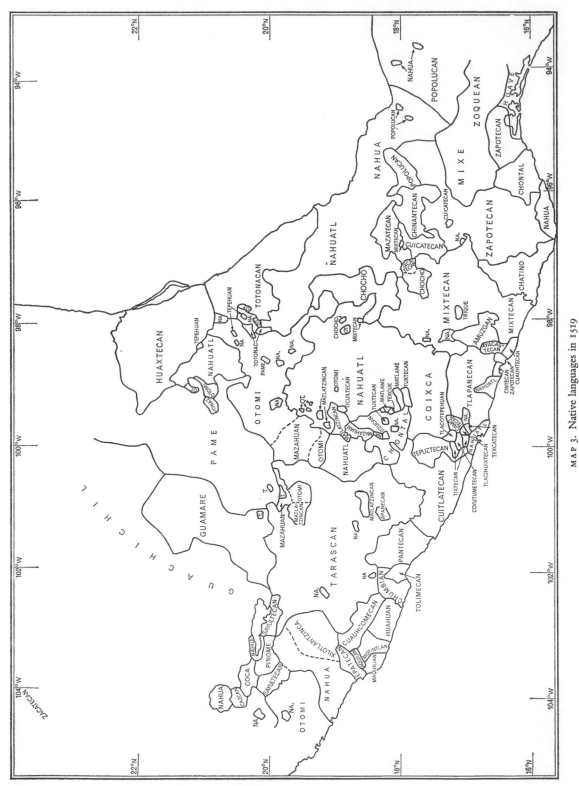

MAP 3. Native languages in 1519

In the individual articles below, native states in each area at the moment of Spanish contact are named wherever possible (for much of the coastal regions the complete record may be forever lost). There is a brief statement of military affiliation and tribute relationship, when known, and an indication of the language or languages spoken (again a matter of conjecture in some areas – we have only scattered linguistic data before 1569).

The Conquest

The pace of Spanish exploration and conquest throughout most of this area was extraordinarily rapid. Juan de Grijalva followed the Gulf coast as far as Cabo Rojo in June and July 1518, leaving Miguel de Zaragoza among the Indians of Cempoala. Between the time that Hernán Cortés and his men landed at Vera Cruz (April 1519) and the fall of Tenochtitlan (August 1521) Europeans explored the country between the Gulf and the valley of Mexico, and a large portion of the regions tributary to the Aztecs. During the conquistadors' first stay in Tenochtitlan (November 1519 to June 1520) numerous expeditions each consisting of two or three Spaniards with Indian guides went out in all directions. We know of such explorations from Mexico northeast to the Gulf, west to the borders of Michoacán, and south into Guerrero and Oaxaca, all in late 1519 or early 1520. Meanwhile, one of Francisco de Garay's ships called twice at the mouth of the Pánuco in those same years.

Most of Nueva España below the Chichimec frontier, including the Pacific coast, was visited by Cortés's armies in the three years following the capture of Tenochtitlan (1521–4). During this brief span nearly all of the components of the Aztec empire accepted the Spaniards as their new rulers, while military expeditions through Michoacán to Colima on the west, north to the Huaxteca, and southeast to Tehuantepec and beyond brought those areas under temporary Spanish control. The Indians were distributed in encomienda (*see below*) after a series of rapid surveys in 1523–5 to determine the population and resources of every corner of the country. Pockets of resistance remained (the Tlapanecs, the mountain Zapotec–Mixe area of Oaxaca,

etc.), and the wild northern parts were still unentered.

Cortés left Mexico in October 1524 on his long overland journey to Honduras, and during the year and a half of his absence Indian rebellions broke out all over the country. Some order was restored after Cortés's return in the spring of 1526, but further revolts marked the confused period of interregnum that followed, and the rule of the first audiencia (1529–30). In general, the period from 1524 to 1530 was one of conflict between the old native rulers, most of them still in power, and the Spanish encomenderos, both groups insisting on their right to the Indian's labor and tribute. A struggle of this nature in Michoacán ended with the execution of the ruler (*cazonci*) in 1530 (Warren, 1963*b*, pp. 78–9). By 1531, with the return of Cortés from Spain and the arrival of the second audiencia, peace was established nearly everywhere south of the Chichimec frontier.

Advancing northward in search of silver, the Spaniards came up against elusive nomadic warriors who found a means of livelihood in raiding the wagon trains and cattle *estancias* that supplied the mines of Zacatecas (1546), Guanajuato (1554), and beyond. Gradually in the sixteenth century the Spanish line of control reached tenuously into the Chichimec domain. Fifty years of raids and repression, with a bloody climax in the Chichimec war of the 1560s, ended in a stalemate and a peace (1590) achieved by providing these Indians with food and relatively kind treatment and by establishing colonies of Tlaxcalan and other farmers in their midst. This made it possible to extend Spanish rule to the mines of San Luis Potosí, the northernmost

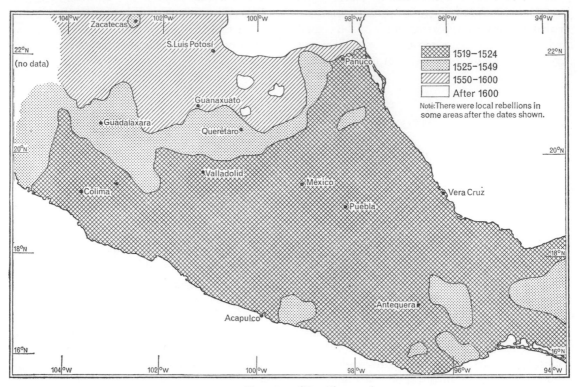

MAP 4. Extension of Spanish control

frontier in the gobierno of Nueva España (Gerhard, 1959; Jiménez Moreno, 1958; Powell, 1952).

Below, under each jurisdiction, the salient facts of first contact and the establishment of Spanish control are summarized.

Encomiendas

From late 1521 to 1524, circumventing an attempt on the part of the Spanish court to make all the natives crown charges, Cortés distributed almost the entire Indian population of central Mexico in *depósito* or encomienda to himself and his conquistador companions. Each native lord with his subjects was placed under the 'protection' of an *encomendero*, who was supposed to see to it that his charges became Christians and vassals of the Spanish king, in return for which he was entitled to their services and tribute. Sometimes a single large native state would be divided into two or more encomiendas, although the opposite

also occurred, a number of states being placed under one encomendero.

During Cortés's absence in Honduras (1524–6) a great many of these profitable grants were annulled by the acting governors and re-distributed among their friends (ENE, I, pp. 89, 92). There was another re-shuffling by governor Alonso de Estrada in 1527–8, and still another by the first *audiencia*, in 1529–30. The second audiencia in 1531 declared null and void all encomienda grants made by the first audiencia confirming many earlier assignments and reserving other places for the crown. Thus in the first

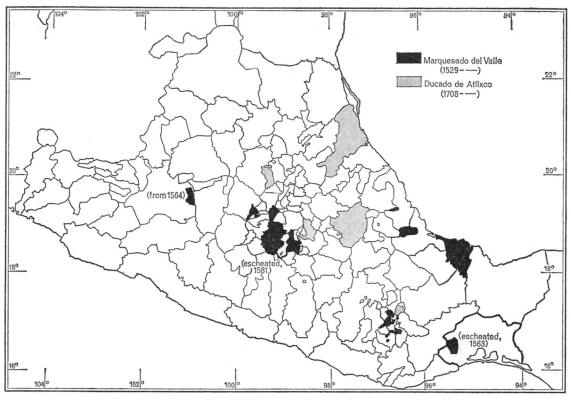

MAP 5. Seignories

decade of the colony most of the native communities changed masters at least two or three times. Information about these first encomenderos can sometimes be found in the records of lawsuits between rival claimants before the audiencia and the council of the Indies. The earliest relatively complete listing we have seen is that of the late 1540s (PNE, 1), by which time the encomenderos had been shorn of much of their wealth and power. The justly celebrated New Laws of that decade and subsequent legislation generally enforced after 1550 denied an encomendero the right to his Indians' labor, forbade him to reside in his encomienda, and limited succession to one lifetime (this last provision was soon repealed; *see below*). Tribute, at first whatever the encomendero could wring from his charges, became regulated by uniform assessment. An order of 1550, implemented within the following two decades, put each encomienda within the jurisdiction of a royal magistrate (*see below*). Thus from the 1550s the holder of an encomienda was entitled only to a yearly head tax, generally a standard amount fixed by a crown inspector, to be collected from a diminishing number of Indians in a specified locality. If the king received this tribute, the Indians were in the *Real Corona* and were directly administered by a crown officer known as a *corregidor*. If the recipient was a private individual, the place appeared in the tribute lists as an encomienda, although it was still ruled by a corregidor as the king's magistrate and justice. Certain areas (e.g. Tlaxcala, most of the Chichimec country) were never given in private encomienda, the Indians being considered wards of the crown from the beginning.

In theory, an encomendero should be a Spaniard, but grants were made to other Europeans, Indians, mestizos, Negroes, and mulattoes. Clearly, only Catholics were eligible, but a good number of conquistadors were accused of practising Judaism (if the charge was 'proven' in most cases their encomiendas were re-assigned). Single women were not supposed to hold encomiendas, which accounts for the rapid re-marriage of many a widow in the sixteenth century. We have mentioned the rule of limited succession, first set at two 'lives', then (1555) three, and finally (1607) four (Gibson, 1966, pp. 58–62). There were frequent exceptions to the law and cases of special privilege. Sometimes, on the death of an encomendero without issue or for other reasons, tributes would revert to the crown, but quite as often this income would be re-assigned to a courtier or favorite or money-lender.

With the decline in native population (*see below*) and increasing demands by crown and church on encomenderos, most of these grants by the late sixteenth century were of greater prestige than monetary value. Mention should be made, however, of two instances where the encomienda was combined with political privileges.

Hernán Cortés, when he was made Marqués del Valle de Oaxaca in 1529, was granted in perpetuity twenty-two separate encomiendas with the right to their tributes, 'lands, vassals, income, pastures, and waters', together with the privilege of exercising civil and criminal jurisdiction (*mero y mixto imperio*), i.e. appointing magistrates. He also received from the Pope the perquisite of nominating priests in his domain, but this was soon revoked as a right belonging only to the crown (*see below*). Cortés's properties were much reduced in size by the second audiencia, and eventually his descendants were forbidden to issue *mercedes* (grants of land and other property) within the Marquesado. On three occasions when Cortés's heirs were in disfavor (1567–93, 1708–26, 1809–16) the estate was sequestered. With all of these restrictions, the Marquesado del Valle for almost three centuries had a special extraterritorial status within Nueva España, and the marquises enjoyed a large income and the right to sell magistracies (cf. García Martínez, 1969).

The Indian and mestizo descendants of Moctezuma also held certain encomiendas in perpetuity. Here as elsewhere the cash value of the tributes declined with the population, and to compensate for this the income from numerous encomiendas which had escheated in the late sixteenth and seventeenth centuries was assigned to the Moctezuma heirs. The first duke of Atlixco, who had married one of these heirs, from 1708 had the privilege of appointing magistrates in several jurisdictions, a right also exercised by his descendants.

Unless further citation is given, the information on encomiendas presented below is derived from the *Suma de visitas* (PNE, 1), the *Diccionario de Conquistadores y Pobladores* (Icaza, 1923), the various *relaciones geográficas* (*see below*), and several listings made between 1560 and 1604.[1] Tribute records of the seventeenth century give further details.[2]

Political history

The Spanish governmental apparatus was divided 'horizontally' into five branches, *Gobierno* (civil administration), *Justicia* (judiciary), *Militar* (military), *Hacienda* (exchequer), and *Eclesiástico* (church affairs).[3] Often authority in the first three of these branches (sometimes in the first four, rarely in all five) was invested in a single person. The inter-workings of this establishment are illustrated in Table B.

Spanish government in Mexico began to function with the auto-establishment of a municipal council (*cabildo, ayuntamiento*) at Vera Cruz in 1519. When Cortés started his march inland to Tenochtitlan, this council elected him 'Governor and Chief Justice' of the country, titles which were confirmed in a royal cédula of 15 October 1522. The effective administrative boundaries of Nueva España, a term which began to be used in 1520, followed the Conquest and by 1524 reached southward to El Salvador and Honduras,

TABLE B. *The Viceregal Government*

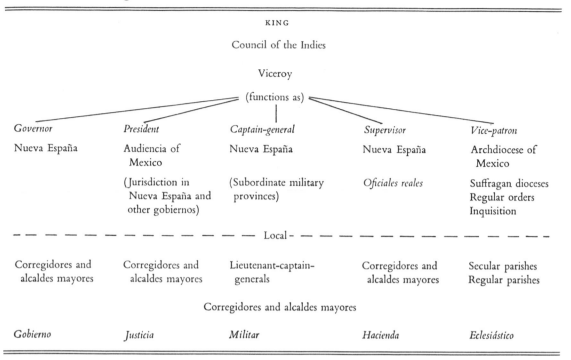

		KING		
		Council of the Indies		
		Viceroy		
		(functions as)		
Governor	*President*	*Captain-general*	*Supervisor*	*Vice-patron*
Nueva España	Audiencia of Mexico	Nueva España	Nueva España	Archdiocese of Mexico
	(Jurisdiction in Nueva España and other gobiernos)	(Subordinate military provinces)	*Oficiales reales*	Suffragan dioceses Regular orders Inquisition
— — — — — — — — — — — — — — Local — — — — — — — — — — — — — — —				
Corregidores and alcaldes mayores	Corregidores and alcaldes mayores	Lieutenant-captain-generals	Corregidores and alcaldes mayores	Secular parishes Regular parishes
		Corregidores and alcaldes mayores		
Gobierno	*Justicia*	*Militar*	*Hacienda*	*Eclesiástico*

northeast to the Huaxteca, and west to Colima. These limits were reduced in 1526 when Honduras received a separate governor, and again in 1527 with the removal of Pánuco and in 1528 with the loss of Yucatán. In 1530 Guatemala (with Chiapa) was detached, and in 1533 newly-conquered Nueva Galicia was lost in the same way (this last gobierno was temporarily re-united with that of Nueva España in 1545–9 and 1572–4). Later adjustments to the south were the separation of Tabasco in 1544 and of Soconusco in 1556. On the north, Pánuco was re-annexed to Nueva España in 1534, while the wild country beyond became *de facto* a separate gobierno, Nuevo León, in 1596. Subsequent external boundary changes were minor and will be discussed below.

Nueva España was ruled by royal governors and deputies until the beginning of 1529, when the first audiencia convened in Mexico city (see Table c). After 1535 matters of government were handled ultimately by the viceroy, while the audiencia continued as the supreme tribunal and as a consultative body, again functioning as the

governing power during interregna. The audiencia of Mexico's judicial authority extended to gobiernos other than that of Nueva España; its jurisdiction included Guatemala and Nueva Galicia until the 1540s when separate tribunals were established in those kingdoms. The audiencia of Nueva Galicia or Guadalaxara was in a sense subordinate to that of Mexico until 1574; four years later it was given jurisdiction in the westernmost part of the gobierno of Nueva España.

During the first decade after the Conquest, each Spanish municipal council had political and judicial powers not only in its immediate vicinity but for many leagues around. Thus in 1519–20 all Mexico was theoretically ruled from Vera Cruz, and a few years later the cabildo of Mexico-Tenochtitlan claimed boundaries extending eastward to meet those of Vera Cruz near Perote, north to Pánuco, and in fact everywhere in Nueva España where there was no other Spanish settlement (*Actas de cabildo*, IV, p. 144). As these settlements proliferated, jurisdictional disputes between

TABLE C. *Rulers of New Spain, 1519–35*

Gobierno	Militar	Justicia
Hernán Cortés, *de facto* governor from 1519, legalized 15 Oct. 1522 (cédula received in Mexico mid-1523) Leaves Mexico for Honduras 22 Oct. 1524	Hernán Cortés, *de facto* captain-general from 1519, legalized 15 Oct. 1522. Leaves Mexico 22 Oct. 1524	Hernán Cortés, *de facto* justicia mayor from 1519, legalized 15 Oct. 1522. Leaves Mexico 22 Oct. 1524
Rodrigo de Albornoz (contador) ⎫ Alonso de Estrada (tesorero) ⎬ Lt.-gs from 22.x.24 Lic. Alonso Zuazo		Lic. Alonso Zuazo. J m from 22.x.24
Pedro Almíndez Chirinos (veedor) ⎫ Lt.-gs from Gonzalo de Salazar (factor) ⎬ 29.xii.24 Lic. Alonso Zuazo		
Albornoz, Chirinos, Estrada, ⎫ Lt.-gs from 25.ii.25 Salazar, Zuazo		
Chirinos, Salazar, Zuazo Lt.-gs from 19.iv.25	Chirinos, Salazar – *de facto* cs-g from 22.viii.25	Chirinos, Salazar, Zuazo. J ms from 19.iv.25
Chirinos, Salazar Lt.-gs from 23.iv.25		Chirinos, Salazar. J ms from 23.iv.25
Albornoz, Estrada Lt.-gs from 23.i.26	Albornoz, Estrada – lieut.cs-g from 23.i.26	Br. Juan de Ortega. Alcalde mayor from 23.i.26
Hernán Cortés, governor, returns to Mexico city 15.vi.26; suspended 4.vii.26	Hernán Cortés, c–g, returns to Mexico city 15.vi.26	Lic. Luis Ponce de León. J m from 4.vii.26. D. 20.vii.26 Lic. Marcos de Aguilar. A m from 16.vii.26; j m from 1.viii.26. D. 23.ii.27
	(Cortés resigns as c–g, 5.ix.26)	
Alonso de Estrada ⎫ Governors from 23.ii.27 Gonzalo de Sandoval ⎰	Cortés again c–g, from 1.iii.27	Alonso de Estrada ⎫ J ms from 23.ii.27 Gonzalo de Sandoval ⎰
Alonso de Estrada Governor from 22.viii.27 (Audiencia governs, from 1.i.29)	(Cortés goes to Spain, 1528; reinstated as c–g, 1.iv.29) (Audiencia commands, from 1.i.29)	Alonso de Estrada. J m from 22.viii.27 (First) Audiencia. Arrives Vera Cruz xii.28; convenes in Mexico city 1.i.29 President: Nuño Beltrán de Guzmán (leaves Mexico city xii.29) Oidores: Francisco Maldonado (d. i.29), Alonso de Parada (d. i.29), Diego Delgadillo, Juan Ortiz de Matienzo
	Cortés recommissioned c–g, 6.vii.29, returns to Vera Cruz 15.vii.30, to Mexico city 1.31	(Second) Audiencia. Convenes in Mexico city 12.i.31 President: Sebastián Ramírez de Fuenleal (bishop of Sto Domingo) (arrives ix.31) Oidores: Francisco Ceynos, Alonso Maldonado, Vasco de Quiroga, Juan de Salmerón
Antonio de Mendoza, viceroy and govnr. Arrives Mexico city 14.xi.35	(Cortés dies, 1547)	Antonio de Mendoza, president of the audiencia from 14.xi.35

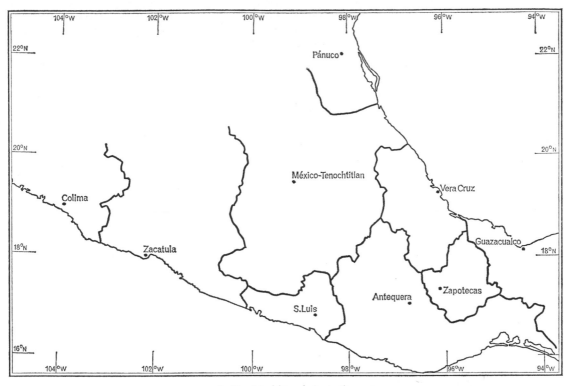

MAP 6. Municipal boundaries in the 1520s

ayuntamientos occurred, and in 1527 the king ordered definite boundaries drawn between them, but this does not seem to have been done. In order of establishment, the ayuntamientos were Villa Rica de la Vera Cruz (1519), Villa Segura de la Frontera (1520, at Tepeaca; moved in 1522 first to the Pacific coast near Tututepec and then to Antequera), Cuyoacán (1521; moved to Mexico–Tenochtitlan, 1523–4), Medellín (1521, near Córdoba; moved to the coast near Vera Cruz in 1523; abandoned, 1528), Espíritu Santo (1522, in Guazacualco), San Luis (*c.* 1522, at Acatlan on the Pacific coast; abandoned, 1531), San Esteban del Puerto (1523, at Pánuco), La Concepción (1523, at Zacatula), Colima (1523), and San Ildefonso de los Zapotecas (1527, at Villa Alta). There were subsequent foundations, but, as we shall see, the matter of municipal boundaries lost much of its significance after the 1520s.

Local officers of justice in these early years were the *alcaldes ordinarios* and constables or *alguaciles*, all dignitaries of the municipal councils. The governors of Nueva España during this period appointed deputies, both to execute specific commissions and to act as permanent lieutenants in outlying areas. These officials generally were given the title of *teniente de gobernador* or *alcalde mayor*. In the mid-1520s there were such deputies resident at Villa Rica, Espíritu Santo, Pánuco, Zacatula, and Colima. They were replaced by appointees of the first audiencia in 1529, at which time additional alcaldes mayores were sent to Antequera, Michoacán, Tasco, Teguantepec, and Villa Alta. In this transitional period, local government and the administration of justice and tribute collection among Indians was, as we have seen, in a chaotic state because of the power struggle between native rulers and Spanish encomenderos, often with the added intervention of the clergy (cf. Ricard, p. 168).

The first effective move to establish royal

13

authority on a local level in Indian communities was the introduction in Mexico of a fourteenth-century Iberian institution, the *corregimiento*. Somewhat more than a hundred corregidores were appointed to crown villages by the audiencia between 1531 and 1535. While in Spain the corregidor was a crown appointee who sat in council with the *regidores* (municipal officers), in Nueva España this official acted as administrator of crown charges, magistrate, tribute collector, and constable, thus concentrating in one person the attributes of the four civil branches of government. At first the encomenderos effectively opposed interference in their domains, but in 1550 a cédula ordered all encomiendas to be assigned to one corregimiento or another, and by 1570 this command had been complied with throughout the country. Thus Nueva España came to be divided into a great many small, contiguous civil jurisdictions each governed by a crown officer. Only in the Marquesado del Valle (and, much later, in the Ducado de Atlixco) did these officers receive their appointments from a private individual rather than from the crown.

Meanwhile, from the 1520s onwards the Spanish settlements continued to be ruled internally by their cabildos with the increasing intervention of alcaldes mayores, who had much the same function here as did the corregidores in Indian settlements. Frequently the alcalde mayor held the additional titles of corregidor in nearby crown Indian villages, and of *justicia mayor* in encomiendas. In some of the older alcaldías mayores (Colima, Guazacualco, Pánuco, Zacatula, Zapotecas) corregimientos were distributed as sinecures to Spanish residents of the capital towns, and in these cases political authority seems to have belonged in reality to the alcaldes mayores.

Each principal Indian community was allowed to retain its internal government (*gobierno, república de indios*) with certain modifications. The old tlatoque or hereditary rulers, now called *caciques*, usually remained, but in most cases their powers were transferred to Indian governors (gobernadores) who, despite a pretense of election, were in effect appointed and controlled by the Spanish authorities. While both cacique and

governor were subordinate to the corregidor, they could (and frequently did) appeal directly to Mexico city. The pre-Conquest nobility retained special privileges for a time, and the calpultin continued to function as local political bodies.

Upon the arrival in Mexico of Antonio de Mendoza in 1535 the privilege of appointing magistrates passed from the audiencia to the viceroy. Mendoza found local administration in a state of chaos. Most of the corregimientos had been entrusted to conquistadores and colonists who considered their posts equivalent to short-term encomiendas and exploited their charges mercilessly. Mendoza wanted to eliminate them all and replace them with carefully chosen *letrados* (men trained in the law) who would be alcaldes mayores in charge of larger and fewer territorial units. This plan was modified in the council of the Indies, and while the corregimientos did not disappear, in the period from 1550 to 1570 Nueva España was divided into some forty *provincias*, each headed by an alcalde mayor who was expected to supervise a number of 'suffragan' corregimientos, making an annual visit to hear appeals and correct abuses.

The greatest political fractionization of Nueva España was reached in the 1570s, when there were some 70 alcaldías mayores and over 200 corregimientos, most of the latter falling in the suffragan category. In this decade the system of intermediate supervisory control began to fall into disuse, and in some areas the corregidores again had considerable autonomy. Elsewhere, the suffragan corregimiento survived well into the seventeenth century. Towards 1600, with a much reduced Indian population gathered in fewer settlements, certain corregimientos were eliminated and annexed to neighboring jurisdictions.

By mid-seventeenth century there was no longer any real difference in function between a corregidor and an alcalde mayor, both terms being used interchangeably, although the latter became more common. In the 1670s and 1680s there was a general consolidation and adjustment of boundaries between alcaldías mayores. Tlaxcala (from 1587), and somewhat later Acapulco, Puebla, and Vera Cruz Nueva achieved the

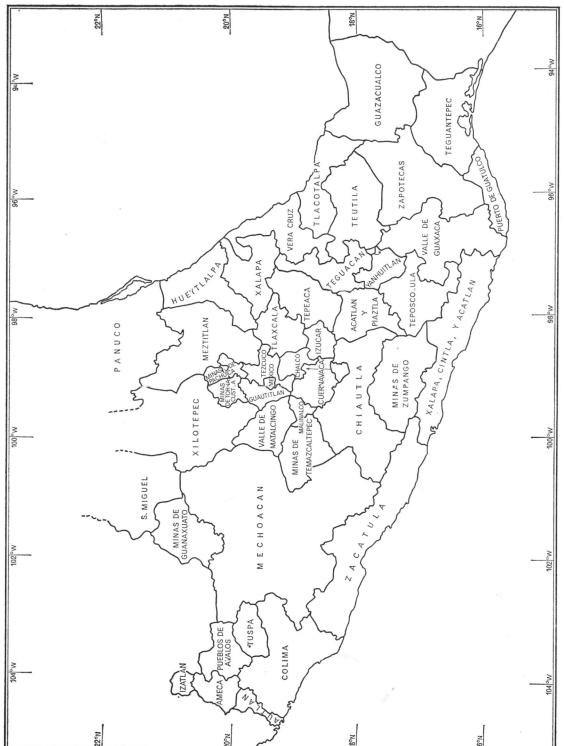

MAP 7. Provincias c. 1570

PANUCO

HUEYTLALPA

XALAPA

VERA CRUZ

MEZTITLAN

TLAXCALA

TEPEACA

TEGUACAN

YANHUITLAN

ACATLAN
Y
PIAZTLA

TEPOSCO-ULA

VALLE DE
GUAXACA

TEUTILA

TLACOTALPA

ZAPOTECAS

GUAZACUALCO

TEGUANTEPEC

PUERTO DE GUATULCO

TEZCUCO

MINAS DE
PACHUCA

MINAS
DE TORNA-
CUSTLA

MEXICO

GUAUTITLAN

CHALCO

IZUCAR

CUERNAVACA

MINAS DE
ZUMPANGO

CHIAUTLA

XALAPA, CINTLA, Y ACATLAN

VALLE DE
MATALCINGO

MINAS DE
TEMAZCALTEPEC

MALINALCO

XILOTEPEC

S. MIGUEL

MINAS DE
GUANAXUATO

MECHOACAN

ZACATULA

IZATLAN

AMECA

PUEBLOS DE
AVALOS

TUSPA

COLIMA

AUTLAN

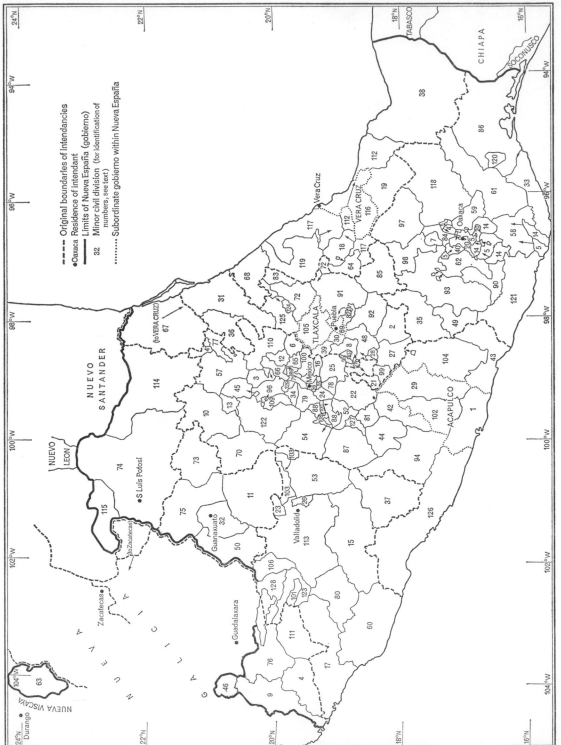

MAP 8. Political divisions in 1786

Legend:
- ---- Original boundaries of intendancies
- ●Oaxaca Residence of intendant
- ——— Limits of Nueva España (gobierno)
- 32 Minor civil division (for identification of numbers, see text)
- .... Subordinate gobierno within Nueva España

NUEVA VISCAYA

Durango●
63

Zacatecas●

(to Zacatecas)

N U E V A   G A L I C I A

NUEVO LEON

●S Luis Potosi

N U E V O   S A N T A N D E R

(to VERA CRUZ)

VERA CRUZ

●Vera Cruz

TABASCO

CHIAPA

SOCONUSCO

Guadalaxara●

Guanaxuato●
32

Valladolid●
113

Oaxaca

TLAXCALA
Puebla

●Mexico

ACAPULCO

16

distinction of being called gobiernos, but the new title of gobernador did not appreciably alter the functions of the magistrate nor diminish his subordination to viceroy and audiencia. Again in 1770 a study of political divisions was made, and a report was submitted to the viceroy recommending changes in inconvenient boundaries, but little seems to have been done at this time.[4]

It was not until 1786 that a supposedly thorough reorganization of the colonial government was ordered. At this time there were 116 civil jurisdictions in Nueva España (see map 8). These were divided between nine intendancies (*intendencias*). Antequera, Guanaxuato, México, Puebla, San Luis Potosí, Valladolid, and Vera Cruz were each headed by an intendant (*intendente*), while the westernmost jurisdictions of Nueva España were placed in the intendancy of Guadalaxara, and Nombre de Dios was assigned to that of Durango. The alcaldías mayores were re-designated *partidos* or *subdelegaciones* ruled by *subdelegados*, whose functions and behavior differed little from those of the alcaldes mayores.

We have mentioned that after 1535 the viceroy had the privilege of appointing local magistrates. Eventually the Spanish court realized the value of this concession and assumed the right to name certain justices, i.e. to sell the magistracies for a specific period. The important corregimiento of Mexico city, established in 1574, was the first such office to be pre-empted by the crown. During the first sequestration of the Marquesado del Valle, in 1583, the king sent appointees from Spain to Toluca, Cuernavaca, and Cuyoacán to fill posts which since 1570 had been controlled by the viceroy. When the third marquis recovered his seignorial rights in 1593, the crown retained the privilege of appointment in the adjoining jurisdictions of Metepec, Cuautla Amilpas, and Tacuba. In the first half of the seventeenth century other jurisdictions were removed from the viceroy's control, and a cedula of 1678 reserved to the king the appointment of all magistrates, although in practise the viceroy was allowed to sell some of the less lucrative posts.

Thus, through most of the three centuries of the colony, Mexico was split into many small political subdivisions, ruled by men with limited terms of office (usually from one to five years) whose concern was to recover and multiply the money they had paid for their posts.[5] The evolution of these minor jurisdictions from 1519 to 1821 will be discussed below, using as a point of reference the situation in 1786.

Ecclesiastical division

The fifth branch of the Spanish governmental apparatus was that concerned with church affairs. The king, in exercise of the *patronato real*, nominated (in effect, appointed) higher church dignitaries, while viceroys and governors as vice-patrons nominated the parish priests. The church had its own judiciary, and considerable political and economic influence. Ten bishops and archbishops served as viceroys of Nueva España. The Inquisition (*Tribunal del Santo Oficio*), with its own minor territorial divisions (*comisarías*) usually entrusted to parish priests, served as an additional link between church and state.

In Mexico there were two principal ecclesiastical establishments, the secular and the regular. The first was headed by an archbishop and bishops, while the second was composed of the mendicant and other orders, all with overlapping provinces.

The Mexican bishoprics with their final colonial boundaries appear on map 9. The 'Carolense' diocese, intended to provide an ecclesiastical legality to the new discoveries, was set up on the island of Cozumel in 1519, but the first bishop to arrive in Nueva España (1527) was assigned to Tlaxcala. Mexico–Tenochtitlan had a resident bishop from 1528, Antequera (Oaxaca) from 1535, and Michoacán from 1538. In 1546–8 Mexico became an archdiocese to which the above-mentioned bishoprics, together with Nueva

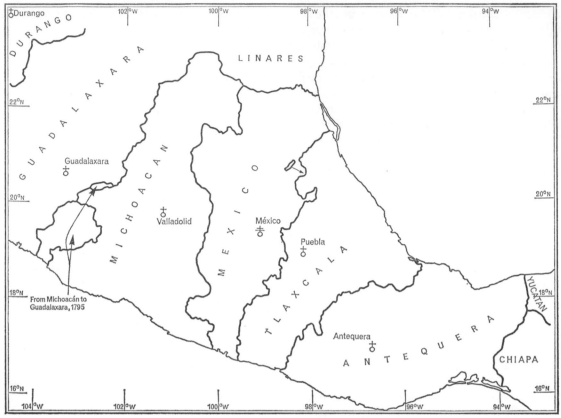

MAP 9. Diocesan boundaries

Galicia and others in Central America, were made suffragan. In early years there was bickering between prelates over vaguely drawn diocesan boundaries, but by the late sixteenth century these were relatively well defined. The archdiocese of Mexico and the bishoprics of Antequera and Tlaxcala were entirely within the gobierno of Nueva España, as was Michoacán except for the parish of La Barca which belonged politically to Nueva Galicia. After 1578 the westernmost jurisdictions of Nueva España were put in the diocese of Nueva Galicia or Guadalaxara; in 1795 parishes in Colima, Tuspa, and La Barca were transferred from Michoacán to Guadalaxara.

Mexico city and Antequera remained episcopal seats, but in other dioceses the cathedrals moved about. In 1543 the see of Tlaxcala was officially transferred to Puebla de los Angeles. The bishop of Michoacán resided briefly at Tzintzuntzan, then

(1538–80) at Pátzcuaro, and from 1580 at Valladolid (Morelia). The official residence of the bishop of Nueva Galicia was at first Compostela, but he preferred Guadalaxara which legally became the cathedral city in 1560. Bravo Ugarte (1965) provides a useful list of Mexican bishops, arranged chronologically for each diocese.

Of the regular orders, that of San Francisco (*orden seráfica, observantes, franciscanos*) was the first to arrive in Mexico, in 1523. Four of its provinces (see map 10) were all or partly within the gobierno of Nueva España: Santo Evangelio de México (1535), San Pedro y San Pablo de Michoacán (1565), Santiago de Jalisco (1606), and San Francisco de Zacatecas (1606).

The second mendicant order, Santo Domingo (*orden de predicadores, dominicos*), reached Mexico in 1526 and founded three provinces in Nueva España (map 11). They were Santiago de México

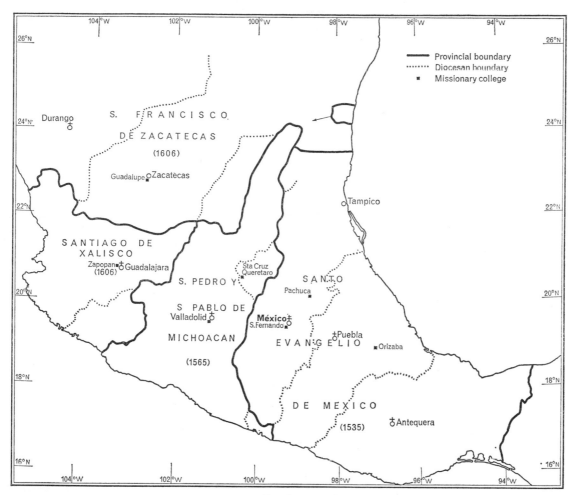

MAP 10. Franciscan provinces

(1532), San Hipólito Mártir de Oaxaca (1592), and Santos Angeles de Puebla (1656).

The Augustinians (*orden de San Agustín, agustinos*) arrived in 1533 and divided their doctrines between two provinces, Nombre de Jesús de México (1535) and San Nicolás de Tolentino de Michoacán (1602) (map 12).

Numerous other regular orders were admitted to Mexico during the colonial period, each with its hierarchy and provincial organization, but none engaged extensively in parochial work within the gobierno of Nueva España. The Jesuits (*Compañía de Jesús*) arrived in 1572, founded many educational institutions, and undertook the conversion of Indians on the northwest frontier. Among the minor orders and their provinces were the Carmelites (*carmelitas*, province of San Alberto, 1585), the Mercedarians (*orden de Nuestra Señora de la Merced*, province of La Visitación de Nuestra Señora, 1594), the Dieguinos (*franciscanos descalzos de la reforma de San Pedro de Alcántara*, province of San Diego de Alcalá, 1599), and the order of San Juan de Dios (1604).

The lesser ecclesiastical divisions of Nueva España were the parishes (*parroquias, doctrinas*). If the parish was ministered by a secular priest (*cura beneficiado, clérigo*) subordinate to a bishop, it was called a *curato colado, beneficio,* or *partido de clérigos*. When the priest in charge belonged to a

2-2

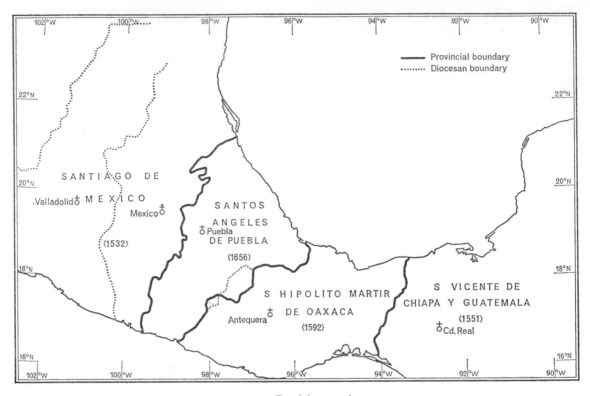

MAP II. Dominican provinces

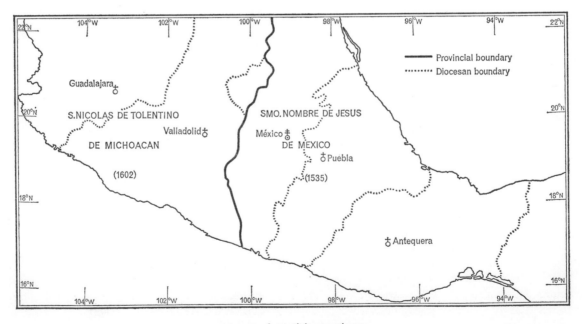

MAP I2. Augustinian provinces

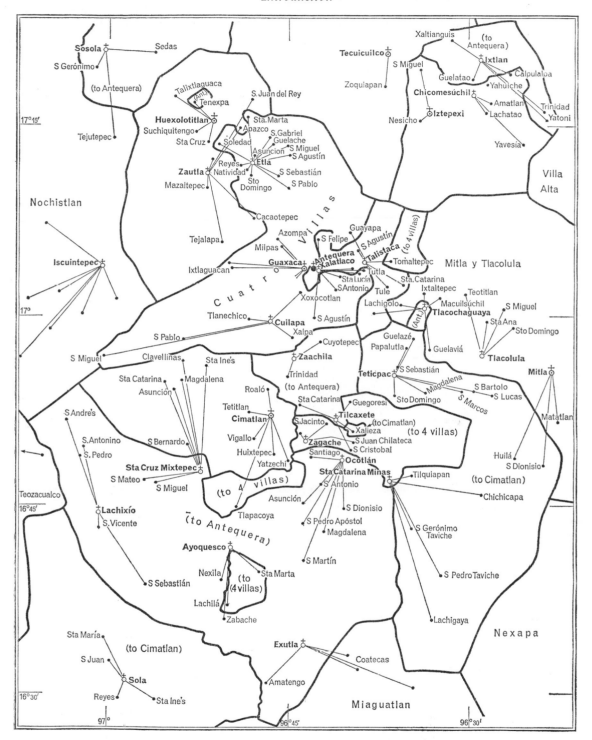

MAP 13. Overlapping of civil and ecclesiastical jurisdictions

regular order, the parish was referred to as a *doctrina de religiosos*; in the latter case, most often the parish church was adjacent to a monastery (*convento, monasterio*), which might be a *vicaría, guardianía, priorato*, or *presidencia*. Parishes were usually smaller in area than corregimientos, but a priest with his headquarters in one corregimiento might visit villages in an adjoining one. Not infrequently, a civil jurisdiction would be split between two dioceses or two regular provinces. Map 13 of central Oaxaca shows how little agreement there was between civil and ecclesiastical jurisdictions.

At the beginning of the colonial period quite a number of Indian parishes were founded by secular priests subsidized by conscientious encomenderos, but within a few decades most of them had been supplanted by regular clergy. Larger towns and cities often were divided into several parishes, Indians attending a regular church, Spaniards and others ministered by secular priests. While the mendicant orders held tenaciously to their privileges and refused to allow bishops to inspect their monasteries, toward the end of the sixteenth century the crown began to exert pressure to transfer parishes from regular to secular control. The first great blow to the regulars came in 1640, when Bishop Palafox seized many of their parishes in his diocese of Puebla and appointed secular priests in their place. The controversy aroused by this move was violent, and the mendicant orders held fast in the other bishoprics until a royal command of 1749 provided that every regular parish in Nueva España should be secularized on the death of the incumbent friar. Thus the transfer took place gradually all over the country during the last half of the eighteenth century. The Franciscans and Dominicans found a more challenging field of activity in the northern missions, especially after the expulsion of the Jesuits in 1767. At the time of Independence, each of the three principal orders by special dispensation kept a handful of parishes in Nueva España, together with a number of monasteries (without parochial functions) and colleges where missionaries were trained for service in the north. Parochial jurisdictions will be discussed below, in each regional study.

Population and settlements

The study of demographic change in colonial Mexico is a complicated matter and one which, for various reasons, has produced bitter controversy among scholars. There are wide divergences of opinion as to the reliability of estimates, the interpretation of data, the extent of *mestizaje*, and other factors. The mixing of Indian, white, and Negro blood began at the time of the Conquest, and while the contemporary material we have to work with was drawn up by men intensely conscious of race, their efforts to subdivide the population along racial lines became increasingly meaningless after the first few generations. Data are given in a bewildering variety of units, and some of the terms used changed significance with time. Large segments of the population, e.g., slaves and others exempt from tribute, are often omitted in the data available. A further source of confusion is the variety of jurisdictions with dissimilar boundaries from which the population is reported (*see above*).

The most serious disagreement concerns the size of the native population at the moment of contact with the Spaniards. For the area we are dealing with here, estimates range from about 3,000,000 to 22,000,000 persons.[6] Clearly there was a dense population in those parts of the central plateau where intensive agriculture with irrigation occurred (cf. Palerm, 1955), and a sparse population in the arid northlands where the land was not cultivated. There is recent evidence that slash-and-burn (swidden) agriculture, used in the tropical coastlands, supported a relatively dense population; irrigation was also used in the lowlands, with resulting urban concentrations.

TABLE D. *Epidemics in Nueva España*

1520–1. *Hueyzáhuatl* (probably smallpox), began on the coast near Vera Cruz in May or June 1520, reaching Tenochtitlan in September and spreading over much of the country. Great mortality.

1530s. Many die from disease, especially in the hot country on both coasts, to a lesser extent inland. Plagues reported in 1531, 1532, 1538.

1545–8. Severe *cocoliztli* spread everywhere, with greater mortality in coastal areas.

1550. Mumps in Tacuba and elsewhere, many deaths.

1559. Plague similar to that of 1545–8 but less serious.

1563–4. Various diseases of epidemic proportions in valley of Mexico; great mortality at Chalco.

1566. *Cocoliztli*, especially on Gulf coast.

1567–68. Plague at Teguantepec.

1576–81. Great *cocoliztli* or *matlazáhuatl* (probably typhus) began in April 1576, spread east–west from Yucatán to Chichimecas. By late 1576 300,000 to 400,000 were dead and the disease was spreading, aided by famine. Affected both lowlands and mountain areas, with greater mortality in latter. By October 1577, the disease was less virulent; in December 1578, it was reported to have stopped altogether. Same disease returned in August 1579, afflicting both Indians and Negroes, but with fewer deaths. Still going on in April 1581; many Negroes dead.

1587–8. *Cocoliztli* at Mexico, Toluca, Tlaxcala.

1590. *Tlatlacistli* (influenza) – many deaths.

1591–2. Plague beginning in the Mixteca, where it was quite virulent, and spreading to Pacific coast.

1592-3. Various diseases in valley of Mexico; many children died.

1595–7. Plague (several diseases?), with many deaths near Toluca; spread, with less mortality, to Oaxaca and Guatemala.

1601–2. *Cocoliztli* at Sochimilco.

1604–7. Epidemic in valley of Mexico, especially among Otomies, with many deaths.

1615–16. Various diseases in valley of Mexico accompanied by drought and famine.

1629–31. *Cocoliztli* with high mortality, especially in valley of Mexico.

1633–4. Plague in Mexico City – many deaths.

1639. Measles in Mexico City – many deaths.

1641–2. *Cocoliztli* with drought; more severe in 1642.

1659. Measles with high mortality in valley of Mexico.

1663. Widespread plague with drought (various diseases), afflicting both Indians and Spaniards.

1667–8. Several diseases in spring of each year, high mortality.

1692–7. Several diseases, beginning in valley of Mexico, with many deaths; spread to Lower California in September 1698.

1714. Widespread fever; over 14,000 deaths in New Spain.

1731. *Matlazáhuatl* reported at Churubusco.

1736–9. Severe *matlazáhuatl* (probably typhus) began in Tacuba late August 1736, reached Cuernavaca early February 1737, spread all over New Spain; notable mortality in Michoacán and Oaxaca, although there were pockets (Nochistlan–Teutila, Guayacocotla–Yagualica) which were not afflicted. It had disappeared in some places by the summer of 1737, but continued in others; reached Lower California, 1742; Sierra Gorda, 1743–4. 200,000 deaths.

1761–4. Typhus and smallpox in Mexico City and elsewhere; 25,000 deaths in Mexico City, 'many' at S Luis Potosí.

1768–9. Measles at Mexico City; many children died.

1772–3. *Matlazáhuatl* in the valley of Mexico with much mortality.

1779–80. Measles and smallpox; 18,000 deaths in Mexico City.

1788. Plague in Mixteca Alta.

1797–8. Smallpox at Mexico City, Puebla, Orizaba, Oaxaca etc. Over 10,000 deaths.

All agree that there was a catastrophic decline in the native population here between 1520 and 1620. Only the extent of the decline is in dispute, and whether it was continuous or interrupted by a period of recovery in the third quarter of the sixteenth century. The 'Berkeley school', with which the present writer is in basic agreement, holds that Nueva España had perhaps 22,000,000 people in 1519, after which the number of Indians dropped without notable respite to less than one million towards 1620.

According to eyewitness accounts of the Conquest, a good many Indians were killed in battle – thousands of deaths occurred in the massacre at Cholula, far more at Tenochtitlan. After the Conquest, many Indians were enslaved and thousands were transported to their death in the Antilles, while others died within Mexico from brutality and hard work. Various and curious reasons were suggested by contemporary Spaniards and Indians for the native decimation – mistreatment or too benign treatment, starvation or rich foods, despondency and drunkenness, unaccustomed liberty, the wearing of clothes, the use of beds, too frequent bathing, divine retribution, etc. – but it is quite certain that the chief cause was death from European diseases to which the Americans had no natural immunity.

During the siege of Tenochtitlan in 1521 the natives were stricken with smallpox, allegedly introduced by a Negro slave at Cempoala. The germ spread within the city and outward to areas still unvisited by the Spaniards, killing millions. In the first two decades after the

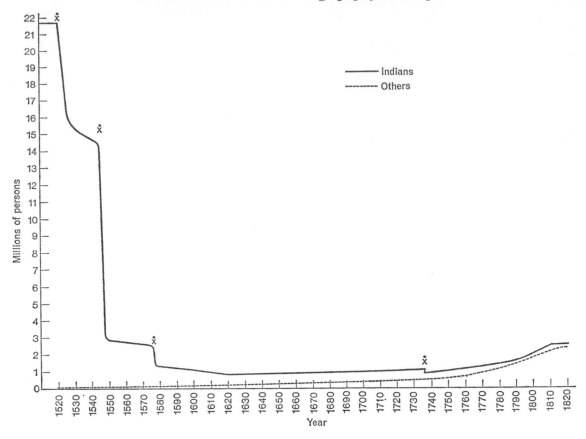

FIGURE I. The decline and recovery of the native population

Conquest vast numbers of Indians, probably in the millions, succumbed in the hot country behind Vera Cruz, and another great de-population occurred along the Pacific coast. We do not know what disease or diseases caused this. The Gulf coastal region had a history in pre-Columbian times of being so plague-ridden that migrants were periodically sent down from the highlands to replace those lost in epidemics (Herrera, 1601–15, 4a década, p. 236; Torquemada, 1723, I, p. 278). It may have been a recurrence of this scourge, or a recently introduced European germ which thrived in the tropics, that wiped out the coastal population in the 1520s and 1530s. For the remainder of the colonial period the hot country of Nueva España had very few Indians.

Subsequent epidemics killed the highland natives as well as those who survived on the coasts. The most serious and widespread of these plagues occurred in 1545–8, 1576–81, 1629–31, 1692–7, and 1736–9, but there were others with less mortality or affecting small areas only (Table D). By 1532 there were perhaps 16,000,000 Indians (Berkeley estimate) in the entire area. In 1570 the number was 2,600,000, from which it appears that the greatest killer of all was the *cocoliztli* (measles?) of 1545–8. After the plague of 1576–81, especially virulent in the highlands, there may have been 1,800,000 Indian survivors, and there was further decline in the last years of the sixteenth and first years of the seventeenth century. From 1620–50 in most areas there was a demographic recovery continuing (with local exceptions and notable setbacks during the plagues of 1692–7 and 1736–9) to the present time. Clearly the surviving Indians, fortified by

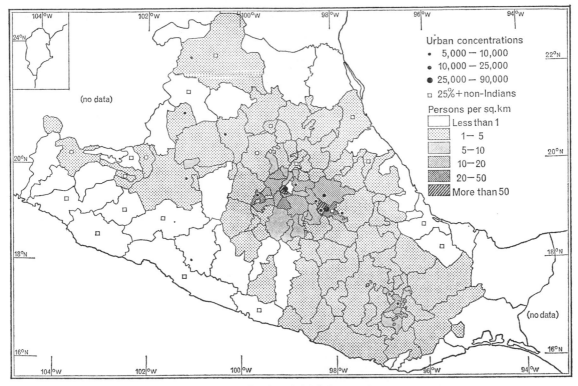

MAP 14. Density of population, *c.* 1620

miscegenation, had acquired considerable immunity to European diseases. At the time of Independence there were perhaps 2,000,000 people of predominantly Indian blood, constituting roughly half the total population.

The whites, almost entirely Spaniards, spread all over Mexico during the three centuries of the colony, although they preferred the highlands. Those of unmixed blood (*españoles, europeos*) formed a very small segment, probably never more than five per cent, of the total population. On the other hand, the number of people of mixed Indian and European blood (*castizos, mestizos*) grew to constitute approximately a third of the total, or about 1,350,000 persons, in 1821.

Negro slaves came with the conquistadors and were brought in increasing numbers, first from the Antilles and later directly from Africa. The flow assumed large proportions after the great decline in Indian manpower in the epidemic of 1545–8, and continued into the nineteenth century. These slaves worked in all parts of Mexico, notably in mines and on sugar plantations. Many took Indian or mestizo mates, and the descendants (*mulatos, pardos, lobos, zambos*, etc.) of those who remained on the central plateau became freedmen and were absorbed into the mixed population (*castas*). Others drifted to the almost deserted lowlands around Vera Cruz and Acapulco where they still form recognizably Negroid communities. The Negroes enjoyed as little immunity to certain Old World diseases as did the Indians, and a great many died in the same epidemics. Yet, at the end of the colonial period, there were probably almost a million individuals with Negro blood (mostly mixed with other races) scattered throughout Nueva España.

There was a small minority of Filipinos (*chinos*) who arrived after 1567 on the Manila galleons and settled at Acapulco and elsewhere on the Pacific coast. Other known minorities, including non-Mexican Indians from Florida and Peru and non-Spanish Europeans, were insignificant in number. Non-Indians in general were referred to as *gente de razón*, while Indians were called simply *indios* or *naturales*.

Map 14 is an effort to show the density of population in Nueva España at its nadir, towards 1620. Based on available tributary and other data, we find a total population at that time of somewhat more than a million persons, roughly eighty per cent Indian and twenty per cent non-Indian. Squares appear in those jurisdictions where non-Indians formed a quarter or more of the total; in only five jurisdictions (Acapulco, Mexico city, Puebla, Vera Cruz Nueva, and Zacatula) did they out-number Indians.

The most commonly used unit for population data was the family, but in the very earliest reports of the 1520s and 1530s the term *casa* was used. This expression in those years clearly meant more than one family, perhaps an entire calpulli or group of families living in the same vicinity. Bishop Ramírez de Fuenleal, writing in 1532, suggested that there might be ten or more families living under the same roof (Chauvet, 1948, p. 123). Later, the terms *indios*, *indios casados*, and *indios vecinos* were all pretty much equivalent and unless defined otherwise meant a married male Indian with his immediate family. This constituted one tributary unit, while Indian bachelors (males and females above fifteen years of age) and widowers and widows, since they paid half the usual amount of tribute, were considered *medios tributarios*. Cook and Borah (1968) have calculated that the ratio of total Indian population to tributaries was 2.8 in the late sixteenth century, 3.4 by mid-seventeenth century, and 3.6 in later years. From the 1790s the proportion changed radically. This and other problems of conversion are intelligently discussed in the paper just cited, to which the interested reader is referred. In the regional descriptions below we give population data as they appear in the documents consulted.

With non-Indians, the term *familia* was generally equivalent to *vecino* and meant a householder and those who live under his roof, i.e. his wife, unmarried children, other relatives, servants, and slaves. Thus a *familia de españoles* generally included elements of different races. The number of slaves was rarely stated, and when it was it

referred to individuals (*piezas*). Slaves and mestizos were exempt from tribute payment, but freed Negroes and mulattoes were tributaries from the 1570s.

While there were local variations, before the Conquest most people in central and southern Mexico lived in a great many small, often contiguous, settlements. Details, where known, of the settlement pattern at contact in each area will be given below.

In general it would seem that large urban concentrations such as Tenochtitlan were rare. The usual pattern was a principal settlement or community center with a market, temple, and the residences of the ruler, priests, and nobility, surrounded by subordinate settlements of commoners. Sometimes the ceremonial centers had no residents other than priests and were separate from the principal settlements. The sites of the latter were often fortress-like strongpoints – hilltops, tongues of land surrounded by ravines, escarpments, islands or peninsulas, etc. – occasionally with additional fortifications, to which the entire population of an area could retreat in wartime (Miranda, 1962b). In some areas there was a nuclear pattern, with density decreasing towards the periphery of a native state, but in general the smaller dependent settlements, often containing a handful of houses each, were rather evenly dispersed near the fields worked by their inhabitants (Sanders, 1968).

At first the Spaniards did little to change the native settlement pattern. A very few of the existing principal settlements (notably Tenochtitlan) were converted into Spanish towns and cities either because the sites suited the conquerors or in spite of their disadvantages. More commonly, Spanish townsites were established in fertile valleys and other places which had been left unoccupied or thinly settled as they were indefensible or inconvenient by Indian standards.

The Spanish missionaries began their activity in the existing principal native communities, which they called *cabeceras*, where they established their first monasteries and parish churches, frequently using the native temple (*teocalli*) as a foundation for a Christian church. Outlying subordinate settlements (cf. calpultin, *above*), if they were adjacent to or near a cabecera, were called by the Spaniards *barrios*; if they were some distance removed, they were more apt to be called *estancias* or *sujetos*. In these early years the Indians were allowed to remain where they had been living in a dispersed fashion, and there was even further proliferation of small estancias in inaccessible places where the natives could avoid tribute and services and continue their old religious practices (Ricard, 1933, p. 163). The friars soon realized the advantages of having their charges nearby, and the encomenderos and crown officers also saw the advisability of gathering the Indians into central communities where they could be controlled and exploited more easily. This common Spanish desire to move the dispersed Indians into consolidated and accessible townsites was given legal force after the epidemic of 1545–8. Royal commands of 1551 and 1558 ordered all the surviving natives to be congregated in *pueblos* of European design near the monasteries. Careful surveys were made to determine the best locations for the latter, and by 1560 most of the old cabeceras had been moved to what the Spaniards considered more satisfactory townsites, generally on lower, level land (Scholes and Adams, 1961, p. 47). At the same time, in the 1550s and 1560s many Indians in outlying estancias were convinced by persuasion or force to abandon their ancestral homesites and move either to a cabecera or to a re-located *pueblo sujeto*.

Hundreds, probably thousands, of estancias disappeared in these first congregations, but in some areas, particularly those ministered by secular priests, the scattered settlement pattern persisted. It was not until after the epidemic of 1576–81 that the crown, under pressure from the clergy and land-hungry Spaniards, began another program of forced congregation. Beginning in the early 1590s, priests and local magistrates together were ordered to re-investigate the possibility of reducing the number of minor settlements. In 1598 most of Nueva España was divided into some thirty congregation districts, to each of which a *juez de congregación* and subordinate officials were sent to examine the area,

choose convenient sites for Indian communities, and send their recommendations to Mexico city. When a decision had been reached, the juez would re-visit the estancias marked for elimination and get the inhabitants to move. The new towns were built by the Indians themselves in the traditional Spanish grid pattern surrounding a central plaza with church and market. The estancias were abandoned, their chapels razed and Indian dwellings burnt (Cline, 1949; Simpson, 1934).

This second program of congregation was carried out in the period 1593–1605. Frequently the Indians objected, the matter was referred to Mexico city, and a new decision was reached on some particular point. Many cases are recorded where the natives refused to abandon their villages, and after they had been forcibly moved and their houses destroyed, they still fled from the new towns and lived more dispersed than before in caves and wild places. After 1607 Indians who still wanted to do so were in theory allowed to return to their old homesites, and some did. Yet thousands of placenames disappeared from the map at this time. Thus, in the first half of the seventeenth century, Nueva España was in a sense urbanized, with compact Spanish towns and cities and Hispanicized Indian villages separated by vast stretches of deserted land, a pattern visible today. As the relatively few surviving Indians were congregated, Spaniards acquired the abandoned village sites with their fields, forests, and waters and converted them into haciendas (Chevalier, 1952). Many Indians at this time ceased to be subsistence farmers when they were hired to work on the Spaniards' estates.

In a special category were the mining centers, *reales de minas*, formed in a haphazard fashion around the mines, some of which became large, multi-racial settlements; these declined in the depression of the 1600s and returned to prosperity in the eighteenth century (Borah, 1951). Another post-Conquest development was the seaport. On the Gulf, Vera Cruz, Pánuco, and Guazacualco were early port settlements, but only Vera Cruz survived as such. Pacific port towns in the 1520s included Teguantepec, Acapulco, and Zacatula.

Guatulco was the terminus of trade with Peru in 1540–75, while the trans-Pacific galleons used Acapulco (1573–1815). Acapulco and Vera Cruz were the only fortified ports, both coasts being left almost deserted and exposed to pirate and contraband activity.

Much about these and other changes in the settlement pattern can be gleaned from the documents at our disposal. Gradually the Chichimec frontier was pushed northward, and rich agricultural zones such as the Bajío received a strong infusion of Spaniards and Indian laborers drawn from older communities in less favored areas (Miranda, 1962*a*).

Sources

Although other sources have been used in its compilation, the present work relies mostly on the *relaciones geográficas*. In the areal descriptions below, where no further citation appears, information is derived from these relaciones and similar documents which are listed and briefly discussed at the end of each description. Mention is also made of published monographic treatment where we have come across it.

One of the Spanish crown's earliest concerns was to determine how the newly discovered lands could best be incorporated into the imperial system, making such changes as were thought necessary or desirable (e.g., replacing the prevailing religion with Christianity, substituting gold for feathers), but without disturbing existing native institutions where continuity was considered useful or harmless. To accomplish this, the crown authorities needed information in detail about the various provinces and peoples. This purpose was thwarted to some extent in early years by native rulers and private encomenderos whose interests were served by withholding or falsifying information, but as the crown gained control over the whole country a mass of trustworthy data was assembled and remitted to the court. We have seen that during the three centuries of the colony fundamental changes occurred in the human and other natural resources on which the king and his subjects depended for their support and prosperity. This called for frequent revaluation, necessarily based on fresh reports drawn up locally and submitted to the crown.

The value of such reports containing information of the most varied nature (see Table E) has been discussed elsewhere. Most were made in answer to inquiries, often in the form of an *instrucción* or questionnaire. Some were drawn up by well educated or intuitive local magistrates or priests, others by myopics or semi-literates, and there were times when no one within a parish or corregimiento was found capable of answering the questions. Many of these documents were no doubt destroyed, but a considerable body has survived in Spanish and Mexican archives and elsewhere, in part published, most still in manuscript. In the following general discussion, reports or series of reports of a geographical nature describing all or portions of the territory covered by the gobierno of Nueva España will be considered, in chronological order. The interested scholar will notice many lacunae, which we hope will stimulate further investigation and bring to light additional documents of this sort (Cline, 1964; Gerhard, 1968; Konetzke, 1948).

Cortés in 1522–3 commissioned inspectors who followed and sometimes accompanied the first Spanish military expeditions as they reduced outlying areas to submission. Each inspector made a more or less careful survey of the region assigned to him, and it was on their reports that Cortés relied in distributing encomiendas to his followers (*see above*). Clearly, these first survey reports showing conditions at or very close to the moment of contact are unique sources, supplementing the few first-hand accounts of the conquistadors with details of the native population and religious–political organization which, in some areas, were soon to disappear. At the moment, we have only fragments (actually, copies) of two of the resulting reports, one made by Antonio de Caravajal in

TABLE E. *Relaciones geográficas*

	1523–5	1531–2	1547–50	1569–71	1579–82	1608–12	1648–50	1743–6	1777–8	1788–92	1822–5
Physical setting											
Geology					×	×			×	×	
Topography	×	×	×		×	×	×	×	×	×	×
Climate	×	×	×		×	×	×	×	×	×	×
Fauna		×			×	×			×		
Flora					×	×			×	×	×
Cultural geography											
Pre-Conquest, contact:											
History					×	×					×
Population	×	×	×		×	×					
Health					×	×					
Languages	×	×			×						
Dress					×	×			×		
Social organization	×				×	×					
Settlements	×	×	×		×						
Government	×	×	×		×	×					
Religion		×			×	×					
Economy	×	×			×						
Warfare	×	×			×	×					
Architecture						×			×		
Artifacts									×		
Conquest, Spanish	×	×	×		×	×					
Post-Conquest, colony:											
History					×	×	×				
Population	×	×	×	×	×	×	×	×	×	×	×
Health				×	×	×		×			
Languages	×	×	×	×	×	×	×		×	×	×
Dress					×	×			×		
Settlements	×	×	×	×	×	×	×	×	×	×	×
Encomiendas	×	×	×	×	×	×		×			
Government	×	×	×	×	×	×	×	×	×	×	×
Religion (parishes)				×	×	×	×	×	×	×	×
Economy	×	×	×		×	×	×	×	×	×	×
Agriculture		×	×		×	×	×	×	×	×	×
Cattle raising		×	×		×	×	×	×	×	×	×
Commerce		×			×	×	×	×	×	×	×
Mining	×	×	×	×	×	×	×	×	×	×	×
Saltworks					×	×	×				×
Textiles and dyes						×		×			
Architecture					×	×	×		×	×	
Communications				×	×	×		×	×	×	×
Revenue			×			×	×			×	

Michoacán in 1523–4 (Warren, 1963*a*), the other describing the region north of Colima in 1525 (BAGN, VIII, pp. 556–72). Under each place visited they show the name of the ruler or tribute collector, subordinate settlements, and the number of houses (*see above*), with observations on topography and natural resources.

A royal command of 5 April 1528, addressed to the first audiencia of Mexico, the bishops (Tlaxcala and Mexico), and the priors of Dominican and Franciscan monasteries in Nueva España, ordered them to submit descriptions of each province with comments on the number of Indians and Spaniards, tributes, natural resources, and topography. Two years later, no reply having been received in Spain, the second audiencia sailed with identical instructions. On 14 August 1531 the tribunal wrote that they had sent out inspectors to gather the required information, and on 5 July of the following year they reported to the empress that they were sending her the completed report. It actually seems to have left Mexico in November 1532, and a duplicate report was sent early in 1533 (ENE II, pp. 180–2; III, p. 91). In its compilation the audiencia had used data submitted by corregidors, religious, encomenderos, and other persons who were familiar with every corner of the country. This 'description y relaçion desta tierra' was accompanied by 'pinturas' which the Indians had made of their lands and villages. Most unfortunately, we have not been able to find the complete report nor the 'pinturas', although part of the former is summarized in the *Décadas* of Antonio de Herrera (Década 4a, pp. 230–7). Even this extract contains valuable information not found elsewhere. Journals of *visitas* or official inspections to gather information for the 'description', which were made to Ocuituco in 1531 and in the gobierno of Pánuco in 1532–3, have also come to light.[7]

On 19 December 1533 the emperor again addressed the audiencia: 'Since we wish to be thoroughly informed about that country and its qualities, we command that you have drawn up a long and particular description of its size, length and breadth and limits, specifically naming the boundary markers. Also the character and special qualities of each individual town, and what sort of people live there, mentioning particularly their religion and customs. Also what Spanish residents there are, and where each one lives, and how many have Spanish wives and Indian, and the number of bachelors. And what ports and rivers exist, what buildings have been constructed, what animals and birds are raised there.... And when it is drawn up and signed by you, you will send this description to us in our council of the Indies.' The emperor further requested 'pinturas' of everything subject to illustration. This order must have reached Mexico sometime in the spring of 1534. Only a few scattered documents have come to light, all undated but apparently drawn up *c.* 1534, answering some of the questions raised here.[8]

Another royal order went out in the early 1540s, this time to certain private subjects in Nueva España. Andrés de Barrios was asked to describe the bishopric of Mexico, Bartolomé de Zárate the dioceses of Antequera and Tlaxcala, and Pedro Almíndez Chirinos and Andrés de Tapia the diocese of Michoacán. Of the three reports, only that of Zárate, dated 1544, has been found; it is brief and rather disorganized, but contains useful information (ENE, IV, pp. 130–48).

The first detailed general survey of New Spain available to us in fairly complete form is the *Suma de Visitas*, a most interesting document compiled towards 1548–50. Mexico had just been shaken by a disastrous epidemic, and there was urgent need for revision of the tribute assessments. Royal commands of 10 and 12 April 1546 ordered the viceroy to have a survey made of all Indian towns and to report on their resources and population. This was done in a series of inspections by different individuals between 1547 and 1550, summarized in a single document, and sent to Spain probably in 1551. It is an uneven production covering slightly more than half the Indian settlements, certain places being described in detail and others quite summarily. Omitted are parts of the Marquesado del Valle, most of the diocese of Tlaxcala, and the province of Guazacualco. Yet the *Suma* is a unique source of demographic, encomienda, and geographical information, showing many places as they were just before the religious congregations of the 1550s.[9]

In 1568 Juan de Ovando was appointed *visitador* of the council of the Indies, and he sent out, under a royal cedula of 23 January 1569, a request for information addressed to various American authorities. A second order later in that year, directed to bishops and provincials of regular orders, called for the answers to some two hundred questions on a variety of subjects. The reports submitted in obedience to these orders, which are cited below, are uneven in treatment and detail. The best, those from the archdiocese of Mexico, the secular clergy of Tlaxcala, and Augustinian monasteries throughout New Spain, were made by the *cordillera* system, in which the questionnaire was circulated among the clerics and priors who each then drew up a description of his parish. Others were compiled by diocesan clerks, and at the Franciscan provincial headquarters of Mexico, and are less detailed. Only partly published, they contain information on settlements and population, native languages, encomiendas, parochial boundaries, and other subjects, compiled in 1569–71. This large body of data was summarized by the royal cosmographer, Juan López de Velasco, in his monumental *Geografía y descripción universal de las Indias*.

Another serious epidemic desolated New Spain in 1576–81, and again there was a need for fresh information. López de Velasco drew up a list of fifty pertinent questions which went out with a cedula of Philip II dated 25 May 1577. The answers to this interrogatory, which embrace a fascinating diversity of subjects, were submitted almost entirely by local magistrates in 1579–82. Relaciones geográficas of this important series have been found for somewhat less than half the civil jurisdictions of Nueva España, and at present are kept in three repositories at Seville, Madrid, and Austin (Texas); most have been published and are widely used by ethno-historians and others. Forty of them are accompanied by maps. Relaciones of twenty-six jurisdictions in Nueva España which were reported in early inventories have since vanished, and no doubt others were destroyed or remain undiscovered.[10]

A useful source of information complementing that found in the 1579–82 relaciones is the *Relación* of Fray Alonso Ponce, a Franciscan commissary-general who covered much of Mexico on foot and horseback in the years 1584–9. His journal, actually written by another religious who accompanied Ponce, displays an extraordinary insight on many phases of colonial life not covered in the official reports of the time.

There is a great deal of correspondence concerning the civil congregations carried out in the 1590s and early 1600s, in some few cases accompanied by actual survey reports and maps. These documents rarely went to Spain, and most of those which have been found are at AGN (Mexico); many of them lie buried in the vast *ramo* (section) of Tierras in that repository. Citations are given below, under each jurisdiction.

The next series of relaciones geográficas was the product of an unwieldy questionnaire covering 355 items, drawn up by the cosmographer García de Céspedes in 1604 and sent out to civil magistrates throughout the Indies. No doubt these local authorities were dismayed by the magnitude of the task. In any case, only twelve replies from minor jurisdictions in Nueva España are listed in a Spanish archival inventory of *c.* 1636, and of these, copies of only five have been discovered and published. Drawn up between 1608 and 1612, and containing data not found elsewhere, they are cited below.

Two general descriptions of the Spanish Indies were compiled by individuals in the first half of the seventeenth century, one a Carmelite friar who knew America firsthand, the other a clerk in the council of the Indies who got his information from official papers. Fray Antonio Vázquez de Espinosa was in Mexico in 1612 and again in the early 1620s, and wrote his *Compendio* in 1628–9. The clerk, Juan Díez de la Calle, published his work in 1646, but many of the data he used were from an earlier period. Useful complementary sources for these years are the journals of pastoral visits made by the archbishop of Mexico in 1646[11] and by two bishops of Tlaxcala in 1609–24[12] and 1643–6.[13]

Two royal cedulas were sent to America in 1648 calling for information. The first, dated 26 April, ordered each bishop to remit a description of his diocese, listing parishes and towns and giving the number of communicants in each. The cedula of 8 November 1648, addressed not only to ecclesiastics but also to viceroys, governors, and audiencias, asked for the same and further information and specified that it was to be used by the royal chronicler, Gil González Dávila, in the compilation of his *Teatro eclesiástico*, a history of the Church in America. From the bishoprics in Nueva España, the only reply to these cedulas that we have seen is that submitted on 25 April 1649 by Dr Francisco Arnaldo Isassi, a long and most interesting 'Demarcación y descripción' of the diocese of Michoacán.[14] Similar documents for remaining areas, if and when discovered, would add immeasurably to our knowledge of Mexico in a period for which organized and accessible data are sadly lacking. González Dávila's work is of little interest in this regard, because he published it before the requested reports had come in.

We have been singularly unsuccessful in finding material from the second half of the seventeenth century. Tributary counts for jurisdictions in the dioceses of Mexico, Tlaxcala, and Michoacán are of some use,[15] while Cook and Borah (1968, p. 34) have unearthed similar information from the bishopric of Antequera. The scholar who one day takes on the thankless task of perusing the charred remnants of the section of Contaduría at AGI (1,945 legajos) should help close this documentary gap, especially if he comes across the answers to two cedulas (21 April 1679 and 5 August 1681) which ordered a detailed census made (Gerhard, 1968, p. 625). For the archdiocese of Mexico, there is a long report (which we have only partly examined) of a *visita* made by the prelate, Francisco de Aguiar y Seixas, in 1683–5.[16]

After a long hiatus, the investigator is treated to a remarkable collection of documents recently discovered by Dr Adèle Kibre in the Archive of the Indies,[17] the result of a cedula of 19 July 1741. The accumulation of geographical data on this occasion was entrusted to the alcaldes mayores, who each received a copy of the cedula and a printed instrucción drawn up in Mexico on 6 March 1743. Of the 129 civil jurisdictions existing at that time in Nueva España, the original reports from seventy-four, prepared between 1743 and 1746, have been found. A very few of them (only five discovered to date) were accompanied by maps. Some go far beyond the scope of the rather simple questionnaire and have complete census lists and other information, while others are quite brief. Before they were sent to Spain these reports, together with others which have since disappeared, were examined by the cosmographer of Mexico, José Antonio de Villaseñor y Sánchez, who prepared and published a summary of them. This published version should be used with caution, as it contains many typographical and factual errors and serious omissions.

In the footsteps of Alonso Ponce, another curious and indefatigable priest, the Capuchin friar Francisco de Ajofrín travelled over much of New Spain in 1763–7 and left a fascinating diary filled with valuable observations and much extraneous material, all copiously illustrated by the author. Ajofrín's wanderings took him from Vera Cruz to Mexico, west to Pátzcuaro and Guanaxuato, and south to Oaxaca.

Towards 1769 the crown prosecutor (*fiscal*) of the audiencia of Mexico sent out a request for information concerning Indian town property, population, local produce, hospitals, and markets. We have seen only one reply, a long and elegant report sent in by the alcalde mayor of Tochimilco in 1770.[18]

In the last quarter of the eighteenth century local officials and priests in Nueva España were bombarded by an almost continuous series of orders from king and viceroy demanding all sorts of information. The same questions were asked repeatedly by different authorities, resulting in such a jumble of reports that it is not always easy to determine which order is being complied with, or to which series a report belongs.

A cedula of 20 October 1776 was accompanied by a 62-point questionnaire covering various subjects, notably topography, weather, geology, antiquities, and native dress. The resulting reports, often referred to as *relaciones topográficas*, were compiled by parish priests. A good many of the original documents written in 1777–8 are found at BNE (Madrid), a few of them accompanied by maps. Copies of many of these, and of others missing in the Madrid collection, are deposited at BNP (Paris). Still other copies which were used in a defective series of publications, together with a few original reports, are in Mexico (full citation will appear below). Complementing the *relaciones topográficas*, which describe only a small portion of the total number of parishes in New Spain, is a series of *padrones* or census lists made in compliance with an order of 10 November 1776. Padrones drawn up in 1777–9 have been found from quite a few parishes in the dioceses of Oaxaca and Puebla.[19]

Reports of uneven value from a few civil *partidos* and parishes were made in answer to a request for information to be used in the *Gazeta de México*, the official organ of the viceregal government. These are dated from 1788 to 1792 and will be cited below.

A separate series easily identifiable was the product of the viceroy's instructions dated 2 January 1790 concerning the preparation of new padrones to determine the number and names of those eligible for military service in each jurisdiction. These census lists of the non-Indian population, drawn up in 1790–3, are generally accompanied by lists of all settlements down to the category of *rancho*, and some have brief geographical descriptions and surprisingly accurate maps. Most are found in the *ramo* of Padrones at AGN. A related group of documents, answering the viceroy's command of 20 August 1792, provides lists of toponyms.[20]

Further reports continued to be requested and submitted during the wars of Independence. As late as 6 October 1812 a rather worried cedula was sent to 'the Americas and islands' with a printed interrogatory asking for observations on the character and religious attitudes of the king's rebellious subjects (we have not seen any answers from Nueva España).[21]

For data reflecting conditions at the end of the colonial period, we are indebted to the Provisional Governing Junta of the newly-independent Mexican nation, which on 1 April 1822 asked the provincial delegations to compile statistical analyses, aided by the ayuntamientos (governing bodies) of the various municipalities. Such an analysis, and an excellent one, was written by Juan José Martínez de Lejarza, describing the province of Michoacán. A more ambitious undertaking was that of José María Murguía y Galardi, who compiled a five-volume *Estadística antigua y moderna* of Oaxaca.[22]

Suggestions for further research

This writer's approach to Mexican historical geography has necessarily been selective. Many of the sources mentioned have only been glanced at and listed as in a catalogue. There are great gaps in our knowledge to be filled by patient archival work.

At AGI (Seville), the twin sections of *Papeles de Justicia de Indias* (*Justicia*, 1,187 legajos) and *Escribanía de Cámara* (1,194 legajos) should yield more such treasures as the Caravajal report of Michoacán (1523–4) and the 1532–3 visita of the Pánuco area, only recently discovered. Both are sixteenth-century transcripts of original documents which have since disappeared, submitted as antecedents of lawsuits. We have mentioned that the badly damaged section of *Contaduría* may well contain demographic and other interesting data from the seventeenth century.

While AGI is the repository of the bulk of official correspondence originating in the overseas possessions and addressed to the Spanish court and the council of the Indies, one must go to AGN (Mexico) for the internal governmental and judicial correspondence of Nueva España, i.e., the handling of business between the viceroy and audiencia on one hand and local magistrates on the other. This is somewhat illogically dispersed in several ramos whose titles give little idea of the wealth of detailed information from every jurisdiction in the land which they contain. The chronological sequence of this correspondence in the sixteenth century is shown in Table F.

AGN still has an undisclosed quantity of unbound and uncatalogued manuscripts which may contain some of the missing *relaciones geográficas*. Frequently original documents of this sort went to Spain, while copies remained in America. In other cases the original reports were filed away in Mexico city, and an extracted summary might be submitted to Spain. The ramo of *Historia* has been and is still being used as a receptacle for such material as it turns up.

Among other collections in Mexico city worth delving into are the Archivo Histórico de Hacienda (now housed at AGN), the Archivo Histórico del Departamento Agrario (much on land disputes between villages), and the Archivo Arquiepiscopal (in the Cathedral – a valuable series of pastoral visits made by archbishops beginning in 1683).

TABLE F. *Internal government correspondence, sixteenth century*

	Archivo General de la Nación				Newberry Library Ayer MSS
	Civil	General de Parte	Indios	Mercedes	
1537	1271				
1538					
1539					
1540					
1541					
1542				1	
1543				2	
1544				↓	
1545					
1546					
1547					
1548					
1549					
1550	↓			3	
1551				↓	
1552					1121
1553					↓
1554				4	
1555				↓	
1556					
1557					
1558				84	
1559					
1560				↓ 5	
1561				↓	
1562					
1563				6 7	
1564				↓	
1565				8	
1566				↓	
1567				9	
1568				↓	
1569					
1570					

	Archivo General de la Nación				Newberry Library Ayer MSS
	Civil	General de Parte	Indios	Mercedes	
1571					
1572					
1573				10	
1574					
1575		1	1		
1576		↓			
1577				↓	
1578					
1579		2			
1580		↓			
1581			↓	11	
1582			2		
1583			↓	12	13
1584					
1585					
1586		3		↓	↓
1587				14	
1588		↓			
1589			4	15	
1590		4	3 5	↓ 16	
1591	↓		↓ 6	17 18	↓ 19
1592				↓	
1593					
1594				20	21
1595				↓ 22	
1596					
1597					
1598				23	
1599	5			↓ 24	↓
1600	↓				

Outside of Mexico city, much remains to be done with the provincial records, which in most cases have been badly cared for and sometimes were totally destroyed. This is a pioneer field requiring courage and perseverance. One of the purposes of the present guide is to point out where such records might logically be found, in the capital cities and towns of intendencias and alcaldías mayores, in diocesan seats and parochial cabeceras.

Some work has been begun in recent years in photographing municipal archives and parish registers (cf. Medina Ascensio, 1966, pp. 243–8).

Another area of which we have scarcely scratched the surface is that of the native pictorial manuscripts and codices, often unique sources of toponymic and other data. A complete list of these documents, with geographical guides, should soon appear in the *Handbook of Middle American Indians*.

A note on spelling of Mexican placenames

It is quite usual to find a toponym spelled two or three different ways in a single colonial document. Sounds in Náhuatl and other native languages were rendered in various forms by scribes attempting to reduce them to Spanish orthography, in itself a highly individualistic matter until the Royal Academy tried to impose conformity in the eighteenth century. To compound the difficulty, the various dialects of Náhuatl, Zapotecan, etc., produced subtle intralingual differences in pronunciation, so that the same toponym would also differ in transliteration from one region to another. Time also caused change, and a name might be pronounced (and spelled) quite differently from one century to another. The suffix *-tépetl* became *-tépeque*, and finally *-tepec*; in general, places ending in *-que* in the sixteenth century ended in *-c* later. While the accent in Náhuatl is normally on the penult, the suffixes *-an* and *-tlan* came to be almost universally stressed by the eighteenth century. The letters *u* and *o* are often interchangeable, as are *g* and *h*; *j*, *s*, and *x*; and *ç*, *s*, and *z*. *B* and *v* are pronounced almost the same in Spanish. An examination of the 1950 census reveals that even to-day there are no fixed rules in the spelling of Mexican toponyms.

This confusion is necessarily reflected in the present work. In discussing the situation at the time of Conquest, a brave attempt is made to reproduce the primitive pronunciation of native toponyms with modern Spanish orthography (for some reason, differences of opinion on how Mexican toponyms should be written and translated reduce competing modern authorities to an unseemly polemical frenzy – cf. Bradomín, 1955; Peñafiel, 1885; Robelo, 1961; Robelo, Olaguibel and Peñafiel, 1966). Subsequently, in mentioning the same and other places in the colonial period, the most frequently used contemporary spelling (somewhat modernized) has been followed, while listing notable variants. Finally, we have tried to provide for each cabecera a modern identification with a place listed in the 1950 census. Thus, 'Cuauhchinanco' at contact becomes 'Guachinango (Quauchinanco, etc.)' during the colony, and '1950: Huauchinango, ciudad'. Variants will be found in the index.

Citations and abbreviations

We have mentioned the omission in this work of individual citation of certain key documents after their first appearance, and of those listed under 'Sources' at the end of each regional description. Extended bibliographical and other comment appears under 'Notes'; otherwise, published works are cited in parentheses within the text, while manuscript sources are cited individually under 'Notes'.

'Corregidor' has been shortened to 'C', and 'alcalde mayor' to 'AM'. Other textual contractions include 'S', 'Sto', and 'Sta' for 'San', 'Santo', and 'Santa', and 'm' for 'meters'. Bibliographical abbreviations are listed preceding the bibliography.

NEW SPAIN
1519–1821

KEY TO MAP SYMBOLS

‡ Seat of archbishop

† Seat of bishop

⊙ Residence of alcalde mayor or corregidor

◎ Residence of gobernador

• Pueblo

∴ Abandoned site

·········· Diocesan boundaries

1 *Acapulco*

Now in southern Guerrero state, Acapulco's late colonial jurisdiction extended from the top of the Sierra Madre del Sur (3,000+ m) to the Pacific coast, centering on the magnificent bay of Acapulco. The area is drained by the Papagayo river and lesser watercourses emptying into lagoons along a narrow coastal plain, mountains occasionally reaching the sea. The climate is semi-arid and hot except in the higher parts, which are forested.

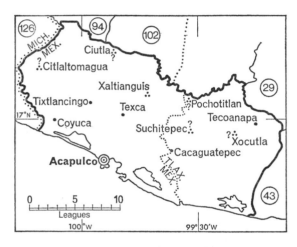

The political situation here at contact can be reconstructed in a rough way with the aid of sixteenth-century documents. Acapulco (which was some distance inland), Acamalutlan, Citlalan, Coyucac, Nahuallan, Tepexóchitl, Tezcatlan, Xaltzapotlan, and Yacapul were probably semi-independent states connected in some way with the neighboring Cuitlatecan kingdom of Mexcaltépec (cf. Zacatula). The same may be said of Anecuilco and Citlaltomahuacan, farther up the slopes of the Sierra Madre (Tlacatépetl). East of the Papagayo (Xiquipila) river were four Yope (Tlapanecan) states, Cacahuatépec, Pochotitlan, Xocotlan, and Xochitépec. The latter maintained their independence, but those west of the Papagayo seem to have paid tribute to the Aztecs. Tlapanecan-speakers extended westward to Aca-

polco, Xaltzapotlan, and Tepexóchitl, but Náhuatl was also spoken in those places, as it was exclusively at Citlalan and Coyucac (thus the coast was a region of Mexican settlement). Inland there was a hodgepodge of languages (some perhaps only dialects) which in 1569 still included Camotecan, Coyutumetecan, Tepuztecan, Texcatecan, Tixtecan, Tlacihuixtecan, and Tlacotepehuan. This variety of tongues, together with the sixteenth-century documentary evidence, suggests a dense contact population dispersed in many rancherías.

Acapulco was perhaps first seen by the expedition of Rodrigo Alvarez Chico in the fall of 1521. Gonzalo de Sandoval's little army brought the Aztec tributary states under control in the spring of 1523 but was less successful with the Yopes (Sauer, pp. 1–17). There were at least three subsequent Yope rebellions, the last that we know of occurring after 1535 (ENE, II, pp. 30–3, 62; Icaza, no. 265).

Encomiendas

Mescaltepec and its dependencies, which included the port of Acapulco, were held by the conquistador Juan Rodríguez de Villafuerte, a resident of Zacatula, from the 1520s (Millares Carlo and Mantecón, no. 1155; ENE, II, pp. 32, 214). In the 1540s Rodríguez was succeeded by a daughter, Aldonza de Villafuerte, who soon afterward married García de Albornoz (Doña Aldonza appears as sole encomendera in 1587–97). Escheatment occurred before 1643.

Citlaltomagua was given to another conquistador, Diego García Xaramillo, but it was taken from him on at least one occasion. On his death the widow, Cecilia Lucero, inherited; the encomienda had escheated by 1550.[1]

The poblador Diego Pardo had a title to Cacaguatepec issued by governor Estrada in the 1520s, although the encomienda was taken by the second audiencia for a year or so (ENE, II, pp. 30–1). Pardo died in the early 1560s and was followed first by a son and then by his widow, Inés de Leiva. In 1597 Esteban de Cisneros appears as encomendero. Later the tributes were re-assigned to the Moctezuma heirs.[2]

Of the three remaining Yope states, Pochotitlan and Suchitepec escheated in the 1530s, while Xocutla seems to have had several encomenderos. Two thirds of the latter grant were taken for the crown at an early date, the other third being assigned to Cristóbal de Monresin (Malresin, Monrosin), still listed in 1548.[3] Later encomenderos were Monresin's widow (in the 1560s), José de Monresin (*c.* 1570), and another Cristóbal de Monresin (1597). By 1626 all the tribute went to the crown.

Government

Cs were appointed to Pochotitlan (with Suchitepec and the crown part of Xocutla) and Citlaltomagua (with Anecuilco) towards 1535. The status of Citlaltomagua in early years is not clear; it appears both as a crown possession and a private encomienda, and perhaps was divided until the final escheatment occurred. In the 1560s this corregimiento was suffragan to the province of Zacatula.[4]

We are told that a settlement was formed at the port of Acapulco in 1550, although a shipyard had functioned there from *c.* 1528 (Brand, 1956, p. 587). Towards 1548 the C of Pochotitlan, Ceutla, Suchitepec y Xocutla was elevated to the rank of AM of Puerto de Acapulco and later he was given jurisdiction in neighbouring encomiendas.[5] Since there was little activity at the port until the arrival of the first galleon with Chinese merchandise in 1573, and since the climate on the coast was considered unhealthy, the AM at first lived in Acamalutla, a mountain village. Even after the beginning of the China trade the magistrate normally resided inland, at Tistla or Cuernavaca or Mexico City, and went to Acapulco only while the galleon was there (usually from December to March; cf. Gerhard, 1960, pp. 36–41). A lieutenant (*teniente*) of the AM remained at the port the rest of the year.[6]

Toward the end of the sixteenth century the jurisdiction was enlarged. Citlaltomagua y Anecuilco ceased to exist as a separate corregimiento, while Tistla (q.v., not to be confused with the estancia mentioned below) was also annexed to Acapulco and henceforth was administered by a *teniente*. Somewhat later, probably in the 1680s, the alcaldía mayor of Chilapa was added to the jurisdiction (both Chilapa and Tistla are considered separately here). Meanwhile the magistrate at Acapulco had acquired the additional titles of castellan (from 1617) and *capitán a guerra* (1633), it being his duty to defend the port from piratical incursions (cf. Gerhard, 1960). From 1628 appointment to this post was made by the king in council, and from *c.* 1710 the AM became a gobernador, although still subordinate to the viceroy. After 1787 the gobierno was in effect divided between three subdelegaciones (Acapulco, Chilapa, Tistla) subordinate to the intendencia of Mexico.[7]

Church

Santos Reyes de Acapulco became a secular parish in the archbishopric of Mexico sometime before 1569, with ecclesiastical jurisdiction at the port, Coyuca, Acamalutla, and Citlaltomagua. Another priest, appointed by the bishop of Tlaxcala, lived at Xocutla in 1570 and visited the surrounding villages. The Papagayo river was both the parochial and diocesan boundary.

By 1611 the curate of Xocutla had moved his headquarters to Santiago Ayutla, in the adjoining jurisdiction of Igualapa (q.v.), leaving a vicar at S Pedro Cacaguatepec. S Miguel Coyuca had become a separate secular parish by 1720, as did Cacaguatepec some years later. There was a Franciscan monastery at Acapulco belonging to the province of Michoacán, without parochial duties.

Population and settlements

The native population was decimated here as elsewhere along the coast in the 1520s and 1530s, and again in the epidemic of 1545–8. Most of the surviving Indians were struck down by the plague of 1576–9, the number of tributaries being reported as 1,589 in 1569 and only 185 in 1643. Later censuses show 541 Indian families in 1743, and 568 Indian tributaries in 1804.

While the cabecera of Mescaltepec was in the neighboring jurisdiction of Zacatula (q.v.), most of its subjects were in that of Acapulco. In 1569 the latter consisted of nine lesser cabeceras (Acamalutla, Acapulco, Citlala, Coyuca, Naguala, Tepezúchil, Tezcatlan, Yacapul, Zalzapotla) and eleven minor estancias, named and approximately located in the report of that year. Indian congregations carried out in 1599–1604 split Acamalutla into two small cabeceras (Acamalutla and Tixtlancingo), collected the survivors of Zalzapotla at its former estancia of Xaltianguis, and left Naguala, Tepezúchil, Tezcatlan, and Yacapul deserted. During the seventeenth century, Acapulco and Coyuca became exclusively non-Indian communities, while Acamalutla, Citlala, and Xaltianguis disappeared altogether. Reports of 1743–92 show only two Indian cabeceras here, Texca (Texcatepec; = former Tezcatlan? 1950: Texca, pueblo) and Tixtlancingo (1950: pueblo).[8]

Citlaltomagua had seven barrios in 1548, only two of which (Tepetistla and Xagualtepec) survived in 1569. After the epidemic of 1576–9 Xagualtepec was abandoned, and about the same time the sub-cabecera of Anecuilco (Anenecuilco) was moved to an estancia higher in the mountains called Ceuhtla (Ciutla). Only the lastnamed place still existed, as a ranchería, in the eighteenth century.

In the Yope country east of the Papagayo, Cacaguatepec, Pochotitlan, and Xocutla each had one subject estancia in 1570, while Suchitepec had none. After the congregations of the 1590s, Suchitepec is no longer mentioned, and Pochotitlan and Xocutla were reduced to a handful of Indians each in 1626. Those of Xocutla were seemingly moved to Tecoanapa (1950: pueblo), which together with Cacaguatepec (1950: Cacahuatepec, pueblo) survived as eighteenth-century cabeceras.[9]

Although the royal shipyard, which was probably first at Puerto del Marqués, employed some Spaniards and Negroes in the 1530s and later, several decades passed before the port of Acapulco was chosen as the eastern terminus of the transPacific trade route. During these years the port of Guatulco (q.v.), far to the south in Oaxaca, was preferred by ships trading with Central America and Perú (Gerhard, 1960, pp. 32–7). Meanwhile, a few Spaniards with Negro slaves drifted into the area and established cacao plantations along the coast. The port settlement came to life in the 1570s and gradually acquired a small, permanent population of Negroes, mulattoes, Filipinos, and a few Spaniards (there was of course a large transient population during the winter when the Manila galleon was in port). Acapulco (1950: Acapulco de Juárez, ciudad) had a fort (castillo de San Diego) with a permanent garrison from 1617; in later years the port settlement was known as Ciudad de los Reyes de Acapulco. The non-Indian population of the jurisdiction increased from fifty families in 1569 to 578 families in 1743, most of them free mulattoes by the latter date living at the port and at Coyuca (1950; Coyuca de Benítez, ciudad). The padrón of 1792 showed a total of 5,679 non-Indians (individuals), made up of 122 Spaniards, 19 castizos, 122 mestizos, 5,307 'pardos' (including Filipinos), and 109 morenos; in that year there were two haciendas and thirty-two ranchos in the jurisdiction.

Sources

Torquemada (1723, I, p. 287) gives important details of the Mescaltepec region at contact. Brief descriptions of certain cabeceras as they were *c.* 1548 are found in the *Suma de Visitas* (PNE, I; nos. 92, 95, 238, 337, 477, 489, 806). Parishes in the archbishopric in 1569 are well covered in a report of the Ovando series,[10] while those in the diocese of Tlaxcala are more summarily described.[11] The relación geográfica submitted by the C of Citlaltomagua y Anecuilco in 1580 has been published,[12] but another in this series from the AM of Acapulco has disappeared.

For the seventeenth century, we have a few tribute lists (cited above), and descriptions of the port of Acapulco written by corsairs and travellers. Among the latter were Speilbergen (pp. 106–9), in 1615; Navarrete (I, pp. 38–45), in 1647; Dampier (pp. 170–2), in 1685; and Gemelli Carreri (I, pp. 22–36), in 1697.

There is a voluminous report submitted by the castellan-gobernador in 1743.[13] Two documents describe the jurisdiction in 1792, one of them accompanied by a padrón of the non-Indian population.[14] Humboldt visited Acapulco in 1803, and has much to say about the port in his *Ensayo político*. There are numerous plans of the port (cf. Calderón Quijano, 1945, figures 151–77), but we

have seen none of interest showing the entire jurisdiction.

The monograph of Alessio Robles has little to our purpose. Gerhard (1960) and Schurz have much to say about the China trade, but little of substance concerning Acapulco.

2 *Acatlan y Piastla*

This is a hot, dry country of barren hills in southernmost Puebla state, at an elevation of 1,000–1,500 m (a few mountains surpass 2,000 m), drained by the Acatlan river, an affluent of the Mexcala.

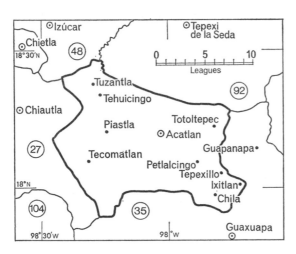

Acatlan (Yucuyuxi in Mixtecan) had a Mexica ruler and perhaps a Náhuatl-speaking minority, although Mixtecan was the more common language; it was an ally of the Aztecs and probably paid some kind of tribute. To the southeast, Chilla, Icxitlan, and Petlaltzinco were Mixtec states tributary to the Aztecs. Piaztlan, to the west, had co-rulers (one of them probably lived at Tozantlan); it was also tributary to the empire and its people spoke a rude form of Náhuatl. Piaztlan was in the region known as Totollan, while the other places fell within the Mixteca Baja (Ñuiñe in Mixtecan). The population was scattered in many small rancherías.

This area probably came under Spanish control in 1521.

Encomiendas
Acatlan was held by the conquistador Juan Bernal, escheating on his death in 1532 (Icaza, 1: p. 131; L de T, p. 5).

Rodrigo de Baeza, a *poblador*, was encomendero of Chila and assigned it in dowry to his daughter, Elvira, who married Lorenzo (Vázquez) Marroquino, sometime before 1550. Marroquino was followed in the 1560s by his widow and a son, Agustín Marroquino. On the latter's death towards 1575 Chila was taken for the crown, but in 1581 Ana Pérez de Zamora appears as encomendera, and fifteen years later another Lorenzo Marroquino is listed. Final escheatment occurred between 1610 and 1626.

Ixitlan was held by the conquistador Francisco Velázquez de Lara, succeeded in the 1570s by a son, Luis, still encomendero in 1604. The place remained a private encomienda well into the seventeenth century.

Santos Hernández was perhaps the first encomendero of Petlalcingo, and is listed as such in the 1530s and 1540s. By 1569 he had been succeeded by Francisco Hernández Guerrero, still mentioned in 1597, although six years later the encomendera was María de Vera. Tributes escheated in the late 1620s, but were subsequently re-assigned.

Piastla seems to have been divided between two encomenderos, Francisco de Olmos and another holder (Fernando Burgueño?), the latter's half passing to the crown in 1532. Olmos died towards 1568 and his share also escheated, but it was recovered by his heirs. One of these, Gaspar de

Burgos, was receiving tribute from the cabecera of Tuzantla in 1603. By 1626 this was entirely a crown possession.

Government

A C was appointed to administer Acatlan and the crown's half of Piastla in September, 1532 (L de T, p. 5). Towards 1558 this magistrate was re-designated AM and put in charge of a province which included Cuyotepexi, Suchitepec, Tezuatlan, and the suffragan C's of Guaxuapa y Tequecistepec, Guapanapa, and Tonalá; this supervisory jurisdiction was much reduced *c.* 1579 when Tonalá became a separate alcaldía mayor (cf. Guaxuapa).[1] Thereafter the AM of Acatlan y Piastla had charge of those places together with Chila, Ixitlan, and Petlalcingo. From 1787 this was a subdelegación in the intendencia of Puebla.

Church

The Dominicans are said to have founded a monastery at Asunción Chila in 1535–6, but it was soon abandoned and not re-occupied until *c.* 1550 (Alvarado, p. 16). By 1569 this parish included Ixitlan and a number of places in the jurisdiction of Guaxuapa, and S Juan Bautista Acatlan had become the residence of a secular priest who visited much of the jurisdiction of Acatlan. Both Santiago Petlalcingo and Asunción Piastla were made secular curacies in 1603, but only the latter survived as a parish. The doctrinas of S Miguel Tehuicingo and Sta María Totoltepec were eighteenth-century creations (before 1766). S Pedro Tecomatlan was the last parish to be founded, after 1777. The Dominicans turned Chila over to the secular clergy between 1743 and 1766. All parishes were in the diocese of Tlaxcala (Puebla).

Population and settlements

Counts of the mid-1560s indicate that there were then about 2,900 Indian tributaries in the jurisdiction (L de T, pp. 5–6, 292). After considerable loss in the epidemic of 1576–81, some 1,290 tributaries survived in 1600; only 470 are recorded in 1626, and 883 in 1696. Then there was an extraordinary recovery, to 2,160 Indian families in 1743, and 3,602 tributaries in 1803.

We have little information on the non-Indian population here. In 1777 there were 243 families of Spaniards and castas in the Acatlan–Tehuicingo area alone. The 1803 *matrícula* shows 193 mulatto tributaries in the jurisdiction.[2]

In 1548 the Indians of Acatlan (1950: Acatlán de Osorio, ciudad) were dispersed in many contiguous settlements along the watercourses, but the 1581 relación names only five *sujetos*. While we have no details of a congregation which was proposed here in 1598,[3] three of the 1581 subject settlements appear as pueblos in the eighteenth century: Tehuicingo, Yeloixtlaguaca (Eloistlahuacan), and Xayacatlan. Four other pueblos, seemingly subject to Acatlan, which appear in the 1792 listing but not in 1581, were perhaps new settlements: Anicano, Atonahuistla, Sta Cruz la Nueva, and Totoltepec.

The cabecera of Chila (1950: pueblo) had only two nearby estancias, Chapultepec and Nochistlan, in 1581. Nochistlan disappeared perhaps *c.* 1600, Chapultepec surviving as a pueblo. Ixitlan (Icxitlan; 1950: S Miguel Ixitlán, pueblo) had no estancias in 1581 or later.

Petlalcingo (Petalzinco; 1950: Petalcingo, pueblo) in 1581 had two estancias, Temascalapa and Tepexic. The congregation report of 1603 mentions a 'quebrada' called Petlalum, ¾ league away, and Sta Ana (Tepexic) at two leagues, which were to be moved to their cabecera together with Guapanapa, a separate cabecera (cf. Guaxuapa). Either this congregation did not take place or it was later undone, as both Guapanapa and Sta Ana Tepexillo appear as pueblos in the eighteenth century.

The 1581 relación names nine estancias around Piastla (Piaztla de la Sal; 1950: Piaxtla, pueblo), but three others are mentioned in the 1603 congregation order. One of them was Huehuepiastla, probably the original cabecera site. In 1603 there were two sub-cabeceras, Chinantla (adjacent to Piastla) and Tuzantla. The Indians of all these places were to be gathered at one of the estancias, Tecomatlan, in that year. Despite this decree, Piastla and eight subjects are listed as pueblos in the 1792 report: Acxustla (S Miguel), Chinantla, Ilamacingo, Tecomatlan, Tecuautitlan, Texalpa, Tlaxcuapan, and Tuzantla.

Sources

Acatlan, Petlalcingo, and Piastla are summarily described in 1548 (PNE, I: nos. 6, 446–7). In the Ovando series (*c.* 1570) there is a brief report from the curate of Acatlan and Piastla (PNE, V: p. 217), as well as the general diocesan description (ENE, XIV: pp. 88–9). A long and most interesting relación geográfica was submitted by the AM in 1581.[4]

The congregation order of 1603 lists estancias of Petlalcingo and Piastla.[5] Bishop Mota y Escobar visited Chila in 1610 and again in 1623; on the second visit he went to Ixitlan and Petlalcingo also.[6] Tributary data for 1623–96 are found in two documents.[7]

A lost relación of *c.* 1743 is condensed in Villa-señor y Sánchez (I: pp. 345–6); in the same series, there is a complete padrón of the village of Tlaxcuapan dated 1745.[8] Fray Ajofrín (II: pp. 135–6) passed through Chila and Totoltepec in 1766. All parishes except Tecomatlan and Totoltepec have padrones drawn up in 1777,[9] and there is a useful list of toponyms dated 1792.[10]

Monographic treatment of this region can be found in Dahlgren de Jordán (1954) and Spores (1965).

3 *Actopan*

Today in south central Hidalgo, this is for the most part a very arid region, cool with slight seasonal rainfall, at 1,600–2,500 m. Drainage is northward into the Amajac and Tula rivers.

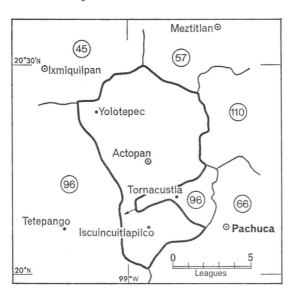

Actopan and Itzcuincuitlapilco, conquered by the Tepaneca in the late fourteenth century and subsequently incorporated in the Triple Alliance tributary province of Hueypochtlan, were Otomí communities, with a Chichimec (Pame) minority in Actopan. The settlement pattern was dispersed.

Visited in late 1519 or early 1520 by the Spaniards, the region came under Spanish control in 1521–2.

Encomiendas

Both Hernando Alonso and Juan González Ponce de León are mentioned as encomenderos of Actopan in the 1520s (Greenleaf, 1961, pp. 90–1. Icaza, I: p. 117). Subsequently the place was assigned to Rodrigo Gómez de Avila, who in 1538 turned over his rights to his son-in-law, Juan Martínez Guerrero (BAGN, X: p. 253). Sometime between 1589 and 1593 the latter was followed by a son, Agustín Guerrero de Luna.[1] The encomienda escheated after 1643, but part of the tribute was re-assigned to the Moctezuma heirs.

Iscuincuitlapilco was held in early years by Pedro Gallego and by Lic. Pedro López de Alcántara (Dorantes de Carranza, p. 309. Icaza, I: p. 208; II: p. 311. Nobiliario, p. 247). Escheatment occurred in April, 1531.[2]

Government

Justice was administered from 1531 by the C of Iscuincuitlapilco, an office which was occasionally combined with the nearby magistracies of Tetepango and Xilotepec.[3] Suffragan to Pachuca in the mid-1560s, the jurisdiction became an alcaldía mayor (Actopan) towards 1568.[4] Its boundaries coincided with those of the two pueblos of Actopan and Iscuincuitlapilco, the latter almost split in two by an intrusion of several other pueblos administered from Tetepango Hueypustla (q.v.); proposals to transfer this enclave to Actopan were made several times but apparently this was not done.[5] From 1787 the AM, who resided at Actopan, was re-designated subdelegado, subject to the intendencia of Mexico.

Church

The Augustinians founded a monastery-parish at S Nicolás Actopan towards 1548 (actually the church was on the dividing line between Actopan and Iscuincuitlapilco). S Juan Yolo (Yolotepec) was an *ayuda de parroquia* with its own minister in the eighteenth century. The parish, secularized *c.* 1750, belonged to the archdiocese of Mexico and included nearby Chicabasco and Tornacustla (cf. Tetepango Hueypustla).

Population and settlements

There must have been a great many Indians here at contact. While there was considerable loss in the epidemic of 1545–8, the jurisdiction still had some 12,000 Indian tributaries in 1570, about two-thirds at Actopan and the rest at Iscuincuitlapilco. Half of these died in the plague of 1576–81, and further loss through disease and emigration reduced the tributary total to 1,092 in 1643. Later counts give 1,509 tributaries in 1688, 2,750 Indian families in 1743, 20,000 Indians (individuals) in 1791, and 4,292 tributaries in 1802.

Spaniards established cattle haciendas here in the sixteenth and seventeenth centuries. Only seventy non-Indian families are mentioned in 1743, but the 1791 padrón shows 1,474 Spaniards (individuals), 2,291 mestizos, and 54 pardos in the jurisdiction. In 1802 there were 243 mulatto tributaries.

Actopan (more often called Atucpa, Atocpan, or Otucpa in early years; 1950: Actopan, ciudad) must once have had a great many rancherías scattered about, although we have no complete list of them nor even an indication of how many there were. The 1571 report mentions the princi-

pal settlement at the monastery, two more (Iztepec, Yolotepec) at two and three leagues respectively, and a fourth (unnamed) four leagues distant, together with an undisclosed number of 'barrios' established to guard the pueblo's boundaries. In 1593 the Indians who had been concentrated in several congregations had abandoned them, returning to their former homesites. Another congregation was proposed in 1598. Ten places which survived as pueblos in 1743–91 can perhaps be identified with former estancias of Actopan: Amaxac, El Potexé, Poxindexé, S Miguel, S Salvador, Sta Bárbara Lagunilla, Sta Mónica, Santiago Tlachichilco (1950: Santiago de Anaya), Suticlan (Suchitlan), and S Juan Yolotepec (Yolo; Otomí, Mamui). The last-named place changed its site after a fire destroyed Yolo el Viejo (= S Miguel Donica) in 1769 (ENE xv: p. 23).

S Mateo Iscuincuitlapilco (Izcuinquitlapilco, Esquincuitlapilco, etc.; 1950: Itzcuinquitlapilco, pueblo) in 1571 had an undisclosed number of estancias and barrios within four leagues of the cabecera, divided into two groups, with Tornacustla and other places in between. Six estancias are named in the 1571 report, one of which (Tenantitlan) was adjacent to the monastery at Actopan. There was an attempted congregation in the 1590s. None of the settlements mentioned in 1571 can be recognized among the pueblos of the eighteenth century: El Arenal, La Magdalena, S Gerónimo, Pueblo Viejo de S Guillermo, S Juan Perdiz, Tlaseaca, and Tlatlacoya (1950: Benito Juárez).

In 1791 there were nine haciendas, three ranchos, seven rancherías, and a mining camp (Minas del Potosí) in the jurisdiction.

Sources

There is a brief but valuable report prepared by the Augustinians of Actopan in 1571.[6] Scattered congregation data for the 1590s[7] are followed by tributary counts of 1588–1623 (Scholes and Adams, 1959, p. 57) and 1643–88.[8] A lost relación of *c.* 1743 is preserved in summary (Villaseñor y Sánchez, 1: pp. 142–3). Other eighteenth-century documents include an Inquisition report of 1754 with a crude map,[9] a short description of Yolotepec in

1789,[10] and a padrón with a useful map dated 1791.[11]

Cook's (1949a) monograph on the Teotlalpan contains additional references, as does Mendizábal's work on the Mezquital. Roquet's little pamphlet describing the monastery reproduces an interesting map of the area, perhaps from the seventeenth century. Fernández (1940–2) gives additional details.

4 *Amula*

A most arid, barren, deeply eroded country, now in southernmost Jalisco, this jurisdiction extended from the twin volcanos of Colima (4,330 m) across the chasm of the Armería river, then over a divide (Cerro Grande, 2,600 m) to follow the Cihuatlán valley almost to the sea. Surface water in the eastern part is found at the bottom of deep *barrancas*,

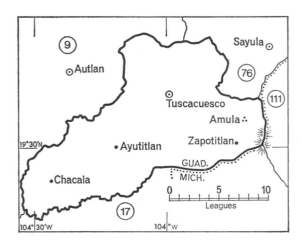

and except in a few irrigated spots vegetation is sparse and xerophytic. The westernmost portion is hot and better watered.

There were probably three major native political units here, Amole or Azmole, Cozolapa, and Tuxcacuexco. Amole seems to have had two dependencies, each perhaps with its ruler, Copalla and Teotlan (Teotitlan?). Tzapotitlan may also have been an autonomous state. Several dialects (Amultecan, Bapame, Pino, Zapoteco) were spoken of a language known as Otomí (its relation, if any, to the Otomí of the central plateau is not known). In spite of a recent attempted invasion

from Michoacán, the rulers of this area were apparently not dominated by the Tarascans.

Spaniards arrived in 1523, and one year later Cortés assigned the region and its people to himself.

Encomienda

Cortés considered Amula and Tuscacuesco to belong to his holdings in neighbouring Tuspa (q.v.), and the encomienda went through the same vicissitudes as that province, escheating in 1531 or thereabouts.[1] It is not clear whether Cuzalapa belonged to this encomienda.

Government

A C was appointed to Amula y Tuscacuesco from the early 1530s. In 1550 this magistrate was ordered to inspect a ship at Puerto de la Navidad (subsequently the AM of Autlan performed that function).[2] The magistracy was suffragan to Colima in early years. Cuzalapa was transferred from the jurisdiction of Autlan to that of Amula sometime after 1551. In the 1570s the C became an AM with residence at Tuscacuesco (at other times he lived at Zapotitlan); in the seventeenth century the designations C and AM were both used.[3]

Although the old cabecera of Amula was deserted towards 1575, the term 'Provincia de Amula' continued to be applied to the jurisdiction throughout the colonial period. From 1787 this was a subdelegación in the intendencia of Guadalaxara.

Church

The area was perhaps first visited by secular clergy from Colima. Franciscans working out of Zapotlan began living in Amula province in the early 1540s, but it was not until 1579 that the first *guardianía*, that of Magdalena Zapotitlan, was founded (Ricard, p. 86). Concepción Chacala and S Antonio Tuscacuesco had resident Franciscan priests assigned in the congregations at the beginning of the seventeenth century, but Chacala was subordinate to the parish of Autlan, and Tuscacuesco to that of Zapotitlan. The latter doctrina was secularized in 1769, at which time Tuscacuesco became the parish seat, but two years later Zapotitlan also received a resident curate. The old Franciscan *vicaría* of Chacala became the secular parish of Concepción Cuautitlan in 1800. All parishes were in the diocese of Guadalaxara.

Population and settlements

Kelly (1945–9, 2: p. 25) postulates an original native population equivalent to five thousand tributaries in eastern Amula. We might add an equal number for the upper Cihuatlan valley, a smaller but denser populated area at contact, giving a total of 10,000 tributary families. By 1548 there were only 1,744, two-thirds of them in the east; the great cause of decline was epidemic disease. Later data are scarce and unreliable (L de T, p. 108). In 1623 the parish of Zapotitlan, including all of eastern Amula, had only 365 tributaries; there were perhaps another hundred in the Chacala region. The 1743 report shows 639 tributaries, 165 of them in the west, while an estimate of 1760 gives about a thousand Indian families in the jurisdiction, and the matrícula of 1801 has 1,097 tributaries.

The non-Indian population included a good many mulattoes, mostly working on sugar haciendas. Ponce records a few Spaniards in 1587. The 1760 count has about 150 'Spanish' families, and there were 519 free Negro and mulatto tributaries in 1801.

There is some confusion about the distribution of settlements under cabeceras here. In 1548 six cabeceras are listed (Amula, Copala, Cuzalapa, Teutlan, Tuscacuesco, Zapotitlan) with a total of twenty subject settlements. By 1579, Amula (Amola, Amole) itself was almost deserted, Copala and Teutlan appear as sujetos of Zapotitlan, and only fourteen of the earlier estancia sites were still occupied, while three other settlements were of recent foundation. A number of villages were abandoned in congregations of *c.* 1600, some of them being re-occupied at a later date.[4] The following places survived as pueblos in the eighteenth century (all were cabeceras in 1801):

Zapotitlan (site changed several times; 1950: pueblo) was a principal cabecera, with Copala, Mazatlan, S Gabriel, Tetapan (Tetlapanic), Teutan (Teuhtlan), Tocin (Toxin, Tolcinic, Teocin), Toliman, and Xiquilpa(n) subject to it.

Ayutitlan (Ayotitlan, Ayutla; 1950: Ayotitlán, pueblo) had taken the place of Cuzalapa as cabecera of the western part of the jurisdiction, although Chacala was long the Franciscan residence. Cuautitlan (Cuatitlan) and Tachichilco (Tlalchichilco) were sujetos. The westernmost point in the jurisdiction was the hacienda of Tesquesquitlan.

Tuscacuesco (1950: Tuxcacuesco, pueblo) had two sujetos, S Juan and Tonaya. The cabecera was moved a half league from its original hillsite in the sixteenth century.

Sources

The cabeceras are described in the *Suma de Visitas* as they were *c.* 1548 (PNE, 1: nos. 40, 168–70, 199, 676–7), and the area was visited by Lebrón de Quiñones a few years later. There is a relación submitted by the AM in 1579.[5] Ponce (2: pp. 97–106) went through here in 1587 and left a valuable account of his visit.

For the seventeenth century, we have seen only a tributary count of 1623 (Scholes and Adams, 1959, p. 67), and a fragment from the lost journal of an episcopal visit in 1648 (Santoscoy).

A brief report from the C, dated 1743,[6] is followed by documents of 1760,[7] 1788,[8] and 1791.[9] The matrícula of 1801[10] is also of interest.

Monographic treatment is especially good, including Sauer (1948), Kelly (1945–9, vol. 2) and Brambila (1962, 1964).

5 Antequera

Geographically this was a most complicated jurisdiction (now in central Oaxaca), split into several non-contiguous segments. Most of it was in the broad, mountain-ringed valley of Oaxaca (1,500–

2,000 m) drained by the southward-flowing Atoyac river, but part lay to the north of the continental divide in the Papaloapan drainage, and it even included a piece of territory far to the south on the Pacific coast. The climate in general is semi-arid,

temperate to cool in the inland parts and quite hot by the sea.

The valley of Oaxaca was inhabited by a Zapotecan-speaking people when, towards the middle of the fourteenth century, it began to be invaded by Mixtecan-speakers from the west. The latter dominated the area for perhaps a century until they came under the hegemony of the Triple Alliance during the reign of Ahuítzotl (1486–1502). There was a Mexican garrison at Huaxyacac (cf. Cuatro Villas), and the valley corresponded roughly to the tributary province of Coyolapan. There is some confusion about the linguistic and political situation here when the Spaniards arrived. Zaachila (Teotzapotlan) had been the seat of a powerful Zapotecan king, and while the Mixtec invasion seems to have much reduced the influence of this kingdom, there were probably dynastic ties linking Zaachila with certain neighboring states. In the area with which we are concerned here, these included Ayoquizco (Guegozunñi in Zapotecan), Coyotépec, Exotla (Lubisaá), Itztépec (Danicahue), Ocotlan, Tlalliztac, and Tlacuechahuayan. The rulers and most of the people in these little kingdoms were most likely Zapotec, but there were Mixtec minorities which, we may assume, had their own local governments.

Two Mixtec communities, Zozollan and Tenexpan, were off to the northwest, straddling the divide between the headwaters of the Atoyac and those of the Tomellín (an affluent of the Papaloapan). These people carried their tribute to the Mexican garrison at distant Coaixtlahuacan. To the northeast, high in a mountain valley, was an independent Zapotecan state, Ixtlan.

Extending from the southern slope of the Sierra Madre del Sur to the Pacific was Colotépec, a dependency of the ruler of Tototépec. The language spoken here was probably Chatino, although this region may once have belonged to the inland Zapotecan kingdom of Coatlan (cf. Miaguatlan).

First visited by Spaniards in 1520, the valley

settlements were subdued with some resistance at the end of 1521 by a force under Francisco de Orozco. Another army led by Pedro de Alvarado conquered the coastal region in the spring of 1522. A general uprising of the valley Indians was quelled by Cortés after his return from Honduras in late 1526.

Encomiendas

In the first assignment of encomiendas, Cortés reserved the valley of Oaxaca to himself, but it was taken from him several times during the next decade. In 1522, certain Spanish *vecinos* from Segura de la Frontera (cf. Tepeaca, Xicayán) settled briefly near Huaxyacac before they were expelled by agents of the governor. During Cortés's absence in 1525 the acting governors re-established a *villa* at this site and assigned the surrounding villages to its settlers. At the end of 1526 Cortés regained possession of the valley and again uprooted the Spanish town. However, the existence of the *villa*, to be called Antequera, had been given royal sanction in a cedula of 14 September 1526, and three years later the place was re-settled by order of the first audiencia.

Thus Cortés returned from Spain as Marqués del Valle de Guaxaca to find his enemies once more entrenched in the middle of his domain, which included the Indian *villas* of Cuilapa, Etla, Guaxaca, and Tecuilabacoya. According to a list submitted by the marquis in 1532, the four *villas* had thirteen 'subjectos', Talistaca, Macuilsuchil, Cimatlan, Tepecimatlan, Ocotlan, Tlacochaguaya, los Peñoles, Huexolotitlan, Cuyotepec, Teozapotlan, Mitla, Tlacolula, and Zapotlan.[1] The claim was clearly based on the pre-Conquest tribute list for the province of Coyolapan, but some of these places had already been given to other encomenderos and others were assigned to the crown by the second audiencia. Cortés's possessions in this area will be discussed below (cf. Cuatro Villas); here we are solely concerned with assignments outside the marquisate and within the final limits of the jurisdiction of Antequera.

The first encomendero of Colotepec, on the South Sea coast, was probably Alonso de Paz, who also held Coatlan (cf. Miaguatlan). By 1545 the tributes had been assigned to the oidor Diego de Loaisa, married to Paz's niece, followed in the 1560s by a son of the latter, Alonso de Loaisa de Paz. Towards 1590 the latter's widow, Doña Juana Calvo, had inherited, while in 1606 the holder was Diego de Loaisa y Paz, a great-grandson of the original holder.[2]

Cuyotepec was given to the conquistador Bartolomé Sánchez at an early date (Dorantes de Carranza, p. 169; Icaza, I, p. 15). A descendant of the same name still held the place in 1597.

Half of Exutla was held by Alonso de Paz and his heirs (cf. Colotepec, *above*). The other half belonged to the conquistador Mateo de Monjaraz, succeeded in the 1550s by a son of the same name, and after 1580 by a grandson, Gregorio de Monjaraz; when the latter died (soon after 1597) this half of the encomienda escheated.

Ixtlan was assigned to a conquistador, Juan Fernández de Mérida, who died *c.* 1544 and was followed by a son, Alonso Martín Muñoz; a grandson of the first holder, also called Juan Fernández de Mérida, is listed from *c.* 1568 to 97.

Ocotlan was first taken from Cortés and was held by the crown for some years until it was assigned in the 1550s to Pedro Zamorano; he was succeeded *c.* 1562 by a son, Nicolás Zamorano de Arrazola, who in turn was followed *c.* 1600 by another Pedro Zamorano.

Sosola and Tenexpa, after being held in the 1520s by Alvaro Maldonado, were given to the conquistador Sebastián de Grijalva. The encomienda was divided between Grijalva's heirs on his death *c.* 1550. Sosola went first to a son, Antonio de Grijalva, followed in the 1580s by Juan de Oseguera, grandson of Sebastián de Grijalva. The holder of Tenexpa in the 1550s was Grijalva's daughter, Rufina, who with her husband, Melchor de Robles, survived in the 1580s; in 1597 Gil de Robles had succeeded (Millares Carlo and Mantecón, no. 16).

Talistaca, claimed by Cortés in the 1530s, was assigned to the first bishop of Antequera, Juan López de Zárate, from *c.* 1537 until it escheated under the New Laws in 1544 (ENE, XV, p. 94).

Tlacochaguaya, according to Burgoa (1934*a*, II, pp. 116–17), was held in encomienda for four lives; these were perhaps Rodrigo Pacheco (*c.* 1550), Gaspar Calderón (1570–80), María Gil (1597), and Diego de Cepeda (1639).

We know nothing about the encomenderos of Ayoquesco, Iztepec, and Teozapotlan (Zaachila); these places were claimed by Cortés and seem to have escheated in 1531.

Government

The confusing encomienda history just described turned the valley of Oaxaca into a patchwork of small jurisdictions and outlying subject villages (see map), a situation which prevailed throughout the colonial period. First were the Cuatro Villas (q.v.) of the Marquesado, governed by an AM appointed by Cortés and his descendants. Then there were other private encomiendas, and the crown villages ruled by Cs. In another category was the Spanish *villa* (a *ciudad* from 1532) of Antequera, surrounded by lands of the Marquesado.

The crown was represented in Antequera by the first audiencia's appointee, an AM (1529), soon redesignated *corregidor justicia mayor* (*c.* 1531–51).[3] Additional Cs were sent in the 1530s to Ocotlan, Talistaca, Teozapotlan e Iztepec, and other nearby crown villages. In 1552 the title of Antequera's chief magistrate was again changed, to AM, and the surrounding corregimientos were grouped in a provincia, Valle de Guaxaca, under his supervision. He was given direct charge of Teozapotlan e Iztepec, and of the encomiendas of Calpulalpa, Colotepec, Cuetlahuistla, Cuyotepec, Chicomesúchil, Exutla, Ixtlan, Iztepexi, Nanalcatepec, Ocotlan, Sosola, Tenexpa, Texotepec, Tlacochaguaya, and Zola. In addition to the corregimientos listed above, others both within and outside the valley were added to the province: Atlatlauca, Cimatlan y Tepecimatlan, Cuicatlan, Chichicapa y Amatlan, Huexolotitlan, Macuilsúchil y Teutitlan, Mitla y Tlacolula, los Peñoles, Tecuicuilco, Teozacualco, Teticpac, and Tetiquipa Río Hondo.[4] The AM was to administer justice personally in the encomiendas and in those corregimientos which had no resident magistrates; elsewhere he was to make a single visit during his term of office.[5]

About 1600 Chichicapa and Teticpac were combined under an AM independent of Antequera (cf. Cimatlan y Chichicapa).[6] Three years later the AM of Antequera was to have been deprived of jurisdiction in all the suffragan corregimientos except Talistaca and Teozapotlan e Iztepec, which were absorbed into his province.[7] However, there are indications that his supervisory function continued as late as the 1630s in some neighboring jurisdictions (Cline, 1946, p. 176).

The title of the king's magistrate at Antequera was changed again, in 1677, from AM to C (Títulos de Indias). Towards 1750 Atlatlauca (q.v.) was annexed to the jurisdiction. At this time tenientes resided at Atlatlauca, Ayoquesco, Colotepec, Exutla, Ixtlan, Ocotlan, Sosola, Talistaca, Tlacochaguaya, and Zaachila. From 1787 the powers of the magistracy were greatly enlarged with the creation of an intendencia corresponding roughly in area to the present state of Oaxaca.

Church

Within a year of its foundation, the villa of Antequera had both a Dominican monastery and a secular curate (Chauvet, p. 38). Parochial duties then and later were shared between the regular and secular clergy. The city, under the patronage of S Marcial, was a bishop's seat from 1537, and it was the headquarters for the Dominican province of S Hipólito Mártir from 1592. The old cathedral was made a separate parish (Sta Catarina) for Indians by 1551; still another Indian doctrina was established by the Jesuits in the suburb of S Matías Xalatlaco in 1595, but it was secularized some years later (Gay, II, p. 58).

During the sixteenth century, monastery-parishes were founded by the Dominicans at Sto Domingo Ocotlan and Sta Cruz Iztepec or Mixtepec (both *c.* 1555), Sta María Teozapotlan or Zaachila (by 1570), S Miguel Talistaca, and S Gerónimo Tlacochaguaya (both in the 1570s). Secular curacies were set up before 1570 at Sta María (Natividad) Exutla and S Juan Sosola. Information about ecclesiastical divisions in the seventeenth century is meager. A Dominican parish founded before 1646 at Sto Tomás Jalieza (cf. Cimatlan y Chichicapa) became in the following century the secular doctrina of S Martín Tilcaxete, while Sto Tomás Ixtlan was separated from the parish of Chicomesúchil (cf. Iztepexi). In the early eighteenth century the old doctrina of Iztepec (Mixtepec) was divided and small monasteries were founded at Sta María Ayoquesco and Sta María (Natividad) Lachixío. Colotepec, on the Pacific, had a curate in 1609 but later belonged to the parish of S Agustín Loxicha (cf. Cimatlan y Chichicapa). The Dominican parishes, with the sole exception of Ocotlan, were secularized within a few years beginning in 1753.

Map 13 shows the complicated pattern of overlapping civil and ecclesiastical jurisdictions here, as they were in the late eighteenth century. All parishes were in the diocese of Antequera.

Population and settlements

The number of native tributaries, estimated at 11,000 in 1550, had dropped to about 8,000 in 1570. After the epidemic of 1576–81 there were perhaps 4,500, and as elsewhere, the nadir was reached early in the seventeenth century. Recovery of the Indian population was slow. The census of 1745 shows 5,300 tributaries, and that of 1794 has 7,640.

The non-Indians, living almost entirely in the city, grew slowly in number from 300 vecinos in 1570 to 400 in 1600, 800 in 1630, and 1,000 (20,000 communicants) in 1766. The census of 1792 has 24,400 inhabitants, most of them mestizos (there were only 340 mulatto tributaries).

Shortly after the Conquest there seems to have been a movement of Mixtecan-speaking people from other valley settlements to those of the Marquesado, with the result that the Indians remaining in the jurisdiction of Antequera were mostly Zapotec. The Sosola area was Mixtec-speaking. Xalatlaco, at least while it remained in the Marquesado, was a Náhuatl community, but by 1590 there were Mixtecs and Zapotecs there also.[8]

The thesis of Schmieder (p. 23) that the valley Zapotecs were already living in concentrated settlements when the Spaniards arrived is not especially convincing. We see no reason to doubt that the usual pattern of central settlements surrounded by a population dispersed in numerous sites prevailed here, and that consolidation in fewer places was a Spanish concept introduced after the Indians had been greatly reduced in number.

Some congregations were undoubtedly carried out by the Dominicans in the 1550s, and other outlying settlements were abandoned in 1600–04.[9] Certain of the old estancia sites were re-occupied in later years. The number of estancias subject to Teozapotlan (Zaachila) dropped from eleven in 1580 to four in 1746. Iztepec (Mixtepec) had twelve estancias in 1603 and eight in 1746.

In the mid-eighteenth century the jurisdiction had thirteen cabeceras and forty-odd subject pueblos which are listed below. Certain places were transferred in the seventeenth century from adjoining jurisdictions to that of Antequera (Guelatao from Iztepexi to Ixtlan in 1632 [Cline, 1946, p. 179], Xalatlaco from Cuatro Villas, Xaltianguis from Tecuicuilco).

Cabeceras	Eighteenth-century sujetos
Antequera (1950: Oaxaca de Juárez, ciudad)	S Felipe del Atarjea, Xalatlaco
Ayoquesco (1950: Sta María Ayoquezco, villa)	Logolaba, Nexiila, Zabache
Colotepec (1950: Sta María Colotepec, pueblo)	
Cuyotepec (1950: S Bartolo Coyotepec, pueblo)	
Exutla (1950: Ejutla de Crespo, ciudad)	S Agustín Amatengo, S Miguel
Ixtlan (1950: Ixtlán de Juárez, villa)	S Pablo Guelatao, Trinidad Viareetoó, Sta María Xaltianguis, S Andrés Yatuni
Lachixío (1950: Sta María Lachixío, pueblo)	S Andrés el alto, S Antonino el alto, S Pedro el alto, S Sebastián de los Fustes, S Vicente Lachixío. (The cabecera was a sujeto of Iztepec, Sta María Ixtlaguaca, in the sixteenth century)
Mixtepec (1950: Sta Cruz Mixtepec, pueblo)	S Mateo, S Miguel. (The cabecera was still called Sta Cruz Iztepec in 1603)
Ocotlan (1950: Ocotlán de Morelos, ciudad)	S Antonino, S Dionisio, S Jacinto, S Lucas, S Martín, S Pedro Apóstol, S Pedro Mártir, S Sebastián, Sta Lucía, Sta María Asunción, Sta María Magdalena, Santiago
Sosola (1950: S Juan Sosola, ranchería)	S Gerónimo, S Mateo, S Sebastián de las Sedas, Santiago, Sta María Tenexpa
Talistaca (1950: Tlalixtac de Cabrera, villa)	S Agustín, Sta Catarina Lanipeo. Sta María del Tule Luguiaga

Cabeceras	Eighteenth-century sujetos
Tlacochaguaya (1950: Tlacochahuaya de Morelos, villa)	S Sebastián (barrio)
Zaachila (1950: villa)	S Felipe (Xuxucuyotltengo in 1580), Sta Catalina Xuchitepec (Quiané), S Martín Tilcaxete (Tlecaxtongo Ticalana), Trinidad. (The cabecera was more often called Teozapotlan in early years)

Sources

Bartolomé de Zárate visited Antequera shortly before 1544 and left a valuable early description (ENE, IV, pp. 141ff.). Most of the cabeceras as they were at mid-century are briefly described in the *Suma de Visitas* (PNE, I: nos. 241, 302, 335, 440, 644, 763, 846, 850). A report of his diocese drawn up by the bishop about 1570 has been published (García Pimentel, 1904, pp. 59ff.). Somewhat less than half the jurisdiction is covered in reports of the 1579–81 series of relaciones geográficas concerning the city of Antequera,[10] Iztepec,[11] Talistaca,[12] and Teozapotlan.[13]

The only detailed congregation report we have seen is that of the Iztepec–Lachixío area.[14] The remainder of the seventeenth century is a documentary blank, although Gage (pp. 111ff.) and

Cobo (pp. 198–201) traversed the valley in 1625–30 and left brief accounts. The Dominican chronicler Burgoa, with priceless information at his disposal, chose to fill four thick volumes with panegyrics of his colleagues and other extraneous material; little of interest to our purpose can be gleaned from his two works, written *c.* 1670.

In Seville there is information on Dominican doctrines in Oaxaca, dated 1706.[15] Villaseñor y Sánchez (II, p. 112) seems to have had access to other material than the brief report submitted by the C in 1746.[16] The Capuchin friar Ajofrín visited Antequera in 1766 and left a valuable description of the city, together with a crude street plan (II, pp. 88ff.). For the year 1777, all but three parishes (Ocotlan, Sosola, Tlacochaguaya) are represented by either a relación topográfica,[17] a padrón,[18] or both. The padrón of the cathedral parish has a fine colored map of the city.[19] In 1792 a census was made of the non-Indian population,[20] and there is further information on Indians and mulatto tributaries in 1794.[21] There are four interesting parochial reports (Ixtlan, Mixtepec, Lachixío, Tlacochaguaya) dated 1802–4.[22] An extraordinarily complete description of the city and jurisdiction at the time of Independence remains unpublished.[23]

Spores (1965) gives an illuminating analysis of the sixteenth century relaciones.

6 *Apa y Tepeapulco*

The *llanos* of Apan occupy a high (2,350–3,000 m) basin in the range separating the Gulf drainage from the valley of Mexico, now in the southeast corner of Hidalgo state. It is a generally flat area with a few isolated hills and numerous hollows which become lakes in the rainy season. The sparse vegetation is dominated by maguey, and the climate is very dry and cold.

Apan was a frontier province which probably had a Triple Alliance garrison to protect the border from hostile Tlaxcallan (Scholes and Adams, 1957, p. 44). It formed a political unit with Tepepolco, and both can perhaps be identified with the Huehue-ichocayan mentioned in certain

annals (Byam Davies, p. 153). Nearby was another state, Tlanalapan, a dependency of Otompa. It is not clear whether Tepepolco paid tribute to Texcoco or to Tenochtitlan (cf. ENE, X, pp. 125–6; XVI, p. 75). Náhuatl was perhaps the chief language, but there was a large population of Otomíes, and a minority of Chichimec (Pame?)-speakers.

Probably visited by Spaniards late in 1519, the region was controlled by them two years later.

Encomiendas

Tepeapulco was claimed by Cortés as part of his encomienda of Otumba.[1] It was seized by the acting governors in 1524, at which time it may have been assigned to Alonso de Navarrete. Cortés held the place again, briefly, but it was taken from him by the first audiencia, and finally escheated in May, 1531.[2]

Tlanalapa and other nearby places (Oxtoticpac, Talistaca) were separated from Otumba and given to Diego de Ocampo, a poblador. Towards 1545 Ocampo's claim to Tlanalapa was contested by the

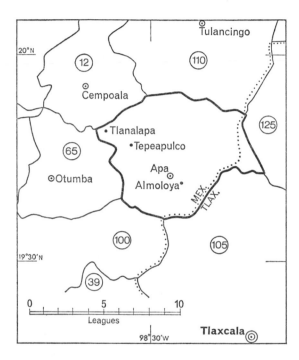

crown, but it passed to an illegitimate daughter married to Ramiro de Arellano, followed in the 1550s by Alonso de Arellano, a grandson of Ocampo. The latter was still encomendero in 1597, but escheatment occurred before 1643.

Government

Tepeapulco was placed in corregimiento on 13 May 1531. A separate C was appointed to Tlanalapa during its brief escheatment *c.* 1545, but this encomienda was attached to the jurisdiction of Tepeapulco from the 1550s; we know of no subsequent change in the jurisdiction's boundaries.

By 1623 the magistrate was being referred to as AM and was living at Apa, keeping a teniente at Tepeapulco (Scholes and Adams, 1959, p. 45). From 1787 Apa y Tepeapulco was a subdelegación in the intendencia of Mexico.

Church

A monastery-parish was founded at S Francisco Tepeapulco by Franciscans from Texcoco perhaps as early as 1527. Towards 1570 another monastery was built at one of the visitas, Asunción Apa. By 1623 there were so few parishioners that a single friar living at Apa ministered the whole area, but later Tepeapulco was reestablished, first as a secular parish (which it was in 1683), then as a Franciscan doctrina. Secularization occurred in 1772. Both parishes were in the archdiocese of Mexico, although in 1743 certain outlying ranchos were being visited from Chignahuapan (cf. Zacatlan), in the diocese of Tlaxcala.

Population and settlements

After two epidemics, the number of tributaries in 1570 was still 6,700 (6,000 at Apa–Tepeapulco, 700 at Tlanalapa). By 1588 it had dropped to 2,512, and later epidemics and perhaps emigration reduced the number to 363 in 1623, 143 in 1643, and 118 in 1688.[3] The census of 1743 shows 297 Indian families in the jurisdiction, while that of 1800 has 1,059 Indian tributaries.[4]

The non-Indian population grew slowly as wheat, cattle and pulque haciendas took over the vacated lands. Only thirty families are reported in 1743, but the padrón of 1792 has a total of 1,295 Spaniards (individuals), 651 mestizos, and 1,059 mulattoes.

At contact the Indians lived in a great many scattered rancherías, although the important religious center of Tepeapulco may have had some concentration (Mendieta, II, p. 110). Reports of 1570–81 give the saints' names and approximate location of forty-four estancias subject to Tepeapulco and Tlanalapa. Congregations in the 1590s and early 1600s reduced these to a handful of pueblos.[5] Tepeapulco (Tepepulco; 1950: Tepeapulco, pueblo) had four subject villages in 1697: S Francisco Achichipica, Concepción Almoloya, S Mateo, and Asunción Apa (by then considered a cabecera). Achichipica and S Mateo were abandoned in the eighteenth century. Tlanalapa (Tlalanapan, etc.; 1950: Tlanalapan, pueblo) had only one subject, Asunción Chiconcuac, by 1697, and it was also deserted soon thereafter. Most of the old sites were taken over by haciendas (there were nineteen in 1792) or survived as ranchos (thirty-seven in 1792). The only Indian pueblos, Almoloya, Apa, Tepeapulco, and Tlanalapa, were all cabeceras in 1800.[6]

Sources

There are two reports in the Ovando series (*c.* 1570),[7] one of which gives the number of tributaries in each estancia. The relación geográfica of 1581 is of considerable interest, although a map

which accompanied it has disappeared (PNE, vi: pp. 291–305). Ponce describes the area as it was in 1585–6 (i, pp. 114, 212).

Various seventeenth-century tributary counts are cited above. The account of an archbishop's visit in 1683[8] is followed by descriptions of the Franciscan doctrines as they were *c.* 1697 (Vetancurt, 4a parte, pp. 64, 86). Villaseñor y Sanchez (i, p. 381) summarizes a lost report of *c.* 1743. Fray Ajofrín spent some time at the hacienda of Tepetates in 1766, and his interesting account includes a map (ii, pp. 193–201). A padrón of 1792 is accompanied by a short description and a map of the jurisdiction.[9] Both the latter document and another of 1794[10] give lists of toponyms.

7 *Atlatlauca*

This small jurisdiction in north central Oaxaca was between the Río Grande and the Río de las Vueltas (= Tomellín, Quiotepec), northward-

flowing affluents of the Papaloapan. It is a rugged country, with elevations from 1,000 to over 2,500 m, very hot and dry along the two rivers, cooler in the mountains.

Atlatlahuca, a community of Cuicatecans, was tributary to the Mexica and was controlled from their garrison at Coaixtlahuacan, as was the neighboring Chinantecan state of Malinaltépec.

A small group of Spanish gold-seekers entered this region early in 1520 and settled at Malinaltépec (Bancroft, i, pp. 321–3; Cortés, pp. 64–5); the little colony was destroyed later in the same year. Francisco de Orozco subdued the region at the end of 1521.

Encomiendas

Atlatlauca was divided between two encomenderos, but half was taken for the crown in 1532. The other half, held by the conquistador Juan de Mancilla, was sold in 1538 to Juan Gallego. The latter (or more likely a son of the same name) appears as encomendero as late as 1597 (BAGN, x, p. 246; L de T, p. 86).

We do not know who was encomendero of Malinaltepec, a crown possession by 1532.

Government

A C for the crown portion of Atlatlauca and for all of Malinaltepec was appointed on 11 October 1532. This unimportant post, suffragan to the alcaldía mayor of Antequera in 1552–1603, had little to attract office-seekers. The viceroy in 1591 ordered the C not to live there because the Indians were too few and too poor to support a magistrate;[1] justice was to be administered by the AM of Antequera. However, C's continued to be appointed in the seventeenth century, and an AM lived at Atlatlauca in 1743.[2] Soon afterwards the office was abolished and the jurisdiction annexed to that of Antequera.

Church

S Juan Bautista Atlatlauca was a secular parish in the diocese of Antequera at latest by 1570. It included several villages (Cuetlahuistla, Nanalcatepec, etc.) outside the political jurisdiction. Malinaltepec was a visita of this parish in the sixteenth century, but later it was transferred to the curacy of Yolos (cf. Tecuicuilco) (Berlín, pp. 74–5).

Population and settlements

There were perhaps a thousand native tributaries at Atlatlauca, and two hundred more at Malinaltepec, in 1560. The number dropped to 950 for the jurisdiction in 1570, and 700 in 1580. Further loss from epidemics, and the transfer of the Chinantec population to Yolos (*see below*), left the area almost deserted in the seventeenth century. Only 172 Indian families are reported in 1743 and there were perhaps 250 at the end of the colonial period.[3]

Atlatlauca (1950: S Juan Bautista Atatlahuca, pueblo) had nine barrios and thirteen subject pueblos in 1548–64, but only six of the latter appear on the 1580 map. Of these, Huitziltengo and Quiotepec seem to have been shifted to the Yolos area (cf. Tecuicuilco) in the congregation of 1599–1603, while only Xayacatlan and Zoquiapan survived as pueblos. The original site of the cabecera, called Ayancua or Cayahua in Cuicatecan, was a half league east of the final site.

Malinaltepec (Marinaltepec; Malama in Chinantecan; 1950: Maninaltepec, rancho?), eight leagues northeast of Atlatlauca in the mountains, had two estancias in the sixteenth century. They were supposed to be congregated at S Pedro Yolos in 1599, and may have been physically moved to the adjoining jurisdiction of Tecuicuilco at that time. In 1699 Malinaltepec and its dependencies, S Juan and S Martín, were visited from Yolos, and we find no further mention of them (Berlín, pp. 74–5).

The non-Indian population here was negligible.

Sources

Both the Suma de Visitas article of *c.* 1548 (PNE, 1: no. 87) and a tribute assessment of 1564 (L de T, p. 86) list the old sujetos of Atlatlauca. Brief mention in a report of 1570 (García Pimentel, 1904, pp. 68, 83–4) is followed by one of the more complete and valuable relaciones geográficas, made by the C and accompanied by a map, dated 1580 (PNE, IV, p. 163).

Congregation data are found in several places.[4] A lost report of *c.* 1743 is summarized in Villaseñor y Sánchez (II, p. 144). Ajofrín (II, pp. 84–5) passed through here in 1766. There is a relación topográfica drawn up by the curate of Atlatlauca in 1777,[5] brief mention of the parish in 1802 (Pérez, end table), and a description of the area *c.* 1820.[6]

Cline (1955) discusses the Yolos congregation.

8 *Atrisco*

Stretching from the snow-crowned peaks of Iztaccíhuatl (5,326 m) and Popocatépetl (5,450 m) southeastward across a broad plain to the edge of the hot country, this is a rather bleak, dry region except where it is irrigated from several streams flowing into the Atoyac system. Most of it is at 1,600–2,500 m. Today it is in westernmost Puebla.

There were two Náhuatl-speaking communities here, Calpan in the north and Cuauhquechollan to the south. Between them was an area known as Acapetlahuacan or Huehuecuauhquechollan, long contested between these neighbors but at contact within the boundaries of Calpan–Huexotzinco (we are told that there was an unoccupied neutral zone separating the two states). Apparently there were close dynastic ties uniting Calpan with Huexotzinco and Cuauhquechollan with Itzocan (Motolinía, pp. 204–7; Ramírez, 1885, p. 83; Torquemada, I, pp. 315–17). According to Durán (II, p. 334) the influence of Cuauhquechollan's ruler extended to several neighboring states.

The first Spaniards to visit the area were Pedro de Alvarado and Bernardino Vázquez de Tapia,

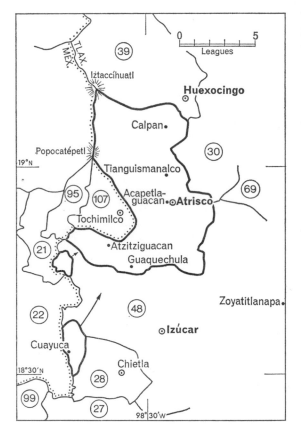

who were sent ahead by Cortés as ambassadors in September 1519, going from Huexotzinco to Cuauhquechollan and across the south slope of Popocatépetl from Tochimilco to Tetelan (Vázquez de Tapia, pp. 35–6). They found the people of Cuauhquechollan friendly to Tlaxcallan, and we know that Huexotzinco and Calpan were allies of that confederation. Cuauhquechollan, however, had to pay tribute to the Aztecs, and had a strong Mexican garrison when Cortés and his allies

arrived there in 1520. The Aztecs, betrayed by the natives of the place, were massacred by the Spanish-led army (Cortés, pp. 106–9).

Encomiendas

Huexocingo and its dependencies, which apparently included Calpan, were assigned by Cortés to himself and were held by him until he left for Honduras in 1524.[1] Later the encomienda was acquired by the conquistador Diego de Ordaz, who died without issue in 1532 (ENE, IV, p. 174; XVI, p. 11; Otte, 1964). The second audiencia then took the tributes for the crown and appointed C's to both Huexocingo (q.v.) and Calpan, but by 1541 the latter place had been re-assigned to Ordaz's nephew, Diego de Ordaz Villagómez, succeeded in the 1570s by a son, Antonio de Ordaz Villagómez.[2] Antonio was followed towards 1600 first by his widow and then by a daughter married to Ruy Díaz de Mendoza (Dorantes de Carranza, pp. 170–1). Part of Calpan's tributes were still privately assigned in the eighteenth century.

Guaquechula was given to the conquistador Jorge de Alvarado, followed on his death in 1540 by a son, and towards 1563 by a grandson, both of the same name. It was still partly a private encomienda in 1696.

Government

Crown control of this area began in 1531–3, when the first Cs arrived at Puebla de los Angeles, Huexocingo, and Calpan. It was at this time that part of the valley of Atrisco (Val de Atlixco, cf. *below*) was annexed to the jurisdiction of Puebla and began to be settled by Spanish cattlemen. There were jurisdictional disputes here in the 1550s, Calpan being claimed by the magistrates of both Huexocingo and Cholula, and Guaquechula by those of Izúcar and Huexocingo. In the provincial division of the following decade, Calpan and the valley of Atrisco were assigned to Huexocingo, while the AM of Izúcar (q.v.) was given charge of Guaquechula.[3]

The Spanish settlement of Val de Atlixco, near Acapetlaguacan, petitioned viceroy Velasco (1550–64) to be made a *villa*, but it was not until the 1570s that a new jurisdiction was created here with land taken from both Huexocingo and Puebla; an AM was appointed from 1579.[4] In the following two decades the same magistrate ruled both Atrisco and Huexocingo, but thereafter they were separated, and the limits of Atrisco were enlarged with the acquisition of Guaquechula (transferred from Izúcar in 1602) and Calpan (annexed from Huexocingo).[5] Certain of Guaquechula's subject villages were separated from their cabecera by others belonging to Izúcar, forming two small enclaves to the southwest.

In the late seventeenth century we find the neighboring jurisdictions of Izúcar and Tochimilco (q.v.) attached as *agregados* to that of Atrisco, a temporary expediency.[6] Somewhat later the village of Zoyatitlanapa, far to the southeast, was annexed to Atrisco, to be returned to the alcaldía mayor of Izúcar late in the eighteenth century.[7]

From 1708 the privilege of appointing the AM belonged to the dukes of Atrisco, a title created two years earlier (BAGN, I, p. 501). This prerogative continued after 1786, although the jurisdiction became part of the intendencia of Puebla.

Church

A Franciscan monastery was established, perhaps in 1524, at Huexocingo, from which this area was visited for some years. By the mid-1540s there were Franciscan houses at S Andrés Calpan and S Martín Guaquechula, and a third house was founded at Sta María Acapetlaguacan by Fray Toribio de Motolinía soon afterward. A secular priest attended to the Spanish congregation at Visitación (S Félix) Atrisco by 1570.[8]

Calpan and Guaquechula were secularized in 1640 (Alegaciones, fol. 90v), and Acapetlaguacan in 1755 (Ocaranza, p. 499). Meanwhile, Santiago Atzitziguacan was detached from Guaquechula and became a secular parish sometime between 1640 and 1697, and S Juan Tianguismanalco was likewise separated from Calpan c. 1750. All the parishes mentioned were in the diocese of Tlaxcala.

Population and settlements

Cortés estimated that in 1520 there were from ten to twelve thousand native families at Guaquechula

and its subject villages. There were perhaps twice as many in the Calpan–Acapetlaguacan territory, even allowing for the uninhabited buffer zone mentioned above, or a total of 35,000 families (Cortés, p. 110). Towards 1570 we find 4,876 tributaries at Calpan, 1,071 at Acapetlaguacan, and 3,665 at Guaquechula, a total of 9,612. These had dwindled to c. 5,230 at the end of that century, and a low point was reached during the seventeenth century with some 2,500 tributaries. 3,845 are reported in 1743, and 4,889 (composed of 13,151 'persons', presumably communicants) in 1755. There were 6,153 Indian tributaries in 1803.

The number of Spanish vecinos at Atrisco was estimated at over 200 in 1577,[9] and 300 in 1662,[10] while the 1743 census gives 660 families of Spaniards, mestizos, and mulattoes; there was probably a considerable number of Negro slaves not counted here. Later censuses show racial proportions within this group:

	1755 (families)	1791 (persons)
Spaniards	396	2,604
Mestizos	383	1,611
Mulattoes (pardos)	230	1,192

There must have been an early consolidation of Indian settlements centering on the Franciscan monasteries. A 1570 report shows only four subject pueblos at Acapetlaguacan, seven at Calpan, and seventeen at Guaquechula. A few of these sites were probably abandoned in another congregation towards 1600.[11]

The first Spanish settlement at Atrisco (Atlixco; 1950: ciudad) seems to have been at a site known as Val de Cristo, two leagues below the Indian village of Acapetlaguacan (= Huehuecuauquechula, S Pedro Atlixco) (Motolinía, p. 204). According to Torquemada, viceroy Velasco had the Spaniards settle at Valsequillo, somewhat closer to Acapetlaguacan, which he identifies with the pueblo of S Baltasar; the Spanish *villa* (also called Villa de Carrión) was later moved a short distance to the south, after an epidemic. Reports from 1697 to 1755 name eight subject pueblos.

Calpan (Calpa; 1950: S Andrés Calpan, pueblo),

after its early congregation, continued to have seven subject pueblos, one of which (Tianguismanalco) achieved cabecera status in the eighteenth century.

The original cabecera of Guaquechula (Quauhquetzolan, Huacachula, etc.; 1950: Huaquechula, pueblo) is said to have been moved by the Spaniards three leagues south of its fortress site (Bancroft, I, p. 528). It had nineteen sujetos in 1697, reduced to sixteen pueblos by 1792.

There were a great many Spanish-owned haciendas here. Cattle raising had largely been replaced by wheat farming in the late sixteenth century.

Sources

Sixteenth-century documents, in chronological order, include descriptions of the valley of Atrisco by Motolinía (pp. 204–7) and Bartolomé de Zárate (ENE, IV, p. 138), both written in the early 1540s, a detailed report on Guaquechula of *c.* 1550 (PNE, I, no. 260), and a census of Calpan and its subjects dated 1559–60.[12] The Ovando reports of *c.* 1570 are preserved in synthesis (Códice Francis-

cano, pp. 23–4; García Pimentel, 1904, pp. 21–3, 28; López de Velasco, pp. 210, 223). The Franciscan monasteries were visited several times between 1585 and 1589 by Father Ponce (I, pp. 154–61, 509; II, pp. 237, 522–4). Torquemada's description of the area, written *c.* 1610, is of considerable interest (I, pp. 315–22).

Two bishops of Tlaxcala left valuable accounts of their pastoral visits here in 1620[13] and 1644.[14] Later seventeenth century data are derived from tribute lists[15] and the work of Vetancurt (1697; 4a parte, pp. 65, 72–3, 87).

The 1743 relación survives only in the summary of Villaseñor y Sánchez (I, p. 346), but there is an excellent report made for the Inquisition in 1755.[16] We also have padrones from the parishes of Atzitziguacan and Guaquechula, dated 1777.[17] For 1792 there are two complete lists of placenames, one of them accompanied by a geographical description.[18]

The only monographic treatment we have seen is that of Díaz Solís.

9 *Autlan*

This jurisdiction, now in southwestern Jalisco, consisted of three distinct areas. Autlan itself lies in what was known in colonial days as the valley or province of Milpa. This valley, as well as those of the Tenamaxtlan region, occupies much of the headwaters of the Armería drainage at an elevation of 1,000–1,600 m, limited by the principal volcanic range on the northeast and the Sierra de Perote on the west (both reach over 2,000 m). Southwest of Autlan, the jurisdiction extended across a low divide into the coastal river valleys of Purificación and Cihuatlan as far as the sea, at the port of Navidad. Far to the north, beyond the Sierra Volcánica, was the valley of Ameca, in the upper reaches of an entirely different drainage system flowing westward toward the Pacific. The climate is quite dry with meager late summer rains resulting in a sparse xerophytic vegetation, although the higher mountains are wooded.

There was a dense native population here speak-

ing a number of languages. The earliest record (1525), describing the Milpa and Purificación areas, groups the people together as 'Otomies' (probably unrelated to the language of that name spoken on the central plateau), with a Nahua-speaking minority in the valley of Milpa. A mid-seventeenth century source states that 'Otomite' was spoken just north of the Cihuatlan river, then 'Bapame', and in the valley of Milpa, 'Auteco'; the first two are identified as Otomí dialects, and Auteco as a Nahua language. In the Tenamaxtlan region the predominant language (in 1648) was 'Cuyoteco', but an Otomí dialect called 'Otontlatolli' was used at Exutla–Ixtlahuacan, and Auteco was spoken at Ayutla. According to the 1579 relación, the original languages at Ameca were Cazcan and Totonac, the first conceivably related to a Chichimec tongue farther north ('Totonac' cannot be classified).

The Milpa valley at contact was a patchwork of

small autonomous states: Aohtlan (with co-rulers), Ayaoquila, Cuetzalan, Epatlan (with subordinate chiefs at Tetlixtla and Tzoquitlan), Milpa (lesser rulers at Aohtlan or Manatlan and Tlacapatlan), Teutlichanga (sub-chief at Tomatlan), Tlacaltexcal (Acapangal, Cuitlatlan, and Zacapala, each with

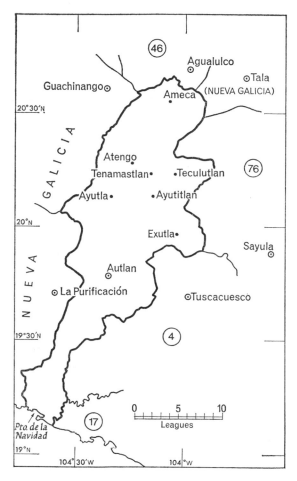

its ruler), Tlaquexpan, and Xiquitlan (two rulers). Ahuacapan, Mixtlan, and Tlilan perhaps should be added to this list. Across the mountains to the west, in the valley of Espuchimilco, was another group of little kingdoms: Apamila–Coyutla, Chipiltitlan, Instlichanga, Tequecistlan (sub-ruler at Acautlan), Xalipanga, Xonacatlan, and perhaps others. On the coast was the populous province of Cihuatlan; among the states on the right bank of

the river were Cihuatlan itself, Maloastla, Ocuil-tépec, Tecuxuacan, and Tlacanáhuac.

Returning to the upper reaches of the Armería on the south slope of the sierra, the royal visitor in 1525 found Ayotlan ruled by two chiefs (with dependent rulers at Tlepantequipa and Tlaquite-tequi), and Nocheztlan and Tenamaxtlan each ruled separately. Other states in this area probably included Atenco, Ayotitlan, Axotla, Ixtlahuacan, and Tecolotla. Ameca can be added to this long list of petty kingdoms.

Sandoval's expedition reached the valley of Cihuatlan in the summer of 1523 (Gardiner, 1961, pp. 123–6). Toward the end of the following year a small army led by Francisco Cortés traversed the area from Espuchimilco through Milpa to Ayutla and Ameca, ravaging these places before continuing north. The various native states here were distributed in 1524–5 among the citizens of the newly-founded *villa* of Colima, but there were rebellions into the 1530s (Icaza, nos. 695, 1137).

Encomiendas

Autlan and a number of sujetos were divided into two parts, one of which escheated before 1545. The remaining half was held from 1526 by Her-nán Ruiz de la Peña, followed in 1562 by a daugh-ter married to Gaspar de Tapia. Diego de Tapia was encomendero in 1597, and half of the tributes were still privately assigned in 1657.

Ayuquila and Zacapala were given successively to Diego de Chávez, Mateo Sánchez, and Juan de Salamanca, followed before 1550 by Chávez's widow, Catalina del Viñar, who then married Antonio de Ortega. This was still a private en-comienda in 1597.

We are told that there were originally twenty-seven encomiendas in the valley of Cihuatlan. By 1534 Cihuatlan itself had escheated, together with Tlacanaguas and other places along the coast. It appears as a crown possession in 1548, but a few years later half was privately held by Alonso López and Juan Alcalde.

Coyutla, Xonacatlan, and Amapila were held by Pedro de Simancas, followed on his death *c.* 1550 by a brother, Cristóbal Moreno.

Chipiltitlan and Aguacatlan belonged from

1528 to the conquistador Bartolomé Chavarrín (Chavarín, Chavarría), followed *c.* 1550 by a son, Antón (Millares Carló and Mantecón, I, no. 1697), who was still alive in 1597.

The cabecera of Milpa with certain subjects were shared between Pedro de Santa Cruz and Diego de Martín de Mérida, the latter followed in 1528 by Rodrigo Guipuzcoano or Lepuzcano. Santa Cruz's half escheated in the late 1540s but was recovered for a time by his heirs (Icaza, I, p. 249). Guipuzcoano was succeeded towards 1550 by a son, Francisco, and not long afterward by a granddaughter of the first holder. Escheatment occurred before 1597.

Rodrigo Alonso and Pedro Gómez held equal shares of Tenamastlan and its dependencies from 1526, but when Alonso died two years later his half was re-assigned to Martín Monje. Gómez was followed perhaps in the 1540s by a daughter married to Juan de Gámez; this half escheated towards 1565 (Icaza, I, p. 51; II, p. 94. L de T, pp. 98–102, 378–80). Monje's share was inherited in the 1560s by a son, Martín Monje de León, still encomendero in 1597.

Presumably all of the native states mentioned above were assigned in encomienda in early years, but for many of them we have no record.

Government

From 1524 this area fell within the limits of the Spanish *villa* of Colima. A number of encomiendas in the valley of Cihuatlan which had escheated were grouped together towards 1534 in a corregimiento, and within the following decade C's suffragan to the AM of Colima were appointed to Cihuatlan y Tlacanaguas, Autlan, Xiquitlan, and Ameca to administer crown interests in those places. In the 1550s these magistrates were given jurisdiction in nearby private encomiendas, and the C of Autlan became AM of Puerto de la Navidad, where there was a shipyard.[1] Perhaps about the same time, the corregimientos of Xiquitlan (Milpa y Manatlan), Espuchimilco y Tecuxuacan, and Cihuatlan y Tlacanaguas were transferred to the suffragan territory of the new AM, although they still appear under Colima in the 1560s. Within that decade, the justice of Ameca was designated AM of Minas

del Palmarejo, and a C at first subordinate to him was appointed to the crown portion of Tenamastlan.

In 1601 Ameca and Tenamastlan were united under a single AM, but within a few years this jurisdiction was abolished and annexed to that of Autlan y Puerto de la Navidad.[2] From 1787 the magistrate was a subdelegado under the intendente of Guadalaxara.

This area was the westernmost part of the gobierno of Nueva España, but in matters of judicial appeal it was disputed between the audiencias of Mexico and Guadalaxara. From 1578, by royal command, Guadalaxara was designated the appeal tribunal, although the order was not always strictly observed in subsequent years.[3]

Church

In early years the southern part of this region was visited by secular clergy working out of Colima, while Ameca was in the Franciscan parish of Izatlan (q.v.). A Franciscan monastery-doctrina was established at Transfiguración (S Salvador) Autlan *c.* 1543, and a second Franciscan parish was founded in 1599 at Trinidad Teculutlan (until then visited from Cocula). Somewhat later Ameca became a secular parish. Secularization of the Franciscan doctrinas occurred in 1799, in which year S Antonio Tenamastlan had recently become a parish. Resident priests were assigned to S Miguel Exutla in 1800, and to S Miguel Ayutla in 1803.

All parishes after 1548 were in the diocese of Nueva Galicia or Guadalaxara, although Autlan was still claimed in the seventeenth century by the bishop of Michoacán. The Franciscan doctrinas belonged to the province of Xalisco.

Population and settlements

When the Spaniards arrived there was probably a denser population in the coastal area than in the upland communities. Lebrón estimated an original population of 15,000 [tributaries] in the vicinity of Cihuatlan, while the report of 1525 gives a total of about 1,000 in Espuchimilco and 8,230 at Milpa. To these we might add 3,000 in the Tenamastlan area and 1,500 at Ameca, making a total of 28,730 tributaries in the whole region. Francisco Cortés's army in 1524 killed a number of Indians, and many others were sent away to death in the mines, but the greatest scourge was undoubtedly epidemic disease, first in the lowlands and later in the mountains. By mid-century the coast was almost literally de-populated and there were perhaps 4,000 tributaries altogether. We are told that the epidemic of 1576–9 was not especially fatal here, and yet at the century's end there were somewhat less than 800 tributaries in the jurisdiction. The 1743 report shows only 280 Indian families, while in 1803 there were 815 Indian tributaries.

As the Indians disappeared, a sparse population of Spaniards and Negroes moved into the vacant lands, occupied in cattle raising, sugar production, and sporadic mining. Ponce reports 'many' Spaniards at Autlan in 1587. By 1743 Autlan and Ameca were predominantly non-Indian and the coast was deserted. The 1760 count shows about 2,000 'Spanish' families, but that of 1788 reduces their number to 957. In 1803 there were 830 mulatto tributaries.

The Milpa valley had about thirty settlements in 1525, nine of them cabeceras. Some of these sites were soon deserted and others disappeared in the congregations of *c.* 1600.[4] Only three places, Autlan (1950: Autlán de Navarro, ciudad), Milpa (Amilpa), and Zacapala, survived as pueblos in the eighteenth century. Of eight settlements in the Espuchimilco valley in 1525, only one (Chipiltitlan) was a pueblo in 1743–88, and it was deserted in 1793. Down on the coast, the valley of Cihuatlan once had twenty-seven cabeceras, reduced to four or five by 1550; there were none at the century's end, and only a single ranch, El Carrizal. The royal shipyard, pearling operations, and saltworks at Puerto de la Navidad kept that bay sparsely inhabited in the sixteenth and seventeenth centuries, but in 1788 the settlement at the port had only seasonal occupation.[5]

The group of mountain villages centering around Tenamastlan (Tenamaztlan; 1950: Tenamaxtlán, pueblo) contained in the sixteenth century some twenty-two settlements, seven of which

were considered cabeceras in 1579. The latter (Atengo, Ayutitlan, Ayutla or Ayuta, Exutla, Ixtlaguacan, Teculutlan or Tecolotlan, and Tenamastlan) were still pueblos in the eighteenth century, as were the former sujetos of Suchitlan (Juchitlan), Tepantla, and Zoyatlan (Soyatlan).

Ameca (1950: ciudad) in 1579 had two subject pueblos and the mining camp of Palmarejo within its limits. Only the cabecera existed as a pueblo in 1743–93.

Sources

A unique record of the first official visita here early in 1525 has been published (BAGN, VII, pp. 556–72). Information of *c.* 1548 in the *Suma de Visitas* (PNE, I, nos. 11, 43, 63, 64, 172, 368, 493, 558, 816) is supplemented by Lebrón de Quiñones' (1951) report of his inspection in 1551–4. In the 1579–81 series, we have valuable reports from the magistrates of Ameca[6] and Tenamastlan,[7] the former accompanied by a map. Ponce's account of his trip through here in 1587 is of interest (Ponce, II, pp. 87–91, 96–7).

For the seventeenth century, we have only a few sparse population data,[8] and an occasional notice of pirate activity at Puerto de la Navidad (Gerhard, 1960, *passim*. Portillo y Díez de Sollano, p. 339). The journal of an episcopal visit in 1648–9 has apparently been retired from circulation, but a few scraps from it have been published (Santoscoy, pp. 309–11).

There is a good report by the AM dated 1743.[9] Later documents include a parochial census of 1760,[10] a most interesting description of Autlan parish in 1777,[11] and lists of toponyms dated *c.* 1788[12] and 1793.[13]

Several scholars have been interested in this area, and have published monographs from which a great deal more can be learned than the few details given here. The admirable studies of Kelly (1945–9) and Sauer (1948) cover the southern part of the jurisdiction, while that of Amaya (1951) discusses the Ameca region. Brambila's history of the diocese of Autlán (1962) contains material not found elsewhere.

10 *Cadereyta*

Most of this is very rugged terrain in what the Spaniards called the Sierra Gorda. It drains in a northeasterly direction into the Extoraz and other tributaries of the Moctezuma (Pánuco) system, which have carved great canyons into the mountains. Elevations range from 400 to over 3,000 m.

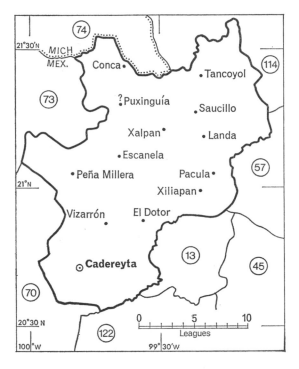

Precipitation is slight and confined to a brief season. The colonial jurisdiction coincided with what is now the eastern half of Querétaro, plus a slice of northwestern Hidalgo.

This was Chichimec country, sparsely inhabited by Pame-speakers with a related group, the Jonaces, in the easternmost part.[1] The Indians, living in dispersed rancherías with a hunting and gathering economy, evaded Spanish rule for over two centuries. There were, however, various attempts at penetration of these mountain refuges, starting perhaps in the late 1520s. Two expeditions, led by Nuño de Guzmán and Cristóbal de Oñate, probably passed through here in 1533 (Jiménez Moreno, 1958, pp. 48, 72). Explorations by the Franciscan Juan de San Miguel and a justice from Xilotepec, Juan Sánchez de Alanís, took place in the 1540s, and the region of Xalpa was entered by Augustinians towards 1550. While Christian settlements were established at both Xalpa and Puxinguía about this time, they were soon abandoned in the face of Chichimec hostility. The first enduring Spanish settlement occurred with the re-establishment of a presidio at Xalpa in 1582, and the discovery of mines at Escanela, probably in 1599.[2] A *villa* was founded at Cadereyta perhaps as early as 1627, but efforts at reduction of the Indians in the 1640s and 1680s were short-lived (Powell, pp. 60, 125, 146. Velázquez, 1946–8, I, pp. 319–20, 476; II, p. 456). It was not until 1742 that the Franciscans, this time supported by a large military force led by José de Escandón, re-occupied the abandoned Indian missions and founded others most of which on this occasion survived.

Encomiendas

We have mentioned that for various reasons the Chichimecs were not given in private encomienda and long escaped the obligation to pay tribute. In the area under discussion, the only exception to this rule that we know of was the encomienda of Xalpa which, with other holdings in the Oxitipa (Valles) region, seems to have been occasionally exploited by Francisco Barrón, succeeded before 1550 by a son of the same name. The Indians of Sichú and Puxinguía (the latter within this jurisdiction) were in theory placed under crown protection in 1552.

Government

In early years the Cadereyta region was considered part of the vast jurisdiction of Xilotepec (q.v.) or *provincia de los chichimecas*. The C of Sichú y Puxinguía (from 1552), suffragan to Michcacán in the 1560s, became AM of Minas de Sichú (cf. San Luis de la Paz) towards 1590. In 1599 the newly-discovered mines of Escanela were assigned to this magistrate, but soon afterward (by 1615) a separate AM was appointed to Minas de Escanela, which included the Puxinguía area and lands taken from Xilotepec and Querétaro.[3]

Probably soon after Cadereyta was founded (1627?), the AM of Escanela moved there. It was not until the eighteenth century that Tilaco (and perhaps Xalpa) were transferred from the jurisdiction of Valles to that of Cadereyta. From 1786 this was a subdelegación in the intendencia of Mexico.

Church

The church history of this area in the first two centuries of the colony is one of ephemeral missions. Xalpa and Tilaco were visited by Augustinians from Xilitla perhaps as early as 1550, but the churches were destroyed by Chichimecs several times before a presidio was re-established at Xalpa in 1582. In that year the Franciscans of the province of Mexico were in charge, but later the place was again visited by Augustinians (in 1693 Xalpa was an Augustinian *cabecera de doctrina*) (Velázquez, 1946–8, I, pp. 312, 319–20; II, p. 298). Puxinguía was visited by the curate of Sichú in the 1570s, and later from the Franciscan monastery at that place (BAGN, IV, p. 579). There was probably a priest at the mines of Escanela from c. 1600.

Franciscans from Río Verde founded a mission at S Juan Tetla in 1617, but it was soon abandoned (Velázquez, P.F., 1946–8, II, pp. 105–6). Towards 1642 friars of the same *custodio* established houses at Cadereyta, S Buenaventura Maconí, S José [Vizarrón], and again at S Juan Tetla; the missions were soon destroyed by the Chichimecs (*ibid.*, p. 473). Beginning in 1682 Maconí was re-founded as a Franciscan center with eight visitas, and about the same time the Dominicans opened missions at Aguacatlan and La Nopalera, and the Augustinians at Pacula (Cuevas, 1946–7, II, p. 173. Espinosa, 1964, p. 228, note 2. Fernandez, 1940–2, II, p. 37. Velázquez, 1946–8, I, pp. 473–7). All these places seem to have been deserted because of Chichimec raids in the early 1700s, with the exception of S Francisco (S Nicolás) Cadereyta, which continued

as a Franciscan parish until it was secularized in 1754 (Revilla Gigedo, p. 92).

In 1742–3 the Franciscans re-opened missions at S Francisco Tilaco, S José Vizarrón, and Santiago Xalpa, and founded new centers at Concepción Landa, S Juan Bautista Pacula, Nuestra Señora de la Luz Tancoyol, and S José Fuenclara de Xiliapan. Pacula and Xiliapan belonged to the missionary college of Pachuca, and the rest to that of San Fernando de México. At the same time, Dominicans re-established their mission of Aguacatlan and founded S Miguel Concá and S Miguelito; before 1753 there was another Dominican parish, S Miguel Puxinguía.[4]

In the late eighteenth century the number of parishes had been reduced to seven, all ministered by secular priests and all in the archdiocese of Mexico. Cadereyta parish included the old missions of Nopalera and Vizarrón. The curate of Escanela had moved to the newer *real* of S José de los Amoles, and visited Aguacatlan. A new curacy founded c. 1766 at S Antonio del Dotor included Maconí and Tetla as visitas. Eight missions were combined in three secular doctrinas, at Landa (with Tancoyol and Tilaco), Pacula (with Xiliapan), and Xalpa (with Conca and Puxinguía). Finally, towards 1790, Sta María Peña Millera became a parish.

Population and settlements

For centuries the Sierra Gorda was a refuge not only for the original Pame population but also for other Chichimec and related groups fleeing from Spanish control in adjoining areas. We know nothing of the fluctuations in this population until it was reduced to mission life in the eighteenth century. Almost immediately, in 1743–4, the Indians were struck by the same epidemic which had ravaged the rest of New Spain several years earlier (Englebert, p. 38). An analysis of the padrones of mission Indians in 1742–3, which we have not attempted, should throw some light on the demographic situation. Later data are incomplete. In 1789 there were 6,314 Otomies (individuals) at the *villa* of Cadereyta, presumably immigrants who had come to work at the mines and haciendas. A census of 1792 shows 3,456

Indian tributaries in the jurisdiction,[5] but it is not clear whether this number included the Otomíes, the mission Pames, or both, nor what proportion was exempt from tribute payment.

Spaniards, mestizos, Negroes, and mulattoes must have begun drifting into the jurisdiction when the mines were opened at the end of the sixteenth century. The 1789 report shows 3,496 non-Indians (persons) at the *villa*. That of 1792 gives 285 mulatto tributaries.

Mention has been made of the Spanish settlements at Xalpan (Xalpa; 1950: Jalpan, ciudad; destroyed in 1581,[6] re-occupied in 1640, again abandoned, re-founded in 1743), at the mines of Escanela (1950: S Pedro Escanela, pueblo) in 1599, and at Cadereyta (1950: Cadereyta de Montes, ciudad). The latter *villa* was probably founded in 1642 (Septién y Villaseñor, p. 436), although another source gives 1627 as the date;[7] it had 300 Spanish vecinos in 1697. Mineral deposits were discovered at Ajuchitlan *c.* 1700, and at S Juan Nepomuceno in 1728, resulting within a few years in the establishment of S Sebastián Bernal and El Dotor, respectively. Presidios were founded at S José Vizarrón (1734) and Peña Millera (*c.* 1776).

The jurisdiction in 1794 had eleven 'Spanish' settlements (those mentioned, plus Amoles or El Pinal, Arroyo Seco, Escanelilla, Maconí, Río Blanco, and the *villa* of Nuestra Señora del Mar de Herrera or Saucillo), thirteen Indian pueblos (Aguacatlán, Conca, Escanela, Landa, Pacula, S Gaspar de los Reyes, Situni, Tancoyol, Tetillas, Tilaco, Tunas Blancas, Xalpan and Xiliapan), fourteen haciendas (mostly in the south, near Cadereyta), and many ranchos. In that year, Arroyo Seco and Peña Millera were still presidios, while Los Amoles, El Dotor, Maconí, and Río Blanco were classified as mining camps, all in a state of decadence.

Sources

There are brief early reports for Xalpa in 1548 (PNE, I, no. 804) and the Puxinguía region in 1552 (L de T, pp. 296–7). The Franciscan parish of Cadereyta as it was in 1697 is summarily described by Vetancurt (4a parte, p. 89).

Villaseñor y Sánchez's description of the jurisdiction *c.* 1743 (I, p. 96) is obviously incomplete, but it is filled out by a good report from Escandón,[8] and censuses of the renovated missions in 1742–3.[9] Two valuable relaciones compiled and sent in by the subdelegado in 1789 and 1794 are filed together, accompanied by an interesting map of the *villa* and its environs.[10]

Additional details about this jurisdiction and its inhabitants are found in Soustelle's essay (1937) on the Otomí-Pame family, as well as in the *Memoria* of Septién y Villaseñor (1875).

11 *Celaya*

Now a rich agricultural and industrial zone in the Bajío of southeastern Guanajuato, this was long a frontier where colonies of Tarascan farmers intruded into the hostile domain of the less civilized Chichimecs. It is a rolling country through which the waters of the Lerma flow from east to west on their long journey to the Pacific. The climate is temperate to cool (1,550–2,900 m), with adequate rainfall.

The *Relación de Michoacán* lists Acámbaro and Yurirapúndaro among the Tarascan conquests of the fifteenth century. It also lists other places in this area which may have had some political autonomy at that time, among them Cazacuaran, Emenguaro, Hiramucuyo, and Tebendaho. The relación of 1580 states that a group of Otomíes from Hueychiapa settled at Acámbaro in the time of Tariácuri, who appointed a Tarascan governor for his own garrison there while also controlling the succession of Otomí and Chichimec governors. This is contradicted by an account written in the 1570s in which it is claimed that the Otomí colonization of Acámbaro did not occur until 1526–8 (Jiménez Moreno, 1958, p. 68).

Be this as it may, we can assume that the area at Spanish contact was inhabited by Chichimecs with

Tarascan rulers at Acámbaro and Yurirapúndaro. There were Tarascan garrisons at both places which, perhaps with the aid of Otomí allies, were defending the cazonci's frontier against enemy Chichimecs on the north and west and the Mexica to the east. Yurirapúndaro was a predominantly Tarascan settlement which may have had Guamare-speakers nearby, while the Chichimecs north of Acámbaro belonged to the Pame family.

We do not know whether Acámbaro was included in the Caravajal visita of 1523-4. An ex-

pedition sent out by Cortés may have passed through here in 1526, and Beaumont says that a mission was established at Acámbaro in September of that year.[1] Both Acámbaro and Yurirapúndaro were paying tribute to encomenderos by April 1528, but a number of years passed before the northern sujetos of these places were reduced, and Chichimec raids continued until 1589.[2] The foundation of a Spanish *villa* at Celaya in 1571 was intended to counteract this menace.

Encomiendas

During Estrada's government in the spring of 1528, Acámbaro was held by Gonzalo Riobó de Sotomayor, while Yurirapúndaro paid tribute to the comendador Tovar (perhaps Juan de Tovar, a

conquistador).[3] The latter place may have belonged to Alonso del Castillo in 1539 (Jiménez Moreno, 1958, p. 75); it had escheated by 1545.

On Riobó's death in 1538, Acámbaro was reassigned to Hernán Pérez de Bocanegra y Córdoba (Chevalier, 1952, p. 67. Dorantes de Carranza, p. 284. ENE, IV, p. 45). Pérez was succeeded first by a son, Bernardino Pacheco de Bocanegra, and then (towards 1565) by the latter's brother, Nuño de Chávez Pacheco de Bocanegra; the next heir, in 1603, was Francisco Pacheco de Bocanegra y Córdoba.[4] In 1625 a son of the latter who had acquired the title of Marquis of Villamayor, Carlos Colón de Córdoba Bocanegra y Pacheco, appears as encomendero (Chevalier, 1952, p. 397). By 1664 more than half the tributes of Acámbaro were going to the crown, the rest being divided between Baltasar de la Cueva Enríquez and Juan Bautista Sauza Navarrete. Certain sujetos (Chamacuero, S Juan de la Vega, Xerécuaro) were still partly private encomiendas in 1698.

Government

As far as we know, the first crown representative to reside in this area was the C of Yurirapúndaro, listed from 1545, who was given jurisdiction as justicia mayor in Acámbaro in the following decade.[5] Celaya was within the boundaries of Acámbaro, and when it became a *villa* in 1571 the C of Yurirapúndaro took on the title of AM of Celaya. Lieutenant justices lived at Acámbaro and Yurirapúndaro in the late sixteenth century.

Another Spanish settlement, Salamanca, was formally assigned to this jurisdiction at the beginning of 1604.[6] Subsequently the viceroy appointed a separate justicia mayor at Salamanca, but by 1649 the AM of Celaya was again in charge. When Guasindeo, still another sujeto of Acámbaro, became the *villa* of Salvatierra towards 1645, it was assigned a C with jurisdiction extending to Acámbaro, but soon afterwards (by 1657) the authority of the AM of Celaya once more extended over the whole area.[7] Each of the three Spanish settlements had its own ayuntamiento.

From 1787 the alcaldía mayor became a subdelegación in the intendencia of Guanaxuato.

Church

The Franciscans seem to have founded a parish at Sta María de Gracia (later, S Francisco) Acámbaro in 1526. S Pedro y S Pablo Yurirapúndaro, first visited by a secular priest from Guango, may have had an Augustinian mission from 1539, although Basalenque gives the foundation date as 1550, and the monastery was still unfinished in 1553 (Basalenque, p. 125. Jiménez Moreno, 1958, pp. 75, 88).[8] A secular priest was living at S Juan Bautista Apaseo in 1571, but a few years later that doctrina had been turned over to the Franciscans. Concepción Celaya also became a Franciscan parish, in 1573.

Seventeenth-century Franciscan foundations were S Andrés Guasindeo (Salvatierra) and S Francisco Chamacuero (both by 1639), and S Miguel Xerécuaro (by 1646). Meanwhile the Augustinians built cloisters at Salamanca (1614–17) and the hacienda of S Nicolás Biscuaro (1620–3), but the parish at Salamanca was ministered by seculars, and S Nicolás was later reduced to a visiting station of Yurirapúndaro. The latest Franciscan establishment was the parish of S Juan de la Vega (by 1743). Valle de Santiago, at first visited from Salamanca, is listed as a secular parish in 1770. S Juan de la Vega, Acámbaro, and Yurirapúndaro were retained by the regular clergy, the other doctrinas being secularized between 1743 and 1770 (León y Gama). All parishes fell within the diocese of Michoacán.

Population and settlements

Early tributary data for this region are perhaps an unreliable indication of the total population, since they necessarily omit the unreduced Chichimecs. Beginning about 1560 there was an influx of Tarascans, Otomies, and Mexicans, accompanied by a retreat northward of the Chichimecs. The number of tributaries fell from *c.* 6,000 in 1570 to 3,500 in 1580, the loss due to the epidemic of that decade. There was a further drop to about 2,000 at the century's end, somewhat more than three-quarters at Acámbaro and the rest at Yurirapúndaro.[9] Subsequently the Indian population of Yurirapúndaro continued to decline (only 285

tributaries are reported in 1623), while that of Acámbaro, helped by immigration, rose to 4,937 tributaries in 1664, 5,612 in 1698, and 7,530 in 1743. In 1802 a census shows 22,000 Indian tributaries in the jurisdiction.[10]

Spaniards, mestizos, and Negroes entered the area in the sixteenth century and soon formed an important part of the total population, mostly living in the *villas* and on haciendas. Four hundred Spanish families are reported in 1649, and 2,700 families of non-Indians in 1743. The padrón of 1792 gives a total of 11,440 Spaniards (persons), 4,935 mestizos, and 3,338 mulattoes (Negro slaves are not included). There were 1,625 mulatto tributaries in 1802.

There must have been a great many small Chichimec rancherías, in addition to the Tarascan and Otomí settlements, in early years. According to the relación of 1580, both regular orders congregated the Indians in 'pueblos formados...en traza' (nuclear settlements) towards 1560. Yet, in the year of the relación, there were still some 44 sujetos of Acámbaro, and 27 grouped around Yurirapúndaro. There were further reductions in the decade beginning in 1593 when many small settlements were eliminated. The documents mention Acámbaro, Aguas Calientes, Apaseo, Celaya, Contepec, Chamacuero, Eménguaro, Iramoco, S Juan de la Vega, Terandacuao, Tepacua, and Xerécuaro as places chosen for Indian congregations in the Acámbaro (1950: ciudad) area. Yurirapúndaro (Orirapundaro, Ururapundaro; 1950: Yuriria, ciudad) had an even greater reduction in 1594–8, when nearly all the Indians were moved into the cabecera or went to work on haciendas.

Spanish settlements were founded at Celaya (Salaya, Zelaya; 1950: Celaya, ciudad) in 1571, Salamanca (originally Sirándaro or Barahona; 1950: Salamanca, ciudad) in 1602, and Salvatierra (Guasindeo; 1950: Salvatierra, ciudad) soon after 1640. In addition, Apaseo and Valle de Santiago had large non-Indian populations by mid-seventeenth century.

Sources

Brief articles describe the two cabeceras as they were *c.* 1548 (PNE, I, nos. 36, 309). In the Ovando series of *c.* 1570 there is a detailed report (the MS is unfortunately mutilated) from Yurirapúndaro,[11] and a shorter description of Acámbaro (García Pimentel, 1904, pp. 35, 44). The AM sent in an excellent report, with maps, in 1580.[12] Ponce (I, p. 526; II, p. 134) describes the region as it was in 1586-7.

Information about congregations in 1593-1604 is found in several places.[13] Reports of 1639[14] and 1649[15] give some interesting details, and other documents provide tributary and encomienda data for the last half of the seventeenth century.[16]

A lost relación of *c.* 1743 is summarized by Villaseñor y Sánchez (II, p. 30). There are several reports drawn up for the Inquisition in 1754-5,[17] and useful descriptions in the journals of Fray Ajofrín (I, pp. 202-3, 255-60, 296-300) and Captain Lafora (pp. 48-50), who visited here in 1764 and 1766 respectively. For 1792, we have padrones of the non-Indian population,[18] and a table listing all settlements.[19]

Velasco y Mendoza's monumental history of Celaya has much additional material.

12 *Cempoala*

Now in southeastern Hidalgo, this is a rolling, maguey-covered country of volcanic cones rising slightly above a plain at 2,180-3,000 m, generally draining westward into the valley of Mexico; only

the northernmost tip belongs to the Amajac (Gulf coast) drainage. The climate is quite cold and dry.

At contact, a population of Pame-speaking Chichimecs and Otomies was mixed with Náhuatl-speakers, and all paid tribute to Texcoco (García Granados, II, p. 45), from which place calpixque

were appointed. Cempoallan, Epazoyucan, and Tlaquilpan were the political divisions, the last-named perhaps connected in some way with neighboring Cuauhquilpan (cf. Pachuca). It is not clear whether these states had Otomí or Acolhua rulers. Tletlixtaca seems to have been a dependency of Otompa (cf. Otumba).

The area was probably visited by Spaniards in 1519 and was controlled by them in 1521.

Encomiendas

As early as 1531 a portion of Cempoala known as Tequipilpan (Tecpilpa) or Zapotlan, which may have been assigned to Francisco Ramírez, was taken for the crown. The other three-quarters of Cempoala were held by Juan Pérez de la Gama (de la Riva), a resident of Puebla in 1534 and of Tenochtitlan in 1537 (ENE, III, p. 139. Millares Carlo and Mantecón, II, no. 2246). Pérez renounced his rights in favor of Lic. Rodrigo de Sandoval, who in turn before 1550 had the encomienda transferred to his son, Lic. Fernando Sánchez de Sandoval (L de T, p. 631). The latter appears in lists of the 1560s and 1570s, and a Luis de Sandoval in 1597. By 1623 this encomienda had escheated.

Epazoyuca was held by Marcos Ruiz until the late 1530s, Lope de Mendoza becoming the new encomendero. When Mendoza died in the late 1540s he was succeeded by his widow, Francisca del Rincón, and on her death in the 1570s tributes were re-assigned to D. Luis de Velasco, the future viceroy, Epazoyuca was still a private encomienda in 1688.[1]

Talistaca, together with nearby Tlanalapa (cf. Apa y Tepeapulco) and Oxtoticpac (cf. Otumba), all were held by Diego de Ocampo, perhaps from the 1520s. Before Ocampo died towards 1545 he divided these encomiendas in dowry between two illegitimate daughters, Talistaca going to María de Ocampo, married to Juan Velázquez Rodríguez. Velázquez was still encomendero in 1570; by 1597 he had been succeeded by Alonso Velázquez. Still later, the tributes were reassigned to the Moctezuma heirs.[2]

Tlaquilpa was also part of a larger encomienda, shared in early years between Antonio (Hernán) Medel and Andrés López; the other part of the encomienda was Guaquilpa (cf. Pachuca). Medel and López sold their rights in the 1540s to Lic. Diego Téllez. By 1560 tributes were divided between two sons of Téllez, those of Guaquilpa going to Diego Téllez *hijo*, and those of Tlaquilpa to Manuel Téllez; half of the latter escheated in January 1562. By 1623 Tlaquilpa was entirely a crown possession.[3]

Zacuala belonged to the encomienda of Axapusco, a sujeto of Otumba, held first by the conquistador Francisco de Santa Cruz. It passed in the 1550s to a son, Alvaro de Santa Cruz, and about the same time the estancia of Zacuala was moved to the source of the Otumba aqueduct at Tecaxete (*see below*). When the second Santa Cruz died *c.* 1569 the tributes were re-assigned to D. Luis de Velasco, by whom they were received until escheatment occurred *c.* 1600.[4]

Government

The crown portions of Cempoala and Tequicistlan (cf. Teotiguacan) were made a corregimiento under a single magistrate in May 1531.[5] Towards 1557 a separate C was assigned to Tequicistlan, while the C of Cempoala took charge of the encomiendas of Epazoyuca, Talistaca, Tlaquilpa, and Zacuala. In the 1560s the C of Tlaquilpa y Cempoala, as he was then called, was suffragan to the AM of Meztitlan. Towards 1640 he was re-designated AM, and from 1786 subdelegado, in the intendencia of Mexico.

Church

Franciscans working out of Texcoco were active here in the first years after the Conquest. Towards 1540 the Augustinian order founded parishes at Todos Santos Cempoala and S Andrés Epazoyuca; the first was soon turned over to the Franciscans, while Epazoyuca remained an Augustinian doctrina which at first included neighboring Zonguiluca (cf. Tulancingo) (ENE, VII, p. 127. Gómez de Orozco). Tepechichilco, an estancia of Talistaca, was visited by Franciscans from Tepeapulco. Both Cempoala and Epazoyuca were secularized *c.* 1753, and both were in the archbishopric of Mexico.

Population and settlements

There were 5,135 Indian tributaries in 1570 (L de T, pp. 182–3). About 2,000 of these died in the epidemic of 1576–81, and subsequent plagues and emigration reduced the number to an estimated 1,780 in 1600, and only 190 in 1643. Later figures show 220 tributaries in 1688, 438 Indian families in 1743, and 896 tributaries (Indian) in 1795. In 1580 somewhat over half the population at Epazoyuca spoke Otomí (there were still a few Chichimec-speakers) and the rest Náhuatl, while in the south the proportions were reversed.

Most of the land here was acquired by cattle and pulque haciendas in the late sixteenth and seventeenth centuries, with a consequent influx of non-Indians. In 1791 there were 400 families 'de rázón' in the jurisdiction, composed of 315 Spaniards (individuals), 638 mestizos, and 736 mulattoes and Negroes.

Cempoala (Senpuala, Zempouallan, etc.; 1950: Zempoala, pueblo) had four barrios, named in the 1580 report, one of which (Quiyahuac) was quite some distance to the north. These were presumably brought in to the cabecera in a congregation proposed in 1598. S Juan Tepemaxalco, listed as a pueblo in the late eighteenth century, was perhaps a later foundation.

Tlaquilpa (1950: Tlaquilpan, pueblo), or S Pablo, was one of three cabeceras which were moved to the vicinity of Cempoala towards 1557 so that its Indians could help build the monastery and the great aqueduct which carried water from

Tecaxete to Otumba, In 1580 it had three outlying sujetos, but these were congregated *c.* 1600 and their lands were taken by haciendas.

Natívitas Zacuala (Saquala, Tzacuala, etc.; also known as Tocastitlas Tlatepozco; 1950: Zacuala, colonia), as we have mentioned, was an estancia of Axapusco which was settled at the spring of Tecaxete, supplying the aqueduct built by Fray Tembleque (this move probably occurred in the 1550s); the Indians were charged with protecting the source from contamination by cattle. Four barrios are named in the 1580 report, and five in a congregation document of 1603. According to the latter, the outlying settlements were to be collected at Tecaxete, but by the late seventeenth century the surviving Indians of Zacuala had moved to the eastern edge of Cempoala where they formed the barrio of S Lorenzo. By 1791–2 the old site at the spring had been re-occupied by a pueblo, Sta María Tecajete.

Santiago Tequipilpan (Tecpilpa) may have been related in some way to the encomienda of Tequepilpa, near Calpulalpa (cf. Texcoco), but in 1531 it was considered part of Cempoala and became a crown possession.[6] In 1580 it was just west of Cempoala, between that place and Tlaquilpa, and had four outlying barrios, some quite far from the cabecera. In 1603 Tequipilpan itself was moved to a deserted barrio (Anazhuatepeque) behind the church in Tlaquilpa, and another settlement was made at S Agustín Zapotlan, south of Cempoala. Four minor barrios, S Bartolomé, S Juan, S Lucas, and Sta María Suchitepec, were moved in to Zapotlan at this time. In the eighteenth century another former barrio of Tequipilpan, S Juan Tizahuapan (Tezaguapa), re-appears as a pueblo, far to the northwest beyond Epazoyuca. Santiago Tepeyahualco, also a pueblo in 1791–2, is shown as an estancia perhaps belonging to Tequipilpan on the 1580 map.

Sto Tomás Talistaca (Telistac, Tletliztaca; 1950: Sto Tomás, pueblo) had three estancias in 1580, all within a half league of the cabecera. Only the latter and one estancia, S Gabriel Tehasoca, seem to have survived as pueblos after the congregation of 1603. Another pueblo, S Mateo (Tlaxomulco), is mentioned in 1683 and later as a sujeto of Sto Tomás.

Epazoyuca (S Andrés Epasoyucan; Tomazquitlac; 1950: Epazoyucan, pueblo) in 1570–80 had a number of dependent settlements, some far removed from their cabecera. Four barrios and four estancias are named in 1580, and five of these places appear on the accompanying map interspersed with estancias of Cempoala and other cabeceras in a most intricate pattern. There was a congregation *c.* 1600, after which two of these dependencies survived as pueblos, Sta María Oztotlatlauca and S Antonio Oztoyuca, both south of the cabecera, the last-named only a *tiro de arcabuz* from Cempoala. One of the old barrios, Tescacoac, is shown as subject to Zacuala in 1791. Sta Rosalía was a later foundation, far to the north near the boundary with Pachuca.

The 1791 report names and locates eleven haciendas and 51 ranchos in the jurisdiction of Cempoala.

Sources

The earliest complete description of the area we have seen is that submitted by the priors of the two monasteries *c.* 1570 (Códice Franciscano, pp. 13–14; García Pimentel, 1904, pp. 107–8; PNE, III, pp. 85–6). There is an excellent relación geográfica drawn up by the C in 1580, with maps of Epazoyuca and Talistaca and a most interesting map of the whole area.[7] Ponce visited Cempoala in 1586 and left a brief account (I, pp. 212–14). Details of the 1598–1604 congregations are found in several documents.[8]

Tributary and toponymic data of the seventeenth century are derived from various sources.[9] The account of an archbishop's visit here in 1683,[10] and a description of the parish of Cempoala towards 1697 (Vetancurt, 4a parte, pp. 70–1), help fill out the picture. A lost document of *c.* 1743 is summarized in Villaseñor y Sánchez (I, p. 147). A brief report dated 1754 has a crude map.[11] Ajofrín's description (II, pp. 195–200) of the aqueduct in 1766 is of interest. For 1791 there is a census of the non-Indian population together with a description and a most useful map.[12] Another report from the subdelegado dated 1792 gives supplementary information.[13]

13 *Cimapan*

The boundaries of this jurisdiction were probably much the same as those of the modern municipality of Zimapán, in the state of Hidalgo. It is a barren, hilly region, draining northward into the Moctezuma (Pánuco) river, with elevations of 1,400–2,800 m. The climate is cool and dry.

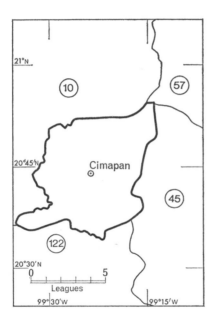

Cimapan (Otomí, Damabuesta), according to the relación of 1579, was at contact part of the Otomí realm of Xilotépec. We rather question this statement, knowing that the natives (and the encomendero) of Xilotépec pushed their boundaries far north into the Chichimec country after the Spanish Conquest. It seems more likely that this region in 1521 was inhabited by wandering Pames, but conceivably there was an Otomí outpost here, facing hostile Metztitlan to the northeast and surrounded by Chichimecs.

The area was probably visited in the 1530s by Franciscans working out of Hueychiapa, and later from Alfaxayuca and Ixmiquilpan. A Spanish mining camp was settled at Cimapan towards 1575, but Chichimec raids continued into the following decade (Powell, p. 183).

Encomienda

Cimapan belonged to the encomienda of Xilotepec (q.v.) although it was claimed as a separate grant by Juan Pérez de Cardona (Icaza, no. 1303).

Government

For some years after its foundation, the real de minas had a local magistrate known as *juez repartidor y justicia mayor*, subordinate to the AM of Xilotepec.[1] The title AM of Minas de Cimapan was in use by 1590, and after 1787 this official became a subdelegado in the intendencia of Mexico.[2]

Church

A 'casa del padre' appears on the plan of the mining camp of S Juan Bautista Cimapan accompanying the 1579 report, from which we gather that a priest resided there at that time, perhaps an Augustinian based at Ixmiquilpan (later it would seem that Cimapan was visited from that monastery). In the eighteenth century, perhaps from 1729, Cimapan was a secular parish in the archdiocese of Mexico (Diccionario Porrúa, p. 1617). The discalced Franciscans (Dieguinos) operated a hospice at Toliman from *c.* 1720 to 1788.

Population and settlements

In 1579 there were 400 'indios', presumably heads of families, living in three settlements. These were mostly Otomies, but some Chichimecs also lived in the cabecera and there were others roaming about. The 1579 report states that the recent epidemic had had little effect here, and that the mines had been gradually populated by Otomies moving up from the south. We guess that the number of Indian families dropped to about 250 in 1600 and recovered to 600 by the end of that century. Later censuses reflect the ups and downs of mining activity: 820 Indian families in 1743, 6,249 Indians (individuals) in 1779, 706 families of Otomies in 1789, and 2,192 Indian tributaries in 1800.

The surnames of Spanish miners are shown on the 1579 map. Towards 1743 there were 200 families of non-Indians, while the 1779 census gives 2,584 individual 'Spaniards', 1,113 mestizos, and 326 mulattoes. The 1789 report mentions 480 families of Spaniards and 35 of mulattoes, and the matrícula of 1800 shows 139 mulatto tributaries.

In the late sixteenth century the Indian cabecera was Santiago Cimapan, separated by a river from the real de minas of S Juan Bautista (Cimapan; 1950: Zimapán, ciudad). Only two other Indian villages, S Juan and S Pedro, are mentioned in 1579, but other natives lived scattered about, and a special magistrate was appointed in that year to reduce them to the three settlements.[3] Another congregation was proposed in 1598.[4] By the late eighteenth century most of the Indians lived at the principal real, but there were five small Indian pueblos, Guadalupe, Los Remedios, S Pedro, Santiago, and Temuté, all quite close to each other. In addition, reports of 1779–92 mention four smaller mining camps (S José del Oro, Verdoza, Cañas, Toliman – the last two completely deserted), an abandoned presidio (Las Adjuntas), six cattle haciendas, and a number of ranches in the jurisdiction.

Sources

The 1579 relación, with a map, has been published (PNE, VI, pp. 1–5). After a long documentary lacuna, there is a brief summary of a report made c. 1743 (Villaseñor y Sánchez, I, p. 132), a census of 1779,[5] and a most interesting topographic description dated 1789.[6] The last-mentioned document is accompanied by two maps, one of the real and another of the whole jurisdiction. Finally, we have a list of toponyms compiled in 1792,[7] and tributary data for 1800.[8]

Fernández (1940–2) has much to say about this area.

14 *Cimatlan y Chichicapa*

In its final form, the jurisdiction known as Cimatlan y Chichicapa was divided into five separate parts, all in what is now south central Oaxaca. Cimatlan (Huyelachi in Zapotecan), Tepecimatlan, and Tetlicpac (Zapotecan, Zeetobaá), in the valley of Huaxyacac, had Zapotecan kings and were tributary to the Aztecs in 1521, as was Chichicapan, which lay beyond a range of hills draining eastward to the Tehuantepec river. Southwest of these places, along the Atoyac and its affluents, was another Zapotec state, Zolla; it is not clear whether it was tributary to the Mexica (it appears as a conquest of Moctezuma II) or to the Mixtec kingdom of Tototépec, or independent of both. Far to the south were two other states, Tetiquipa (also called Xaltenco; Yegoyuxi in Zapotecan) and Cozauhtépec, the first extending from the summit of the Sierra Madre to the Pacific coastal plain, the second along the sea, both tributary to Tototépec. Zapotecan in one form or another was spoken throughout, a special dialect (perhaps Chatino) at Zolla, the mountain variety at Tetiquipa, and Valley Zapotecan elsewhere. Elevations range from sea level to over 3,000 m (near Tetiquipa); Zolla lay at 800–2,500 m, and the valley states at 1,500–2,500 m. The climate is temperate and dry inland, cold with greater precipitation in the mountains, and hot and dry on the coast.

The Spanish Conquest of these places occurred between late 1521 and early 1522. Chichicapa is said to have been reduced by Pedro de Alvarado, and Teticpac by Juan Esteban Colmenero. We know of two subsequent uprisings, a general one in 1525–6, and a more localized rebellion at Tetiquipa beginning in May 1547, and ending the following year (ENE, v, pp. 37–41; Herrera, Dec. 8, p. 131; PNE, IV, pp. 291–2).

Encomiendas

Cimatlan, and perhaps Tepecimatlan as well, were claimed by Cortés as part of his holdings in the valley of Guaxaca,[1] although a secondary source (Gay, I, p. 392) shows first Martín de la Mezquita and later Gerónimo de Salinas as encomenderos. Both places were taken for the crown in October, 1532 (L de T, p. 636).

Cozautepec, held by Martín Rodríguez, escheated in November 1535.[2]

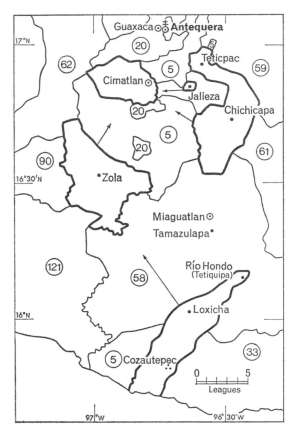

Chichicapa and Tetiquipa, mentioned together in early documents although quite far from each other, seem to have been held by Cortés until they escheated sometime before 1534.

There are hints that Teticpac was assigned either to Juan Esteban Colmenero or García de Llerena, or both, before it became crown property in April, 1531 (Icaza, II, p. 68; L de T, p. 435).

The only encomienda in this area which remained in private hands for some time was Zola. It was first assigned to Bartolomé Sánchez, then given (by Cortés) to another conquistador, Román

López, followed *c.* 1565 by the latter's son, Cristóbal López de Solís (Icaza, I, p. 15). When the last-named encomendero died towards 1598 he was succeeded by a son, Juan de Guzmán Sotomayor (Dorantes de Carranza, p. 228).

Government

C's were appointed as the various encomiendas escheated, at Teticpac (1531), Cimatlan y Tepecimatlan (1532), Chichicapa y Tetiquipa (by 1534), and Cozautepec y Amatlan (1535). There was some re-shuffling in the 1550s, when Tetiquipa and Cozautepec were put in a single corregimiento, and the C of Chichicapa was given jurisdiction in Amatlan and the neighboring encomiendas of Coatlan, Miaguatlan, and Ocelotepec; the encomienda of Zola was attached at this time to the alcaldía mayor of Antequera, whose magistrate had supervisory power in all of the corregimientos mentioned. In 1579 the C of Tetiquipa Río Hondo, as it was by then called, was ordered not to live in his jurisdiction (it was to be administered by the AM of Guatulco), but appointments continued to be made to this office for some years.[3]

At the end of 1599 a separate AM was sent to the mines of Chichicapa; he was given jurisdiction at Teticpac, but Miaguatlan (together with Amatlan, Coatlan, and Ocelotepec) was detached and placed under another C (cf. Miaguatlan).[4] Zola by 1609 was administered by the C of Cimatlan (PNE, IV, p. 308), whose territory was enlarged by the absorption of the old corregimiento of Tetiquipa Río Hondo a year or so later. In the jurisdictional reforms of 1676–1687 Cimatlan and Chichicapa were combined under a single AM with residence at Cimatlan.[5]

From 1787 Cimatlan y Chichicapa formed a subdelegación in the intendencia of Oaxaca.

Church

There was a secular priest at S Mateo Tetiquipa (Río Hondo) by 1547 (ENE, V, p. 37), and ten years later a small Dominican convent subordinate to Ocotlan had been founded at S Baltasar Chichicapa.[6] By 1570 there was a second Dominican parish, at S Sebastián Teticpac, while a secular priest lived at S Miguel Zola. S Lorenzo Cimatlan, until then visited from Zaachila, became a separate Dominican doctrina in 1579.[7] Towards 1600 the parish of Chichicapa was divided between two *cabeceras de doctrina*, Sta Catarina Minas (cf. Cuatro Villas) and Sto Tomás Jalieza, both ministered by Dominicans. Jalieza seems to have been secularized and the parish seat moved to Tilcaxete (cf. Antequera) in 1707.[8] Another secular doctrina, S Agustín Loxicha, was established sometime before 1743. Cimatlan was transferred to secular clergy in 1753, but Teticpac remained in Dominican hands until after Independence. All parishes were in the diocese of Antequera.

The reader is referred to map 13, which shows the complex overlapping of political and ecclesiastical jurisdictions here.

Population and settlements

The number of native tributaries dropped from *c.* 7,600 in 1548 to 4,810 in 1570, *c.* 3,250 in 1600, and *c.* 2,400 in 1623. Here as elsewhere the coastal region was depopulated at an early date, Cozautepec having only 38 tributaries in 1565. The 1743 report shows 2,871 Indian families in the jurisdiction, while a count of 1800 gives 4,380 Indian tributaries.[9] The few non-Indians, mostly mestizos and Negroes, lived first (in the late sixteenth century) at the mines of Teticpac and Chichicapa, and later on cattle haciendas.

Cimatlan (1950: Zimatlán de Alvarez, *villa*) and Tepecimatlan (1950: S Bernardo Mixtepec, pueblo) were long considered separate cabeceras, and in fact the latter in 1548 had twelve estancias each of which paid tribute separately, which may indicate a further pre-Columbian political division. A congregation was proposed here in 1599 to be centered in three cabeceras, S Lorenzo Cimatlan, S Bernardo, and Sta María Magdalena Tepecimatlan (Mixtepec). In addition to these places, ten other settlements existed as pueblos in the eighteenth century (Asunción, Huixtepec, Roaló, S Cristóbal, Sta Catarina, Sta Inés del Monte, Santiago Clavellinas, Tetitlan, Vigalló, Yacuche).

Zola (Sola, Tzola; 1950: S Miguel Sola de Vega, *villa*) had twelve estancias, one of them eight leagues from the cabecera, when they were to be congregated in 1599. The more distant dependencies were perhaps abandoned at this time, six or seven estancias surviving as pueblos.

Six subjects of Chichicapa (1950: S Baltasar Chichicapan, pueblo) are named in the 1548 report, and seven in 1580. Five of them (Lachigaya, S Gerónimo and S Pedro Taviche, Tilquiapan, and Jalieza [Xalieza, or Acatepec]) were pueblos in the eighteenth century; the last-named place seems to have been surrounded by lands belonging to the Marquesado del Valle. Mineral deposits were discovered within Chichicapa's limits in July, 1599.[10]

Teticpac (Titicapa, Tectipac, etc.; frequently confused with Tetiquipa, *see below*; 1950: S Juan Teítipac, pueblo) was surrounded by a number of dependent settlements which apparently escaped congregation. Only six are named in 1548, but there were ten estancias in 1580 and ten subject pueblos in 1777–1820. The most distant was S Dionisio Ocotepec (Lachiguise), on the road to Guatemala. The cabecera was at both S Juan and S Sebastián at different times. Silver mines were being worked at Magdalena Taba as early as 1580.

Tetiquipa (Titiquipa, Tetiquepaque, etc.; also known as Xaltengo and Río Hondo; 1950: S Mateo Río Hondo, pueblo), on the road from Antequera to the port of Guatulco, had seventeen estancias in 1580, most of which disappeared in a congregation proposed in 1594.[11] The surviving Indians were all supposed to settle at S Mateo, but other communities appear subsequently: La Galera, S Agustín and S Bartolomé Loxicha, and Tamazulapa (the latter was annexed to Miaguatlan sometime after 1609) (ENE, v, p. 37).

We have mentioned that the native population of Cozautepec (Coxualtepec in 1803; 1950: S Francisco Cozoaltepec, ranchería) had practically disappeared by 1565 (L de T, p. 34). There was one subject estancia in 1580 which later was abandoned.

Sources

There are brief articles in the Suma de Visitas (*c.* 1548) describing Cimatlan-Tepecimatlan, Chichicapa, and Teticpac (PNE, I, nos. 230, 762, 844–5). All cabeceras appear in the truncated 1570 report (García Pimentel, 1904, pp. 65, 70–1, 88–90). We have not examined a long legal investigation of pagan beliefs at Teticpac in 1574.[12] 1580–1 relaciones cover Chichicapa (PNE, IV, pp. 115–43), Teticpac (*ibid.*, pp. 109–14), Tepecimatlan,[13] and Tetiquipa.[14] There are congregation documents dated 1599 for Tepecimatlan[15] and Zola.[16]

Burgoa (1934*a*, II, pp. 22–70), writing *c.* 1670, gives a few details of the Dominican missions here. A lost 1743 report is summarized in Villa-señor y Sánchez (II, p. 123). For 1777, we have padrones of Cimatlan and Loxicha parishes,[17] a topographic report from the curate of Teticpac,[18] and a few other data.[19] There are parochial reports of uneven value for 1802–3.[20] The *Estadística* of *c.* 1820 has valuable information not fully utilized here.[21]

Spores (1965) analyzes a number of sixteenth-century documents concerning this area.

15 *Cinagua y la Guacana*

This region in southern Michoacán drops from the south escarpment of the Sierra Volcánica (2,000+ m) to the Balsas–Tepalcatepec basin (less than 100 m). The climate is dry and extremely hot except around Ario, which occupies an elevated plain surrounded by gorges. The volcano of Jorullo was created here in 1759. Much of the lowland area is now covered by the waters of Infiernillo reservoir.

The Tarascans settled Ario, part of their original domain, in the fourteenth century. Somewhat later the lord of Guacanan, an ally of the cazonci, conquered the hot country at least as far as the Balsas. Native states tributary to the cazonci were Guacanan (which included within its limits the famed copper mines of Inguaran), Toricato, and Tzinagua. Tarascan was the predominant language at contact, but there were traces of another language, perhaps Nahua, spoken by earlier inhabitants.

Rodríguez de Villafuerte probably went through here in late 1522. Spanish control, established after a survey made at the beginning of 1524, was interrupted by native uprisings in 1526–8 (*Relación de . . . Michoacán*).

Encomiendas

Ario was part of the encomienda of Tzintzuntzan, held by Cortés from 1524 and taken for the crown in 1529.

Cinagua and its dependencies were paying tribute to Juan de la Plaza in April, 1528, but the encomienda escheated sometime before 1533. Another early encomendero may have been Antonio de Godoy, who sued for possession of Cinagua in 1542.[1]

La Guacana was perhaps first assigned to the conquistador, Juan Pantoja (listed in 1528–33). He died about 1565 and was followed by a son, Pedro, and towards 1600 by a grandson, Juan Pantoja. Escheatment occurred after 1657.[2]

The first encomendero of Turicato was Antonio de Oliver. In the 1540s Diego Hernández Nieto claimed possession, and thereafter shared the tributes with Oliver, and with the crown when Oliver's half escheated *c.* 1563. Sometime between 1571 and 1597 Hernández Nieto was succeeded by a son, Bartolomé Gallegos, who seems to have survived until *c.* 1660.[3]

Government

While Cinagua became a corregimiento when it escheated in the early 1530s, most of the area under consideration here was administered by the AM of Michoacán (cf. Valladolid) until the end of the century, either directly or through various subordinate magistrates.[4] The C of Cinagua was suffragan to the province of Zacatula in early years (1534–6). Towards 1544 a separate C was appointed to Guanaxo, with jurisdiction in Ario, La Guacana, Urapa, and Turicato. For a time in the 1550s the C of Tiripitio governed the whole *tierra caliente*, including Cinagua, La Guacana, and Turicato.[5] But Cs continued to be appointed to both Cinagua and Guanaxo until *c.* 1600 when the corregimiento of Cinagua was enlarged to include Ario, La Guacana, and Turicato (Guanaxo and Urapa at

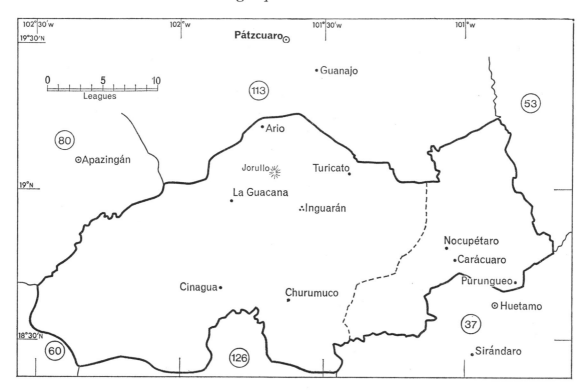

this time remained in the alcaldía mayor of Valladolid). By 1649 the magistrate, now AM, of 'Cinagua y Minas de la Guacana' (a reference to the copper mines of Inguaran) was living at Ario, and had temporary jurisdiction in Sta Clara de los Cobres.[6]

Sometime between 1713 and 1744 the jurisdiction of Cinagua y la Guacana was attached to the adjoining alcaldía mayor of Tancítaro (*Títulos de Indias*, p. 213). From 1787 the former corregimiento, now generally called Santiago Ario, was a subdelegación in the intendencia of Valladolid. Perhaps about the same time, certain distant sujetos of Turicato (Acuyo, Carácuaro, Nocupétaro) were transferred from this jurisdiction to that of Guaymeo y Sirándaro. Carácuaro appears as a separate partido in 1799, but by 1822 this distant area had been annexed to the tenencia of Tacámbaro. For convenience, we include Carácuaro here in the jurisdiction of Cinagua y la Guacana.

Church

While there may have been priests provided in early years by the encomenderos of this area, and it was visited by Augustinians from Tacámbaro and Tiripitio in 1540–67, the first parishes of which we have notice were founded in the late 1560s by secular clergy at Santiago Ario, Santa María (Concepción) de la Guacana, and Sta Ana Turicato (Basalenque, pp. 46–58). Cinagua was visited by the curate of La Guacana. By 1639 the seat of Ario parish had moved to Sta Clara de los Cobres, Ario remaining a visita of that place until after Independence. In the 1640s a secular parish was founded at Sta Catarina Purungueo, and the priest of Turicato moved his headquarters temporarily to Sta Catarina Nocupétaro.

After the volcano of Jorullo destroyed La Guacana in 1759 (*see below*), the parish seat moved to S Pedro Churumuco, returning to La Guacana in 1813. Another parish was founded at S Agustín Carácuaro before 1770 (León y Gama). All parishes were in the diocese of Michoacán.

Population and settlements

The number of Tarascan-speaking tributaries in the entire jurisdiction as described above fell from *c.* 2,500 in 1550 to 1,750 in 1570, 620 in 1600, 200 in 1668, and 160 in 1698. Later counts show some recovery, to 328 tributaries in 1744, 330 in 1789, and 603 in 1799 (89 of these were in the Carácuaro area).

Beginning in the sixteenth century, Negroes were brought in to work on the cattle ranches and sugar and indigo haciendas. By 1744 there were 104 families of 'Spaniards' and 327 of castas. The 1799 census shows 927 mulatto tributaries.

Turicato (1950: pueblo) had twenty-three barrios named in the 1570 report, some of them far southeast of the cabecera in the vicinity of Huetamo. In the same report (1570), Ario (1950: Ario de Rosales, *villa*) had but one barrio, La Guacana (1950: La Huacana, pueblo) three, and Cinagua (1950: Sinagua, rancho) four. In the congregations of 1592–1604, Turicato was left with only five sujetos (Acuyo, Carácuaro, Etucuarillo, Nocupétaro, Purungueo), La Guacana with none, and Cinagua with one (Churumuco). All these places survived as pueblos in mid-eighteenth century. La Guacana was buried in the eruption of Jorullo in 1759 and its inhabitants moved to nearby Tamácuaro, but the original site was re-occupied in 1813.

In 1789 there were seventy-four haciendas (cattle, sugar cane, indigo), 63 ranchos, and two small reales de minas in the jurisdiction.

Sources

A copy of the report of Antonio de Caravajal's visit to Turicato in 1524 has been preserved.[7] There are brief articles in the *Suma de Visitas* (*c.* 1548) on each of the cabeceras (PNE, I, nos. 167, 272, 674, 788), and several tribute assessments for the 1550s and 1560s.[8] Two Ovando reports (*c.* 1570) have been published (García Pimentel, 1904, pp. 33, 39, 47–8; Miranda Godinez, 9/33, 9/35–9/36). A very brief relación from Cinagua dated 1581 describes only that cabecera and its estancias.[9] Brief references to congregations here in 1592–8[10] are supplemented by a detailed report from the juez congregador of Cinagua and La Guacana (Turicato and Ario are not included) dated 1605 (Lemoine V., 1962b). We have further descriptions of the region as it was in 1639[11] and 1649[12], and tributary data for the period 1657–98.[13]

There is an excellent unpublished relación by the AM dated 1744.[14] The birth of Jorullo volcano in 1759 is described in several places (Ajofrín, I, pp. 231–44; Humboldt, pp. 163–7, N.Y. ed. vol. 2, pp. 219 ff.). For the late colonial period, there is a detailed report of 1789,[15] another of 1793,[16] and still another of 1822 (Martínez de Lejarza, pp. 121–34.)

Further citations are found in the monograph of Aguirre Beltrán (1952) on the Tepalcatepec basin.

16 *Coatepec*

Most of it lying in the eastern part of the valley of Mexico (now part of the state of Mexico), Coatepec's small jurisdiction extended from the shore of Lake Texcoco (2,200 m) to the volcano of Tláloc (4,150 m) and beyond to include certain headwaters (Río Frío) of the Atoyac. The climate is temperate to cold, with moderate seasonal rainfall.

At contact the region was divided between several states subordinate to the Acolhuaque of Texcoco, only one of which, Chimalhoacan

Atenco, had its own tlatoani. Coatépec itself was ruled by a calpixqui appointed from Texcoco, and Chicoloapan belonged to neighboring Coatlichan. While the predominant language was Náhuatl, there was an Otomí minority. The lower elevations were densely populated, with many contiguous settlements.

First seen by Spaniards in October, 1519, Coatépec surrendered to Cortés without resistance in December, 1520.

Encomiendas

We do not know the early encomenderos of Coatepec, which was taken for the crown by 1534, was re-assigned in 1537 to the treasurer Juan Alonso de Sosa, and again escheated in April, 1544 (CDI, II, p. 190).

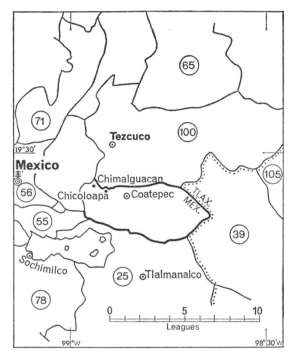

Chimalguacan Atenco was given by Cortés to the conquistador Juan de Cuéllar Verdugo (el Gitano), a grant confirmed by governor Estrada in 1528. Sometime before 1547 Cuéllar sold his rights to Blas de Bustamante, who was succeeded in the 1570s by a son, Gerónimo. By 1597 the encomienda had passed to Gerónimo's daughter, María de Bustamante, and her husband, Felipe de la Cueva. In 1628 Nuño de Villavicencio was encomendero. Half of the encomienda escheated before 1643, and the remaining half in 1670.

Cortés made Chicoloapa a separate encomienda which he assigned to the *protomédico* Pedro López (de Alcántara?), followed *c.* 1550 by a son, Gaspar. Escheatment occurred on the latter's death between 1580 and 1597.

Government

Coatepec had a C in 1534–7, and again from 1544 when the encomienda escheated.[1] After 1550 this corregimiento, considered suffragan to Texcoco for some years, was enlarged to include the encomiendas of Chimalguacan and Chicoloapa. The magistrate, whose title alternated between C and AM in the seventeenth century, became a subdelegado in the intendencia of Mexico after 1786.[2]

Church

Sta María (Natividad) Coatepec was visited by Franciscans from Texcoco in the 1520s and became a separate parish perhaps as early as 1527. By 1560 administration had been transferred to the Dominicans, and about the same time a separate Dominican parish was founded at Sto Domingo Chimalguacan Atenco.[3] Coatepec was secularized in 1752, and Chimalguacan in 1770. Both were in the archdiocese of Mexico.

Population and settlements

At first densely populated, the area was ravaged in early epidemics, especially that of 1545–8. The number of tributaries was 1,800 in 1570, 1,150 in 1579, 560 in 1623, and only 171½ in 1643.[4] Forty years later there were 700 Indian communicants. The 1743 census shows 827 Indian families, while that of 1799 has 1,319 Indian tributaries.[5]

There were 143 non-Indian communicants in 1683, 49 families in 1743, and 461 persons (mostly Spaniards and mestizos living on haciendas) in 1791.

The relación of 1579 shows the natives scattered in fifty-three small settlements (named in the document) beside the three main cabeceras. In that year, Coatepec itself (Guatepec, etc.; 1950: Coatepec, pueblo) had four sub-cabeceras (Acuauhtla, Cuatlapanca, Tepetlapa, Tetitlan) with sixteen estancias, Chicoloapa (1950: Chicoloapan de Juárez, villa) had only two estancias, and Chimalguacan (Chimalguacanejo; 1950: Sta María Chimalhuacán, pueblo) had thirty-one estancias, all within two leagues of the cabecera.

Towards 1604 the Indians were reduced to six pueblos; these were the three cabeceras, together with Acuautla, Aticpac, and Atlapulco. With the demographic recovery in the eighteenth century, two more places (S Sebastián, Jesús Tecamachalco) acquired the status of pueblo, and two barrios (S Lorenzo, Xuchiaca) are listed. The padrón of 1791 mentions a ranchería (Río Frío), nine haciendas, and two ranchos in the jurisdiction.

Sources

Reports in the Ovando series (*c.* 1570) are disappointingly brief,[6] but this is compensated by a long, detailed relación submitted by the C in 1579, accompanied by three large colored maps.[7]

Data on the congregations of *c.* 1604 are found in an unpublished document.[8] The journal of an archbishop's visit in 1683 contains valuable information.[9]

For the eighteenth century, there is a summary of a lost 1743 report (Villaseñor y Sánchez, I, p. 163), a census of the non-Indian population in 1791 (with an excellent map)[10] and a list of place-names dated 1792.[11]

Gibson (1964) gives a great many more details and citations. Colín's documentary listings for the state of Mexico are also of interest.

17 *Colima*

The western part of this area, now comprising most of the state of Colima, is a coastal plain drained by three rivers, the Cihuatlán and the Coahuayana bounding it on the north and southeast and the Armería cutting through the center, with low mountains sometimes reaching the coast. Farther inland, the Xilotlan region (today in southernmost Jalisco) falls in the upper Tepalcatepec basin, draining southeastward into the Balsas river. Elevations range from sea level to almost 4,000 m at the Volcán de Fuego. The climate is hot and semi-arid except in the higher mountains.

Colímotl, on the south slope of the volcano in the Armería valley, seems to have been the dominant native state here. Among the other political units were Apatlan, Tepetitango, Tecoman, and Alima along the coast, and Apapatlan and Xilotlan inland. In addition, we can assume that most or all of the encomiendas listed in sixteenth-century documents (*see below*) represent native kingdoms at contact. Judging from the earlier and more complete records available for the neighboring jurisdiction of Autlan (q.v.), it seems likely that there were a number of states in Colima which had disappeared by 1550. An archaic Nahua may have been spoken at Colímotl and elsewhere, although Donald Brand feels that Náhuatl was introduced here as a lingua franca after the Conquest, many

languages being spoken at contact. Here again, if Brand's thesis is correct, the record is probably forever lost. A tongue known as 'Otomí' was prevalent along the northern border, and Xilotlantzinca (perhaps a form of Nahua) was spoken in the east. The region was densely populated, particularly along the coast where irrigation agriculture was practised. Archaeological evidence points to settlements of almost urban proportions at Alima and Tecoman. The Xilotlan area, less densely settled, was under Tarascan control, and sporadic warfare was engaged in between Tarascans and Colimans.

A Spanish–Tarascan expedition led by Rodríguez de Villafuerte raided the area and withdrew early in 1523, meeting some resistance at Tecoman. Later in that year Gonzalo de Sandoval subdued the country as far as Ciguatlan and founded a Spanish settlement in the vicinity of Tecoman.

Encomiendas

During the first decade after Conquest, when the Spaniards in this region were engaged in extensive gold placer mining with slave labor, the natives were divided among a great many (probably more than a hundred) encomenderos of whom we have almost no record. Depletion of the gold placers was accompanied by drastic depopulation (*see below*). In the 1530s many encomenderos deserted

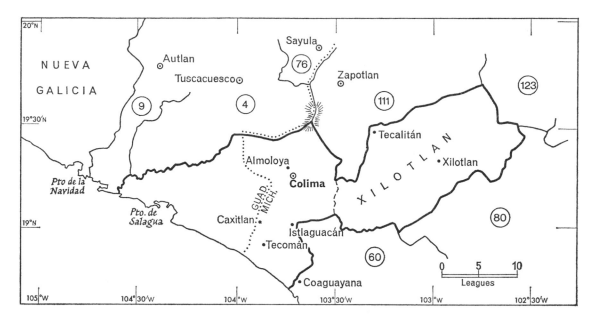

the area, and those of their villages which still existed were taken for the crown. The first relatively complete listings of encomiendas here are those found in the *Suma de Visitas* (*c.* 1548) and in the report of Lebrón de Quiñones's inspection (1551–3). This and later information is summarized in Table G.[1] By 1657 all encomiendas had escheated.

Government

The jurisdiction of the Spanish *villa* of Colima, which had an AM appointed by Cortés in 1524 and subsequently replaced by appointees of the acting governors, the audiencia, and the viceroy, at first extended along the Pacific coast from the Motines (q.v.) region (where it met the limits of the *villa* of Zacatula) northward to encompass the conquests of Francisco Cortés as far as Tepic, and inland to Lake Chapala. In 1530–3 the northern and western boundaries of this vast province were much reduced by the intrusion of Nuño de Guzmán's forces, culminating in the creation of a new gobierno, Nueva Galicia, which reached southward to the valley of Purificación and the Pacific coast, only a few leagues from Colima. Still, until mid-sixteenth century, the AM of Colima ruled a large territory, from the sea north to Ameca and Izatlan, south along the coast to the

Motines, and inland to Tuspa and the province of Avalos.

Beginning in 1531, the crown villages within the alcaldía mayor were grouped in corregimientos, which were assigned to Spanish residents of the *villa* of Colima, giving preference to those who had no encomiendas and could use the offices as a means of subsistence. Some of these magistracies suffragan to the AM were beyond the final limits of Colima and will be listed elsewhere (cf. Amula, Autlan, Izatlan, Motines, Sayula, Tuspa). Within the territory under consideration here, Cs were appointed in the 1530s to Alima (Pochotitlan), Escayamoca, Istlaguaca (Malacatlan), Tamala, Tecoman, Tepetitango, Xilotlan, and Zalagua y Tlacatipa. As other encomiendas escheated, more corregimientos were created: Acautlan y Chapula, Chiametla, Ixtapa, Quezalapa, Tecpa y Tepetlazuneca, and Xocotlan (Caxitlan), together with those already mentioned, appear in a list of 1545. The *visitador* Lebrón (1551–3) recommended doing away with these offices, but appointments continued to be made into the 1580s. The C of Tamala became C of Ecatlan y Contla, Tecoman and Zalagua were joined with Chiametla, and Xuluapa became a corregimiento, all by 1567. There was a conflict

TABLE G. *Encomenderos of Colima*

Pueblos	1520s–30s	c. 1550	1560s
Aguacatitlan	Benito Gallego	Gallego's widow	Diego de Velasco (mar. widow)★
Alcozahui, with Mixtlan	Martín Jiménez	Martín Jiménez	Juan Jiménez, son★
Alima, Pochotitlan, Tlacuahuan	Sancho de Horna; RC by 1532		
Aquixtlan	?	Diego de Almodóvar	
Comala, Cecamachantla	Pedro de Simancas, Bartolomé López	Alonso Carrillo (mar. widow)	Son of Carrillo★
Contla	?	Pedro de Sta Cruz	
Cueyatlan	Martín Monje	Martín Monje	Son of Monje★
Gualata	Francisco de Cifontes	Francisco de Cifontes	
Moyutla, Ixtapa	?	Alonso López; RC by 1551	
Nagualapa, Mispan	Martín Ruiz de Monjarraz	Martín Ruiz de Monjarraz	Son of Monjarraz★
Ocotlan, Ospanaguastla	Juan Fernández de Ocampo	Juan Fernández	Juan Fernández★
Pascoatlan	?	Francisco Lepuzcano	
Petatlan	Ginés Pinzón	Hernando de Gamboa (mar. widow)	Hernando de Gamboa
Pomayagua, Chapula	Gómez Gutiérrez	Juan Buriezo (mar. widow)	Son of Buriezo
Popoyutla	Juan de Almesto	Bartolomé Sánchez (son-in-law)	Son of Almesto★
Tecociapa, Atliacapan, Temecatipan, Xaltepozotlan	Cristóbal de Valderrama; Juan Pinzón from 1526	Ginesa López, widow of Pinzón	
Tecolapa	Juan Bautista de Rapalo	Juan Martel (mar. widow)	
Tecoman	Francisco Cortés; RC by 1532		
Tecucitlan, Chiapa	Jorge Carrillo	Jorge Carrillo	Alonso Carrillo, son★
Tepeguacan	Diego de Chávez; Mateo Sánchez	Antonio de Ortega (mar. widow of Chávez)	
Tepetitango	Gerónimo López; RC by 1532		
Tlacoloastla, Almoloya	Francisco Santos	Sons of Santos	Son of Santos★
Totolmaloya	Juan Bautista (de Rapalo?)	Juan Bautista; RC by 1553	
Tototlan, Tlapistlan	Manuel de Cáceres	Gonzalo de Cáceres, son	RC by 1560
Xicotlan, Cuautecomatlan, Xonacatlan	Manuel de Cáceres; Juan de Aguilar	Juan de Aguilar	Cristóbal de Solórzano, son of Aguilar★
Xilotlan	Pedro Sánchez; RC by 1532		
Xuluapa	Gómez de Hoyos	RC	Widow of Hoyos; RC by 1567
Zalagua, Tlacatipa	Francisco Cortés RC by 1532		
Zapotlanejo, Suchitlan	Diego Garrido	Francisco Preciado (mar. widow)	Juan Preciado, son (?)

Explanation: RC, crown village; mar., married; ★, still private encomienda in 1597.

over Miaguatlan and Xilotlan, which were annexed to the jurisdiction of Tuspa (q.v.) in the 1570s.[2] Towards 1590 or perhaps somewhat later, the suffragan corregimientos within Colima were eliminated, and henceforth the jurisdiction was administered by the AM directly and through various tenientes whom he appointed.

Meanwhile, the AM's once considerable domain had been much reduced in size. Izatlan became a separate alcaldía mayor in the 1540s, followed by Ameca, Autlan y Puerto de la Navidad, and the province of Avalos in the following decade. Motines and Tuspa (with Tamazula and Zapotlan) had their own AMs from c. 1560, as did the province of Amula from the 1570s. After this, there were minor adjustments in the jurisdiction's boundaries. The valley of Alima, long disputed between Colima and Motines, was divided between them in 1603–4; from this time Alima remained in Colima while Xolotlan and its dependencies were given to Motines.[3] Somewhat later, the old corregimiento of Xilotlan, far to the east, was assigned as an agregado to the jurisdiction of Colima.

While in an administrative sense Colima belonged to the gobierno of Nueva España and its AM was appointed by the viceroy, in matters of judicial appeal the region was disputed between the audiencias of Mexico and Guadalaxara. In 1578 a royal order fixed the boundary between the two audiencias, giving neighboring Autlan to Guadalaxara and Colima to Mexico.[4] From 1787 Colima was a subdelegación in the intendencia of Valladolid, although the first subdelegado did not replace the AM until 1790. Five years later the jurisdiction was transferred to the intendencia of Guadalaxara, but judicial appeals continued to go to Mexico.

Church

A secular curate resided at S Sebastián (Santiago from 1554; S Felipe de Jesús from 1668) Colima as early as 1525 (Chauvet, p. 38). Franciscans from the province of Xalisco in 1554 founded a monastery just outside the *villa* at S Francisco Almoloya for the ministration of the Indians.[5] The two parishes, secular and regular, continued until 1767 when Almoloya was secularized. In 1789 parochial duties within the *villa* were being shared between secular clergy and the orders of La Merced, S Francisco, and S Juan de Dios.

Another secular parish was established sometime before 1571 in the valley of Caxitlan at S José Tecolapa. The priest moved his headquarters in the 1640s to S Francisco Caxitlan, and again in 1806 to Santiago Tecomán.

S Salvador Chamila, in the neighboring jurisdiction of Motines, became the residence of a secular curate as a result of the congregations of c. 1600. This priest visited the entire Alima–Coahuayana valley, and by 1738 he was living at Concepción Istlaguacán. Two more parishes (secular) were created in 1803, at Guadalupe Tecalitán and S Miguel Xilotlan, until then visitas of Tuspa and Tepalcatepec, respectively.

There was an early jurisdictional dispute here between the bishops of Michoacán and Nueva Galicia (Guadalaxara). It was resolved in 1550, when the alcaldía mayor was divided ecclesiastic-

ally along the Armería river, the western half being assigned to Nueva Galicia and the rest to Michoacán. The few settlements west of the Armería were still being visited in the eighteenth century by Franciscans from Autlan and Chacala. In 1795 the eastern part of the jurisdiction was transferred from the diocese of Michoacán to that of Guadalaxara (cf. *Colección de documentos...
Guadalajara*, I, pp. 150–1).

Population and settlements

Epidemics reduced the native population of this area from about 300,000 persons at contact to perhaps 1,800 tributaries in 1570. The greatest loss seems to have occurred in a series of plagues between 1531 and 1540, and in the great *cocoliztli* of 1545–8. Contributing factors other than disease (e.g., mistreatment) were probably responsible for a small part of this decline. Here, as elsewhere, the lowlands were depopulated first and the higher areas later. There were probably about a thousand Indian tributaries in the jurisdiction in 1600. Later censuses show 400 tributaries in 1657 and 459 in 1698, 796 Indian families in 1744, 957 in 1789, and 1,084 Indian tributaries in 1802.

A considerable number of Indian communities, particularly in the lowlands, disappeared within a relatively short time, some because all their inhabitants had died and others as a result of combining two or more settlements in a single congregation. Slightly more than a hundred pueblos survived at the time of Lebrón's inspection (1553), but many of these had only a handful of residents. There were forty-four Indian pueblos in the parishes of Colima and Tecolapa in 1571, plus a few west of the Armería and at Xilotlan, say a total of fifty. Congregations in the 1590s and early 1600s reduced the number to about twenty-five.[6] These were mostly some distance inland, perhaps a result of repeated orders to leave the coast uninhabited and thus reduce the incentive for piratical incursions (Gerhard, 1960, p. 79). Three places, Alcozahui, Alima, and Tlacuaguayan, were deserted between 1639 and 1657. Five more, Coatlan, Tecocitlan, Tecolapa, Xiloteupa, and Zumpalmani, had disappeared by 1744, and another, Nagualapa, was destroyed by a flood in

1773. By the late eighteenth century the erstwhile Indian pueblos of Almoloya and Caxitlan had become mestizo settlements, and only twelve Indian communities (all considered cabeceras) survived: Acautlan, Comala, Coquimatlan, Istlaguacán, Quezalapa, Tamala, Tecomán, Totolmaloya, Xilotlan, Xuchitlan, Xuluapa, and Zacualpa.

The Spanish *villa* of Colima (1950: ciudad, Col.), founded in the fall of 1523 near Tecoman, was moved to a new townsite (the present location) some leagues farther inland in 1525. The Indians occupying the second site are said to have emigrated to Tuspa at this time.[7] Originally there were 145 Spanish vecinos, but there was a general exodus in the 1530s (*Actas de cabildo...*, III, p. 89), and Lebrón states that only ten families lived there in 1551. Later sources show 60 vecinos in 1571, 40 in 1580,[8] 70 in 1587, 150 in 1649, and 322 (Spanish and mestizo families) in 1744. In 1789 the *villa* had 2,117 Spanish and mestizo and 1,580 mulatto communicants.

Elsewhere in the jurisdiction, non-Indian immigrants, especially Negroes brought to work on the cattle haciendas and cacao and coco plantations, and a number of 'chinos' (Filipinos), began to appear in the second half of the sixteenth century (ENE, VI, p. 149). By the late eighteenth century mulattoes were the largest element (43 per cent) in the total population; there were almost equal numbers of 'Spaniards' and Indians, and relatively few 'mestizos', according to the padrones (many of mixed ancestry must have acquired *limpieza de sangre* certificates). The census of 1802 has 1,221 mulatto tributaries.[9]

An energetic AM in the 1770s founded a number of non-Indian communities in the old corregimiento of Xilotlan, an area which had been almost deserted since the sixteenth century. Tecalitán (1950: Tecalitlán, pueblo, Jal.), established in 1774, had a population of over 1,500, mostly 'Spanish', fifteen years later. The mining camps of Sta María del Favor, El Oro, and El Sombrero, revived at this time, exploited ores perhaps first worked by the Tarascans and later by Cortés.

In addition to the settlements mentioned, in 1793 there were twenty-four haciendas and thirty-eight ranchos in the jurisdiction.

Sources

What may have been a valuable document describing Colima in 1532 is unfortunately sadly garbled in a nineteenth-century copy.[10] Entries for this area in the *Suma de Visitas* of *c.* 1548 (PNE, I, *passim*) are supplemented by the report of Lebrón de Quiñones's visit in 1551–3. The *Libro de las Tasaciones* has numerous tribute assessments of places in Colima, mostly from the 1560s. Reports in the Ovando series (1571) are disappointingly brief (López de Velasco, p. 244; Miranda Godínez), and a relación of *c.* 1580 has disappeared. Father Ponce's journal (II, pp. 106–9) describes Colima as he saw it in 1587.

Two most interesting reports dated 1639[11] and 1649[12] are followed by tributary data of 1657–98.[13] Villaseñor y Sánchez (II, p. 83) omitted many details of interest in his summary of a document submitted by the AM in 1744.[14] A description of the corregimiento of Xilotlan in 1776 has been misplaced, but the map which accompanied it has been preserved.[15] The parish of Istlaguacán is represented by an excellent report in the 'topographic' series sent in by the curate in 1777.[16] For the late eighteenth century, we have valuable descriptions dated 1789[17] and 1793[18] (the first with two maps), and a list of settlements in 1793.[19]

The harbors and littoral are described in several illustrated coast pilots and pirate accounts.[20]

Much further information about Colima in the sixteenth century is found in Sauer's exemplary monograph (1948). Brambila (1964) gives details of ecclesiastical foundations.

18 Córdoba

Roughly coterminous with the Aztec tributary province of Cuauhtochco, this jurisdiction extended from the slopes of snow-capped Citaltépetl (Pico de Orizaba) to the gulf coastal plain. The inhabited part is at an elevation of 250–2,000+

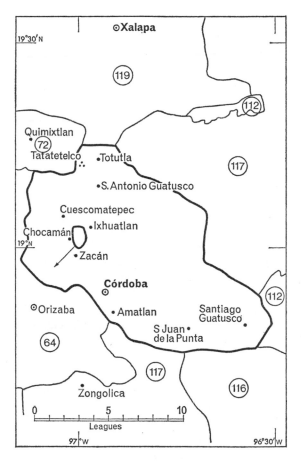

m and thus there is a wide temperature variation with rain much of the year producing an exuberant flora. The area is now in Veracruz state.

The Náhuatl-speaking people here were grouped at contact into at least six states, Cuauhtochco, Itzteyocan, Teohzoltzapotlan, Tlatlactetelco (= Cuauhtetelco), Tototlan, and Tuchzonco. Axocapan and Tenexapan may also have

had a certain autonomy. There were Triple Alliance garrisons at Atzacan, Cuauhtochco, and Itzteyocan. On the side of the volcano near Tuchzonco were vast granaries (Cuexcomatépec) where the Aztecs stored their corn. The native population must have been considerable, over 20,000 'casas' being reported at Tlatlactetelco alone (Aguilar, p. 88).

The Mexican garrisons remained loyal to Moctezuma, and were defeated by Gonzalo de Sandoval in November 1521 (Bancroft, II, p. 32; Gardiner, 1958, p. 54; 1961, p. 103). Sandoval then founded the Spanish *villa* of Medellín at or near Tlatlactetelco, but it was moved to the coast in 1523 (Cortés, p. 233; ENE, I, p. 84).

Encomiendas

Guatusco and Istayuca were held by Francisco de Bonal until they were taken for the crown *c.* 1535.[1]

In 1525 the ayuntamiento of Medellín asked to be given the encomienda of Tatatetelco, but apparently the place was assigned to Diego de Ocampo instead (ENE, I, p. 84). Half of this grant escheated in June 1545, while later it was re-assigned to two daughters of Ocampo married to Ramiro de Arellano and Juan Velázquez Rodríguez. D. Alonso de Arellano succeeded on his father's death in 1552. Final escheatment occurred before the end of the century.[2]

The remaining encomiendas in this jurisdiction have no apparent relationship to the pre-Columbian political divisions mentioned above. Some of these places, such as Tozongo-Cuescomatepec, were perhaps re-born with new names. Tezulzapotla (Teohzoltzapotlan) may have formed part of the encomienda of Guatusco.

Two small villages, Cintla and Tepetlachco, belonged to Martín de Mafra *c.* 1569 and were still held by him in 1597; they seem to have escheated soon afterward.

The first encomendero of Chocaman and Tozongo (= Cuescomatepec?) was the conquistador Sebastián Rodríguez, succeeded before 1560

6-2

by his widow, María de Villanueva. Escheatment occurred on the latter's death in 1606, but tributes were re-assigned in the seventeenth century.[3]

Ixguatlan was held by Gregorio de Villalobos, a conquistador and resident of Puebla, followed towards 1550 by a son. When the latter died *c.* 1565 the tributes were assigned to D. Luis de Velasco, continuing after Velasco's death (1617) as part of the holdings of the Marquesado de Salinas.[4]

Otlaquistla (= Acatepec, or S Antonio Guatusco) was given by Cortés to the conquistador Juan López de Ximena (a vecino of Vera Cruz), succeeded on his death (by 1540) by a son, Pedro de Nava. In 1597–1604 Diego de Nava, grandson of the first holder, was encomendero; he was followed in 1628 by a daughter, Juana de Nava. By 1664 the tributes had been re-assigned to one of the Moctezuma heirs.[5]

Government

A C was first appointed to Guatusco e Istayuca when that encomienda escheated towards 1535. The jurisdiction, to which other encomiendas were added in the 1550s, survived intact until Independence, with lapses. In 1560, for example, the C of distant Ayutla y Tepeapa (cf. Teutila) administered justice here,[6] and in 1580–81 royal authority in 'San Antonio' was temporarily given to the C of Tustepec y Quimistlan (cf. San Juan de los Llanos) because the regular magistrate was absent.[7] In the 1560s and later Guatusco was suffragan to Vera Cruz, and in 1575 a single C was in charge of Guatusco and Chichiquila (cf. Orizaba).[8]

When the *villa* of Córdoba was founded, apparently on land belonging to S Antonio, in 1618, the C of Guatusco became justice and eventually AM of Córdoba. During the eighteenth century the magistrate lived at Córdoba and kept tenientes at Cuescomatepec, S Antonio Guatusco, and Zacán. After 1787 he was designated sub-delegado, under the intendente of Vera Cruz.

Church

In the earliest ecclesiastical division known to us, towards 1569, there was a secular priest at Santiago Guatusco who visited most of the jurisdiction; S Antonio Guatusco (Acatepec) at that time was a visita of Quimixtlan (cf. S Juan de los Llanos). By 1609 S Antonio had become a separate parish, and in 1617 a curate also lived at S Juan Cuescomatepec. The parish seat of Santiago Guatusco was moved to Córdoba after 1618.

By 1744 the three parishes mentioned had been divided into six, curates residing at S Pedro Ixhuatlan, S Juan de la Punta, and Sta Ana Zacán. In 1777 there were two more, Amatlan de los Reyes and Santiago Totutla. All were in the diocese of Tlaxcala.

Population and settlements

By mid-sixteenth century most of the native population here had been wiped out by European diseases. Aguilar, writing about 1560, states that only 200 tributaries then survived at Tatatetelco, a hundredth of the original total (Aguilar, p. 88). Reports of *c.* 1570 show some 1,400 tributaries in the jurisdiction, but these were further reduced to 440 in 1626. Subsequent data give 850 tributaries in 1643, 1,391 in 1696, 2,423 in 1744, and 2,354 in 1800.

We have no complete list of sixteenth-century settlements, which would enable us to determine cabecera-sujeto relationships. Santiago Guatusco (1950: El Tamarindo, congregación?) is listed with two dependencies, Istayuca and Tezulzapotla, in 1560.[9] In 1626–9 Guatusco and Ocotitlan (perhaps the same as S Juan Tetitlan, a barrio in or near Córdoba) are mentioned together.

What became known as S Antonio Guatusco (1950: Huatusco de Chicuellar, ciudad) has a most confusing toponymic history. In the sixteenth century it is variously referred to as Acatepec, Utlaquiquistla, Xicayan, or simply S Antonio (we are not sure that all these names apply to the same place). In 1609 what is now Huatusco was called S Antonio Acatepec, while later in that century the town was known as S Antonio Otlaquiquistlan or Otlaquistlan. 'S Antonio Guatusco' appears towards 1615 and was the usual designation in the eighteenth century (Vázquez de Espinosa, 1948, p. 267).

Certain Indian communities either were moved about or disappeared in the congregations of 1598–1604.[10] Istayuca (Ixteyuca) and Tezulzapotla, together with S Juan Tenexapa(n), may have been abandoned at this time (cf. Barlow, 1949, p. 90). Tlatlactetelco (Tatatetelco, Tatatetela; 1950: Tlaltetela, pueblo?) appears to have been reduced to S Diego (Metitlan).

Fourteen places survived as Indian pueblos in the eighteenth century: Alpatlagua, Amatlan, S Bartolomé Axocoapa, S Salvador Calcagualco, Comapan, Cuescomatepec, Chocaman, S Antonio Guatusco, Santiago Guatusco, Ixhuatlan, S Diego Metitlan, Santiago Totutla, Zacan, and Zentla.

The *villa* of Medellín was more a legalistic than a real foundation, probably not more than a handful of Spaniards residing at the first site at Tatatetelco (1521–3). Some years later in the same century cattle and sugar haciendas were formed on the deserted Indian lands, with both Indian and Negro laborers, and many of the latter escaped from servitude and for some years maintained a virtually independent existence on the slopes of the Pico de Orizaba under the leadership of the *caudillo* Yanga, assaulting haciendas and travellers. An expedition was sent against them in 1609, a truce was arranged, and they were settled in a predominantly Negro community, S Lorenzo (Cerralvo; 1950: Yanga, pueblo). The Spanish *villa* of Córdoba (founded in 1618) was intended to defend the area against future uprisings, but as late as 1744 the AM asked for troops to quell some Negro insurgents. The *villa* had fifty Spanish vecinos in 1643. A century later it had grown to 258 families of Spaniards, 126 of mestizos, 79 of mulattoes, and 273 of Indians, the latter living in three barrios. In the whole jurisdiction in 1744 there were 600 families of Spaniards and mestizos and 633 of Negroes and mulattoes, not counting Negro slaves; in that year 33 sugar cane *trapiches* were being operated.

Sources

We know very little about this jurisdiction in the sixteenth century, beyond a few details provided in two reports of the Ovando series (*c.* 1570) (García Pimentel, 1904, p. 16. PNE, v, pp. 244–5). The journals of episcopal visits here in 1609,[11] 1617,[12] and 1643[13] show the area at a crucial point in its history. The tributary population in 1626–96 has been calculated from tax records.[14]

A useful report by the AM dated 1744[15] is summarized by Villaseñor y Sánchez (I, p. 264). Fray Ajofrín (II, pp. 31–5) left a description of the *villa*, which he visited in 1766. There are padrones, drawn up in 1777, from the parishes of Amatlan, Guatusco, and Totutla.[16] Later statistics can be found in a post-Independence publication (*Estadística...de Veracruz*, Cuaderno Primero).

Monographs include the work of Domínguez (1943) on Coscomatepec, and that of Aguirre Beltrán (1940).

19 *Cozamaloapa*

Occupying the broad coastal plain in the lower reaches of the Papaloapan (Alvarado) river, with elevations nowhere exceeding 150 m, this is a hot, humid region, much of it clothed in tropical rain forest. Now partly controlled by massive irrigation works, the great river and its tributaries annually overflowed and covered much of the land. Settlements are on natural levees today as they were in the colonial period and before.

The area at contact was tributary to the Aztec garrison at Tochtépec, with the probable exception of Cuauhcuetzpaltépec, a large and prosperous Popolucan kingdom. These people spoke a Mayan language related to the neighboring Mixe; Tlacoapan and Mixtlan may have been autonomous Popolucan states. Along the Papaloapan was a string of Nahua-speaking communities, Otlatitlan, Cozamaloapan, Ixmatlatlan, and Puctlan. Icpactepec was either a separate state or a dependency of Cozamaloapan. The 'Misteca' spoken along the river at Cozamaloapan and elsewhere seems to have been rather an archaic Nahua dialect.[1] All sources agree that this was a rich and densely populated region (Aguilar, p. 88. Motolinía, pp. 173–4).

A ship under the command of Pedro de Alvarado

entered the river which later bore his name in 1518, and may have reached the vicinity of Cozamaloapan. There were probably other Spanish visits here before Sandoval and his army overcame the Mexica of Tochtépec and occupied the province towards the end of 1521.

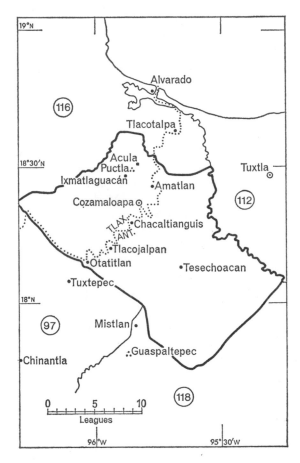

Encomiendas

It would seem that Gonzalo de Sandoval made the first *repartimiento* of Indians here in 1522, not unexpectedly assigning the richest of the native states, Guaspaltepec, to himself. This encomienda was exploited by Sandoval, perhaps with interruptions, until he went to Spain in 1528. The first audiencia gave Guaspaltepec first to the ayuntamiento of Vera Cruz and then to the *contador* Rodrigo de Albornoz, in 1529, but the second audiencia took it for the crown in March, 1531.

Then or not long afterwards the encomienda was divided, half going to the conquistador Jorge de Alvarado (brother of Pedro). Alvarado was followed on his death in 1540 by a son, and towards 1563 by a grandson, both of the same name. The grandson was still encomendero in 1597.[2]

Amatlan (perhaps the same as Ixmatlatlan) was first given to the conquistador Pedro Moreno Cendejas, succeeded by a son, Martín de Mafra, towards 1565. It escheated sometime between 1597 and 1609.

We do not know the encomendero of Cuzamaluava, as it was called in early years; it became crown property sometime before 1534.

Juan de Limpias Carvajal, perhaps the first holder of Otatitlan, died *c.* 1565, and tributes were assigned to his son. The latter was also called Juan de Limpias (Dorantes de Carranza, p. 209), although a Fernando de Carvajal is listed as encomendero in 1597.

Puctla is said to have been first held by Alonso Vázquez, but it was re-assigned by the second audiencia to Rodrigo de Castañeda. The latter was succeeded soon after 1560 by a son of the same name. The place was still a private encomienda held by Xicoténcatl Castañeda (the mestizo grandson of Rodrigo de Castañeda) in 1609, but it escheated by 1626.

Government

C's were appointed in the early 1530s to administer both Cuzamaluava and the crown half of Guaspaltepec (ENE, II, p. 58). In January, 1560, the C of Zoyaltepec y Coyatlan (Zoyatla?) (cf. Teutila) was ordered to reside at Cozamaloapa and to govern there and in neighboring encomiendas.[3] Soon afterwards the C of Guaspaltepec was made suffragan to the AM of Teutila and was given jurisdiction throughout the lower Alvarado, from Amatlan–Puctla to Oxitlan.[4]

In the seventeenth century the C of Guaspaltepec was re-designated AM and resided in Cozamaloapa. The abandoned village of Guaspaltepec, together with Tesechoacan, was transferred to the jurisdiction of Villa Alta towards 1740, while the Oxitlan–Tuxtepec area was absorbed by Teutila. Perhaps to compensate for this loss, the old corregimiento of Chinantla–Ucila was for a time attached to Cozamaloapa, but by 1770 it had been annexed to Teutila. There was a lengthy dispute between the AMs of Cozamaloapa and Villa Alta over the Tesechoacan–Guaspaltepec–Sochiapan area, which was eventually divided between the two (only Tesechoacan remained in the jurisdiction of Cozamaloapa).⁵

After 1787 Cozamaloapa was a subdelegación in the intendencia of Vera Cruz.

Church

In 1570 there were secular priests at S Martín Cozamaloapa and Guaspaltepec who visited the entire area and parts of adjoining jurisdictions. The parish seat of Guaspaltepec was moved to S Juan Bautista Chacaltianguis(co) towards 1600 (*see below*). Sometime between 1743 and 1777 a new secular parish was founded at S Pedro Amatlan, and by 1802 S Andrés Otatitlan had its own priest. The Alvarado river was the diocesan boundary, Chacaltianguis and Otatitlan belonging to Antequera, and Amatlan and Cozamaloapa to Tlaxcala.

Population and settlements

The mysterious plague which decimated the gulf coast was felt here very soon after the Conquest, especially on the lower river. In 1536 the tribute of Cozamaloapa was halved, and three years later the survivors there were granted total if temporary exemption from tribute payment, 'por...estar despoblado el dicho pueblo y sus estancias de pestilencia e anbre' (L de T, p. 161); only 67 'casas' are reported there in 1548. Puctla, Amatlan, and Otatitlan were struck by the same disease. Guaspaltepec, which Aguilar (p. 88) says had 80,000 casas at contact, was reported to still have a 'población recia' in 1544 (ENE, IV, p. 140), but Aguilar's 1560 estimate is only 200 casas. 350 tributaries are mentioned at Guaspaltepec in 1570, when there were perhaps a thousand in the whole jurisdiction. There was further loss, to 537 tributaries in 1600, and perhaps 300 in 1629. The 1743 count shows 800 Indian families, the greatest increase being registered in the Amatlan–Puctla area. In 1796 there were 1,014 Indian tributaries.⁶

By 1743 many of the Indians on the lower river spoke Spanish, but they also used 'mexicana masorral que antiguamente llamaron misteca'. In the old Guaspaltepec area, Náhuatl had replaced Popoluca.

Non-Indians, especially Negroes, began arriving in the sixteenth century to work on the vast cattle haciendas that were established on the Alvarado plains. In 1743 there were 48 families of Spaniards, five of mestizos, and 233 of freed Negroes and mulattoes in the jurisdiction; Cozamaloapa and Tesechoacan were by then predominantly Negroid communities.

Cozamaloapa (Cuzamaluava, etc.; 1950: Cosamaloapan de Carpio, ciudad) had ten estancias in 1548, only one of which, Cipactepec, was inhabited in 1570. By 1600 Cipactepec had disappeared.

Amatlan (Acatlan; 1950: Amatitlan, *villa*) was associated in the 1560s with another place, Cuzamasernaca. In 1570 four estancias are named, all of which seem to have been congregated at the cabecera towards 1600.

Puctla (1950: ?), also known as Istayuca in the sixteenth century, had three estancias in 1570–1600. One of them, Tatayan, with the cabecera itself, disappeared in the congregation of 1600, while the others, Acula and Ixmatlaguacan, survived as pueblos.

The cabecera of Guaspaltepec (1950: Guaxpala, ranchería?) must have had many dependent settlements in early years, but we have no record of them. Only a handful remained in the late sixteenth century. One of these, Tecxuchuacan, was to be the center of a congregation which included Mistlan, Tecoloapa, and Tlatlahuicapa in 1594. Shortly before 1600 the few Indians remaining at the cabecera of Guaspaltepec were moved to Mistlan. In that year a congregation was proposed in which all the Indians (81½ tributaries) of this vast province, together with those of Otatitlan (*see below*), were to move to a place called Cacaguaxuchitlan, a league east of Otatitlan. While this reduction seems to have been largely thwarted by the curate, who did not approve of the selected townsite, we have no further news of the Indians of Guaspaltepec. The place is mentioned as a ranchería in the neighboring jurisdiction of Villa Alta in 1777. The old estancia of Tesechoacan, as we have mentioned, survived as a mulatto village.

Otatitlan (Utlatitlan; 1950: Otatitlán, pueblo) had three estancias in 1548, two of which, Chacaltianguis(co) and Tlacojalpan, were to have been congregated near the cabecera (*see above*) in 1600. All three places existed as pueblos in the eighteenth century.

Sources

Of the five cabeceras, only Cozamaloapa and Otatitlan are described in the *Suma de Visitas* (*c.* 1548) (PNE, I, nos. 232, 441). There are two brief reports in the Ovando series (*c.* 1570) for the parish of Cozamaloapa (García Pimentel, 1904, p. 17. PNE, v, pp. 235–7), and another for Guaspaltepec (García Pimentel, 1904, pp. 67, 81–2). Congregations in 1594–1603 are discussed in several documents.[7]

Bishop Mota y Escobar described the area as it was in 1609 and 1618,[8] while Palafox was there in 1646.[9] Tributary data of 1626–96 for the Tlaxcalan portion alone are contained in another source.[10]

A most illuminating report by the AM written in 1743[11] is poorly summarized by Villaseñor y Sánchez (I, p. 371). We have found censuses drawn up by the curates of Amatlan and Cozamaloapa,[12] and a valuable topographic report written by the parish priest of Chacaltianguis,[13] all dated 1777. The Oaxacan parishes are summarily described in a document of 1802 (E. Pérez, table at end), while the whole jurisdiction is covered in a post-Independence publication (*Estadística...de Veracruz*, Cuaderno Primero).

Syntheses of these and other documents are found in the works of Mariano Espinosa and Scholes and Warren (1965).

20 *Cuatro Villas*

The region under consideration here – i.e., that part of the valley of Oaxaca which, after intrusions and lawsuits with the crown and private encomenderos, remained subject to the Marquesado del Valle de Guaxaca – consisted of several unconnected pieces of territory in the upper Atoyac basin. Elevations range from 1,200 to 3,000 m, the climate being temperate and semi-arid.

The intricate political maneuvering which began here soon after the conquest, part of which involved moving the Mixtec-speaking population of the whole valley to the Marquesado, makes it difficult to determine the actual situation at contact. We have mentioned (cf. Antequera) that Huaxyácac (Mixtec, Ñuhundúa; Zapotec, Luhulaa) was the seat of an Aztec garrison charged with the enforcement of tribute collection in a large and wealthy province known as Coyolapan (= Cuitlapan?). The immediate political influence of Huaxyácac was apparently confined to the garrison settlement, where Náhuatl was spoken, and a few nearby communities in the center of the valley, from Ixtlahuaca to Xallat-

lauhco. Huaxyácac was surrounded by, and probably founded on, lands belonging to the Mixtec kingdom of Cuitlapan or Coyolapan (Mixtec, Sahayuco), a large and important state with subordinate settlements scattered throughout the valley. The principal settlement of Cuitlapan lay at the foot of the sacred mountain which the Mixtecs called Yucu-ocoñaña (Monte Albán) (cf. Bradomín, pp. 16–19). Nearby, occupying the valley and hillsides to the northwest, was a Zapotec state, Etla (Zapotec, Loovhana). Some distance to the south was a Zapotec community called Tecuilabacoya (the earliest spelling known to us; Zapotec, Esdánayoo), which may either have been an autonomous state or a dependency of Cuitlapan.

The Aztecs of Huaxyácac and their tributary vassals were defeated by a Spanish and allied army at the end of 1521. A subsequent rebellion was put down in late 1526.

Encomienda and government

We have discussed elsewhere (Antequera, *see above*) the early vicissitudes of Hernando Cortés's holdings here, which at first embraced the entire valley of Oaxaca and certain neighboring areas. Among the '*villas*' mentioned in Cortés's grant of 1529 were Cuilapa, Etla, Guaxaca, and Tecuilabacoya. The usual arguments arose as to how far the limits of these places extended, and which settlements had been subordinate to them 'from time immemorial', as the phrase went. By 1534 the Cuatro Villas had been reduced almost to their

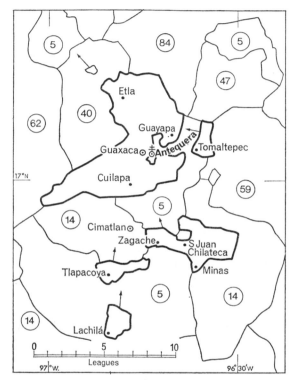

final boundaries, and henceforth were ruled by an AM appointed by Cortés and his descendants.

There were, however, further efforts on the part of the crown to narrow the extent of this jurisdiction, and there were also interruptions in the political control of Cortés's heirs. In 1552 the viceroy recommended unsuccessfully placing Cuilapa and Guaxaca under the crown. The *oidor* Quesada complained two years later that the second marquis had illegally enlarged his domain through the purchase of land surrounding the city of Antequera.[1] In 1565 the crown pro-

secutor claimed that certain villages considered subject to Cuilapa were 'cabeceras de por sí' and should be removed from the marquisate.[2] From 1570 to 1594, in retaliation for the second marquis's involvement in an alleged conspiracy, the jurisdictions controlled by him were administered by crown officers, Cuatro Villas being attached at this time to the alcaldía mayor of Antequera (actually, the viceroy named subordinate magistrates to Cuatro Villas during part of this period).[3] In this time of troubles for the marquisate, the royal agents pressed their territorial claims with more than usual success. Among other places, the suburbs of Xalatlaco and S Felipe del Atarjea seem to have been transferred sometime about 1574 from Cuatro Villas to Antequera.[4] Again in 1710–1725 the marquisate was sequestered and the council of the Indies appointed AMs (*Títulos de Indias*, p. 152).

The official residence of the AM of Cuatro Villas was the *villa* of Guaxaca, also called *villa del Marquesado*, adjoining the city of Antequera on the west. After 1787, although the jurisdiction was within the intendencia of Oaxaca, its magistrate continued to be called AM rather than subdelegado (Beleña, II, p. vi).

Church

The first parish here was perhaps Natividad Etla, where the Dominicans founded a monastery in the 1530s; after the church collapsed in 1575 it was rebuilt in nearby S Pedro Etla.[5] Santiago Cuilapa may have been a secular parish before the Dominicans took charge there *c.* 1555. The *villa* of Sta María Guaxaca was visited for many years by Dominicans from their convent in Antequera before it became a parish, probably early in the eighteenth century. The fourth *villa*, Sta Ana Tecuilabacoya (later, Tlapacoya), belonged first to the Dominican parish of Sta Cruz Iztepec (cf. Antequera) and later to that of Cimatlan; it is listed as a separate curacy in 1813 (Navarro y Noriega, p. 22). Sta Ana Zagache and Sta Catarina Minas, beginning as visitas of Cuilapa, had resident Dominican ministers from *c.* 1600 (Burgoa, 1934*a*, II, pp. 56, 59–60.) Cuilapa and Etla, and perhaps the remaining parishes, were secularized in 1753 (Gay, II, pp. 410–11). All were in the bishopric of Antequera.

Map 13 shows the complex pattern of overlapping political and ecclesiastical jurisdictions here.

Population and settlements

At mid-sixteenth century this jurisdiction probably had close to 12,000 tributaries. Two-thirds of these were Mixtecs living at Cuilapa and its dependencies. Etla and Tecuilabacoya (the latter almost depopulated by 1544) were Zapotec with Mixtec barrios, while the *villa* of Guaxaca was Náhuatl-speaking until other elements settled there. The Indian population was reduced drastically in the epidemic of 1576–81, and continued to decline in the seventeenth century; the tributary count fell from 11,517 in 1563 to 8,950 in 1570, 4,816 in 1597, 3,290 in 1676, and 3,006 in 1693. A century later it had recovered somewhat, 4,235 Indian tributaries being reported in 1793.[6]

We do not know what the settlement pattern was at contact, and only in the case of Cuilapa do we have a complete list of late sixteenth-century communities. In general, it would seem that efforts to collect the Indians in a limited number of congregations were opposed by the agents of the Marquesado, who managed to keep the dwindling population scattered in many small settlements, probably in order to claim as much land as possible. Cuilapa, for example, had fourteen estancias in 1570, but seventeen are named in 1580, and twenty-one in 1743. Shortly before 1611 four new Marquesado villages were founded in the environs of Antequera for the purpose of thwarting an attempt to extend the limits of that crowded city.[7]

Subject to Cuilapa (1950: Cuilapan de Guerrero, *villa*) in the late eighteenth century were Sta María Azompa, S Jacinto and S Juan Chilateca, S Pedro Guegoresi, S Agustín de las Juntas, S Antonio de la Cal, S Miguel de las Peras (Yucucua, Jiuyace, Cozautepec), S Pablo de las Peras (Idzucun, Cuatro Venados), Sta Catarina de las Minas, Sta Lucía del Camino, S Lucas Tlanichico, Sto Domingo Tomaltepec, S Francisco and S Sebastián Tutla, S Raymundo Xalpa, Sta Cruz Xoxocotlan, Sta Ana Zagache (Xuchitepec), S Gerónimo Zagache, and S Andrés Guayapa. Some of these places were far removed from their cabecera, cut off from it by intrusions of other pueblos in an intricate pattern. The cabecera was moved to its final site *c.* 1555. Sta Ana Tecuilabacoya (Teuquilapacoya, Tlacolabacoya, Tlapalaguacoya, in the sixteenth century; Cuitlapacoya in 1676; Tlapacoya in 1693 and later; 1950: Sta Ana Tlapacoyan, pueblo), although one of the original four *villas*, seems to have lost its cabecera status and appears as a pueblo subject to Cuilapa in some reports of the eighteenth century. Tlapacoya had two dependencies, which are also occasionally listed under Cuilapa, forming a distant enclave southeast of Ayoquesco: Sta Marta Chichigualtepec and S Martín Lachilá.

The cabecera de doctrina of Etla (and probably the political center as well) was moved in the 1580s from Natividad to S Pedro y S Pablo (1950: S Pedro y S Pablo Etla, *villa*). The subject pueblos in the eighteenth century were Asunción, Guadalupe, Jesús Nazareno, Natividad, S Agustín, S Gabriel, S Miguel, S Pablo, S Sebastián, Sta Marta, Santiago, Sto Domingo, Soledad, Stos Reyes (all named thus far had the cognomen *Etla*), and S Juan Guelache.

The *villa* of Guaxaca (Villa del Marquesado; 1950; part of Oaxaca de Juárez, ciudad) had six dependencies in the late eighteenth century: S Juan and Sta Ana Chapultepec, S Pedro Ixtlaguaca, S Martín Mexicapa, S Jacinto Milpas, and Sto Tomás Xuchimilco. A former estancia, S Matías Xalatlaco, was lost to Antequera in the sixteenth century.

There were a number of cattle haciendas in this jurisdiction, whose claimed limits provided a source of dispute with neighboring justices. They were tended by a relatively insignificant number of non-Indians, mostly mulattoes.

Sources

The region is summarily described in Zárate's relación of 1544 (ENE, IV, p. 141). Population data for 1563 are derived by comparing a tribute assessment for that year (L de T, p. 186) with the report made by an accountant in 1570 (ENE, XI, p. 5).

Alburquerque's description of his diocese in 1570 gives further information concerning parishes and tributaries (García Pimentel, 1904, pp. 59 ff.).

Two of the four villas, Cuilapa[8] and Tlapacoya,[9] are represented in the 1580 series of relaciones geográficas; both reports were prepared by Dominican friars.

Some details can be gleaned from the journals of three clergymen who visited Oaxaca, the Franciscan Ponce in 1586 (Ponce, I, pp. 271–2, 496), the Dominican Gage in 1625 (Gage, pp. 111–14), and the Jesuit Cobo in 1630 (Cobo, p. 201). Population data for the late seventeenth century are found in the accounting records of the marquisate preserved at AGN,[10] a source which would reveal far more if properly investigated.

The much disputed boundaries of the Marquesado can be traced in reports of actual surveys made in 1686 (BAGN, 1a ser., III, pp. 488–511), 1717,[11] and 1746.[12] The first two marked the division between Cuatro Villas and the city of Antequera, while the third fixed the boundary between Cuilapa and the Peñoles villages (the latter has a map). In the 1743 series, we have a report made by the AM of Cuatro Villas, accompanied by a compass diagram showing places in the jurisdiction.[13] Ajofrín, who visited Oaxaca in 1766, gives a list of cabeceras and sujetos in the Marquesado, and a description of the monastery at Cuilapa (Ajofrín, II, pp. 104–7). We have seen censuses from the parishes of Cuilapa, Oaxaca, Sta Catalina Minas, and Zagache,[14] and topographic descriptions of Cuilapa and Oaxaca,[15] all prepared in 1777. The parishes as they were in 1802 are summarily described (Eutimio Pérez, table at end), and there is a deficient report from the curate of Etla dated 1804.[16]

The jurisdiction at the time of Independence is described in detail by Murguía y Galardi.[17]

Spores (1965) summarizes various sixteenth-century sources. The interesting work of García Martínez (1969) has much to add about the Marquesado del Valle, but little about the jurisdiction of Cuatro Villas.

21 *Cuautla Amilpas*

This jurisdiction, now in eastern Morelos state, was split by an intrusion of that of Cuernavaca into two sections. Drainage is southward from the volcanic escarpment into affluents of the Atoyac (Balsas), with elevations of 800–2,500 m. The climate is generally temperate and dry; precipitation, nearly confined to June–October, increases from south to north.

On the southern slope of Popocatépetl was a state ruled by the lord of Ocuiltuco, which included Acatcinco, Tetellan, and Ximiltépec. Related to the kings of Xochimilco, this tlatoani supplied the Mexican court with flowers. Below to the south lived the four tlatoque of Tlacotépec, Zacoalpan, Cuauhzolco, and Temoac, probably also of Xochimilcan lineage and subject to the Triple Alliance. Still further down in the hot country were a number of small states (Ahuehuepan, Anenecuilco, Cuauhtlan, Cuahuitlixco, Olintépec, Tzompanco, Xochimilcatzinco) known collectively as Amilpanecapan, which perhaps were directly subordinate to the Aztec military governor of Huaxtépec (cf. Cuernavaca). Beyond Amilpanecapan was a wild region of barren mountains and gullies belonging to Huaxtépec. The people lived dispersed in many small rancherías and spoke the Xochimilca dialect of Náhuatl. Water was taken from the rivers in irrigation canals to grow cotton in the flat country.

Pedro de Alvarado and Bernardino Vázquez de Tapia visited Tlacotépec and Ocuiltuco in September–October 1519, but the area was not subjected by the Spaniards until April 1521 (Vázquez de Tapia, p. 36).

Encomiendas

Cortés considered the Amilpas villages subject to his *villa* of Guastepec, but a crown suit begun in the 1560s contended that they were separate cabeceras. The final decision in the council of the Indies was against the marquis, and the Amilpas were taken for the crown in 1581.[1]

Soon after the Conquest, the *señorío* of Ocuituco was divided into four parts (cf. Gerhard, 1970). Perhaps the first encomenderos were Bartolomé Hernández at Ocuituco (replaced by Hernando Medel in 1528), Rodrigo Martín at Xumiltepec (Alonso de Escobar from 1526), and Pedro Sánchez

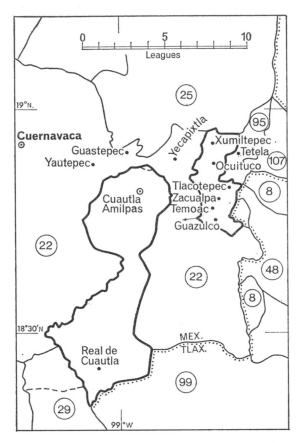

Farfán at Tetela; Acacingo was annexed to the province of Chalco. On Medel's death in 1531 Ocuituco escheated, but by March, 1535, it had been re-assigned to the bishop of Mexico, D. Juan de Zumárraga, who remained in possession until final escheatment occurred in 1544.[2] When Escobar died (early 1540s) his estate was disputed between two women each claiming to be the widow; tributes of Xumiltepec were collected by the crown until in 1551 the suit was won by Francisca de Loaisa and her new husband,

Antonio Velázquez.[3] The latter died in the 1570s, when the tribute was divided between Martín de Cuéllar and the crown; as late as the 1740s part of Xumiltepec's tribute was going to the Moctezuma heirs.[4]

The first holder of the four cabeceras of Zacualpa, Tlacotepec, Temoac, and Guazulco was the conquistador Francisco de Solís. He was succeeded in 1550 by a son, Miguel, who still appears in 1604 as encomendero.[5] In 1688–1743 Temoac and Zacualpa were paying tribute to the Marquesa de la Conquista.

Government

Ocuituco had a C during its brief period of escheatment in the early 1530s, and again from 1544, as did Xumiltepec in 1545–8.[6] In 1550 the C of Ocuituco was given jurisdiction in Xumiltepec and the Solís encomiendas, under the supervision of the AM of Chalco.[7] His territory was enlarged during the sequestration of the marquisate in 1570, when he acquired the additional title of AM of the 'Cuatro *villas* del Marquesado' (these were not the Cuatro Villas (q.v.) of Guaxaca, but rather those of Guastepec, Tepuztlan, Yautepec, and Yecapistla [cf. Cuernavaca]). These places were returned to the jurisdiction of Cuernavaca in 1583, but meanwhile the Amilpas and another group of Marquesado villages known as Las Tlalnaguas had come under crown control in 1581–2.[8] The C of Ocuituco thereafter acted as justicia mayor in this recently-escheated area. When the Tlalnaguas were reincorporated in the Marquesado in 1594, Ocuituco's magistrate was left with a divided jurisdiction consisting of the Amilpas to the west and the corregimiento of Ocuituco in the east, a situation which prevailed to the end of the colonial period.[9] In the late sixteenth century silver mines were opened in the mountains south of Cuautla, and the justice began to be referred to as AM of Minas de Cuautla, or Guautla, residing first at the mines and eventually at Cuautla Amilpas.[10] The right of appointing this AM was preempted by the council of the Indies in 1609.

Meanwhile, Ocuituco continued for many years to be called a corregimiento, and had a teniente appointed by the AM of Cuautla Amilpas. The nearby corregimiento of Tetela del Volcán (q.v.), while actually administered from Cuautla in the seventeenth century, had a separate magistrate until it was annexed to Cuautla Amilpas towards 1780. In the reforms of 1787 Cuautla became a subdelegación in the intendencia of Puebla; it was transferred to that of Mexico in February, 1793.[11]

Church

Dominicans from Guastepec visited the area from 1528.[12] The Augustinians founded a monastery at Ocuituco (Santiago) in 1534, but after a row with the bishop they abandoned the place to a secular priest for a few years. There was an Augustinian visita at Rosario Zacualpa from 1535 which soon became a separate parish. Another Augustinian monastery was in operation at S Andrés Xumiltepec by 1570 (Gómez de Orozco, pp. 40–54. Greenleaf, 1961, p. 60. Ricard, pp. 297–8).

The Amilpas were visited from Guastepec until a Dominican house was built at Santiago Cuautla in the 1580s.[13] Parochial duties here were later shared with Franciscans of the province of S Diego de Alcalá (Dieguinos), who had their own monastery from 1640. The mining camp of Cuautla occasionally had a resident priest, but most of the time it was visited from other parishes (Cuautla, Atenango del Río). Certain important haciendas maintained resident curates at times.

The Augustinian parishes were secularized, first Xumiltepec (1752), then Ocuituco (1775), and finally Zacualpa. The doctrina of Cuautla, however, remained in charge of the two regular orders to the end of the colony. All parishes were in the archdiocese of Mexico. (Navarro y Noriega. Vera, p. 117.)

Population and settlements

The epidemic of 1576–81 wiped out more than half the native population of the Amilpas, and two-thirds in the mountain villages. Records for the whole jurisdiction show 7,052 tributaries in 1570, 3,028 in 1588, 2,240 in 1600, and 849 in 1643.[14] In 1743 there were 1,408 Indian families (614 in the Amilpas, 794 elsewhere), while the census of 1801 gives 2,130 Indian tributaries.[15]

Negro slaves arrived here in the sixteenth century, and their offspring came to rival the Indians in number. By mid-eighteenth century the population of the Amilpas was perhaps mostly Negroid, while Zacualpa also had considerable Negro and mestizo elements. The census of 1743 shows 508 families of free non-Indians (mostly mulattoes) in the jurisdiction; in 1801 there were 814 mulatto tributaries. Ocuituco and Xumiltepec remained predominantly Indian. The Spanish population was insignificant.

A good many small settlements in the Amilpas region were eliminated in congregations carried out by the Dominicans, probably in the 1550s (Cruz y Moya, II, p. 133). A document of 1552 mentions sixteen *barrios* here which are not heard of thereafter.[16] Of six cabeceras and six estancias named in 1570, only four Indian communities survived a second round of congregations in 1603. The resulting pueblos were Cuautla Amilpas (Guautla, etc.; 1950: Cuautla Morelos, ciudad), Ahuehuepa, Anenecuilco, and Tetelcingo (the latter was also claimed as a sujeto of Guastepec, as was Cocoyoc, and jurisdiction in both places was long disputed between Cuautla and Cuernavaca). At this time, Amilcingo and Cuautlixco became barrios of Cuautla, while Olintepec continued as a ranchería. The lands vacated in these congregations were swallowed up by sugar haciendas. The *real de minas* of Cuautla (Guautla; 1950: Huautla, pueblo) also survived, as a mestizo settlement, in the eighteenth century.

The four cabeceras of Guazulco (1950: Huazulco, pueblo), Temoac (1950: pueblo), Tlacotepec (1950: pueblo), and Zacualpa (1950: Zacualpan de Amilpas, pueblo) remained *in situ* in the 1603 congregation. Popotlan, one of two estancias subject to Temoac which were ordered abandoned at this time, reappears as a pueblo in the eighteenth century. Cuautepec and Chicomocelo, both Jesuit haciendas near Zacualpa, began as a single *huerta* owned by the first encomendero in 1548.

Ocuituco (1950: pueblo) had ten estancias which in 1550 were divided between two barrios, Tlalnepantla and Tlaltengo. These were all ordered to be congregated at the cabecera and Tlamimilulpa in 1603, but another place, Guapalcalco, also survived as a pueblo.

Seven estancias of Xumiltepec (Ximiltepec in the earliest documents; 1950: Jumiltepec, pueblo) were reduced to two townsites, the cabecera and Ocoxaltepec, in 1603. Another estancia, Cuauhuecahuasco, was perhaps the same as Huecahuasco, an eighteenth-century pueblo.

Sources

There is an interesting series of documents concerning Ocuituco and Xumiltepec in 1536, which includes a copy of a rare 1531 *visita* of those places.[17] Of special value is an Inquisition report on idolatry at Ocuituco in 1539.[18] Ocuituco, Xumiltepec, and the Solís encomiendas are tersely described as they were *c.* 1548 in the Suma de Visitas (PNE, I, nos. 122–3, 421, 503–4, 800). For the late sixteenth century, we have reports in the Ovando series made *c.* 1570,[19] a map of Ocuituco in 1578,[20] and a brief description of the Amilpas in 1580.[21]

Unusually complete details of the 1603 congregations have survived.[22] The journal of an archbishop's visit here in 1646 contains valuable data on pueblos and haciendas.[23] There is an excellent on-the-spot report by the AM in 1743, accompanied by a map.[24] For 1791 there is a census of the non-Indian population with a fine map showing the jurisdiction in great detail,[25] and a separate list of placenames.[26]

Much further information about the Amilpas in the sixteenth century will be found in the ramo of Hospital de Jesús at AGN. Solís Martínez's little monograph on Cuautla is of interest, but those of Díez and Urbán Aguirre are worthless for the colonial period.

22 *Cuernavaca*

Now almost entirely within the state of Morelos, this is a well-watered region of fertile valleys descending from the slopes of Ajusco and Popocatépetl to the hot country (800–3,400 m). Watercourses are tributary to the Atoyac (Balsas) system. The climate is semi-arid and temperate with adequate seasonal rainfall.

This area was controlled by the Aztec garrison settlements of Cuauhnáhuac and Huaxtépec. The tlatoani of Cuauhnáhuac, a relative of Moctezuma, seems to have had precedence over a number of lesser tlatoque in the province of Tlálhuic, namely the lords of Acatlicpac, Amacoztitla, Atlicholoayan, Atlpoyecan, Coatlan, Cohuintépec, Huitzilapan, Itztépec, Ixtlan, Mazatépec, Miacatlan, Molotla, Ocpayucan, Panchimalco, Teocaltzinco, Tlaquiltenanco, Xiuhtépec, Xochitépec, and Xoxouhtla. The Tlálhuica, who spoke a Náhuatl dialect, sent tribute to the lord of Texcoco. To the east, the people were predominantly Xochimilca, also Náhuatl-speakers. Tepuztlan seems to have had co-rulers, while the tlatoani of Yauhtépec dominated the lesser lords of Atlhuelic, Coacalco, Huitzilan, Itzamatitlan, and Tlaltizapan. Huaxtépec probably had a native ruler, as well as a military governor, whose domain extended far to the south and who may have controlled the Amilpanecapan region (cf. Cuautla Amilpas). On the south slope of Popocatépetl was the state of Yacapichtlan, whose tlatoani claimed the services of several autonomous communities (Ayoxochapan, Tecpantzinco, Tlayacac, Xalostoc) on the plains below, known collectively as Tlalnáhuac. Outside the principal settlements, which were well-defended fortresses, the people lived scattered in numerous small rancherías. This was a rich and densely inhabited region. Irrigation was widely used, canals for cotton (the principal tribute item) and terracing for subsistence crops.

Probably first seen by Spaniards in 1520, the area was invaded by an army led by Cortés in April, 1521, at which time the garrisons at Huaxtépec and Cuauhnáhuac were defeated.

Encomiendas

Hernando Cortés set aside this and adjoining regions as part of his personal fief, at latest by 1524. Clearly the grant involved a number of native states, but Cortés claimed (probably with some reason) that they were all 'subject' to the five principal rulers of Cuauhnáhuac (Cuernavaca), Tepuztlan, Yauhtépec (Yautepec), Huaxtépcc (Guastepec), and Yacapichtlan (Yecapixtla).

1529 named all five cabeceras mentioned above among the *villas* given him in perpetual encomienda. After his return to Mexico in 1531 Cortés took possession of these places, although Burgos and Villarroel continued to claim the validity of

These multiple encomiendas were seized by the acting governors in October 1525, and when Cortés returned to Mexico the following year he found Antonio Villarroel (alias Antonio Serrano de Cardona) in possession of Cuernavaca, while Yautepec and Tepuztlan were divided between Francisco Verdugo and Diego de Ordaz. Unable at first to dislodge these rivals, Cortés regained control of Guastepec and Yecapixtla; shortly before he went to Spain, early in 1528, he 'deposited' Guastepec with Juan de Burgos and Yecapixtla with Diego de Holguín and Francisco de Solís. Cortés's grant as Marqués del Valle in

their grants in suits which dragged on for years in the council of the Indies.[1]

Government

Here as in other parts of the Marquesado, the crown's agents questioned the extent of Cortés's holdings. Totolapa, together with Atlatlauca, Nepopualco, Tehuizco, and Tlayacapa, were first claimed for the crown, despite Cortés's assertion that they belonged to his *villas* of Guastepec and Yecapixtla; they were all placed under a C in 1532 (cf. Chalco).[2] Two more protracted crown suits were directed against Cortés's descendants. In

1565, when the second marquis was in disfavor, the royal prosecutor laid claim to two groups of villages, comprising the entire south-eastern quarter of the jurisdiction, Las Amilpas (until then considered subject to Guastepec) and Las Tlalnaguas (subject to Yecapixtla).[3] The crown alleged that these places had always been 'cabeceras por sí', that they were not mentioned in the grant, and that the first marquis had appropriated them illegally. Both suits were won by the crown in review sentences of the audiencia in 1581–2.[4] Meanwhile, in 1567 the estate of the marquis had been sequestered, magistrates being appointed first by the viceroy and later by the king. From the early 1570s the four *villas* of Yecapixtla, Guastepec, Yautepec, and Tepuztlan were attached for administration to the corregimiento of Ocuituco (cf. Cuautla Amilpas). In 1583 these 'Cuatro Villas' were returned to the AM of Cuernavaca, but the Amilpas and Tlalnaguas were united with Ocuituco in a new royal jurisdiction.[5] The old suit was appealed to the council of the Indies, and while the Amilpas henceforth remained crown property, the 'Catorce pueblos de las Tlalnaguas' were given back to the third marquis in 1587.[6] Thus at the end of the sixteenth century the alcaldía mayor of Cuernavaca acquired the irregular shape which it retained to the end of the colonial period. The cabeceras of Cuernavaca, Tepuztlan, and Yautepec in the west were joined to the eastern dependencies (Yecapixtla, Tlalnaguas) by a narrow corridor at Guastepec. Minor boundary disputes continued. Teocalcingo was claimed by both Cuernavaca and Chilapa, while certain estancias (Cocoyoc, Tetelcingo, etc.) of Guastepec were disputed between Cuernavaca and Cuautla.

Except during the various periods of sequestration (1570–94, 1710–26, 1810–15), appointment of the AM of Cuernavaca was a prerogative of the marquis, although in later years the privilege was in some measure shared with the crown. While considered part of the intendencia of Mexico after 1787, Cuernavaca retained a special position as a province of the Marquesado, and its magistrate continued to be called AM rather than subdelegado. The *villa* of Cuernavaca was the seat of justice,

while tenientes lived elsewhere (in 1743 they resided at Xoxutla, Yautepec, and Xonacatepec).[7]

Church

A monastery-mission was begun by Franciscans at Asunción Cuernavaca in 1525. Within a decade, the other mendicant orders founded similar houses at Sto Domingo Guastepec (Dominican, 1528), and S Juan Bautista Yecapixtla (Augustinian, 1535). Subsequently the doctrina of Cuernavaca was divided with Franciscan parishes at Tlaquiltenango (*c.* 1540; transferred to the Dominicans in 1580, when the patron became Sto Domingo), Santiago Xiutepec (1570s), S Lucas Mazatepec and S Juan Evangelista Xochitepec (the last two in 1694). The primitive parish of Guastepec was partitioned with the erection of Dominican monasteries at Asunción Yautepec (*c.* 1550), Natividad Tepuztlan (*c.* 1556), and S Miguel Tlaltizapan (by 1591). S Agustín Xonacatepec (*c.* 1557) and S Pedro Xantetelco (by 1565) were offspring of the Augustinian doctrina of Yecapixtla. There were other temporary foundations, such as S Marcos Tlayacac (listed as an Augustinian house in 1646), and certain important haciendas had resident priests (Cruz y Moya, II, p. 133. Dávila Padilla, p. 64. Grijalva, p. 66. Vera, *passim*).

All parishes were secularized in 1750–70, and new curacies were formed from visitas of Yecapixtla (S Sebastián Achichipico, 1767) and Xonacatepec (S Martín Tepancingo in the 1790s, S Miguel Atlacahualoya in 1807). The jurisdiction fell within the archdiocese of Mexico.

Population and settlements

The oidor Dr. Quesada in 1551, after a personal inspection of this jurisdiction, estimated that there were 15,000 tributaries in Cuernavaca and its estancias, 5,500 in Yautepec and Tepoztlan, 4,500 in Guastepec and the Amilpas, and 5,000 in Yecapixtla and the Tlalnaguas. To this total of 30,000 he added another 6,000 tributaries to account for 'los que los yndios encubren'.[8] From this, we must deduct perhaps 3,500 in the Amilpas, leaving 32,500 tributaries at mid-century, just after a disastrous epidemic (Quesada mentions 'great loss' at Guastepec) and just before the reforms which added many tribute-exempt Indians to the lists.

Later counts show 27,008 tributaries in 1570, 15,568 in 1597, 8,084 in 1620, 5,258 in 1643, and 4,326 in 1680.[9] Only 4,954 Indian families are recorded in 1743 (after another epidemic), while the census of 1800 gives 9,353 Indian tributaries.[10]

Negro slaves were brought to work in the sugar haciendas in the sixteenth century and later; many married Indian women, resulting in a large zambo population, especially in the hot country. Non-Indians in 1743 numbered 2,690 families, including 1,600 slaves. In 1800 there were 1,655 mulatto tributaries.[11] The Spanish population was insignificant.

We have only hints of the first congregations in the 1550s, in which many small Indian settlements undoubtedly disappeared (Cruz y Moya, II, p. 133). The number was further reduced in the 1600–1605 congregations.

The *villa* of Cuernavaca (Quauhnahuac, etc.; 1950: Cuernavaca, ciudad) had eighty-two subject estancias in 1532, and seventy-odd in 1570. Somewhat over thirty settlements disappeared from the map in the reductions of 1603–5, but some of these sites were reoccupied later. Lands belonging to the extinct villages were acquired by sugar haciendas. Surviving as pueblos in the eighteenth century were Acatlipa, Ahuehuecingo, Alpuyeca, Amacuzac, Amatitlan, Atlacholoaya, Coatlan, Cuauchichinola, Cuautetelco, Cuautla (Tlaxutla; 1950: Cuatlita), Cuauxomulco, Cuentepec, Guaxintlan, Huitzilac, Ixtla, Mazatepec, Miacatlan, Nexpa, Panchimalco, Tehuixtla, Temimilcingo, Teocalcingo (1950: Teocaltzingo, Gro.), Tequesquitengo, S Francisco Tetecala, S Mateo Tetecala (1950: Tetecalita), Tetelpa, Tetlama, Tezoyuca, Tlaquiltenango, Tlatenchi, Xiutepec, Xochitepec, Xoxocotla, Xoxutla, and Zacualpa (1950: Emiliano Zapata). Most of these places were eventually given cabecera status.[12]

In 1570 the *villa* of Yautepec (1950: ciudad) had thirteen estancias, some of them far south of the cabecera.[13] Guacalco (Coacalco, Oacalco), Izamatitlan, Ticuman, and Tlaltizapan remained pueblos after the congregations of *c.* 1600.

Tepuztlan (1950: Tepoztlán, villa) had five

subject villages in 1532, six in 1570–80, and a seventh (Ixcatepec) from the 1730s, seemingly a reversal of the congregation process. They are still inhabited today, probably at their original sites all within a league of the cabecera: Acacueyecan (S Andrés de la Cal), Amatlan (Magdalena), Ixcatepec, Tepecuitlapilco (S Juanico, Tlacotenco), Tepetlapan (Santiago), Xocotitlan (Sto Domingo), and Zacatepetlac (Sta Catalina). In addition, there were a number of outlying barrios which seem to have been deserted in the eighteenth century.[14]

Guastepec (Huaxtepec, etc.; 1950: Oaxtepec, pueblo), apart from its claim to the Amilpas (*see above*), in 1570–91 had seven estancias, three nearby and four far to the south, beyond the Amilpas. A document of 1591 shows Tetelcingo as a sub-cabecera to which the other estancias were subject.[15] There was a long-standing boundary dispute between Guastepec and Cuautla Amilpas in the course of which all these places seem to have been annexed to the latter jurisdiction, although the status of Tetelcingo appears in doubt as late as 1791.[16]

Yecapixtla (Acapistla, etc.; 1950: Yecapixtla, villa) in 1570–80 had seventeen estancias all within three leagues of the cabecera, most of which disappeared in a congregation of 1603–4. The cabecera and Pazulco are mentioned as the sites chosen in 1604, while three other pueblos which survived in 1743 (Achichipico, Texcala, Xochitlan) were perhaps abandoned and reoccupied.

We have mentioned above the controversy over 'Las Tlalnaguas'. In 1558 a commission representing fifteen Tlalnaguas villages declared that they had 'always' been subject to Cuernavaca and refused to help build an aqueduct at Yecapixtla.[17] According to the 1580 report, there were originally only two cabeceras in the Tlalnaguas, Tecpancingo (Tepazinco; 1950: Tepalcingo, *villa*) and Tlayacac (Tlayecac; 1950: Tlayecac, pueblo), but afterwards 'they all became cabeceras'. Separate listing in the Matrícula de Tributos suggests that Ayoxochiapa (Aosuchapan, etc.; 1950: Axochapan, *villa*) and Xalostoc (1950: Jaloxtoc, pueblo) were pre-Columbian political units as well. In 1602–4 congregations were formed at several places here, including Xalostoc, Xantetelco (Santetelco; 1950: Jantetelco, *villa*), and Xonacatepec (1950: Jonacatepec, *ciudad*); it was probably at this time that three settlements were abandoned, Teuhamac, Tizoyuca, and Tenango (the latter was an hacienda in the eighteenth century). A sujeto of Tlayacac called Huisilaque or Huichililla (1950: Huitzililla, pueblo) became a separate cabecera shortly before 1673. The remaining Tlalnaguas villages, all of which survived as pueblo-cabeceras, were Amacuitlapilco, Amayuca, Atlacagualoya (Atlicahualoya), Atotonilco, Chalcacingo, Tetela (Tetelilla), and Tetliztaca (Tlalixtac, Telixtac).

In addition to the Indian pueblos, in 1792 there were thirty-two haciendas, most of them producing sugar cane, and fifty-four ranchos in the jurisdiction.

Sources

Both the Matrícula de Tributos (cf. Barlow, 1949, pp. 75–82) and a list drawn up at Cortés's command in 1532[18] name cabeceras and principal sujetos. Probably dating from the late 1530s is a detailed census (in Náhuatl) of Tepuztlan, a brief summary of which has been published (Carrasco, 1964). The so-called 'Códice Municipal de Cuernavaca', containing disjointed information about barrios and sujetos, may date from the 1530s or much later.[19] In the Ovando series (1569–71) there are descriptions of each monastery-parish with valuable data on estancias and population.[20] The AM of Cuatro Villas towards 1580

submitted separate reports describing Guastepec, Tepuztlan, Yecapixtla, and Yautepec, although the Yautepec relación has been lost; those concerning Guastepec and Yecapixtla have large colored maps made by native artists.[21]

For the period of congregations, there are both a 1597 listing of tributary counts for the cabeceras and further data from 1603–4.[22] Various sources give demographic information for the seventeenth century,[23] and there are interesting details of parishes and haciendas in the account of an archbishop's visit in 1646.[24] Vetancurt (4a parte, pp. 59–60, 83) describes the Franciscan doctrines as they were towards 1697.

There is an excellent report made in 1743 by the AM with a wealth of detail, together with a small map of the jurisdiction.[25] Dated 1777 is a topographic description of the parish of Mazatepec.[26] For 1791–2 we have an extraordinarily good map of the jurisdiction, both detailed and accurate,[27] and a complete list of toponyms with a brief geographical description.[28] We have also seen a collection of census lists covering Guastepec, Yautepec, and parts of Tepuztlan and Yecapixtla, dated 1807.[29]

The ramo of Hospital de Jesús, at AGN, should yield much further information about Cuernavaca. Monographic treatment includes the essays of Lewis (1963) and Redfield on Tepoztlán; the works of Díez and Urbán Aguirre are of little interest to our purposes, but that of García Martínez (1969) adds important details, as do those of Berthe (1966) and Riley (1968).

23 *Cuiseo de la Laguna*

Lake Cuitzeo, in northernmost Michoacán, is a shallow volcanic basin at an elevation of 1,880 m surrounded by low hills. The climate is temperate, with scant precipitation.

Cuitzeo was a Tarascan outpost on the Chichimec frontier, and we may assume that both Tarascan and Chichimec (probably Pame) were spoken there at contact. Several small states, all

tributary to the cazonci, shared the lake waters and surrounding lands. Among them, Huandacareo, Jeruco, and Uriparao seem to have been subordinate to Cuitzeo itself, which was perhaps ruled by a military governor.

The area submitted to the Spaniards in the early 1520s.

Encomienda

Gonzalo López (el Camarero) held Cuiseo as early as 1528; escheatment occurred between 1553 and 1560.[1]

Government

A C was assigned to Cuiseo from the 1550s. This magistrate was suffragan to the AM of Michoacán in the late sixteenth century. In 1657–76 we find the jurisdiction attached for purposes of tribute collection to nearby Celaya, but magistrates

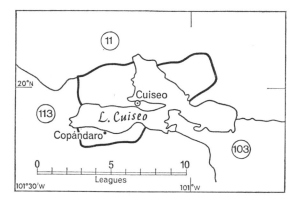

(AMs) were assigned to Cuiseo during those years and later. From 1787 this justice was referred to as a C, subordinate to the intendencia of Valladolid.[2]

Church

Cuiseo was visited by the curate of neighboring Guango until 1550, when an Augustinian monastery dedicated to Sta María Magdalena was founded there. Santiago Copándaro became a separate Augustinian parish in 1566 (Basalenque, pp. 143–6). S Gerónimo Guandacareo and Sta Ana Maya were subordinate vicariates in the eighteenth century. Copándaro was secularized sometime after 1777, but Cuiseo remained an Augustinian parish. Both were in the diocese of Michoacán.

Population and settlements

After a considerable loss from disease in 1545–7, there were 4,379 persons above four years of age in Cuiseo and its dependencies towards 1548. An estimate of 1554 gives two thousand 'hombres de carga' (BAGN, III, p. 42). In early years many Indian servants of the monastery were exempt from tribute payment, a privilege withdrawn in the 1560s (Scholes and Adams, 1961, p. 69); thus the number of tributaries had increased to c. 2,500 before the epidemic of 1576–9, in which a third of the population is said to have perished. Much of the subsequent loss may have resulted from emigration to haciendas in the Bajío. 1,900 tributaries are reported in 1579, 1,545 in 1588, 1,019 in 1601, 624 in 1623, 383 in 1657, and 315 in 1698. Despite further decimation in the cocoliztli of 1736–7, a census of 1743 shows 446 Indian families. There were 1,400 Indian tributaries by 1799.[3]

The 1743 report mentions 285 non-Indian families (more than a third of the total), while that of 1799 gives 258 mulatto tributaries in the jurisdiction.

In 1548 the population of Cuiseo (Cuseo; 1950: Cuitzeo del Porvenir, *villa*) was dispersed in four cabeceras (Cuiseo, Guandacareo, Jeruco, Uriparao) and thirty-six estancias. By 1571 the number of estancias had been reduced to twenty-seven, visited from the two monasteries, and other settlements were abandoned after the epidemic of 1576. There were subsequent congregations in which most of the estancias were combined in a half dozen pueblos. One such reduction occurred c. 1593, when six or seven outlying communities were moved in to Cuiseo, and Sta Ana Maya became a center of congregation.[4] Another may have taken place in 1599–1604.[5] In 1639 the surviving sujetos were Capamacutiro (=Capacho), Chocandiro (=Tararameo?), Guandacareo, Maya, S Lorenzo, and S Miguel. A century later the two last-named places had disappeared, their place taken by a new pueblo, S Buenaventura Guacao. The 1791 padrón lists the cabecera, Cuiseo, with two barrios, three pueblos (Copándaro, Guandacareo, Maya), nine rancherías, and three haciendas.

Sources

A brief description of c. 1548 (PNE, I, no. 154) is followed by two reports in the Ovando series, only one of them published (García Pimentel, 1904, pp. 34–5); the second, dated 1571, gives more detailed information.[6] There is an interesting report submitted by the C of Cuiseo in 1579.[7]

Tributary data for the period 1588–1698 are derived from several sources.[8] A general description of Michoacán dated 1639 gives useful details about settlements at Cuiseo.[9]

The MS relación of 1743 is badly mutilated,[10] but a résumé is found in Villaseñor y Sánchez (II, p. 71). There is a good report sent in by the Augustinian prior in 1777,[11] a census of *c.* 1791,[12] a list of settlements in 1793,[13] and finally, a description of Cuiseo as it was *c.* 1821 (Martínez de Lejarza, pp. 270–9).

24 *Cuyoacan*

Now occupying the southwest quadrant of the Distrito Federal and of the valley of Mexico, this jurisdiction extended from the shore of Lake Texcoco to the valley's rim at Cerro Ajusco (2,200–3,952 m). The climate is cool with moderate rainfall.

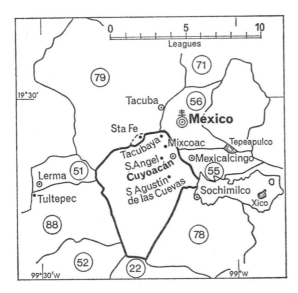

Cuyoacan was ruled by a tlatoani of Tepaneca lineage. It can perhaps be identified with the 'Quahuacan' of the Codex Mendocino, a center of tribute collection for the Triple Alliance. It probably included Tlacobayan, and perhaps had other subject states outside the valley to the west. Tlalpan belonged to neighboring Xochimilco. Náhuatl was the predominant language, but there was an Otomí minority.

First seen by the Spaniards in the fall of 1519,

Cuyoacan was re-occupied by them in April, 1521.

Encomienda

Cortés established his headquarters at Cuyoacan after the capture of Tenochtitlan and kept the place as a personal fief when the Spanish ayuntamiento moved to Mexico city in 1524. Although Cortés's rights were infringed on in early years, both Cuyoacan and Tacubaya were named in the 1529 grant of the Marquesado. They remained in encomienda to the descendants of Cortés, except during the various periods of sequestration.

Government

The first Spanish settlement with its ayuntamiento in the valley of Mexico was founded at Cuyoacan in 1521 and remained there until it was moved to Tenochtitlan at the beginning of 1524. From 1530 the jurisdiction had a magistrate (C, sometimes AM) appointed by the Marqués del Valle, although this privilege was revoked in 1570–95, 1710–25, and 1814–15. During the first of these sequestrations Cuyoacan was attached to the alcaldía mayor of Tenayuca (cf. Tacuba). From 1787 the magistrate was in a sense subordinate to the intendente of Mexico.

In a petition of 1532 Cortés claimed various places (Atlapulco, Capulhuac, Ocelotepec, Texcalyacac, Xalatlaco) as sujetos of Cuyoacan,[1] but the audiencia gave these places in encomienda to other persons, leaving Cuyoacan with approximately its final limits. There were minor border disputes between Cuyoacan and Sochimilco (which lost Tlalpan in the 1540s) and Mexico city (which acquired Chapultepec). We might mention here two small enclaves belonging to Cortés and his descendants. The *peñoles* (hills) of Xico and Tepeapulco, which were at the time islands in the lakes of Chalco and Texcoco, together with certain properties in Mexico city, were included in the 1529 Marquesado grant (Cortés, p. 546. ENE, XI, pp. 56–7).

Santa Fé, the hospital settlement founded with royal protection by Vasco de Quiroga in 1532, was in a special jurisdictional category. The land which was acquired to form the settlement was taken from three contiguous villages, Tacuba, Guajimalpa, and Tacubaya, the last two belonging to Cuyoacan (most of the area seems to have corresponded to an estancia of Tacubaya called Acasúchil). In addition, the city of Mexico claimed that its own limits included Santa Fé. Yet from the 1530s, despite attempts to annex it to Cuyoacan, Mexico, and Tacuba, and in fact profiting from the conflicting claims, Santa Fé retained its autonomy and was governed by its own native officers. The hospital's jurisdiction came to include Tultepec, a small island in the Lerma river some distance to the southwest (cf. Tenango del Valle) (Martin, p. 143. Warren, 1963*b*, pp. 43–73).

Church

While there was apparently some early Franciscan activity there, the parish of S Juan Bautista Cuyoacan began with the establishment of a Dominican monastery in 1528. By 1570 there was a second Dominican parish at S José Tacubaya, and before the end of that century two more had been founded, Sto Domingo Mixcoac and S Agustín de las Cuevas (Tlalpan).[2] The discalced Carmelites built two monasteries in the jurisdiction; that of the Santo Desierto de los Leones or La Soledad (1606–11) was a cloister only, while S Angel (1615–27, also known for a time as Sta Ana and S Jacinto) became a Dominican parish. All were secularized in 1752–6 except Tacubaya, which remained Dominican until 1765. These parishes were in the archdiocese of Mexico (cf. Vera, *passim*).

Santa Fé was in a special position ecclesiastically as well as politically. In the 1530s there was a small Augustinian cloister there, but by 1542 parochial functions were being performed by a secular priest. The curate was first appointed by the bishop of Michoacán; after 1565 appointment was controlled by the dean and cabildo of the cathedral of Michoacán, although in later years this priest, once he had taken office, was considered subordinate to the archbishop of Mexico (Navarro y Noriega, p. 40. Vera, p. 54. Warren, 1963*b*, pp. 53, 61–2).

Population and settlements

The number of Indian tributaries is given as 4,000 in 1551,[3] 5,670 in 1563, *c.* 5,200 in 1570,[4] 3,975 in 1597, 1,781 in 1644, 2,168 in 1692,[5] 3,430 in 1736, 2,887 in 1763, and 3,722 in 1799.[6] Not included here are the residents of Santa Fé, who paid no tribute; the number of vecinos was estimated at 300 in 1556, 130 (500 communicants) towards 1570, and only 70 or 80 after the epidemic of 1576–81 (Warren, 1963*b*, p. 119).

Quite a number of Spaniards lived at Cuyoacan in 1521–3, but later Cortés tried to keep them out (there were disputes between Cortés's descendants and the cabildo of Mexico city concerning who had the right to dispose of land and water here). By 1552 there were a number of mestizos and mulattoes in the jurisdiction, most of them living in haciendas and huertas.[7] In 1790 twenty per cent of the total population, consisting of 3,931 persons, was non-Indian.

We have no complete list of sixteenth-century settlements, nor do we know how Cuyoacán was affected by the congregations of 1600–4.[8] The 1570 report names only the two *villa-cabeceras* of Cuyoacan (1950: Coyoacán, *villa*) and Tacubaya (Atlacuvaya, etc.; 1950: part of Mexico city), and ten estancias (saints' names) subject to Cuyoacan. Three places were later made cabeceras: S Angel (1950: Villa Obregón), Mixcoac, and S Agustín de las Cuevas (1950: Tlalpan, ciudad). A number of places considered barrios or estancias in the sixteenth century survived as pueblos. Reports of 1791–4 name nineteen subject pueblos (some of these were late foundations), ten barrios, twenty-three haciendas, a rancho, and two inns (*ventas*) within the jurisdiction.

There is a brief report of *c.* 1570 on the two Dominican monasteries,[9] after which we have no satisfactory description of the jurisdiction until the late eighteenth century. Two archbishops who visited Cuyoacan in 1646[10] and 1683[11] give some information in their journals. A missing 1743 report is summarized by Villaseñor y Sánchez (I, p. 69). There is a map, a list of toponyms, and a census of non-Indians made *c.* 1791,[12] and another report for 1794.[13]

Gibson (1964) cites many unpublished documents, and a great many more will be found in the ramo of Hospital de Jesús at AGN. Warren (1963*b*) has produced a fine monograph on the hospital of Santa Fé. The textile industry at Cuyoacan as revealed in seventeenth-century documents is discussed by Greenleaf (1968) and O'Gorman (1940). Special mention should be made of García Martínez's (1969) work on the Marquesado.

25 *Chalco*

This area, economically and strategically among the most important in New Spain, included the southeastern part of the valley of Mexico (today partly in the Distrito Federal and the state of

Mexico) with a section beyond the escarpment limiting that valley on the south (now in the state of Morelos). Elevations range from 1,600 m at Tlayacapa to 5,450 m at Popocatépetl, and the climate is cool to frigid with moderate precipitation.

At contact there were a number of native states here, all inhabited by Náhuatl-speaking people (there may well have been a few Otomíes) tributary to the Aztecs. The largest part, the land of the Chalca, stretched from the lake shore up the slopes of the two snow-capped volcanoes, with five principal political divisions, Chalco, Tenanco, Chimalhuacan, Tlalmanalco, and Amaquemecan. Each of the first three was ruled by a tlatoani, while the others were divided into multiple governments. Tlalmanalco contained the semi-independent states of Opochuacan, Itzcahuacan, and Acxotlan Cihuateopan. Amaquemecan was governed by the five tlatoque of Itzlacocauhcan, Tlallotlacan, Tzacualtitlan Tenanco, Tecuanipan, and Panohuayan. Geographically within the Chalca area but directly subject to Tenochtitlan–Tlatelolco were a number of small settlements including Acatlixcoacan, Coxtocan, Tepopula, and Tepoxtlan.

Other places outside the Chalca territory were for various reasons added to the colonial jurisdiction. Among these were Cuitláhuac, Mixquic, and Ixtapalocan, three small communities on the shore and islands of Lake Chalco. Mixquic had its own tlatoani, while Cuitláhuac had four tlatoque governments, Tizic, Teopancalcan, Atenchicalcan, and Tecpan (cf. Ramírez, 1885, p. 83); both were peopled by Xochimilca. Ixtapalocan was an Acolhua settlement subject to Texcoco. Far to the southeast was Acatcinco, which belonged to the lord of Ocuiltuco. On the southern slope of the escarpment ruled the lord of Cuauhtenco or Totolapan, with subordinate tlatoque or perhaps calpixque at Atlatlauhcan, Nepopoalco, Tlayacapan, and Tehuitzco. The people of Totolapan and Acatcinco were Xochimilca in origin. Totolapan was an important center of trade with the hot country and delivered its tribute to the Aztec garrison at Huaxtépec.

This area was crossed by Pedro de Alvarado and Bernardino Vázquez de Tapia in the fall of 1519. The Chalca turned against the Aztecs and joined Cortés at the beginning of 1521, but Moctezuma's forces refused to surrender until they were defeated in a series of engagements in April of that year (Bancroft, I, p. 596. Vázquez de Tapia, p. 36).

Encomiendas

The Chalca territory (Chalco, Tlalmanalco, Tenango, Chimalguacan, and Amecameca), with the addition of Ecatzingo, was claimed for himself by Hernando Cortés. During his absences from Mexico (1524–6, 1528–30) the province was re-assigned several times, being held on one occasion by Nuño de Guzmán. It was not included in the Marquesado del Valle, and by 1533 it was considered a crown possession, although Cortés was assigned part of the tributes.

Perhaps on the basis of pre-Columbian tribute records, Cortés insisted that the Atlatlauca–Totolapa–Tlayacapa area was subject to his possessions of Guastepec and Yecapixtla. These places were briefly controlled by Diego de Holguín and Francisco de Solís (Atlatlauca–Totolapa), and Juan de Burgos (Tlayacapa) in 1528–30, regained by Cortés in 1531, and seized for the crown in 1532. They were re-assigned to the contador Rodrigo de Albornoz in 1538–44, after which they remained in the crown.[1]

The early encomienda history of Cuitláhuac is not known to us. We have mentioned that the island of Xico, which probably belonged to Cuitláhuac, was assigned to Cortés in 1529 (cf. Cuyoacan); it was still considered part of the Marquesado as late as 1743. The rest of this encomienda was acquired by the *escribano de minas*

Juan de Cuevas sometime before 1544. When Cuevas died in the 1560s he was succeeded by a son, Alonso, who still appears as encomendero in 1606. After 1678 Cuitláhuac was re-assigned; in 1743 tributes were going to the Duquesa de Atlixco.

Mixquic was given to Bartolomé de Zárate, who renounced it before 1550 in favor of his daughter Ana. She married Gil Ramírez de Avalos, who lost the encomienda when he went to Perú, but by 1570 it had been regained by their son of the same name. Before 1586 tributes were re-assigned to Luis de Velasco, whose heirs continued to receive them for many years (Mixquic was still a private encomienda in 1743).

Cortés assigned Ixtapaluca to Juan de Cuéllar in the 1520s. It was inherited *c.* 1551 by his widow, Ana Ruiz, and his son, Andrés de Cuéllar. The latter died without issue sometime before 1565 and the encomienda passed to his younger brother, Martín. This was contested by the royal prosecutor, and in 1574 Ixtapaluca became a crown possession. Later, it was re-assigned to Luis de Velasco.

Government

A C was first appointed in 1532 to administer Totolapa, and by the following year Chalco was a corregimiento. Mixquic and Huichilobusco (cf. Mexicalcingo) had a crown magistrate in the 1530s, but both places soon reverted to private encomienda, as did Totolapa in 1538–44.[2] In 1550 the corregidor of Chalco was ordered to administer justice in neighboring encomienda villages, and within a few years he was re-designated AM, with supervisory functions in the corregimientos of Ocopetlayuca (cf. Tochimilco), Ocuituco (cf. Cuautla Amilpas), Tetela del Volcán (q.v.), Teutlalco (q.v.), and Totolapa.[3] This suffragan arrangement ended towards the end of the sixteenth century. Totolapa (Tlayacapa) continued to have its own justice, variously referred to as C or AM, until it was annexed to the jurisdiction of Chalco in the 1670s.[4]

The residence of the AM moved about, but most often he lived at Tlalmanalco. In the eighteenth century there were tenientes at

Amecameca, Ayotzingo, Chalco, Ozumba, Totolapa, and Tlayacapa. From 1787 Chalco was a subdelegación in the intendencia of Mexico.

Church

The Franciscans, soon after their arrival in Mexico in 1524, began work in the Chalco area. They were joined by the other mendicant orders, and within twelve years or so each had established a doctrina. Excluding for the moment the Totolapa region, these were S Vicente Chimalguacan (Dominican, 1528), S Luis Tlalmanalco (Franciscan, 1531), and S Andrés Mixquic (Augustinian, 1536?). Towards 1550 a Dominican monastery was founded at Asunción Amecameca, and by 1570 there were others at S Pedro Cuitláhuac and S Juan Bautista Tenango (all these places had previously been visited by Franciscans). By 1558 the Franciscans had a resident priest at Santiago Chalco, and in the early 1580s the Augustinians started a separate doctrina at Sta Catalina Ayotzingo (Ponce, I, p. 77).

S Guillermo Totolapa was first visited by Dominicans from Guastepec, but in 1535 it was assigned to the Augustinians, who founded additional houses at S Juan Bautista Tlayacapa (1554), S Mateo Atlatlauca (*c.* 1570), and Purificación Tlalnepantla (soon after 1600).

With the congregations early in the seventeenth century several new parishes were created. Sto Domingo Xuchitepec (Dominican) and S Juan Bautista Temamatla (Franciscan) were separated from Tenango and Tlalmanalco, respectively, in 1603. About the same time, Dominican monasteries were placed at S Pedro Ecatzingo and S Juan Bautista Ixtapaluca (the latter until then a visita of Coatepec), and by 1640 Concepción Ozumba was a Franciscan parish.

Between 1745 and 1789 these parishes, all in the archbishopric of Mexico, were secularized. Two new curacies were formed in 1769 from former visitas of Tlalmanalco, Santiago Ayapango and S Gregorio Cuautzingo (cf. Vera, *passim*).

Population and settlements

Apart from the epidemics which de-populated New Spain in general, plagues of a more local extent afflicted the Chalco area in 1563–4 and 1604–7. The number of native tributaries dropped from 18,496 (4,879 of these were in the corregimiento of Totolapa) in 1570 to perhaps 9,000 at the end of that century, further declined to 4,316 in 1643, and then recovered slightly to 4,919 in 1688. The census of 1743 shows 4,593 Indian families in Chalco proper and 2,091 in the Totolapa area, a total of 6,684, while that of 1800–3 gives 12,318 Indian tributaries in the whole jurisdiction. The non-Indian population was relatively small – 253 mulatto tributaries are reported in 1800.[5]

There were at least two attempts at congregation of Indian settlements in this region. We have seen notices of early reductions at Chimalguacan in 1553,[6] and five years later at Chalco, Ixtapaluca, Tlalmanalco, and again at Chimalguacan.[7] In 1598–1604 many estancias were abandoned or moved closer to congregation sites.[8]

Five outlying settlements subject to Chalco (Chalcoatengo; 1950: Chalco de Díaz Covarrubias, *villa*) were to be concentrated at the cabecera in 1558. Eleven visitas are mentioned in the 1570 report, but some of these places were politically subject to other cabeceras. In 1604 the five surviving estancias of Chalco seem to have been moved in to the monastery.

Amecameca (Amaquemecan; 1950: Amecameca de Juárez, ciudad) probably had an early congregation in the 1550s, although it still had twelve dependant settlements (they are named and located on the congregation map and report) in 1599; only S Miguel Atlauhcan (Atlautla, Tlautla) seems to have survived this last reduction as a subject pueblo.[9]

Cuitláhuac (Cuitlaguaca, Tláhuac in later years; 1950: Tláhuac, pueblo) had its cabecera on an island in Lake Chalco, with estancias scattered about on the north shore and on other islands, perhaps a dozen settlements altogether in the 1570s. Most of the latter disappeared in the congregation of 1603,[10] but four subject pueblos survived in the eighteenth century: Sta Catarina Mártir, S Francisco Tlaltenco, S Martín Xico, and Santiago Zapotitlan.

There was an early border dispute between

Chimalguacan (Chimaloacan; 1950: Chimalhuacán Chalco, pueblo) and Ocuituco involving the village of Acacingo or Ecatzingo, but by 1535 the place had been 'usurped' by Chimalguacan.[11] Some twenty estancias were reduced in the congregations we have mentioned to eight pueblos (Ecatzingo, Mamalhuazuca, Ozumba or Atzompan, Tecalco, Tecomaxusco, Tepecoculco, Tepetlixpa, Tlalamac).

Ixtapaluca (Estapalucan, etc.; 1950: Ixtapaluca, pueblo) had nine or ten estancias on the shores and islands of Lake Chalco before the congregations of 1558 and 1603-4. Ayotla, Tlalpizagua, and Tlapacoya were subject to this cabecera in the eighteenth century.

Mixquic (Mezquic, Amesquique, etc.; 1950: Mixquic, pueblo) in 1571 had five 'barrios' and six 'cabeceras sujetas' (all named in the report) within a half league of the principal settlement on the south shore and islands of Lake Chalco. Tetelco (Cuicatetelco) and Tezompa survived as pueblos.

According to a document of 1571, the old site of Tenango (Tenanco Tepopula; 1950: Tenango del Aire, pueblo) was five leagues south of Ayotzingo, although towards 1552 it was moved to its new site at Tepopula, two leagues east of Ayotzingo. This would place the original location high in the mountains above Tlalnepantla, near the present boundary between Mexico and Morelos. The political and ecclesiastical affiliations of this area were most complicated. Tepopula itself was shared between the two wards of Tenochtitlan and Tlatelolco in Mexico city, a situation which continued to the late eighteenth century. Nearby Tepostlan (Poxtla, Santiago Tepopula) was subject to Tlatelolco, while Acatlixcoacan and Ochtocansul (S Juan Coxtocán) belonged politically to Tenochtitlan. Two estancias of Tenango, Ayapango and Ayotzingo, were long subject in matters of doctrine to Tlalmanalco and Mixquic respectively. Another, Cuautzotzongo (Guazozongo), which must have been near the original site of Tenango's cabecera, was claimed in 1532 by Cortés as an estancia of Yecapixtla.[12] In 1603-4 it was determined to make two congregations, one centered at the monastery of Tenango Tepopula and another at the newly-founded doctrine of Sto

Domingo Xuchitepec, a league from Cuautzotzongo. We have record of twenty-four Indian communities, most of them quite small, which apparently disappeared at this time.[13] Still in existence in the eighteenth century were the former estancias, now pueblos, of Ayapango, Ayotzingo, Costocán, Cuautenco, Chalcatepehuacán, Chalma, Mihuacatzinco (Mihuacán), Pahuacán, Puxtla, Tepopula, Tepostlan (Tlatelulco), Tlaltehuacán, Tlamapa, Xuchitepec, Zentlalpan, and Zoyatzingo.

Tlalmanalco (1950: Tlalmanalco de Velázquez, *villa*), the principal cabecera of the jurisdiction of Chalco, had a great many dependent settlements. In 1558 the Indians of sixteen estancias were ordered to move to Tlalmanalco, but most of these places continue to appear in later reports.[14] Ten sujetos seem to have been congregated in 1603-4, while seventeen survived as pueblos: Acatlixhuaya, Amalinalpa, Atlaxalpa, Atzacualoya, Atzingo, Cocotitlan, Cuatlalpan, Cuautzingo (Cuazilzingo), Huexoculco, Huistoco, Huitzilzingo, Metla, S Mateo de los Molinos, Temamatla, Tlalmimilolpan, Tlapala, and Zula.

There was an acrid dispute in the sixteenth century between Totolapa(n) (1950: Totolapan, pueblo, Mor.) and certain of its sujetos which claimed to be cabeceras.[15] Two of them, Atlatlauca and Tlayacapa, were successful in obtaining cabecera status, each taking with it a number of smaller estancias. Three or four of the sites remaining to Totolapa were deserted in a congregation of *c.* 1600, and three others were moved to the new monastery of Purificación Tlalnepantla (Cuauhtenca) at that time. Still other estancias (Aguatlan, S Miguel Metepec, Nepopualco, S Lucas Tehuizco) were pueblos in the eighteenth century, together with two later foundations, S Nicolás and S Sebastián.

Atlatlauca (1950: Atlatlahucan, pueblo, Mor.) was considered a separate cabecera by 1579. There was a congregation here in 1604, at which time Tepetlixpa and Tonalá were abandoned, while S Juan Texcalpan remained inhabited. Tepetlixpa el Chico re-appears as a pueblo in the 1790s.[16]

Tlayacapa(n) (1950: Tlayacapan, *villa*, Mor.) had at least thirteen estancias, eight of which seem to have been congregated at the cabecera in 1601–4 (here as elsewhere the cabecera itself was moved at an early date from its hillsite to the valley below). S Agustín (Atocpa), S José (Iscuitepec), S Andrés (Nonopala), S Pablo (Texoacan), and Sta Catarina (Tlalhuica, Zacatiliucan) all were pueblos in the eighteenth century.

Sources

The pre-Conquest and early colonial history of this area is related in Chimalpahin Cuauhtlehuanitzin (1965). Additional details are found in a 1554 history of Chimalguacan (ENE, VII, pp. 259–66), and a valuable document concerning the corregimiento of Totolapa dated 1559 (ENE, VIII, pp. 232–44). The original land titles of Cuitláhuac[17] and Tlayacapan[18] have been preserved.

In the Ovando series (*c.* 1570), there is a general report on the entire area,[19] together with individual and more detailed reports concerning Tlayacapa[20] and Mixquic and Totolapa[21] (cf. *Códice Franciscano*, p. 10). Only the jurisdiction of Totolapa is described in a relación geográfica of

1579.[22] Scattered data on the congregations of 1592–1604 are cited above, but special mention should be made of two more detailed reports concerning Amecameca (with a map)[23] and Tenango.[24]

For the seventeenth century, we have population data for the period 1623–88,[25] the journal of an archbishop's visit in 1646,[26] and descriptions of the Franciscan doctrinas as they were *c.* 1697 (Vetancurt, 4a parte, pp. 62, 79, 84, 87).

Two detailed reports from the AM and his teniente describe Chalco[27] and Tlayacapa-Totolapa[28] in 1743. There is a useful list of pueblos with population data for 1770,[29] accompanied by a map of part of the jurisdiction.[30] Only two parishes, Ayapango[31] and Tlalnepantla,[32] are represented in the 1777–8 series of topographic reports. A complete list of placenames dates from 1792.[33] The latest document seen is the baptism register of Tlayacapa for the years 1815–18.[34]

Much more concerning Chalco (excluding Totolapa-Tlayacapa) can be found in the work of Gibson (1964), and in the indices of Colín (1966, 1967).

26 Charo

Charo (Tarascan) or Matlatcinco (Náhuatl) straddles the Sierra de Ozumatlán in northeast Michoacán, with drainage northward towards the Cuitzeo basin and south into affluents of the Balsas. Temperatures are temperate to cool depending on the elevation (1,500–2,500 m); rainfall is heavier on the southern exposure, and the sierra is covered with pine–oak forest.

This was an enclave of Otomí migrants from the region of Toluca, surrounded by Tarascans. These people, known as Pirinda or Matlatzinca, arrived in Michoacán in the fifteenth century and were given lands by the cazonci, whom they served as mercenaries. Their territory included neighboring Necotlan (cf. Valladolid). Along with the Tarascans, they submitted without known resistance to Olid's expedition in mid-1522.

Encomienda

Matalcingo (the name most used in the sixteenth century) and its dependency, Necotlan, were assigned by Cortés to the contador Rodrigo de Albornoz in July, 1524 (Warren, 1963 *a*, p. 409). Possession was being contested by Juan Fernández Infante in 1531, and five years later the encomendero was Jorge Cerón Saavedra (Millares Carlo and Mantecón, II, no. 1989). Sometime between 1536 and 1545 the encomienda escheated; it was perhaps at this time that Necotlan was made a separate cabecera.[1]

When the second Marqués del Valle, Martín Cortés, arrived in Mexico he brought suit for the possession of Matalcingo, pointing out that it was named in the grant made to his father in 1529. The royal prosecutor countered that there were two Matalcingos, one which he identified with Toluca (long recognized as part of the marquisate), and that of Michoacán which had never been held by the first marquis. However, the audiencia decided against the crown, and the '*villa*' of Matalcingo Charo was annexed to the Marquesado, probably in 1564.[2]

Government

Cs appointed by the viceroy ruled Matalcingo during the first period of escheatment. In 1565–9 the magistrate was an appointee of the Marqués del

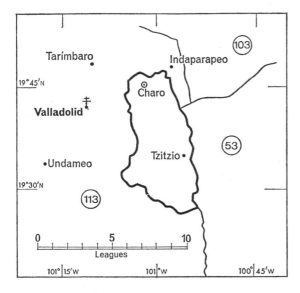

Valle, but during the first sequestration of the Cortés holdings (1570–95) the jurisdiction was administered by the C of Jaso y Teremendo (cf. Valladolid).[3] The third marquis recovered the privilege of appointment in 1595 and his descendants continued to name Cs here, interrupted only by the sequestrations of 1710–25 and 1814–15.[4] From 1787 the corregimiento was included in the intendencia of Valladolid.

Church

A secular priest appointed by the bishop of Mexico and paid by the encomendero agreed to take up residence at Matalcingo in October, 1536 (Millares Carlo and Mantecón, II, no. 1989). Subsequently the place was visited by the curate of Indaparapeo

until an Augustinian monastery was founded at S Miguel Matalcingo Charo in 1550 (Basalenque, p. 150). This parish, which belonged to the diocese of Michoacán, was secularized by 1764.

Population and settlements

The *Suma de Visitas* (*c.* 1548) gives 963 persons above three years of age at Matalcingo, while 600 'hombres de carga' are reported in 1554, and the same number of tributaries is given in 1573.[5] This total dropped to 351 in 1597, and 254 in 1657. There were 296 tributaries in 1698, 425 in 1706, 430 Indian families in 1743, and 462 Indian tributaries in 1798.[6] Forty to fifty non-Indian families are reported in 1743, and forty mulatto tributaries in 1798.

Nine places, some of them later removed from the jurisdiction, are named in the 1524 encomienda grant of Matalcingo: Coyzola, Maratuhaco, Maritaro, Moquenzan, Necotan, Totula, Uritla, Vichitepeque, and Yrapeo (Warren, 1963*a*, p. 409). We are told that the original Pirinda cabecera was in the highland of Surumbeneo, and that the curate of Indaparapeo collected his charges some distance below at Los Capulines where a chapel was built. When the Augustinians arrived, the settlement was moved first to Los Reyes, and later to its final site on a low hill (Matalcingo, Charo; 1950: Charo, pueblo).[7]

The Augustinian report of 1571 mentions six estancias, the most distant being five leagues south of the cabecera, while another document of about the same date lists eight. Only two of these settlements, Sta María Patamoro (Patámbaro) and S Guillermo Tzitzio (Checheo), apparently survived the congregation of *c.* 1604 as pueblos. Two places listed as sujetos of Tarímbaro in 1604, Irapeo and Acerumbenio (Surumbeneo), appear in the jurisdiction of Charo in the eighteenth century, the first an hacienda and the second a ranchería.

Sources

Warren (1963*a*, p. 409) cites the 1524 grant of Charo Matalcingo, and the area is succinctly described as it was *c.* 1548 (PNE, I, no. 365). One of the Ovando reports (1571),[8] although badly mutilated, is more detailed than another in the same series (García Pimentel, 1904, p. 42). Congregation data appear in two documents.[9]

A lost report of *c.* 1743 is summarized in Villaseñor y Sánchez (II, p. 29). The Capuchin friar Ajofrín has little to say about Charo, which he visited in 1764 (Ajofrín, I, pp. 207–8). There is an excellent report submitted by the curate in 1778 with a map of his parish.[10] For 1790–1 there are two documents, one a brief description,[11] the other a census of non-Indians.[12] Further details are given in the work of Martínez Lejarza (pp. 36–41), corresponding to *c.* 1822.

27 *Chiautla*

Chiautla, now in southwestern Puebla (with a small part of Guerrero), is a region of low hills and watercourses draining into the Mexcala (Balsas)

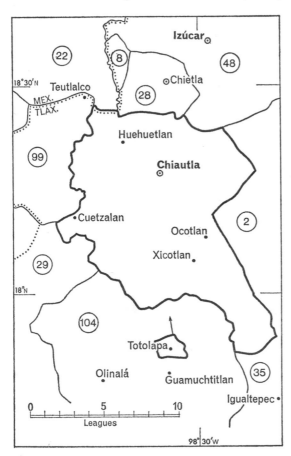

river, which crosses it from east to west. Elevations are 800–1,600 m, and the climate is quite dry and hot, producing a xerophytic vegetation.

Chiyauhtla was the dominant state here, with Cuetzallan, Ocotlan, and Tzontecomapan either entirely subject to it or semi-autonomous. There was an Aztec garrison at Ichcaatoyac (=Ichcamillpan? Cf. Guaxuapa) where tribute was collected. Cotton, copal incense, and salt were produced. The people spoke Náhuatl and lived in a great many scattered settlements.

Spaniards visited this area in search of gold perhaps before the end of 1519, and it came under their control late in 1520.

Encomienda

Diego de Ordaz was given Chiautla in the early 1520s and was followed as encomendero by Alonso de Grado, who died in 1527, and then by Diego Becerra de Mendoza. Becerra was killed on the west coast in 1533 or 1534. The second audiencia made Chiautla a crown possession at this time, although Gerónimo López claimed possession (Cortés, p. 522. ENE, IV, pp. 172–5. Gibson, 1964, p. 423. Millares Carlo and Mantecón, I, no. 606).

Government

A corregimiento by 1534, Chiautla became an alcaldía mayor in the late 1540s after rich silver deposits were discovered in the south.[1] The province was known in these early years as Minas de Ayoteco, and in the sixteenth century included Igualtepec, Guamuchtitlan, and Olinalá as well as Chiautla.[2] In the provincial division of the 1560s the AM supervised a number of suffragan Cs along the Mexcala river as far as Iscateupa. In the late seventeenth century (probably in the jurisdictional re-arrangement of the 1670s) Olinalá and Guamuchtitlan were transferred to Tlapa (q.v.), Igualtepec to Tonalá (cf. Guaxuapa), and Papalutla to Chilapa (q.v.), leaving Chiautla with approximately its final boundaries. One of Chiautla's sujetos, Totolapa, formed an enclave off to the south (see map).

Teutlalco (q.v.) was attached to this jurisdiction sometime between 1743 and 1770, but we will consider it separately here.[3] After 1787 the AM of Chiautla became a subdelegado in the intendencia of Puebla.

Church

Chiautla may well have had a secular priest before the foundation of an Augustinian monastery-parish (S Agustín Chiautla) in 1550. We may assume there was a curate at the mines of Ayoteco in early years. The whole jurisdiction was subsequently visited from the monastery until additional secular parishes were created at S Juan Xicotlan (before 1743) and Sta María Cuetzala (after 1743). Chiautla itself was secularized by 1777. All parishes were in the bishopric of Tlaxcala.

Population and settlements

Chiautla may have had 6,000 tributaries just before the great plague of 1545–8. A new count was made in 1554, at which time the province was 'much destroyed by famine and drought', giving a total of 3,800 tributaries. Subsequent loss from death and emigration reduced the number to 2,816 in 1571, 2,348 in 1588, 1,050 in 1610, and 525 in 1626. By 1696 there were 655 tributaries, in 1743 there were 915 Indian families, and the census of 1800 shows some 2,290 Indian tributaries here.[4]

There must have been a good number of non-Indian miners at Ayoteco (the first word we have seen of these mines is in 1542) and Apizalo (mentioned in 1552) during the sixteenth century.[5] There were 'many' cattle haciendas in the jurisdiction in 1604, which we assume were run by Spaniards and castas (Chevalier, 1952, p. 138). The padrón of Chiautla parish in 1777 shows 768

families of Indians and 302 of non-Indians, mostly mulattoes.

The 1571 report names sixteen estancias subject to Chiautla with a total of eighty-one 'barrios'. A congregation proposed in 1598 was probably carried out in 1603–4 resulting in the abandonment of most of these small settlements.[6] Only sixteen toponyms from the 1571 list appear as pueblos in 1792: Acaixtlaguacan, Ayoxochtlan (Ayosustla), Centeocala (Tzinteocalan), Cuacalco (Cuauhcalco), Sta María Cuetzalan (Quezala), Chila (de la Sal), Huehuetlan, Ixcamilpa, Nahuitochco (Nahuituxco), Ocotlan, Pilcaya (Acatelpilcayan), Tlancualpican, Totolapa(n), Tulcingo (Toltzinco), Tzicatlan, and Xicotlan. Four other 1792 pueblos may be later foundations: Sta Mónica Cuetzalan, S Juan del Río, Tlaltepexi, and Xicingo. Three settlements had cabecera status in 1770: Chiautla (1950: Chiautla de Tapia, villa), Huehuetlan (1950: Huehuetlán el Chico, pueblo), and Xicotlan (1950: pueblo).[7]

Sources

Interesting details of this area are given in an excerpt from the 1532 'Description de la tierra' (Herrera, Déc. 4a, p. 230). A very brief entry in the *Suma* of c. 1548 (PNE, I, no. 243) is followed by a report of the 1554 visita carried out by Gonzalo Díaz de Vargas (ENE, VIII, pp. 114–18). There is an unusually detailed relación drawn up by the Augustinian prior in 1571 (García Pimentel, 1904, pp. 109–15).

For the period 1588–1623 we have a valuable document concerning tributes and tributaries (Scholes and Adams, 1959). Bishop Mota y Escobar visited Chiautla in 1620.[8] There is additional tributary information for 1626–96,[9] a summary of a lost 1743 relación (Villaseñor y Sánchez, I, p. 343), a padrón of Chiautla parish dated 1777,[10] and a list of placenames dated 1792.[11]

28 Chietla

Adjoining Chiautla to the north was the small corregimiento of Chietla. This is a rather hot, arid region at 980–1,800 m, irrigated now as in pre-Conquest times by the waters of the Nexapa, which drains southwesterly into the Mexcala (Balsas). Today it is in the state of Puebla along its western border with Morelos.

Chietlan (Chiyetlan?) was the westernmost state in the Aztec tributary zone of Tepeyacac. Its ruler may have been related or subordinate in some way to that of Itzocan, and his realm perhaps formed

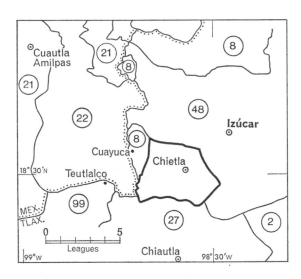

part of what was known as Coatlalpan. Ahuehuet-cinco, Atlchichica, Ayacatic, and Tenexcalco, while subject to Chietlan, may have had a certain autonomy. The people spoke Náhuatl and were dispersed in many settlements.

The area submitted to the Spaniards along with neighboring Itzocan in September, 1520.

Encomienda

Chietla seems to have been included among the holdings of the Alvarado family at Izúcar (q.v.). It escheated in the early 1540s (Icaza, I, p. 103. Sherman, 1969, p. 201).

Government

By 1545 Chietla was a corregimiento, which in the provincial division of the 1560s was considered suffragan to the alcaldía mayor of Izúcar. In 1576, however, the magistrate of Izúcar was reprimanded for sending constables to Chietla and was ordered not to interfere in the administration of justice there as long as the C was in residence.[1] In the seventeenth century Chietla continued to have its own magistrate (he was referred to as AM in 1667, C on other occasions), although tributes were sent to Izúcar. In 1743 the jurisdiction had 'recently' been annexed to that of Izúcar, but again from 1756 it had its own C. After 1787 Chietla was a subdelegación in the intendencia of Puebla.

Church

A Franciscan monastery was being built at Chietla in 1550 (BAGN, x, p. 270). Seventeen years later the parish was transferred to the Augustinians, who administered it until they were replaced by a secular curate in 1640 (*Alegaciones en favor del clero...*, fol. 37v, 69). As late as 1792 there was an Augustinian friar in residence, but he had no parochial duties. The patron saint, at first S Francisco, became S Agustín under that order, S Andrés upon secularization, and again S Francisco by 1743. The parish, in the diocese of Tlaxcala, included certain villages (Cuayuca, Zumpaguacan) in the jurisdiction of Atrisco in the seventeenth century, but later these places were transferred to the doctrina of Teutlalco (q.v.).

Population and settlements

There is such a wide discrepancy in the number of tributaries given in the *Suma de visitas* (1,718) and that reported in 1571 (906) that we suspect the former count was made before the epidemic of 1545–8. Further loss brought the total down to 553 in 1592,[2] and only 169 in 1626; later censuses show 238 tributaries in 1644, 327 in 1696, 356 Indian families in 1743, and 466 Indian tributaries in 1800.[3]

By 1644 there were a good many mulattoes and other castas living at three sugar-cane haciendas. In the late eighteenth century non-Indians comprised perhaps half the total population, and included 216 mulatto tributaries.

The *Suma de visitas* (c. 1548 or earlier in this case) names twenty settlements under Chietla, six barrios and fourteen estancias. Only ten estancias are listed in 1571, and most of these disappeared in the congregation of c. 1603. Ahuehuecingo, Azala, and Ayacatic were visitas in 1644. At the end of the eighteenth century settlements included the cabecera of Chietla (1950: *villa*), the pueblos of Ahuehuecingo, Azala, and Tenexcalco, one barrio, two ranchos, and three haciendas.[4]

Sources

An unusually detailed entry in the *Suma de visitas* (PNE, I, no. 108) describes Chietla as it was perhaps in the early 1540s. In the Ovando series (1571) is a brief report written by the Augustinian in charge of Chietla.[5] There is a brief reference to the congregation of c. 1603,[6] and another concerning the population decline in 1588–1623 (Scholes and Adams, 1959, p. 59).

Bishop Palafox visited Chietla in 1644 and described the doctrina in his journal.[7] A report from the AM of Izúcar dated 1743 includes interesting data on Chietla.[8] The padrón of 1791 is accompanied by an informative relación drawn up by the C,[9] who the following year sent in a list of placenames in his jurisdiction.[10]

29 *Chilapa*

This is a country of barren hills with some rugged mountains and canyons, drained in the north by the Mexcala (Balsas) and its affluents and in the south by tributaries of the Papagayo river. Now in eastern Guerrero state, it is crossed by the Sierra Madre del Sur in one of its lower parts, with elevations of 400–2,000 m producing a variety of climates (mostly hot and dry).

At contact, this was the heart of Coixcatlalpan, most of the people speaking a form of Náhuatl known as Coixca. Smaller groups in the north spoke Matlame (=Matlatzincan?) and Tuxtecan (=Chontal?), while Tlapanecan or Yope predominated in the south along the Omitlán river. The Mexica were in control of the entire region except in the south where they had a frontier with the belligerent Yope; Quecholtenanco was an Aztec fortress protecting this southern border. The states of Chilapan and Atenanco sent their tribute to Tepecoacuilco. Tlalcozauhtitlan was a separate state and a Mexica tributary center to which the lords of Ahuacicinco (Ahuacuauhtzinco), Cuauhtecomaccinco, Ichcatlan, Mictlantcinco, Tepuztitlan, Tolimani, and Zacatlan were subject. Other communities which may have been autonomous to some extent were in the north, in the vicinity of Atenanco: Acacuila, Acuauhtcinco, Comala, Cuetlaxochitlan, Mezquitlan, Ostotla, Papalotla, Tecoacuilco, Tetlauhco, Zacango, and Zacuantla. In general, this seems to have been a rich, populous agricultural zone with many independent or semi-independent communities, the largest being Chilapan.

The Mexcala basin was explored by Spanish gold-seekers in 1520. Spanish control in Coixcatlalpan was imposed in the summer of 1521 (Oviedo y Valdés, III, p. 406).

Encomiendas

Chilapa was perhaps first held by Cristóbal Flores and somewhat later by Diego de Ordaz (another early holder may have been Alonso Grado). The place was crown property in 1532–6, but by 1541 it had been assigned to Diego de Ordaz Villagómez, nephew of the conquistador. Sometime between 1573 and 1582 the latter was succeeded by a son, Antonio de Ordaz Villagómez (cf. Dorantes de Carranza, p. 171). Chilapa was still a private encomienda in the mid-eighteenth century, by which time it had been re-assigned to the countess of Moctezuma (ENE, II, p. 176; IV, p. 174).

The first encomendero that we hear of at Tlalcozautitlan was the conquistador Ruy González. The second audiencia divided this enco-

mienda, assigning half to another conquistador, Vasco Porcallo, who by 1551 had been followed by a son, Lorenzo Porcallo de Figueroa (de la Cerda). When González died towards 1559 his half escheated (Gardiner, 1958, p. 155). The other half was still held by a Lorenzo Porcallo in 1611. In 1743 the encomendera was the marquesa de la Bañera.

Papalutla was perhaps first held by Alonso de

Aguilar, succeeded in the 1550s by a son, Baltasar. Escheatment seems to have occurred towards 1566.

We know little else about encomiendas here. Mezquitlan and Ostutla, long privately held, were crown property by 1548. Atenango and Zacango were claimed by the encomendero of neighboring Huizuco (cf. Iguala) in the 1590s, but before and after that time they appear as crown villages.[1] Other places in the north were crown cabeceras in 1570 and may once have been private encomiendas: Acaquila, Acuaucingo, Comala, Cuetlaxochitlan, Tecuacuilco, Tetlauco, and Zacuantla; more likely, they were attached to one or another of the encomiendas mentioned above.

Government

While a C was assigned to Chilapa during its brief escheatment in the 1530s, it was not until *c.* 1552 that crown control was re-established with the creation of a provincial alcaldía mayor, generally designated Minas de Zumpango.[2] The jurisdiction of this magistrate, whose residence was at times Chilapa, included the cabeceras of Chilapa, Huiciltepec, Muchitlan, Tistla, Tlapa, and Zumpango.[3] North of the Mexcala, the villages of Atenango, Mezquitlan, Zacango, and perhaps Tlalcozautitlan were attached to the corregimiento of Iscateupa (q.v.) until a C arrived at Tlalcozautitlan towards 1560 (L de T, p. 63). Meanwhile the AM of 'provincia de Chilapa y Minas de Zumpango' functioned also as C of Tlapa (q.v.) until the latter became a separate jurisdiction in 1579.[4]

Sometime around 1600, Tistla (q.v.), Zumpango, Huiciltepec, and Muchitlan were annexed to the alcaldía mayor of Acapulco, while the corregimiento of Tlalcozautitlan was combined with the jurisdiction of Chilapa.[5] During the seventeenth century the magistrate here was generally called AM of 'Tlalcozautitlan, provincia de Chilapa'; in this same period, Ostutla was acquired from Teutlalco, and Papalutla from Chiautla.

Sometime before 1743, likely in the jurisdictional reforms of the 1680s, the province of Chilapa–Tlalcozautitlan was made subordinate to that of Acapulco and was henceforth administered by a teniente of the castellan of that port. From 1787 this was a subdelegación in the intendencia of Mexico.

Church

The Augustinians entered this area late in 1533 and founded a doctrina at Asunción Chilapa (Gómez de Orozco. Grijalva, p. 49). There was a secular priest from the diocese of Tlaxcala at S Lucas Tlalcozautitlan by 1569, while the Atenango–Zacango region remained in the archdiocese of Mexico, first visited from Huizuco; from *c.* 1600 a secular curate lived at S Juan Atenango del Río.[6] As another result of the congregations of *c.* 1600, the doctrina of Chilapa was divided and two new Augustinian parishes were founded, Santiago Quecholtenango and S Nicolás Zitlala. At the same time, a secular priest was assigned to S Antonio Aguacuaucingo. By 1743 there was another Augustinian doctrina, at S Gerónimo Chacalinitla. The regular parishes were secularized between 1743 and 1777, at which time a priest was assigned to S Miguel Ayagualtempa.

Thus at Independence there were seven parishes here subject to the bishop of Puebla, and one (Atenango) in the archbishopric of Mexico. A few villages were visited from adjoining jurisdictions.

Population and settlements

There are indications that this area once supported a considerable native population, among them the fact that as late as 1570 residues of Tuxtecan- and Matlatzincan-speaking groups survived in five estancias of Tlalcozautitlan.[7] In that year there were some 7,440 tributaries in the jurisdiction, 4,000 at Chilapa, 1,970 at Tlalcozautitlan, and the rest spread among the smaller cabeceras (L de T, pp. 504–5). Later estimates show *c.* 4,390 tributaries in 1600, 1,480 in 1630, 2,000 in 1700, 2,494 in 1743, and 4,373 Indian tributaries in 1800.[8]

The non-Indian element was not significant in early years. There were only ten Spanish vecinos at Chilapa in 1582. The 1743 census shows 56 Spanish, 94 mestizo, and 35 mulatto families, most of them occupied in commerce and sugar-cane cultivation. Yet the padrón of 1792 has somewhat over 4,000 non-Indian individuals, nearly all mestizos and mulattoes.

The pre-Conquest settlement pattern was one of great dispersion, especially in the north. Chilapa (1950: Chilapa de Alvarez, ciudad) had over forty sujetos in 1570, after an early reduction by the Augustinians; most of them disappeared in the congregations of 1598–1604.[9] Seventeen places appear as pueblos in the eighteenth century: Acatlan, Ayagualtempa, Ayagualulco, Azacualoya, Colotlipan, Cualmecatitlan, Chacalinitla, Mazapa (S Juan de la Brea), Nancintla, Palantla, Petatlan, Quecholtenango (Cacholtenanco), Tehuitzingo, Teocintla, Xicuiltepec, Xocutla, and Zitlala.

Tlalcozautitlan (Tlacosautitlan, etc.; 1950: Tlalcozotitlán, pueblo) in 1570 had seven subcabeceras, forty-one estancias, and numerous barrios. These were reduced in 1593–1603 to the principal cabecera and eleven subordinate pueblos: Aguacuaucingo (Ahuacatzinco, etc.), Alpoyeca (Almiyeca), Copalillo (=Copalxocotitlan in 1570?), Mitlancingo, Pochotla, Tehuastitlan, Tepostlan, Tlaquilcingo, Tulimani (Toliman), Xitopontla (Xiutopuntlan), and Zacanguillo or Zacango.[10]

Atenango (Tenango, Atenanco; 1950: Atenango del Río, pueblo) had seven other cabeceras nearby, with a total of eighteen estancias, in a report of 1570. Most of these places were congregated at Atenango towards 1600.[11] Only the principal cabecera together with Comala and Zacango survived as pueblos in the eighteenth century.[12] Another place to the north, S Juan Teocalcingo, was disputed between Cuernavaca (q.v.) and Chilapa.

Mezquitlan (Mixquitlan; 1950: Mezquitlán, pueblo) is listed in 1570 with four estancias, one of which, Temalac(a), survived as a pueblo. The six estancias of Ostutla (Hoztotla, etc.; 1950: Oztutla, pueblo), and the five estancias of Papalutla (1950: pueblo) disappeared in the congregations of *c.* 1600.[13]

In 1792 there were 11 haciendas and 38 ranchos in the jurisdiction.

Sources

Herrera (Década 4a, p. 231) gives a summary of conditions here in 1532. There are brief articles in the *Suma* (*c*. 1548) for some of the cabeceras (PNE, I, nos. 236, 398, 443, 774), and a report of Papalutla as it was in 1554 (ENE, VIII, p. 119). Unusually detailed and useful relaciones in the Ovando series (*c*. 1570) were drawn up by clerics.[14] There is a report from the AM describing Chilapa and its immediate dependencies, dated 1582, the value of which is lessened by the loss of a map which originally accompanied it.[15] Among other related documents (*cited above*) is one which lists estancias and tributaries to be congregated in the Chilapa region in 1603.[16]

Bishop Mota y Escobar left an account of his visit here in 1611.[17] We have tributary data for places in the diocese of Tlaxcala (1626–96),[18] as well as the archbishopric (1643–88).[19]

Eighteenth-century documents include a useful report from the teniente of Chilapa dated 1743,[20] censuses of Tlalcozautitlan and Zitlala parishes in 1777,[21] a topographic report by the priest at Tlalcozautitlan in 1777,[22] and two lists of place-names, one accompanying a census of the non-Indian population, dated 1791–2.[23]

30 *Cholula*

This small jurisdiction was in the broad Atoyac valley at the base of Iztaccíhuatl (present state of Puebla), with elevations of 2,000–2,400 m. The climate is dry and cold.

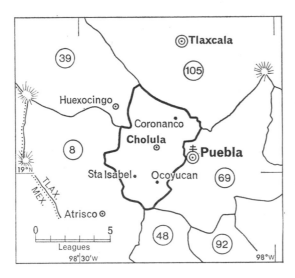

Cholollan was a large urban concentration with a great market-place next to what was perhaps the most extensive religious-ceremonial complex in America. According to one account, the government was headed by co-rulers, temporal and spiritual, with a council of six (other sources say four) nobles, each of whom ruled a section of the city and its dependent settlements. One of the

calpultin, Tenanquiáhuac, seems to have had preference over the others. Although once allied with Tlaxcallan, when the Spaniards arrived the city supported the Triple Alliance. The language spoken was Náhuatl (Torquemada, II, pp. 350–1).

Pedro de Alvarado and Bernardino Vázquez de Tapia visited Cholollan in September 1519, and a month later Cortés arrived with his army and native allies (Vázquez de Tapia, p. 36). Feeling the Chololtecans' hostility, and fearing an ambush, the Spaniards assembled all the leaders they could find in a courtyard and killed them, after which they reduced the city to rubble.

Encomienda

The conquistador Andrés de Tapia was granted Cholula by Cortés, after which the place seems to have been held for a time by Rodrigo Rangel. In 1529 the first audiencia divided the encomienda between Diego Fernández de Proaño and Diego Pacheco. These grants were revoked by the second audiencia, which placed Cholula in corregimiento early in 1531 (Cedulario Cortesiano, p. 230. ENE, II, p. 61; IV, p. 20. García Payón, p. 56).

Government

The C of Cholula, first appointed by March 1531, also governed Tlaxcala until 1545 (Gibson, 1952, p. 68). In the first year of the corregimiento land was taken from Cholula to form the Spanish settlement of Puebla (q.v.). In the 1550s the nearby encomienda of Calpan was annexed to Cholula's jurisdiction, but it was removed in 1558.[1]

From 1646 the council of the Indies controlled appointment of the magistrate (thereafter he was more often called AM). Cholula became a subdelegación in the intendencia of Puebla from 1787.

Church

At first visited from Huexocingo, Cholula was a Franciscan doctrina probably from the early 1530s, the original patron being S Pedro. A large monastery dedicated to S Gabriel was built there in 1549–52 (McAndrew, p. 401); a smaller one in a nearby barrio, S Andrés Collomochco (S Andrés Cholula), was a separate parish perhaps by 1585. Both doctrinas were secularized in 1640, when the monastery of S Gabriel seems to have been replaced as the parochial center by the church of S Pedro Apóstol (*Alegaciones*... fol. 90v).

By 1743 Sta Isabel and Sta María Coronanco had become separate parishes. Somewhat later (by 1790) Sta Clara Ocoyucan had a resident curate. All parishes were in the diocese of Tlaxcala. Two villages within the civil jurisdiction of Cholula, S Gerónimo de las Caleras and S Pablo Zochimehuacan, belonged to the parish of S José in the city of Puebla.

Population and settlements

Contemporary estimates give a native population at contact of 40,000 to 100,000 families (Aguilar, p. 89; Herrera, Década 1a, p. 360; Torquemada, I, p. 281). Thousands were killed in the 1519 massacre, and further loss from epidemics and other causes reduced the number of tributaries to 20,000 in 1531, 13,640 in 1564, 12,000 in 1570, 9,000 in 1581, and 8,114 in 1588 (ENE, x, p. 22; XVI, p. 9; Scholes and Adams, 1959, p. 48). A census of 1623 shows 6,496 tributaries, while another only three years later gives 3,644 (perhaps different definitions of tributary were used). Later counts have 2,873 tributaries in 1643, 3,550 in 1696, 3,715 Indian families in 1743, 4,100 tributaries in 1790, and 4,896 in 1800.[2]

'Many' Spaniards lived here in 1585, and figures

from the mid-seventeenth century range from 300 to 400 non-Indian vecinos.[3] In 1743 there were sixty Spanish families and 530 of mestizos, mulattoes, and Negroes (excluding slaves); most of the latter probably lived in the fifty-eight haciendas and ranchos which the jurisdiction had at that time.

According to the Suma de Visitas (*c.* 1548), Cholula then had thirty-five estancias distributed among six cabeceras; the latter seem to have been wards or barrios within the city. In the following table the names of these barrios are compared according to three different sixteenth-century sources.

c. 1548	1564	1593
S Andrés Tequepan	S Andrés Collomochco	S Andrés
Sta María Ocotlan	Sta María Quauhtlan	Sta María
Santiago Yzquitlan	S Diego Izquitlan	Santiago
Santiago Mexico		
Tequepa	S Miguel Tecpan	S Miguel
S Juan Tequepan	S Juan Tespolco	S Juan
	S Pablo Tlayllochoyan	S Pablo

A greater discrepancy is observed when we compare the lists of estancias in 1548, 1593, and the eighteenth century. The first gives only Náhuatl toponyms, with a single exception. The second has saints' names for fifty-three sujetos, with Náhuatl cognomens for ten of these; none of the latter corresponds to a 1548 name. In the interim, in 1558, there had been a congregation in which the Indians were reluctant to cooperate.[4] We guess that in this unpopular 'reduction' a number of settlements experienced a change of site in which new toponyms were adopted.

The next complete listing we have is in the 1743 relación, which names four cabeceras (S Pedro Cholula, S Andrés Cholula, Sta María Coronanco, Sta Isabel) and thirty-seven pueblos. At least sixteen places either were abandoned as settlement sites or were re-named between 1593 and 1743, some perhaps in a congregation of *c.* 1600. We are told that in 1640, when the Franciscans left, there were four 'barrios', eighteen 'ermitas', and thirty-three 'pueblos de visita', and that certain places were deserted soon afterwards.

Cholula (1950: Cholula de Rivadabia, ciudad) received the title of ciudad in 1535 or 1537. The following places survived as pueblos in the eighteenth century: S Francisco Acatepec, Sta Ana Acosautla, S Pablo Aguatempa, Sta Bárbara Almoloya, S Gregorio Atzompa, S Antonio Cacalotepec, Sta María Coronanco, S Francisco Cuapa, S Diego Cuauchayotla, S Juan Cuautlacingo, Sta María Cuescomate, S Bernardino Chalchuapa (Chalchiguapa), S Andrés Cholula, Sta Isabel Cholula, S Mateo Guanalá, Sta María Malacatepec, S Antonio Miguacan, Santiago Momoxpa, S Lucas Nextetelco, S Francisco Ocotlan (de los Pinillos), Sta Clara Ocoyuca, S Lorenzo Omecatla (Almecatlan), S Gabriel Ometoxtlan, S Miguel Papalotla (Papaxtla), Sta Marta Petlachucan, Santos Reyes, S Cosme, S Gerónimo de las Caleras, S Sebastián, Santorum (Todos Santos), S Gerónimo Tecuanipan, S Luis Tehuiloyucan, S Bernabé Temoxtitlan (Texmititlan), S Pedro Tlaltenango, S Martín Tlamapa, S Juan Tlautla, S Bernardo Tlaxcalancingo, Sta María Tonantzintla, S Miguel Xostla, S Gregorio Zacapexpan, Sta María Zacatepec, S Pablo Zochimeguacan, and S Martín Zoquiapan.

Sources

The Suma de Visitas article (PNE, I, no. 114) on Cholula *c.* 1548 is among the more detailed in this series. Cabeceras in 1564 appear in another document (Scholes and Adams, 1958, p. 133). There are two brief descriptions from *c.* 1570 (Códice Franciscano, p. 22. García Pimentel, 1904, p. 28). The report submitted by the C in 1581 has a map with interesting details.[5] Ponce (I, pp. 161–3) describes the place as it was in 1585. A document of 1593 gives a list of estancias in the jurisdiction.[6]

Two bishops left accounts of visits here in 1610,[7] 1620,[8] and 1644,[9] while data on tributaries are available for 1626–96.[10] Vetancurt (4a parte, pp. 31, 55–6, 90), writing in 1697, gives details of the former Franciscan doctrinas here. The AM in 1743–4 submitted a complete census with his report.[11] We have seen another report dated 1754, made for the Inquisition,[12] and a most useful description with a plan of the city by Fray Ajofrín (II, pp. 201–18), who lived there for some months in 1766–7. There is another census made in 1790,[13] and a list of settlements dated 1792.[14]

Mention should be made here of Maza's work on Cholula and its churches, together with the monographs of Kubler (1968) and Simons (1967, 1970).

31 *Guachinango*

Now in northern Veracruz and northernmost Puebla states, this was a large jurisdiction extending from the eastern slopes of the Sierra Madre Oriental down to a broad coastal plain and the Gulf shore (Barra de Cazones to Tamiahua lagoon). Elevations range from sea level to over 2,000 m. Heavy precipitation much of the year in the mountains supports a dense vegetation, mostly tropical savanna behind the coast and temperate in the highlands. Drainage is generally into the Pantepec–Tuxpan and Cazones rivers.

Both the political division and the distribution of languages here at contact were quite complex. The whole area was tributary to the Triple Alliance, except the shores of Tamiahua lagoon which were occupied by unreduced Huaxtecans. There were Aztec garrisons at Atlan and Tezapotitlan. In the mountainous region to the south were the states of Cuauhchinanco, Xicotépec, and Pahuatlan, with Acolhuaque (Texcocan) rulers whose subjects spoke Náhuatl, Otomí, and Totonac. Next to the northeast was the Aztec province of Atlan (=Huitzilpopocatlan = Metlateyocan?), where people speaking the same three languages together with Tepehuan were ruled by a military governor (tlacochteuhctli) (van Zantwijk, p. 152). East of here, on the coast, was the province of Tochpan, where Totonacs in the south

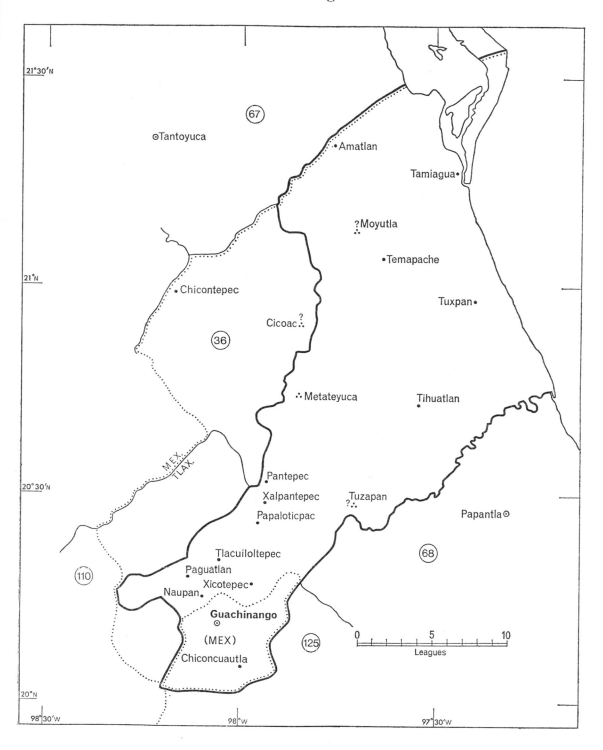

21°30′N

(67)

⊙Tantoyuca

•Amatlan

Tamiagua•

?Moyutla
∴

•Temapache

21°N

•Chicontepec

Cicoac∴?

Tuxpan•

(36)

∴Metateyuca

Tihuatlan
•

M.EX.
TLAX.

20°30′N

•Pantepec

Xalpantepec•

Tuzapan
? ∴

Papantla⊙

Papaloticpac•

(68)

Tlacuiloltepec•

(110)

Paguatlan
Xicotepec•

Naupan•

Guachinango
⊙

(MEX)

Chiconcuautla
•

(125)

0   5   10

Leagues

20°N

98°30′W   98°W   97°30′W

and Huaxtecans in the north lived alongside Náhuatl-speakers; there may have been another Totonac-speaking state, Tuzapan (which included Xalpantépec), in the southern part of this area. Inland from Tochpan was the province of Xiuhcoac (Tzicoac), where Náhuatl and Huaxtecan were spoken; most of Xiuhcoac was beyond the limits of this jurisdiction to the west (cf. Guayacocotla).

The coast was seen by ships of the Grijalva expedition in June, 1518. Other contacts occurred in 1519–20, and the Tuxpan–Tuzapan area was subdued by an expedition led by Andrés de Tapia early in 1520. The highlands came under Spanish control probably the following year, while the Tamiahua region was reduced from Pánuco in 1523.

Encomiendas

Guachinango was briefly held by Juan de Jaso in the early 1520s, after which it was re-assigned to the conquistador Alonso de Villanueva, succeeded on his death in the 1550s by a son, Agustín de Villanueva Cervantes; the latter died between 1573 and 1597, and tributes then went to his widow, Catalina de Peralta. In the 1640s the recipient was the count of Moctezuma; by 1688 part of this encomienda had escheated.[1]

Early encomenderos of Atlan and Metateyuca (which may have included Huicilpopocatlan and Tezapotitlan) were Francisco (Juan?) de Hinojosa and Juan de Nájera. Escheatment occurred by 1534 (Icaza, I, p. 92; II, p. 18).

A poblador, Luis de la Torre, controlled a string of villages including Paguatlan, Papaloticpac, Tlacuiloltepec, and Acasuchitlan (cf. Tulancingo). When he died *c.* 1550 his widow, Luisa de Acuña (who soon married Lope Cherinos) inherited Paguatlan and Acasuchitlan, while tributes from the other places went to a nephew, Juan de la Torre. Doña Luisa still appears as encomendera of Paguatlan in 1597, but by 1610 the grant had escheated; soon afterward it was re-assigned to the Moctezuma heirs. In 1597 Papaloticpac and Tlacuiloltepec were held by Luis de la Torre, a nephew of the first encomendero; both places became crown possessions between 1604 and 1610 and were subsequently re-assigned.[2]

We do not know who was the encomendero of Pantepec, which seems to have included Epuxutlan.

Xicotepec was held by a conquistador, Alvaro Maldonado, but it was taken from his widow by the governor, Estrada, *c.* 1528 and became a corregimiento early in 1531 (Icaza, I, p. 130). Part reverted to private encomienda early in the seventeenth century.

Hernando Cortés claimed both Cicoac and Tuxpan for himself in 1526 (Cortés, p. 471). The first of these places, together with Chicontepec, was soon reassigned to two conquistadors, Francisco de Ramírez and Diego de Coria. Since most if not all of this encomienda in later years was in the neighboring jurisdiction of Guayacocotla, its history will be summarized there.

Tuxpan, after it was taken from Cortés, formed part of a large multiple encomienda which included Xalpantepec, Tiguatlan, Tuzapan, and Papantla (q.v.). Estrada gave it to Lope de Saavedra, a resident of Pánuco, towards 1528. Soon afterward it was acquired by Andrés de Tapia y Sosa, succeeded in 1561 by a son, Cristóbal. The latter was still alive in 1604, but later tributes were re-assigned to the Moctezuma heirs.

Tamiagua and Tenesticpac were long held by Juan de Villagómez, listed in 1548–70. By 1587 the encomienda had been assigned to D. Luis de Velasco, together with nearby Tamaos, which may have had another earlier encomendero. Tamiagua and Tamaos remained privately held, in part, to the late seventeenth century.

Temapache seems to have had some connection with the encomienda of Moyutla, in the jurisdiction of Pánuco (q.v.), a cabecera which may have been moved to the Temapache vicinity towards 1600. It was still privately held in 1696.

Government

The first crown officers here were the Cs of Xicotepec (from April 1531) and Metateyuca (by 1534). In the 1550s these magistrates were given jurisdiction in adjacent encomiendas, including Tamiagua–Tenesticpac, formerly claimed by the province of Pánuco. By 1565 Metateyuca and Xicotepec were ruled by a single C, suffragan to Meztitlan. The coast from Tuxpan to Tuzapan was at first attached to the corregimiento of Hueytlalpa (cf. Zacatlan), but by the 1570s it had been transferred to that of Metateyuca and the Cazones river was made the southern boundary with Papantla. In 1575–83 Tututepec and Acasuchitlan were lost to Tulancingo. Towards 1580 the C of Metateyuca was re-designated AM of Guachinango, which became his residence, a teniente living at distant Tamiagua. There was a dispute over Chicontepec, which was being visited by the magistrate of Guachinango in 1583, but eventually it was attached to Guayacocotla.³

There is a puzzling reference in 1609 to the four 'suffragan corregimientos' of Paguatlan, Tamiagua, Xalpantepec, and Xicotepec within the alcaldía mayor of Guachinango. It could well be that all these places were under crown control at that time, but the concept of subordinate or suffragan jurisdictions (cf. Introduction, *above*) was no longer much observed in New Spain. At any rate, the four places mentioned were soon re-assigned in private encomienda.

From 1708 Guachinango formed part of the appointive dominion of the dukes of Atlixco. After 1786 this jurisdiction was a subdelegación in the intendencia of Puebla, although the coastal area of Tamiagua subsequently became a separate partido attached to the intendencia of Veracruz.

Church

We are told that Augustinian doctrinas were founded at Asunción Guachinango in 1543 and at Santiago Paguatlan in 1552 (Grijalva, pp. 191, 250), although construction of the monasteries at both places did not begin until 1553.⁴ By 1570 there were in addition two secular parishes, S Juan Bautista Xicotepec (including Papaloticpac) and Chicontepec (cf. Guayacocotla); the curate of Chicontepec visited Metateyuca, Tuxpan, and Tamiagua. The congregations of 1598–1606 spawned several new parishes. Augustinians founded houses at S Marcos Naupan and Papaloticpac (soon afterward the cabecera de doctrina was moved to S Bartolomé Tlacuiloltepec), and took charge of Xicotepec. At the same time, secular clergy began to reside at S Juan Pantepec and Santiago Tamiagua, and in 1610 the last-mentioned doctrina was divided with a priest at Santiago y S Vicente Temapache; by 1646 the curate of Pantepec had moved his headquarters to S Bartolomé Xalpantepec.

A century later, in 1743, we find the same parishes with a few additions. The Augustinians had founded (after 1684) small monasteries at S Pedro Chiconcuautla and Sta María Tlaola, while Pantepec had become a separate secular parish. By 1777 most if not all of the regular doctrinas were secularized, and there was a priest living at Tuxpan. In 1791 the curacies of Amatlan and Sta Mónica Cihuateutla had been added to the list, making a total of fourteen parishes in the jurisdiction. Cihuateutla, Chiconcuautla, Guachinango, and Tlaola were in the archdiocese of Mexico, the others in the bishopric of Tlaxcala or Puebla. Two sujetos of Paguatlan, Guaxtla and Tlasco, were in a neighboring parish, Huehuetlan (cf. Tulancingo).

Population and settlements

The native population of the lowlands was decimated at an early date. Metateyuca-Huitzilpopocatlan was being de-populated in 1537 and again in 1545 (L de T, pp. 229, 475), and we guess that the Cicoac-Tamiagua-Tuxpan area had a similar loss in the 1520s and 1530s. By 1570 there were some 7,800 tributaries in the jurisdiction, about nine tenths of them in the relatively small highland area. The latter was hit by the plague of 1576–81 and later epidemics. The nadir was reached towards 1635, when there were perhaps 1,900 tributaries. Later censuses show 4,483 Indian families in 1743, and 8,033 in 1791.

The almost deserted coastal region was gradually if sparsely settled with Spaniards, mestizos, and mulattoes, especially the latter. In 1791 there were 1,598 non-Indian families in the jurisdiction, the Negroid element predominating on the coast, with mestizo concentrations at Guachinango and Paguatlan.

Guachinango (Quauchinanco, etc.; 1950: Huauchinango, ciudad, Pue.) in 1571 had sixty-five estancias (named in the report), some of which disappeared in the congregation of 1598–1604. In 1571 all of these dependencies were in the archbishopric of Mexico, but by 1610 a group north of the cabecera called the Cinco Estancias (Naupan, Atlan, Chachaguantla, Tlaxpanaloyan, Xolotlan) had been transferred to the diocese of Tlaxcala.[5] In 1684 there were still four barrios and forty-five estancias within the archdiocese; forty-six settlements survived in 1791 as pueblos, grouped around the cabeceras de doctrina of Guachinango, Cihuateutla, Chiconcuautla, and Tlaola. The five estancias centering around Naupan had increased to nine in 1743, but only seven were considered pueblos in 1791.

The 1570 report shows twenty-three dependencies under Xicotepec (1950: Villa Juárez, Pue.), the most distant being 5½ leagues from the cabecera. Only a handful survived the congregation of 1598–1603. One of them, S Agustín Atenancan, is perhaps the Atenango of a seventeenth-century document and the S Agustín Teotihuacán of 1791. Three other places were pueblos in the late eighteenth century. Totonac was the language spoken here.

Paguatlan (Pauatlan, etc.; 1950: Pahuatlán de Valle, *villa*, Pue.) had twenty-four estancias in 1571, one to seven leagues from the cabecera. Otomí and Náhuatl were the chief languages, although Totonac was spoken by some. There was a congregation here in 1606–7 in which two centers were designated, Paguatlan and S Agustín Cuautlapegualco. The latter disappeared, but nine other places are named as subject pueblos in 1791.[6]

Tlacuiloltepec (Tlalculultepec; 1950: Tlacuilotepec, pueblo, Pue.) had fifteen visitas in 1571, most quite close to the cabecera. Since none of those listed is recognizable in eighteenth-century documents, we assume they disappeared in the congregation of *c.* 1600.[7]

Three of the ten estancias belonging in 1571 to Papaloticpac (1950: Pápalo, pueblo, Pue.) survived as pueblos.

Four cabeceras in the lowlands, all belonging to the Tapia encomienda in the sixteenth century, lost most of their native population at an early date. Only two, Xalpantepec (1950: Jalpan, pueblo, Pue.) and Tihuatlan (Atlihuitlan; 1950: Tihuatlán, pueblo, Ver.) remained predominantly Indian communities throughout the colonial period.

Xalpantepec had ten estancias in 1569, all ordered to be congregated at the cabecera and Reyes Cupiltitlan towards 1600. There was some immigration of Otomies to this area shortly before 1646, at which time Totonac and Tepehuan were the principal languages. By 1743 Cupiltitlan had disappeared, but there were five other villages in the vicinity. Tihuatlan survived as a Náhuatl-speaking pueblo.

One of the other Tapia cabeceras, Tuzapan (1950: S Diego, ranchería, Pue. (?)), which had eleven estancias in 1548, was deserted by 1581.[8] The fourth was Tuxpan (Tuspa, etc.; more often called Tabuco or Tapoco in the late sixteenth and seventeenth centuries; 1950: Tuxpan, ciudad, Ver.), which also once had eleven estancias. Towards 1548 the cabecera had been abandoned, and the few surviving Indians had moved to Tomilco. In 1777–91 Tuxpan–Tabuco had almost equal numbers of mulattoes and Náhuatl-speaking Indians.

Pantepec (1950: pueblo, Pue.) survived as a pueblo in the eighteenth century, as did certain of its old estancias (Mecapalapa, El Pozo, Tenexco).

Moyutla (1950: ranchería, Ver.) was still a cabecera in 1610 but is not heard from thereafter. Two former estancias, Temapache and Tepesintla, were Indian-mulatto settlements in 1743-91. Huaxtecan was spoken by the Indians.

The ephemeral Cicoac (Tzicoaque, Xiuhcoac, etc.) may have been in this jurisdiction, and indeed there was an hacienda called Cicuaque on the Tuxpan river south of Temapache in 1646. In later years, however, the place was equated with Chicontepec in the neighboring jurisdiction of Guayacocotla (q.v.) (Byam Davies, pp. 34–5).

Tamiagua (1950: Tamiahua, *villa*, Ver.) and Tamaos (Tamahox, etc.) were two cabeceras which shared the same church, the center of an encomienda containing a number of outlying estancias. The cabeceras had become non-Indian settlements by 1646, but several sujetos inland survived as Indian (Huaxtecan) pueblos in the eighteenth century: Acala, Amatlan, Ixtlachinampa, Tancoco.

Other cabeceras disappeared entirely. We find no mention of Metateyuca (1950: Metlaltoyuca, pueblo, Pue.) as a pueblo after 1598, when it was supposed to be reduced to a congregation; in 1609 this place which 'solía ser cabeza de los pueblos de Guauchinango' was deserted, and in 1791 it was an hacienda. Tezapotitlan by 1570 had lost its cabecera status to a former sujeto, Huitzilpopocatlan (Uzilpupucatlan, etc.; 1950: Huitzilac, ranchería, Pue.?), which still existed in 1646, although its Indians may have been moved in to Xalpantepec; it had only three tributaries in 1696, and is no longer mentioned in 1743.

Sources

Information for the first half of the sixteenth century is found in various documents (L de T, pp. 76–9, 229–35, 284, 474–7. PNE, I, nos. 269, 525–6, 530, 803, 842. Scholes and Adams, 1957, pp. 57–8). There is an interesting manuscript about Xalpantepec dated 1569.[9] In the Ovando series (c. 1570) we have rather detailed reports from both dioceses.[10]

There are scattered data on the 1598–1606 congregations.[11] A rare answer to the Céspedes questionnaire, drawn up by the AM in 1609, survives in a MS copy.[12] Two bishops of Tlaxcala went through this area in 1610[13] and 1646,[14] leaving illuminating remarks in their journals, while an archbishop of Mexico who visited Guachinango in 1684 also provided valuable information.[15] Tributary figures, by cabecera, from the seventeenth century are available for both dioceses.[16]

A most useful report sent in by the AM in 1743[17] is followed by complete censuses of three Tlaxcalan parishes (Naupan, Tlacuiloltepec, Tuxpan) dated 1777.[18] There is a good description of the entire jurisdiction,[19] together with a padrón of the partido of Tamiagua,[20] both from 1791. Finally, we have a list of toponyms in 1792.[21]

Williams García (1963) deals with the ethnography of the Tepehuas.

32 *Guanaxuato*

Guanajuato, now a state capital, lies in a canyon surrounded by low, barren mountains. The colonial jurisdiction, for the most part draining southward into the Río Grande (Lerma) with elevations of 1,500–2,500 m, included Silao and Irapuato. Temperatures are moderate to cool, precipitation is slight and seasonal.

Although there is evidence of an early Tarascan penetration, when the Spaniards arrived this region was thinly occupied by Guamare-speaking Chichimecs, hunters and gatherers living in small dispersed rancherías with a primitive political organization.[1]

Perhaps the first Spanish contact was in 1530, when certain members of the Guzmán expedition probed northward from Pénjamo in the direction of Irapuato. In the 1540s the area was visited by Franciscans from S Miguel, and a cattle estancia seems to have been established near Guanaxuato in 1546 (Jiménez Moreno, 1958, p. 76). Mineral deposits at the latter place, discovered in 1552,

began to be worked several years later and a real de minas was founded in 1557 (Powell, p. 17; Jiménez Moreno, 1958, pp. 57, 81, 93). Gradually the region was taken over by Spanish settlements and cattle haciendas worked by Otomí and Tarascan immigrants, although harassment by Chichimec raiding parties continued until 1590.

Encomienda

We have no information on encomiendas in this jurisdiction. The encomendero of Puruándiro and Pénjamo, Juan de Villaseñor, may have had some claims on the Indians in early years, but in general they were exempt from tribute payment until the late eighteenth century.

Government

From the 1540s the justicia mayor of Xilotepec (q.v.) and Chichimecas had jurisdiction here, although there was some conflict between him and the AM of Michoacán, and further claims to the area were made by the audiencia of Nueva Galicia and the AM of S Miguel. Towards 1559 the viceroy appointed an AM for Minas de Guanaxuato, whose realm in the early 1560s extended to Comanja in the north and Guaniqueo in the south.[2] Comanja was soon annexed to

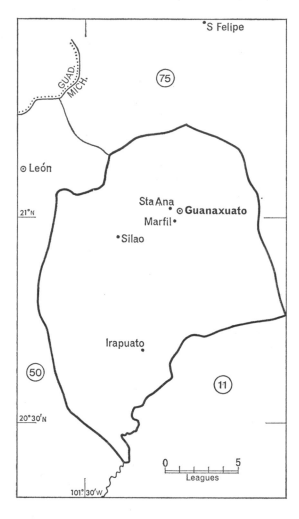

Nueva Galicia, Guaniqueo was returned to Michoacán, and León (q.v.) was made a separate alcaldía mayor in 1579, leaving Guanaxuato with approximately its final boundaries. The AM had tenientes at Irapuato and Silao, and somewhat later at Marfil; these continued as subdelegados after the AM was replaced by an intendente-corregidor in October, 1787.

Church

While the Franciscans were probably the first religious in this area, and kept a monastery at Guanaxuato until after Independence, the parishes there seem to have been ministered by secular clergy from their inception. It is not clear whether the original parish at the mines was that of Sta Ana or Sta Fé, both of which were benefices in 1571; whichever it was, it probably dated from *c.* 1560. Santiago Silao, S Marcos Irapuato, and Santiago Marfil, first visited from Guanaxuato, each had a resident priest early in the seventeenth century. The region fell within the diocese of Michoacán.

Population and settlements

The size of the Chichimec population here at contact is a matter of conjecture; we guess that it did not exceed seven thousand persons. While some Chichimecs remained as gañanes and mine workers, most moved northward out of the area and were replaced (beginning in the 1550s) by Tarascans, Otomies (including Mazahuans and Matlatzincans), and Mexicans. Most of these worked on haciendas and in the mines, and a careful examination of parish records (which we have not attempted) might yield a clue to their numbers. The decline in mining activity in the early seventeenth century would be accompanied by a population loss, and subsequent recovery by a corresponding gain. The 1639 report mentions three Indian settlements near Silao: Comanxa, Cuicillo, and Nápoles. That of 1754–5 shows 9,000 adult Indians at thirty haciendas near Silao, plus 1,265 at Guanaxuato. A 1772 census shows 4,427 Indian tributaries in the *partido* of Guanaxuato (presumably the mines alone), while that of 1801–2 has 3,374 Indian tributaries at Irapuato, 807 at Marfil, and 3,256 at Silao.[3]

The real de minas at Guanaxuato (1950: Guanajuato, ciudad) began to be settled in 1553–4, and by 1570 was reported to have 600 Spanish miners in the two camps of Sta Fé and Sta Ana, Marfil being founded somewhat later. Only 85 vecinos are reported in 1639, and 150 (together with 1,330 *operarios*) in 1649. Somewhat over 5,000 families of Spaniards and castas lived in the three reales in 1743, and the total non-Indian population of Guanaxuato–Marfil–Sta Ana in 1791 was 39,694 persons.

Irapuato (Iricuato? 1950: Irapuato, ciudad) and Llanos de Silao (1950: Silao, ciudad) both began in the sixteenth century as dispersed farming and cattle raising settlements for supplying the mines. Each became a congregación centered around a parish church in the midst of the haciendas and farms. In 1649 Irapuato had some 30 Spanish *vecinos*, only half of whom lived in the congregación, with 815 gañanes and other servants. Silao in the same year had 14 Spanish families and 500-odd servants. The non-Indian population in 1791 was 7,564 persons at Irapuato and 5,039 at Silao; of these, over half were considered Spaniards, and the rest divided between mestizos and a large minority of mulattoes.

Sources

We have seen two brief descriptions of Guanaxuato deriving from reports in the Ovando series (1570–1) (López de Velasco, p. 242. Miranda Godínez, 1967). Reports on the diocese of Michoacán dated 1639[4] and 1649[5] give valuable data. There is a good relación from the AM in 1743–4,[6] followed by two reports drawn up by clerics for the Inquisition in 1754–5 (with a map showing the various mining camps),[7] and the accounts of travelers who passed through here in 1764 (Ajofrín, I, pp. 262–90) and 1766 (Lafora, p. 50). The parish of Sta Ana is described as it was in 1778.[8] For the early 1790s, we have a list of toponyms,[9] and several censuses of the jurisdiction.[10]

There is a local history of Irapuato by Martínez de la Rosa.

33 *Guatulco y Guamelula*

This, the southernmost jurisdiction in Nueva España, includes a long littoral on the Pacific, the coastal plain (somewhat reduced), and foothills of the Sierra Madre del Sur, with elevations to 1,600 m. The coast is an alternation of rocky headlands and sand beaches, with occasional tidal estuaries where watercourses reach the sea. The bay of Guatulco (now called Sta Cruz) is the best natural harbor between Acapulco and Central America. The climate is hot and dry, although rains in July–October produce a dense vegetation.

The western part of this area was inhabited by a people speaking archaic Nahua, perhaps the descendants of Toltec colonists (Boas, 1917. Brasseur de Bourbourg, I, pp. 420–1). The native states here (Tonamilca, Pochotla, Coatulco, Cimatlan, Cacalotépec) were tributary to the king of Tototépec. To the northeast, in the foothills, was a small Zapotecan state, Xadani (Axochitépec), also subject to Tototépec. Just beyond Xadani began the country of the Chontals, a wild people speaking a language distantly related to Yuman, occupying the coast and mountains

north and east to Tequixistlan and Mazatlan. From all accounts the Chontals lived in small, scattered rancherías without a centralized political system; the fact that certain Chontal communities (Aztatlan, Huaumimilollan, Mazatlan) were selected as encomienda centers after the Conquest may indicate that they had some pre-Conquest predominance. At the moment of contact a state of war existed between Tototépec and Tecoantépec.

Pedro de Alvarado, after subjugating Tototépec in the spring of 1522, continued with his army along the coast through Coatulco and Aztatlan to Tecoantépec (Herrera, década 1a, p. 26. Martínez Gracida, pp. 134–5). Spanish control in the west was interrupted by at least one rebellion of Tototépec, put down with great cruelty in 1523, and perhaps again in 1525–6. We are told that the Chontals also rebelled and were reconquered in 1527. This and later Chontal revolts in the 1560s may have been rather resistance to Spanish slaving expeditions, and other extreme forms of exploitation.

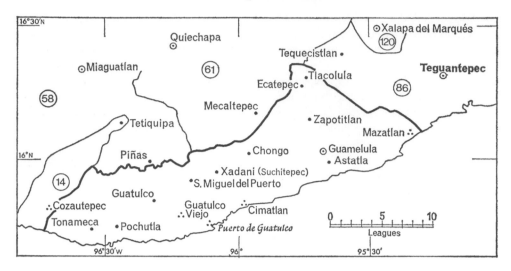

Encomiendas

In the Nahua area, Pochutla and Tonameca were held by Diego de Ocampo in September, 1528; this encomienda escheated in July, 1531 (L de T, p. 294. Millares Carlo and Mantecón, I, no. 1499).

Guatulco was granted in the early 1520s to Antonio Gutiérrez de Ahumada, a conquistador who accompanied Alvarado. He died towards 1549 and was followed by a son, Diego Gutiérrez, and *c.* 1565 by a granddaughter who married Bernardino López. Escheatment occurred on the latter's death, between 1580 and 1597.[1]

Cimatlan and Cacalotepec, which included the port of Guatulco, were assigned to Pedro de Pantoja, perhaps in 1525. Pantoja went to Spain in 1553, and his encomienda was taken for the crown.[2]

Francisco de Vargas may have been encomendero of Suchitepec, a place which was a crown possession from *c.* 1537 (BAGN, VI, pp. 15–16. Icaza, I, p. 22).

There were at least three encomiendas in the Chontal country. Astatla was held from 1528 by the conquistador Juan Bello, followed in the 1550s by a daughter who married Gil González de Avila. It escheated when González was executed in August, 1566.[3]

Guamelula was taken for the crown from Juan Hernández de Prado in April 1531.[4]

Cortés seems to have claimed Mazatlan as a dependency of Teguantepec, but it was included in the corregimiento of Guamelula in 1531. Towards 1540 Mazatlan was granted to Alvaro de Zamora, the official interpreter of the audiencia. Zamora died in the late 1560s, and after some problems with his heirs this encomienda was again put in the crown (before 1580).[5]

Government

Cs were appointed to Guamelula and Pochutla y Tonameca in 1531, and to Suchitepec (at first included in the province of Zapotecas) towards 1537. Perhaps in 1550 the C of Pochutla y Tonameca was redesignated AM of the port of Guatulco (*see below*).[6] Then or very soon afterwards the magistrates of Suchitepec and Guamelula were placed under the supervisory control of this AM.[7] Another area to the west, Tetiquipa – Río Hondo and Cozautepec, was attached to Guatulco from 1579 but later was transferred to the jurisdiction of Cimatlan (q.v.).[8]

In 1599 the corregimiento of Suchitepec was abolished and added to the alcaldía mayor of Guatulco, and it was probably about the same time that Guamelula ceased to exist as a separate jurisdiction.[9] The AM, first resident at the port, moved inland to the pueblo of Guatulco in 1616; in later years his residence was Guamelula, although Pochutla appears as the seat of government in

1789. From 1787 Guatulco y Guamelula was a subdelegación in the intendencia of Oaxaca.

Church

There must have been a priest at the port of Guatulco at latest by the 1550s. In 1552 we find a secular curate living at Mazatlan who visited the Chontal coastal area together with Suchitepec.[10] In 1570 there were secular parishes at Sta María Guatulco (including the port and pueblo of that name, and Suchitepec) and S Pedro Guamelula (including Astatla and Mazatlan); in that year Pochutla and Tonameca were visited from Tetiquipa, while the mountain Chontals and Tlacolula belonged to the Dominican doctrina of Tequecistlan (cf. Teguantepec). Ten years later the curate of Guatulco was visiting Pochutla and Tonameca.

In the 1680s the old parish seat of Guatulco was abandoned as a result of pirate raids and the curate moved his headquarters inland, first to S Miguel del Puerto and later (1699) to S Mateo Piñas in the jurisdiction of Miaguatlan; subsequently this priest visited the region from Tonameca to Suchitepec, a situation which prevailed until after Independence (an assistant lived at Pochutla in the late eighteenth century). Guamelula continued as a secular parish which included Astatla. Asunción Tlacolula by 1745 had a vicar subordinate to the curate of Tequecistlan who visited Alotepec, Ecatepec, and Zapotitlan. S Miguel Chongo in the eighteenth century was visited from Tepalcatepec (later, Mecaltepec), in the jurisdiction of Nexapa.

The area was in the diocese of Antequera.

Population and settlements

The natives here began to disappear very soon after the Conquest. The greatest loss occurred before 1550, but later plagues took many lives in 1566–7, 1576–7, 1591–7, and 1737–8. The number of Indian tributaries is estimated at 3,000 in 1550, 2,000 in 1570, and 600 towards 1650. Recovery was interrupted by the epidemic of 1737–8 in which many Chontals died. In the west, the Nahua-speaking population was largely replaced with Zapotecans who moved down from the mountains to the coastal plain. A count of 1786

shows 660 Indian tributaries, while the report of 1789 has 3,283 (persons).[11]

There was a sixteenth-century invasion of Negroes, some of whom came to work at the port of Guatulco, others fleeing from servitude and settling near Pochutla and Tonameca and elsewhere.[12] Their numbers were not great, but by 1699 Tonameca was a predominantly Negroid settlement, and mulattoes were scattered along the coast as far as Astatla and Guamelula (Berlín, p. 78). The 1786 census has $52\frac{1}{2}$ mulatto tributaries in the jurisdiction, while that of 1789 shows 219 individual mulattoes. In addition, there was a sprinkling of Spaniards, mestizos, Filipinos ('chinos'), and Peruvians ('peruleros'), a thoroughly mixed-up racial situation.[13]

There is a good deal of scattered information on settlements here which it would be worthwhile to unravel. Many lands were deserted after the early de-population and were taken for cattle ranches; a number of these grants (mercedes) are recorded in the 1550s and 1560s.[14]

The pueblo of Guatulco (its first site was three leagues from the sea) had six or eight estancias in the latter half of the sixteenth century, only one of which, Cuixtepec (Huistepec, etc.) seems to have survived the congregation of 1598–1604.[15] The cabecera was destroyed by pirates in 1687, its inhabitants being dispersed for some years until they re-settled at the present site (1950: Sta María Huatulco, pueblo), further inland, towards 1700.[16] Another pueblo, Magdalena Piñas, was founded nearby as a sujeto sometime before 1699.

Southeast of Guatulco was Cimatlan, a cabecera which included within its limits the port of Guatulco. This sheltered bay began to be used in the late 1530s as the northern terminus of maritime traffic between New Spain and Central America and Perú. For several decades it was a busy settlement, but it declined after 1573 when Acapulco became the official port for trade with the Orient. The place was rummaged by Drake (1579) and Cavendish (1587), and in 1616 the viceroy ordered it to be deserted.[17] However, the bay continued to be used for contraband traffic (Borah, 1954; Lynch, 1969, p. 226). Cimatlan itself had no inhabitants by 1580, and of six former estancias only the port of Guatulco and Copalita were inhabited in that year.

Pochutla (1950: S Pedro Pochutla, *villa*) and Tonameca (1950: Sta María Tonameca, pueblo) still had a few estancias in 1550, but only the two cabeceras survived in 1580.

Suchitepec, re-baptised Xanatanij or Xadani (1950: Sta María Xadani, pueblo) in the eighteenth century, had four subject estancias in 1550–80; Zapotecan was then spoken in the cabecera and Chontal in the estancias. Three places besides the cabecera seem to have survived the congregation proposed here in 1598: S Miguel Macupilco (= Chongo), S Bartolomé Tamagaztepec, and S Lorenzo; the last two communities were wiped out in the epidemic of 1737. Another village in this area, S Miguel del Puerto, was settled *c.* 1687. In the eighteenth century the Chontals were concentrated at Chongo, and Zapotecans at Xadani and S Miguel del Puerto.[18]

Guamelula (1950: S Pedro Huamelula, pueblo) must have had dependent settlements in the sixteenth century, but we have no list of them, a relación of *c.* 1580 having disappeared. Most probably their number was reduced in a congregation towards 1600. Santiago Pijutla (Xutla), in the mountains, was abandoned *c.* 1675. Alotepec, Ecatepec, Tilzapotitlan (Zapotitlan), and Tlacolula, which may or may not have been subject to Guamelula, were pueblos in the eighteenth century.[19]

The cabecera of Astatla (1950: Santiago Astata, pueblo) had five estancias in 1550, all seemingly congregated *c.* 1600. Pirate raids in the 1680s caused a removal of all the inhabitants to Guamelula, but Astatla was re-settled in 1708 at a new site somewhat further inland.[20]

We have no record of the estancias of Mazatlan (1950: Morro de Mazatán, ranchería.) The cabecera was abandoned after the epidemic of 1737.

Sources

A few details can be gleaned from the various articles in the Suma de Visitas (*c.* 1550) (PNE, I, nos. 233–4, 284, 334, 396, 476, 758, 766–7, 847–8), and the Ovando report (*c.* 1570) on Oaxaca (García Pimentel, 1904, pp. 65, 67, 90–1. Cf. López de Velasco, pp. 232–9). There is a useful relación, drawn up *c.* 1580 by the AM of Guatulco, describing the western part of the jurisdiction (PNE, IV, pp. 232–51), and a most interesting one in the same series (1579) from the C of Suchitepec (PNE, IV, pp. 24–8), the latter accompanied by five map-drawings in the native tradition. Accounts of the coast and port of Guatulco were written by chroniclers of the Drake (1579) (Fletcher) and Cavendish (1587) (Pretty) expeditions; the latter is supplemented by an interesting document concerning the Spanish fleet sent from Peru in pursuit of Cavendish (*Gobernantes del Perú*, XI, pp. 132–4).

For the seventeenth century, we have a few scattered references about the port,[21] some sailing directions and charts of the coast,[22] and descriptions left by English (Dampier, Funnell), Dutch (Speilbergen), and French (Lussan) pirates and privateers. There is good information on languages in a 1699 document from the priest of S Mateo Piñas (Berlín, pp. 78–9).

A table made by the AM in 1745 is of interest,[23] while the description in Villaseñor y Sánchez (II, p. 177) was taken from another source. There is an excellent report made by the subdelegado in 1789,[24] and a padrón of the non-Indian population in 1792.[25]

For the final years of the colony, we have a report drawn up by the curate of Piñas in 1803,[26] and a statistical summary of the jurisdiction as it was *c.* 1820.[27]

Spores (1965) and Byam Davies analyze sixteenth-century sources in an attempt to reconstruct the situation at contact, while Martínez Gracida in his work on the Chontal area seems to have had access to other material mixed with traditions. Borah (1954) and Gerhard (1960) give further details on the port of Guatulco.

34 Guautitlan

Now in north central Mexico state, on the northwest edge of the valley of Mexico, this is a high (2,200–2,900 m), dry region which includes the trench (*desagüe*) excavated in 1608–1789 to provide an outlet for the valley's lakes and protect Mexico city from floods.

At contact the area was shared between Cuauhtitlan and Tepozotlan, with Tepanecan rulers. Huehuetocan once had its own dynasty, but in 1519 was under the tlatoani of Cuauhtitlan (Gibson, 1964, p. 41). Náhuatl was predominant in the south and Otomí at Huehuetocan.

Cuauhtitlan came under Spanish rule in early 1521, when Cortés's forces occupied it without resistance.

Encomiendas

The first encomendero of Guautitlan was the conquistador Alonso de Avila, who received the grant from Cortés. It included Huehuetoca, Xaltocan, Zumpango, and other communities. On his departure from Mexico in the early 1520s, Avila left his holdings with a brother, Gil González de Avila (Benavides). The latter died in 1544 and was followed by a son, Alonso de Avila Alvarado. Escheatment occurred in 1566 when the last encomendero was executed (ENE, IV, pp. 21, 48. Gibson, 1964, pp. 416–17).

Tepozotlan was held by the bachelor Juan de Ortega until his death in 1546 when it escheated (L de T, p. 415).

Government

In 1546 the newly appointed C of Tepozotlan was ordered to look after the Indians of Guautitlan as well. On at least two other occasions this magistrate was specifically given jurisdiction in the encomienda of Guautitlan to hear the Indians' complaints of mistreatment, in 1555 and 1560. In 1566 an AM was appointed to administer the province, to which were assigned the suffragan corregimientos of Tepozotlan (a post usually filled by the AM), Citlaltepec (cf. Zumpango de la Laguna), Xaltocan, and Tenayuca (cf. Tacuba). By 1572 Tenayuca had its own AM, and toward the end of the century the suffragan relationship with Citlaltepec–Zumpango was terminated. The status of Xaltocan was disputed for some years until it was annexed to Zumpango. Sometime before 1643 Tepoxaco and other villages were transferred from the jurisdiction of Guautitlan to that of Tacuba. In 1676 we find Guautitlan attached to the nearby alcaldía mayor of S Cristóbal Ecatepec, a temporary situation. From 1786 Guautitlan was a subdelegación in the intendencia of Mexico.[1]

Church

Franciscans founded a monastery in 1525 at S Buenaventura Guautitlan, a doctrina which remained in their care until it was secularized in 1754–56. Secular clergy were resident at both S Pablo Huehuetoca and S Pedro Tepozotlan by

1569, and at S Mateo Teoloyuca from *c.* 1603. From 1582 to 1767 the Jesuits maintained a church and seminary at Tepozotlan. All parishes were in the archdiocese of Mexico.

Population and settlements

Of the 10,600 Indian tributaries in the area towards 1570, perhaps half died in the epidemic of 1576–81; further mortality and emigration brought the number down to 1,193 in 1643. Recovery was slow, to 1,866 in 1688, 2,231 (families) in 1743, and 3,978 in 1797; in the latter year non-Indians formed *c.* sixteen per cent of the total population.[2]

Guautitlan (Huauhtitlan, etc.; 1950: Cuautitlan de Romero Rubio, *villa*) had a large number of estancias, some of which may have been deserted in an early congregation. In the 1560s there were, beside the principal cabecera, six sub-cabeceras, Coyotepec, Huehuetoca, Tehuiloyuca (Teoloyuca), Tultepec, Xaltocan, and Zumpango. The two last named eventually were put in a separate political jurisdiction (*see above*), while the others had some twenty-five estancias among them in 1570. Most of these were reduced to eight congregation centers in 1603–4, the five old cabeceras and three new ones, S Martín, Santiago Tlatepoxco, and S Miguel de los Jagüeyes. Several other places remained *in situ*, and other former estancia sites were re-occupied and became pueblos in the seventeenth century.

Tepozotlan (1950: Tepotzotlán, pueblo) in 1570 had thirteen subordinate settlements, all within 2½ leagues of the cabecera. These were ordered reduced to three sites in 1593, but certain estancias survived or were later re-occupied. The subject of Tepoxaco (Tepuxaco) was transferred to Tacuba.

Sources

A brief article on Guautitlan in the Suma de Visitas (PNE, I, no. 487), and tribute records of the 1560s (L de T, p. 149) are followed by detailed reports in the Ovando series dated 1569–70.[3] Much on the region in the 1580s and earlier can be gleaned from three thick volumes dealing with land disputes, with several maps.[4]

Scattered data on the congregations of 1593–1604 are found at AGN.[5] Population figures and other information for the seventeenth century are derived from the Moderación de Doctrinas (Scholes and Adams, 1959, pp. 43–4), tribute records,[6] the journal of an archbishop's visit in 1685,[7] and the work of Vetancurt (4a parte, pp. 60–1).

A lost document of 1743 is summarized in Villaseñor y Sánchez (I, p. 78). For 1792 there is a brief report describing the jurisdiction,[8] and another description accompanied by a padrón of the non-Indian population and a map.[9]

Monographic treatment with further citation is found in Galarza (1963) and Gibson (1964). The indices of Colín (1966, 1967) should be consulted.

35 *Guaxuapa*

The center of the Mixteca Baja (Ñuiñe in Mixtecan), this is mostly a hot, dry country of eroded mountains with scanty vegetation at 1,000–1,700 m, rising in the south to over 3,000 m at the summit of the Sierra Madre del Sur. Now in northwesternmost Oaxaca state, it is drained by the Mixteco and Tlapaneco rivers, affluents of the Mexcala.

The region contained a number of Mixtecan states of disparate size, most if not all of which

paid tribute to the Triple Alliance. The largest were Guaxoapan (Mixtecan, Ñudée), Igualtépec or Yocaltépec, Tequicistépec (Yucundiachi), and Tonalla (Ñuhuni). Others were perhaps Calihualan, Coyotepexic (Yucuñaña), Huepanapan (Ñutunvito), Patlanalan, Tezoatlan, Tuctlan, Tzilacayoapan, Xochicuitlapilco, and Xochitépec (Yucuitahino). There is some doubt whether the center of Aztec tribute collection was Yocaltépec or Ichcaatoyac, and whether the last-named is

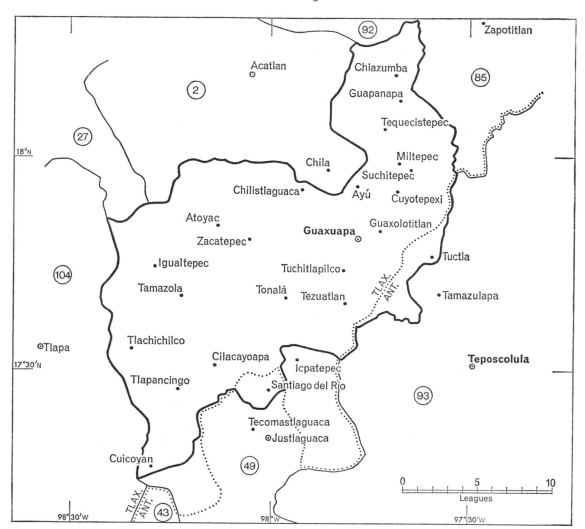

identifiable with modern S Pedro Atoyac or a community in neighboring Chiautla (q.v.). Mixtecan was the predominant language, with a sprinkling of Náhuatl in the southwest, and a Popolocan intrusion at Huepanapan.

Gonzalo de Umbria traversed this area in 1520, and it probably came under Spanish control a year or so later.

Encomiendas

Cuyotepexi, together with Guaxolotitlan, Miltepec, Suchitepetongo, and Yeitepec were held by the conquistador Juan Tello de Medina, succeeded before 1550 by a son of the same name. When the latter entered the priesthood in the 1560s his rights passed to his mother, by this time re-married to Pedro Calderón. Escheatment occurred between 1570 and 1597.

We do not know the encomenderos of Guapanapa and Tequecistepec, which were crown possessions by 1534.

Juan Tello de Medina (*see above*) also appears as first holder of Guaxuapa and Tuctla. All of Tuctla and half of Guaxuapa were taken for the crown by 1534, while the other half of Guaxuapa was re-assigned to Juan de Arriaga. In two lists dated 1560, we find the original Arriaga still encomendero of his share, but one source shows the remaining half of Guaxuapa plus Tuctla recovered by the son of Tello de Medina (the other lists them as crown property); at any rate, Tello became a priest towards 1566. Arriaga died in the 1560s and his part was inherited by a son of the same name. By 1597 the Arriaga share had escheated.[1]

The tributes of Igualtepec were divided at an early date between two conquistadors, García de Aguilar and Francisco de Terrazas. This was a large encomienda extending southward to Ayusuchiquilazala (cf. Justlaguaca). The Terrazas share was inherited towards 1548 by a son, Francisco (the poet), and towards 1600 by a grandson of the same name. Aguilar died in the 1570s and was followed by a daughter, Juana, married to Felipe de Arellano; in 1604 Juan Ramírez de Arellano, a grandson of the first holder, was encomendero. Final escheatment occurred after 1696 (Icaza, I, pp. 7, 49. L de T, p. 574).

Juan de Morales was perhaps the original holder of Suchitepec, succeeded in 1566 by his widow, Ana de Agüero. By 1597 the place had been reassigned to D. Luis de Velasco, but it was a crown village in 1626 (Icaza, I, p. 80. L de T, p. 307).

Tezuatlan was assigned by viceroy Mendoza to Martín de Peralta, succeeded before 1552 by his widow, Beatriz de Zayas. Alonso de Peralta was a later encomendero. Escheatment occurred between 1629 and 1664 (Icaza, I, p. 143).

Tonalá, which included Cilacayoapan and perhaps Patlanalá, was taken for the crown in 1531, but six years later it was given by the viceroy to Juan Alonso de Sosa, the treasurer. It escheated in accordance with the New Laws in April, 1544 (CDI, II, p. 190. ENE, xv, p. 93. Icaza, II, p. 357. L de T, p. 524).

A small place called Tuchitlapilco (see below for variant spellings), perhaps once an estancia of Guaxuapa, seems to have been assigned in encomienda to an Indian governor, Juan Sánchez. On his death, sometime before 1568, it escheated (L de T, p. 534).

The following places appear separately as crown cabeceras in a tribute list of 1626: Atoyac,

Tulistlauaca (Chilistlaguaca). It is not certain, however, whether these were once private encomiendas or former sujetos which had achieved cabecera status.

Government

Cs were appointed in the early 1530s to Guapanapa, Guaxuapa y Tequecistepec, Tonalá, and Tuctla. We have mentioned that Tonalá reverted to private encomienda in 1537–44, while Tuctla (or perhaps Tuchitlapilco) was annexed to the corregimiento of Guaxuapa y Tequecistepec in 1555.[2] Towards 1558 the three remaining Cs were made suffragan to the AM of Acatlan y Piastla, whose jurisdiction included Cuyotepexi, Guaxolotitlan, Suchitepec, Tezuatlan, and Tuchitlapilco.[3] However, the C of Guaxuapa also claimed these places, and by the late 1580s he was administering them. In these early years Igualtepec belonged to the jurisdiction of Chiautla.

Cilacayoapa, a sujeto of Tonalá, was made a separate corregimiento briefly in the 1570s, perhaps because mineral deposits were discovered near there.[4] The magistrate of Tonalá was redesignated AM *c.* 1579 and thereafter lived much of the time at Cilacayoapa.[5]

Meanwhile, early in the seventeenth century the corregimiento of Guaxuapa shed its suffragan status and was enlarged by the absorption of Guapanapa. In the jurisdictional reforms of the 1680s Guaxuapa and Minas de Tonalá were united under a single AM whose territory now included the Igualtepec area, transferred from Chiautla.[6] From 1787 Guaxuapa was a subdelegación in the intendancy of Oaxaca. Sometime later certain villages within the jurisdiction of Guaxuapa seem to have been put in the intendencia of Puebla.

Church

In the early 1550s the Dominicans founded a monastery–parish at Sto Domingo Tonalá (Alvarado, pp. 11–18). In 1570 this was the only doctrina with its cabecera within the civil jurisdiction we are concerned with here. The region from Tezuatlan to Tequecistepec in that year was being visited by Dominicans working out of Chila (cf. Acatlan y Piastla), while Chiazumba and Guapanapa were visitas of a secular priest based at Zapotitlan (cf. Teguacán). To the south, the curate of Icpatepec (cf. Justlaguaca) visited the Cilacayoapa area, but eventually the latter became a separate parish. Meanwhile, Dominican doctrinas were established at S Pedro y S Pablo Tequecistepec (by 1576), Guaxuapa (by 1578), and S Juan Bautista Igualtepec (by 1596) (Scholes and Adams, 1959, p. 33).

By 1603 there was another Dominican parish at S Juan Tezuatlan, and before 1610 a secular priest was appointed to S Francisco Tlapancingo. Between 1743 and 1777 most if not all of the regular doctrinas were secularized, and new parochial centers were created at Santiago Chiazumba, S Francisco Guapanapa, Santiago Guaxolotitlan, and S Juan Tlachichilco. A further division was effected, perhaps somewhat later, with parishes at Santiago Cuicoyan, Santiago Tamazola, and S Martín Zacatepec.

All of these parishes belonged to the diocese of Tlaxcala, while the Dominicans were subject to their province of Santiago de México until 1656, and to that of Santos Angeles de Puebla thereafter. The parishes of Cilacayoapa and Guapanapa included portions of the neighboring civil jurisdictions of Justlaguaca and Teguacán respectively.[7] Certain villages politically subject to Guaxuapa belonged to parishes whose centers were in adjoining jurisdictions. Ayhú, Ahuehuetitlan, Ayuquila, Ayuquililla, Chilistlaguaca, and Tetaltepec were visited from Chila. Tuctla and its dependencies were in the diocese of Antequera, visited from Tamazulapa, while Santiago del Río was a visita of Tecomastlaguaca, also an Antequera parish.

Population and settlements

We have few data on native population here before the 1560s, in which decade new tribute assessments were made and have been found for some, but not all, of the numerous cabeceras. By interpolation, we estimate there were 8,000 tributaries in 1565, 5,000 in 1595, and 2,100 in 1626. The loss was due both to disease and emigration. Later counts give 2,700 tributaries in 1696, 3,710 Indian families in 1743, and 6,308 Indian tributaries in 1795–7.[8]

There were relatively few non-Indians at any period. Mines in the Cilacayoapan–Tlapancingo area attracted Spaniards and mulattoes in the late sixteenth and seventeenth centuries (60 vecinos in 1610, 40 in 1662), until they were abandoned.[9] Guaxuapa itself had eight Spanish families in 1610, and 'many' in 1820. The 1795 census shows 368 mulatto tributaries in the jurisdiction.

The post-Conquest tendency of subject pueblos to break away from their cabeceras, common to many parts of New Spain, was accentuated here. There were probably not more than a dozen native states at contact, while forty-nine settlements were considered cabeceras in the late eighteenth century.

Guaxuapa (Huexoapam, etc.; 1950: Huajuapan de León, ciudad) had a large number of estancias which disappeared towards 1600. Cacalostepec, S Gerónimo Cilacayoapilla, and Zapotitlan seem to have survived as pueblos. Nearby was Xochicuitlapilco (Tuchitlapilco, Zochicotlapilco, Tlachicostlapilco, Tuchcuitlapilco, etc.; 1950: Sta María Xochixtlapilco, ranchería), which acquired cabecera status as a separate encomienda in the sixteenth century, although it also appears as a sujeto of Guaxuapa.[10] S Pedro Cotlalpan (= Yodoyuxi?) was to have been congregated at Xochicuitlapilco in 1604, but was still a pueblo in 1820.[11]

Igualtepec (Yoaltepec, Yocaltepec; 1950: S Juan Igualtepec, pueblo) probably included the sujetos of Tamazola and Tlachichilco, although we are not sure of this (cf. Miranda, 1968, p. 144).

We are fortunate in having a complete congregation record of S Pedro y S Pablo Tequecistepec (Tequisistepec, etc.; 1950: S Pedro y S Pablo Tequixtepec, pueblo), often confused with a homonym (S Miguel Tequecistepec) in the neighboring jurisdiction of Teposcolula (q.v.). It had thirteen estancias which were ordered moved into the cabecera in 1600, together with a place called S Luis Papalutla.[12] Most of them either survived as pueblos or were re-occupied, and one, Chiazumba (Chazumba), was soon made a cabecera.

The *Suma de Visitas* gives Náhuatl names of eight sujetos of Tezuatlan (Teshoatlan, etc.; 1950:

Tezoatlán de Segura y Luna, *villa*). Four or five of them survived a congregation of 1603–4.[13]

Tonala(n) (1950: Sto Domingo Tonalá, pueblo) had three sujetos and twenty-four estancias in 1548. Among these were Cilacayoapa(n) (Silacayoapan), Tlapancingo, and Patlanala. Many disappeared after 1600.

Sta María Tuctla (Tustla, Tutlan; 1950: Sta María Tutla, ranchería) had five sujetos, of which three (Cuitito, Dinicuiti, Yodoino) survived a congregation in 1604.[14]

We have no information about dependent settlements belonging to Ayú (Ayhu, Suchitepetongo; 1950: Sta María Ayú, ranchería), Cuyotepexi (1950: Asunción Cuyotepeji, pueblo), Chilistlaguaca (Tulistlauaca; 1950: Santiago Chilixtlahuaca, ranchería), Guapanapa (Huepanapa, etc.; 1950: S Francisco Huapanapan, ranchería), Guaxolotitlan (1950: Santiago Huajolotitlán, pueblo), Miltepec (1950: Santiago Miltepec, pueblo), and Suchitepec (Xuchiltepec; 1950: S Juan Bautista Suchitepec, pueblo). If they had estancias, they presumably were congregated in 1598–1603.[15] It was proposed to combine Cuyotepexi and Suchitepec at one site, Xuliaca, in 1600, while Guapanapa was to be moved to Petlalcingo in 1603, but all these places survived as cabeceras in the eighteenth century.[16]

Sources

There are brief *Suma* articles (*c.* 1548) (PNE, I, nos. 131, 659, 753, 784), and tributary data for the 1560s (L de T, pp. 156–7, 307–8, 422–4, 524–5, 534–5, 574–8), followed by the Ovando report on the diocese of Tlaxcala (García Pimentel, 1904, pp. 18–21) and a separate relación from the curate of Icpatepec–Cilacayoapa (PNE, v, pp. 237–8), both written *c.* 1570. We have seen a most interesting congregation document concerning Tequecistepec in 1600.[17]

Bishop Mota y Escobar went through here twice, in 1610 and 1623, leaving a valuable description.[18] Population data for the seventeenth century are derived from two sources.[19]

A report of *c.* 1743 is summarized in Villaseñor y Sánchez (I, p. 325). Fray Ajofrín went through Guaxuapa in 1766 (Ajofrín, II, pp. 132–5). For the year 1777, we have padrones from the parishes of Chiazumba, Guapanapa, Guaxolotitlan, Igualtepec, Tequecistepec, Tezuatlan, Tlachichilco, Tlapancingo, and Tonalá.[20] There is a topographic description sent in by the curate of Chiazumba in 1778,[21] as well as a detailed statistical summary of *c.* 1820.[22]

36 *Guayacocotla*

This is a most rugged area on the east slope of the Sierra Madre Oriental, facing the Gulf and drained by affluents of the Tuxpan and Pánuco rivers. Rains most of the year support a heavy vegetation which, together with the temperature, varies widely depending on the altitude (200–2,600 m). The boundaries of the colonial jurisdiction coincide with two westerly bulges in the modern state of Veracruz, plus the village of Tehuitzila in Hidalgo.

The political situation of Hueyacocotlan is a bit of a mystery. It nowhere appears as a conquest or tributary of the Aztecs, and yet we are told that it was at war with Metztitlan; if it was not an ally

of the Mexicans, at least Hueyacocotlan seems to have allowed them passage through its territory, strategically placed between Metztitlan and Tototépec. People speaking three languages, Náhuatl, Otomí, and Tepehuan, lived here. Subordinate to Hueyacocotlan were Hueytliltipan, Patlachiuhcan, and Tzontecomatlan, which may have been semiautonomous communities.

Adjoining Tzontecomatlan on the northwest were two small Náhuatl-speaking states, Ilamatlan and Atlihuetzian, both allies of and perhaps subject to the lord of Metztitlan. In the hot country off to the northeast was the Aztec tributary province of Xiuhcoac, which included Chicontépec.

Náhuatl, Otomí, Tepehuan, and (in the north) Huaxtecan were all spoken there.

While it may have been visited by Spaniards as early as 1520, this inaccessible area was not secured by them until about 1526.

Encomiendas

The conquistador Guillén de la Loa (de Lalo, de la Lua) held Guayacocotla until his death sometime before 1550. Then the tributes were divided between two sons of the first holder, Julián de

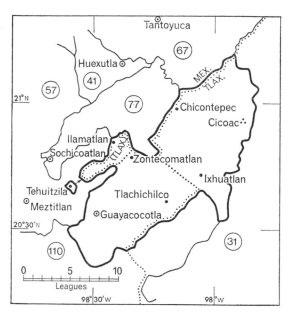

la Lóa and Gómez de Alvarado. By 1560 both were dead, and the encomienda was shared between Isabel de Alvarado (widow of Guillén de la Loa, now married to a Midinilla) and a son of Gómez de Alvarado. Escheatment occurred sometime between 1568 and 1594.[1]

Ilamatlan and Atlehuecian were assigned to Juan de Cervantes, followed in 1564 by his eldest son, Leonel. The latter was still encomendero in 1598, and Ilamatlan did not escheat until the late seventeenth century.[2]

Cicoac was claimed by Hernando Cortés in 1526, but two years later it was given to Francisco Ramírez. Sometime before 1550 Diego de Coria acquired a third of this encomienda, which in-

cluded Chicontepec, while Ramírez sold his share to Pedro de Meneses. Both encomenderos died in the 1560s and were succeeded by sons, Pedro Bermúdez de Meneses and Hernando de Coria. By 1592 the Meneses share had been acquired through marriage by Lic. Miguel de Chávez (five years later the holder was Agustina de Meneses, presumably the widow), while Francisco de Coria held the other third. Cicoac-Chicontepec is listed as a crown possession in 1626, and again as a private encomienda in 1629–96.[3]

Government

For most of the sixteenth century this region formed part of the jurisdiction of Molango y Malila or Meztitlan (q.v.).[4] It was perhaps in the 1590s that Guayacocotla became a crown possession to which a C was assigned, although it may have had a separate magistrate some years earlier.[5] Chicontepec (until then administered from Meztitlan, Huexutla, and Guachinango on different occasions) and Ilamatlan were added to the new jurisdiction.[6] In the seventeenth century the magistrate was re-designated AM and resided at times in Guayacocotla, at others in Chicontepec. In 1787 the region became a subdelegación in the intendencia of Puebla.

Church

First visited by Augustinians from Meztitlan, S Pedro Guayacocotla had a separate Augustinian monastery from 1558 which became a secular parish in 1569.[7] Another visita, Santiago Ilamatlan, was an Augustinian parish from 1572 until it was secularized in 1640. Sta Catarina Chicontepec in 1570 had a secular priest.

S Agustín Tlachichilco and S Francisco Zontecomatlan had resident secular clergy from c. 1600. S Cristóbal Ixhuatlan seems to have become a separate doctrina late in the seventeenth century, while S Francisco Xocholoco was likewise separated from Chicontepec towards the end of the colonial period.

Of these parishes, three (Guayacocotla, Tlachichilco, and Zontecomatlan) were in the archdiocese of Mexico, the remaining four belonging to the bishopric of Tlaxcala.

Guayacocotla

Population and settlements

We have no useable data on the native population before *c.* 1565, by which time there had been a considerable loss, especially in the lowlands. In that year there were some 2,000 tributaries at Guayacocotla, 1,650 in Ilamatlan–Atlehuecian, and 700 at Chicontepec, a total of perhaps 4,350. This number had dropped to *c.* 2,700 in 1597, many deaths occurring in the epidemic of 1576–81, especially in the mountains. There were subsequent plagues and movements to and from the jurisdiction. Towards 1640 there were probably not more than 1,300 tributaries, after which (1646) we are told that a thousand families moved from neighboring Tututepec to Chicontepec (*Alegaciones...*, fol. 160v). Interpolation of later censuses gives 1,350 tributaries in 1690, 3,558 Indian families in 1743, and 4,289 Indian tributaries in 1800.

The white and mixed population was largely confined to the lowlands. In 1791 there were 239 Spaniards (persons), 576 mestizos, and 380 mulattoes in the jurisdiction.

Guayacocotla (Hueyacocotla; 1950: Huayacocotla, *villa*) towards 1548 had three subject pueblos (Patlachiucan or Patlachihuacan, Hueytliltipan, Zontecomatlan) with an undisclosed number of estancias. Thirty-three of the latter are named in the 1569 report, but the list seems to be incomplete as there were fifty estancias when it was proposed to reduce them to four congregations in 1592; the Náhuatl-speakers were to gather at Zontecomatlan, the Otomies at Tezcatepec, and the Tepehuas at Pataloyan. Later in the same year settlements of Otomies were authorized at Atlistaca and Chila, while Alahuaco or Tlachichilco was set aside as the center of the Tepehuas. These reductions, if carried out at all, were later broken up, twenty-three pueblos surviving in 1792.[8]

Ilamatlan (1950: pueblo) had twenty-seven estancias in 1569 and 34 in 1599, when they were to be reduced to five congregations. The 1792 report names seven pueblos in addition to the cabecera. An eighth, S Nicolás Tehuitzila, may be the old cabecera of Atlehuecian (Atlihuetzian, Tlehuicilan, etc.; 1950: Tehuitzila, pueblo, Hgo.), which formed an enclave surrounded by lands of Meztitlan; Atlehuecian had seven estancias of its own in 1569.

The cabecera of Cicoac (Tzicoac, Xiuhcoac, etc.) was moved at an early date to Chicontepec (1950: ciudad), but the old name continued to be used well into the seventeenth century. The original Cicoac was most likely on the Vinasco river near its junction with the Tuxpan, although other locations have been postulated in the jurisdiction of Guachinango (q.v.). Cicoac-Chicontepec, with perhaps 300 tributaries, still had thirty-two small estancias in 1592, when they were to be reduced to four congregations, Chicontepec, S Juan, S Cristóbal Ixhuatlan, and S Francisco Xocholoco. These places and four others are listed as pueblos in 1792 (Byam Davies, pp. 34–5. Williams García, p. 62).

Sources

Scanty information in the Suma de Visitas (PNE, I, nos. 20, 285, 299) is filled out in several reports of *c.* 1570 (PNE, III, p. 113; V, p. 220). There are documents concerning the congregations at Chicontepec (1592)[9] and Ilamatlan (1599).[10]

Two bishops of Tlaxcala left valuable descriptions of this area as it was in 1610[11] and 1646.[12] The part corresponding to the archbishopric was visited in 1684.[13] Tributary data for the seventeenth century are derived from several documents.[14]

The jurisdiction in 1743 is described in Villaseñor y Sánchez (I, p. 378). We have seen padrones dated 1777 from the parishes of Chicontepec, Ilamatlan, and Ixhuatlan.[15] For the late eighteenth century, there is a report of 1781,[16] a brief description with a census of non-Indians dated 1791,[17] and a list of toponyms made in 1792.[18]

Further details are found in the works of Meade (1962) and Williams García.

37 Guaymeo y Sirándaro

This is a very hot, semi-arid region along the Balsas river, much of it at 100–400 m, although the southern part reaches over 2,000 m in the Sierra Madre del Sur. It is today in southeastern Michoacán and northwestern Guerrero.

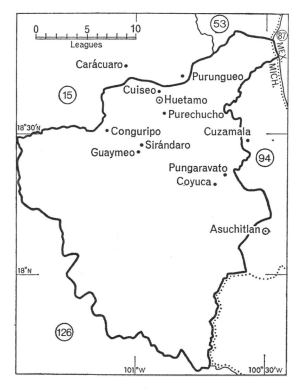

We do not know what people lived here when the area was invaded by Tarascans in the fifteenth century. They may have been Nahua-speakers who were driven out. At least three languages were spoken when the Spaniards arrived, the predominant Tarascan, Matlatzincan (Pirinda) at Huetamo, and Apaneca (=Pantecan?) at Huayameo. The last two groups are said to have immigrated to those places at the invitation of Tzitzipandácuare (two generations before the Spanish Conquest), the Pirindas coming from the vicinity of Toluca, the Apanecas from the Pacific

coast. This infusion of foreign colonists leads one to think that here, as in parts of the Gulf coastal region, there may have been some pre-Columbian disease which decimated the population (Herrera, 4a Década, p. 236).

Principal native states tributary to the cazonci were Cutzío, Cuyucan, Huayameo, Pungarahuato, and Sirándaro (=Zarandancho?). This was a frontier region, at war with the Mexica and their allies to the east.

The area submitted without resistance to a small group led by Antonio de Caravajal, perhaps in 1523 (Warren, 1963 a, p. 407). There may have been an attempt at rebellion in 1526–8.

Encomiendas

Cortés gave Cuiseo to Nicolás López de Palacios Rubios, but the place was re-assigned and was a crown possession in 1533–6. Gonzalo Ruiz was the holder in the 1540s, succeeded shortly before 1560 by his widow, Juana de Torres. When the latter died the tributes escheated, in March, 1566, but they were soon re-assigned to D. Luis de Velasco the younger, and were held by his descendants, the marquises of Salinas, in the seventeenth century.[1]

Coyuca, held in 1528–33 by Guillén de la Loa, was acquired within the next decade by Pedro de Meneses, followed towards 1567 by a son, Cristóbal de Soto. The latter died very soon afterwards and was succeeded first by a son, Rodrigo de Meneses, and later by Agustina de Meneses (still in 1603). Escheatment occurred before 1657, but part of the tributes were subsequently re-assigned.

Gil González de Avila (Benavides) acquired title to Guaymeo y Sirándaro in 1527, and was succeeded by a son, Alonso de Avila Alvarado, in 1544. The encomienda escheated when Avila Alvarado was executed in August, 1566.[2]

Pungaravato may have been first given by Cortés to Juan Velázquez, although by early 1528 it was divided between two encomenderos, Fernando Alonso and Pedro Bazán. Alonso was executed as a relapsed Jew later in 1528, after which Bazán acquired the vacant half (Millares Carlo and Mantecón, I, no. 1695). Both Antonio Anguiano and Luis Sánchez claimed the encomienda in the 1540s after Bazán's death, but Hernando de Bazán (a son) held title until he became a priest shortly after 1579, at which time Pungaravato escheated.[3]

Government

The area was occasionally visited in early years by the Cs of Cuiseo and neighboring Asuchitlan and Capulalcolulco (cf. Tetela del Río),[4] but there was little interference with the encomenderos until 1554, when the C of Tiripitio, far to the north, was given jurisdiction there 'since there is no magistrate in those villages'.[5] In 1566 both Guaymeo y Sirándaro and Cuiseo escheated, and when Cuiseo was re-assigned in private encomienda it was assigned to the jurisdiction of the C of Guaymeo y Sirándaro, who also held the title of AM of Minas del Espíritu Santo. Meanwhile, Coyuca, Cuzamala, and Pungaravato were placed in the corregimiento of Asuchitlan.[6]

In 1599 or very soon afterwards a new jurisdiction was created with its center at Minas de Tetela (cf. Tetela del Río), at which time the corregimiento of Asuchitlan was partitioned, Coyuca and Pungaravato being assigned to Guaymeo y Sirándaro, and the rest going to Tetela.[7] However, Coyuca and its dependencies were disputed for some years and were still claimed by the magistrate of Tetela as late as 1743.

The justice was living at Cuiseo in 1649, and at nearby Huetamo in 1789. From 1787 the jurisdiction became a subdelegación in the intendencia of Valladolid. It was perhaps at this time that the Acuyo–Carácuaro–Purungueo area was transferred from Cinagua y la Guacana to the jurisdiction of Huetamo, a temporary move (cf. Cinagua).

Church

Visited by Augustinians working out of Tiripitio and Tacámbaro from *c.* 1540, the towns of this jurisdiction were divided between three secular curacies in the 1560s: Asunción Cuiseo (which included Huetamo and Purechucho), S Juan Bautista Pungaravato (including Coyuca), and S Nicolás Sirándaro (with Guaymeo). The curate of Cuiseo moved to S Juan Huetamo after 1789. All three parishes were in the diocese of Michoacán.[8]

Population and settlements

The native population dropped from 5,468 'persons' (=tributaries?) in 1548 to 2,300 tributaries in 1579, 1,175 in 1603, and 416 in 1649, after which it recovered to 528 in 1657, 915 in 1743, 1,620 in 1789, and 1,859 Indian tributaries in 1800.[9] Beside the three languages (Tarascan, Pirinda, Apaneca) mentioned in the sixteenth century, a report of 1649 says that some people spoke Náhuatl at Cuiseo, while a minority spoke Cuicatecan and Chontal at Pungaravato. Thus, in addition to epidemic disease, and an earthquake which caused some mortality shortly before 1559, migration should be considered as a cause of the above fluctuations (L de T, p. 147).

Cuiseo (Cuseo; 1950: Cutzío, pueblo, Mich.) and Huetamo (Güetamo; 1950: Huetamo de Núñez, *villa*, Mich.), joint cabeceras, had a large number of sujetos, twenty-one of which were presumably eliminated in a congregation carried out by the Augustinians in 1558. Twenty or more estancias survived in 1579, but these were reduced to four sites including the cabeceras in 1603. Purechucho and S Lucas Turepecuao were the other two congregations, and all four were still pueblos in the late eighteenth century.

Sta Lucía Coyuca (Cuyuca; 1950: Coyuca de Catalán, ciudad, Gro.) had twelve sujetos in 1579, all of which were moved to the cabecera in 1603.

Pungaravato (Pungarabato, Pungarahuato, etc.; 1950: Ciudad Altamirano, Gro.) had thirteen estancias in 1548, and eight or ten in 1603–4 when a congregation was carried out. They were all supposed to be eliminated, but Asunción Acasécuaro (Tlapeguala) and Santiago Tanguenguato (Tanganhuato) survived as pueblos.

Guaymeo (Güimeo, Huayameo; 1950: S Agustín, cuadrilla, Gro.?) and Sirándaro (Cirandaro; =Zarandancho? 1950: Zirándaro, pueblo, Gro.) together had ten sujetos, some of them nine leagues away, in 1579. The two cabeceras were so near each other that they were ordered to be joined in a single settlement in 1603, and the estancias were also to be moved in at that time, but three of the latter (Capeo, Cicunduato or Conguripo, Mazán) appear as pueblos in 1649. Capeo was abandoned somewhat later.

This area did not particularly attract Europeans, although there were a few at the mines of Espíritu Santo in the 1540s (they had much declined by 1579). At mid-seventeenth century there were six cattle ranches with a total of four Spanish and two mulatto families. There was a brief revival of mining activity (Minas de Oromucho) in the early eighteenth century. In 1743, 240 'Spanish' families are reported, with 146 of mestizos and mulattoes and 218 mulatto vagrants. The 1789 census shows 123 Spanish families and 504 mulatto tributaries, most of them living in twenty-nine haciendas and cattle ranches and twenty-seven

ranchos. 990 mulatto tributaries were counted in 1800.

Sources

There is a brief description of each cabecera in the Suma of *c.* 1548 (PNE, I, nos. 164–6, 461, 492). A rare congregation report of 1558[10] is followed by tribute assessments for the 1560s (L de T, pp. 190–2) and the Ovando summary of *c.* 1570 (García Pimentel, 1904, pp. 43–9; cf. Miranda Godínez, 9/37). The Cs of both Asuchitlan[11] and Guaymeo y Sirándaro[12] submitted valuable relaciones geográficas in 1579–80. Congregation data for 1593–1604 are found in several places.[13]

The jurisdiction is described in 1639[14] and 1649,[15] and we have tributary data for the period 1657–98.[16] In 1743 the AM sent in a complete matrícula with his report.[17] There is a detailed analysis of settlements and communal lands of *c.* 1789,[18] and a brief report dated 1792.[19] Martínez de Lejarza (pp. 96–107) describes the jurisdiction as it was *c.* 1822.

38 *Guazacualco*

Most of this extensive jurisdiction, which now occupies the easternmost part of the state of Veracruz and western Tabasco, is a broad plain stretching from the Gulf coast, bordered with lagoons and mangrove swamps, southward to the middle of the Tehuantepec isthmus. Elevations of over 1,000 m are reached on the continental divide and at the volcano of S Martín Pajapan. Unusually heavy and year-around rains feed numerous rivers (the largest are the Coatzacoalcos, Mezcalapa or Grijalva, and Tonalá) pouring into the Gulf and flooding the low country in summer. In the higher parts there is a dense rain forest.

Natural levees in the lowlands here were the scene of the remarkable culture known to modern anthropologists as Olmec, and according to some this was the place of origin of all Middle American civilization. Here as elsewhere, when the Spaniards arrived the Olmec ceremonial sites were long since covered by the jungle or buried under

more recent settlements. The area was densely inhabited by Nahua- and Popolucan-speaking people dispersed in a great many villages and divided into numerous independent states. Some idea of the political complexity here can be had from the mid-sixteenth-century list of encomiendas (*see below*), but there were undoubtedly chiefdoms which had disappeared by that time. Perhaps the realm of the lord of Coatzacualco, which seems to have comprised an extensive area of settlement ('grandes poblaciones') along the river of that name, was larger and more important than the other states (Cervantes de Salazar, p. 364); here and to the west an archaic variety of Nahua was spoken, although there may well have been a Popolucan minority. The situation was reversed in the area east of Coatzacualco known as Yahualulco, where there were more Popolucan than Nahua speakers. Mixtec and Zapotec minorities are reported in 1580, but these may have been post-Conquest immigrants. The region was just beyond the limit of the Mexica tributary hegemony, and there had been recent warfare between Coatzacualco and the Aztec garrison of Tochtépec, but the *pochteca* of Tenochtitlan were allowed passage through the area to their trading posts in Tabasco.

Grijalva sailed along this coast in June, 1518, and entered the Tonalá river the following month. The ships of Cortés went by without landing in 1519. Another naval expedition led by Diego de

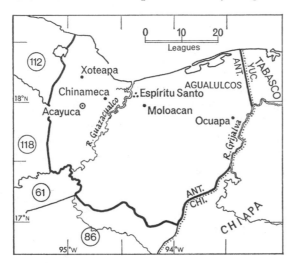

Ordaz entered the Coatzacualco in 1520, established friendly relations with the ruler, and explored ten leagues upstream. Later in the same year Juan Velázquez de León and Rodrigo Rangel founded a Spanish settlement at the mouth of the river, but it was soon abandoned. It was not until May, 1522, that an army commanded by Gonzalo de Sandoval defeated the natives in a battle and established the *villa* of Espíritu Santo on the bank of the Coatzacualco four leagues from its mouth (Bancroft, II, p. 35. Cervantes de Salazar, pp. 364–6, 805. Oviedo y Valdés, III, p. 437). During the next few years, Espíritu Santo served as a base for further Spanish penetration towards Tabasco, Chiapa, and Yucatán. Cortés passed through at the end of 1524 on his way to Honduras, taking with him many of the Spanish settlers, after which there was a native rebellion quelled with vigor in 1525–6 (Herrera, 3a década, pp. 121, 268–70).

Encomiendas

The Indians of Guazacualco and Agualulcos were soon distributed among the Spanish vecinos of Espíritu Santo, with re-assignments on the accession of successive governors in Mexico in the 1520s and early 1530s. We have no information concerning encomiendas here before mid-century, by which time the population had greatly diminished and about half the surviving native communities had escheated.

Available data for the second half of the sixteenth century are summarized in Table H.

Government

The *villa* of Espíritu Santo had an ayuntamiento from its foundation in 1522, and an AM appointed from Mexico by 1525. This magistrate was ruler of the province of Guazacualco, and in early years he and the ayuntamiento laid claim to a vast jurisdiction, a pretension successfully disputed by neighboring municipalities (Díaz del Castillo, II, p. 97). This territorial war was largely resolved to Guazacualco's loss by 1531. The Alvarado basin went to Vera Cruz, Tuxtla was put in the Marquesado del Valle, the Zapotecas were made a separate municipality as was Chiapa, and the Zimatán-Copilco region was given to Tabasco. Espíritu Santo–Guazacualco was left with a very large but economically relatively worthless jurisdiction.

From *c.* 1550 the AM was also C of certain villages which had come under crown control.[1] Gradually, as the encomiendas escheated, new corregimientos were created and were assigned annually to vecinos of Espíritu Santo, presumably those who did not have encomiendas. The earliest C of whom we have record was that of Aguataco (1545). In 1550 Yagualulcos (Los Agualulcos) appears as a corregimiento, and by 1554 there were Cs at Ataco y Ocelotepec, Hueytlan y Tilzapoapa, Miaguatlan y Zapotancingo, Tapalan, and Tonalá. Other communities passed to the crown in the late 1550s and 1560s: Chicuitlan y Ostuacan, Taquilapas, and Zacualpa y Cayaco. Thus by 1580 the jurisdiction contained ten Cs, all suffragan to the AM. Most of these posts were

TABLE H. *Encomenderos of Guazacualco*

Pueblos	1554	1560–7	1597–9
Acalapa, Tacotalpa (Tatatuytalpa)	Alonso García	Same	Francisco del Caso
Acayuca, Chacalapa, Olutla, Tequecistepec, Tetiquipa, Xaltepec, Xaltipa, Zayultepec	Luis Marín, followed by a son, Francisco	Sons of Francisco Marín	Luis Marín
Agualulco (1/2), Guacuilapa, Cosoliacac, Guazacualco (1/2), Mecatepec, Ocuapa	Gonzalo Gallego Hernández de Alconchel	Gonzalo Hernández, son	Gonzalo Hernández de Alconchel
Cotastan, Cempoala, Pechucalco	Bartolomé Sánchez	Same	Juan López de Frías
Chinameca, Mistecas	Cristóbal de Herrera	Cristóbal de Herrera, son	
Huestepec, Quezaltepec, Teotalco	Juan Enamorado, followed by daughter married to Luis Alvarez	Alvarez dead, widow marries Luis Velázquez	
Mechoacan	Bernal Díaz del Castillo, Teresa Díaz de Padilla	Daughter of Díaz married to Juan de Fuentes	Bernardino del Castillo; Bernardo de Estrada
Miaguatlan, Guatepec	Teresa Méndez	Same	
Minzapa	Lorenzo Genovés, followed by Gonzalo Rodríguez de Villafuerte and Juan de España	Rodríguez and España; latter dies, widow inherits	Alonso de Horta
Monzapa, Chacalapa, Pichucalco, Zolcuautla	Juan López Frías	Same	Juan López Frías and Catalina del Castillo (Monzapa)
Suchititlan, Guatepec, Milpancingo	Gaspar de Hita, followed by son of same name	Same	Catalina de Hita
Xoteapa, Quinamulapa	Juan Martín de Valencia	Same	Luis Guillén
Zapotitlan, Ostopilla	Widow of first holder married to Diego de Lizana	Diego de Lizana	Same

abolished towards 1600, but Agualulcos had its own magistrate until it was absorbed by Guazacualco *c.* 1680.[2] Other places which may have survived for a time as suffragan jurisdictions appear in a badly transcribed list of 1676: 'Ataco y Tejapa y ocolotepeque' (Ataco y Ocelotepec), 'Chuicatlan' (= Chicuitlan?), and 'Tonala proua de Guazaqualco'.[3]

The AM lived at Espíritu Santo until that place was deserted (*see below*), after which his residence was Acayuca. From 1787 Guazacualco, or Acayuca, as the jurisdiction was called in later years, became a subdelegación in the intendencia of Veracruz.

Church

There was a secular curate at Espíritu Santo as early as 1527 (Millares Carlo and Mantecón, 1, no. 833). This man and his successors were to visit the entire jurisdiction, although there may have been other clergy employed by individual encomenderos in early years. In the 1570s four secular parishes were founded at S Martín Acayuca, S Juan Bautista Mecatepec, and two unnamed places; there was a complaint about the last two priests in 1583, and they were removed.[4]

Sometime before 1743 (perhaps long before, when Espíritu Santo was abandoned) a secular doctrina was founded at S Juan Tenantitlan or Chinameca. In the eighteenth century Santiago Moloacan had a vicar subordinate to the curate of S Francisco Ocuapa, which had replaced Mecatepec as the parish center of Agualulcos. Towards the end of the colony (after 1802) S Pedro Xoteapa was separated from Acayuca and made a parish.

The area came first within the diocese of Tlaxcala. Guazacualco was to be the center of a new diocese proposed in 1532, but the bishop's seat was established three years later at Antequera, and the province remained in that ecclesiastical jurisdiction.

Population and settlements

According to the 1580 relación, there were originally 50,000 tributaries in the province, a conservative estimate. There was much loss in the earliest epidemics which desolated the coastal region, and by 1568 the number had dropped to 3,200. Later counts show 3,000 native tributaries in 1580, and 1,638 in 1743 (the nadir must have been reached in the seventeenth century). In the latter year, the language most used by the Indians was 'mexicano masorral', although some spoke Popolucan. A census of 1777 gives 10,595 Indian communicants, 182 Spaniards, and 3,567 pardos (mostly mulattoes). In 1800 there were 3,100 Indian tributaries.[5]

The Villa del Espíritu Santo, first capital of the province, was never a large settlement. It was almost deserted in the 1530s, and had only twenty Spanish vecinos in 1570–80 (*Actas de Cabildo...*, III, p. 89). In 1587 the AM proposed moving the *villa* one league upstream to a healthier site, and it was perhaps not too long afterwards that the place was altogether abandoned, Acayuca becoming the new seat of government.[6] Most of the non-Indians lived scattered in cattle haciendas created from abandoned Indian lands.

Of seventy-six Indian communities which still existed in 1580 (they are named in the document), only a few survived the congregations of 1598–1603.[7] In the eighteenth century there were three clusters of pueblos. West of the Coatzacoalcos were two parish seats, Acayuca (1950: Acayucan, ciudad, Ver.) and Tenantitlan or Chinameca (1950: Chinameca, pueblo, Ver.), from which the villages of Cosoliacaque, Macayapa, Minzapa, Olutla (Huilotlan), Oteapa, Sayultepeque, Soconusco, Tecistepeque (Texistepec), Xaltipa, and Xoteapa were visited. Just east of the river were Moloacan (1950: pueblo, Ver.) and Ixguatlan (1950: Chapopotla, pueblo, Ver.), to which two other places, Pochutla and Acalapa, were annexed. At the mouth of the river, on the left side of the bar, was (in 1748) a sentinel's shack and the abandoned battery of S Felipe de Guazacualco.

Far to the east, near the border with Tabasco, were what remained of the Agualulcos pueblos, Ocuapa(n) (1950: pueblo, Tab.), Huimanguillo, Mecatepec, Ostitan, and Tecominuacan. The original Agualulcos cabecera may have been on or near the coast, but in 1599 Mecatepec was the chief town, and by 1743 Ocuapa had this distinction. Since Tonalá appears as a corregimiento in 1676, it may have survived the congregations of *c.* 1600, but it no longer was a pueblo in the eighteenth century.

The rest of this vast area was largely uninhabited after 1600, except for an occasional country house belonging to a cattle hacienda or a cacao plantation. Guazacualco, while never used extensively as a port, was the northern terminus of a trade route across the isthmus, linking the two oceans with river craft and wagons (cf. Teguantepec).

Sources

The *Suma de Visitas*, as it has come down to us, does not include descriptions of places in Guazacualco, but there is a companion document giving the results of a visit made by Gasco (Gastón) de Herrera in 1554 (L de T, pp. 18–19, 62–3, 145, 203–4, 207, 242, 247–8, 257–8, 289–90, 311, 346–7, 531–2, 570, 611).

Brief mention of the province in a report of the Ovando series dating from 1571 (García Pimentel, 1904, pp. 67, 69, 79–80) is followed by a short relación geográfica submitted in 1580 by the AM, together with a chart of the river.[8] There is a valuable document concerning the congregation of the Agualulcos villages in 1599, with nine maps.[9]

The few references that we have found to Guazacualco in the seventeenth century are given above. There is a good report made by the AM in 1743,[10] another (with a map) concerning the shipyard and lumber industry along the river of Guazacualco in 1748,[11] and still another with demographic information drawn up for the Inquisition in 1754.[12] The parish of Acayucan is the only curacy represented by a padrón in the 1777 series,[13] but there are two 'topographical' reports made in the same year, one by the priest at

Tenantitlan–Chinameca[14] and the other covering the whole jurisdiction.[15] A brief document describes the parish of Agualulcos (Ocuapa) in 1792.[16] Further information is derived from an ecclesi-

astical survey of *c.* 1802 (Pérez, 1888, table at end).

Scholes and Warren (1965) provide a terse analysis of the situation in this area at contact.

39 *Huexocingo*

Huexocingo is on the east slope of Iztaccíhuatl volcano in the upper Atoyac valley (western Puebla). That part of the jurisdiction which is inhabited today lies at 2,200–2,600 m (settlements went higher at contact) and is a series of well-eroded, eastward-flowing watercourses with a

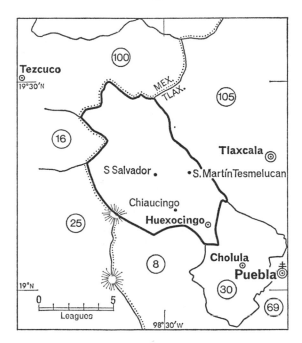

cold, semi-arid climate. Above are extensive pine forests, followed by tundra and perpetual snow.

The Huexotzinca were Náhuatl-speakers (there was an Otomí minority) allied with Tlaxcallan, and thus enemies of the Triple Alliance. The principal settlement and ceremonial center was an elevated site protected by deep canyons. The influence of the tlatoani extended to neighboring Calpan (where there seems to have been a related dynasty) and Acapetlahuacan (cf. Atrisco).

Pedro de Alvarado and Bernardino Vázquez de Tapia passed through here in September 1519, followed within a few weeks by Cortés and his army who were joined by the Huexotzinca warriors; the latter fought on the Spaniards' side in numerous engagements (Vázquez de Tapia, pp. 35–6).

Encomienda

Huexocingo, which may then have included the Calpan–Acapetlaguacan area, was taken for himself by Hernán Cortés and held by him until his departure in late 1524.[1] During the next few years the encomienda was taken for the crown (1526), seized by Gonzalo de Salazar (1528), used by the oidores of the first audiencia (1529), and assigned to the conquistador Diego de Ordaz (1530) (ENE, I, p. 141; IV, p. 174. García Granados and MacGregor, p. 82. Herrera, 3a década, p. 366). On the latter's death without issue in 1532, the encomienda again escheated.

Government

A C was first appointed to Huexocingo probably in 1532. Calpan had a separate magistrate in the 1530s, but in the following decade the jurisdiction of Huexocingo extended southward to include Calpan, Acapetlaguacan, and Guaquechula. In the 1550s there was trouble between the Indians of Huexocingo and Calpan, and the latter place was transferred briefly to the magistrate of Cholula.[2] A decade later we find Calpan–Acapetlaguacan once more under the C of Huexocingo, who in turn was subordinate to the AM of Tlaxcala.

A separate AM was assigned to Acapetlaguacan (cf. Atrisco) in 1579, and for some years Huexocingo was included in his jurisdiction. In the 1590s the southern dependencies were definitely separated, leaving Huexocingo with more or less its final boundaries, minus Calpan. The magistrate was variously referred to as C or AM, more often AM after 1643. In that year S Salvador Tesmelucan was made a separate jurisdiction, but it was soon attached again to Huexocingo (*Alegaciones...*, fol. 160). Both S Salvador and S Martín Tesmelucan had resident tenientes in the eighteenth century. From 1787 Huexocingo was a sub-delegación in the intendencia of Puebla.

Church

The Franciscans entered this area in 1524 and erected a provisional church and monastery atop a pre-Conquest temple at the original cabecera (ENE, xv, p. 187). A more permanent structure was built at the final site, S Miguel Huexocingo, in the 1540s and 1550s, according to McAndrew (pp. 33, 135, 180; cf. below). A subordinate Franciscan doctrina at S Salvador Tesmelucan was transferred to secular clergy sometime before 1569. Huexocingo itself was secularized in 1640, although the Franciscans maintained cloisters there and at S Martín Tesmelucan (which became a secular parish *c.* 1678) for some years (Ajofrín, I, p. 59). S Lorenzo Chiaucingo became a parish, separated from S Salvador, sometime after 1743. All were in the diocese of Tlaxcala.

Population and settlements

Various sources estimate the original native population at from 35,000 to over 100,000 vecinos, but Indians living in the Atrisco area were perhaps included in these figures as well as in later censuses. (Aguilar, p. 69. Herrera, 1a década, p. 360. Torquemada, II, p. 282). There was great mortality in 1528–9, after which a count of 1531 gives 30,000 men, presumably heads of families (ENE, I, p. 141; XVI, pp. 9–10). What appears to be a careful census in 1558, after the severe epidemic of the 1540s, shows 11,318 vecinos of all categories, including caciques, macehuales, widows, etc. (Scholes and Adams, 1958, pp. 79–81). Further loss in the epidemics of 1563–4 and 1576–81 brought the number of tributaries down to 6,270 in 1570, and 5,543 in 1588 (ENE, x, p. 38). The figure given in 1623 (4,008 **tributaries**) probably

covers a larger area than that of 1627 (2,047 tributaries) and subsequent counts (2,583 in 1696, 2,553 in 1743, 3,430 in 1790, and 4,129 Indian tributaries in 1799).[3]

The non-Indian population, Spaniards and mestizos with some mulattoes, ranged between 200 and 450 families in the seventeenth century.[4] In 1743 there were 513 families of 'Spaniards' and 360 of 'castas' living at Huexocingo, S Salvador, and numerous haciendas. Only 29½ mulatto tributaries are recorded in 1799.

The ciudad of Huexocingo (Guaxozingo, Bexosinco, etc.; 1950: Huejotzingo, ciudad), which was granted arms in 1553, was moved in 1529 or 1530 from its fortress site to what the Franciscans considered a more convenient location a league or so below in the plain (García Granados and MacGregor, p. 11). We do not know whether the city's division into four *parcialidades*, referred to in later documents, reflects a pre-Columbian political condition or was a post-Conquest innovation. The final monastery structure is said to have been laid out in the early 1540s and completed during the next 20 or 30 years (McAndrew, p. 135). However, there is evidence that the cabecera was again moved, in 1552. A document dating from August of that year states succinctly, 'se dio licencia y facultad al gouernador prençipales y naturales del pueblo de guajocingo para que puedan pasarse...el dho pueblo en vn sitio que se llama texoquipan'.[5] (The governor and Indians of Goajocingo were given permission to move that pueblo to a site called Texoquipan.) The sources at our disposal give a puzzling picture of the dependent settlement pattern in this area. Reports of *c.* 1570 mention between 20 and 30 subject pueblos, including the sub-cabecera of S Salvador Tesmelucan (= Tlalnepantla? 1950: S Salvador el Verde, villa). Congregation studies beginning in 1598 may have resulted in some consolidation, and yet the number of settlements of pueblo category increased to thirty-one in 1743, and to thirty-seven by 1791.[6] S Martín Tesmelucan (1950: Texmelucan, ciudad) was given cabecera status in the seventeenth century.

There is a good deal of sixteenth-century material on tributes, tributaries, and settlements here, most of it unexplored by this writer.[7] Reports of the Ovando series (*c.* 1570) are reproduced in four different versions (Códice Franciscano, pp. 22–3. García Pimentel, 1904, p. 28. López de Velasco, pp. 221, 223. PNE, v, pp. 263–4). Huexocingo was visited by Father Ponce in 1585 (Ponce, I, p. 151), by Gage (p. 51) in 1625, and by Cobo (p. 204) in 1630, each of whom left a brief description.

Seventeenth-century population data are taken from two sources.[8] The AM drew up a valuable description of his jurisdiction in 1743.[9] For 1791 we have a relación accompanying a census of the non-Indian population,[10] and a separate list of toponyms.[11]

Further references and speculations are found in the interesting work of García Granados and MacGregor (1934).

40 *Huexolotitlan*

This small jurisdiction straddled the continental divide, having within it headwaters of the Atoyac and Papaloapan systems, although most of it was and is in the upper Atoyac or valley of Oaxaca.

The climate is dry and temperate to cold, with elevations of 1,500–2,400 m.

Huexolotitlan (Zapotecan, Huijazoo; the Náhuatl name was perhaps Cuauhxilotitlan), whose extensive ruins indicate that it was once an important Zapotec religious center, at contact was sending tribute to the Aztec garrison at Coaixtlahuacan. The ruling dynasty seems to have been Mixtecan, while the people spoke both Mixtecan and the valley dialect of Zapotecan, in separate communities.

First visited by Spaniards perhaps in 1520, Huexolotitlan submitted to the Orozco expedition in late 1521.

Encomienda

Cortés claimed Huexolotitlan as part of his valley of Guaxaca possessions, but it was not named in the Marquesado grant, and the second audiencia took the place for the crown in 1531.[1]

Government

The first C was appointed October 2 1531.[2] In the 1550s and later this magistrate was subordinate to the AM of Antequera, but the jurisdiction became independent early in the seventeenth century. From 1787 it was a subdelegación in the intendencia of Oaxaca.

Church

S Pablo Huexolotitlan (Huizoo), at first a secular curacy, was turned over to the Dominicans in 1554 (Alvarado, pp. 15–16). S Andrés Zautla became a separate Dominican parish towards 1714. Both doctrinas were in the diocese of Antequera, and were secularized sometime after 1777.

Population and settlements

A great many Indians are said to have died here in the first epidemic in 1520, a year before Spanish control was established. The number of tributaries was 1,793 in 1548, 1,200 in 1570, 834 in 1588, 639 in 1608, and about 600 in 1670 (Scholes and Adams, 1959, p. 38). Later counts show 1,130 Indian families in 1745, and 1,222 tributaries in 1792. Zapotecan was the dominant language, but there were pockets of Mixtecans. The non-Indian population was insignificant.

The original site of the cabecera was a hilltop near S Juan del Rey; it was probably moved down into the valley soon after the Conquest. While a congregation was proposed here in 1599, little if anything seems to have been done, and there were more subject pueblos in the eighteenth than in the sixteenth century. Some of those listed in 1777–1820, however, were new settlements: Magdalena Apazco, S Lorenzo Cacaotepec, Santiago (Itz)tenango, Sto Tomás Mazatepec (Mazaltepec), S Juan del Rey, S Lázaro, Sta Cruz Castizos, S Felipe Tejalapa, S Francisco Huizo or Talixtlahuaca, Sto Domingo (Tlaltenango), Santiago Xochiquitongo (Suchiquitongo), S Andrés Zautla.

The cabecera, S Pablo Huexolotitlan (Guaxilotitlan, Quauhxolotitlan, etc.; 1950: S Pablo Huitzo, pueblo), seems to have split into two settlements about a half mile apart, both Guaxolotitlan and Huizóo appearing in the parish registers in the 1720s and 1730s. The southernmost settlement where the church and convent are was probably Huexolotitlan, the other being Huizo.

Sources

There are brief references in the *Suma de Visitas* of *c.* 1548 (PNE, I, no. 286), and an Ovando report of 1571 (García Pimentel, 1904, pp. 65, 73), as well as a relación submitted by the C in 1581 (PNE, IV, pp. 196–205). Father Ponce (I, p. 271) went through here in 1586. For 1599 we have a congregation document,[3] as well as a land dispute record accompanied by a map.[4]

Burgoa (1934*a*, II, pp. 9–21) relates the history of the Dominican doctrine here. There is a brief report from the AM dated 1745,[5] supplemented by other information in Villaseñor y Sánchez (II, p. 126). Ajofrín (II, pp. 85–7) visited the jurisdiction in 1766. For the late colonial period, we have seen censuses of both parishes,[6] dated 1777, a topographic description written by the friar in charge of Huexolotitlan also in 1777,[7] a report made for the bishop in 1803,[8] and a description of *c.* 1821.[9]

The area is covered in the works of Dahlgren de Jordán (1954) and Spores (1965).

41 *Huexutla*

This is hot country, in the foothills of the Sierra Madre (150–600 m) facing the plains of the Huaxteca on the north. Rainfall is excessive much of the year. Huexutla is now in the northeast corner of Hidalgo state.

According to the relación of 1580, Huexotla had a ruler who was much respected in the surrounding region because of his ability to control the rain. Huaxtecan, Tepehuan, and Náhuatl were all spoken here. Tepehuacan and Tlacuilula perhaps had tlatoque subordinate to the lord of Huexotla, and another state, Nexpa, lay to the northwest. We have no evidence linking Huexotla with the Triple Alliance, although one source claims that it was at war with Metztitlan.

Cortés went through here on his way to Pánuco in late 1522 or early 1523. We do not know whether Huexotla participated in subsequent revolts of the Huaxtecans.

Encomienda

Bernardino Iñiguez held Huexutla in 1527–33, while subsequently the encomienda was claimed by Juan Rodríguez and Gabriel de Aguilera (Chipman, pp. 154, 292. ENE, XIV, p. 107). Escheatment occurred towards 1545–8 (ENE, VII, pp. 15–27).

The encomienda of Nespa (cf. Valles) may have been in this area.

Government

In early years jurisdiction at Huexutla was disputed, first between the ayuntamientos of Tenochtitlan and S Esteban del Puerto, then between the gobiernos of Nueva España and Pánuco (*Actas de Cabildo*, I, p. 160). From 1537 the place was considered part of the alcaldía mayor of Pánuco, but by 1550 it was a separate corregimiento. In the 1550s and 1560s the C of Huexutla was suffragan at times to Pánuco and at others to Meztitlan. What perhaps corresponded to the old corregimiento

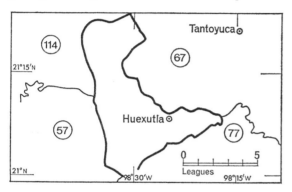

of Nespa y Tauzán was disputed for many years between the magistrates of Huexutla and Valles or Pánuco.

In 1676 we find Huexutla attached to the alcaldía mayor of Guayacocotla, and somewhat later it was being administered from Pánuco and Valles, but in intervening and subsequent periods a C or AM with residence at Huexutla continued to be appointed. According to a document of 1770, the jurisdiction had until recently been attached to Pánuco; it was recommended at that time that Xaltocan and Chiconamel–Coyutla be transferred to Huexutla from Valles and Pánuco respectively, and the suggestion seems to have been accepted in the case of Xaltocan.[1] After 1787 the AM of Huexutla became a subdelegado in the intendencia of Mexico.

Church

S Agustín Huexutla was chosen towards 1545–8 as the site of an Augustinian monastery from which

a number of places in surrounding jurisdictions were visited (ENE, VII, pp. 15–27). The archbishop in 1684 wanted to divide this parish by assigning a resident priest to Paguatlan, and in 1743 there was an Augustinian vicar at S Nicolás Ixcatlan, but only the original parish survived. It was secularized towards 1750 and belonged to the archdiocese of Mexico.

Population and settlements

Differences in the area covered by the civil and ecclesiastical jurisdictions here probably account in part for the fluctuations reported in the native population. 700 casas are mentioned at Huexutla in 1532, representing a considerably greater number of tributaries. There were 609 married Indians in 1548, and 814 tributaries were visited from the monastery in 1571. The C in 1580 stated that three-quarters of the macehuales had died from 'hunger and disease' within the previous twenty years, leaving 500 tributaries. Another document, referring to the parish of Huexutla, shows a drop in tributaries from 800 in 1588 to 372 in 1623. Huexutla, Tlacolula, and Nespa y Tauzan altogether had 251 tributaries in 1643 and 196½ in 1688.[2] In 1684 there were 1,724 communicants, mostly Náhuatl- and Huaxtecan-speaking, in the parish. Eight hundred and fifty-two Indian families are reported in 1743 and 1,761 Indian tributaries in the jurisdiction in 1797.[3]

Several large haciendas were set up within the jurisdiction, operated by a steadily growing number of non-Indians. According to the 1791 census, there were 685 Spaniards (persons), 180 mestizos, and 457 mulattoes and Negroes; by that time the cabecera of Huexutla had only gente de razón.

There is considerable confusion in the early toponymy of this area. Huexutla (Guaxutla, etc.; 1950: Huejutla de Reyes, ciudad) appears in 1548 with only three estancias (Tacolula, Teguacan, Xiquilan). The 1571 report shows three cabeceras (Guexutla, Tepeguacan, Tlacuilula) with two estancias each (Xiquilan was subject to Tepeguacan), while the relación of 1580 names nine estancias, only three of which correspond to those of 1571. To these, we should perhaps add Nespa and Tauzan (=Xaltocan?) and their dependencies.

There was a congregation here towards 1600, after which the cabecera, Ixcatlan, Macustepetla (Macuextepetlapa in 1571–80), Paguatlan (= Tepeguacan, Pahuaca?), Tehuetlan, Tomatlan, and Xaltocan seem to have survived as pueblos.[4] In 1794, besides the seven pueblos, there were ten Indian barrios (all near the cabecera) and numerous haciendas and ranchos.

Sources

A brief notice dating from *c.* 1548 (PNE, I, no. 265) is followed by a detailed report drawn up by the Augustinian prior in 1571 (García Pimentel, 1904, p. 132. PNE, III, p. 136). The relación submitted by the C in 1580 (PNE, VI, pp. 183–92) is, as Barlow puts it, rather myopic, and omits the Nespa–Tauzan area; it is accompanied by a map.

The few late sixteenth- and early seventeenth-century documents that we have seen are mentioned above. Archbishop Aguiar y Seixas visited Huexutla in 1684 and left some valuable observations in his report.[5]

For the eighteenth century, there is a 1743 description sent in by the AM,[6] somewhat enlarged upon by Villaseñor y Sánchez (I, p. 120), together with a census of the non-Indian population made in 1791,[7] and another report of 1794.[8]

Some further details are found in Fernández (1940–42).

42 *Iguala*

Iguala's jurisdiction covered a hot, semi-arid region (now in north central Guerrero) with perennial streams flowing into the Mexcala (Balsas) from either side. It is mostly at 700–1,400 m, with extreme elevations of 400–2,500 m. Vegetation is xerophytic except in the higher mountains which are forested.

The linguistic and political situation at contact was quite complicated. Cocolan, Huitzoco, Tepecuacuilco, Tlachmalacac, and Yoallan were the native states; Mayanalan either belonged to Tlachmalacac (from which it was separated by lands of Tepecuacuilco) or had a semi-independent status. There was an Aztec garrison at Tepecuacuilco where tribute was collected from the whole area and adjoining regions; its ruler seems to have had lesser tlatoque or calpixque governing an extensive territory which stretched southward to the Sierra Madre. At least six languages were spoken. Coixcan (a rustic Náhuatl) was used at Huitzoco, Tlachmalacac, and Mayanalan, and to a lesser degree elsewhere, but Chontal predominated at Cocolan, Yoallan, and Tepecuacuilco. Minor language groups included Matlame, Matlatzincan, Texome, and Tuxtecan, all north of the Balsas.

The area was probably visited by Spaniards in late 1519, and was finally subdued in 1521–2.

Encomiendas

Francisco Flores was perhaps the holder of Iguala, which escheated *c.* 1535 (Boyd-Bowman, I, no. 1724).

Cocula was held by Gonzalo Cerezo, *alguacil mayor* of the audiencia. The crown claimed this encomienda in 1564, and there was a dispute soon thereafter between the royal prosecutor and Cerezo's widow, María de Espinosa (ENE, X, p. 56). Escheatment definitely occurred before 1579.

The conquistador Isidro Moreno was granted Huizuco and was followed in the 1550s by a son, Bernardino (Moreno) de Casasola, still listed in 1597. Tributes escheated sometime after 1643.

Mayanala and Tasmalaca were assigned to the conquistador Juan de Cisneros, who died in 1542 in the Mixton war (Icaza, I, p. 117). Cisneros was succeeded first by his widow, María de Medina, and then by a son, Mateo Vázquez de Cisneros, still alive in 1604. This was still a private encomienda in 1688.

Juan de la Torre seems to have been the first holder of Tepecuacuilco, with a grant from Cortés. He was replaced by Hernando de Torres, another conquistador, followed sometime before 1548 by a daughter, Bernardina de Torres. This encomendera first married Pedro de Osorio (listed in 1548 as co-holder with Antonio de Almaguer), and then Luis de Godoy (listed in 1560–70), and seems to have outlived both husbands (she is listed as sole holder in 1579). Francisco Enríquez Magariño, perhaps a grandson of Hernando de Torres, was encomendero in 1591–6, while

María de Godoy appears in the 1597 listing. Partial escheatment occurred by 1688.[1]

Government

The corregimiento of Iguala, created when that encomienda escheated *c.* 1535, was much enlarged in 1556 when its C was given jurisdiction in Mayanala, Tasmalaca, Tepecuacuilco, Huizuco, Cocula, Cuatepec, and Cuesala (the last two were later transferred to Iscateupa).[2] Neighboring Oapa was assigned to this corregimiento in the

sixteenth century, while the distant estancias of Tepecuacuilco south of the Balsas were administered by the magistrate of Zumpango (cf. Tistla), probably as a matter of convenience; shortly before 1593 this situation was reversed, Oapa going to Tistla and the southern estancias returning to Iguala.[3]

After *c.* 1650 the magistrate here was more often referred to as AM. The office was abolished towards 1780 when the jurisdiction of Iguala was annexed to that of Tasco.

Church

The first clergy here were in all likelihood secular priests hired by the encomenderos, although we are told that the Augustinians in 1545 founded a monastery at Tepecuacuilco which was secularized in 1563 or 1566 (Gómez de Orozco). By 1570 there were secular parishes at Veracruz Huizuco, S Francisco Iguala, Sta Ana Tasmalaca (later visited from Huizuco), and Asunción (Concepción) Tepecuacuilco. In the late eighteenth century S Cristóbal Mexcala was a *vicaría fija*. All parishes were in the archdiocese of Mexico.

Population and settlements

This was a rich farming area in 1531, with a large population dispersed in many settlements. There were still some 10,225 Indian tributaries in 1548, but their number dropped to 4,970 in 1570, 2,400 in 1597, 376 in 1643, and only 297 in 1688 (L de T, pp. 210, 572–4). Some of this decline was no doubt due to emigration. By 1743 there were 532 Indian families, and these had more than doubled by the end of the century.

We do not know when non-Indians became an important element here, but in 1794 Tepecuacuilco was a 'Spanish' town with only a few Indians, and both Huizuco and Iguala had many families of Spaniards and castas as well as Indians.

Iguala (Yohualan, etc.; 1950: Iguala, ciudad) had six estancias within three leagues of the cabecera in 1579, but all seem to have been abandoned in the congregations of 1593–1604. Cocula (Coaculan, etc.; 1950: Cocula, pueblo) lost six or seven nearby estancias at the same time. Huizuco (Isuco; 1950: Huitzuco de los Figueroa, pueblo) had fifteen estancias in 1570 and eleven in 1579, all within 2½ leagues; none survived the congregation. The six sujetos of Mayanala (1950: Mayanalan, pueblo) were also congregated. Tasmalaca (Tlazmalaca; 1950; Tlaxmalac, pueblo) was reduced from eleven estancias to the cabecera and one other pueblo, S Andrés Tuxpan.

In 1579 Tepecuacuilco (1950: Tepecoacuilco de Trujano, pueblo) had over fifty small dependencies, most of them near the cabecera but others extending far to the southwest on the far side of the Balsas; in early years they were grouped under six subject cabeceras. All were supposed to be collected at the cabecera in 1604, but two of the southern estancias, Mexcala (Mescala) and Xochipalan (Suchipala), were re-occupied and survived as Indian pueblos.

A great many rancherías (most of them old estancia sites), together with a few haciendas and mining camps, are named in the 1794 report.

Sources

The 'Prouinçia de Cuexco' is described in a much abbreviated version of the 1531 description of New Spain (Herrera, 4a década, p. 231). Only Cocula, Iguala, and Tepecuacuilco are covered by the *Suma* of *c.* 1548 (PNE, I, nos. 231, 336, 764). Both the Ovando report of *c.* 1570[4] and the relación of 1579[5] are of considerable interest; the so-called *Mapa de Tepecuacuilco*[6] may have been drawn to accompany the 1579 document.

Several sources are concerned with the 1593–1604 congregations here.[7] Tributary data for the seventeenth century[8] are followed by an interesting map of the region, partly in the native tradition, showing many toponyms.[9] A lost report of *c.* 1743 is summarized in Villaseñor y Sánchez (I, p. 239). For 1794 we have a valuable geographical description submitted by the subdelegado of Tasco.[10]

43 *Igualapa*

On what is now called the Costa Chica in southeastern Guerrero state, this is a hot, dry region most of the year with heavy rains in September–October. It extends from the sea across a coastal plain to elevations occasionally exceeding 1,600 m in the foothills of the Sierra Madre del Sur. There are no good harbors, and numerous rivers interrupt communication in the rainy season.

There was a dense native population here speaking numerous languages, if we are to believe the most detailed sixteenth century source available to us, a truncated relación drawn up sixty years after the Conquest when few Indians survived. According to this document, the dominant state in the west was Ayotlan, a Tlapanecan community from which a large coastal area was controlled. The rulers of Ayotlan and its dependencies were in turn held in line by a Mexican garrison at Totoépec which faced the belligerent and independent Yopes on the west and north. Among the 'subjects' of Ayotlan which probably had a certain autonomy in domestic affairs were the Yope

(Tlapanecan) states of Acatlan, Xochitonallan, and Cuilutla, and the Náhuatl-speaking communities of Xalapan, Cuauhtépec, Copalitech, and Nexpan. To this list should be added Tzintla (where 'Cinteco' was spoken in the chief settlement and Zapotecan in a dependency called Cuauhtzapotla) and Cuauhitlan (where 'Quahutecan' was the language in 1582).

The allegiance of the eastern part of this region is not at all clear, and there may have been a number of independent buffer states here separating the Triple Alliance forces from those of the independent kingdom of Tototépec (cf. Xicayan). Nearest the coast were three large communities, Tlacolula, Ometépec (Ometepal), and Yohualapa, known collectively as Ayacastla, with their own language (Ayacastecan). There was a complicated multi-lingual situation here in 1582 which may not accurately reflect conditions at contact. In that year Náhuatl is reported at Tlacolula and 'Huehuetecan' at Huehuetlan (one of Tlacolula's dependencies), while Amuzgan in

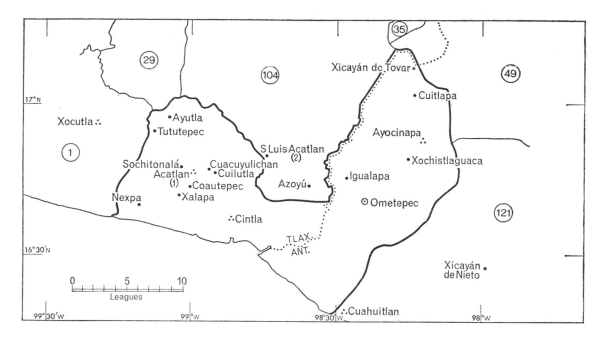

addition to Ayacastecan was heard at Yohualapa and Ometépec. Farther inland, Amuzgan (a Mixtecan language) was spoken in the states of Xochixtlahuacan, Ayocinapan, Acuitlapan, and Xicayan. The last two were mountain communities which paid tribute to the Aztecs; Acuitlapan was perhaps connected politically to Tlapan (cf. Tlapa), while Xicayan (=Ixicayan?) sent its tribute to Yocaltépec (cf. Guaxuapa).

Pedro de Alvarado seems to have entered this area from the east in the summer of 1522, meeting little resistance until he reached the Yope country. There was a general rebellion put down in 1523, with several further insurrections of the Yopes, the last recorded occurring after 1535 (ENE, II, pp. 29–33, 62).

Encomiendas

Cortés gave Pedro de Alvarado title to the Indians of Tututepec and Xalapa in November, 1522 (Gay, I, p. 386). These places were re-assigned several times, being separated, combined with other pueblos, etc. Diego de Olvera held Acatlan, Cintla, and Xalapa from 1528 to 1531 or 1532 when they were taken for the crown (Icaza, I, p. 128. Millares Carlo and Mantecón, I, no. 1743). Pedro

(Francisco) Lozano, encomendero of 'Cuscotitlan' in 1531, held Ayutla, Tututepec, and Suchitonalá a few years later (ENE, II, p. 31. Icaza, I, p. 165). Tributes from these last three villages continued to go to the Lozano family, the first encomendero being succeeded by a son, Francisco, before 1548, and by a grandson, Pedro Lozano, listed in 1597; the latter was still alive in 1626, but very soon thereafter the encomienda escheated. Somewhat later it was re-assigned to the Moctezuma heirs.

Cuautepec and Cuacuyulichan were given to Gaspar de Avila Quiñones, followed towards 1550 by a son, Pedro, still alive in 1579. Cuacuyulichan escheated by 1626, and Cuautepec before 1664.

Copalitas and perhaps Cuilutla in 1531 belonged to Juan Larios, but the encomienda was taken from him by viceroy Mendoza (ENE, II, pp. 30–33. Icaza, II, p. 341).

Nexpa was first held by Antonio de Guadalaxara; it was re-assigned, perhaps in 1531, to Gutierre de Badajoz, who already held nearby Tlacolula and Huehuetlan. Towards 1565 Badajoz was followed by a son, Gabriel de Chávez, who still appears as encomendero in 1599–1604.[1]

The three cabeceras of Igualapa, Ometepec,

and Suchistlaguaca were given *c.* 1528 in joint encomienda, half of each, to Francisco de Herrera and Alonso de Castillo (Francisco de Orduña appears in place of Castillo in some documents). By 1548 these encomenderos had been replaced by Gonzalo Hernández de Herrera and Bernardino del Castillo. In the 1560s we find the encomienda divided geographically, Igualapa's tributes going to Castillo and those of Ometepec – Suchistlaguaca to Hernández. Igualapa escheated before 1597, at which time the other places were held by a Pedro Fajardo.

Pierres Gómez, a conquistador, is listed as the first encomendero of Ayocinapa. He was succeeded *c.* 1550 by a son, the alguacil mayor Baltasar Mejía Salmerón, who still appears in 1597–1604 (L de T, p. 604).

Xicayan, in 1548, was jointly held by Juan de Tovar and Francisco Guillén, two conquistadors who seem to have been the original encomenderos. Both died in the 1550s and were followed by sons, Juan Hipólito de Tovar and Antonio (Cristóbal) Guillén. The second Guillén died before 1597, and the son of Tovar in 1600, after which both halves presumably escheated.

Cuitlapa may have belonged to the complicated encomienda of Tlapa (q.v.).

Government

Sometime before 1534 a C arrived to administer Xalapa, Cintla y Acatlan, the first places to be taken from private encomienda. This magistrate's jurisdiction perhaps coincided with that of a short-lived Spanish municipality, S Luis (see below). After 1550 the various encomienda villages nearby were attached to this corregimiento, while the Igualapa–Ometepec region was administered by the C of Cuahuitlan (cf. Xicayan). Perhaps about the same time, Xicayan (de Tovar) was assigned to the C of Justlaguaca, and Cuitlapa to that of Tlapa. In 1555 the neighboring C of Xicayan (de Pedro Nieto) took charge of Igualapa–Ometepec.[2]

Towards 1558 the magistrate of Xalapa, Cintla y Acatlan was made AM of a large province which included the whole coastal area from Ayutla and Nexpa to Igualapa and Ayocinapa.[3]

In 1579 Azoyuc and its dependencies were transferred to the new alcaldía mayor of Tlapa, and a year or so later Xicayan de Tovar was annexed from Justlaguaca.[4] Somewhat later Cuitlapa was acquired, while the Indians of Acatlan moved to the site of S Luis in the jurisdiction of Tlapa. Henceforth the boundaries of Xalapa de la Costa, or the province of Igualapa, as it came to be called, experienced only minor alterations. The AM lived at Igualapa for many years, but had moved to Ometepec by 1777. From 1786 he was a subdelegado, first in the intendencia of Mexico, then (from 1792) in that of Puebla.[5]

Church

There was a priest at the villa of S Luis in 1531, and he may have stayed on in the Indian village of Acatlan after the Spanish settlement was abandoned (ENE, II, p. 33). Towards 1570 the secular parish of S Luis Acatlan included much of the coastal area, while another curate at Xocutla (cf. Acapulco) visited Ayutla, Tututepec, and Suchitonalá. Augustinians working out of Tlapa were active here in early years, but by 1570 additional secular parishes had been founded at S Juan Igualapa and Santiago Ometepec. This last doctrina extended northward to Xicayan de Tovar, although in 1576 the Indians of Xicayan complained that they had to attend mass at Zacatepec, several days distant.[6] Their problem was made somewhat less acute by establishing a closer parish center at S Miguel Suchistlaguaca (*c.* 1604).

In the west, the curate of Xocutla moved to Santiago Ayutla sometime before 1611, but his parish continued to include places in the jurisdiction of Acapulco. An auxiliary doctrina at Santiago Coautepec (sometimes at S Agustín Cuilutla) became independent of Acatlan by 1760.

Xocutla–Ayutla and Acatlan–Coautepec belonged to the diocese of Tlaxcala, while the remaining parishes were in that of Antequera.

Population and settlements

The native population here was decimated before 1550 and continued to decline, at a slower rate, for another century. There were perhaps 3,000 Indian tributaries in 1570. Later estimates and censuses give 1,900 tributaries at *c.* 1600, 1,250 in 1626, 1,400 in 1700, and 2,075 in 1801.[7] Most of the languages mentioned above disappeared. There seems to have been a migration of people from the east speaking Mixtecan, which had replaced Tlapanecan in the Acatlan–Ayutla area by 1611, while there was some extension of Náhuatl throughout the jurisdiction.

The villa of S Luis, founded in the early 1520s just north of the boundary between this jurisdiction and that of Tlapa, was abandoned by its Spanish vecinos after the Yope rebellion of 1530–31. A few Spaniards remained and settled on cacao plantations and cattle estancias. Negro slaves were brought in to work on these estates, and free or fugitive Negroes and mulattoes settled along the coast where they still form noticeably Negroid communities. The 1791 census shows a total of 235 Spaniards (persons), 594 mestizos, and 5,206 Negroes and mulattoes in the jurisdiction. Inland the settlements remained predominantly Indian.

We have no complete list of the estancias or sujetos, of which there must have been a great many in early years. Sixty or seventy of these dependencies still existed when the congregations were carried out in 1598–1604.[8] About forty of them were abandoned at this time, along with the cabeceras of Ayocinapa (Ixcatoyac), Cintla, Cuahuitlan, Tepetlapa, and Tlacolula. In the west, Ayutla (1950: Ayutla de los Libres, ciudad), Coautepec, Caucuyulichan, Cuilutla, Sochitonalá, Tututepec, and Xalapa survived as Indian communities in the eighteenth century. The Indians of Acatlan moved to S Luis, outside the jurisdiction, sometime after 1611. Nexpa (Nespa) became a mulatto settlement, while Copalitas (reduced to six tributaries in 1626) became an hacienda.

In the east, many of the old estancia sites deserted in the congregations were subsequently re-occupied by Indians. Igualapa (1950: pueblo) had ten estancias in 1582 and nine in 1706; three of these disappeared in the epidemic of 1737, leaving Alcamani, Chacalapa, Popoyuapa, and Quesalapa as pueblos. Six Indian towns survived near Ometepec (1950: ciudad): Acatepec, Asunción, Cochuapa, Guajintepec, Huistepec, and Zacualpa. Xochistlaguaca (Suchistlahuaca; 1950: pueblo) in 1706–92 was the center for eight pueblos, some of which had been estancias of Ayocinapa and Ometepec. Three of these were abandoned in 1737, while five survived: Cosoyuapa, Huehuetono, Papaloapa (Minas), S Cristóbal, and Tlacochistlaguaca. Farther north, Cuitlapa and Xicayan de Tovar were still pueblos in the eighteenth century, as were two former estancias, S Martín et Alto and S Miguel (de la Montaña) Elotepec.

Sources

An abbreviated fragment of the lost 1531 'Descripción de la tierra' gives tantalizing hints about this region very soon after the Conquest (Herrera, 4a década, pp. 230–1). Most of the cabeceras are described in the Suma of *c.* 1548 (PNE, I, nos. 28, 96–7, 217, 239–40, 303–4, 406, 427, 479, 490, 499, 647, 775, 807, 810). We have seen two brief Diocesan reports of *c.* 1570 (García Pimentel, 1904, pp. 26–7, 65, 86–7, 106), and there is another most interesting geographical description, available only in a faulty English translation, probably made about the same time (Tlalocan, V, pp. 85–96). The relación geográfica of 1582 seems to be incomplete (PNE, IV, pp. 252–66); additional data for Xicayan de Tovar appear in the relación of Justlaguaca.[9]

A bishop of Tlaxcala left an account of his trip through Acatlan and Ayutla in 1611.[10] There are tributary data for 1626–96, for Tlaxcala cabeceras only.[11] For the early eighteenth century, we have a document concerning parishes in the diocese of Antequera in 1706,[12] and a census report from the AM dated 1743.[13] These are followed by censuses of two parishes, Coautepec and Ometepec, in 1777.[14] There is a statistical table of the jurisdiction dated 1789,[15] together with a good description submitted by the subdelegado in 1792,[16] and a non-Indian padrón of 1791.[17]

Scanty information on the parishes of Ometepec and Xochistlaguaca is contained in an 1802 listing (E. Pérez, table at end). We have also seen an interesting report made in 1804 concerning coastal defenses here, accompanied by a map.[18]

44 *Iscateupa*

Now in north central Guerrero, this is a much eroded country of barren hills and perennial watercourses draining southward into the Mexcala (Balsas) river. The climate is hot and rather dry, temperatures varying with elevation (360–2,500 m).

This had been a battleground for a century before the Spanish Conquest. From the reign of Itzcoatl (1427–40) the Aztecs had waged war both against the local people and the Tarascans on the west. In the 1490s some 9,000 Náhuatl-speaking colonists were sent from the central plateau to

Alahuiztlan, Oztoman, and Teloloapan, from which we gather that the native population of those places had declined due to disease or warfare or both. At Spanish contact there were Triple Alliance fortresses at Oztoman, Acapetlahuayan, Totoltépec, and Cuetzalan; at the latter, war was in progress between the Mexicans and the Chontals of Apaxtlan. Oztoman and Acapetlahuayan were ruled by two Mexica governors, a *tlacatécatl* and a *tlacochteuhctli*.

The linguistic and tributary situation at contact can be derived from sixteenth century sources in a general way. Both Chontal and Náhuatl were spoken at Alahuiztlan and Oztoman. Going southeast from those places, the same two languages prevailed at Ichcateopan, Teloloapan, and Totoltépec, but there were smaller groups speaking Tuxtecan at Ichcateopan and Itzucan at Teloloapan. Cuetzalan was still a Náhuatl community, while Chilacachapan was Chontal. All these states gave services to the Triple Alliance or tribute which was sent to Tepecuacuilco. People speaking 'Mazateco' (=Mazahuan?) lived in the north around Tzicaputzalco and paid tribute to the Aztec garrison at Tlachco; pockets of 'Mazateco'-speakers extended southward to Cuetzalan. Off to the south were two seemingly independent and hostile states, Chontal-speaking Apaxtlan, and a Cuitlatecan community called Tlalnexpantlan. Barlow (1949, pp. 15–23) and van Zantwijk (1967) have more to say about this thoroughly confusing picture.

Probably visited by Spaniards before the end of 1519, the various native states here capitulated without known resistance in 1521–2.

Encomiendas

Both Alahuistlan and Ostuma were granted by Cortés to a conquistador named López, who held them for a year. Then or later they were assigned to Blas de Monterroso, succeeded first by his widow and then (before 1548) by a daughter,

152

Francisca de Xexa, married to Juan del Aguila. The latter appears as sole encomendero in 1550–67. Escheatment occurred by 1597.

Cicapuzalco was held at latest from 1532 by the conquistador Juan de Manzanilla, followed in the 1540s by a son, Juan de Caravallar (Manzanilla) (Icaza, I, p. 110). Towards 1600 the encomienda was claimed by the first Manzanilla's daughter, María de Caravallar, married to Gonzalo de Aguilar (el Portugués), but it escheated at this time or shortly thereafter (Dorantes de Carranza, p. 212).

Francisco Rodríguez Magariño held a number of cabeceras here by virtue of a grant from Cortés. They included Chilacachapa (Coatepec) and Cuezala (with Apastla and Tlanexpatla), as well as neighboring Tlacotepec (cf. Tetela del Río). A son, Juan Rodríguez (Enríquez) Magariño, was encomendero in 1550–64. Towards 1568 the widow of the latter, Polonia de la Serna, inherited despite crown opposition. Doña Polonia died after 1597, and escheatment occurred after 1643.

Iscateupa was held by the *maestre* Martín de Sepúlveda, on whose death (*c.* 1535) it was taken for the crown. We do not know the encomenderos of Teloloapa and Totoltepec, which escheated early in 1531.

Government

The cabeceras of Teloloapa and Totoltepec (Tululuava y Tultebeque) were placed in corregimiento in March, 1531, as were Iscateupa and Atenango some four years later (L de T, p. 545). In the provincial division of 1556, Coatepec and Cuezala were attached to the jurisdiction of Iguala, and about the same time a group of encomiendas stretching from Tetela and Utlatlan to Mezquitlan were assigned to the C of Iscateupa.[1] Towards 1560 the Atenango–Mezquitlan region was transferred to a new corregimiento, Tlalcozautitlan (cf. Chilapa), and by 1579 Iscateupa had acquired Cuezala and Coatepec; in the latter year the corregimiento of Teloloapa was annexed to that of Iscateupa, although Teloloapa actually became the residence of the magistrate. Towards 1600, Tetela, Tlacotepec, and Utlatlan were detached to form a new jurisdiction (cf. Tetela del Río).

In the 1680's the partido of Iscateupa, by then an alcaldía mayor which had greatly declined in population and importance, was annexed to neighboring Zacualpa.[2] This arrangement continued into the final years of the colony when the combined jurisdiction was a subdelegación in the intendencia of Mexico.

Church

There was some early activity here by Franciscans, who are said to have been the first to proselytize in Cuezala, but their place was taken by secular clergy who by 1570 had founded parishes at S Juan Bautista Cuezala, Sto Tomás (Asunción) Iscateupa, and Asunción Teloloapa. Later the parish seat of Cuezala was moved to S Francisco Coatepec, and additional secular doctrinas were established at S Juan Bautista Acapetlaguaya, S Juan Bautista Alahuistlan (*c.* 1723), and Purificación (Asunción) Apastla. All were in the archdiocese of Mexico.

Population and settlements

There must have been considerable loss in the native population before 1570, when some 2,800 tributaries lived in the area (L de T, p. 546). This total dropped to *c.* 1,500 at the end of that century, 800 in 1643, and 735 in 1688. 1,725 Indian families are reported in 1743, and there were perhaps 4,000 tributaries in 1800. The non-Indian population was negligible, except during brief early periods of mining activity. There were some Spaniards and mulattoes living at haciendas in the late eighteenth century.

Alahuistlan (Alahuixtla, Alaustlan; 1950: Alahuistlán, pueblo) had fifteen estancias in 1579, all rather close to the cabecera. A congregation proposed in 1594 seems to have eliminated most of these settlements, only Alahuistlan and Ixcapaneca surviving as pueblos.

Cicapuzalco (Zicaputzalco, Sicapusalco, Ixcapuzalco, etc.; 1950: Ixcapuzalco, pueblo) had fourteen *barrios* in 1548, nine of which are named in the 1579 report. In 1595 congregations were recommended at the cabecera and the estancia of Tlacotepec, where a salt deposit was being worked, but none of the estancias appear as pueblos in 1791. A silver mine at Azulaques was nearly abandoned in 1579 and is listed as a barrio in 1791.

The old cabecera of Chilacachapan was replaced at an early date by an erstwhile estancia, Coatepec (Quatepec de los Costales; 1950: Coatepec Costales, pueblo). There were five or six sujetos in 1570–9, all within a league of the new cabecera. In 1594 the Indians were to be collected at Chilacachapa, but in fact both cabeceras survived as pueblos.

Cuezala (Quetzalan; 1950: Cuetzala de Progreso, pueblo) was originally on a hill two leagues from the final site chosen by Franciscan missionaries. In 1570–9 it had two sub-cabeceras, Apastla (1950: Apaxtla, pueblo) and Tlanexpatla (Tlalnecpantlan, Tenepantla, Tlanipatlan; 1950: Tlanipatlán, pueblo), with twenty-odd estancias between them, spread over a distance of eight leagues. In 1594 congregations were planned at the three cabeceras and at two other sites, Ostotitlan (an estancia of Apastla) and Zozocolpa (Tzotzocoltzinco, Zozocolcochiuhcan, subject to Tlanexpatla). Five of these survived as pueblos, but Zozocolpa disappeared.

Iscateupa (Escateopan, Ixcatiopa, etc.; 1950: Ixcateopan, pueblo) had nine nearby estancias in 1579, all of which seem to have been collected at the cabecera towards 1600.

Ostuma (Oxtomac; 1950: S Simón Ostumba, pueblo) was at first on a *peñol* half a league from its final (?) site. The people here were Chontal except for the remnants of the Náhuatl garrison at Acapetlaguaya (1950: Acapetlahuaya, pueblo), which was considered a sub-cabecera. There were a dozen or more estancias, congregated in the late 1590s at the two cabeceras and at a place called Zahualapa (Saulapa is listed as a *barrio* in 1791).

Teloloapa (Tololoava, etc.; 1950: Teloloapan, ciudad) had thirteen estancias named in the 1548 report and nine in 1579. Several of them are recognizable as *barrios*, and one (Acatempa) as a pueblo, after the congregation of the late 1590s.

There may have been an early congregation at Totoltepec (Tutultepec; 1950: Totoltepec, pueblo), which had twenty estancias in 1548 and only eight in 1579. Two of the latter, Almolonga (Almoloya) and Ixcatepec, survived as pueblos in the eighteenth century.

In 1791 there were a total of thirteen barrios, four haciendas (cattle and sugar cane), one cuadrilla, and twenty-two ranchos in the jurisdiction.

Sources

The *Suma de Visitas* of *c.* 1548 only partly describes this area, omitting Coatepec and Cuezala (PNE, I, nos. 7, 162, 420, 544–5). The Ovando reports of *c.* 1570 are also incomplete,[3] but there is an unusually long and useful relación compiled by the C in 1579 (PNE, VI, pp. 87–152).

Information concerning congregations here is scattered.[4] Tributary data from the seventeenth century[5] is followed by the journal of an archbishop's visit in 1684.[6]

Villaseñor y Sánchez (I, pp. 230–1) summarizes a lost report of *c.* 1743. For the late eighteenth century, there is a file concerning Indian community finances in 1785–1809,[7] a description of Alahuistlan parish in 1789,[8] a list of toponyms dated 1791,[9] and censuses made in 1800.[10]

45 *Ixmiquilpan*

The southern part of this jurisdiction, today in central Hidalgo state at 1,000–3,000 m, lay on the central plateau draining westerly into the Tula river, a generally flat, barren countryside, very dry and temperate. North of Ixmiquilpan is a range of mountains and an abrupt descent into the canyon of the Amaxac, like the Tula a tributary of the Pánuco system.

Itzmiquilpan (Otomí, Zecteccani) was a large Otomí state with dependencies extending quite some distance north of the principal settlement to Itztactlachco, on the frontier of hostile Metztitlan.

While Otomí was predominant, there was a sizable Chichimec (Pame) minority. Off to the south was a smaller Otomí community, Chilcuauhtla. Both states were tributary to the Aztecs.

We do not know just when the Spaniards arrived here. The region was under their control in the mid-1520s.

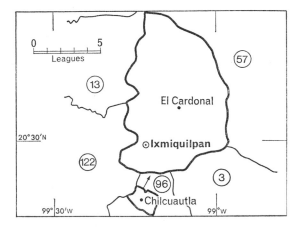

Encomiendas

Among the early holders of Ixmiquilpan were Pedro Rodríguez de Escobar (who had a grant from Cortés), Juan Gómez de Almazán (from 1525), and Juan Bello (Dorantes de Carranza, p. 222. Icaza, I, pp. 21, 64). On October 15, 1535, the encomienda was divided, half (Ixmiquilpan) being assigned to Bello and the other half (Tlacintla) to the crown (L de T, pp. 604–5). Bello's share was inherited in the 1550s by a daughter who married Gil González de Avila, and it escheated on the latter's death in August, 1566.[1]

Chilcuautla may have been held first by Martín Vázquez, but towards the end of 1528 governor Estrada assigned it to Juan de Avila (Dávila), 'el tuerto', followed (between 1548 and 1560) by a son, Juan de Cuéllar Verdugo (Icaza, I, p. 46. Millares Carlo and Mantecón, I, nos. 1601–2). Cuéllar was succeeded towards 1570 by his widow, María de Garao, and then by a son, Pablo de Vargas (listed in 1597–1604).[2] Chilcuautla was still a private encomienda in 1688.

Government

A C was appointed for the crown portion of Ixmiquilpan in 1535. When mines began to be worked nearby, perhaps in the late 1540s, an AM took up residence there. Thus in 1556–60 and later we find two crown officials here, one for the real de minas and the other handling Indian affairs, although eventually the offices were combined in a single individual who also had charge of Chilcuautla.[3] The latter encomienda was separated from the rest of the jurisdiction by lands belonging to the estancia of Tlacotlapilco, subject to Hueypustla. After 1787 the AM was a subdelegado in the intendencia of Mexico.

Church

1550 is the date given for the founding of an Augustinian mission among the Otomies at Ixmiquilpan (Gómez de Orozco). The adjacent mining camp, by 1550 at the latest, had a secular priest but somewhat later the two parishes were combined in a single Augustinian doctrina, Sta María Ixmiquilpan. Asunción Chilcuautla, an Augustinian visita at first, became a separate parish towards 1600, and Concepción del Cardonal acquired equal rank some years later.[4] Secularization of the three parishes, all in the archdiocese of Mexico, occurred in the early 1750s. Certain villages belonging politically to Meztitlan were visited from parish centers in Ixmiquilpan.

Population and settlements

The 1570 reports show 4,027 tributaries in Ixmiquilpan–Tlacintla and 1,218 at Chilcuautla, to which we must add the equivalent of 320 Indian communicants at the mines, giving a total of c. 5,400 tributaries (L de T, p. 174). There was perhaps fifty per cent mortality in the epidemic of 1576–81, and further loss brought the tributary number down to 2,300 in 1600. After other plagues, including that of 1604–7, there were only 790 tributaries in 1643 (Indian mine workers may not be included here). Later data show 1,521 tributaries in 1688, 2,387 in 1744, 3,714 in 1751, 5,240 in 1780, 3,602 in 1791, and 4,315 in 1804.[5]

In 1569 there were 34 adult Spaniards and 118

Negro slaves in two mining camps. 447 families of non-Indians are reported in 1744. The 1791 padrón lists 1,471 Spaniards, 2,422 mestizos, and 47 pardos.

The Indian government of Ixmiquilpan (Esmiquilpa, Izmiquilpa, etc.; 1950: Ixmiquilpan, ciudad) was divided for tribute purposes in two parts, Ixmiquilpan and Tlacintla (even when both became crown possessions they were listed separately in the tribute registers). These were apparently barrios fairly close to each other, and the monastery was placed between the two. In 1548–71 only four outlying estancias are mentioned, all Chichimec settlements off to the north, but clearly there were others nearby. They were supposed to be congregated in the 1590s.[6] Twelve subject Indian pueblos existed in the late eighteenth century. Aguacatlan (1548) may be the same as Cuyametepeque (1571), which became Cuyometepec or Tixqui in 1791–2. Sixteenth-century Guayactepexic (Hueytepexe) is recognizable as eighteenth-century Sta María Tepexi, Istactlachco (Iztequetlasco) as S Agustín Ixtatlaxco, and Junacapa (Xonacapa) as S Miguel Juanacapa. The other 1791–2 pueblos were Sta Cruz Alberto, Espíritu Santo Palma Gorda, Sta Clara Nequetejé, S Miguel Nopalera, Orizaba, Los Remedios Sabana, S Antón Sabanilla, and S Juan Bautista (S Juanico). Tlacintla (Tlatzintla) survived as one of six barrios in Ixmiquilpan in 1744–91.

In 1548 the mines of Sto Tomé are mentioned, while in 1569 there were two reales, Sta María and S Juan, a half league apart. Silver deposits discovered towards the end of the sixteenth century were responsible for the founding of a new real, El Cardonal (Bargalló, p. 204). Other mining camps in the jurisdiction include Chalchiutepec (far to the north beyond Ixtatlaxco, abandoned by 1744) and Sta Cruz de los Alamos or Pechuga.

Chilcuautla (Chilguauhtla, etc.; 1950: Chilcuautla, pueblo), which formed an enclave off to the south, had four estancias according to the 1548 report, but these were congregated at their cabecera by 1571. One of these old sites was reoccupied and appears as a pueblo, Tuni, in 1791.

In addition to the places mentioned here, a number of haciendas, ranchos, rancherías, and mines are named in the reports.

Sources

Both cabeceras as they were c. 1548 are described in the *Suma* (PNE, I, nos. 112, 293). The Ovando reports of c. 1570 are of great interest.[7] A relación of c. 1580 has disappeared. We have seen two sources of seventeenth-century demographic data.[8]

A relación prepared by the AM in 1744 is accompanied by a census list and a map.[9] The non-Indian padrón of 1791 also has a good map of the jurisdiction, and a geographical description.[10] There is still another useful report dated 1792.[11]

Additional sources and an analysis of demographic change here are provided in a monograph of José Miranda (1966). Mendizábal's work (1947, VI) on the Mezquital should be consulted, as should the *Catálogo* of Fernández (1940–2).

46 *Izatlan*

A low volcanic range traverses this area in central Jalisco, the most notable feature of which is a basin which until recently contained a group of fresh-water lakes. Outside the basin drainage is westward into the Ameca river and northward to the Río Grande de Santiago. The climate is dry and temperate, with extreme elevations of 1,300–2,890 m.

Etzatlan was an independent state on bad terms with the Tarascan satellites to the southeast. Most of the people spoke a Nahua language, but there was an Otomí (western variety) minority. Perhaps subordinate to Etzalan was Ocotitlan, with its own ruler. Settlements were scattered about the lake shores and on islands.

Francisco Cortés and his party passed through here in 1524, apparently meeting little resistance, and claimed the area for Colima.

Encomienda

In 1524 the Indians of Izatlan were assigned to two residents of Colima (Sauer, p. 21). Six years later, when Guzmán and Oñate visited the area, the encomendero was Juan de Escarcena (Escacena). Escheatment occurred towards 1535 (Torres, pp. 13, 37–8).

Government

Izatlan's magistrate, a C appointed from Mexico city from *c.* 1535, became an AM in the 1540s when silver and lead mines began to be exploited nearby. Perhaps because of its strategic importance as the northwesternmost extension of Nueva

España in the heart of Nueva Galicia, the jurisdiction was made a separate province in the division of the 1560s.[1] For a time in the 1590s, before it was absorbed by the alcaldía mayor of Autlan, Ameca was administered from Izatlan.[2] In the eighteenth century the magistrate lived at Agualulco and kept deputies at Izatlan and Magdalena. He remained subordinate to the viceroy until 1787, when Izatlan (Agualulco) became a subdelegación in the intendencia of Guadalaxara.

Church

A Franciscan is said to have stayed at Izatlan when the Cortés party went through in 1524, and a monastery (Concepción Izatlan) was established not long afterwards, perhaps in 1534 (Torres,

pp. 37–9. Vázquez Vázquez, p. 58). Somewhat later there was a secular priest attending to the Spanish miner-population, but he does not seem to have remained for long. In 1605 there were Franciscan doctrinas, subordinate to that of Izatlan, at Sta María Magdalena and S Miguel Oconagua. By 1744 Oconagua was only a visita, but there was another monastery-parish at S Francisco Agualulco. While Agualulco and Magdalena were secularized sometime after 1760, Izatlan was still a Franciscan parish at Independence. The area fell within the diocese of Guadalaxara and the custody (province from 1606) of Santiago de Xalisco.

Population and settlements

The count of 1525, clearly incomplete, showed 1,055 *casas* and 2,070 *hombres* in the province of Izatlan. The first of two inspections recorded in the *Suma de visitas* (*c.* 1548) gave a tributary equivalent of 1,498, while the second found 2,483 tributaries, 165 married men working on the monastery who were excused from paying tribute, and 972 other Indians exempt from tribute; the latter report further mentioned that there were 'many others' at Agualulco who did not pay tribute, from which we gather that nearly half the native population (perhaps 4,000 families altogether) enjoyed a special tribute-free status at mid-century.

An assessment of 1556 gives 2,000 tributaries, reduced to 1,000 in 1569 and 436 in 1623 (Códice Franciscano, p. 152. L de T, p. 603. Scholes and Adams, 1959, p. 66). Later censuses show much fluctuation, 335 Indian families (1,289 persons) in 1760, 1,745 tributaries in 1788, and only 783 Indian tributaries in 1804.[3] The Otomí minority disappeared, the surviving Indians speaking 'Nahuatlaca', although in 1587 many also understood and spoke ordinary Náhuatl.

The non-Indian population also varied greatly, depending on mining activity and other factors. Ponce noted that 'many' Spaniards lived at the mines in 1587. The census of 1744 has only 20 Spanish families with some mulattoes, while that of 1760 shows 1,294 non-Indian families. In 1804 there were 946 mulatto tributaries.

The nine dispersed settlements mentioned in the 1525 inspection of this area were perhaps somewhat centralized and moved about in an early Franciscan congregation. Further reduction occurred towards 1600, when the Indians of S Juan and perhaps S Andrés (Atlitic?) were moved into the new doctrina of Magdalena; Santiago and Tezontepec also disappeared at this time.[4] Some of the abandoned sites were later re-occupied, such as the island of S Juan, and by the early eighteenth century there were six Indian pueblos, Agualulco (1950: Ahualulco de Mercado, ciudad), Izatlan (1950: Etzatlán, *villa*), Magdalena, Oconahua, S Juan, and S Marcos. The 1792 report also names seventeen haciendas and eight ranchos in the jurisdiction.

Sources

This is one of the very few areas where we have details of the first Spanish visita, made in February, 1525.[5] There are four entries (apparently the result of two separate inspections) in the *Suma* of *c.* 1548 describing places in the jurisdiction (PNE, I, nos. 61, 295, 318, 432). Father Ponce traveled through here in 1587 (Ponce, II, pp. 46–8, 84–6). The description of Mota y Escobar (pp. 74–5) dates from *c.* 1605, and that of Arregui (pp. 72–3) from *c.* 1620.

The 1744 report by the AM is greatly mutilated,[6] but a summary is preserved in Villaseñor y Sánchez (II, p. 242). For the last part of the eighteenth century, there are useful documents dated 1760,[7] 1788,[8] and 1792.[9]

47 *Iztepexi*

This small jurisdiction occupied several mountain valleys on the north slope of the Sierra de Ixtlán or Juárez, drained by headwaters of the Río Grande, in north central Oaxaca. Elevations are 1,500–2,400 m. The climate is temperate to cold, with heavy precipitation from May to October.

Although Chicomexóchitl (Zapotecan: Xaguia) was said to have been founded by Cuicatecs shortly before the Spanish Conquest, the whole area by 1570 was inhabited by people speaking the mountain dialect of Zapotecan. Itztepexic (Zapotecan: Yaxitza Latziyela), whose founders came from the Yolos area, was tributary to the Aztecs. Calpulalpan and Chicomexóchitl were at war with Itztepexic and thus may have been beyond the reach of the Triple Alliance.

According to a native pictorial document, perhaps the Lienzo de Chicomesúchil, there was a battle between Spaniards and Indians near that place in which the warriors of Calpulalpa and Ixtlan were defeated, while those of Chicomesúchil submitted peaceably; this may have occurred in 1525 or 1526 (Cortés, p. 227).

Encomiendas

Iztepexi was assigned to Pedro de Aragón, a blacksmith by trade and a conquistador. He was succeeded by a son, Juan de Aragón; escheatment occurred in 1554.

The first holder of Calpulalpa was Juan Núñez Sedeño, followed *c.* 1550 by a son, Pedro. The encomienda escheated sometime after 1570.

Chicomesúchil was first held by Gaspar de Tarifa, a conquistador, succeeded by 1548 by a son, Diego de Vargas. In 1597 the encomendero was Melchor de Vargas, a grandson of Tarifa.

Government

A corregimiento from 27 February 1554, Iztepexi was suffragan to the alcaldía mayor of Antequera as late as the 1630s (Cline, 1946, p. 176). The magistrate's jurisdiction was enlarged in 1600 with the acquisition of Calpulalpa and Chicomesúchil, previously administered by the AM of Antequera. The village of Guelatao was lost to neighboring Ixtlan in 1632 (Cline, 1946, p. 179).

Tecuicuilco (q.v.) was attached to this jurisdiction for a time in the seventeenth century. By

1669 the C had been re-designated AM, and in 1707 the right of appointment was granted to the dukes of Atlixco. In later years the capital of the jurisdiction was Chicomesúchil. Iztepexi became a subdelegación in the intendencia of Oaxaca from 1787.[1]

Church

The Dominicans visited the area from the 1530s, and there is a vague reference to a monastery at Iztepexi before 1556 (Ricard, p. 91). By 1570 there

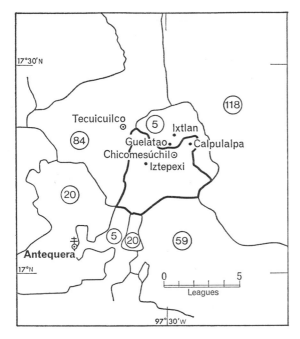

were secular priests at S Juan Chicomesúchil and Sta Catarina Iztepexi, each of whom visited places in adjoining political jurisdictions. Subsequently the curate of Chicomesúchil moved to Ixtlan, but in 1702 the former place became a separate parish again. Calpulalpa and Yahuiche were visited from Ixtlan. The parishes belonged to the diocese of Antequera.

Population and settlements

We know of a mass emigration from Iztepexi to other jurisdictions in the 1550s (ENE, VIII, pp. 230–1), and there was a severe drop in the native population during the epidemic of 1576–9. There were 1,250 tributaries in 1570 and perhaps half that number at the century's end. The low point was probably reached in the seventeenth century. The 1745 census shows 1,280 Indian families, while that of 1801 lists 1,146 Indian tributaries.[2] There were very few non-Indians except during a brief period of mining activity beginning in 1787.

Iztepexi (Yxtepexe, etc.; 1950: Sta Catarina Ixtepeji, *villa*) had five estancias in 1548, but only two are mentioned in 1579; one of them, S Miguel del Río Laatziguía (Amacuautitlan), survived as a pueblo, while S Pedro Nesicho was perhaps re-occupied after a congregation in 1603.[3] The cabecera was moved in 1575 from a hilltop to its final site across the river half a league to the east.

Calpulalpa (Capulalpa; 1950: Calpulalpan de Méndez, pueblo) had four barrios in 1548, all of which seem to have been moved into the cabecera towards 1600. However, one estancia site (Guelatao) was re-occupied, and in 1632 it was made a sujeto of Ixtlan in the jurisdiction of Antequera (q.v.) (Cline, 1946).

Chicomesúchil (Xaguía; 1950: S Juan Chicomezúchil, pueblo), originally the most populous of the three communities, in 1548 had eleven estancias, most of which seem to have been abandoned towards 1600.[4] One of them, Sta María Yahuiche, was made a separate cabecera at this time (Cline, 1946, p. 168), and other sites were re-settled in later years. In the eighteenth century there were two barrios (S Sebastián, Xobaia) and four subject pueblos (Amatlan, Lachatao, Yahuiche or Macuiltepec, and Yavesía). The cabecera of Chicomesúchil was moved a short distance ('unas pocas quadras') to a new site *c.* 1687.

All nine of the surviving pueblos had cabecera status in 1801. The language spoken at that time was 'Zapoteco serrano de Ixtepeji', presumably a dialect.

Sources

For the sixteenth century, we have brief *Suma* articles (*c.* 1548) for each cabecera (PNE, I, nos. 149, 151, 301), the Ovando reports of *c.* 1570 (García Pimentel, 1904, pp. 65, 92), and a valuable relación submitted by the C in 1579 (PNE, IV, pp. 9–23); the latter, which describes only Iztepexi and its estancias, is accompanied by an interesting pintura. There is also a pictorial manuscript concerning Chicomesúchil, data from which seem to make up part of the 1777 report (*see below*).

There is a brief relación by the AM dated 1745.[5] We have seen two documents drawn up by the curate of Chicomesúchil in 1777, a parochial census[6] and a most interesting 'topographical' description.[7] Both parishes are summarily described in 1802 (Pérez, 1888, table at end), and the jurisdiction is covered in detail by a report of *c.* 1820.[8]

Monographic treatment includes Cline (1946), Schmieder (1930), and Spores (1965).

48 *Izúcar*

Occupying a broad plain in southwestern Puebla draining from the lower slopes of Popocatépetl southward to the Atoyac river, with elevations of 1,100–2,200 m, this is mostly a dry, hot area of rich volcanic soil irrigated by several streams.

Itzocan, or Itzyocan, was a large and important kingdom with a dynasty related to those of Tenochtitlan and neighboring Cuauhquechollan. Cortés described the principal settlement as 'muy concertada en sus calles y tratos', with a hundred *teocaltin* and from three to four thousand families, a truly urban concentration; most of the people, however, were dispersed in a great many smaller settlements. Cotton was grown with the aid of irrigation canals. Smaller states in the region were Ahuatlan, Coatzinco, Epatlan, Nacochtlan, Teonochtitlan, and Teopantlan. Texalocan, within the limits of Ahuatlan, had a military ruler (*tlacatécatl*) appointed by Moctezuma. All were subordinate to the Aztec garrison at Tepeyacac. Náhuatl was spoken throughout this area which was collectively known as Coatlalpan.

Small groups of Spaniards must have entered this region in late 1519 or early 1520. In the latter year the Mexica sent a large force to Itzocan, which was protected by a river on one side and a fortified hill on another. This stronghold fell to the Spaniards and their allies in September, 1520.

Encomiendas

Izúcar was assigned to the conquistador Pedro de Alvarado, but the tributes were impounded by the first audiencia in 1529 (ENE, I, p. 146). When both Alvarado and his widow died in 1541, the encomienda was again claimed for the crown. Perhaps it was at this time that tributes were divided, those from the principal cabecera and its immediate dependencies being assigned to the crown, while the erstwhile estancia of Tepapayeca and a number of other settlements were granted to the widow (Luisa de Estrada) and sons of Jorge de Alvarado, brother of Pedro. The eldest son, also named Jorge, died *c.* 1563 and was succeeded by a grandson of the conquistador. Tepapayeca was still a private encomienda in 1696.

We do not know the encomendero of Aguatlan–Texaluca, which escheated in 1532.

Coacingo and Zoyatitlanapa, originally a single state, were granted by Cortés to two separate encomenderos. Zoyatitlanapa was taken for the crown in 1532, while Coacingo was held by Diego Quixada. Quixada left Mexico in the early 1540s, after which tributes were collected for some years by Pedro Núñez. Coacingo appears as a crown possession in 1550 and had definitely escheated in July 1553 (L de T, p. 136).

Epatlan seems to have been divided between Juan Pérez de Herrera and his brother, Pedro Hernández, although Diego Garrido also appears as an early holder. In 1530 the first audiencia assigned Hernández's half to Pérez de Herrera, but the second took this half for the crown (ENE, XV, p. 159). Pérez's half escheated sometime after 1570. This encomienda included Nacuchtlan.

Teonochtitlan included the sub-cabeceras of Teyucan and Tepexoxuma, the last-named being the usual designation by 1548. The encomendero here was Martín de Calahorra, followed in the

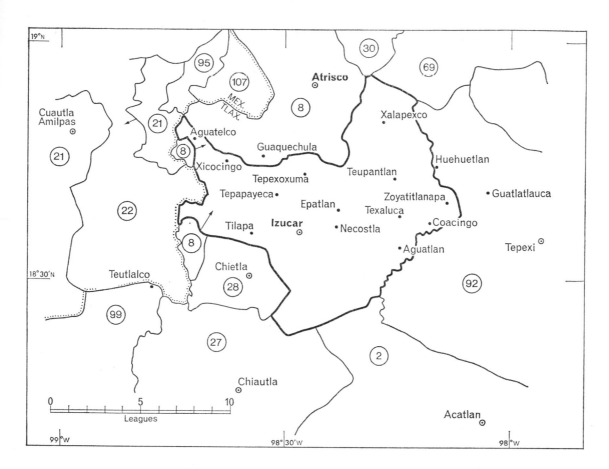

1550s by a son, Cristóbal de Acunada (still listed in 1597). Escheatment occurred between 1626 and 1664, although Teyucan was re-assigned to the Moctezuma heirs at this time.

Teupantlan was shared between two encomenderos, one half escheating by 1534. The other share was held by Alonso González, followed soon after 1560 by his widow, Isabel de Bolaños, who in turn was replaced *c.* 1600 by Diego de Bolaños, a grandson of González. Final escheatment occurred in the late seventeenth century.

Government

Cs were appointed to the crown possessions here, first (May 1532) at Aguatlan y Zoyatitlanapa, then (by 1534) at Epatlan y Teupantlan, and finally (probably in 1541) at Izúcar.[1] The last-mentioned magistrate became a provincial AM in 1559 or 1560, with supervisory jurisdiction at Aguatlan and Epatlan, together with the corregimiento of Chietla and adjoining encomiendas (Guaquechula, Tepapayeca, Tepexoxuma).

In 1602 Guaquechula was transferred to the jurisdiction of Atrisco, while the corregimiento of Epatlan was annexed to that of Izúcar.[2] This left two small enclaves (subjects of Guaquechula) separated from their cabecera (see map), an anomaly which continued into the eighteenth century.[3] Chietla (q.v.) and Aguatlan continued to have separate Cs until they were absorbed by Izúcar towards 1680 (Chietla again became a corregimiento in 1756). Perhaps in this same reorganization, the Teupantlan–Zoyatitlanapa area was assigned to the AM of Atrisco, but it seems to have returned to Izúcar in the 1770s. From 1787 Izúcar was a subdelegación in the intendencia of Puebla.

Church

The Dominicans founded a monastery-parish at Asunción Izúcar towards 1530, although it did not become a vicaría until a decade later (Greenleaf, 1961, p. 62. McAndrew, p. 477). One of its visitas, Sta María Tepapayeca, was made a separate doctrina *c.* 1550 (Ricard, p. 88). Twenty years later, besides the two regular parishes, there was a secular priest at Asunción (S Cristóbal) Tepexoxuma who visited the villages of Aguatlan, Epatlan, and Teupantlan. By 1581 S Juan Epatlan had its own priest, and still another secular parish was established at Santiago Teupantlan towards 1600. S Miguel Tilapa, long a Dominican visita of Izúcar, was secularized in 1640 and appears four years later as a Franciscan doctrina, but not long afterwards it was returned to the Dominicans. Also in 1640 the Dominicans were supposed to be replaced by secular clergy at Izúcar and Tepapayeca (*Alegaciones...*, fol. 91); while a secular curate continued to minister the non-Indian residents of Izúcar and the surrounding haciendas, the Indian congregations remained in Dominican hands at this time.

A separate Dominican parish existed at S Andrés Aguatelco by 1743. Shortly afterward, the regular doctrinas were secularized. S Miguel Xicocingo was a visita of Aguatelco until it became a parish sometime after 1777. The area fell entirely within the diocese of Tlaxcala.

As so often happened, parishes extended across the boundaries of political divisions. In 1581 Coacingo was being visited by Dominicans from Huehuetlan, and Zoyatitlanapa by Augustinians from Guatlatlauca (cf. Tepexi de la Seda); other places outside the civil jurisdiction belonged to parishes within it.

Population and settlements

After much initial loss, in 1548 there were still some 9,852 tributaries, of whom 7,156 were in Izúcar-Tepapayeca and their many dependencies. The total dropped to 6,175 in 1570, 3,000 in 1600, and 1,625 in 1626. Later counts show 2,029 tributaries in 1696, 2,975 Indian families in 1743, and 3,679 in 1754. There were 4,398 Indian tributaries in 1800.[4]

Only thirteen Spanish residents are reported in Izúcar in 1548, but many more came in later years to establish sugar and cattle haciendas, bringing with them Negro slaves. In 1662 there were 100 families of Spaniards, and by 1743 a total of 627 non-Indian families (almost a fifth of the total population) lived in the jurisdiction. The 1754 census shows 118 families (461 persons) of Spaniards and 622 (2,535 persons) of 'color quebrado' (mostly Negro and mulatto) living at Izúcar (the population there was predominantly Negroid at this time) and at numerous haciendas and trapiches. The padrón of 1791 gives 1,028 Spaniards, 2,121 mestizos, and 3,850 mulattoes, excluding slaves.

By 1548 the cabecera of Izúcar (Ysucar, etc.; 1950: Izúcar de Matamoros, ciudad) had lost control over a number of its sujetos. Cuilucan (later, Colucan), Tlatequetlan (Tlatectla, Tatetla), and Tlilapan (Tilapa) had achieved cabecera status, while Tepapayeca (1950: pueblo) had become a separate encomienda with sub-cabeceras at Coatepec, Chalma, and Tlapanala. There were a great many estancias (fifty are listed in 1548) scattered between the Atoyac river and Aguatelco. Most of them disappeared in the congregations of 1598–1604, although some were reoccupied at a later date. In the eighteenth century, in addition to the cabeceras mentioned, three old estancias directly subject to Izúcar (Ayutla, Mazaco, Puctla) survived as Indian pueblos, while thirteen (Aguatelco, Atzitzintla, Ayotlichan or Ayotzintichan, Cohuecan, Cuespala, Choaco, Tecatzoc or Catzo, Teolco, Tepemaxalco, Tepexco, Tetla, Toctlan, Xicotzinco) existed in the Tepapayeca area. Still another, Calmecatitlan, was formerly a subject estancia of Guaquechula.

Aguatlan (1950: Ahuatlán, pueblo) in 1548 had two estancias which had been abandoned by 1581. The cabecera was moved to a new site towards 1560. Texaluca (Texalocan), once subject to Aguatlan, was a cabecera by 1548 and survived as a pueblo.

Coacingo (Coatzinco; 1950: Coatzingo, pueblo) had no known estancias. Its sister-cabecera, Zoyatitlanapa (Cihuatitlanapa, Xoyaltlipanapa) had two small estancias in 1581 both of which were eliminated *c.* 1600.

Epatlan (Yepatlan; 1950: S Juan Epatlan, pueblo) had eleven barrios in 1548. From other sixteenth-century sources, we learn that S Miguel Ayotlan (Ayutla) and S Mateo Ostotlan were subject to Epatlan;[5] both survived as pueblos in the eighteenth century, as did Totoltepec (S Martín de la Laguna) and Xicosingo (S Felipe de la Laguna). Nacuchtlan (Necuchtla, Necostla; 1950: Necoxtla, pueblo), a former state united in encomienda with Epatlan, claimed cabecera status in 1552 and also survived.[6]

The ancient state of Teonochtitlan (Teunuchtitlan) disappears after 1548, its place taken by adjacent Tepexoxuma (Tepexuxumac; 1950: Tepeojuma, pueblo), which, together with Teocan (Teuçan, Teyuca) had been subordinate cabeceras. Between the three places, thirteen estancias are named in the 1548 report. All these sites were deserted in the congregations of *c.* 1600, only Tepexoxuma and Teyuca surviving as native communities.

Teupantlan (1950: Teopantlán, pueblo) in 1548 had five barrios or estancias (eight are mentioned in 1570), reduced to two barrios in 1777. S Francisco Xalapexco, listed as a pueblo in 1754–92, was probably within the limits of Teupantlan.

Sources

Cortés, in his letter of October 30, 1520, gives a valuable description of Izúcar as he saw it only a month before (Cortés, pp. 110–11; cf. Mártir de Angleria, II, pp. 502–3). The various cabeceras are listed in the *Suma de Visitas* of *c.* 1548 in an unusually useful group of articles (PNE, I, nos. 14, 107, 119–20, 248, 292, 399, 521, 540–2, 553, 559). Reports in the Ovando series are less satisfactory (García Pimentel, 1904, pp. 21–2. PNE, V, pp. 245–6), and only the corregimiento of Aguatlan is described in a relación of 1581 (PNE, V, pp. 81–98).

There are sparse details of the 1598–1604 congregations here,[7] followed by a bishop's report on the area in 1610.[8] Other seventeenth-century documents include tributary data for 1626–96[9] and another report of an episcopal visit in 1644.[10]

We have a good description sent in by the AM in 1743,[11] and a report drawn up for the Inquisition in 1754.[12] The parishes of Aguatelco (including Xicocingo), Epatlan, Teupantlan, and Tepapayeca are represented by padrones made in 1777.[13] There is an excellent description of the area written in 1791 to accompany another census report,[14] and a complete list of toponyms submitted in 1792.[15]

49 *Justlaguaca*

Straddling the Sierra Madre del Sur, this rugged area in the Mixteca Baja (western Oaxaca) drains both northward into the Balsas system and south toward the Pacific. Elevations range from 800–3,200 m, but most of the region lies at 1,200–2,000 m. While the higher mountains are forested, elsewhere vegetation is sparse and rainfall deficient.

Shortly before the arrival of the Spaniards, Triple Alliance forces led by Moctezuma II invaded this area from the north until they met the armies of Tototépec. At this time the Aztecs seem to have secured the mountain passes and established garrisons at Ayoxochiquilatzallan and Poctla to defend their recent conquests from the enemy to the south.[1] Among the states mentioned in the Aztec conquest lists were Icpactépec (Mixtecan: Yocoyúa), Quimichtépec or Mixtépec (Yosonohuico), and Cuczcomaixtlahuacan or Tecomaixtlahuacan (Yodzoyáa). Other places tributary to the Mexica, which were probably separate chiefdoms, were Xohuixtlahuacan (Yosocuya) and Tepexicoapan (Ñucahua). Another community which may have had some autonomy was Tlacotépec.

We suspect that all of these were Mixtecan-speaking states at the time of Moctezuma's invasion, although there may have been an older Náhuatl minority; either explanation would account for the fact that both languages were spoken in the sixteenth century. There were also some Amuzgan-speakers at Ayoxochiquilatzallan, and perhaps an intrusion of Triques between Poctla and Xohuixtlahuacan. Mixtépec is said to have been subordinate politically to Tlachquiauco (cf. Teposcolula), and Tlacotépec to Tecomaixtlahuacan (Icaza, I, p. 47), while Ayoxochiquilatzallan was apparently connected in some way with Igualtépec or Yocaltépec (cf. Guaxuapa).

This area came under Spanish control in the early 1520s, but subsequently there was a rebellion

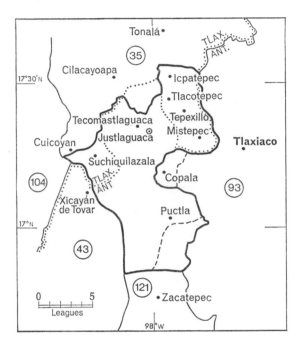

which was quelled by an army under Bernardino Vázquez de Tapia in late 1523 or 1524 (Vázquez de Tapia, p. 52).

Encomiendas

Ayusuchiquilazala formed part of the encomienda of Igualtepec (cf. Guaxuapa), with final escheatment after 1696.

Justlaguaca seems to have been first held by Bartolomé de Valdés, although Antonio de Aznar may have shared the encomienda in early years (Millares Carlo and Mantecón, I, nos. 71–2). Tristán de Arellano held half of this encomienda in 1548–50, by which time the other half had escheated. Francisco Valadés appears as encomen-

dero of the private half in 1580, but by the end of the century Justlaguaca was entirely a crown possession (Icaza, I, p. 253).

The first holder of Mistepec was perhaps Martín Vázquez, followed towards 1528 by Alonso García Bravo (Albani), who died c. 1565. García's daughter, who succeeded, married Melchor Xuárez or Suárez. Between 1580 and 1597 Suárez was replaced by a son, Lázaro. Escheatment occurred sometime after 1665 (Icaza, I, p. 5).

Puctla was held by the conquistador Antonio de Aznar, followed towards 1559 by a son of the same name. The latter seems to have died c. 1570, when the encomienda escheated (L de T, p. 296).

Tecomastlaguaca was one of many places in the Mixteca granted by Cortés to Francisco Maldonado, who died c. 1548. Maldonado's widow, Isabel de Rojas, then married Tristán de Luna y Arellano, who was succeeded as encomendero on his death in 1573 by a son, Carlos. Further details are given below (cf. Teposcolula).[2]

Tepexicoapan (Tepexillo) was assigned to Lázaro (Alvaro) Guerrero, a conquistador. When he died (before 1550) the encomienda passed to a daughter married to Andrés Tello, listed in 1560–70. In 1597–1604 a Diego Tello (grandson of the first holder) was encomendero. Escheatment occurred between 1629 and 1664.

Perhaps originally an estancia of Tecomastlaguaca, Tlacotepec was granted sometime before 1550 to Gabriel Bosque, followed (1565–70) by a son, Juan Bosque. Tributes had escheated by 1597 (Icaza, I, p. 47).

The encomienda history of Icpatepec is somewhat of a mystery. Clearly it was a cabecera at contact, but no place of that name appears in the early lists of crown and private encomiendas at our disposal, from which we gather that either it was attached to another place as a sujeto or was known by another name. By 1550 it was a crown cabecera.

Government

Half of Justlaguaca became crown property, administered by a C, on June 6, 1548.[3] During the following decade this magistrate was given jurisdiction in the encomiendas of Ayusuchiquilazala,

Mistepec, Puctla, and Tecomastlaguaca, together with Xicayán de Tovar and Zacatepec.[4] Icpatepec was a separate corregimiento from perhaps 1570; its C was ordered not to live there in 1582, and it was annexed to the jurisdiction of Justlaguaca in the 1590s.[5] In the provincial distribution of the 1560s and later, Justlaguaca was suffragan to the AM of Teposcolula.

Xicayán de Tovar was transferred to Igualapa (q.v.) late in the sixteenth century, and not long afterward Zacatepec was assigned to the jurisdiction of Xicayán (q.v.) de Pedro Nieto. There seems to have been a dispute between the magistrates of Justlaguaca and Teposcolula over the Trique villages of Copala.[6]

Toward the end of the seventeenth century the C of Justlaguaca was re-designated AM. From 1786 he was a subdelegado in the intendencia of Oaxaca.

Church

Perhaps first visited by Dominicans from Teposcolula and Tlaxiaco, Santiago Justlaguaca became a separate Dominican doctrina towards 1557.[7] Icpatepec and Mistepec apparently belonged to this parish for a few years (a Dominican monastery is recorded at Mistepec in 1560), but both had secular priests by 1570 (Alvarado, p. 17). When S Sebastián Tecomastlaguaca was moved to its final site towards 1582 it also became a Dominican parish.

Sometime between 1646 and 1745 the curate of S Juan Icpatepec moved his headquarters to S Miguel Tlacotepec de las Nieves (*Alegaciones...,* fol. 90). This parish, together with that of S Juan Mistepec, belonged to the diocese of Tlaxcala, while Justlaguaca and Tecomastlaguaca were in the bishopric of Antequera. Copala was visited from Justlaguaca, and Puctla and Santiago del Río (the latter in the civil jurisdiction of Guaxuapa) from Tecomastlaguaca. Suchiquilazala and nearby villages belonged first to the doctrina of Tlapancingo, and eventually to that of Cuicoyan (cf. Guaxuapa), thus falling within the diocese of Tlaxcala.

The Dominicans were replaced by secular clergy soon after 1706.[8]

Population and settlements

If we accept Burgoa's figure (3,000+ families) for Justlaguaca–Tecomastlaguaca on the arrival of the Dominicans about 1555, and work backward from the 1570 census, we arrive at a total of 6,800 tributaries in the jurisdiction towards 1555, reduced to 3,625 in 1570, 2,160 after the epidemic of 1576–9, and *c.* 1,200 in 1626 (Burgoa, 1934*a*, I, p. 355. L de T, pp. 296, 574–8. Scholes and Adams, 1959, p. 35). Recovery was slow, due to further plagues and emigration. There were 1,381 Indian families in 1745, and 1,699 Indian tributaries in 1795.[9] The 1777 census has 6,479 Indians (persons), 174 Spaniards, 591 mestizos, and 116 mulattoes.

Justlaguaca (Xiustlauaca, Juxtlabaca, etc.; Yosocuya; 1950: Santiago Juxtlahuaca, *villa*), according to the 1777 relación, was originally located on a hilltop to the east. It was moved (presumably by the Dominicans in the 1550s) down into the plain, and again towards 1633 the cabecera was shifted some 12 or 14 *cuadras* northward to its final site. In 1600 the estancias were so close to the monastery that no further congregation was thought necessary.[10] The 1745 report lists six sujetos within three leagues; five of these survived as pueblos in 1777 (their Mixtecan names are given in the report of that year).[11]

Tecomastlaguaca (Tecomastláhuac, etc.; Yodzoyáa; 1950: S Sebastián Tecomaxtlahuaca, *villa*) also had two changes of cabecera site. Burgoa writes that it was first a league downstream from Justlaguaca. The Dominicans moved it *c.* 1572 to the outskirts of Justlaguaca ('a stone's throw', or 'two harquebus shots' away, according to two different documents), but in 1582 the Indians requested and were given permission to return to the old site.[12] According to Burgoa, they actually moved at this time to a new and final site a half league northwest of Justlaguaca. A congregation was proposed here in 1598, but there were still six sujetos in 1670, most or all of which seem to have survived as pueblos. Mixtecan toponyms are given in the 1803 report.

Puctla (Poctlan, Putla; Nucáa; 1950: Putla de Guerrero, pueblo) had six estancias some of which disappeared in a congregation proposed in 1598. We are not sure whether S Juan Copala was subject to Puctla, Justlaguaca, Tecomastlaguaca, or Tlaxiaco; in 1600 this Trique community had two small estancias which were to be moved to Puctla.[13] The Trique name for Copala was Sahatnuncuti. Sta María Pueblo Nuevo, in the Puctla vicinity, seems to have been settled in the late eighteenth century.

In the bishopric of Tlaxcala, Mistepec (Mixtepec; Yosonohuico; 1950: S Juan Mixtepec Juxtlahuaca, pueblo) had six estancias before a proposed congregation in 1598, and four or five subject pueblos in the eighteenth century.

Tepexicoapan (Tepexi, more often Tepexillo after the sixteenth century; 1950: Stos Reyes Tepejillo, pueblo) had no dependencies in 1570 or later. Icpatepec (Yepatepec, Icpactepec, Ixpaltepec, Ipantepec; Yocoyua; 1950: Nieves Ixpantepec, pueblo) in 1570–80 had three subordinate settlements nearby; the original site of the cabecera was perhaps a hilltop ceremonial center recently discovered to the northeast of its present location (*Cuadernos Americanos*, CXXXVIII, pp. 157–66). One source states that Tlacotepec (de las Nieves; 1950: S Miguel Tlacotepec, pueblo) was an estancia of Tecomastlaguaca until it became a cabecera, perhaps in the 1540s; it had two estancias in 1570 (Icaza, I, p. 47).

Suchiquilazala (more often Ayusuchiquilazala in the sixteenth century; Zuchiquilatzan, etc.; 1950: Zochiquilazala, pueblo) had three estancias in 1580, at least one of which, Tilapa, survived as a pueblo.

Sources

Only Justlaguaca and Puctla are described in brief articles in the *Suma* of *c.* 1548 (PNE, I, nos. 452, 835). The area is covered summarily in reports of the 1570 Ovando series (García Pimentel, 1904, pp. 20, 75–6. PNE, V, pp. 238, 263). There is a lengthy relación sent in by the C of Justlaguaca in 1580,[14] and another, undated, from the C of Icpatepec (PNE, IV, pp. 155–62).

Data on the congregations of *c.* 1600 are scattered and fragmentary.[15] For the Tlaxcalan part of the jurisdiction, we have the journal of bishop Mota y Escobar in 1610[16] and tributary data for 1626–96.[17] The history of the Dominican monasteries up to 1670 is given by Burgoa (1934*a*, I, pp. 353–68), who worked in this area.

A brief 1745 report from the AM covers only Justlaguaca and Tecomastlaguaca,[18] but it is filled out by Villaseñor y Sánchez (I, pp. 340–2). There is a padrón of the jurisdiction,[19] together with parochial censuses of Mistepec and Tlacotepec,[20] all dated 1777. The parish of Justlaguaca is described in a most interesting report of the 'topographic' series, also made in 1777.[21] A statistical summary of 1792[22] is followed by parochial descriptions from Justlaguaca and Tecomastlaguaca dated 1803.[23] The entire jurisdiction as it was *c.* 1820 is covered in another document.[24]

The works of Dahlgren de Jordán (1954) and Spores (1965) touch on this region only incidentally.

50 *León*

Now the southwestern corner of the state of Guanajuato, León's jurisdiction extended from the Sierra de Comanja on the north to the Lerma river on the south; most of it is drained by the Turbio river. The climate is semi-arid and cool, with elevations of 1,690–2,400 m.

At contact this was wild Chichimec country, although there may have been Tarascan outposts in the south. Guamare-speakers predominated in the south, and Guachichiles in the north, living in scattered rancherías.[1]

When Nuño de Guzmán passed through Pénjamo on his way from Michoacán to Jalisco in 1530, he may have been crossing territory already visited by Juan de Villaseñor, the encomendero of Guango and Puruándiro (cf. Valladolid). Villaseñor founded a settlement of Tarascans, Otomíes, and Christianized Guamares at Pénjamo towards 1549 (Bancroft, II, p. 471. Jiménez Moreno, 1958, pp. 55, 77. Velázquez, 1946–8, I, p. 375). During the following years cattle ranches were established throughout the area to supply the mines nearby. At Huastatillos (Valle de la Señora), a site already

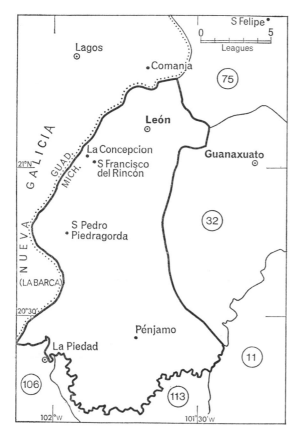

occupied by cattlemen, the *villa* of León was established in 1576 as a defensive settlement against Indian attacks (Jiménez Moreno, 1958, p. 57. Powell, pp. 153–4). Chichimec harassment continued until 1590.

Encomienda

Puruándiro, in Michoacán, was held in encomienda by Juan de Villaseñor as early as 1528.[2] Either the limits of this grant were extended north of the river or a separate assignment of the

Pénjamo region was made to Villaseñor in 1544 (Jiménez Moreno, 1958, p. 77). In any case, the Indians of Pénjamo seem to have been included in the tributary quotas of Puruándiro in the seventeenth century, although for a time they were exempt from tribute payment.

Government

The area was disputed in early years between the magistrates of Michoacán, Nueva Galicia, and Chichimecas (cf. Xilotepec), and from 1559 there was still another claimant, the AM of Guanaxuato (Jiménez Moreno, 1958, pp. 83–4). In the following decade the last-named justice seems to have exercised jurisdiction from Comanja to Guaniqueo, but in 1563, the boundary was defined leaving Comanja in Nueva Galicia, and soon afterwards the Río Grande became the border between Guanaxuato and Michoacán. At the end of 1575, in ordering the foundation of the new *villa* of León, the viceroy set its southern limit at the Río Grande, and in 1579 a separate AM was appointed.[3]

Towards 1670 the province of Zacatula (q.v.) was placed under a teniente of the AM of León, an arrangement which continued off and on for a century.[4] Deputies also resided at Pénjamo and S Pedro Piedragorda. From 1787 the last two *tenientazgos*, as well as León, became subdelegaciones in the intendencia of Guanaxuato.

Church

There was a secular priest at S Francisco Pénjamo in the 1560s at the latest, and while the place does not appear in a list of curacies dated 1571, it had achieved parochial status by the following decade (Jiménez Moreno, 1958, p. 87. Powell, p. 249, note 19. Velázquez, 1946–8, I, p. 375). In 1589 Numarán, south of the Río Grande in the alcaldía mayor of Michoacán, was added to this parish.[5]

S Diego (S Sebastián) León from 1582 had a secular curate, replaced in 1589 by Franciscans (Jiménez Moreno, 1958, pp. 90–1). The parish was again secularized between 1743 and 1770.

A priest (secular) who had until recently ministered the nearby mining camp of Comanja was resident at S Francisco del Rincón in 1649. This parish was divided (before 1743) with the erection of another secular curacy, S Pedro Piedragorda. All these doctrinas were in the diocese of Michoacán.

Population and settlements

The relatively sparse Chichimec population here was gradually Christianized or driven out and replaced by Tarascan, Otomí, and Náhuatl immigrants, beginning with a trickle in the sixteenth century. In 1649 only some 150 Indian families are reported in the three parishes. Their number had increased to somewhat over 1,000 by 1743, and the census of 1801–2 shows 6,762 Indian tributaries in the three subdelegaciones, most of them working on haciendas.

Pénjamo (1950: ciudad), as we have mentioned, seems to have been the first (c. 1549) settlement of Tarascans and Otomies; it was raided and perhaps destroyed by Chichimecs at least twice in the 1560s. More immigrants subsequently arrived to form the congregations of Cuerámoro, S Francisco del Cuecillo, and S Miguel. By 1649 S Francisco del Rincón (1950: ciudad) had been established as a predominantly Indian settlement of Mexicans and Otomies. S Pedro Piedragorda (1950: Ciudad Manuel Doblado) was founded

towards 1683, and Pueblo Nuevo de la Concepción (1950: Purísima del Rincón, pueblo) somewhat later.

León (1950: ciudad) grew from 50 Spanish vecinos in 1639 to 521 in 1743. From its foundation it had a large Negro and mulatto element, some in the town and more on surrounding haciendas. In 1649 there were some fifty haciendas, *labores*, and *hatos* in the jurisdiction.

In 1743 there were 1,302 families of 'Spaniards', 735 of mestizos, and at least 800 of Negroes and mulattoes, excluding slaves. The 1801–2 census shows 3,295 mulatto tributaries in the jurisdiction.[6]

Sources

There are two brief reports on Indian congregations in this area in 1595–1601.[7] Two documents of considerable interest describe the jurisdiction as it was in 1639[8] and 1649.[9] A defective relación of 1743[10] is supplemented by Villaseñor y Sánchez (II, p. 42). Lafora (pp. 50–1) passed through here in 1766, as did Morfi (p. 381) in 1781. For 1792 there is a list of toponyms down to the category of rancho,[11] and a padrón of the Pénjamo area.[12]

Jiménez Moreno (1958) and Powell (1952) give details of the early history of this region.

51 *Lerma*

This tiny jurisdiction occupied a high (2,580 m) swampy area and a tributary valley near the headwaters of the Lerma river, now in central Mexico state. It has a cold, rather moist climate.

Tlalachco, or Tlallahco, according to a sixteenth-century petition of the cacique and *pipiltin* of Tlacopan, was in pre-Conquest times an estancia or minor dependency of that realm (ENE, XVI, pp. 71–3). Náhuatl, Otomí, and Matlatzincan were all spoken there in 1570. First contact with the Spaniards was probably in 1519, and final subjugation in 1521.

Encomienda

The conquistador Diego Sánchez de Sopuerta held Talasco, apparently considered a separate

cabecera by the Spaniards, until his death towards 1534 when the encomienda escheated (ENE, XIV, p. 150. Icaza, II, pp. 237, 240).

Government

Talasco appears in a list of corregimientos of c. 1534. In the 1560s the C was suffragan to the AM of Valle de Matalcingo (cf. Metepec); in the following decade he not only maintained his independence but was attempting to annex part of the AM's jurisdiction.[1]

In 1611–13 Martín Rolín Varejón seems to have obtained permission to found a settlement within the limits of Talasco, to be called the city of Lerma. In return for this service, Rolín was to be given the privilege of serving as or appointing the local magistrate. By 1640 Cs are listed for both Lerma and Tarasquillo, as Talasco had begun to be called. A document of 1676, however, states that '25 or 30 years ago' the king had granted the right of appointment for three 'lives' to Diego López Jardon with the condition that he establish a city called Lerma in the vicinity, and that this had not yet been accomplished.[2] By 1743 the jurisdiction was known as Lerma and included the village of Tarasquillo. After 1786 it was a subdelegación in the intendencia of Mexico.

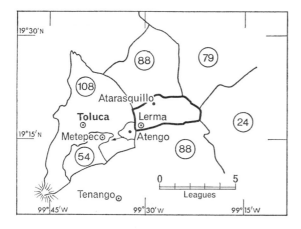

Church

In the sixteenth century Talasco was visited by the curate of Huicicilapa. A secular priest was living at Sta María (Asunción) Tarasquillo in 1646, and perhaps from 1693 there was another parish at Sta Clara de Lerma (*Diccionario Porrúa*, p. 821). Towards 1750 the two parishes were combined under a single curate at Lerma, who also had jurisdiction in Tianguistengo (cf. Tenango del Valle).[3] Lerma was in the archbishopric of Mexico.

Population and settlements

The number of tributaries dropped from 596 in 1564 to 463 in 1570 and 130 in 1643. By 1688 it had risen to $323\frac{1}{2}$, and the census of 1743 shows 643 Indian families, 57 of Spaniards, and 133 of mestizos and mulattoes. According to the padrón of 1791, there were 821 individual Spaniards, 283 mestizos, and 87 mulattoes. In 1801 there were 800 Indian tributaries.[4]

The 1570 report lists only the cabecera of Talasco (Tlalachco, etc.) and the nearby estancias of S Miguel and Santiago. Outlying settlements were to have been abandoned in 1593, and while there was some moving about, the Indians resisted these efforts at congregation. The original cabecera apparently came to be known as Sta María Atarasquillo. Three other villages, S Mateo, S Miguel, and S Miguelito, together with three haciendas and six ranchos are listed in the eighteenth century. The ciudad of Lerma (1950: Lerma de Villada, ciudad), as we have mentioned, was probably not founded until the late seventeenth century, and never amounted to much.

Sources

A few early tribute records are available (L de T, pp. 319–21), followed by the 1570 report.[5] There are references to congregations in 1593–8.[6] Much has been written about the foundation of Lerma in the seventeenth century.[7] We have the diaries of two archbishops' visits, in 1646[8] and 1685,[9] and tribute records for the same period.[10]

A long report sent in by the C in 1743[11] is summarized in Villaseñor y Sánchez (I, p. 217). There is a brief description of the jurisdiction, accompanied by a padrón, dated 1791,[12] together with a list of toponyms made in 1792.[13]

The indices of Colín (1966, 1967) cite other documents.

52 Malinalco

While a corner of this area (now in the state of Mexico) reaches to the Chiuhnauhtzin or Nevado de Toluca (4,560 m), most of it is cool, dry country at 1,600–2,800 m on the slopes of that volcano, cut by deep barrancas draining southward toward the Balsas. It also includes headwaters of the Lerma.

Malinalco and Ocuilan were important religious and political centers, each a center of tribute collection for the Triple Alliance. Other native states were Coatépec, Tenantzinco (with sub-rulers at Tecualoyan and Tonatiuhco), Zoquitzinco, and Tzompahuacan (with a dependency, Cincozcatlan or Cincozcac). Náhuatl was predominant at Malinalco and Tzompahuacan, and Matlatzincan elsewhere; Ocuiltecan, a close relative of Matlatzincan, was spoken at Ocuila. Both Matlatzincans and Otomies lived at Coatépec.

Probably first visited by Spaniards in early 1520, Malinalco rose in rebellion in the spring of 1521. By the end of that year, following a punitive expedition led by Andrés de Tapia, the region was under Spanish control (Bancroft, I, pp. 662–5. Cortés, pp. 172–3. Oviedo y Valdés, III, p. 403).

Encomiendas

Malinalco was shared between two encomenderos, the half belonging to Cristóbal Romero escheating at the end of 1532.[1] The other half was held by Cristóbal (Sebastián) Rodríguez de Avalos, a conquistador, whose widow married Cristóbal Hidalgo *c.* 1545. A son of the conquistador, Cristóbal Rodríguez de Avalos, is listed in 1560–97, while a grandson, Agustín de Villasana, was receiving the tribute in 1604. Malinalco was still half private encomienda in 1688.[2]

Ocuila was given by Cortés de Juan de Morales, but in 1527 it was divided between Serván Bejarano and Pedro Zamorano. By 1548 Bejarano had died, and his widow, Francisca Calderón, had married Antonio de la Torre. In the 1560s Zamorano was succeeded by a son, while Doña Francisca, again a widow, was married to Diego de Ocampo Saavedra. Ocampo and Zamorano were still encomenderos at the century's end. By 1623 half of Ocuila had escheated; twenty years later the private half was held by one of the Moctezuma heirs.[3]

Coatepec was entirely held by Serván Bejarano from 1527, and suffered the same fate as his half of Ocuila.[4]

A conquistador, Juan de Salcedo, held Tenancingo until he was succeeded by a son, Pedro, in 1536. The latter was followed by his son, Ruiz López de Salcedo, between 1570 and 1591. In 1647 the Conde de Moctezuma was getting the tribute, or rather a portion of it, the rest having escheated.[5]

Zumpaguacan and Zoquicingo belonged to Alonso de la Serna, followed in the 1560s by a son, Antonio Velázquez de la Serna. In 1595 the latter's widow, Isabel de Cárdenas, is listed, but Juana de la Cuadra appears two years later as encomendera. Luis del Castillo, a son-in-law of the first holder,

was receiving the tribute in 1604, but the encomienda was later re-assigned.[6]

Government

A C administered the crown half of Malinalco
from December 29, 1532, and during the 1550s
he was given charge of nearby encomiendas and
re-designated AM of a province which included
the suffragan corregimiento of Atlatlauca y
Suchiaca (cf. Tenango del Valle). The seat of
government, first at Malinalco, moved to Tenancingo before 1580.[7] From 1787 the magistrate was
a subdelegado in the intendencia of Mexico, with
deputies at Malinalco and Tecualoya.

Church

Augustinians entered this area in the late 1530s and
founded doctrinas at Santiago Ocuila and S
Salvador (Transfiguración) Malinalco; monasteries
were being built at both places in 1552.[8] By 1569
secular clergy were living at S Francisco Tenancingo and Sta María (Asunción, Natividad)
Zumpaguacan. The latter parish was divided in
the 1690s with another priest at Sta Bárbara
Tecualoya.[9] Somewhat earlier, in 1680-3, a small
hermitage was built by the Augustinians at S
Miguel Chalma, a famous sanctuary subordinate
to the doctrina of Ocuila (Vera, p. 123). Malinalco
remained an Augustinian parish until after Independence and Chalma continued as an Augustinian
cloister, but Ocuila was secularized between 1743
and 1791.

Coatepec and Texcaliacac belonged to the
parish of Capuluac in the late colonial period, while
Zoquicingo and its dependencies were visited from
Tenango (cf. Tenango del Valle). All parishes
here were in the archdiocese of Mexico.

Population and settlements

Indian tributaries dropped from 6,985 in 1570 to
3,035 in 1597, and only 1,405 in 1643.[10] There was
some emigration in this period, notably to
neighboring Cuernavaca in the 1570s and later.[11]
Subsequent counts show 1,667 tributaries in 1688,
2,657 in 1743, and 4,163 in 1801.[12] Matlatzincan,
still spoken at Tenancingo in 1646, had become a
dead language here by 1791, but Ocuiltecan con-

tinued to be used near Ocuila; elsewhere Náhuatl
was spoken.

The non-Indian population settled at Malinalco,
Tenancingo, Tecualoya, and numerous haciendas.
In 1791 there were 2,935 Spaniards (persons), 2,639
mestizos, and 358 mulattoes in the jurisdiction.

Malinalco (Marinalco; 1950: Malinalco, pueblo)
had ten estancias from one to six leagues from the
cabecera in 1548-71 (forty barrios are also mentioned in the latter year). S Martín, S Miguel
Tecomatlan, and S Simón Tesquitipan were the
subject pueblos in the eighteenth century.

Coatepec (Quatepec, etc.; 1950: S Nicolás
Coatepec de las Bateas, pueblo) had only two
nearby estancias in 1548-71, one of which, Texcaliacac, survived the congregation.

Seventeen estancias were subject to Ocuila
(1950: Ocuilan de Arteaga, pueblo) in 1548,
fourteen of which still existed in 1580. These were
ordered to be gathered in two settlements, Ocuila
and Chalma, in 1604; the latter place was moved
closer to the cabecera, surviving in the eighteenth
century as S Ambrosio Chalmita. S Juan Atzingo,
a pueblo in the 1790s, perhaps corresponded to the
1580 estancia Acahualtzingo.

Tenancingo (1950: Tenancingo de Degollado,
ciudad) had nine estancias, named in the 1548
report. One of them was the pre-Columbian
cabecera of Tecualoya (1950: Villa Guerrero), and
we suspect that another was Tonatiuhco or
Tonatico, although the latter may have been in
the neighboring jurisdiction of Zacualpa (q.v.).
A congregation here in the 1590s was thwarted,
the Indians returning to their abandoned homesites. Ixtlahuacingo, Tecualoya, Tlaxomulco,
Santiago, S Mateo, and S Lucas all survived as
pueblos in the eighteenth century.

Zumpaguacan (Tzumpahuacan, Tzompahuac;
1950: Zumpahuacán, pueblo) was reduced from
twenty-two estancias in 1548 to fourteen in 1580.
The Indians fled from another congregation in the
1590s, many emigrating to other jurisdictions.
Only S Gaspar Totoltepec, in addition to the
cabecera, acquired the status of pueblo.

Zoquicingo (Xuquitzinco, etc.; 1950: Joqui-
cingo, pueblo) was a cabecera with three nearby
estancias in 1570. All were ordered congregated

at Cepayautla (cf. Tenango del Valle) in 1603, but Zoquicingo, Cuaxuchco, and Tepexuxuca were still (or again) pueblos in 1791-2.

Twenty-eight haciendas, three cattle estancias, and fifteen ranchos are named in the 1792 report.

Sources

There are detailed *Suma de Visitas* (*c.* 1548) articles for this area, giving Náhuatl names of most of the settlements (PNE, I, nos. 101, 256, 346, 419, 531). However, these are not easy to identify with the saints' names listed in various reports of the 1570–71 Ovando series.[13] There are additional toponymic data for Ocuila and Zumpaguacan in 1580.[14]

Congregation documents (1593–1604) are scattered.[15] We have valuable journals of two archbishops' visits in 1646[16] and 1685,[17] and tributary data for 1623–88.[18]

The 1743 relación is very badly drawn up;[19] we have not checked details against the summary in Villaseñor y Sánchez (I, p. 198). A scanty report from the aged friar in charge of Malinalco in 1777[20] is filled out with an excellent description sent in, with a map, by the subdelegado in 1791.[21] There is also a complete list of placenames dated 1792.[22]

A great many other documents are cited in the archival guides of Colín (1966, 1967).

53 *Maravatio*

This extensive region in easternmost Michoacán traverses the main volcanic range, draining both northward into the Lerma and south toward the Balsas. The northern part, at 1,600–3,600 m, is cool and has greater precipitation than the south, which is semi-arid and quite hot at 400–1,600 m.

The political divisions at contact, from north to south, were Maravatio, Taximaroa (Tlaximaloyan), and Tuzantla (Tarascan, Cusaro). Each of these states was ruled by a military governor appointed by the cazonci of Michoacán in charge of carrying on war with the neighboring Mexica and their allies. According to the earliest record we have, Tarascan was spoken exclusively (in 1571) at Maravatio, both Tarascan and Otomí at Taximaroa, and Tarascan and Náhuatl at Tuzantla. On the north, the area was bounded by Mazahuans and Pame-speaking Chichimecs.

Spaniards reached Taximaroa in 1521; the Tarascan forces there submitted without resistance to the expedition led by Cristóbal de Olid in July, 1522. The region may have participated in the rebellions and repressions of the 1520s (Warren, 1963*b*, pp. 75–7).

Encomiendas

Cortés seems to have included at least part of this area among his own holdings; while he was in Honduras, Taximaroa was taken by the *factor* and *veedor*, Salazar and Almíndez. After some early litigation, Gonzalo de Salazar retained possession until his death *c.* 1553, to be succeeded by a son, Juan Velázquez de Salazar, who in turn died shortly before 1612. Tributes were then reassigned, and Taximaroa (including Tuxpan and Zitácuaro) was still part private encomienda as late as 1698.[1]

In 1528 Maravatio was held by 'Ocaño' (perhaps Diego de Ocaña, a Jew and an enemy of Cortés), but he was soon replaced by Pedro Juárez or Suárez. When the latter died, the encomienda escheated on 20 August 1550.[2]

Francisco de Santa Cruz held Tuzantla with a grant from Cortés (Millares Carlo and Mantecón, I, no. 497. Icaza, I, p. 66). In the early 1540s there was a three-way dispute over the revenues between Santa Cruz, Alonso de Mata, and Juan de Ortega. Escheatment occurred after Ortega's death, on 2 August 1546.[3]

Government

The Maravatio–Taximaroa area was looked after by the C of Ucareo (cf. Tlalpuxagua) until Maravatio escheated (it appears in a list of corregimientos dated 1550). Subsequently Taximaroa remained in the jurisdiction of the AM of Minas de Tlalpuxagua until the end of the century; during this period, the C of Maravatio was suffragan to Valladolid or Michoacán. Meanwhile, Tuzantla, which became a corregimiento in 1546, was

administered by the AM of Minas de Temazcaltepec during most of the sixteenth and seventeenth centuries.

Towards 1600 Taximaroa was transferred to the corregimiento of Maravatio and became the residence of the magistrate, soon re-designated AM. It was probably in the reforms of the 1680s that Tuzantla was attached to the jurisdiction of Maravatio. From 1692 distant Zamora y Xacona was also an *anexo* of this alcaldía mayor, an anomalous situation which prevailed until at

least 1759; the AM of the joint jurisdiction took up residence at Zitácuaro, which became the capital. From 1787 ('Zitácuaro y Angangueo' was a subdelegación in the intendencia of Valladolid.[4]

Church

S José Taximaroa may have been a secular parish before it was taken over by the Franciscans *c.* 1550 (Romero, 1861, IX, p. 1). By 1570 there were also secular doctrinas at S Juan Maravatio and S Francisco Tuzantla. In 1585 and later the curate of Maravatio was living at S Mateo Irimbo, but before 1700 each place had a resident priest. Meanwhile, the Franciscans established additional monastery-parishes at S Juan Bautista Zitácuaro (*c.* 1580), Santiago Tuxpan (*c.* 1602), and S Sebastián Chapatuato (by 1649; later abandoned). Secularization had occurred by 1770, although Tuxpan and Zitácuaro continued to have Franciscan cloisters until after Independence. S Mateo del Rincón appears as a separate Franciscan doctrina in 1743 but soon reverted to visita status.

Tarimangacho, a subject of Maravatio, was in the parish of Tlalpuxagua (q.v.), while Tiquichio (a dependency of Tuzantla) was visited in 1649–1743 from Purungueo (cf. Guaymeo y Sirándaro). The whole area was in the diocese of Michoacán.

Population and settlements

The native population, rather evenly distributed at contact, had the greatest early loss in the hot country. By 1570 it was reduced to 4,148 tributaries, 3,800 in Maravatio-Taximaroa and the rest at Tuzantla. The higher regions were more affected by subsequent epidemics and emigration. in 1600 there were *c.* 2,000 tributaries. Later censuses show 803 tributaries in 1657, 1,942 in 1698, 3,231 Indian families in 1743, and 5,845 Indian tributaries in 1801.[5] The language pattern here is most confusing. The original Tarascan population of Maravatio had been mostly replaced in 1649 by Mazahuan-speakers. Ponce in 1585 found four languages spoken at Zitácuaro, Tarascan, Otomí, Mazahuan, and Matlatzincan. In the Tuzantla area, alongside the original Tarascans and Náhuatl-speakers, Mazahuan immigrants are recorded in 1579 and later.

With the establishment of numerous haciendas, the non-Indian element became important in the seventeenth century. By 1743 there were 586 families of Spaniards and castas in Maravatio, 867 in Taximaroa, and 680 in Tuzantla (a large number of Negro slaves were omitted in this census). The 1801 count shows 1,203 mulatto tributaries in the jurisdiction.

At Taximaroa (1950: Ciudad Hidalgo) there may have been an attempt at congregation around the Franciscan monastery in the 1550s, and there was further concentration here in 1593–1604 when a number of settlements were eliminated and others moved closer to the centers of Taximaroa, Queréndaro, Tuxpan, and Zitácuaro. The last-mentioned place became a cabecera in the seventeenth century, at which time or soon afterward a Spanish *villa* was founded adjacent to the Indian town, with the name of Peñaranda de Bracamonte; since royal approval was withheld, the old name of Zitácuaro prevailed.

Maravatio (Maroatio, Marbatio; 1950: Maravatío, *villa*) also had a congregation in 1598–1604. The lands of at least two Otomí settlements, Pateo and Puchichamuco, were converted into haciendas at this time, while other places were abandoned. Angangueo became first an hacienda and later a mining center.

Far to the south in the hot country, Tuzantla (1950: pueblo) had fourteen small sujetos in 1579. Many of these were eliminated in a forced reduc-tion in 1594–1603, although in the latter year the congregation was 'falling apart', most Indians having fled to the old sites. By 1639 there were only four Indian pueblos here, the cabecera, Copándaro, Susupuato, and distant Tiquicheo; most of the others had been swallowed up by haciendas, including the vast Tiripetío sugar estate of the Jesuits. Only 88 Indian tributaries are registered in 1657. By 1743 there was an additional settlement, Chiranguengueo, a copper mining center.[6]

Sources

Tuzantla is omitted in the 1548 reports of the *Suma de Visitas* (PNE, I, nos. 366, 665), but its tribute assessments in 1545–66 survive (L de T, pp. 553–5). The jurisdiction is described briefly in two documents of the Ovando (1570–71) series (García Pimentel, 1904, pp. 45–6. Miranda Godínez, 9/36–9/37). There is an interesting relación, with map, of the corregimiento of Tuzantla, dated 1579.[7] Father Ponce (I, pp. 35–8, 54–5; II, pp. 151–2) went through the northern part of this area several times in 1585–7.

Congregation data can be gleaned from several sources.[8] We have valuable reports dated 1639[9] and 1649,[10] and tributary information for 1657–98.[11]

The AM's account of his jurisdiction in 1743 is of great interest.[12] This is followed by a list of pueblos dated 1793,[13] and the statistical summary of 1821 (Martínez de Lejarza, pp. 67–95).

54 *Metepec*

As will be seen, the extent of this jurisdiction underwent important changes, but in general it can be said that it comprised the upper reaches of the Lerma river, known during most of the colonial period as the valley of Matalcingo, together with certain headwaters of the Balsas system near Valle de Bravo, all in what is today the western part of the state of Mexico. Elevations range from 1,700 to 4,560 m (Nevado de Toluca), with most of the settlements at 2,400–3,000 m. The climate is cold with moderate rainfall.

The Matlatzinca, who had once been powerful here, were defeated by the Aztecs in a series of battles in the fifteenth century, the survivors emigrating to other places. At contact there were still Matlatzincan-speakers at Metépec, while the rest of the area was settled by Otomies and their relatives, the Mazahuans; there were also Náhuatl-speaking minorities. Metépec, Tlacotépec, Tlalchichilpan, and Tzinacantépec were native states subordinate, at least for tribute-collecting purposes, to Calixtlahuacan (cf. Toluca), where there was an Aztec garrison. Xiquipilco and Xocotitlan formed another Aztec tributary province which probably included the Mazahuan states of Ixtlahuacan and Atlacomulco. Four of these states (Atlacomulco, Xocotitlan, Ixtlahuacan, Tlalchichilpan) stretched westward from their principal settlements to the hostile Tarascan frontier; Atlacomulco was perhaps subject to incursions of Chichimecs on the northwest.

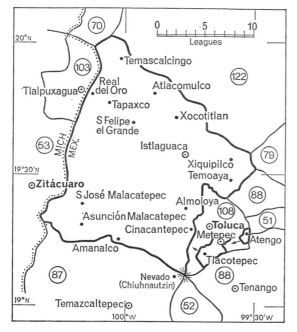

While the Otomies surrendered peaceably to the Spaniards, perhaps in 1520, there was a rebellion seemingly of Mazahuans led by Mexican garrison forces which was put down by an army under the command of Gonzalo de Sandoval in the late summer of 1521 (Gardiner, 1961, pp. 93–4. Herrera, 4a década, p. 231. Oviedo y Valdés, III, pp. 404–6).

Encomiendas

Both Atlacomulco and Xocotitlan were held by Francisco de Villegas until his death *c.* 1552 when he was succeeded by a son, Manuel, followed sometime between 1570 and 1593 by Pedro Villegas y Peralta. The encomienda escheated before 1597, but was subsequently re-assigned.[1]

Cinacantepec, which Cortés in 1532 claimed was subject to Toluca, was eventually assigned to the poblador and alguacil mayor Juan de Sámano, followed towards 1564 by a son, Juan de Sámano Turcios, who was still alive in 1626. Partial escheatment occurred before 1688.[2]

Istlaguaca was granted by Cortés to Juan de la Torre, on whose death *c.* 1535 it was taken for the crown. Soon afterward tributes were assigned to the royal mint, but they again escheated in 1544 (Dorantes de Carranza, p. 291. ENE, XV, pp. 94–5. Icaza, II, pp. 5, 35).

Metepec and Tepemaxalco (cf. Tenango del Valle), first claimed by Cortés, appear in 1534–6 as crown possessions, although they seem to have been held since 1528 in succession by Lic. Juan Gutiérrez Altamirano, Lope de Samaniego, Cristóbal de Cisneros, and Alonso de Avila.[3] Gutiérrez Altamirano recovered possession in 1536 and was succeeded in 1558 by a son, Hernán. By 1594 the holder was Juan Gutiérrez Altamirano, followed in 1610 by Fernando Altamirano y Velasco, who became first count of Santiago de Calimaya. Tributes were still going to this family in the eighteenth century.[4]

Tlacotepec, another place claimed in 1532 by Cortés as a subject of Toluca, was divided between two conquistadors, Gaspar de Garnica and Alonso de la Serna. Garnica's half was inherited before 1550 by his widow, and then (by 1560) by a son of the same name, and finally (towards 1600) by a grandson, Antonio de Garnica. De la Serna died in the 1560s and was followed by a son, Antonio Velázquez de la Serna; in 1595 Velázquez's widow, Isabel de Cárdenas, was encomendera. In 1597 Juana de la Cuadra is listed. Both parts of this encomienda seem to have been re-assigned, partial escheatment occurring before 1688.

Tlalchichilpa (also claimed by Cortés) was given to the conquistador Alonso de Avila, possibly a grant from viceroy Mendoza (Icaza, I, p. 83). A son, Antonio, inherited before 1550 and was still alive in 1597. Part of this encomienda escheated after 1643.

After an unknown early history and a brief crown tenure in 1534–6, Xiquipilco was held by Pedro Núñez, Maese de Roa, until his death between 1570 and 1597; in the latter year, Pedro Núñez de Chávez is listed. Escheatment occurred between 1643 and 1688.

Government

The first magistrates in the valley of Matalcingo may well have been appointees of Cortés (cf. Toluca), although the second audiencia sent Cs to Xiquipilco and Metepec y Tepemaxalco by 1534 at the latest. When these places reverted to private encomienda later in the 1530s, crown interests in the area were represented by the Cs of Talasco and Teutenango (cf. Lerma, Tenango del Valle). In 1551–5 we find a single magistrate administering the valley with the title of AM del valle de Matalcingo (or Toluca) and C of Istlaguaca.[5] It is not clear whether this official was named by the viceroy or the marquis, but evidently his jurisdiction included the crown and encomienda villages mentioned above, together with the suffragan corregimientos of Huicicilapa, Talasco, and Teutenango, and the encomiendas of Atlapulco, Calimaya, Capuluac, Cuapanoaya, Chichicuautla, Ocelotepec, Ocoyoacac, Tepexoyuca, Tepemaxalco, and Xalatlaco. In most sixteenth-century documents the jurisdiction is called Valle de Matalcingo.[6]

During the first sequestration of the marquisate, from 1570 to 1583, the AM was appointed by the viceroy. In 1583 an appointee arrived from Spain, and thereafter AMs were subject to royal appointment with a six-year tenure.[7] S Mateo Atengo, meanwhile, had been removed from the marquisate and made a crown village (*Memorial de los pleitos...*). Towards 1595 the third marquis regained the right to name magistrates in Toluca, after which the crown jurisdiction was generally referred to as Istlaguaca y Metepec.[8]

Seemingly in 1762 it was decided to name separate AMs in Istlaguaca (including Atlacomulco, Xiquipilco, and Xocotitlan) and Metepec y Cinacantepec (with Almoloya, Atengo, and Tlacotepec); at the same time, Huicicilapa and ten other cabeceras were transferred to the neighboring alcaldía mayor of Tenango del Valle.[9] From 1787 both Istlaguaca and Metepec were subdelegaciones in the intendencia of Mexico.

Metepec (see map) was divided, by the intrusion of Toluca, into various segments.

Church

The area was first visited by Franciscans who, working out of Toluca, founded doctrinas at S Juan Bautista Metepec and S Miguel Cinacantepec, probably in the 1550s. Cinacantepec was briefly (c. 1565–70) under secular clergy. By 1569 secular parishes had been established at S Miguel (later, Sta María, Guadalupe) Atlacomulco, S Francisco Istlaguaca, S Mateo Tlalchichilpa, and Santiago (S Juan) Xiquipilco. S Lucas Xocotitlan appears in a list of parishes held by seculars in 1575, and seems to have been definitely separated from Atlacomulco towards 1600, as was S Miguel Temascalcingo.[10] The parish center of Tlalchichilpa was moved to S Miguel Almoloya about the same time. S Mateo Atengo, a visita of Metepec, was a separate Franciscan doctrina for a time in the seventeenth century (Vera, p. 91).

We have no record of the founding of S Felipe Istlaguaca and Santiago Temoaya, both secular parishes in 1743. The two Malacatepecs, Asunción and S José, erstwhile visitas of Almoloya, together with S Gerónimo Amanalco, seem to have become parish centers after 1754, the year in which the Franciscan doctrinas were secularized. All parishes were in the archdiocese of Mexico.

Population and settlements

The number of tributaries is reported as 17,430 in 1570. Epidemics in 1576–81 and 1595–7 caused a drop to perhaps 8,470 at the century's end.[11] Further loss to 4,380 in 1643 may have been partly due to emigration, but there was a notable increase (7,555 tributaries in 1688, 14,150 Indian families in 1743, 20,558 Indian tributaries in 1801–4) with the establishment of new settlements in the northwestern part of the jurisdiction.[12]

The valley of Matalcingo was chosen by Cortés, very soon after the Conquest, as the chief center of experimentation in cattle breeding. Undoubtedly many Spaniards and castas went to live there, but we have practically no indication of their numbers. Only 207 mulatto tributaries are recorded in 1801–4.

S Mateo Atengo (1950: Atenco, pueblo) is said to have been the site of Cortés's first cattle estancia in 1528 (*Memorial de los pleitos...*). It was separated from Toluca, after a lengthy suit, in 1575.

Only three estancias are listed for Atlacomulco (1950: pueblo) in 1548–69, but there must have been many others. A congregation was proposed here in 1593. By 1643 there were two cabeceras, Atlacomulco (with six subject pueblos) and Temascalcingo (seven *sujetos*). Most of the people spoke Mazahuan.

S Miguel Cinacantepec (Tzinacantepec, etc.; 1950: Zinacantepec, *villa*), just west of Toluca, had some twenty-four estancias inhabited by Otomies in the sixteenth century. An attempted congregation in 1593 was a failure.[13] In 1603–4 it was proposed to collect twelve estancias at the cabecera, and twelve others at S Francisco Iztacapan, a half league away. Six of the latter, known as the estancias del Monte, were some five leagues west of Cinacantepec, and they were again ordered in 1604 to move, this time to S Gerónimo Amanalco. In the eighteenth century Amanalco and Cinacantepec each had eight subject pueblos.

Reports of 1569–94 list ten to twelve estancias near Istlaguaca (Ixtlahuaca; 1950: Ixtlahuaca de Rayón, *villa*), but there were others off to the west. Here again there were abortive congregations in 1593 and 1604. In 1792 there were two cabeceras, Istlaguaca (thirteen subject pueblos) and S Felipe el Grande del Obraje (eight pueblos).

Metepec (1950: *villa*) had five or six estancias, all nearby, in 1569. Of these, Magdalena (Sta María Ocotitlan), S Felipe, and S Francisco Cuaxusco survived a congregation in 1603. Two other pueblos listed in 1792, S Gaspar and Sta María Yancuitlalpa, may be later foundations.

Very close to Metepec was Tlacotepec (1950: pueblo), for which five estancias are listed in 1580.[14] They were all congregated in the quarter league between the cabecera and S Juan Ictzotitlan in 1603.

S Mateo Tlalchichilpa (1950: pueblo) had twenty-five estancias in 1569, some far to the west on the Michoacán border. The cabecera itself was moved to Almoloya (1950: Almoloya de Juárez, *villa*), an erstwhile estancia, while other congregations were made at Asunción Malacatepec (1950: Asunción Donato Guerra, *villa*) and S José Malacatepec (1950: S José Allende, *villa*), in 1604. Quite a number of settlements either remained *in situ* or were re-occupied, and new communities were founded. In 1792 the cabeceras here were Almoloya (seven sujetos), Asunción Malacatepec (ten), and S José (five sujetos).

In 1548, Xiquipilco (1950: S Juan Jiquipilco, pueblo) had twenty-three estancias, the cabecera being in a place called Ahuazhuatepeque. Permission was obtained in 1594 to move the cabecera half a league to a new site, Matlaguacala, in which the distant estancias were to be gathered.[15] A dissident group fled this congregation and set up a rival cabecera, at first called Santiago del Nuevo Xiquipilco, which later became Santiago Temoaya. In 1792 Xiquipilco had five subject pueblos, and Temoaya four.

Xocotitlan (1950: Jocotitlán, pueblo) formed a wedge between Atlacomulco and Istlaguaca, all three bordering on Michoacán. The principal western estancias of Xocotitlan were Tapaxco (Tapasco) and Cuauxumulco (Goajomulco), where congregations were made in 1604 of all the Analco settlements, as they were collectively called. In 1792 Xocotitlan had three subject pueblos and Tapaxco six, in addition to the recently (1787) discovered mines of Real del Oro.

The 1792 reports name 110 haciendas, mostly of *ganado mayor*, together with numerous ranchos and other places in the jurisdiction.

Sources

Alonso de Zorita (pp. 263–71) discusses land tenure and other subjects in the valley of Matalcingo before and after the Conquest. Not all the cabeceras are described in the 1548 *Suma de Visitas* (PNE, I, nos. 12, 117, 296, 562, 799, 801), but there is a good series of reports in 1569–71.[16] Father Ponce (I, pp. 30–34, 512–15; II, pp. 152–4) passed through here several times in 1585–6.

The congregations of 1593–1604 are discussed in several documents.[17] We have tribute assessments of 1623–88,[18] the journals of archiepiscopal visits in 1646[19] and 1685[20], and a description of the Franciscan doctrinas as they were *c.* 1697 (Vetancurt, 4a parte, pp. 73, 80, 85).

Villaseñor y Sánchez (I, p. 232*a*) summarizes a missing relación of *c.* 1743. There is a brief report drawn up for the Inquisition in 1754,[21] and there are lists of toponyms in the two *partidos* dated 1792.[22]

Other sources will be found in the indices of Colín (1966, 1967).

55 *Mexicalcingo*

Occupying part of a peninsula, or rather an isthmus between Lakes Texcoco and Xochimilco, with *chinampas* along the shore of the latter, this was the much reduced territory of the Colhuaque, masters of the valley of Mexico until they were defeated by the Mexica in the fourteenth century.

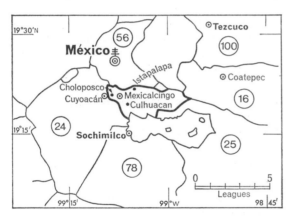

In 1519 there were four tlatoque, known collectively as the Nauhtecuhtli, all related to the Tenochtitlan dynasty, rulers of Colhuacan, Huitzilopochco, Iztapalapan, and Mexicaltzinco. Náhuatl was the predominant language, Otomí being spoken by a minority. Elevations range from 2,200 m at the lakeside to 2,460 m at Huixachtécatl (Cerro de la Estrella), between Colhuacan and Iztapalapan, where the 'New Fire' ceremony was held every 52 years (the last one was in 1507). The area is now in the Distrito Federal with the exception of Los Reyes, which belongs to the state of Mexico. The climate is cool with moderate rainfall.

First visited by Spaniards in late 1519, this region was occupied by them in the summer of 1521.

Encomiendas

Very soon after the fall of Tenochtitlan, the new Spanish city was given by Cortés the right to the tribute and labor of the four Colhua towns, together with nearby Cuitláhuac and Mixquic. However, in 1525 or shortly thereafter Mexicalcingo was made a crown holding, and the other places were re-distributed to private encomenderos with the exception of Istapalapa, which continued to serve the city of Mexico until it was taken by the crown in 1582.

The first encomendero of Culhuacan was Cristóbal de Oñate, followed on his death in 1568 by a son, Hernando. The latter was succeeded by a son, and perhaps a grandson, of the same name until the encomienda escheated *c.* 1659. It was later re-assigned, and in 1688 was held by the Count of Palma.

Huitzilopochco was given by Cortés to the conquistador Bernardino Vázquez de Tapia, but by 1529 it had escheated. After 1536 it was returned to the same encomendero, followed in 1559 by a son, and after 1604 by a grandson, both of the same name. It was still a private encomienda in 1688 (Teresa Maldonado Zapata was receiving tributes then) and later.

Government

Huitzilopochco and Mexicalcingo both became corregimientos under the second audiencia, the first combined with Mixquic, and Mexicalcingo joined with Zayula, far to the north. We have seen that Huitzilopochco reverted to private encomienda in the 1530s, and in the 1550s Mexicalcingo, now separated from Zayula, had a C with jurisdiction in adjacent encomiendas; in the following decade this magistrate was suffragan to the AM of Tezcuco. Los Reyes and Sta Marta, estancias of Tenochtitlan, were annexed somewhat later, perhaps in the late seventeenth century.

The magistrate was referred to as both C and AM, the latter title being more common after 1640. From 1786 he was a subdelegado in the intendencia of Mexico.

Church

The area was first visited by Franciscans from their monastery in Mexico city, from the 1520s. Two of their visitas became secular parishes at an early date, S Mateo Huitzilopochco (by 1548) and S Lucas Istapalapa (by 1570). Meanwhile, construction had begun in 1552 on an Augustinian monastery at S Juan Evangelista Culhuacan; this remained a regular establishment until 1756.[1] There was also a cloister of discalced Franciscans (Dieguinos) at Huitzilopochco from 1580.[2]

The Franciscans had small houses at S Marcos Mexicalcingo (by 1580), Sta Marta, and Natívitas Tepetlacinco (1682), the latter in the jurisdiction of Mexico city. These three were long only vicariates subordinate to the parish of S José de los Naturales, but Mexicalcingo survived as a separate doctrina (which included Natívitas) in the eighteenth century. The Franciscans were replaced by secular clergy in 1770, at which time Sta Marta seems to have been annexed to the parish of Istapalapa. All parishes were in the archdiocese of Mexico (Vera, *passim*).

Population and settlements

The earliest population data we have seen are for 1552, following a serious epidemic; in that year Culhuacan had 817 tributaries and Mexicalcingo 260. In 1570, when a larger proportion of the Indians was classified as tributary, there were 2,420 in the jurisdiction. Later censuses show c. 1,800 tributaries in 1580, 462 in 1644, 318 in 1692, 892 Indian families in 1743 (after the annexation of Sta Marta and Los Reyes), 1,761 in 1782, and 2,223 in 1801.[3]

Non-Indian residents here were few. In 1743 there were only 80 families, 31 of Spaniards and the rest castas.

We have what may be a complete list of sixteenth-century estancias in Culhuacan, partial lists for Istapalapa and Huitzilopochco, and nothing for Mexicalcingo; it is not always clear in these documents whether the places mentioned were sujetos in a political sense or visitas de doctrina.

Mexicalcingo (Mexicaltzinco; 1950: Mexicaltzingo, pueblo) and Huitzilopochco (which becomes Ocholopuchco, then [1743] Choloposco and [1792] Churubusco) had the smallest population and the fewest number of estancias. The latter in 1569 had eleven barrios and three estancias, all within a half league of the cabecera; the estancias survived as visitas of Mexicalcingo (Asunción, S Juan Nexticpac, Sta Cruz) in 1697, but in 1743 only the two cabeceras are mentioned.

The map accompanying the 1580 relación of Culhuacan (Culguacan; 1950: Culhuacán, pueblo) shows eighteen estancias surrounding the cabecera. While it gives only saints' names, the baptism register of 1588 has also the Náhuatl cognomens of most, with the addition of another barrio, Otomites. Most of these places seem to have disappeared in a congregation of 1599–1604.[4] Surviving as pueblos in 1743 were S Lorenzo Tesonco and Santiago Cagualtepec (Acahualtepec).

Istapalapa (Eztapalapa, Itztapalapa, etc.; 1950: Ixtapalapa) had fifteen barrios in 1570, but only five saints' names appear on the 1580 map; one of them, Sta María Astaguacan (Ixtahuacan) was a pueblo in 1743.

Two communities politically subject to Tenochtitlan, Sta Marta (Tequesquite, Tequesquiatenco; 1950: Sta Marta Acatitla, pueblo) and Los Reyes (Caxahuacan in 1697, Acaquilca in 1792; 1950: Los Reyes, pueblo), appear in the jurisdiction of Mexicalcingo in the eighteenth century. In 1792 there were three haciendas and two ranchos.

Sources

Of the four cabeceras, only Huitzilopochco has a brief article in the 1548 *Suma de Visitas* (PNE, I, no. 444), but there are tribute records for Mexicalcingo (1531–63) and Culhuacan (1552–65) (L de T, pp. 156, 239–41). The three parishes of 1570 are described in a partly published document.[5] For

1580, there are separate relaciones of the cabeceras of Culhuacan,[6] Istapalapa,[7] and Mexicalcingo (PNE, VI, pp. 193–8). A baptism register of Culhuacan, beginning in 1588, survives.[8]

Information about this area appears in the journal of an archbishop's visit in 1683,[9] and there are further data on the Franciscan vicariates in 1697 (Vetancurt, 4a parte, pp. 86, 88). In another series of documents tributary and encomienda information are found,[10] covering the period 1643–88.

There is a valuable report submitted by the AM in 1743,[11] followed by a relación of the 'topographic' series describing Mexicalcingo parish *c.* 1790,[12] and a list of toponyms dated 1792.[13]

Many further citations are found in Gibson (1964).

56 *Mexico*

In the center of the basin or 'valley' of México, 2,280 m above sea level, most of this area in 1519 was covered by the saline waters of Lake Texcoco. The final colonial jurisdiction is roughly conterminous with the modern city of México, D. F., which has a cool, dry climate much of the year,

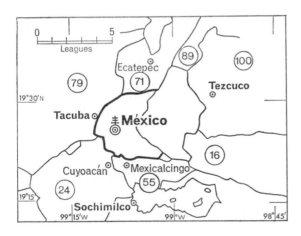

precipitation generally being confined to June–October.

The twin island-city of Tenochtitlan–Tlaltelolco was connected by causeways with the shore of the lake at Tepeyac on the north, Tlacopan and Chapultépec on the west, and Cuyoacan and Iztapalapan on the south. Tenochtitlan was the residence of the *hueytlatoani* or supreme ruler of the Mexica, an aggressive tribe which had dominated its neighbors for almost a century and was the leading member of the so-called Triple Alliance (the others were the Tepaneca of Tlacopan [cf. Tacuba] and the Acolhuaque of Texcoco [q.v.]), a military confederation to which most of central Mexico paid tribute (see Map 2). Tlaltelolco, adjoining Tenochtitlan to the north, was a division of the Mexica with its own hereditary ruler until it was subjugated by its neighbor in the 1470s; thereafter it had a military governor (*cuauhtlatoani*) appointed from Tenochtitlan. The immediate political influence of these two states did not extend very far, being confined to a number of villages on the lake shore and the surrounding mountain slopes. The Mexica spoke Náhuatl, but other languages must have been heard, notably Otomí. This was probably the largest urban concentration in the world (outside the Far East) when first seen by the Spaniards.

Hernando Cortés and his followers reached Tenochtitlan on November 8, 1519, but were expelled from the city the following June. The Mexica were defeated, and Tenochtitlan was occupied by the Spaniards after a prolonged siege in August 1521.

Encomiendas

While Indian tributes of Tenochtitlan seem to have reached private hands in the years immediately following the Conquest, they were assigned to the crown *c.* 1525 (Gibson, 1964, p. 427). Tlaltelolco was at first a crown possession, then was briefly held by Diego de Ocampo and by Cortés himself before escheating (by 1529) (*ibid.*, 432–3).

Government

The Spanish ayuntamiento, established in Cuyoacan immediately after the capture of the Mexica capital, moved to Tenochtitlan at the beginning of 1524. This body had vast jurisdictional pretensions, claiming that its limits included all of New Spain where there was no other Spanish settlement (*Actas de cabildo*..., I, p. 160; II, pp. 14, 34; IV, p. 144). In 1532 the audiencia declared that the municipal jurisdiction extended only five leagues from the city (ENE, II, p. 221. Puga, fol. 86). Seven years later this was increased to fifteen leagues, but by this time the real boundaries of the city, surrounded as it was by encomiendas and corregimientos, were established (see map) (*Actas de cabildo*..., IV, p. 207). Still the Spanish ayuntamiento attempted for some years more to extend its influence by sending out alguaciles and issuing land grants in other jurisdictions. Furthermore, the native governments of Tenochtitlan and Tlatelolco continued to control their distant dependencies (*see below*).

México-Tenochtitlan was the residence first of the *gobernador* of Nueva España (from 1524), then of the royal audiencia (from 1529) and the viceroy (from November 1535). Locally, justice was administered in the Spanish part of the city at first by alcaldes ordinarios elected annually in the cabildo, while each of the two Indian parts, S Juan Tenochtitlan and Santiago Tlatelolco, had its own governor (until 1565 the Indian governor of Tenochtitlan was a descendant of the pre-Conquest dynasty). Native cabildos were introduced in the 1540s.[1]

1574 marks the arrival of the first C of Mexico city, sent out by the council of the Indies.[2] Thereafter, with occasional lapses when the ordinary alcaldes took charge, the C was the chief municipal magistrate.[3] Appointment to this office was almost always made in Spain. From 1787 the C of Mexico became an intendente, with a considerably enlarged supervisory jurisdiction (Beleña, II, pp. iv–v).

Church

In 1524 the secular parish of Santiago Tenochtitlan was founded for the Spaniards, and the Franciscan doctrina of S José de los Naturales for the Indians. Each had numerous visitas, some of which later became separate parishes. Santiago became a cathedral parish (Nuestra Señora de los Remedios, Asunción) when the first bishop arrived in 1528 (there was a legalistic argument about this until the bishop, Zumárraga, was consecrated in 1533). Additional secular parishes dating from the sixteenth century were Sta Catalina Mártir (1537) and Sta Vera Cruz (1568). Each of the four Indian barrios of Tenochtitlan (see below) was made a Franciscan visita. Of these, S Juan Bautista retained that category; S Pablo was secularized in the 1560s and then (1575) turned over to the Augustinians; S Sebastián was ministered by Carmelite friars from 1585 and by Augustinians in 1607–36, after which it was a secular parish; and Sta María de la Redonda became a separate Franciscan doctrina. Two other regular parishes were created in the sixteenth century, Santiago Tlatelolco (Franciscan from 1543?) and Sta Cruz Cotzinco (Augustinian).

S Miguel was a secular parish from 1692, Nuestra Señora de Guadalupe from 1702, and S Antonio de las Huertas (until then a Franciscan visita) from 1762. In the early 1770s the regular orders were relieved of parochial duties and all doctrinas were secularized, although the cloisters continued in operation. Sta Cruz Acatlan, S Matías Ixtacalco, and Sta Ana, all former Franciscan visitas, became secular parishes at this time, as did Sto Tomás de la Palma (formerly an Augustinian visita of Cotzinco parish) and Concepción Salto de Agua (a visita of Vera Cruz).[4]

The city of Mexico was the residence of the bishop (1528–47) and archbishop (from 1547), and a provincial center of the various regular orders.

Population and settlements

Gibson (1964, p. 378) guesses that the native population of Tenochtitlan–Tlatelolco in 1519 was between 250,000 and 400,000 persons. A great many died from smallpox in 1520, and more during the siege of 1521. Thereafter there were considerable fluctuations caused by migrations and periodic epidemics. There was usually a large floating population of Indians from all over the country. The number of native tributaries is estimated at 20,000 in 1560, 9,952 in 1569, 7,349 in 1581, 7,630 in 1644, 8,400 in 1743, and 9,672 in 1800–1.[5] Within the city, there was a movement of Indians from Tlatelolco to Tenochtitlan in the late seventeenth century (Gibson, 1964, pp. 378–9).

Mexico city had the greatest concentration of Europeans, mestizos, and mulattoes in New Spain, although their number also varied greatly from one period to another. Householders (vecinos) classified as Spanish numbered perhaps 2,000 in 1550, 3,000 in 1560–70, 4,000 in 1580, 7,000 in 1610, and 12,000 (60,872 persons) in 1790 (*Gazeta de México*, tomo v, no. 1, 10 Jan. 1792). Figures for mestizos and mulattoes, quite unreliable, show 3,000 persons in 1560, and 26,450 in 1790. In 1800 there were 418 mulatto tributaries. Other minorities (e.g. non-Spanish Europeans, Filipinos) were insignificant, but there were probably a good many Negro slaves.

On several occasions there were temporary losses of magnitude. In 1534, while the Indian population was increasing, the Spaniards were 'less than half what they had been', many having left for Spain and Perú (*Actas de cabildo...*, iii, p. 89. Gibson, 1964, p. 378). After a series of floods in the early 1630s the city was almost abandoned, and a great many (perhaps 40,000 persons) died in the epidemic of 1736–9. Cooper (1965, pp. 185–6) estimates that there were at least 50,000 premature deaths in various epidemics between 1761 and 1813. The late eighteenth-century plagues, unlike earlier ones, affected both whites and castas as well as Indians.

In 1519–21 Tenochtitlan and Tlatelolco shared an island which occupied about four square miles in Lake Texcoco. It was only a few feet above the lake level, but Tlatelolco was slightly higher than its neighbor. Each was composed of greater and lesser subdivisions, and each had subordinate villages scattered about on the shores of the lake and elsewhere, some of them in what became neighboring jurisdictions (cf. Gibson, 1964, maps on pp. 374–5).

Tenochtitlan was divided into four sections, Atzacualco, Cuepopan or Tlaquechiuhcan, Moyotlan, and Teopan or Zoquipan. Under the Spaniards, these became the barrios of S Sebastián, Sta María, S Juan, and S Pablo, respectively. The Spaniards placed their quarter in the very center, taking slices of each barrio. In later years, despite orders to maintain racial segregation, the distinction between Indian and non-Indian quarters was not strictly adhered to. Certain groups of Indians from distant areas, notably Otomíes, Tarascans, and Tlaxcalans, settled within the city in sufficient numbers to form distinct political units which were recognized by the Spanish authorities.

For reasons not entirely clear, the level of Lake Texcoco began dropping in the early 1520s, and by 1550 it was so low that the shore had receded to some distance east of the city, leaving it surrounded no longer by water but with marshy lowlands. Thereafter heavy rains brought occasional disastrous floods, such as that of 1555 and those beginning in 1629 which covered most of the valley for four years and hastened the construction of the famous desagüe (actually begun in 1608 and finished in 1789), through which the waters of the valley's lakes were given an outlet northward to the Tula river. Despite their precarious situation, numerous suburban villages were established in the flat country on all sides of the city. Among the outer settlements which survived as pueblos in the eighteenth century were S Andrés Ahuehuetepanco, Acatlan (Sta Cruz de los Rastreros), Atlapahuaca, Atzacualco, Coatlayuca, Cuezcontitlan (S Lucas de los Carniceros), Chapultepec, Ixtacalco, Macuitlapilco, Natívitas Tepetlatzinco, Nonoalco, Popotla, Guadalupe Tepeyac, and Sta Ana Zacatlalmanco; another was S Antonio de las Huertas, re-named Villa de Mancera in 1667. Popotla was in the neighboring jurisdiction of Tacuba until the eighteenth century, and Chapultepec was claimed by Cuyoacan.

Sources

Scholarly attention has long been directed to Mexico city's past, and because so much has been published on the subject, this jurisdiction has been given only summary treatment here. Gibson's (1964) excellent monograph is perhaps the best general treatment. Caso (1956) discusses the old barrios, and Gardiner (1956) has much original material in his essay on the siege of Tenochtitlan.

Some of the more notable maps and plans of the city and its environs are described and reproduced in another publication (Toussaint, Gómez de Orozco, and Fernández, 1938). The Actas de Cabildo, beginning in 1524, have been published (1889–1916). There is still a vast amount of unexploited material in the archives, especially at AGN.

In the Ovando series (1569–71), we have reports from both secular and regular parishes.[6] The Náhuatl 'Códice del Tecpan de Santiago Tlatelolco (1576–1581)' has been translated and published (Fernández and Leicht, 1939). A relación geográfica and map made *c.* 1580 remain undiscovered.

Several reports of parochial visits, the earliest made in 1683–5, are found in the Archiepiscopal Archive in the cathedral.[7] The Franciscan parishes *c.* 1697 are described by Vetancurt (4a parte, 42, 67, 83, 87–8). Villaseñor y Sánchez (I, pp. 31–61, seems to have based his description of the city as it was *c.* 1744 on personal observation and access to official sources.

There are useful accounts by travelers who visited Mexico city at different periods. Among them were Ponce (I, pp. 174–82) in 1585, Cobo (pp. 205–7) in 1630, Gemelli Carreri (I, pp. 41–8) in 1697, and Ajofrín (I, pp. 61–94) in 1763–4.

57 *Meztitlan*

This area, now in northern Hidalgo state, is bisected by the Sierra Madre Oriental (Sierra de Metztitlán, elevations to 2,600 m) into two principal drainage systems, the Amajac and the Claro rivers, which flow northward and eventually meet and join the Moctezuma (Pánuco) river; the land in the north falls to 200 m. Other streams in the northeast also eventually reach the Pánuco. The climate is most varied, with precipitation increasing from the extremely arid southwest to the quite rainy northeast, and with notable extremes of temperature depending on the altitude. It is a very broken, mountainous country of difficult communication (most of it can still be reached only on foot or horseback), some of it heavily forested.

Not much is known of the political structure of Metztitlan as the Spaniards found it, but all sources agree that it was a militarily powerful state, or more likely a confederation, unsubdued by and frequently at war with the Triple Alliance. Metztitlan itself was hemmed in on the west, south, and east by hostile territory, Ixmiquilpan, Actopan, Atotonilco, and Hueyacocotlan. To the north and northeast, Malilla, Mollanco, Tlachinolticpac, Xochicuauhtlan, Cuezalinco, Yahualiuhcan, and Ilamatlan were most probably autonomous states either tributary to or allied with the tlatoani of Metztitlan; farther to the north were the hostile Huaxtecans. Atlihuetzian and Tianguistenco were either directly subject to Metztitlan or autonomous regions under its hegemony. On the northern frontier, the rulers of Huexotla and Macuilxóchitl were unfriendly to Metztitlan. At Macuilxóchitl a sedentary population of Nahua- and Otomí-speakers was mixed with Chichimec (Pame) nomads (ENE, II, pp. 20–21). Between Macuilxóchitl and Metztitlan was a wild, rugged area known variously as Tenanco, Cuezalatenco, or Chichicaxtla, inhabited by Pame Chichimecs seemingly dominated by Metztitlan. Except for Tenanco, the people of Metztitlan and its allies spoke an archaic variety of Náhuatl. They lived dispersed in a great many settlements.

Soon after the fall of Tenochtitlan, the tlatoque of Metztitlan and its allies sent a peace embassy to Cortés, but subsequently (in 1523?) they rebelled. A Spanish-led army reduced the area after several battles (Cortés, p. 206). By mid-1524 resistance had ceased, but Chichimecs were still raiding here in the 1580s.[1]

Encomiendas

Perhaps the first holders of Meztitlan were Miguel Díaz (Díez) de Aux and Alonso Lucas, both conquistadors. In 1525 the acting governors reassigned Díaz's share, which subsequently was given to Andrés de Barrios, a poblador and brother-in-law of Cortés. Towards 1535 Lucas sold his half to Alonso de Mérida (ENE, VII, p. 82). Meanwhile, Díaz de Aux sued Barrios for recovery of his share, and after years of litigation the council of the Indies decided that a third of the

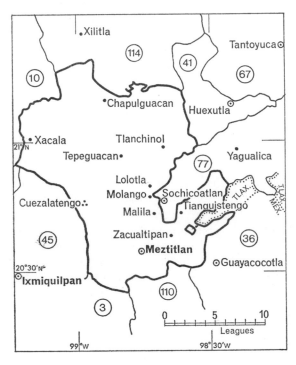

Barrios half of the tributes should go to Díaz de Aux (Díaz del Castillo, I, pp. 421–2. Dorantes de Carranza, p. 216. ENE, VII, p. 115. Millares Carlo and Mantecón, II, no. 1839). On Barrios's death *c.* 1550 his part of the encomienda (with the Díaz de Aux deduction) was inherited by a daughter, Isabel de Barrios, married to Diego de Guevara (ENE, VI, p. 125. Simpson, 1950, pp. 146–7). In 1553 the royal visitador Diego Ramírez, in a combination of zeal and pique, took the Guevara and Mérida shares for the crown, but his action was revoked by the audiencia early the following year. Very soon after this, Alonso de Mérida died and was succeeded by a son, Francisco de Mérida y Molina, who in turn was followed *c.* 1600 by his daughter, Mariana de Mérida, married to Fran-

cisco de Quintana Dueñas (Dorantes de Carranza, p. 269). Doña Mariana died shortly before 1623, at which time the Mérida half escheated (Scholes and Adams, 1959, p. 65). In the meantime, the Barrios share continued to be held by Doña Isabel after Guevara's death (by 1604 she had remarried, to Diego de Guzmán); in the 1560s a third of this share was going to Rodrigo Maldonado, who had married Luisa de Aux, daughter of the deceased conquistador. Part of Meztitlan's tributes were still in private encomienda in the eighteenth century.

Tenango and Cuezalatengo (Chichicastla) were included in the encomienda of Meztitlan during the sixteenth century, although they had a separate tribute assessment. By 1643 the crown's share of the tributes was going to Juan de Andrada Moctezuma.

Macuilsúchil, later known as Chapulguacán, while it may once have been held by Hernán Martín, was included in the patrimony of Isabel Moctezuma, the emperor's daughter and wife first of Cuauhtémoc, then of Alonso de Grado, Pedro Gallego, and Juan Cano (Gibson, 1964, p. 423. Icaza, I, pp. 31, 253). Isabel died *c.* 1550, and Juan Cano turned his rights over to a mestizo son, Pedro, in 1560. Pedro Cano was followed by his daughter, María, in the 1570s (she is still listed in 1597). Escheatment occurred after 1643.

Governor Estrada towards 1526 assigned Molango and Malila to Gerónimo de Aguilar, a Spaniard who had been shipwrecked in Yucatán and lived for years among the Indians until he was rescued by Cortés in 1519. When Aguilar died without issue, his encomiendas escheated on 7 November 1531.[2]

Tianguistengo was granted to Alonso Gutiérrez de Badajoz, followed before 1548 by his widow, who seems to have then married successively Hontañón de Angulo and Francisco de Temiño or Tremino; the latter appears as encomendero from 1551 into the late 1570s. María Mosquera was encomendera in 1597–1604. Tributes escheated between 1643 and 1688.

The encomienda of Tlanchinolticpac was disputed in early years between Pánuco and Nueva España. Gil González Trujillo was the holder in

1527 when Nuño de Guzmán had him executed and assigned the place to Andrés de Inero (Chipman, pp. 151–5). The second audiencia later (before 1534) split the encomienda, assigning Cuimantlan and a group of estancias to Alonso Ortiz de Zúñiga, and the principal cabecera to Gerónimo de Medina (L de T, p. 339). Each was succeeded by a son of the same name, Medina in the 1550s and Ortiz in 1568. The second Gerónimo de Medina was followed towards 1565 by a daughter, Ana, who married Juan de Montejo (listed in 1580–97). A third Alonso Ortiz de Zúñiga is mentioned in 1597–1604 (Dorantes de Carranza, p. 159). Both shares escheated before 1643, but part of the tributes were re-assigned to the Moctezuma heirs.

Government

In late 1527 and early 1528 there was a brief but acrimonious border dispute between the gobiernos of Nueva España and Pánuco concerning jurisdiction in Tlanchinolticpac and adjacent encomiendas (cf. Sochicoatlan) (Chipman, pp. 151–5). After 1533, when Pánuco was annexed to Nueva España, the conflict ended.

Meanwhile, in November, 1531, a C was sent to the first crown encomienda here, Molango y Malila. In 1550 this magistrate was given jurisdiction as justicia mayor in nearby private encomiendas with instructions to remedy abuses, but when visitador Ramírez arrived at Meztitlan three years later he found that the C had been suborned by the powerful encomenderos there.[3] Ramírez then seized Meztitlan for the crown. The audiencia, however, soon returned it to its former holders. In the 1560s and 1570s the C of Molango y Malila was referred to as AM of the province of Meztitlan, with suffragan jurisdiction in numerous adjoining corregimientos. The AM directly administered Atlehuecian, Cicoac–Chicontepec, Chapulguacan, Chichicastla, Guautla, Guayacocotla, Guazalingo, Ilamatlan, Meztitlan, Molango y Malila, Tianguistengo, and Tlanchinolticpac. The limits of this realm were much reduced with the separation of Guayacocotla in the 1590s, of Sochicoatlan and Yagualica a decade later, and the loss of suffragan powers and transference of

encomiendas to neighboring jurisdictions.[4] Early in the seventeenth century the final boundaries of Meztitlan were fairly well established; perhaps the latest change was the loss of Xilitla to Valles.[5] From 1787 'Meztitlan de la Sierra' was a subdelegación in the intendencia of Mexico.

Church

Augustinians entered the Sierra de Meztitlan in 1536, their first doctrina being that of Sta María (Nuestra Señora de Loreto) Molango. Stos Reyes (later, S Antonio) Meztitlan dates as an Augustinian parish from c. 1537. S Agustín Tlanchinolticpac, S Pedro Chapulguacan, and Nuestra Señora de Monserrate Chichicastla became separate doctrinas in 1545–8, c. 1557, and before 1570, respectively.[6] Sta María Zacualtipan was made a priorate in 1578, while Sta Catarina Lolotla had resident friars from 1593. Santiago Tepeguacan and Sta Ana Tianguistengo seem to have been seventeenth-century Augustinian foundations, while Chichicastla was abandoned. The parish center of Chapulguacan was moved to the mining center of S Antonió Xacala and was secularized in 1770. Secularization of the remaining regular doctrinas began in the 1750s, although Meztitlan was kept by the Augustinians until after Independence. All parishes were in the archdiocese of Mexico.

Population and settlements

The number of Indian tributaries fell from 17,900 in 1560 to 15,800 in 1570, 12,750 at the end of the century, 3,570 in 1643, and only 2,190 in 1688 (ENE, VII, p. 123. L de T, p. 340. Scholes and Adams, 1959, pp. 60–61, 65). The 1743 count shows 5,458 Indian families, while in 1797 there were 7,313 Indian tributaries.[7]

Only '15 to 20' non-Indian families are reported at Meztitlan in 1743, but there were 607 mulatto tributaries in the jurisdiction in 1797.

According to the 1579 relación, the realm of Meztitlan was divided after the Conquest by Cortés, who distributed the various parts in encomienda. We find no reason to believe, however, that Cortés did not follow, here as elsewhere, an already established division, and we assume that the relationship of outlying estancias to cabeceras which prevailed at mid-sixteenth century in most cases faithfully reflected the pre-Conquest political arrangement. The settlement pattern was remarkably dispersed. There were probably at least two attempts at congregation, first in the 1550s or 1560s and again in the 1590s and early 1600s.

Meztitlan (Metztitlan, Mestitlan de la Sierra; 1950: Metztitlán, *villa*) in 1573 had somewhat more than 120 dependent settlements, although the 1570 report names only seventy-four of them (the visita of *c.* 1548 gives forty estancia names, nine of which do not appear in the 1570 list); some were as much as 14 leagues from the cabecera. The latter was moved towards 1539, by the Augustinians, from the bank of a river where it had been destroyed in a flood to a ledge levelled off on the cliffside above (McAndrew, p. 269). A congregation was proposed here in 1593 and again in 1599, but we do not know the results. Some twenty-four places mentioned as estancias in 1548–70 appear as pueblos in the 1950 census; one of them at least, Tlahuelumpa, became a separate cabecera.

Documents of 1548–53 mention a cabecera of Tenango, a name often coupled with that of Cuezalatengo (Quetzalatengo) (ENE, VII, pp. 116–17). This was a dependency of Meztitlan consisting of a number of Chichimec rancherías in the Sierra of Cuyamatepec, bounded by Meztitlan, Macuilsúchil, and Ixmiquilpan. When the Augustinians founded a mission here towards 1565 they built their monastery in one of the rancherías, Chichicastla (Cicicastla, Tzitzicaxtla; 1950: Chichicaxtla, pueblo). The 1548 visita gives Náhuatl names of eleven estancias and mentions nine others, while a report of 1570 names Chichicastla, Tenango, and ten other places (only the saints' names are given) within five leagues. Some of these can be identified with 1950 census toponyms, among them seven pueblos.

At Macuilsúchil, also, the Augustinians chose an estancia, Chapulguacan (1950: Chapulhuacán), for their monastery site. In 1548 there were nine estancias (named in the report) together with fifty-four lesser settlements. The 1570 report names eighteen places within 12 leagues of the cabecera, while that of 1573 says there were twenty-one. These had been reduced to three pueblos and three rancherías by 1684. Subsequently the real de minas of Xacala was founded at or near Sta Catarina Xacalan, a former estancia; the surviving pueblos were perhaps Acapa, S Nicolás, and Tlahuitecpan (Tlahuiltepa).

Malila (1950: pueblo) had many estancias within ten leagues of the cabecera, interspersed with settlements subject to Molango. The names of nine are given in 1548, and twenty-two in 1571, by which time the cabecera had been moved to Lolotla (Loloctlan; 1950: Lolotla, pueblo). A congregation document of 1599 lists five sujetos not mentioned in 1548–71. In 1684 the Augustinians visited sixteen pueblos from Lolotla, but we cannot be certain that these were all politically subject to Lolotla–Malila. Besides the two cabeceras, four places identifiable with former estancias appear in the 1950 census.

The estancias of Molango (1950: pueblo) are named in the reports of 1548 and 1571, but in the former ten places are repeated under Malila! Conceivably they were divided between the two cabeceras. Three others in the 1548 list can be added to the eighteen toponyms mentioned in 1571, the most distant being 8½ leagues from its cabecera. The latter was moved *c.* 1545 when the Augustinians chose for their monastery a higher site, on the boundary between Molango and Malila (McAndrew, p. 224). Thirteen pueblos de visita are mentioned but not named in 1684, and ten or eleven survived as pueblos in 1950.

Tianguistengo (Tianguiztenco, etc.; 1950: Tianguistengo, pueblo) in 1548 had 16 dependencies, some of which are further identified in documents of 1570 and 1604; they were spread out in a line reaching ten leagues from the cabecera, sandwiched in between Sochicoatlan and Ilamatlan. A congregation seems to have occurred here towards 1604–5 in which certain of these places were abandoned. Mastlatla, Ochpantla, and Zoyatla were among the surviving settlements, as were Tenexco, Tlacuechac, and Zacatipan, which in the sixteenth century were listed as estancias under both Tianguistengo and Sochicoatlan. Tlacolula, a cabecera in the eighteenth century, was perhaps within the limits of Tianguistengo.

We have mentioned that Tlanchinolticpac (Tlachinoltipac; Tlanchinol in 1604 and later; 1950: Tlanchinol, pueblo) was divided in the 1530s into two parts, perhaps for convenience in separating the tributes between two encomenderos. Both parts, Tlanchinolticpac and Cuimantlan (1950: Acuimantla, pueblo), appear as cabeceras in 1548, but subsequently Cuimantlan and its estancias are listed under the main cabecera. In 1573 there were more than eighty *sujetos*, seventy of which are named in the 1570 report; they were scattered around in the mountains and below in the hot country, up to 12 leagues from the cabecera. Several attempts were made to reduce their number in the 1590s and later. Only twenty-four pueblos de doctrina are named in 1684, although others of the old estancias are recognizable as pueblos in the 1950 census. Among them, Ihuitepec and Tepeguacan were considered cabeceras in the eighteenth century.

Sources

All cabeceras as they were *c.* 1548 are described in the *Suma* (PNE, I, nos. 132, 352–5, 516–18). There is a good deal of material about the Ramírez visit in 1553–4 (ENE, VII and VIII, *passim*. Scholes, 1946), and a friar's report dated 1554 gives valuable details about the situation at contact (ENE, XVI, pp. 56–62). The various Augustinian doctrinas are covered in several documents of the Ovando series (*c.* 1570–1),[8] and in another report of 1573.[9] The 1579 relación submitted by the AM, accompanied by a map, while deficient in some details, is of interest for the pre-Conquest period.[10]

For the congregations of 1593–1605, we have detailed reports concerning Malila-Lolotla[11] and part of Tlanchinol,[12] with some other scattered data.[13] Several sources give seventeenth-century tributary information.[14] The journal of an archbishop's visit in 1684 is of interest.[15]

We have been singularly unsuccessful in unearthing documents describing Meztitlan in the late colonial period. Only the résumé of a lost relación (*c.* 1743) in Villaseñor y Sánchez (I, pp. 129–32) and a partial census of 1809[16] have come to light.

Byam Davies (1968) analyzes numerous sources to determine the pre-Conquest extent of Meztitlan. The massive work of Fernández (1940–2) is a mine of information about this area.

58 *Miaguatlan*

This region in south central Oaxaca has both inland and seaward slopes of the Sierra Madre del Sur, draining northwest into the Atoyac, northeast to the Tehuantepec river, and southward directly to the Pacific. Elevations range from 150 to over 3,000 m. There is heavy seasonal rainfall in the higher mountains, which are forested, while the lower parts are dry and barren on the north, and covered with a dense xerophytic growth on the south.

There were four populous Zapotec states here at contact. Miahuatlan (Zapotecan, Guichitoo, or Pelopenitza) and Coatlan (Huihuogui) were within the Aztec sphere of influence, with rulers appointed from Tenochtitlan. Miahuatlan was a great market center, and Coatlan had a garrison to defend the frontier against hostile Tototépec.

Farther east in the mountains were Amatlan (Coatila) and Ocelotépec (Quiahuechi), the former perhaps independent. Quiahuechi was a Zapotec colony with a ruler related to the dynasty of Pelopenitza, in a rugged area which had belonged to the Chontales three generations earlier; according to the 1580 relación, it was tributary to the Aztecs and on bad terms with its Chontal, Mixe, and Nahua neighbors, the last-mentioned being dominated from Tototépec. The Zapotecan spoken by these people was 'corrupt' except at Amatlan, where the natives spoke the 'polished' language of the valley of Huaxyacac, having originally come from Cimatlan.

Pedro de Alvarado is credited with subduing this area in 1522–3, but there was a serious rebellion at Coatlan beginning in 1525 and lasting two years (Díaz del Castillo, II, p. 247. ENE, I, p. 94. Herrera, 3a década, pp. 284–5). This, together with an uprising in neighboring Tetiquipa in 1547–8 which spread to Miahuatlan, seem to have been motivated by pre-Christian religious fervor, although another reason adduced for the Coatlan revolt was the encomendero's ill-treatment of his charges.

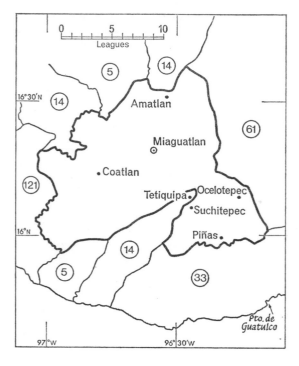

Encomiendas

Amatlan was assigned to a 'Gallardo' (perhaps Pedro Gallardo, a conquistador and resident of Los Angeles in 1534), and escheated *c.* 1535.

Coatlan and Miaguatlan are linked in a confusing encomienda history. Both may have been assigned by Cortés to a favorite and kinsman, Diego Becerra de Mendoza, whose encomiendas were taken from him by the first audiencia on the pretext that he was the grandson of a heretic, and re-assigned to Andrés de Monjarraz (ENE, I, pp. 143–4). According to the 1580 relación, the double encomienda was shared between two conquistador brothers, Gregorio ('el sordo') and Pedro de Monjarraz, until the latter lost his half

because of his cruel treatment of the Indians. Another source mentions that Gregorio's brother was the captain Andrés de Monjarraz (Dorantes de Carranza, p. 197). From still another, we learn that Coatlan was shared in April, 1528, between Alonso de Paz and his brother-in-law, Cristóbal de Salamanca (Millares Carlo and Mantecón, I, nos. 96, 1207). By 1545 Paz's share had been given in dowry to a niece, the daughter of Juan de Salamanca, when she married the oidor Diego de Loaisa (Berlín, 1947, p. 35). Three years later, we find both Coatlan and Miaguatlan divided equally between Loaisa and Mateo de Monjarraz, the latter identified in 1560 as a son of the 'first' holder. In the early 1560s Diego de Loaisa renounced his rights in favor of a son, Alonso de Loaisa de Paz, who in turn was succeeded (before 1592) by his widow, Juana Calvo, and in 1606 by Diego de Loaisa y Paz, son of Alonso and grandson of the oidor.[1] Meanwhile, by 1597 the Monjarraz share had been inherited by Gregorio de Monjarraz, son of Mateo, and it escheated on the latter's death before 1609.

Cortés assigned Ocelotepec to Alonso Martín Rieros or Riberos (ENE, IV, pp. 46–7). Rieros was killed by the Indians of his encomienda towards 1540, at which time the place escheated, but it was soon re-assigned by viceroy Mendoza to Alonso Ruiz, doorkeeper of the audiencia. Shortly after 1560, Ruiz died and was followed by a son, Andrés Ruiz de Rosas, still listed as encomendero in 1609.

Government

A C was first appointed to Amatlan y Cozautepec on 7 November 1535 (L de T, p. 34). As a result of the apostasies uncovered at Coatlan (1544) and Tetiquipa (1547) (*see below*), crown officers from Antequera controlled the area for some years. In the 1550s Chichicapa and Amatlan were put under a single C who also administered Coatlan, Miaguatlan, and Ocelotepec (the latter had briefly been a corregimiento in the 1540s). This magistrate, who lived at Miaguatlan from 1577, was subordinate to the AM of Antequera until the early seventeenth century. Towards 1600 Chichicapa became a separate alcaldía mayor; Miaguatlan,

Amatlan, Coatlan, and Ocelotepec thereafter had their own magistrate, re-designated AM *c.*1640, and subdelegado (intendencia of Oaxaca) from 1787.

Church

The Dominicans visited this area in early years, relinquishing S Pablo Coatlan to the secular clergy towards 1538, and S Andrés Miaguatlan in 1568; S Juan Ocelotepec had a secular priest from the 1540s. S Luis Amatlan, visited from Miaguatlan in 1570 and from Zoquitlan (cf. Nexapa) in 1580-2, became a secular parish as a result of the congregations soon after 1600, as did Sta María (Asunción) Ocelotepec in 1607. This last doctrina was further divided in 1699, when a priest was assigned to S Mateo Piñas. All parishes were in the diocese of Antequera.

Certain villages politically subject to Miaguatlan were visited from parish seats (Exutla, Loxicha, Río Hondo) in adjoining jurisdictions. The parish of Piñas included places subject to Guatulco.

Population and settlements

More than most of New Spain, this area was affected by violent death in early years. The Indians of Coatlan reportedly killed 50 Spaniards and from 8,000 to 10,000 Indian slaves in the 1525 revolt, and a great many of the rebels in turn died in the ensuing repression. In 1547 the insurgents of Tetiquipa and Ocelotepec descended on Miaguatlan and are said to have killed more than 10,000 Indians. There were 4,100 tributaries in the entire jurisdiction in 1580, 3,490 in 1597, and 2,434 in 1609. The 1745 census has 2,944 Indian families. Despite a smallpox epidemic in 1798, the number of Indian tributaries stood at 3,251 by 1803.[2]

The few non-Indians lived mostly on cattle haciendas near Miaguatlan and Amatlan. Forty-one mulatto tributaries are recorded in 1803.

The Dominicans were the first to attempt to change the extremely dispersed settlement pattern. The natives of Amatlan 'were living in some high mountains to the east, and the Spaniards drove them out of there and settled them where they now [1580] are'. In another congregation towards 1600, nine barrios were collected at the cabecera of S Luis Amatlan (1950: pueblo) and the three pueblos of S Francisco Logueche, S Pedro, and S Cristóbal. Three other places here, S Estéban, S Ildefonso, and Sto Domingo, were classified as pueblos in the eighteenth century.

S Pablo Coatlan (1950: pueblo) still had thirty-three estancias scattered about in 1548, and twenty-six when they were congregated *c.* 1600 at two sites, sixteen at the principal cabecera and ten at S Baltasar Loxicha (Icha). By 1609 the congregation of S Pablo had begun to disintegrate, with houses spread out for two leagues along an arroyo. Subsequently this dispersion continued, and in 1745-1803 there were eleven pueblos in addition to the two cabeceras (Coatecas Altas, Coatecas Bajas, S Miguel Excoo, Sto Domingo Hielveo, S Sebastián Hielvi, Sta María Lachixí, S Vicente Latenda, S Francisco Latenixi, Sta Catarina Loxicha, S Gerónimo Toblá, S Pedro Tzezon).

Before the Conquest, the people of Miaguatlan lived 'each one where he wanted, in canyons and on mountaintops'. They were collected in two groups of villages, fourteen of them within 3 leagues of S Andrés (1950: Miahuatlán de Porfirio Díaz, ciudad), and four at a distance of 10-12 leagues south of that cabecera, in the mountains beyond Tetiquipa (the latter group of estancias may well have been transferred from Tetiquipa to Miaguatlan in recompense for the losses suffered in the war of 1547-8). Only four subject pueblos are mentioned after the congregation of *c.* 1600, but here as elsewhere the natives were allowed to return to the old sites. In the eighteenth century, thirteen pueblos can be identified either as former estancias or later subject settlements. In the vicinity of S Andrés Miaguatlan, these were S Simón Almolongas, S Miguel and Sta Catarina Cuistla, Roatina, Rooquitlla, Sta Lucía, Sto Tomás Tamazulapan (formerly subject to Tetiquipa), and Sta Cruz Xiitla or Xixo. The southern enclave was headed by S Miguel Suchitepec and included S Ildefonso, S Pedro el Alto, S Sebastián, and Santiago La Galera (subject to Tetiquipa in 1609).[3]

The saints' names of twenty-five estancias appear under Ocelotepec (Ozolotepec, etc.; 1950: S Juan Ozolotepec, pueblo) in the 1580 report. Towards 1600 these were reduced to two cabeceras, S Juan and Sta María (Asunción) but nine years later ten of the old sites had been re-occupied, and other settlements were formed later. One of these, S Mateo Piñas, became a cabecera de doctrina in 1699, and in this region there seems to have been a considerable migration of Zapotecans southward into the neighboring jurisdiction of Guatulco in the seventeenth century. There were twenty-four subject pueblos under Ocelotepec in 1745, reduced to sixteen at the century's end (these included Sta Catarina Xanaguía and Santiago Xanica). The sites of certain villages were moved after an earthquake in 1801.

Sources

Worthy of further study is the revival of pre-Columbian religious practices (including human sacrifice) in the mountain fastnesses of Coatlan and Tetiquipa in 1544–7, of which we have a few details (Berlin, 1947, pp. 34–8. ENE, V, pp. 37–41). All the cabeceras but Amatlan are described as they were c. 1550 (PNE, I, nos. 791, 849, 851). A disappointingly brief report of c. 1570 (García Pimentel, 1904, pp. 65, 80–90, 92) is compensated with two excellent relaciones sent in by the magistrates in 1580 and 1609 (PNE, IV, pp. 119–143, 289–319); the latter gives details of congregations.

An interesting item from the parish of S Mateo Piñas dated 1699 (Berlín, 1947, pp. 78–9) is followed by a good report submitted by the AM in 1745.[4] For the late eighteenth and early nineteenth centuries, we have censuses of the parishes of Amatlan, Coatlan, Miaguatlan, and S Juan Ocelotepec,[5] and topographic descriptions of Coatlan and Miaguatlan,[6] all dated 1777; reports from all the parishes made in connexion with the bishop's visit in 1803;[7] and the invaluable statistical survey of c. 1821.[8]

The monographs of Byam Davies (1968) and Spores (1965) discuss the situation here at contact.

59 *Mitla y Tlacolula*

This jurisdiction includes most of the valley of Tlacolula (an eastern tributary of that of Oaxaca), bounded on the north by the Sierra of Ixtlán or Juárez rising 2,600 m, and on the south by a lower range. To the east it extends across a low divide to headwaters of the Tehuantepec river. The settled part of the valley lies at 1,600–1,800 m, and the climate is dry and temperate.

There were four native states here, ruled autonomously but falling within the Aztec tributary province of Coyolapan since the reign of Ahuízotl (1486–1502).

They probably all had Zapotecan hereditary rulers. The largest was Mictlan or Miquetlan (Zapotecan, Liobaa or Yoopaa), a religious complex of wide influence, followed by Tlacuilollan (Zapotecan, Paca?), Macuilxóchitl (Quiabelagayo), and Teocuitlatlan (Paguia or Xaquija). Off to the east, Hueyactépec (Quiaduni) was an important religious center. Valley Zapotecan was the predominant language, although there was perhaps a Mixtecan minority.

The area came under Spanish control in late 1521.

Encomiendas

Macuilsúchil, Mitla, and Tlacolula were claimed by Cortés as subjects of one of his valley cabeceras, probably Cuilapa, but they all seem to have been assigned to other encomenderos in the 1520s.[1] Macuilsúchil was perhaps briefly held by Hernán Martín, the blacksmith-conquistador (Icaza, I, pp. 31, 253), although the reference may be to a homonym (cf. Meztitlan). Mitla and Tlacolula towards 1529 were held by a regidor called Zamora, presumably Francisco de Zamora, a conquistador (Cuevas, 1946–7, I, pp. 516–17). The last two places escheated in August 1531, as did Macuilsúchil and Teotitlan in May 1532 (L de T, pp. 219, 245).

Government

The Cs of Macuilsúchil y Teotitlan and Mitla y Tlacolula, appointed from 1531–2, were made suffragan to the AM of Antequera *c.* 1552, a situation which ended apparently in 1603.[2] The Guayactepec area seems to have formed a separate corregimiento in the Zapotecas, and in the late sixteenth century was administered from Nexapa (PNE, IV, p. 36); we do not know just when it was transferred to Mitla.

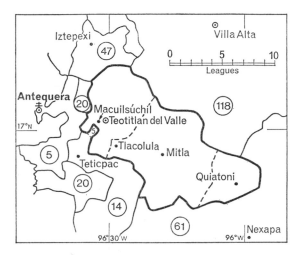

Towards 1680 the two jurisdictions were combined under a single magistrate (AM) with residence at Teotitlan del Valle. From 1787 this was a subdelegación in the intendencia of Oaxaca.

Church

In the 1550s there was a secular priest at S Pablo Mitla, while the rest of the jurisdiction was visited by 1570 from the Dominican monastery at Teticpac. A few years later Macuilsúchil and Teotitlan were put in the new Dominican parish of Tlacochaguaya. Then, early in the seventeenth century, Natividad Teotitlan became a Dominican doctrina which included Asunción Tlacolula, but Macuilsúchil continued to be visited from Tlacochaguaya.[3] By mid-eighteenth century there was a resident priest at S Pedro Quiatoni, and the Dominicans had moved their parish seat from Teotitlan to Tlacolula. The latter doctrina was secularized after 1777. All parishes were in the bishopric of Antequera.

Population and settlements.

2,231 tributaries are reported in 1548, 2,271 in 1564, and 1,700 in 1570 (L de T, pp. 219–20, 246–7). Presumably these figures do not include the Quiatoni region (Guayactepec). We assume there was considerable loss in the epidemic of 1576–9, further decline in subsequent decades, and gradual recovery in the seventeenth century. There were 1,891 Indian families *c.* 1743, and 2,760 Indian tributaries in 1797.[4]

Non-Indians were few, living mostly on haciendas, of which there were eight in 1743. The 1797 count shows 43 mulatto tributaries.

At contact the principal settlements were on hilltops, but the Spaniards soon moved them to flat country below. There were probably two attempts at reduction in the number of dependent settlements, the second *c.* 1600.[5]

Mitla (Mictlan, Miquitla; 1950: S Pablo Mitla, *villa*) in 1580 had eleven sujetos within eight leagues of the cabecera. Some of these places (S Juan del Río Quelaa, S Lorenzo Albarradas Lachibize, S Miguel Albarradas Cunzeche, Santiago Matatlan Sabaje, Sta Ana del Río Toagui, Sta Catalina Paquiec, Sta María Lachiato, Sto Domingo Cuilapa) can be paired off with eighteenth-century pueblos. Three other places (S Luis del Río, S Pablo Lachiriega, Sto Tomás) had pueblo status in 1777–1820. S Pedro Quiatoni, most likely a separate cabecera from contact, was a pueblo with four barrios in 1777.

Macuilsúchil (1950: S Mateo Macuilxóchitl, ranchería) had three outlying estancias in 1580, all of which survived as eighteenth-century pueblos: Santiago Ixtaltepec (Iztactepetitlan in 1580), S Juan Guelavia (Apazco), and S Francisco Lachigoló (Iztlayutlan).

The 1580 estancias of Teotitlan (Teutitlan del Valle; 1950: pueblo) were pueblos, Sta Ana and S Miguel del Valle, in the eighteenth century.

Tlacolula (Taculula; 1950: Tlacolula de Matamoros, ciudad) had one estancia in 1548–80, Atengo, which by 1777 had become the pueblo of Sto Domingo del Valle (Niguigo; 1950: Díaz Ordaz, *villa*).

Sources

Brief articles of *c.* 1548 in the *Suma* (PNE, I, nos. 348, 361, 645) are followed by a succinct report of 1570 (García Pimentel, 1904, pp. 65, 71, 91). Both corregimientos are described in relaciones dated 1580; that of Macuilsúchil y Teotitlan is accompanied by a map in the native tradition (PNE, IV, pp. 100–8, 144–54).

Burgoa (1934*a*, II, pp. 119–27), writing *c.* 1670, describes the Dominican doctrinas and their history. A missing report of *c.* 1743 is condensed in Villaseñor y Sánchez (II, pp. 165–8). Fray Ajofrín (II, pp. 109–17) left an account of his visit here in 1766.

For 1777, there are 'topographic' reports drawn up by the priests of Quiatoni[6] and Teotitlan,[7] and padrones of all three parishes.[8] Only Macuilsúchil is covered by the Bergosa y Jordán visit of 1803.[9] There is a detailed statistical treatment for *c.* 1820.[10]

Monographs include Schmieder (1930) and Spores (1965).

60 *Motines*

This is a wild, mountainous country (now in Michoacán, with a slice of Colima), stretching along the Pacific shore between the Coahuayana and Carrizal rivers and inland to the ridge dividing it from the Tepalcatepec basin. The higher parts

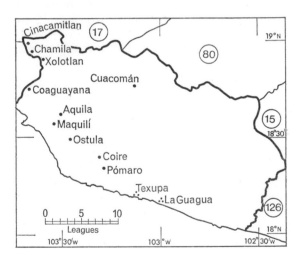

(2,000+ m) are cool, rather well-watered, and forested, but in general the climate is hot and semi-arid.

Tarascan power extended to Cuauhcoman, an inland state tributary to the cazonci, and Tarascan merchants seem to have frequented the coast and may have had a trading post at Epatlan. The area was densely inhabited. Brand (1960, pp. 129–30) thinks there were perhaps six unclassified languages spoken: Cuauhcomeca (inland), Epateca, Aquilan, Motintlan, Maquilian, and Huahuan (the last five along the coast). There were at least a dozen (perhaps many more) political units here, probably quite independent of each other.

The Motines may have been entered by Gonzalo de Sandoval in the summer of 1523. Its renowned gold placers were exploited from 1524 into the 1530s by Spanish residents of Colima and Zacatula and elsewhere. Indian revolts, which may have been rather a reluctance to die in the mines, are reported in 1526–8 and 1530–2.

Encomiendas

For 35 years the area known as Motines was divided between the 'provinces' of Colima and Zacatula, and its Indians were assigned in encomienda to Spaniards most of whom lived in the two *villas*. We have only sporadic records of grants before 1550, by which time some of the contact communities had no doubt disappeared.

Amatlan (=Tecomatlan?), with Motenpacoya, was held in 1524–53 by Jorge Carrillo, who may have been followed by a son, Alonso, in the 1560s (Icaza, I, p. 195; Lebrón de Quiñones, p. 39).

Epatlan (with Alimanci, Huitontlan, Suchicinque, and Xocotlan) was held by Diego Garrido, succeeded by his widow, Elvira de Arévalo, who then married Francisco Preciado (listed in 1548–

53). By 1568 Preciado's son, Juan, was encomendero, and he appears in the 1597 list.

Giroma or Ziroma (with Huitzitzila, Totontlan, and Turiaque) was assigned by an ordinary alcalde of Colima in 1529 to Juan Fernández, still listed in the 1560s; escheatment occurred after 1597 (Lebrón de Quiñones, p. 38).

Guacoman can perhaps be identified with 'Cuycoran', held by Andrés de Ecija in 1528.[1] Brand (1960, p. 67) says it was crown property in the 1530s.

Antonio de Ortega was the holder of Huiztlan in 1553, and Gerónimo Flores in 1580.

Pedro Ruiz de Guadalcanal claimed to have a title from Cortés to La Guagua. When Ruiz died in 1553, his son-in-law, Francisco de Castrejón, inherited. The tributes escheated after 1580.[2]

Perhaps the original holder of Maquilí (with Cuzcacuautla, Gualoxa, and Tlatictla), Manuel de Cáceres, was succeeded *c.* 1550 by a son, Gonzalo. Maquilí was a crown possession by 1560 (García Pimentel, 1904, p. 57).

Ostutla (with Coxumatlan) was held by Rodrigo d'Evia (Heredia) from *c.* 1529, followed by his widow (*c.* 1550) who then married Juan Alcalde. Escheatment occurred between 1568 and 1580.

Xolotlan (with Anamila, Apapatlan, Cinacamitlan, Chapula, Chinayo y Loli, Miaguatlan, Tepenocantitlan, Tlaxinastla, Umitlan, etc.) belonged, probably from the 1520s, to Alonso de Arévalo, a vecino of Colima. Sometime before 1552 Arévalo was succeeded by his widow, Beatriz López, and a son, Pedro. The last encomendero died between 1573 and 1578, when Xolotlan escheated.[3]

In 1649 there was still at least one private encomienda in the jurisdiction, but eight years later there were none.

Government

The Motines area was shared by the AMs of Colima and Zacatula until *c.* 1560, when a separate AM was appointed to the Motines de Colima, west and north of the Cachán river. Four corregimientos until then suffragan to Colima (Aquila, Cuacomán, Maquilí y Tlatictla, Motín y Maruata [Pómaro]) were transferred to the new jurisdiction. The AM was also C of Cuacomán, where he lived until the capital was moved to Maquilí sometime between 1604 and 1639.[4]

Meantime the Motines de Zacatula continued under the AM of that province (q.v.). Early corregimientos in that area were Nexpa, Arimao y Borona, and Texupa y Topetina (all from the 1530s), and Cuacuatlan (by 1545).

Towards 1600 the suffragan corregimientos in both Motines areas seem to have been abolished, and the boundary of Motines de Colima was extended northward with the annexation (from Colima) of Xolotlan and its dependencies.[5] Sometime after 1649 most of the old Motines de Zacatula or La Guagua area east of the Cachán river was transferred from the alcaldía mayor of Zacatula to that of Motines. It was perhaps because of this that the capital of Motines was moved to Pómaro, and later to La Guagua.

In the jurisdictional reforms of the late 1770s it was decided to annex Motines to the alcaldía mayor of Tancítaro (q.v.). However, after 1787 the old jurisdiction was re-constituted as a sub-delegación in the intendencia of Valladolid, with its capital at Coaguayana. In the 1790s and later the partido was generally called Motines del Oro, or Coaguayana.

Church

In early years secular priests were occasionally provided by encomenderos (one is said to have lived at Aquila in the 1530s), and both Franciscans and Augustinians visited the area (Brand, 1960, pp. 131, 133). There was a curate at Texupa in 1553, and seven years later bishop Quiroga sent a secular priest to S Pedro (Soledad) Maquilí.[6] By 1571 the parish seats had been moved to La Guagua (Motines de Zacatula) and Santiago Cuacomán (Motines de Colima), although for a time the curate of Cuacomán seems to have retreated to Tepalcatepec. Towards 1600 the Xolotlan area was assigned a priest resident at S Salvador Chamila; previously it had been visited from Tecolapa (cf. Colima). The parish of Maquilí seems to have been re-constituted *c.* 1600.

By 1738 the curate of Chamila had moved out

of the jurisdiction, to Istlaguacán, and about the same time the parish center of La Guagua was changed to Stos Reyes Pómaro. The Xolotlan region continued to be visited from Istlaguacán until *c.* 1795, when a priest was assigned to S José Coaguayana. All parishes were in the diocese of Michoacán.

Population and settlements

The Spaniards found a relatively large native population here, and there may well have been over a hundred principal settlements before the Indians were decimated by disease and mistreatment. The greatest loss occurred perhaps in the 1530s and in the great epidemic of 1544–8, but there were subsequent plagues. We estimate the tributary number at 2,500 in 1560, 2,200 in 1571 and 1,200 in 1580. Later counts show only 227 Indian tributaries in 1657, 186 in 1698, 326 (families) in 1743, and 362 in 1800.[7] Factors other than disease (cf. Zacatula) may have had something to do with these fluctuations.

The non-Indian population here was never great, but it came to rival that of the disappearing natives with the introduction of Negro slaves and Filipinos ('chinos') to work on cacao plantations in the Alima valley and on the coast, and on cattle ranches.[8] In the 1790s, Brand (1960, p. 123) finds 32 families of Spaniards and 200 of mestizos and mulattoes in the jurisdiction. The census of 1800 has 165 free Negro and mulatto tributaries.

A great many Indian settlements had disappeared by mid-sixteenth century, and others in the congregations ordered by Lebrón de Quiñones in 1553. Yet, in 1571, there were still fifty-seven pueblos and '*poblezuelos*' in the two parishes of La Guagua and Cuacomán, to which we should add a dozen or so in the Alima valley visited from Tecolapa, say seventy in all within the final boundaries of the jurisdiction. These were reduced to about twenty (named in the 1639–49 reports)

after the congregations of 1598–1604. Only nine Indian pueblos survived in the late eighteenth century: Aquila (1950: pueblo), Cinacamitlan, Coire, Cuacomán (Guacomán, etc.; 1950: Coalcomán de Matamoros, *villa*), Chamila, Maquilí, Ostula, Pómaro (1950: pueblo), and Xolotlan. Coaguayana (1950: Coahuayana, pueblo) was a non-Indian settlement founded *c.* 1767.

Beginning in the sixteenth century, lands taken from the languishing Indian communities were acquired by Spanish cattle haciendas and cacao plantations, the latter mostly converted to coconuts by 1650. In later years, cotton and salt were the chief products.

Sources

The region at mid-sixteenth century is described in the *Suma de visitas* (PNE, I, *passim*) and the 1553 report of Lebrón de Quiñones. There are several records of tribute assessments in the 1560s and 1570s (L de T, *passim*), together with a most valuable description in the Ovando series, dated 1571 (Miranda Godínez, 1967, 9/38–9/39). Relaciones of 1580 cover both Coliman[9] and Zacatulan[10] Motines. Congregation data of 1598–1604 are found in several documents.[11]

General descriptions of the diocese of Michoacán in 1639[12] and 1649[13] cover the area under consideration here, and there are tributary counts of 1657–98.[14]

A lost report of *c.* 1743 is badly garbled by Villaseñor y Sánchez (II, p. 98). For the late eighteenth century, there are descriptions of uneven value dated 1778 (parish of Istlaguacán),[15] 1789,[16] 1791 (incomplete),[17] 1792,[18] 1793,[19] and 1798.[20] Finally, we have a statistical summary of 1822 (Martínez de Lejarza, pp. 144–55).

Many other sources are mentioned in the admirable studies by Brand et al. (1957–8, 1960). Sauer's (1948) map and comments on the Motines de Colima should also be consulted.

61 *Nexapa*

This large territory, now in eastern Oaxaca, straddling the continental divide has a most varied topography and climate. Beginning at the summit (3,000+ m) of the Sierra Madre del Sur in the southwest, it crosses the basin of the Tehuantepec river (Río Grande) and includes much of the Sierra de los Mixes, dropping off in the northeast to the Gulf plains (150 m) drained by tributaries of the Coatzacoalcos. The side facing the Pacific is generally dry with xerophytic flora, but there is considerable seasonal rainfall in the mountains, which are forested in the higher parts. The Gulf exposure has vast rain forests.

At contact, the area was divided almost equally by three language groups, Zapotecan, Mixe, and Chontal, quite unrelated. Zapotec-speakers occupied the northern slopes of the Sierra Madre del Sur and the upper Río Grande, the chief political divisions being Azuntépec, Ixpuxtépec, Necotépec, Nexapa, Olintépec, Tepexistépec, Tizatépec, Tonacayotépec, Totolapa, Xochitépec, and Zoquitlan. There were Zapotec strongpoints at Nexapa, Maxaltépec, Quievicusas, Quiechapa, and Quiecolani (the Zapotecan names may correspond to some of the Náhuatl toponyms given above) (Burgoa, 1934a, II, p. 236). These fortresses seem to have been controlled by the Zapotecan ruler of Tecuantépec (*ibid.*, pp. 272–3).

The Chontal had a fragmented political structure with many autonomous rancherías. The rulers of Centecomaltépec (Chontal, Gualaexpitzua), Petlacaltépec (Gualacjuopo), Pilcintépec, Tlapalcatépec (Gualaquepacuae), Topiltépec (Gualacpalu), and Xilotépec (Gualaquixióm) may have had some precedence over lesser chiefs.

To the north were the Mixe, fierce mountain warriors feared by their neighbors. The lord of Mixitlan (cf. Villa Alta), outside this area, was perhaps the strongest of the Mixe rulers. Others ruled Cacalotépec, Coatlan, Chimaltépec, Malacatépec, Ocotépec, and Totolapa (Totolapilla). It is not clear whether Nanacatépec, a large state down in the hot country, was Mixe or Zapotecan.

Spaniards traversed this area, following the Río Grande to Tecuantépec, in late 1521, but it was many years before they brought all of its people under control. While the Zapotecan states were reduced by Rodrigo Rangel in 1524, a rebellion broke out the following year (Cortés, p. 227. ENE, I, p. 142. Herrera, 3a década, p. 213). An expedition was led by Diego de Figueroa and Gaspar Pacheco against the Zapotec, Mixe, and Chontal in late 1526 or early 1527, and another under Francisco Maldonado in the Nexapa area towards 1533 (Burgoa, 1934a, II, p. 147. ENE, III, p. 111). There were subsequent uprisings, including a widespread revolt in 1550, Chontal resistance in the 1550s and later, and a rebellion of the Mixe in 1570.[1]

Encomiendas

There was an early distribution of encomiendas by Cortés, and Gaspar Pacheco assigned a number of communities in this area to residents of Villa Alta at the beginning of 1527 (ENE, XV, p. 83). The first audiencia in 1529–30 removed the Nexapa region from the control of Villa Alta by reassigning these grants to other Spaniards living at Antequera, and there was another general reshuffling under the second audiencia towards 1533.

Cortés claimed that the entire Chontal–Zapotec area was subject to his encomienda of Teguantepec; specifically, he listed Nexapa, Xilotepec, and Maxaltepec as dependencies.[2] These places were considered cabeceras by the second audiencia and were taken for the crown, perhaps in the 1530s.

The choicest grant here in early years was the 'province' of Xaltepec, a vast and populous Zapotecan kingdom in the low country between the Sierra de los Mixes and Guazacualco. Gonzalo de Sandoval assigned it to one of his captains, Luis Marín, in 1522 (Díaz del Castillo, II, pp. 94–5.

Gardiner, 1961, p. 109). We know nothing of subsequent re-assignments until 1534, when half of Xaltepec appears as a crown possession together with all of Nanacatepec and Quezalapa, seemingly dependencies of Xaltepec (PNE, I, no. 832). The old cabecera of Xaltepec was in the jurisdiction of Villa Alta (q.v.), but Nanacatepec belonged to Nexapa, at least in the late sixteenth century.

A conquistador, Francisco Flores, held a group of Zapotecan communities, Azuntepec, Epustepec, Necotepec, Olintepec, Tepexistepec, and Zoquitlan. Flores was a powerful man, a regidor of Mexico city with cattle haciendas and mines in his encomiendas (Millares Carlo and Mantecón, II, no. 1999). Between 1537 and 1548 he was succeeded first by his widow, Francisca de la Cueva, and then by a son, Francisco Flores de la Cueva, who lived in Antequera. These encomiendas seem to have escheated towards 1600 on the death of the latter (Scholes and Adams, 1959, p. 37).

Two Chontal villages, Centecomaltepec and Tecpa, were held by Francisco (Diego?) de Leiva, followed by a son, Diego. The encomienda was inherited *c.* 1565 by Juana de Cabrera, the latter's widow, soon re-married to Alonso de Olivares. Escheatment occurred before 1597.

Chicomeaguatepec (Totolapa, Totolapilla) was in the grant made by Cortés to the conquistador Francisco Maldonado, inherited by his widow, Isabel de Rojas, who in 1548 married Tristán de Luna y Arellano; the latter was followed by his son Carlos de Luna y Arellano, in 1573 (he is still listed in 1597).

Ocotepec, Quezaltepec, Acatlan, Xuquila, and other Mixe villages were held by Juan Bautista Oliver, followed towards 1565 by a son of the same name who was still alive in 1597.

Petlacaltepec may have escheated on the death of its encomendero, Pedro Martín de Coria, in 1525, although it seems likely that it was held for a second 'life' (L de T, p. 288. Millares Carlo and Mantecón, I, no. 135).

Juan Gallego, a resident of Antequera, held a number of villages (Lapaguia, Pilcintepec, Tizatepec, Topiltepec, Xolotepec) until they were taken for the crown in 1553 (L de T, p. 498).

Totolapa (Asunción) was held by Antonio de Villarroel, succeeded c. 1565 by a son, Francisco, still alive in 1604.

Government

There was a municipal council from 1527 at Villa Alta (q.v.) de los Zapotecas which lay claim to the area under consideration here, but as we have mentioned this claim was contested in early years by both Cortés and the settlers of Antequera (ENE, III, p. 58). While a Spanish *villa* seems to have been founded in the vicinity of Nexapa towards 1533 it was soon abandoned (*ibid.*, p. 111). The second audiencia sent a C to administer the recently escheated crown possessions in the Nanacatepec–Xaltepec region sometime before 1534. Additional corregimientos were organized then or soon afterwards at Nexapa, Peñol de Huelamos (Maxaltepec, Tonacayotepec, Xilotepec), and Tlapalcatepec.[3]

In 1550 a petition from the cabildo of Villa Alta implies that the Nexapa–Chontal area fell outside their effective jurisdiction, but ten years later the AM of Zapotecas was authorized to administer justice in the newly-founded *villa* of Santiago de Nexapa both in person and through the appoint-

ment of Cs.[4] The latter, according to a list of c. 1567, were Coatlan e Ixpaltepec, Chimaltepec, Malacatepec y Camotlan, Nanacatepec y Quezalapa, Nexapa, Peñol de Huelamos (Maxaltepec), Quiabecuza, Tizatepec, Tlahuitoltepec, and Tlapalcatepec. Towards 1570 the jurisdiction of Nexapa was separated from that of Villa Alta and henceforth had its own AM, who in turn received the right to appoint suffragan Cs subject to the approval of the viceroy; these posts were in fact sinecures rotated among the Spanish residents of Nexapa, and they were eliminated towards 1600.[5]

In 1579 Tlahuitoltepec was transferred from the jurisdiction of Nexapa to that of Villa Alta.[6] Somewhat later, Quiatoni was lost to Mitla y Tlacolula, after which boundaries seem to have remained unchanged. The residence of the AM was moved from Nexapa to Quiechapa towards the end of the seventeenth century. From 1787 Nexapa was governed by a subdelegado, and a year later the southern part of this jurisdiction was made a separate subdelegación called Chontales, with its center at Sta María Ecatepec; both partidos were in the intendencia of Oaxaca.[7]

Church

The northern part of this area was visited in the 1530s and 1540s by secular priests from Villa Alta, while the southern portion was perhaps shared between the parishes of Antequera and Teguantepec in those years. Towards 1550 the Dominicans founded a monastery at Santiago (later, Sto Domingo) Nexapa, until then occasionally visited by a priest from Mitla (Burgoa, 1934a, II, p. 237. Gay, I, p. 559). From 1558 Dominican missionaries took charge of Villa Alta and its many visitas, while the Chontal country began to be proselytized from Nexapa and (by 1570) from a new monastery at Tequecistlan (cf. Teguantepec).[8] In 1570 Nexapa was still the only parish with its center in the jurisdiction; the Nanacatepec–Totolapilla region was being visited by Dominicans from Xalapa del Marqués (q.v.), Lapaguía and Pilcintepec were visitas of a secular priest at Ocelotepec (cf. Miaguatlan), and Totolapa–Zoquitlan were in the parish of Mitla. Within the next decade, a separate Dominican doctrina was founded at S Juan Bautista Xuquila, and a secular parish at Sta María Zoquitlan (this parish center was subsequently moved to Asunción [Concepción] Totolapa). In the 1590s the Dominicans began a small monastery at S Pedro Quiechapa.

The congregations of 1600–05 caused the founding of three new parishes, two of them (Asunción Quiegolani and S Miguel Quezaltepec) Dominican and the other (S Juan [later at S Agustín and S Pedro] Mixtepec) secular. In 1620 Dominicans started a mission among the Chontal at S Pedro Tlapalcatepec (until then visited from Tequecistlan), and perhaps about the same time a secular curate was assigned to Santiago Lapaguía. Tlapalcatepec, Nexapa, and Quiechapa were secularized in 1707, although Quiechapa appears again as a Dominican doctrina in 1743–77.

By 1743 there was a Dominican house at Sta María (Asunción) Ecatepec (secularized before 1777), together with new secular doctrinas at S Pedro Acatlan and S Pedro Xilotepec. In 1777 Sta Lucía Mecaltepec became the residence of a secular curate (Tlapalcatepec was annexed to this parish in 1793), while Quezaltepec was secularized sometime between 1743 and 1777. Later in the eighteenth century, Quiegolani, Quiechapa, and Xuquila were transferred to secular clergy, and S Juan Lachixila became a separate doctrina, the last of fourteen parishes (all in the diocese of Antequera) to be erected here in the colonial period.

Population and settlements

The once populous kingdom of Xaltepec apparently was hit by the same scourge which devastated the Gulf coastal region within a very few years after the Spaniards' arrival. That part of it known as Nanacatepec was reduced to only 370 tributaries by 1548, although the visitor's report says 'it is thought there are more people'; in 1570 the number had dropped to 200, and later reports indicate that the whole tierra caliente on the north side of the mountains was almost uninhabited.

As for the rest of the jurisdiction, the AM in 1580 stated 'a sido tierra muy poblada de yndios y aora no ay tantos'. (This was a land densely peopled with Indians, but now there are not as many.) In 1570 the total number of tributaries was 6,550 (3,150 Zapotec, 1,300 Mixe, 2,100 Chontal). The Zapotec villages in private encomienda altogether had a slight increase in population between 1570 and 1600, but elsewhere there was continued decline. At Nexapa itself, the tributary count fell from 786 in 1569 to 189 in 1623 (Scholes and Adams, 1959, pp. 37–8); of the latter, almost half were recent Náhuatl-speaking immigrants.[9] In the late seventeenth century there was a gradual recovery, especially among the Mixe. The Zapotec and Chontal suffered more in the great plague of 1737–9, when a number of their villages were entirely wiped out. The census of 1743 shows 4,284 Indian families (1,254 Zapotec, 1,864 Mixe, 1,166 Chontal), while that of 1794 has 4,380 Indian tributaries in Nexapa-Chontales.[10]

The non-Indian population here was inconsequential. The *villa* of Nexapa had 20 or 30 Spanish residents in 1560–1670, but only half that number of Negroes and mulattoes in 1743. At mid-eighteenth century there were perhaps 50 families altogether of Spaniards and mestizos living in the Zapotec area, not counting the clergy. There were 142 free Negro and mulatto tributaries in 1794.

All three language groups here probably lived in a great many small rancherías on mountaintops and other defensible sites when the Spaniards arrived. The 1579 relación says that 'their nature was to live on windswept peaks', from which they had been obliged to move down into valleys. There was some attempt at congregation here in the 1590s and later, but since we have no complete list of sixteenth-century settlements we cannot determine whether there was a great reduction in their number. Reports of 1743–1821 name seventy-three places in the jurisdiction with the category of pueblo (including forty-seven cabeceras), some of them old settlements and others recent foundations.

Among the places which disappeared entirely, most likely in the congregations of *c*. 1600, was Nanacatepec. The six pueblos of the Flores encomienda were reduced to a single cabecera, Zoquitlan. The Indians of Pilcintepec, Tizatepec, and Xolotepec were perhaps gathered at Topiltepec. Other placenames underwent change through the years. Sixteenth-century Centeco-maltepec became Chontecomaltepec and finally Chontecomatlan. Chicomeguatepec seems to be a later version of Totolapa (Totolapilla), and Ixpaltepec turned into Ixcuintepec. Tecpa became Teipa, and Tlapalcatepec by 1743 was Tapal-catepec and later Tepalcatepec. A place listed in 1548–70 as Tonacayotepec or Los Tonacayos was later called Latectrina, and by 1743 had become S Bartolomé Yautepec.

The original Dominican monastery at Nexapa (1950: Nejapa de Madero, pueblo) seems to have been on a hillside on the south bank of the Río Grande, with the Indian settlement spread out on the plain below. When the Spanish *villa* of Santiago de Nexapa was resettled in 1560, its first site was on low ground on the north bank of the river, but sometime after 1580 it was moved across to the hill adjoining the monastery. By 1614, when the Indian population had been reduced to 76 families living nearby in the 'pueblo de los mexicanos' or barrio of S Sebastián, the Spanish residents asked permission to move their *villa* down to the now vacant plain (we do not know whether this was done).[11] In the eighteenth century the place was still a *villa*, Sto Domingo Nexapa, although a predominantly Negroid community.

Sources

There is a brief but graphic description of the Mixe, extracted from the 'description de la tierra' of 1531 (Herrera, 4a década, pp. 234–5).

Interesting details about the Nexapa area can be gleaned from a *testimonio* drawn up at Villa Alta in 1533 (ENE, III, pp. 48–78). Most of the cabeceras are summarily described in the 1548 Suma de Visitas (PNE, I, nos. 147–8, 226, 300, 332–3, 345, 394, 405, 415–16, 426, 439, 472–3, 641–2, 745–7, 749–50, 833–4), and the bishop's report of 1570 is useful (García Pimentel, 1904, pp. 59–94). A relación sent in by the AM in 1580 would be of far greater value if the accompanying map had not been lost (PNE, IV, pp. 29–44). Ponce went through here in 1586 (I, pp. 284–6, 493–5).

Data on the congregations of 1592–1604 are scattered.[12] The Jesuit Cobo was here in 1630 (Cobo, p. 198). Details of the Dominican founda-tions are given in Burgoa (1934a, II, pp. 232–90).

The parish of Xuquila is described with a map in a document of 1706–7.[13] There is a very brief report of c. 1743,[14] summarized in Villaseñor y Sánchez (II, pp. 148–59). For 1777–8, parochial censuses have been found from Ecatepec, Lapa-guía, Mixtepec, and Quezaltepec,[15] and indivi-dual 'topographic' descriptions from the curates of Acatlan,[16] Lapaguía,[17] Mecaltepec,[18] Quezal-tepec,[19] Quiechapa,[20] Quiegolani,[21] Tepalcate-pec,[22] Totolapa,[23] and Xilotepec.[24] The 1802–3 visit of bishop Bergosa y Jordán covers the parishes of Acatlan, Ecatepec, Mecaltepec, Mixtepec, Nexapa, Quiechapa, Quiegolani, and Totolapa.[25] Those lacking are briefly described elsewhere (E. Pérez, 1888, table at end). There is a detailed statistical summary of c. 1821.[26]

62 *Nochistlan*

In the Mixteca Alta (Ñuñuma, 'the cloud country', in Mixtecan) of north central Oaxaca, this is a high (1,500–2,400 m) plateau with much eroded moun-tains and a very dry, cool climate. Arroyos drain mostly into the Verde or Atoyac system, although a small part is in the Papaloapan drainage, Nochist-lan itself being almost on the continental divide. The higher mountains have oak–pine forests.

Ñuutnoo, or Yucnoo (Tlillantonco) was the most prestigious state here at contact, exercising a certain hegemony through dynastic relationships over much of the surrounding country. The lord of nearby Añute (Xaltépec) was subordinate to that of Ñuutnoo, but he paid tribute to the Aztec garrison at Coayxtlahuacan, as did the rulers of Anduhcu (Nocheztlan), Andzayas (Mictlantonco), and Ñuyahua (Tamazola); Andzayas had co-rulers who were brothers, and the ruler of Ñuyahua was also lord of Yutañani (Chalchiuhapan). Other small city-states here were probably Yucunduchi (Etlantonco), Yucundec(u) (Guautla), and Yucutnoho (Tliltépec), all tributary to the Aztecs. The language spoken in these places was Mixtecan. Lords and nobles lived in fortified ceremonial

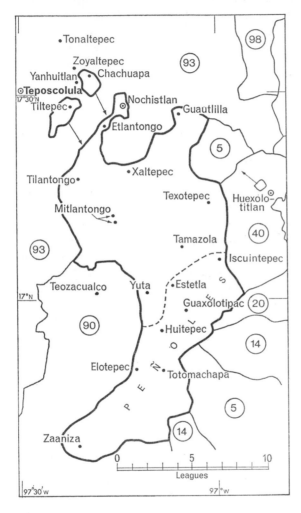

centers on hilltops or other defensible sites, while commoners were dispersed in numerous small settlements. Anduhcu (Nocheztlan) was an important trade center.

To the south, facing hostile Tototépec, was another group of hilltop fortress states which paid tribute to the Mexica. Ñundoho (Cuauhxoloticpac), Ñuniña (Itzcuintépec), Ñuchiña (Itztetlan),

and Yucuyata (Huitztépec) were Mixtecan-speaking, while the people of Yucundedzi (Elotépec) and Yñuu (Totomachapa) spoke a Zapotec dialect, probably Chatino.

The area, or at least the northern part of it, was traversed by Gonzalo de Umbría and other Spaniards in 1520. Offering considerable resistance, the Mexicans and Mixtecans were defeated by an army under Francisco de Orozco at Itzcuintépec towards the end of 1521. There seems to have been another rebellion in 1523–4 (Vázquez de Tapia, p. 52).

Encomiendas

Pedro de Maya held Nochistlan as early as 1528 and was still living at Antequera in 1537, but the encomienda had escheated by 1545 (Millares Carlo and Mantecón, I, no. 1349; II, no. 2272).

Iscuintepec and Elotepec and the other villages known as Los Peñoles were claimed by Hernán Cortés as part of his Valley of Guaxaca holdings in 1532, but they were apparently held by another encomendero until they escheated (by 1545).[1]

Chachuapa was assigned to Rufio (Nuflo) de Benavides, a conquistador, followed shortly before 1550 by a son, Juan. The latter, still alive in 1570, had been replaced by García de Benavides in 1590. Chachuapa escheated before 1597 but tributes were subsequently re-assigned.[2]

Another conquistador, Juan de Valdivieso, is listed as first encomendero of Etlantongo and Guautla (Guautlilla), together with half of Tamazola. On his death in the 1530s Valdivieso's holdings passed to a son, Juan Vázquez de Valdivieso, who was still alive in 1597 (a grandson is mentioned in 1604). The other half of Tamazola was held by Alonso de Contreras, followed in 1559 by a son, García de Contreras, who appears as joint encomendero of both Tamazola and Etlantongo in 1597–1604, Guautla being held by Valdivieso alone. Guautla at least was still privately held in 1623 (ENE, XIV, p. 153. L de T, pp. 321–4. Scholes and Adams, 1959, p. 33).

Mitlantongo was given to Gerónimo Ruiz de la Mota Zárate, succeeded on his death *c.* 1560 by a son, Antonio de la Mota. A grandson, Antonio, is listed in 1597–1604; tributes were still privately assigned in 1623 (ENE, XII, p. 146. Scholes and Adams, 1959, p. 34).

Texotepec and other nearby villages (cf. Antequera) were given to Sebastián de Grijalva, who died *c.* 1552. A son, Antonio, held the place in 1567–81; by 1597 Juan de Oseguera, a grandson of the first encomendero, is listed, but he died a year or so later.

We do not know who was the first encomendero of Tilantongo, listed as a crown possession in 1536. Soon afterward it was assigned to Luis de Guzmán Saavedra, succeeded (by 1543) by a son, Alonso (Saavedra) de Estrada y Guzmán. Escheatment occurred in 1566 (L de T, pp. 516–18).

The conquistador Gerónimo de Salinas held Tiltepec until his death shortly after 1560. His son, Agustín, was still encomendero in 1597, but by 1623 the place had escheated.

Juan de la Torre was encomendero of Xaltepec in 1525 (Millares Carlo and Mantecón, I, no. 131). The place was then held, probably in 1529–30, by the oidor Lic. Juan Ortiz de Matienzo (Icaza, I, p. 242). The second audiencia re-assigned it to Angel de Villafañe, followed on his death *c.* 1567 by a son, Juan. Shortly before 1578 the tributes passed to D. Luis de Velasco, and they continued to be paid to his descendants for many years.[3]

Government

Crown affairs in this region were at first handled by the Cs of Teposcolula and Antequera, although corregimientos of Tamazola y Tilantongo and Yanhuitlan also existed for a time in the 1530s. By 1545 Cs were administering Nochistlan and the Peñoles (Iscuintepec y Elotepec) area.

As part of the provincial division of New Spain, in 1553 the villages of Chachuapa, Etlantongo, Guautla, Nochistlan, Tiltepec, and Xaltepec (among others, cf. Teposcolula) were assigned to the C of Tonaltepec y Zoyaltepec; those of Mitlantongo, Tamazola, and Tilantongo were to be administered by the AM of Teposcolula, and the C of Iscuintepec y Elotepec was made suffragan to the AM of Antequera.[4] In this division, the C of Nochistlan was subordinate to what soon became the alcaldía mayor of Yanhuitlan, while the new AM administered the encomiendas which had

been assigned to him as C of Zoyaltepec. The boundaries of Yanhuitlan's jurisdiction as defined in 1553 remained essentially unchanged for over a century.

When Tilantongo escheated in May 1566, its new C was given charge of Mitlantongo and Tamazola as well. The subordination of Nochistlan to Yanhuitlan, Tilantongo to Teposcolula, and Iscuintepec to Antequera probably ceased early in the seventeenth century. In 1676 we find Tilantongo being administered, perhaps as a temporary measure, by the AM of Yanhuitlan, and the Peñoles (Iscuintepec, etc.) attached in a similar way to Antequera.[5]

There was a total readjustment of civil boundaries here in 1688–9, when the northern part of the old 'provincia' of Yanhuitlan, including its cabecera, was annexed to the alcaldía mayor of Teposcolula.[6] At the same time, an AM was assigned to Nochistlan and assumed jurisdiction there and in the former corregimiento of Tilantongo, together with the villages of Chachuapa, Etlantongo, Guautlilla, Texotepec, Tiltepec, and Xaltepec. Somewhat later (between 1743 and 1770) the jurisdiction of Iscuintepec Peñoles was annexed to Nochistlan, doubling its area.

From 1787 Nochistlan was a subdelegación in the intendencia of Oaxaca. It had a most irregular outline (see map), with several enclaves separated from Nochistlan by villages belonging to Teposcolula.

Church

The secular clergy began conversion in this region, a curate residing at Tilantongo perhaps as early as 1532, although Dominicans from Yanhuitlan and elsewhere also visited the area. Xaltepec had a secular priest by 1560, as did Nochistlan by 1563 and Sta María (Santiago) Iscuintepec Peñoles by 1571 (Scholes and Adams, 1961, p. 298). Dominican friars then assumed parochial duties at Asunción (Ascensión) Nochistlan *c.* 1566, Magdalen Xaltepec *c.* 1568, and Santiago Tilantongo in 1572. S Juan Elotepec, first visited from Iscuintepec and later from Teozacualco, became a separate parish (secular) in 1692. All these doctrinas were in the diocese of Antequera. The Dominican parishes were secularized between 1743 and 1777.

There seems to be a deliberate lack of coincidence between civil and ecclesiastical boundaries here. Villages in adjoining jurisdictions were visited from several of the abovementioned parochial centers, while places belonging to the alcaldía mayor of Nochistlan were attached to parishes whose seats were outside that jurisdiction.

Population and settlements

Using the estimates of Cook and Borah (1968, pp. 22–32) for the Mixteca Alta in general, we find a decline in the number of native tributaries in the area under consideration here from *c.* 44,000 at contact to 6,330 in 1570. There was further loss to *c.* 3,000 tributaries in 1600, following the plagues of 1576–81 and 1591–2. There were perhaps half as many at the nadir in the seventeenth century, then a recovery interrupted by the *matlazáhuatl* (typhus?) of 1736–9 and the plague of 1788. Towards 1743 there were 1,526 Indian families. The 1791 report has 2,193 Indian families, while the count of 1792–3 shows only 1,686 Indian tributaries.[7]

Non-Indians were few here. In 1791 only nine Spanish families and 75 of mestizos and mulattoes are reported, nearly all of them at Nochistlan and Chachuapa.

Chachuapa (Yutañani; 1950: Sta María Chachoapan, pueblo), with a very small territory, had no sujetos in 1550 or later.

Etlantongo (Yeltlatongo; Yucunduchi; 1950: S Mateo Etlatongo, pueblo) had seven or eight sujetos, named in the 1550 report, which probably disappeared in a congregation of *c.* 1600.[8]

Guautla at an early date became known as Guautlilla (Huauctlilla, etc.; Yucundecu; 1950: Santiago Huauclilla, pueblo), probably to distinguish it from another Guautla nearby (cf. Teposcolula). In 1550 it had three barrios, but no estancias.

Mitlatongo (Andzayas; 1950: Sta Cruz and Santiago Mitlatongo, rancherías) in 1550 had five barrios and five estancias (named). By 1579 the population was concentrated in twin cabeceras, Sta Cruz and Santiago, quite close to each other; both survived as pueblos.

The cabecera of Nochistlan (Nuchiztlan, etc.;

Anduhcu, Atoco, Nuanduco; 1950: Asunción Nochixtlán, *villa*) was originally atop a low hill, but was moved *c.* 1561 to its final site in the valley below. Within a very small area were four estancias (named in 1550) which were congregated at the new site.

Tamazola (Ñuyahua, Yagua; 1950: S Juan Tamazola, pueblo) had a large territory, seven by eight leagues, within which there were fourteen estancias in 1550, reduced to five by 1579. Only one seems to have survived the congregation of *c.* 1600 and appears as a pueblo, S Juan Yuta, in the eighteenth century.

Texotepec (Texutepec, etc.; 1950: Sta María Tejotepec, rancho) had no recorded estancias and was still a pueblo in 1743–1820. It may at one time have been in the jurisdiction of Antequera.

Only five sujetos are mentioned under Tilantongo (Tlilantonco; Yucuno, Yucnoo, Ñuutnoo, etc.; 1950: Santiago Tilantongo, pueblo) in 1550, but eight within four leagues are named in the 1579 relación, and there were at least two others in 1600 when they were all probably moved in to the cabecera. The latter was moved shortly after the Conquest, two 'long' leagues from its original fortress site (Burgoa, 1934a, I, p. 372. Cf. Spores, 1967, p. 43).

While Tiltepec (Tliltepec; Yucutnoho; 1950: Sta María Tiltepec, ranchería) had no known sujetos, there was another pueblo nearby in the eighteenth century, Santiago Nejapilla (Yudzuyaa), which was perhaps a late offshoot; together they formed an enclave separated from the rest of Nochistlan's jurisdiction.

Xaltepec (Añute; 1950: Magdalena Jaltepec, pueblo) had six 'barrios' within an area four by eight leagues in 1550. Eight subject estancias are named in the congregation report of *c.* 1600, when it was proposed to leave *in situ* four of these places, Xaltepec itself, Sta Catarina Juancatajucu, Sta Inés Tyheje, and S Andrés Ñunjino. The cabecera, S Andrés Nusino, Sta Inés, and Sto Domingo Ñuhusaa appear as pueblos in 1777–1821.

The 'pueblos de los Peñoles' formed a region apart. In 1571–80 there were six cabeceras here: Cuauxoloticpac (Guaxolotipac; Ñundoho; 1950:

Santiago Huajolotipac, ranchería), Elotepec (Yucundedzi; 1950: S Juan Elotepec, ranchería), Estetla (Ñuchiña; 1950: Sta Catarina Estetla, ranchería), Huictepec (Huitepec, Cuiquitepec; Yucuyata; 1950: S Antonio Huitepec, pueblo), Iscuintepec (Itzquintepec Peñoles, Ñuniña; 1950: Sta María Peñoles, pueblo), and Totomachapa (Yñuu; 1950: S Pedro Totomachapan, ranchería). A congregation proposed in 1599 seemingly had little effect, as there were twice as many settlements, all classified as pueblos, in the late eighteenth century.[9] The new ones were S Pedro Cholula, S Sebastián Río Dulce (Guiegojxij), S Mateo Tepantepec (Yucuñunii), Santiago Teytitlan (Naquiee), Santiago Tlazoyaltepec (Ñusaca), and Sta María Zaaniza (Ceniza). In 1592 a petition from the Indians of Iscuintepec to move their village to a higher location was approved by the curate.[10]

Sources

The famous Mixtecan screenfolds (Códices Bodley, Muro, Nuttall, Selden, Vienna), some of them pre-Columbian, besides telling the dynastic history of the lords of Tilantongo, should add much to our knowledge of placenames in this area when they are deciphered.

Brief entires in the *Suma* of *c.* 1550 (PNE, I, nos. 153, 249, 291, 395, 408, 655–6, 757, 836) are followed by a summary report of *c.* 1571 in the Ovando group (García Pimentel, 1904, pp. 64, 74, 84–6). Relaciones geográficas dated 1579–81 have been found for the corregimientos of Nochistlan (PNE, IV, pp. 206–12, with map), Peñoles,[11] and Tilantongo (PNE, IV, pp. 69–87), but another submitted by the AM of Yanhuitlan has disappeared. For the congregations of *c.* 1600, there is a document (with map) concerning Nochistlan, Guautlilla, and Chachuapa,[12] and another concerning Tilantongo and Xaltepec.[13]

Burgoa (1934*a*, I, pp. 369–83) gives details of the history of the Dominican doctrinas here, and their condition *c.* 1670.

Missing reports sent in by the AMs of Nochistlan and Peñoles towards 1743 are summarized in Villaseñor y Sánchez (II, pp. 142–3, 169–71). There are descriptions of their parishes from the curates of Elotepec[14] and Xaltepec,[15] and censuses from Elotepec and Nochistlan,[16] all dated 1777. Two reports were submitted in 1791, a brief description of Elotepec parish[17] and a detailed one covering the whole jurisdiction.[18]

All parishes but Xaltepec are described in response to a questionnaire in 1803–4.[19] The statistical analysis of *c.* 1821 is of special interest.[20]

Monographic treatment of this area includes the admirable work of Spores (1965, 1967), the treatise of Dahlgren y Jordán (1954), and a penetrating study of the population by Cook and Borah (1968).

63 *Nombre de Dios*

Now in southeastern Durango on the border with Zacatecas, the basins or valleys of Poanas and Súchil at 1,600–2,000 m flow southward into the Mezquital (S Pedro), which eventually reaches the Pacific. To the southeast is a mountain range (2,500 m), while on the north is a volcanic badlands (*malpaís*). The climate is quite dry, with seasonal extremes of temperature.

A relatively advanced culture of farmers and artisans which once flourished in these fertile valleys had disappeared, apparently driven southward, some two centuries before the Spaniards arrived. At contact, the region was occupied by hunters and gatherers speaking Zacatecan, a Nahuan language.

In 1558 Pedro de Quiroga, a Spaniard from the mines of S Martín, seems to have begun raising cattle in this area. He and his men were killed and the ranch was destroyed by Indians in 1560. In June 1562, a Franciscan mission was established here with Mexican, Tarascan, and friendly Zacatecan colonists, and in the fall of 1563 the viceroy ordered the foundation of a Spanish *villa* to be called Nombre de Dios. Gradually settled by farmers and cattlemen, the settlement was harassed by Chichimec raiders until the early years of the seventeenth century. We know of no encomienda here.

Government

According to a report from the audiencia of Guadalaxara dated February 15 1564, the AM of

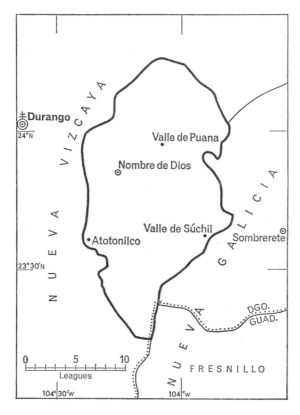

Minas de S Martín had exercised jurisdiction in 'Valles de la Puana' for the past six years and even had a teniente there until the ayuntamiento of Nombre de Dios was organized in 1563.[1] At the same time, Francisco de Ibarra considered the settlement part of his new gobierno of Nueva Vizcaya, and appointed the municipal officials when he and his party passed through in that year (Saravia, p. 114). The jurisdictional dispute between Nueva Galicia and Nueva Vizcaya was more or less resolved in 1579 when the viceroy appointed an AM to administer Nombre de Dios,

and while there were subsequent attempts on the part of both gobiernos to control the area, it remained a distant enclave of Nueva España until the late eighteenth century.[2] From 1579 to 1787, with occasional lapses, the AM was controlled from Mexico city and generally was appointed by the viceroy; after 1787 he was re-designated a sub-delegado, subordinate to the intendente of Durango.

The jurisdiction extended for some six to ten leagues around the *villa* except on the west where it soon met that of Durango. It included the valleys of Puana and Súchil, part of the malpaís, the mines of Santiago and S Buenaventura, and probably the Indian village of Atotonilco.

Church

We have mentioned that the Franciscans had a missionary parish here from mid-1562, and while their monastery was temporarily deserted in 1572 they remained in charge of the Indian population for many years (Jiménez Moreno, 1958, pp. 59, 141). The parish, known as S Francisco del Malpaís, belonged to the custodia of Zacatecas (a province from 1606). Meanwhile, as early as 1572 we find a secular beneficiary sent out from Guadalaxara who was attending to the Spaniards and others in the *villa* and surrounding farms. Later, the curate was appointed by the viceroy in his capacity of vice-patron. The secular parish, S Pedro del Nombre de Dios, nevertheless continued to belong to the diocese of Guadalaxara, and after 1620 to that of Guadiana or Durango.

Shortly before 1761 the Franciscans were relieved of parochial duties, and henceforth the beneficiary kept vicars at the valleys of Puana and Súchil and in each of the two Indian villages.

Population and settlements

Beginning in 1562, the Chichimec (Zacatecan) population was gradually replaced by immigrants, mostly Mexicans but with a Tarascan minority in early years. The unreduced Indians retreated to the Malpaís and eventually left the area altogether, while the Christianized natives were collected in two settlements, S Francisco del Malpaís (adjoining the *villa*) and Atotonilco. By 1605 there were 70 or 80 Indian vecinos, of whom 20 are identified as 'Chichimecos' living at Atotonilco, but the 1608 report claims that all the Indians were recent arrivals ('*advenedizos*'). In 1761 there were 194 Indian families (929 persons) of Mexican origin.

The number of Spanish vecinos dwindled from fifty in 1572 (20 in the *villa* and Puana valley, 30 at Súchil and the Santiago mines) to thirty in 1585, and only eighteen in 1608; there were a few Negroes and mulattoes in the latter year. By 1761 there were 936 families of Spaniards and 'gente de razón' in the jurisdiction, most of them living on haciendas.

Sixteenth-century settlements included the *villa* itself (1950: Nombre de Dios, ciudad) and two small mining camps, S Buenaventura and Santiago, which were soon abandoned. The 1778 padrón lists eighteen haciendas (mostly wheat-producing) and 15 ranchos.

Sources

Barlow and Smisor (1943) have published a number of documents (two of them translated from Náhuatl) concerning the foundation of Nombre de Dios and its history in the sixteenth century. Another source, unfortunately much mutilated, describes the boundaries of the *villa* as they were laid out in 1563 (Tamarón y Romeral, pp. 185–7). There is a brief mention of the area in two reports of the Ovando series dated *c.* 1570 (López de Velasco, p. 270) and 1572,[3] and further data are given in the 1585 relación of Sombrerete.[4]

Mota y Escobar's report (pp. 178–81) on his diocese (*c.* 1605) is followed by a valuable description submitted by the AM in 1608.[5] Several travelers left accounts of their visits here, including Rivera in 1725, Tamarón y Romeral (pp. 183–4) in 1761, Lafora (pp. 57–8) in 1766, and Morfi (pp. 15–16) in 1777. In the latter year a useful 'topographic' description was sent in by the priest of Nombre de Dios,[6] and the same curate submitted padrones dated 1778 and 1779.[7]

64 *Orizaba*

Perched on the Gulf side of the continental divide, on the southeast slope of the massive Citlaltépetl volcano (Pico de Orizaba) in central Veracruz, this area has rain much of the year which produces a dense vegetation in the lower parts. Since elevations range from 800 to 5,700 m, temperatures are torrid to frigid, but most of the inhabited part is temperate.

The native states here at contact were most likely Ahahuializapan, Acoltzinco, Matlatlan, Poxcauhtlan, and Quecholtenanco. They were all probably subordinate in some way to the Triple Alliance, although Ahahuializapan (Ahuilizapan) alone appears in the tributary province of Cuauhtochco in the Codex Mendoza. Quecholtenanco is mentioned in that document as an Aztec fortress, with a *tlacateuhctli* appointed by the Mexica, but this may be an entirely different place near Chilapa (q.v.). Náhuatl was the language spoken.

The region submitted to Spanish rule in late 1521.

Encomiendas

Aculcingo was assigned to the conquistador Francisco de Montalvo, followed *c.* 1550 by a son, Diego. When the latter died *c.* 1570 the tributes went to his widow, Juana Ruiz de Bozbuena. Another Diego de Montalvo is listed as encomendero in 1597, and the place escheated between 1629 and 1664.

Orizaba was held by Juan Coronel, who died in the 1550s to be succeeded by a son, Matías (listed in 1560–1604). Escheatment occurred after 1665 with a partial re-assignment of tributes.

Part of the encomienda of Ixguatlan may have been within this jurisdiction (cf. Córdoba).

We know nothing of the encomenderos of Poxcauhtlan (Tequila), Cachultenango (Tomatlan), or Matlatlan. The first two of these places had escheated by 1536, and Matlatlan two years later (L de T, p. 222).

Government

Cs were appointed in the 1530s to Chapultepec y Matlatlan and Cachultenango, Tequila y Chichiquila. In the provincial division of the early 1550s, Chapultepec was annexed to Xalapa (q.v.), while

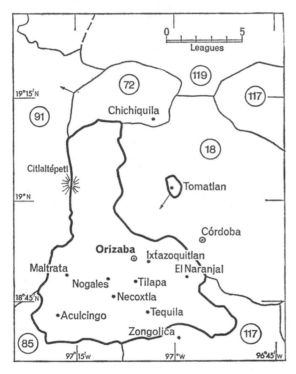

Matlatlan and the encomiendas of Aculcingo and Orizaba were placed in the jurisdiction of Tequila, which in turn was made suffragan to the AM of Teguacan. Chichiquila seems to have been transferred to the neighboring corregimiento of Guatusco (cf. Córdoba) in the 1570s. In 1579 the C of Tequila claimed jurisdiction as far north as Cuescomatepec and kept a deputy at Chocaman, but both of these places were soon being administered by the C of Guatusco. Orizaba was the residence of the magistrate of Tequila as early as 1575.[1]

In the seventeenth century the corregimiento of Tequila became the alcaldía mayor of Orizaba.

Jursidictional boundaries do not seem to have changed further, although for a time the tributes of Aculcingo were collected by the AM of Teguacan. In 1743 there were tenientes at Tequila, Maltrata, Nogales, and distant Tomatlan, the latter place forming a small enclave within the jurisdiction of Córdoba (see map). From 1787 the AM was a subdelegado in the intendencia of Vera Cruz.

Church

In 1570 there was but one secular parish here, S Miguel Orizaba, the Tequila region being visited from Zongolica (cf. Vera Cruz Vieja). Sometime before 1610 a priest at the sugar hacienda of D. Rodrigo de Vivero acquired the status of curate, the parish being known as Ingenio del Conde in 1643 and S Juan Bautista Nogales later. By 1643 the curate of Zongolica was living at S Pedro Tequila. A century later there were two more secular parishes, S Pedro Maltrata and S Cristóbal del Naranjal, and not long afterward the parish seat of Nogales was moved to S Francisco Necoxtla. Concepción Ixtazoquitlan and Santiago Tilapa became separate doctrinas toward the end of the colonial period. S Miguel Tomatlan was visited from Ixhuatlan (cf. Córdoba). All parishes were in the diocese of Tlaxcala.

Population and settlements

The native population had dropped considerably by 1565, when there were perhaps 1,300 tributaries (L de T, pp. 124–5, 222–3, 424–7). Later counts show 1,140 tributaries in 1570, 500 in 1626, 1,740 in 1696, 3,392 in 1743, and 7,532 in 1802. Náhuatl remained the language, although Maltrata in 1610 had a few recently-immigrated Popolocans.

Non-Indians, including Negro slaves, arrived in the sixteenth century, many of them to work at the great sugar plantation founded in the 1530s by viceroy Mendoza within the limits of Orizaba (*see below*). The town of Orizaba itself had 80 Spanish vecinos in 1643, and a century later it was a predominantly non-Indian settlement. The 1791 census has 1,827 Spaniards and 3,533 mestizos in the jurisdiction, while another in 1802 shows 617 mulatto tributaries.[2]

S Juan Aculcingo (Acoltzinco; 1950: Acultzingo, pueblo), if it had any estancias, lost them in a congregation *c.* 1600.[3]

Cachultenango (Quechultenango) had practically ceased to exist by 1558, when it had only 16 tributaries (L de T, p. 124). In 1579 the surviving Indians were given permission to move to the plain of Tomatlan (1950: pueblo), presumably some distance north of the original cabecera.[4]

Matlatlan (Matatla, Maltrata in later years; 1950: Maltrata, pueblo) had but one sujeto in the seventeenth century and later, Sta María Aquila.

We know little about the dependencies of Orizaba (Ahuilizapan, Huitzilapan, Ulizabal, Olizaua, etc.; 1950: Orizaba, ciudad), a multi-racial settlement which was considered a *villa* by 1777. Mendoza's sugar hacienda (Ingenio de Orizaba, Ingenio del Conde; S Juan Bautista Nogales by 1743; 1950: Nogales, *villa*), on land taken from Orizaba, was acquired in 1580 by D. Rodrigo de Vivero and was held by his descendants, the counts of Orizaba (Chevalier, 1952, pp. 91, 93–4, 97, 100, 161, 378, 398, with ample citation. ENE, xv, p. 134). Ixtazoquitlan and Nocochtlan (Necoxtla), together with Tenanco (Tenango) and Zopiloapan (Huiluapan, Huilapa) may have been estancias of Orizaba which survived a congregation in 1601 and were pueblos in the period 1643–1791; Tlilapan (Tilapa) was supposed to be moved in to the cabecera in 1601, but either this was not done or the site was re-occupied (Trens, II, p. 256). S Juan del Río was a pueblo founded by viceroy Palafox in 1642. The status of Ixhuatlancillo del Monte (Ixhuatlan in 1743) is not clear; it may have been a sujeto of S Pedro Ixhuatlan, in neighboring Córdoba jurisdiction.

Of eight estancias listed at Tequila (1950: *villa*) in 1570, only Temimilocan is recognizable as a post-congregation pueblo. Among those which disappeared was Paxcautlan, a near homonym (Poxcauhtlan) of which appears in various Aztec conquest lists, leading us to believe that it was the original cabecera, two leagues below Tequila. Atlahuilco, Atlanca, S Cristóbal del Naranjal, and Tenexapan (Nexapa), all eighteenth-century pueblos, were perhaps in the territory of Tequila.

Sources

Other than the documents cited above, we have found little concerning Orizaba in the sixteenth century, only the *Suma* reports of *c.* 1548 (PNE, I, nos. 17, 350, 423, 511) and others of *c.* 1570 (García Pimentel, 1904, p. 15. PNE, V, pp. 230–32). Chevalier (1952) cites some interesting material on the Ingenio del Conde.

For the seventeenth century, we have accounts of two bishops' visits here, those of Mota y Escobar in 1610 and 1618,[5] and that of Palafox in 1643.[6] There are also tributary data for 1626–96.[7]

A relación drawn up in 1743 by the AM[8] is summarized in Villaseñor y Sánchez (I, p. 258). The description of Ajofrín, who visited Orizaba in 1766, is accompanied by a crude map of the town (Ajofrín, II, pp. 36–9). There is another map of the parish of Orizaba made in 1770,[9] and we have seen padrones of Naranjal, Necoxtla, Orizaba, and Tequila dated 1777.[10] A census of non-Indians in 1791 has an excellent map of the whole jurisdiction.[11]

A paper of Lemoine (1962a) is of interest.

65 *Otumba*

This small jurisdiction was on the northeast rim of the valley of Mexico (modern state of Mexico) at 2,300–2,600 m. The climate is dry and cold.

Otompan at contact was a satellite state of the Acolhuaque of Texcoco, although it had had its own tlatoque since the fifteenth century. Both Otomí and Náhuatl were spoken. The population was dense and dispersed in many contiguous rancherías, although the principal settlement had perhaps 3,000 houses.

Shortly before the Spaniards' arrival, the Acolhua tlatoani Ixtlilxóchitl rebelled against his brother, the ruler of Texcoco, and made himself lord of Otompan. This dispute, partly resolved with a truce between the brothers, had brought Ixtlilxóchitl into conflict with the Triple Alliance and made him inclined to become an ally of Cortés, in 1519. After their expulsion from Tenochtitlan in July 1520, the Spaniards retreated through this area and defeated a large Aztec force in a crucial battle; when they returned at the beginning of 1521, Otompan capitulated without

resistance (Gibson, 1964, pp. 18–19. Herrera, 3a década, p. 4).

Encomiendas

Cortés made himself encomendero of Otumba, but it was taken from him in 1528, and became a corregimiento in 1531 (part of the tributes were assigned to Cortés for some years).[1] Meanwhile, two sujetos of Otumba were separated from their cabecera and were granted as individual encomiendas.

Axapusco (Achichilacachoca) was given to the conquistador Francisco de Santa Cruz, followed in the 1550s by a son, Alvaro. On the latter's death *c.* 1569 it was re-assigned to Luis de Velasco the younger, who still held it in 1597. By 1603 Axapusco had escheated.

The other sujeto, Ostoticpac, was assigned to Diego de Ocampo. Taken for the crown in 1545,

it was re-assigned within a year or so to Ocampo's daughter, who held it with her husband, Juan Velázquez Rodríguez. The latter appears as encomendero in the 1560s, followed by Alonso Velázquez (1597). In the 1640s tributes were going to the count of Moctezuma; partial escheatment occurred by 1688.

Government

Cs were first appointed to Otumba in 1531 and to Ostoticpac in 1545. Within the next decade, the C of Otumba was given charge of Axapusco and Ostoticapac. After 1640 the magistrate was generally called AM, and from 1787 he was a subdelegado in the intendencia of Mexico.[2]

Church

The Franciscans began work here in 1527 and soon had a monastery at Concepción Otumba, which they administered until the parish was secularized in 1756. S Esteban Axapusco, a visita of Otumba, became a separate secular doctrina in the second half of the eighteenth century. The area was in the archdiocese of Mexico.

Population and settlements

Towards 1570 the three cabeceras here had 6,472 tributaries. More than half died in the epidemic of 1576–81, and subsequent plagues and emigration brought the tributary count down to 2,474 in 1588, 2,090 in 1600, 350 in 1643, and 281 in 1688. 709 Indian families are reported in 1743, and 1,362 Indian tributaries in 1800. There were 34 non-Indian families in 1743, and 2,183 persons (24 per cent of the total) in 1790.[3]

While there may have been an early congregation, in 1603 there were still sixty-one settlements in the jurisdiction, including the three cabeceras. Many of these estancias disappeared at that time when it was decided to group them in seven congregations, Otumba (1950: Otumba de Gómez Farías, ciudad), Cuatlacingo (Cuautlalcingo), Ostoticpac (Uztoticpac, etc.), Axapusco (Axapotzco, Axapuchco), Aguatepec, Tizayuca (Tesayuca), and Tlamapa. Two pairs of pueblos, Axapusco–Tlamapa and Aguatepec–Tizayuca, were each combined in one continuous settlement. Other sites either remained occupied or were resettled and appear as pueblos in the seventeenth and eighteenth centuries: Acatepec (=Tiotitlan in 1603?) Astacameca (Hastacuemeca, Ixtacamecan, etc.), Izquitlan, Nopaltepec, Tecalco, Tepetitlan, Tilmatlan (Tlicmatlan, disappears after 1697), Tlaxuchico, Xalmimilolpa, and Xaltepec. S Francisco Tlalpica is listed as a pueblo from 1697. There were eleven haciendas and twenty-seven ranchos in the jurisdiction in 1791.

Sources

Brief reports in the 1570 series[4] are filled out with an unusually complete record of the 1603 congregation.[5] Another document gives population and estancia data for 1588–1623 (Scholes and Adams, 1959, pp. 44–5), and an unpublished source provides the same information for 1643–88.[6] For the late seventeenth century, we have the journal of an archbishop's visit in 1683,[7] and a report on the monastery-parish of *c.* 1697 (Vetancurt, 4a parte, p. 63).

A lost relación of *c.* 1743 is summarized in Villaseñor y Sánchez (I, p. 143). There is a census of non-Indians for 1791, accompanied by a map,[8] and a list of toponyms dated 1792.[9]

Much further citation is given by Gibson (1964), and in the archival guides of Colín (1966, 1967).

66 *Pachuca*

Pachuca, now in southern Hidalgo, is near the divide between the valley of Mexico on the south and the headwaters of the Amajac (a tributary of the Pánuco) on the north. The colonial jurisdiction extended from the Gulf side of this divide south-

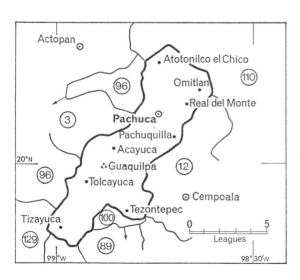

west across the plain of Cuauhquilpan to the shores of Lake Zumpango (elevations of 1,700–3,000+ m). There is a good deal of precipitation in the mountains north of Pachuca, but the rest of the area is in a rain shadow.

This was Otomí territory, with a Náhuatl-speaking minority and perhaps a sprinkling of Pame Chichimecs. It was the eastern limit of what was known as Teotlalpan. The political situation at contact is far from clear, but it would seem that Acayocan, Cuauhquilpan, Pachucan, Tezontépec, Tizayocan, Tolcuauhyocan, and Zapotlan were at least semi-autonomous communities, most if not all of them ruled by calpixque appointed by one or another of the Triple Alliance rulers.

Spaniards were first seen here in late 1519, and controlled the region in the spring of 1521.

Encomiendas

Acayuca was held by Pedro Hernández de Navarrete, succeeded before 1550 by his widow, Ana de Reboledo, and a son, García de Navarrete. Escheatment occurred on the latter's death without issue *c.* 1568.[1]

Guaquilpa seems to have been connected in early years with neighboring Tlaquilpa (cf. Cempoala). It was first shared between Antonio (Hernán) Medel and Andrés López, who sold their rights sometime before 1547 to Lic. Diego Téllez. Téllez's sons, Diego and Manuel, were joint holders in 1560, but the first brother died within a year or so and his share (which apparently corresponded to Guaquilpa) escheated (Icaza, I, p. 205).

Pachuca was held by the conquistador Bachiller Pedro Díaz de Sotomayor, who in 1537 gave his rights in dowry to his daughter, Francisca, married to Antonio de la Cadena. Cadena was followed *c.* 1565 by a son, Baltasar, still listed in 1604. Part of Pachuca had escheated by 1688 (BAGN, x, p. 229. Icaza, I, p. 225).

A poblador, Rodrigo de Baeza, was given Tezontepec and was followed sometime before 1548 by a son, and towards 1565 by a grandson, both called Baltasar de Obregón. When the second Obregón died after 1573 the tributes escheated, but they were re-assigned by 1597 to Francisco Tello de Orozco. Final escheatment occurred by 1623.

Tizayuca and Zapotlan were perhaps originally subject to Ecatepec and as such were first included in that encomienda, but they were made separate crown cabeceras in 1531 (L de T, p. 471).

Tolcayuca was granted to the conquistador Alonso Pérez de Zamora, but half was taken for the crown at an early date. A son, Alonso or Alvaro, inherited the private half soon after 1560, and an Alonso Pérez de Zamora is still listed in 1597, although by 1643 Tolcayuca was entirely a crown possession (Icaza, I, p. 85).

Government

On 1 April 1531, Tizayuca y Zapotlan became a corregimiento to which Tolcayuca was subsequently added (L de T, p. 471). When the Pachuca mines were opened in 1552, the magistrate acquired the additional title of AM and was given charge of the private encomiendas nearby.[2] A decade later Guaquilpa became a corregimiento suffragan to the province of Minas de Pachuca, which also included at this time Iscuincuitlapilco (cf. Actopan) and Tecama (cf. S Cristóbal Ecatepec).[3] From *c.* 1569 the jurisdiction of Pachuca had more or less reached its final boundaries, although Guaquilpa retained a separate C for some years.[4]

At mid-eighteenth century the AM kept deputies at Real del Monte, Tizayuca, and Atotonilco el Chico. From 1787 he was a subdelegado in the intendencia of Mexico.

Church

Franciscans were most likely the first religious here, followed in the 1540s by Augustinians working out of Acolman who founded a doctrina at S Pedro Tezontepec towards 1554. Our first notice of secular activity comes with the founding (*c.* 1560) of a parish at the mines of Pachuca (Asunción). By 1569 there were additional secular priests at Real de Arriba and Asunción Real del Monte, and in the village of Transfiguración Tizayuca; six years later S Juan Bautista Tolcayuca had a curate.[5] By 1608 the priest from Real de Arriba had moved to another mining camp, Rosario Atotonilco el Chico (cf. Vera, *passim*).

In 1754 we find the same parishes, Tezontepec now secularized, and one more, Omitlan. The curate of Atotonilco el Chico had charge of the Real de Capula (cf. Tetepango).[6] All parishes were in the archdiocese of Mexico.

Population and settlements

A report of 1569 says that there were 6,233 Indian families in the jurisdiction, but some of these were tribute-exempt mine workers. There was severe loss from the plague of 1576–81 and later, contributing to the curtailment of mining activity in the seventeenth century. In 1643 there were only 136 tributaries in the seven Indian communities; again it should be remembered that there were Indians working in the mines not included in these figures, although much of the labor, now on a reduced scale, was done by Negro slaves. Later counts show 322 tributaries in 1688, 479 Indian families in 1743, and 1,047 Indian tributaries in 1804.[7] Both Otomí and Náhuatl continued to be spoken in the eighteenth century.

The non-Indian population fluctuated greatly according to the state of prosperity of the mines. There were 70 married and 48 unmarried Spaniards in 1569. A bonanza in the late seventeenth century caused a great influx – 12,000 people at Real del Monte alone – most of them of 'color quebrado' and Indians. The census of *c.* 1791 has 2,755 Spaniards (persons), 3,821 mestizos, and 3,039 mulattoes in the jurisdiction.

Silver deposits were discovered here early in

1552, probably near what later became known as Real de Arriba, within the limits of the pueblo of Acayuca at the estancia of S Bartolomé.[8] By 1569 the principal real was that of Santiago Tlahuililpa, an estancia of Pachuca, while other camps had sprung up at Atotonilco el Chico (Molexuchitlan) and Real del Monte. By the late eighteenth century, Pachuca (1950: Pachuca de Soto, ciudad) was considered a ciudad, while Atotonilco el Chico, La Estanzuela, Omitlan, and Real del Monte were subordinate settlements.

The Indian community of Magdalena Pachuca, later called Pachuquilla (1950: pueblo), had two estancias in 1548–69, one of which (Tlahuililpa) as we have seen became the principal mining center, while the other disappeared. The eighteenth-century pueblo of Asoyacla was perhaps within Pachuca's limits.

S Francisco Acayuca (1950: pueblo) also had two estancias, S Bartolomé and Santiago, in 1569; they were probably moved to the cabecera in the 1590s, although S Bartolomé survived as a pueblo.[9]

S Pedro Guaquilpa (Cuauhquilpan, Vauquilpa, etc.; 1950: S Pedro Huaquilpan, pueblo) had a single estancia, S Martín, nearby to the northwest in 1569, which had disappeared by 1581. A congregation was proposed here in 1603 in which Acayuca (*see above*) and Zapotlan (1950: Zapotlan de Juárez, pueblo) were to be moved to the outskirts of Guaquilpa.[10] Both Guaquilpa and Zapotlan were almost depopulated in the seventeenth century (they had a total of 14 tributaries in 1643), and they are not even mentioned in the 1791 report.

Two sujetos are listed in 1548 as subject to Tezontepec (1950: *villa*), but they seem to have been moved to the cabecera by the Augustinians before 1569.

According to the 1569 report, Tizayuca (Tesayucan; 1950: Tizayuca, pueblo) had seven estancias within a league of the cabecera; they probably disappeared after the epidemic of 1576–81. A similar end was met by the two barrios of Tolcayuca (Tolguayuca, Tolcuauhyucan; 1950: Tolcayuca, pueblo).

Most of the lands relinquished by these dying villages were acquired in the 1580s by the vast Jesuit hacienda of Sta Lucía, in the jurisdiction of S Cristóbal Ecatepec (Chevalier, 1952, pp. 318–19). In 1791 there were twenty-three haciendas and nine ranchos in the partido of Pachuca.

Sources

All of the cabeceras here, except Acayuca, are summarily described in the 1548 *Suma de Visitas* (PNE, I, nos. 121, 262, 448, 523–4). There are several versions of the 1569–70 Ovando reports.[11] The C of Guaquilpa submitted a relación dated 1581 (PNE, VI, pp. 306–12).

For the seventeenth century, we have a useful description of Pachuca as it was in 1608,[12] tributary data for 1623–88,[13] an account of an archbishop's visit in 1684,[14] and a vivid description of the mines by an Italian who was in Pachuca in 1697 (Gemelli Carreri, I, pp. 129–41).

A missing report of *c.* 1743 is condensed in Villaseñor y Sánchez (I, p. 145). There is an interesting document, accompanied by a crude map, drawn up for the Inquisition in 1754,[15] together with a census, description, and map made *c.* 1791.[16]

Fernández (1940–2) should be consulted for further details.

67 *Pánuco*

In its final form, this jurisdiction (now the northernmost part of Veracruz state) extended southward from the Tamesí river across the floodplain of the Pánuco, ending in low hills (200 m) on the south, and including part of the Gulf coast and Tamiahua lagoon. The climate is hot but tempered by north winds with moderate rainfall much of the year.

The Huaxtecans, linguistically related to the Mayans, lived in numerous dispersed settlements on levees and other sites protected from flooding. These communities, often individually but sometimes including subordinate rancherías, were ruled by hereditary lords (ENE, XVI, pp. 56–7). There was warfare between villages, but occasionally two or more rulers would unite to repel foreign invasions (e.g., against Metztitlan or the Triple Alliance forces, neither of which controlled the area). The people lived from agriculture, hunting, fishing, and gathering. Although they went naked, they produced cotton cloth for trade with the

mountain Indians to the south. There may have been some intrusion of Náhuatl-speakers along the southern edge, while north of the Pánuco were wandering Chichimecs who spoke Tamaulipecan (a Hokaltecan language) and other tongues; since the Huaxtecans took Chichimec slaves when they could, there was a minority of these groups within the Huaxteca.

While the coast may have been sighted by Europeans in 1497–8 (the controversial Vespucci expedition), contact with Spaniards did not begin until 1519, when a ship sent out by Francisco de Garay under the command of Alonso Alvarez de Pineda entered the Pánuco and spent over a month trading. Alvarez returned the following year and founded a colony which was wiped out by the Indians. Hernando Cortés marched over-

land from Tenochtitlan with a large force of Spaniards and Mexican allies and defeated the Huaxtecans after considerable resistance at the beginning of 1523, founding the *villa* of S Esteban. A revolt of the Huaxtecans in October–December, 1523, was put down with great cruelty, and another rebellion occurred in 1525–6 (Bancroft, II, p. 226). After this, the Chichimecs, both those north of the Pánuco and others from the western mountains, raided Christianized settlements, notably in 1547 and 1579.[1] The country to the north remained unconquered until mid-eighteenth century.

Encomiendas

As soon as he controlled the area, in the spring of 1523, Cortés distributed the Huaxtecan communities among the Spaniards whom he left as colonists at S Esteban (Cortés, p. 211). Many of these grants were re-assigned by the acting governors in 1525, and in 1527 all of them were revoked by Nuño de Guzmán (*cf. below*) and were given to his men. Finally, in 1534 and subsequently, a fresh distribution was made by the audiencia and viceroy. The Spaniards considered each of the many native states a cabecera, thus affording nearly all the early colonists a comfortable living, and incidentally providing us with a list of principal communities which reflects the complex political situation at contact. A résumé of available information on encomiendas here will be given below, under 'Population and settlements'. Some of these grants escheated when the encomendero died or for other reasons, but many ceased to exist because there were no more Indians to pay tribute. By 1643 there were only two private encomiendas in the jurisdiction.

Government

On the heels of Cortés's conquest of Pánuco, Francisco de Garay, lieutenant-governor of Jamaica, arrived at the river in June 1523, with a royal commission to govern and colonize the area, which he called Vitoria Garayana. His men were disarmed by those of Cortés, and Garay soon afterward died in Mexico city. While there was some confusion in Spain over the status of the colony, it remained *de facto* part of the gobierno of Nueva España until May 1527, when Nuño de Guzmán arrived at Pánuco as royal governor. Guzmán's subsequent adventures took him to Mexico city (late 1528) and Nueva Galicia, but during his absence he continued to rule Pánuco through deputies as a separate gobierno, and in the spring of 1533 he crossed the continent through un-reduced Chichimec country, founded a settlement at Valles (q.v.) which he then annexed to Nueva Galicia, and re-appeared at S Esteban in July of that year, remaining there several months. Mean-while, a cedula of 20 April 1533 ordered Pánuco re-united with Nueva España; this order reached America and was carried out at the beginning of 1534.

For several years the province was governed by the cabildo of S Esteban, but in 1537 an AM was appointed by viceroy Mendoza (Puga, fol. 82). Subordinate to this magistrate were a growing number of Cs in charge of those encomiendas which had escheated. There were over a dozen corregimientos towards 1570, assigned to residents of S Esteban. In the following list, the earliest known date of crown administration is indicated. Acececa (1545), Cuzcatlan (1536), Chachapala y Tanquian (1545), Guaxutla (1548), Nanaguautla (1545), Nexpa y Tauzan (1555), Piastla y Ciguala (1548), Tamahol y Tamatlan (1545), Tamaholipa (1547), Tamintla (1548), Tamohi or Tamoin (with Tampico, 1543), Tancuiche y Texupespa (1545), Tancuiname (1545), Tanchinamol y Huesco (1545), Tanchoy y Mesquitlan (1545), Tanhuis (1565), Tempoal (1564), Tlacolula (1545), Xilitla (1536), Xocutla (1545), Yagualica (1545). In addition, a teniente or justicia subordinate to the AM of Pánuco lived at Santiago de los Valles at an early date, as did another at the villa of Tampico from 1556.[2]

Thus the borders of Pánuco at this time extended westward to Valles and a considerable distance to the south, in the Sierra de Meztitlan (Actas de cabildo..., I, p. 160). We have discussed (cf. Huexutla, Meztitlan) the early border dispute between Pánuco and Nueva España. It was not until rather late in the sixteenth century that the mountain villages (Guautla, Guazalingo, Huexutla, Xilitla, Yagualica) were definitely assigned to other jurisdictions.[3] Western Pánuco became a separate alcaldía mayor with its capital at Valles (q.v.) towards 1579.[4]

While the southern and western boundaries of Pánuco were defined with the usual amount of inter-jurisdictional haggling, the wild Chichimec country to the north was another matter. The Tamesí branch of the Pánuco river was the effec-tive northern limit of Spanish control for over two centuries. During this period frontier missions were established and abandoned, and Chichimec raids menaced villages and haciendas south of the Tamesí and even extended to the villas of Pánuco and Tampico. Much of this unsettled condition can be blamed on slave-hunting expeditions into the Chichimec country, beginning with the Sancho de Caniego *entrada* to Río de las Palmas late in 1527. In 1579 Luis de Carvajal y de la Cueva was commissioned to found a gobierno called Nuevo León, which was to extend 200 leagues north and the same distance west of the Pánuco's mouth. He and his party seem to have arrived at the beginning of 1581 and spent the next five years taking slaves and waging a little border war with the AMs of Pánuco and Valles. In 1586 the viceroy ordered Carvajal to stay north of the Tamesí, and to return the area south of that river to the jurisdiction of Nueva España.[5] Two or three years later Carvajal was arrested as a relapsed Jew and was taken to Mexico where he died in prison. When a new governor was sent to Nuevo León in 1596, he established his seat far to the northwest, at Monterrey. No further effort was made to occupy the coastal area north of Pánuco until 1749, when José de Escandón founded a series of mission-presidios in what came to be known as Nuevo Santander. The southern-most of these settlements was Altamira, and the boundary with Nueva España was fixed at the Tamesí-Pánuco river.

Towards 1600 the AM of Pánuco moved his headquarters to Tantoyuca, keeping deputies at the villas of Pánuco and Tampico; it was probably about the same time that the suffragan corregi-mientos were done away with. Another teniente was stationed at Ozuluama in 1743. Generally referred to as Pánuco y Tampico in later years, the jurisdiction was a subdelegación in the intendencia of Veracruz from 1787.

Church

Cortés may have taken a priest to the *villa* of S Esteban de Pánuco in 1523, but the earliest resident curate of whom we have record was a Carmelite, Fray Gregorio de Santa María, who arrived in 1527 and stayed into the 1530s (cf. Chauvet, p. 38). There also seems to have been a short-lived Dominican mission during this period (Chipman, pp. 190–91). By 1538 the parish had been taken over by a secular priest (Meade, 1962, I, p. 290).

Missionaries of the Franciscan and Augustinian orders were active here from the early 1540s, at first operating out of S Esteban. The Augustinians had a monastery at nearby Huexutla (q.v.) by 1548, nine years later founding another house at Santiago Metatepec (Tantoyuca); the latter, which became a priory in 1562, was for some time the center of a large parish including Indian villages as far as Tampico. The Franciscan Andrés de Olmos apparently founded, in the 1540s, a mission (Asunción or Concepción Tamaholipa) on the Chichimec frontier, and another in 1555 at Tampico, but both were soon abandoned. In 1570, in addition to the Augustinian doctrina, secular priests were living at S Esteban, S Luis de Tampico, and Concepción Tempoal.[6] In 1575 the Franciscans returned to found (or re-found) the custodia of Tampico, which had seven missions by 1586 (ENE, XI, pp. 244–7. Ponce, I, p. 87).

By *c.* 1605, Tamaholipa had been re-established as a Franciscan mission, although perhaps in a different site, Tampico had been taken over by the same order, and Asunción Ozuluama was a Franciscan doctrina. Tamaholipa was again deserted, re-occupied by Franciscans from the college of Querétaro in 1686, and returned to the custodia of Tampico two years later (Espinosa, 1964, p. 225. León, Chapa, and Sánchez, pp. 101–2, 223).

In 1743 the same parishes existed with the exception of old Tamaholipa, now called S José Tancasnequi, which had been abandoned after a Chichimec raid 14 years previously. S Francisco Tantima (S Juan Tenancusco) at this time was an Augustinian vicariate under Tantoyuca, but by 1759 the Augustinians were replaced by secular priests living at Tantima and Tantoyuca. Franciscans continued to minister Ozuluama and Tampico until after Independence.

All these parishes were in the archdiocese of Mexico.

Population and settlements

The native population here at contact probably approached 1,000,000. There was a tremendous decline in the first decade of Spanish rule, some killed in battle, many shipped off as slaves to the Antilles, and others (perhaps most) wiped out in epidemics. The number of tributaries was *c.* 11,700 in 1532, 5,140 in 1570, 1,220 in 1610, 600 in 1643, and only 338 in 1688.[7] That a good many Indians were exempt from tribute payment can be deduced from the count of archbishop Aguiar y Seixas, who in 1683 found 4,009 *feligreses* (= communicants?) in the five parishes; of these, perhaps 3,200 were Indians, say 1,000 families. The 1743 report shows 1,423 Indian families, while in 1802 there were 3,566 Indian tributaries.[8] By 1683 there were a good many Náhuatl-speakers, but Huaxtecan was still the predominant language. There was also a small group of Olives or Maguaos, said to have been brought from Florida by Andrés de Olmos in the 1540s (Meade, 1962, I, pp. 289, 336).

The number of non-Indians fluctuated a good deal with changes in the political situation and for other reasons. When no mines were discovered and the taking of Indian slaves was curtailed some Spaniards left the province, while others established cattle haciendas and introduced Negro slaves. There were perhaps 60 or 70 Spanish vecinos in 1530, but only 26 are reported in 1570 (Chipman, p. 175). In 1610 there were 200 non-Indian families, and in 1743 there were 481, the majority mulattoes living at Pánuco, Tampico, and Ozuluama.

The villa of S Esteban del Puerto de Pánuco (1950: Pánuco, ciudad) was founded in early 1523, and that of S Luis de Tampico (Pueblo Viejo; 1950: Villa Cuauhtémoc) on the right bank near the mouth of the Pánuco in 1554–60; most of the residents of the latter settlement seem to have moved in 1754 some distance south to Tampico el Alto (1950: Tampico Alto, *villa*).

It is not always possible to determine which of the many Indian communities mentioned in sixteenth-century documents fell within the final boundaries of the jurisdiction of Pánuco, as so many of them have quite disappeared from the map. Changes of site were frequent, some were moved and combined in congregations of *c.* 1560 and *c.* 1600, most simply ceased to exist.[9] Sources of 1532–70 name some forty-four cabeceras and twenty-two estancias in this general area. Only sixteen settlements of Indians survived in 1610, and the same number in 1743; twelve of them were considered cabeceras in 1802. We will condense available data below, with the warning that certain places mentioned may properly belong in adjoining jurisdictions, and that there were undoubtedly others of which we have no record.

Acececa (Asiseca), just southwest of Tantoyuca, was held by Pedro Sánchez in 1532 but had escheated by 1545. It had two estancias which disappeared in a congregation *c.* 1600. The few tributaries who survived in 1643 may have moved to Tantoyuca.

Apaztlan, downstream of Pánuco, was a crown village in 1548–70, probably moved to the *villa* *c.* 1600.

Ciguala, near Chiconamel, was a crown possession in 1548 and is last heard from in 1570.

S Pedro Coyutla (1950: congregación), also near Chiconamel, was given by Guzmán to Juan Romero, who in 1550 had been succeeded by a son of the same name; a Juan Romero was still encomendero in 1597. There were three estancias in 1571, but they with their cabecera drop from the record, to reappear as a pueblo subject to Chiconamel in 1743.

Chachapala, near Tempoal to the north, belonged to Rodrigo de Bustamante in 1533. It escheated before 1545, and was probably moved into Tempoal *c.* 1600.[10]

Chiconamel (1950: pueblo) was given by Guzmán to Héctor Méndez, followed by his widow who married Alonso de Audelo. A son of the first holder, Juan Méndez de Sotomayor, is listed in 1553–97, and Chiconamel, together with Tanta (near Pánuco), was still privately held in 1688. It survived as a pueblo in 1743 (ENE, VII, pp. 24–5; XV, p. 28).

Chila, southeast of Pánuco, was held by Benito de Cuenca, followed in the early 1560s by a son, Pedro, who died within a year or so; the latter's widow, María de Porras, is listed in 1597. Chila disappeared in the congregations.

Las Laxas, held by Alonso García in 1548, was four leagues south of Pánuco, had escheated by 1570, and disappears thereafter.

Moyutla was held in 1532 by Francisco Gutiérrez, who soon afterward sold his rights to Gregorio de Saldaña. In 1548–97 the holder was Saldaña's widow, María de Campos. This place was two leagues from Metatepec in 1571, but it seems to have been moved *c.* 1600 far to the southeast to a neighboring jurisdiction (cf. Guachinango).

Juan(es) de Azpeitia is listed as encomendero of Nanaguatlan in 1532–53, but the place escheated before 1570 and disappears thereafter (ENE, XV, p. 217).

Ozuluama (Oceloamatl; 1950: Ozuluama, ciudad) had the same encomenderos as Moyutla, escheating soon after 1597. The center of a congregation in 1600, it survived as a pueblo.[11]

Piastla, near Pánuco, was a crown village in 1548–69.

Tamaholipa, somewhere to the north of Pánuco, escheated on the death of its encomendero, Juan Ortiz, in 1547.

Three places, Tamante, Tamos, and Tanzaquila, all near Pánuco, were held by Vicencio Corzo, succeeded *c.* 1553 by a son, Francisco. Tamante and Tamaos were still privately held in 1643; the latter site is said to have been abandoned *c.* 1660 (Meade, 1962, I, p. 351).

Tamateque (Tamacte) was a crown village visited from Pánuco in 1548–70.

S Miguel Tamboate (Tanbohat), a crown pueblo upstream from Pánuco, disappeared after 1612 (Meade, 1962, I, p. 347).

Tamintla, northwest of Tempoal, had two encomenderos in 1533, a Maya and Ginés Martín. It was congregated at Tancuiche *c.* 1600, but appears as Tlamintla en las Laxas in 1643–88.

Tampachiche, between Ozuluama and Tampico, was held by Cristóbal de Frías in 1571. There was a congregation there in 1594, and no more is heard of the place (Meade, 1962, I, pp. 391–7).

The Indian pueblo of Tampico seems to have been some distance north of the *villa* of that name. It was claimed for himself by Guzmán, but later was included in the encomienda of Tamoin (cf. Valles), escheating in 1543 (L de T, p. 341).

Tampuche, very near Pánuco, was held by Cristóbal de Frías, followed *c.* 1550 by his widow and a son of the same name. In 1597 Juan Ramírez is listed. It was congregated at the *villa* (ENE, xv, p. 217).

The encomendero of Tancetuco (Tasetuco) in 1533, Ramiro de Guzmán, sold his rights to Juan de Busto, listed in 1548–1612. It was near Acececa, and had three estancias in 1571. By 1612 it had been congregated at Acececa.

Tancolol, near Pánuco, was held in 1533 by Juan de Villagrán and Alonso Navarrete, and then by Diego de las Roelas, followed by his widow, Isabel de Escobar (listed in 1548); when the widow died in 1564 escheatment occurred. The Indians were moved to Pánuco *c.* 1600 (ENE, xv, p. 217).

Tancoso, seven leagues from Pánuco, was held in 1592–1612 by Andrés Muñoz in the third 'life'; it moved to the *villa c.* 1600.

Santiago Tancuiche (Tancubichi, etc.; 1950: Tancuiche, rancho), a crown village as early as 1545, was the center of a congregation *c.* 1600 and was still an Indian cabecera in 1743.[12]

Santiago Tancuiname (Tencuinan, Tanquinon), a crown pueblo by 1545, was moved near Pánuco *c.* 1600 but remained a separate cabecera and was still considered such in 1743 (Meade, 1962, I, p. 391).

Tanchachahual (Chachavala) and Tanchicuin (Tanxicuy), between Pánuco and Tampico, were held by Lucas Ginovés in 1533, a son, Alonso Ginovés (de Alvarado), following him (1548–64). Alonso's widow inherited before 1568, and another Alonso de Alvarado appears in 1597. Both places were probably abandoned *c.* 1600 (ENE, vii, p. 18; viii, p. 157).

Tanjuco (Tanxuco, Tanjuxuco), a crown village

upstream from Pánuco in 1570, survived as an Indian cabecera and presidio in 1684–1743.

Tanlucuc, a cabecera near Tantohon in 1569, disappeared when both places were moved to Tancuiche *c.* 1600; Tantohon was still a crown cabecera in 1643.

Tantomol was granted by Guzmán to Gonzalo de Avila; on his death *c.* 1569 it escheated, and towards 1600 it was incorporated in Tantoyuca.

The largest encomienda in the area was Metatepec, later known as Santiago Tantoyuca (1950: Tantoyuca, ciudad). It was given by Cortés to his AM, Francisco Ramírez, and by Guzmán to his deputies Lic. Pedro de Mondragón (died 1530) and Lope de Mendoza (to *c.* 1537). Then it was re-assigned to the conquistador Marcos Ruiz (*c.* 1539–43), followed by his widow Beatriz de Escobar who married Pedro de Fuentes. The latter was encomendero from *c.* 1544 until his death shortly after 1560, when Beatriz de Escobar and a son by Fuentes inherited. In 1597 a Juan Hernández is listed, but within a few years the encomienda escheated. Tantoyuca appears as an estancia of Metatepec in 1548–60, but it was chosen as the site of the monastery, and thus became the cabecera. Six estancias, one of them six leagues distant, are named in 1571; they were congregated at Tantoyuca towards 1600, and it was perhaps about the same time that the AM began living there.[13]

Juan Azedo is listed in 1548 as encomendero of Tanxohol, some distance west of Pánuco. Still an encomienda in 1570, it is not heard of thereafter (Icaza, i, p. 238).

Tanzalichoc was a private encomienda visited from Pánuco in 1570 and seems to have been moved in to the *villa c.* 1600 (Meade, 1962, I, p. 391). By 1643 it was a crown possession, and it was still a cabecera, adjacent to the *villa*, in 1743.

Tempoal (1950: *villa*) was granted by Cortés to Miguel Díaz de Aux in 1524. In May of the following year the acting governors revoked Díaz's grant and assigned the place to Rodrigo de Añasco and Hernando Ruiz, but Díaz de Aux recovered possession in September 1526. Under Guzmán, in 1527, Tempoal was re-assigned to Juan de Villagrán, replaced *c.* 1534 by Diego de las Roelas. Roelas's widow, Isabel de Escobar, was encomendera in 1548; escheatment occurred on her death in 1564 (L de T, pp. 389–90). In 1569 Tempoal had six estancias, two of them some distance away and the others clustered about the cabecera, a congregation having occurred eight years before; they were reduced to one settlement towards 1600. Tempoal was still an Indian cabecera in 1743, although by then the natives were outnumbered by 'pardos libres' (Chipman, pp. 92–5).

Guzmán's encomendero at Tenacusco and Tantima was Baltasar de Torquemada. By 1548 Torquemada was dead and his widow had married Rodrigo Bezos, who in turn died after 1571; by 1597 the encomienda had escheated. While originally both places were cabeceras, in 1571 Tantima was one of three estancias subject to Tenacusco. Shortly after 1600 it was proposed to reduce these places in two congregations, at S Juan Otontepec (= Tenacusco?) and S Gerónimo Citlaltepec, two leagues apart. Otontepec (1950: Juan N. Troncoso, ranchería) seems to have been predominantly Náhuatl-speaking and survived as a pueblo in the eighteenth century. The other congregation by 1612 had become centered at S Francisco Tantima, a Huaxtecan community. In 1743 Tantima (1950: *villa*) was a cabecera with five 'distant' barrios and two subject pueblos, S Nicolás and Tamalintoho.[14]

Texupespa was held in 1532 by Juan de Medina but had escheated by 1545. It disappeared, perhaps moved to Tempoal or Tancuiche, after 1569 (ENE, VIII, p. 157).

There were two places called Tlacolula (Tacolula), both within a league of the *villa* of Pánuco. In 1548 they were known as Tacolula and Taculilla, both crown villages, the former having been settled only recently on an estancia owned by Juan de Busto. Twenty years later they appear as Taculula de los Maguaos and Tacuilola de los Guastecos, and both seem to have been congregated at Pánuco *c.* 1600 (Meade, 1962, I, p. 391). Tlacolula de los Maguaos, presumably inhabited by the descendants of the Maguaos or Olives who came from Florida a century before, continues to

be listed in the seventeenth century. The surviving Olives were living at Horcasitas, in Nuevo Santander, in 1755.

Xicayan (Chicayan) was perhaps granted by Cortés to Juan López de Ximénez. It was held by Diego Castañeda in 1532 and had escheated by 1553 (ENE, VII, p. 26. Meade, 1962, I, p. 333). Last mentioned in 1571, it was moved to Ozuluama *c.* 1600.

Sources

An Augustinian friar in 1554 wrote an illuminating essay on social and political conditions in the Huaxteca in pre-Conquest times (ENE, XVI, pp. 56–62). There is an excellent summary of documentary data for the period 1518–33 in Chipman (1967). Much additional information covering a somewhat greater time span (from the Mesozoic era to the present time!) is presented in the ambitious work of Joaquín Meade (1962). Meade's (1939) shorter study on Tampico is also useful.

A rare early (1532–3) *visita* of native communities[15] is synthesized in Chipman (1967), and is supplemented by numerous articles describing Huaxtecan communities as they were *c.* 1548 (PNE, I, *passim*). There are two principal reports of interest dated 1569–71, only one of them published.[16] Ortelius in 1584 published a most useful and detailed map of this region (Cline, 1962, p. 104).

One of the few surviving copies of the reports called for by the Céspedes questionnaire of 1604, that submitted by the AM of Pánuco and Tampico, bears the date 1612 in an inventory but may have been written several years earlier.[17] We also have tributary data for 1643–88,[18] the journal of an archiepiscopal visit in 1684,[19] and information concerning the Franciscan missions *c.* 1697 (Vetancurt, 4a parte, pp. 92–4).

Censuses dated 1738–1744 were sent in by the AM[20] and contain important details omitted for reasons of state in the published summary of Villaseñor y Sánchez (I, pp. 122–7). For the rest of the colonial period, we have seen only a few tables on the Franciscan custody of Tampico.[21]

68 Papantla

This jurisdiction, now in central Veracruz, occupied part of the coastal plain extending from the Gulf to foothills (800 m) of the Sierra Madre Oriental, crossed by numerous short rivers flowing northeastward. The Cazones and Nautla form the northern and southern limits, while the Tecolutla (S Pedro y S Pablo) goes through the middle. The climate is hot, with moderate to abundant rainfall all year.

There seem to have been many small chiefdoms here inhabited by a Totonac-speaking people, all

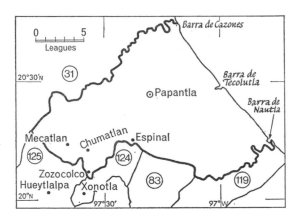

within the Triple Alliance hegemony. Eighteen little states which appear in various lists of Aztec conquests can be roughly identified in sixteenth-century documents describing the colonial cabeceras and their dependencies: Achachalintlan, Atlxoxouhcan, Cihuateopan, Conzoquitlan, Cuauhcalco, Ixicayan, Miquetlan, Ocelotépec (Ocelotlan), Papantlan, Polotlan, Pouazantlan, Tecolotlan, Tenexticpac, Tlaltizapan, Tlapolintlan, Tonatiuhco, Xochumitlan, and Yeitzcuintlan (Anonymous, 1897. ENE, xiv, pp. 118–22. Motolinía, pp. 353–6). Still others which we cannot identify may have been in this area. Papantlan and Nauhtlan were garrison towns with military governors. Cetuchco, Mactlactonatiuhco, and Tlapotonco were perhaps separate states.

The coast was visited by Grijalva in 1518, and the Papantla region probably came under Spanish control early in 1520 (Kelly and Palerm, p. 30. Vázquez de Tapia, p. 51).

Encomiendas

Most of the native states here were combined with others after the first great drop in population (*see below*).

Cetusco seems to have formed part of the Portillo–Salazar holdings (cf. S Juan de los Llanos), escheating in 1533.

Achachalintla, which included Chumatlan and Mecatlan, was given to Diego de Porras, succeeded *c.* 1550 by his daughter María, who married Juan de Cuenca (listed in 1553–81) (ENE, vii, p. 1; xv, p. 212. Icaza, ii, p. 152). By the end of the century, tributes were going to Ana María de Porras, who is identified in 1619 as the widow of Fernando de Tovar.[1] Partial escheatment occurred by 1664.

Matlactonatico was held from the 1520s by Alonso de Avila and Diego de Villapadierna. Avila's share was acquired *c.* 1543 by Gonzalo de Salazar, who had married his daughter, while Villapadierna's half was inherited by a son of the same name *c.* 1565. Tributes were still privately assigned in 1626 (Boyd-Bowman, ii, no. 6204. ENE, vii, p. 4. Icaza, i, pp. 68, 144).

Papantla's tributes belonged to the conquistador Andrés de Tapia, although they had been received in the late 1520s by Lope de Saavedra. The encomienda was inherited in 1561 by Cristóbal de Tapia, and towards 1600 by Andrés de Tapia Sosa, grandson of the original holder (Dorantes de Carranza, p. 158. ENE, iv, p. 20. Icaza, ii, p. 59). Escheatment may have occurred by 1610, although we suspect that Papantla's tributes were combined with those of Tuzantla (cf. Guachinango) in the seventeenth century.

Tlapotongo, perhaps first held by an Italian conquistador, Tomás de Rijoles, was sold in the 1540s to Jorge González, and was inherited *c.* 1565 by the latter's son. By the late 1560s the place was deserted (Boyd-Bowman, I, no. 5234. ENE, xv, p. 212).

The first audiencia gave Tonatico to Dr. Blas de Bustamante, and the second re-assigned it to Rodrigo de Guzmán (from 1531–2). Guzmán left New Spain, and the encomienda escheated in April 1544 (Icaza, I, p. 213. L de T, pp. 528–9).

Government

A C was first appointed to Cetusco and other nearby places which had escheated in May 1533, and in 1544 Cetusco and Tonatico were joined in one corregimiento.[2] Presumably this jurisdiction included neighboring encomiendas after 1550, although in 1556 the AM of Hueytlalpa (cf. Zacatlan) was put in charge of Tonatico, Matlactonatico, Papantla, and Tumilco because there was no resident magistrate in those places.[3] In the 1560s Tonatico y Cetusco had a C subordinate to the AM of Hueytlalpa; the latter made an annual visit, and was directly responsible for the Papantla-Tecolutla area. A deputy of the AM lived at Tenampulco (cf. Xonotla y Tetela).[4]

By 1570 Cetusco had disappeared and Tonatico had been re-located at Zozocolco, although the old title of the jurisdiction continued to be used. It was probably toward the end of the century that the boundaries of the corregimiento, no longer suffragan to Hueytlalpa, were enlarged to include Papantla, which became the capital of the jurisdiction. By 1633 the magistrate was being addressed as AM of Papantla, and Tenampulco had been transferred to Xonotla y Tetela. From 1787 Papantla was a subdelegación in the intendencia of Veracruz.

Church

First visited by Franciscans, the area in 1569 had a secular priest living at Mecatlan, although his predecessor had lived at the old cabecera of Achachalintla. Zozocolco in that year was visited from Xonotla, while Papantla was claimed by the curates of both Mecatlan and distant Chicontepec (cf. Guayacocotla). In 1581 Papantla was in the parish of Xonotla. By 1610 there were priests resident at Papantla, Mecatlan, and Natividad Chumatlan; the latter visited Xonotla and Zozocolco and had a rectory which had been built by Franciscans ('fue de frailes'). Nine years later, Chumatlan and Mecatlan had been combined in a single parish with its center at Mecatlan, from which Zozocolco and perhaps Xonotla were visited.[5] Somewhat later (1646) Zozocolco (S Miguel) had its own priest who visited Chumatlan, while Mecatlan and Papantla remained parish centers to the end of the colonial period. Espinal became a parish separate from Papantla after 1743. The area was in the diocese of Tlaxcala.

Population and settlements

The population was greatly decimated within a few years of the Conquest. By 1570 there were only 1,750 tributaries, and these were reduced to 835 in 1626 (L de T, pp. 217–18, 226, 528–30). Towards 1640 there seems to have been considerable immigration from neighboring jurisdictions ('over 700' families arrived at Zozocolco), and yet the total number of tributaries at the end of that century is given as 942 (*Alegaciones...*, fol. 160v). The 1743 count shows 1,543 Indian families, nearly all Totonacs although many spoke Náhuatl as well. In 1795 there were 2,269 Indian tributaries.[6]

A few Spaniards lived at Papantla, and other non-Indians (mostly mulattoes) settled there and elsewhere on cattle ranches. In 1743 the number of Spanish and casta families was 215.

We have mentioned above the possibility that there were at contact a considerable number of native states in this area, each of which would have been considered a cabecera by the Spaniards. By 1550 there were only six cabeceras, and it is not certain that all of them were within the final limits of Papantla's jurisdiction.

Achachalintla (Chichilintla, Chachalintla) had twenty-one estancias in 1569, by which time the cabecera had been moved to Mecatlan (1950: pueblo). Six of these dependencies, Azozolco, Chapolintlan, Chomatlan, Itzcuintlan, Mecatlan, and Ocelotlan, were perhaps former cabeceras. In the congregations of *c.* 1600, six estancias were assembled at Chumatlan, while the others seemingly were distributed between Coyutla, Cuahuitlan, and Mecatlan, all pueblos in 1743. Another

1743 pueblo, Sto Domingo (1950: Filomeno Mata, pueblo), may have been within Achachalintla's boundaries.[7]

Cetusco (Setusco, Zetusco), when visited by visitador Ramírez in 1553, had only 10 tributaries (ENE, VIII, p. 156). The old cabecera site can perhaps be identified with Mesa de Zetuco, a Spanish cattle ranch in the parish of Papantla in 1610.

The names of fifteen estancias subject to Papantla (1950: Papantla de Olarte, ciudad) are given in the *Suma* of *c.* 1548. Guacalco, Palotla, Puzantla, Tacolutla, Tenuxtepec, Xicayan, and Zoquitla may have been old cabeceras. There must have been a congregation here before 1581, when there were only three sujetos (shown but not named on the map). One of these was Cuacintla, and the others may have been Chicualoque and Espinal (all pueblos in 1743), although we are not sure about this. The limits of Papantla extended to the Gulf coast and may have included ancient Nauhtlan; one of the old estancias survived as a ranchería of fishermen, Barra de Tecolutla, in 1743.

Tonatico seems to have been replaced before 1570 by one of its estancias, Zozocolco (1950: Zozocolco de Hidalgo, pueblo). Iztaczoquitlan was a nearby dependency, and there were undoubtedly others.[8] In 1642 viceroy Palafox formed a congregation of Indians who had 'fled' from Augustinian doctrines at S Juan Bautista Comalteco (these were probably the '700' families mentioned above). A century later Comalteco was only a rancho, but Zozocolco had five rancherías within five leagues, and there was an Indian pueblo at S Miguel Coxquihui, two leagues north.

We are not sure that Matlactonatico and Tlapotongo were in this jurisdiction. The latter had only 10 tributaries in 1567 and is not heard from thereafter. Matlactonatico, in the same general area, was reduced to 14 tributaries in 1626 and is not listed in subsequent counts; the survivors may well have moved to Zozocolco.

Sources

The jurisdiction is described in the 1548 *Suma de Visitas* (PNE, I, nos. 116, 449, 528–9), in reports of the 1570 Ovando series (PNE, V, pp. 210–13, 218–21, 232–4), and in part by a relación of 1581,[9] the last-mentioned accompanied by several maps. There is a document concerning the congregation of Chumatlan dated 1599.[10]

We have most interesting accounts of bishops' visits here in 1610,[11] 1622–3,[12] and 1646,[13] as well as tributary data for 1626–96.[14] An *expediente* running from 1607 to 1738 is concerned with a boundary dispute between Chumatlan and Zozocolco.[15]

Other eighteenth-century material includes a valuable report from the AM dated 1743,[16] and a 1777 padrón of Zozocolco parish.[17]

Kelly and Palerm (1952) have much to say about this area in the colonial period.

69 *Puebla*

The immediate jurisdiction of Puebla de los Angeles in a political sense extended from the peak of Matlalcuéyatl (Malinche, 4,460 m) on the Tlaxcala border southward to the Atoyac river and a short distance beyond, with a small enclave (Hueyotlipan) off to the south-east. The inhabited part in the Atoyac valley is at 1,900–2,400 m and has a cool, dry climate.

At contact there were three political units here, all more or less under the hegemony of the Triple Alliance. Cholollan (cf. Cholula) was perhaps the most independent of the lot. Totomihuacan was a rather belligerent state which had been defeated in a disastrous war with Tepeaca in the fifteenth century. Cuauhtinchan was an autonomous community which paid tribute to the Aztec garrison at Tepeyacac. Náhuatl was the predominant language, although Otomí was also spoken at Totomihuacan, and Popolocan at Cuauhtinchan (ENE, XVI, p. 12).

The Spaniards led by Cortés entered Cholollan in October, 1519. Tepeyacac and its satellites were defeated in an engagement with a joint Spanish–Tlaxcalan force in the summer of 1520, at which time we assume both Cuauhtinchan and Totomihuacan fell under Spanish control.

Encomiendas

The confused early encomienda history of Cholula has been discussed above; it would seem that it was crown property from early 1531.

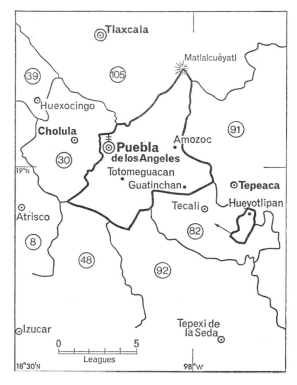

Guatinchan may once have formed part of the encomienda of Tecali, held by Francisco de Orduña Loyando (*Historia Tolteca–Chichimeca*, p. 124). In 1522 it was divided between two Spaniards, perhaps Diego de Colio and Juan Pérez de Arteaga (Icaza, I, p. 16). Colio's share apparently was re-assigned, first to Pedro de Alvarado and then to Alonso de Valencia (Alonso Valiente?), before escheating in 1542 (Icaza, I, p. 19. L de T, p. 371). Pérez de Arteaga, a conquistador and resident of Puebla, was succeeded in

the 1550s by a mestizo son of the same name, then by a grandson, and finally towards 1600 by a great-grandson, Francisco de Arteaga Pacheco (Dorantes de Carranza, p. 206). Half of Guatinchan's tributes were still privately assigned, to the marquis of Ariza, in 1696.

The first encomendero of Totomeguacan was probably Alonso de Avila, but it was soon acquired in a trade by the conquistador Alonso Galeote. In the 1560s Galeote died and was followed in rapid succession by a son, Juan, and a grandson, Alonso Galeote. When the latter died shortly before 1610 the encomienda escheated, but it was re-assigned to the Moctezuma heirs and was still privately held in 1801 (ENE, XIV, p. 148; XVI, pp. 12–13).

Government

Crown government, loosely exercised from Mexico city in the decade after the Conquest, was established locally with the founding of a Spanish settlement in 1531 at Cuetlaxcohuapan, soon re-baptized the city of Los Angeles. While the actual site was within the limits of Cholula, land was also taken from Tepeaca (Guatinchan), Totomeguacan, and Huexocingo (Atrisco) to form the city's jurisdiction (ENE, II, p. 225; XVI, pp. 11–13). In 1531–8 the crown was represented by a C who administered Cholula and Tlaxcala as well. By royal dispensation Puebla de los Angeles was permitted to govern itself through its cabildo from 1538 to 1550, after which it had a C, re-designated AM in 1555.[1]

Guatinchan seems to have had a separate C from 1542, an office which was eventually (by 1575) combined with that of the AM of Puebla who also administered Totomeguacan. Meanwhile Tepeaca, until then vaguely subordinate to the magistrate of Puebla, became a separate alcaldía mayor in 1555, and in the 1570s the boundary with Huexocingo was revised to Puebla's detriment when Atrisco became a separate jurisdiction.[2]

In 1755 the AM of Puebla was re-designated gobernador, a title which did not greatly change his duties and prerogatives nor his subordination to the viceroy. After 1786 Puebla was the capital of an intendencia, headed by a gobernador-intendente, but at the same time the former tenientazgos of Amozoc (Guatinchan) and Toto-meguacan were detached from the city's immediate jurisdiction and became subdelegaciones.[3]

Church

There was a secular parish at Puebla de los Angeles from 1531. Eight years later the bishop of Tlaxcala and part of his cabildo were residing at Puebla, but it was not until 1543 that royal approval was given to move the diocesan seat from Tlaxcala (Gibson, 1952, pp. 55–6).

In 1570 there were monasteries of all three mendicant orders in the city. Parochial duties in that year were shared between the curates of the cathedral and the Augustinians and Franciscans, each of the latter ministering an Indian barrio, and the construction of four churches (Los Remedios, S José, S Sebastián, Vera Cruz) 'which might become parishes' was under way. These did in fact become parishes within the city, although Los Remedios was rebaptized Angel Custodio. By 1746, in addition to those mentioned, there was a suffragan parish of S Marcos, and by 1777 there was still another, La Resurrección del Señor.

S Juan Bautista Guatinchan, a visita of Tepeaca from 1530, was a separate Franciscan doctrina by 1533, relinquished temporarily to the Dominicans, and re-occupied by Franciscans from c. 1557. Sto Tomás Hueyotlipan was made a separate parish sometime between 1746 and 1777 (Mendieta, III, pp. 333–47).

Additional Franciscan houses were founded at S Francisco Totomeguacan (by 1569) and Asunción Amozoc (by 1585). The regular parishes were secularized in 1640–1 with the exception of Totomeguacan, where Franciscans shared the doctrina with a secular priest as late as 1746 (*Alegaciones...*, fol. 90v).

Parts of the political jurisdiction of Puebla belonged to parishes with their seats in Tlaxcala and Tecali, while the doctrina of Hueyotlipan extended into the jurisdictions of Tecali and Tepeaca.

Population and settlements

We are told that Totomeguacan was almost depopulated in a war with Tepeaca c. 1470, before which it had 30,000 'men' and afterwards only 50 or 60 'casas' scattered about; ten years after the Spanish Conquest it was still sparsely inhabited. Quite a number of Totomihuaque who had been living in Tlaxcala seem to have returned to their ancestral homesites within the next few decades. Towards 1548 644 tributaries were counted at Totomihuacan, and 1,000 are reported in 1570. The part of Cholula occupied by the Spanish founders of Puebla in 1530 also seems to have been sparsely populated, perhaps partly because it had been a frontier region with hostile neighbors. When the city was founded, some Chololteca were moved west of the Atoyac but others remained to build the Spaniards' houses and serve them; in 1570 there were c. 1,000 Indian tributaries in the city and its environs. In that year Guatinchan had 2,570 tributaries, making a total of 4,570 in the whole jurisdiction in 1570.[4]

Epidemic disease and other factors caused a severe drop in the native population in succeeding years, although immigration to the city of Puebla left it with more than half the total in 1626 and later. Also, there were a good many Indians in Puebla who did not pay tribute. Available data show 3,760 tributaries for the whole jurisdiction in 1588, 3,275 in 1600, 2,622 in 1626, and 4,387 in 1696. In 1746 there were 3,200 Indian families in Puebla, 865 in Guatinchan–Amozoc, and 421 in Totomeguacan, a total of 4,486. The 1801 count gives 5,072 Indian tributaries.[5]

Puebla de los Angeles (1950: Puebla de Zaragoza, ciudad), which acquired the title of ciudad in a cédula of 20 March 1532, was organized to accommodate Spaniards who had arrived in Mexico after the Conquest, too late to participate in the distribution of encomiendas; others, however, including encomenderos, settled there, Their number grew from 50 vecinos in 1531 to 81 in 1534 ('many' had gone away to Perú and other parts in that year), 500 in 1570, 1,500 towards 1600, and perhaps 3,000 by 1620 (*Actas de cabildo...*, III, p. 89. ENE, III, pp. 137–44; XVI, p. 8. Vázquez de Espinosa, p. 124). By 1746 there were perhaps 15,000 non-Indian families in the jurisdiction, nearly all within the city and most of them mestizos and mulattoes.

An idea of the dispersed native settlement pattern in this area can be gleaned from the *Suma* (*c.* 1548) report on Totomeguacan (Totomihuacan; 1950: Totimehuacán, pueblo). At that time, presumably before any congregation had been made and before the population had entirely recovered from its pre-Conquest decimation (*see above*), there were thirty *barrios* divided into four *partes* and four *estancias*, or thirty-four settlements altogether within three leagues of the cabecera; these are named (Náhuatl toponyms) in the report. By 1569 these had been reduced to nine *sujetos* visited from the newly-founded monastery, although there may have been other inhabited sites. A century later there were seven visitas, and by the late eighteenth century we find only five subject pueblos, Azumiatla, Sto Tomás (Chautla), Tecola, Tetela, and Xacachimalco.

At Guatinchan (Coatinchan, etc.; 1950: Cuautinchán, pueblo) the natives were also scattered in many outlying estancias. We have confusing reports on their congregation. In 1552 visitador Ramírez ordered them all moved to the cabecera.[6] At this time we are told that the cabecera itself was moved to a better site, and in 1555 there was a proposal to move everyone to Amozoc, one of the sujetos.[7] Whatever happened, nine estancias of Guatinchan were still inhabited in 1580.[8] There may have been another congregation *c.* 1600, since reports of 1643 and 1777–92 list only the two cabeceras (Guatinchan and Amozoc) and three subject pueblos, Acuapan and Hueyotlipan (which formed an isolated pocket off to the east between Tecali and Tepeaca) and Chachapancingo.[9] In the padrones of 1777, the names of eight barrios in Guatinchan and an equal number at Amozoc may well correspond to those of some of the old estancias, moved in to the cabeceras.

We have mentioned that the city of Puebla was founded in 1530–1 on land belonging to Cholula, at a place called Cuetlaxcohuapan. Other sixteenth-century estancias of Cholula which fell within the immediate jurisdiction of Puebla were perhaps Achichipico, Amatlan, Analco, Tecuanipan, Xonacatepec, and Yancuitlalpan, although some of these may have been post-Conquest settlements. In the late eighteenth century we find three Indian pueblos here, La Resurrección, S Felipe de Jesús (Hueyotlipan), and S Miguel del Monte Canoa.

Besides the settlements mentioned, in 1792 the jurisdiction had forty-five haciendas and twenty-six ranchos.

Sources

The pre-Conquest history of Guatinchan is given in the *Historia Tolteca-Chichimeca*, also useful for the period 1519–44. The *Suma de Visitas* (PNE, I, nos. 257, 539) describes the area as it was *c.* 1548. There is another document concerning Dr. Vasco de Puga's inspection of Guatinchan in 1563 (Scholes and Adams, 1958, pp. 120–2). In the Ovando series (1569–71) there are brief descriptions of the monastery-parishes (*Códice Franciscano*, pp. 20, 24. García Pimentel, 1904, pp. 1–3, 121). A Náhuatl codex (*Códice de Cholula*) dated *c.* 1586, concerned with Cholula's forced donation of land here, has been translated and published (*Tlalocan*, V, pp. 267–88). Father Ponce spent some time in Puebla in 1585–7 and left a description of the city and environs (I, pp. 70–1, 135–9, 168, 205, 258–9; II, pp. 238–301).

The journals of two bishops, Mota y Escobar (1609–23)[10] and Palafox y Mendoza (1643),[11] contain valuable details about this region. The city of Puebla was visited by Thomas Gage (pp. 49–51) in 1625, Bernabé Cobo (pp. 203–4) in 1630, and Gemelli Carreri (II, pp. 231–8) in 1697. The Franciscan doctrinas as they survived *c.* 1697 are described in Vetancurt (4a parte, pp. 84, 87).

A long description of the city by a Dominican priest in 1746[12] was probably not used by Villaseñor y Sánchez (I, pp. 241–8) when he wrote about Puebla. Ajofrín, who was there in 1763, tells much about the city (I, pp. 42–55) but little about the rest of the jurisdiction. There is a padrón for each parish drawn up by the priest in charge in 1777.[13] All placenames are listed in a report dated 1792.[14]

Monographic treatment of Puebla and its history is voluminous, and includes Carrión (1896), López de Villaseñor (1961), and Zerón Zapata (1945).

70 Querétaro

Most of this region, now the southwest half of Querétaro state, is made up of hills and broad valleys draining northeastward into the Moctezuma (Pánuco) system; part, however, lies southwest of the continental divide in the Lerma basin. Elevations range from 1,500–2,800 m, and the climate is generally cool and quite dry, with short seasonal rains.

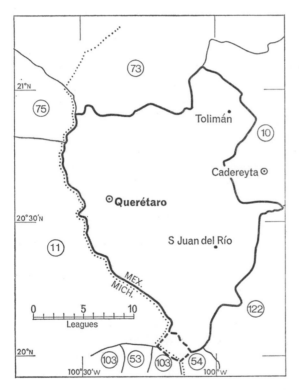

This area was held by Pame-speaking Chichimecs, a nomadic people living from hunting and gathering in dispersed rancherías. Perhaps the first Spanish party to arrive was one sent out by Cortés in 1526 (Cortés, p. 321). Sometime later, in 1531 and subsequent years, Otomies from Xilotépec founded colonies amidst the Chichimecs at Querétaro (Tarascan, Queréndaro; Otomí, Andamaxei; Náhuatl, Tlachco), S Juan del Río,

and elsewhere. Expeditions from Nueva Galicia passed through in 1532–3, and while there was some missionary activity by Franciscans working out of Acámbaro and Xilotépec, it was not until 1550 that Querétaro acquired importance with the opening of a road to the Zacatecas mines (Jiménez Moreno, 1958, pp. 56, 71–2, 84). After that date, Spanish cattlemen and farmers gradually moved in, but both their haciendas and the friendly Indian settlements suffered periodic Chichimec raids until 1589.[1]

Encomienda

Because it had been settled by Otomí colonists from Xilotepec (q.v.), Querétaro was considered to form part of that encomienda. It was still a third private encomienda in 1688.

Government

From its founding, Querétaro belonged to the province of Xilotepec, which by the late 1540s had a magistrate known as justicia mayor (later, AM) of Chichimecas. At various times from the early 1550s this officer had a deputy resident at Querétaro.[2] Towards 1577 a separate C, very soon re-designated AM, was appointed with jurisdiction at Querétaro, S Juan del Río, and the Chichimec frontier to the north.[3] Boundaries were defined at the end of the sixteenth century, S Pedro Toliman being assigned to Querétaro, and the Escanela–Cadereyta area being first attached to Sichú, and soon after made a separate jurisdiction (cf. Cadereyta).[4]

For some reason, the title of the justice here was changed to C by 1662.[5] Tenientes lived at S Juan del Río and Toliman. From 1787 Querétaro was a subdelegación in the intendencia of Mexico.

Church

First visited from the monasteries at Xilotepec and Acámbaro, Santiago Querétaro became a Franciscan parish towards 1570, subject to the province of Michoacán. Perhaps about the same time (at latest by 1575) a secular priest was assigned to S Juan del Río, later replaced by a Franciscan, and later still by a Dominican monastery.[6] In 1583 a Franciscan house was opened at S Pedro Toliman.

A secular parish, Nuestra Señora de Guadalupe, was organized in Querétaro *c.* 1680, and soon afterward a Dominican mission began at Sto Domingo Soriano (Jiménez Moreno, 1958, p. 98). By 1743 Sta María (Asunción) Tequisquiapan had become a secular doctrina, and parochial duties at S Juan had been assumed by a curate, although the Dominicans continued to maintain a cloister there. There was a small Franciscan monastery at S Francisco Galileo (Nuestra Señora del Pueblito) in 1764, but fourteen years later the parish had a secular curate, as did S Pedro de la Cañada, Sta María Amealco, Sta Rosa, and S Francisco Tolimanejo. By this time the Franciscan doctrinas at Querétaro and Toliman had been secularized, while the Dominican mission of Soriano had been absorbed by the parish of Tolimanejo. Within the city of Querétaro were the additional parishes of Espíritu Santo and S Sebastián.

In the sixteenth century there was a jurisdictional dispute here between the bishopric of Michoacán and the archdiocese of Mexico. Both sees sent curates in early years, and in 1568 S Juan del Río was assigned to México and Querétaro to Michoacán, but in 1586 the whole jurisdiction was placed in the archbishopric; the Franciscan convent, however, remained in the province of S Pedro y S Pablo de Michoacán (Bravo Ugarte, 1963, II, pp. 64–5).

Population and settlements

There must have been a sizable Otomí population, although outnumbered by the Chichimecs, by the time the Spaniards began to colonize here in the 1550s. In 1582 there were eighteen Otomí settlements of which seven or more had 'recently' been abandoned because of Chichimec hostility. At that time the Chichimecs in fact seem to have overrun most of the province, a situation which continued until peace was achieved in 1589. There was a Chichimec stronghold in the mountains just four leagues north of Querétaro, and sporadic raids from the Sierra Gorda (cf. Cadereyta) continued for many years. After 1590 the Otomí population grew, at first slowly and then with increased immigration from the south; there were minorities of Christianized Pames ('*mecos*' are reported at Soriano in 1754), Mexicans, and Tarascans. The number of tributaries is given as 770 in 1643, 2,193 in 1688, 5,506 (Indian families) in 1743, and 13,185 in 1802.[7] In 1778 there were 47,430 Indians (individuals).

The 1582 relación states that only fifty Spanish families were in the jurisdiction. They had increased to 200 in 1605, 1,000 in 1662, and 1,430 by 1743; in the latter year there were also 2,236 families of mestizos, mulattoes, and Negroes (including slaves), plus an estimated 1,200 non-Indian individuals among clergy, servants, etc. The 1778 census shows 15,421 Spaniards (persons), 11,185 mestizos, and 12,382 Negroes and mulattoes, many living on haciendas. There were 687 mulatto tributaries in 1802.

We know little about the development of settlements here. Querétaro (1950: ciudad) and S Juan del Río (1950: ciudad) were the only towns with Spaniards in the late sixteenth century (the former became a ciudad in 1656). Of the early Otomí pueblos, some disappeared in congregations *c.* 1600 while others were founded as the Chichimec frontier retreated.[8] In 1743 there were three cabeceras, Querétaro, S Juan del Río, and Tolimán (1950: ciudad). Subject to Querétaro were S Pedro de la Cañada, S Francisco Galileo (El Pueblito), and S Pedro Huimilpan, all Indian villages. By the late eighteenth century Sta María Magdalena and Sta Rosa had achieved pueblo status.

Subject to S Juan del Río were Aguacatlan, Amealco, S Juan Deguedó, S Miguel Detí, S Bartolomé del Pino, S Sebastián, and Tequisquiapan.

S Pedro Toliman (Tulimán) had five subject pueblos in 1743–94, S Antonio Bernal, S Miguelito, S Pablo, Sto Domingo Soriano, and S Francisco Tolimanejo.

In addition to these settlements, the jurisdiction in 1743 had ninety-one haciendas, a number which had increased to 104 (with eighteen ranchos) by 1794.

Sources

There is an interesting *testimonio* beginning in 1557 which throws some light on the Otomí foundations here (Fernández de Recas, pp. 305–15). While Querétaro is scarcely mentioned in documents of the 1569–71 Ovando series (*Códice Franciscano*, pp. 2, 17. López de Velasco, p. 197), the relación submitted by the AM in 1582 is of considerable interest.[9] Ponce (I, pp. 535–6), although he did not visit Querétaro, left a brief description of the Franciscan parish as it was *c.* 1586.

For the seventeenth century, we have tributary data in 1643 and 1688.[10] There is a lengthy and valuable report from the C sent in in 1743,[11] as well as a brief description drawn up for the Inquisition in 1754.[12] The accounts of their visits left by Ajofrín (I, pp. 183–201) and Morfi (pp. 5–9), who went through here in 1764 and 1777 respectively, are of interest. A complete padrón of the jurisdiction dated 1777–8 has survived.[13] Documents of the late colonial period include a non-Indian census of 1791,[14] two general descriptions dated 1794,[15] and another report of 1796–1802.[16]

Jiménez Moreno (1958, pp. 95–8) writes about the foundation and growth of the city of Querétaro, and Chevalier (1952, *passim*) has much to say about haciendas in this area. Many additional details are found in the work of Septién y Villaseñor.

71 *San Cristóbal Ecatepec*

Now in the outskirts of Mexico City, in northern Mexico state, this is a high (2,200–2,600 m), rather dry and cold area, on the shores of lakes Texcoco and Xaltocan in the northern part of the valley of Mexico.

Chiconauhtlan (= Chiuhnauhtlan?) was an independent Acolhua state, while Ehecatépec was ruled by a Mexica dynasty related to that of Tenochtitlan. The people of these communities lived in numerous scattered settlements; interspersed with them were lands and settlements belonging to Tenochtitlan and Tlaltelolco. Náhuatl was spoken by most, but there were Otomies also (Gibson, 1964, pp. 37–8, 43).

While Spaniards visited this region in 1519, it was not reduced until the summer of 1521.

Encomiendas

We are ignorant of the early encomienda history of Chiconautla. Towards 1530 it seems to have been given to a quarrier or stonemason (*cantero*) called Diego Díaz in reward for teaching the Indians his trade, but it was taken for the crown on 17 May 1532.[1] There may have been another private assignment before 1536, at which time Chiconautla had definitely escheated.

Ecatepec was first held by Cortés, who in 1527 granted it in perpetuity to Leonor, a daughter of the emperor Moctezuma. Leonor married the conquistador Juan Paz, and after his death married another Spaniard, Cristóbal de Valderrama, who died in 1537. The mestiza daughter of this last matrimony, Leonor de Valderrama y Moctezuma, also married a Spaniard, Diego Arias de Sotelo, who appears as encomendero until 1568, when he was exiled from New Spain. His son by Leonor, Fernando Sotelo de Moctezuma, was sole encomendero until 1593, when he relinquished a third of the tribute to a brother, Cristóbal de Sotelo Valderrama. Cristóbal died in 1607, and the sons of Fernando sold their two-thirds of the encomienda in 1618, but the tributes continued to be distributed among a maze of encomenderos until the end of the colonial period. Until 1531 Tizayuca and Zapotlan (cf. Pachuca) belonged to this encomienda. Certain places originally subject to Tlatelolco (Acalhuacan, Coatitlan, Tolpetlac) became sub-cabeceras here, as did Coacalco (Gibson, 1964, pp. 74–5, 418–20).

Another sujeto of Tlatelolco, Tecama, was granted in separate encomienda *c.* 1522 to the conquistador Juan (González) Ponce de León, succeeded *c.* 1540 by his son, Juan Ponce de León. Tecama appears in a list of crown pueblos dated 1550, but it was soon recovered by its encomendero.[2] Ponce de León died in 1552, his widow was sent into exile, and final escheatment occurred in 1554 (Gibson, 1964, pp. 426–7).

Government

Chiconautla became a corregimiento in the spring of 1532 (*see above*). When Tecama escheated in 1554 a C was appointed there, but this office was held for some years by the AM of Pachuca.[3]

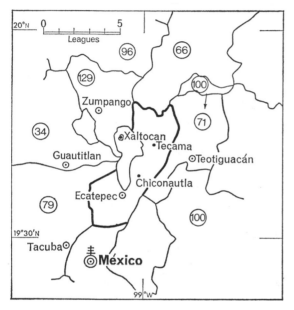

Meanwhile, in the late 1550s the C of Chiconautla was given jurisdiction in Ecatepec and Xaltocan, together with the outlying sujetos of Tenochtitlan and Tlatelolco, and in the following decade Tecama also came under his control. In the provincial division of the 1560s Chiconautla was suffragan to Tezcuco. Xaltocan was later transferred to Zumpango de la Laguna (q.v.).

Towards 1640 the designation AM, rather than C, became more common, and the magistrate established residence at S Cristóbal Ecatepec. After 1786 this jurisdiction was a subdelegación in the intendencia of Mexico.

Church

The area for many years fell within the Franciscan doctrina of Guautitlan. By 1562 S Cristóbal Ecatepec had a Dominican monastery, soon (in 1567) transferred to the Franciscans.[4] A second parish was founded in the early 1600s by the Augustinians at Sta Cruz Tecama, until then visited from Zumpango and Acolman. Axoloapan and Xoloc belonged to the doctrina of Tizayuca (cf. Pachuca), while Coacalco was visited from Toltitlan (cf. Tacuba). Ecatepec was secularized in 1761, and Tecama *c.* 1768; both parishes were in the archdiocese of Mexico.

Population and settlements

The number of Indian tributaries dropped from 2,600 in 1570 to perhaps 1,000 at the century's end, 443 in 1643, and only 284 in 1688. In 1743 there were 1,024 Indian families, and in 1803 a census showed 2,574 Indian tributaries.[5] In the latter year non-Indians, mostly mestizos and mulattoes, comprised 12 per cent of the total population.

In the late sixteenth century there were still sixty or seventy villages in the jurisdiction, although we assume that some effort had been made to congregate them. Chiconautla (1950: Sta María Chiconautla, pueblo) had four or five estancias, all nearby. Ecatepec (1950: Ecatepec Morelos, *villa*) had perhaps ten or twelve estancias, some quite far from the cabecera; these included the places disputed with Tlatelolco (*see above*), and the recalcitrant Coacalco, which claimed cabecera status as early as 1550.[6] Twenty or thirty dependencies, quite spread out, belonged to Tecama (1950: Sta Cruz Tecamac, pueblo). The other estancias were still considered subject to Tenochtitlan and Tlatelolco.[7]

Most of the dependent settlements disappeared in the congregations of *c.* 1600–4. The old cabeceras and sixteen other places survived as pueblos in the eighteenth century; they had all achieved cabecera status by 1803.

Sources

Chiconautla and Tecama, but not Ecatepec, are very briefly described as they were *c.* 1548 (PNE,

I, nos. 244, 513). A valuable report of *c.* 1570 showing the parochial division and listing the many visitas is published only in part.[8] The relación sent in by the C of Chiconautla in 1580 is rather disappointing (PNE, VI, pp. 167–77). Three volumes of litigation on land disputes in this area, most of the documents dating from the 1580s, have been preserved.[9]

There are scattered data, worthy of further study, on the congregations of 1603–4.[10] For the rest of the seventeenth century, we have a series of tribute records,[11] the journal of an arch-bishop's visit in 1684,[12] and a report on the Franciscan doctrina of Ecatepec towards 1697 (Vetancurt, 4a parte, pp. 74, 80).

A lost document of *c.* 1743 is summarized in Villaseñor y Sánchez (I, pp. 81–3). There is a brief description of the jurisdiction accompanying a padrón of non-Indians, undated but drawn up *c.* 1791.[13]

Gibson (1964) has much to add to these notes, which in fact rely greatly on his research. The documentary guides of Colín (1966, 1967) are of considerable value.

72 *San Juan de los Llanos*

As finally constituted, this jurisdiction was split in two quite unrelated parts. The first and largest of these sections, in the Sierra Madre Oriental of central Puebla state, drains partly northeast towards the Gulf and partly southward into the Llanos de S Juan, a basin with no outlet. The Gulf exposure has excessive rainfall and wide temperature variation depending on the altitude (200–2,600 m). The Llanos, at somewhat over 2,000 m, are quite dry and deeply eroded, with generally low temperatures. The Quimichtlan area formed an enclave off to the southeast, where Puebla now bulges into Veracruz state (Elotepec, belonging to S Juan, is now in Veracruz); this is a rugged, much broken region on the Gulf side of the Sierra Volcánica (1,200–3,800 m) with heavy precipitation.

The two largest states here seem to have been Iztaquimaxtitlan (with Tlalxocoapan) in the south, and Tlatlauhquitépec (with Nauhtzontlan, Yauhnáhuac, Yayauhquitlapan, and Zacapoaxtlan) in the north; the subjects mentioned may have had some political autonomy. Between the two was another community, Tzaóctlan. Chichiquillan, Quimixtlan, and Tuxtéhuec each probably had a tlatoani. Most if not all of the area was tributary to the Aztecs (Tlatlauhquitépec was a center of tribute collection), although Iztaquimaxtitlan's contribution was more likely limited to military support. The latter place was a mountain-top garrison city with perhaps 5,000 families and had a fortified boundary with hostile Tlaxcallan. Tzaóctlan was also a relatively large and concentrated settlement, but elsewhere the population was dispersed. While the language was Náhuatl, there may have been a Totonac minority in the north.

Cortés and his men passed through here in August, 1519, and spent a week at Iztaquimaxtitlan, whose ruler (perhaps a military governor) was a loyal ally of Moctezuma. Some Spaniards were killed here after the retreat from Tenochtitlan, as a result of which Iztaquimaxtitlan was stormed and taken by a force under Gonzalo de Sandoval late in 1520 (Díaz del Castillo, I, pp. 426–7). There was another revolt after 1524 (Icaza, no. 382).

Encomiendas

Iztaquimaxtitlan was divided at an early date between two conquistadores, Francisco Montaño and Pedro de Vargas. Montaño sold his half to Bartolomé Hernández de Nava (one source calls him Diego Muñoz), who *c.* 1540 was succeeded by a son, Hernando de Nava. The latter still appears as encomendero in 1570; in 1597 a Francisco de Nava is listed, and in 1604 the holder was Martín de Nava Guevara, grandson of Bartolomé Hernández. Vargas gave his share in dowry to a daughter who in the late 1540s was married to Juan Ortiz de Arriaga. The latter was followed

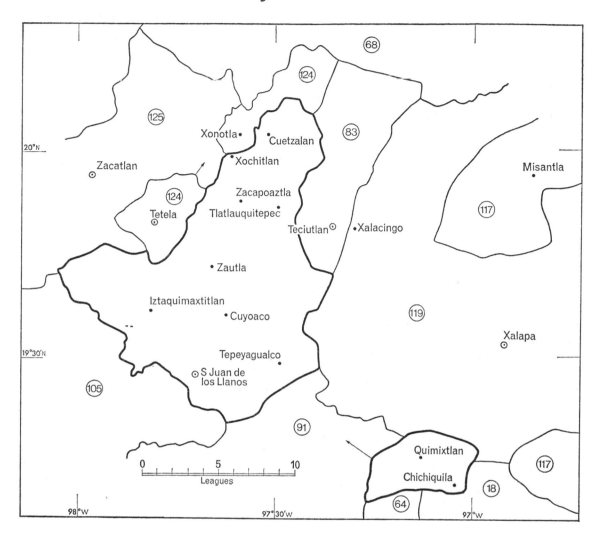

c. 1560 by a son, Diego de Arriaga, and in 1597 the holder was another Juan Ortiz de Arriaga. One of these halves escheated before 1664.[1]

Hernando de Salazar and Pedro Cindos de Portillo were early encomenderos of Tlatlauquitepec. Portillo gave up his rights when he entered the Franciscan order (*c.* 1528), and Salazar's share passed to the crown in June, 1535 (Icaza, II, p. 292. L de T, pp. 520 f. Mendieta, IV, pp. 127–8).

Zautla (Xonacatlan) was held by a Portuguese conquistador, Francisco de Oliveros, followed on his death in the 1550s by a son, Martín, and later

by a grandson. Tributes were still privately assigned in 1696 (Icaza, I, p. 47. L de T, p. 609).

We have no record of the encomenderos at Chichiquila, Quimixtlan, and Tustebec (Tustepec), although Juan de Cuéllar claimed that he once held Quimixtlan (Icaza, I, p. 222). Tustebec seems to have escheated in 1531.[2] Both Tustebec and Quimistlan were crown villages in 1534 and were apparently re-assigned for a few years before final escheatment in July, 1538 (L de T, pp. 543–4). Chichiquila was a crown possession by 1536.

Government

Appointed from 1535, the C of Tlatlauquitepec administered nearby Teciutlan and Atempa until they were made a separate jurisdiction towards 1553. In that year the magistrate of Tlatlauquitepec was given charge of all crown and encomienda villages within ten leagues, including Iztaquimaxtitlan, and at the same time Ixcoyamec and Zoncozcatlan were transferred from his jurisdiction to that of Hueytlalpa (cf. Zacatlan).[3] By 1579 the C was living at Tlalxocoapan (S Juan de los Llanos).[4]

Meanwhile, Tustepec y Quimixtlan had a C in 1531–4 and again from 1538. Chichiquila was administered variously from Tequila and Guatusco until it was annexed to Tustepec late in the sixteenth century.[5] Both S Juan de los Llanos and Tustepec y Quimixtlan appear as alcaldías mayores from the 1640s, but by 1676 the latter had been attached to S Juan.[6] After 1787 S Juan de los Llanos became a subdelegación in the intendencia of Puebla. In 1791 there were tenientes at Cuyoaco, Iztaquimaxtitlan, Quimixtlan, Tepeyagualco, Tlatlauquitepec, and Zacapoaztla.

Church

By 1548 the Franciscans had monastery-parishes at Sta María Tlatlauquitepec and S Francisco Iztaquimaxtitlan, and perhaps smaller houses at S Juan Tlalxocoapan, Xonacatlan, and S Pedro Zacapoaztla, all of which were turned over to secular clergy towards 1567 (*Alegaciones...*, fol. 23). Two years later we find priests resident at all these places except Iztaquimaxtitlan, which was visited from both Tlalxocoapan and nearby Tetela; in 1569 there was also a priest at S Juan Quimixtlan.

By 1609 S Francisco Iztaquimaxtitlan and S Francisco Cuetzalan were separate secular doctrinas, while the priest of Xonacatlan had moved to Santiago Zautla. Parishes were founded in the eighteenth century at Sta María Cuyoaco, S Mateo Chichiquila, S Pedro y S Pablo Tepeyagualco, and S Bartolomé Xochitlan. The area was within the diocese of Tlaxcala.

For most of the colonial period the curate of Tlatlauquitepec visited Atempa (cf. Teciutlan y Atempa), that of Tepeyagualco visited Perote (cf. Xalapa de la Feria), and S Francisco Elotepec belonged to the parish of S Antonio Guatusco (cf. Córdoba).

Population and settlements

The number of tributaries in 1570 was *c.* 5,000 (500 of these were in the Chichiquila–Quimixtlan area) and dropped to 1,840 in 1609, 1,444 in 1626, and perhaps somewhat less by mid-century. There were 3,453 tributaries in 1696, *c.* 4,500 Indian families in 1743, and 30,166 Indians (individuals) in 1791; eight years later a census showed 8,313 Indian tributaries.[7]

The non-Indian population was mostly confined to the *llanos*, at S Juan and nearby haciendas. There were 40 or 50 Spanish vecinos in 1662, and 300-odd non-Indian families in 1743. The 1791 padrón has 3,484 Spaniards, 4,649 mestizos, and 165 mulattoes (individuals).

S Francisco Iztaquimaxtitlan (Istac-ymachtitlan, Estacquimestitlan, Itztaquimitztitlan, etc.; frequently called Castilblanco in early accounts; 1950: Ixtacamaxtitlán, *villa*) was moved in the 1560s from its hilltop site to the valley below where a congregation was effected, bitterly opposed by the Indians.[8] In 1569 there were two cabeceras, Iztaquimaxtitlan and S Juan Tlalxocoapan (Tlajocoapan, S Juan de los Llanos; 1950: Libres, *villa*) and an undisclosed number of estancias. Certain barrios mentioned in the eighteenth century (Huiscolotla, S Andrés, Sta María, Xocoxiutla) may be relics of a congregation carried out here *c.* 1600.[9] Some old estancia sites became haciendas (Ajuluapa, Almonamiqui, etc.).

Tlatlauquitepec (1950: *villa*) in 1548 had twenty estancias, two of which were lost to Hueytlalpa in 1553–4 (*see above*). By 1569 the estancia of Zacapoaztla (Zacapustla; 1950: Zacapoaxtla, ciudad) was considered a cabecera, and there were eight subject estancias altogether. Seven other places survived as pueblos in the eighteenth century: Cuetzalan (Quezala), Hueyapan, Nauzontla (Naotzontlan), Los Teteles, Suchitlan, Yancuitlalpan, and Yaonáhuac. Eleven 'barrios' are also named in the 1791 report.

Santiago Zautla (Tzauctlan, Zacotla, etc.; 1950: Santiago Zautla, pueblo) was replaced for a while as cabecera by one of its estancias, Xonacatlan (five other estancias are named in the 1569 report). Two sites were chosen as congregation centers *c.* 1600, Zautla and S Miguel Huitzitzilapa (Tenextlatiloyan). Xonacatlan re-appears as a pueblo with a new name, Cuyoaco, in the eighteenth century, by which time Tenextlatiloyan is listed as one of five barrios. Far out on the llanos, Tepeyagualco was by 1613 an inn on the highroad from Vera Cruz to Mexico to accommodate viceroys on their journeys; eventually it became an Indian cabecera.

There is much confusion about early settlements in the Quimixtlan region.[10] Originally there seem to have been three cabeceras here, Quimixtlan (Quimichtlan, etc.; 1950: Quimixtlán, *villa*), Chichiquila (1950: pueblo), and Tustepec (Tuxteueque, Tustebec, etc.; 1950: Tozihuic, ranchería?). Congregations were proposed at Quimixtlan and Chichiquila in the early 1590s, then the Indians of Chichiquila were moved to Quimixtlan, but by 1609 the old sites were re-occupied. Of the pueblos surviving in the eighteenth century, Chilchotla, Huescaleca, and Patlanalá apparently were former estancias of

Quimixtlan, while Elotepec may have been subject to Chichiquila. 'Tusteueque' still appears as a cabecera in 1696, but we find no further mention of it.

In 1792, besides the places mentioned, there were thirty-six haciendas and fifty-seven ranchos in the jurisdiction.

Sources

The area at first contact is described by Cortés (pp. 38–9) and Díaz del Castillo (I, pp. 182–5). Of the various cabeceras, only Tlatlauquitepec is represented in the *c.* 1548 visit (PNE, I, no 522), while the Ovando reports (1569–70) are quite succinct (PNE, v, pp. 207–8, 243–5, 247, 266, 269–70).

There is much of interest in the journal of bishop Mota y Escobar, who passed through here in 1609–10 and later.[11] We have tributary data for 1626–96,[12] and the report of further episcopal visits in 1643–6.[13] A missing relación of *c.* 1743 is condensed in Villaseñor y Sánchez (I, pp. 302–6). Padrones drawn up in 1777 by the priests of all but two parishes (Cuyoaco and S Juan) have been found.[14] A valuable description dated 1791 is accompanied by a good map and a padrón,[15] and there is another list of toponyms made in 1792.[16]

73 *San Luis de la Paz*

Today occupying the northeast corner of Guanajuato state, this is an extremely arid, mountainous region (800–2,600 m), most of it draining eastward into the Pánuco system through great, eroded canyons.

This was part of what was known as the Sierra Gorda, the home of Chichimecs, hunters and gatherers living in isolated rancherías. Guamare was spoken in the west, Pame in the east. If there was an early Tarascan penetration, it was no longer evident when the Spaniards arrived.[1]

This area was left to the Indians for several decades. It was explored from the mid-1540s by the Franciscan Fray Juan de San Miguel and by Juan Sánchez de Alanís, a magistrate of Xilotepec,

who established Otomí outposts with a few friendly Chichimecs at Sichú and Puxinguía (Jiménez Moreno, 1958, pp. 81–4. Powell, p. 162. Velázquez, 1946–8, I, p. 358). Sánchez de Alanís became a priest and lived among the Indians for many years. In the 1580s Franciscans took over the doctrina of Sichú, protected by a few soldiers, and in 1590 the Jesuits established themselves at S Luis de la Paz with a mission of Otomies, Mexicans, and Tarascans. Very soon afterward the mines of Sichú began to be exploited, and the jurisdiction was gradually occupied by Spanish miners and cattlemen, although Chichimec raids and uprisings continued well into the seventeenth century (Jiménez Moreno, 1958, p. 91. Powell, p. 209).

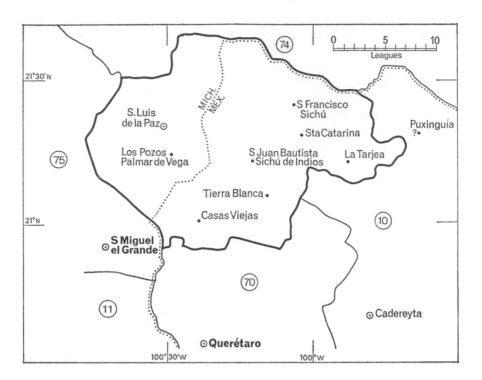

No attempt was made to distribute encomiendas here, although in early years the Indians paid a nominal tribute.

Government

Sichú y Puxinguía appear in a list of crown possessions dated 1550, although the order for organizing a corregimiento does not seem to have been issued until April, 1552.[2] The first C was Juan Sánchez de Alanís, justice of Xilotepec, who with the additional title of *Justicia mayor en los chichimecas* spent much of his time in this frontier area in the 1550s, continuing as a missionary (*see below*) into the 1570s.[3] In a list of *c.* 1567 Sichú y Puxinguía appear as a corregimiento suffragan to Michoacán. The area was nominally attached to the gobierno of Nuevo León in 1579, but we do not know that the governor, Carvajal, visited it (Velázquez, 1946–8, I, pp. 326, 328, 335). In the 1590s, with the opening of the mines, the C became AM of Minas de Sichú.[4]

In 1595 the newly-opened mines of Palmar de Vega were attached to the jurisdiction of S Miguel el Grande, and four years later the AM of Sichú took charge of the real of Escanela.[5] Early in the seventeenth century there was an adjustment of boundaries here by which Palmar de Vega and S Luis de la Paz were transferred to the alcaldía mayor of Sichú, and the mines of Escanela were put under a separate AM (cf. Cadereyta) whose jurisdiction included Puxinguía. For some time the commander of the garrison at S Luis functioned as a local magistrate, but toward the end of the seventeenth century the jurisdiction began to be called S Luis de la Paz, an indication that the AM had moved his residence there from Sichú (*Títulos de Indias*). After 1787 the alcaldía mayor became a subdelegación in the intendencia of Guanaxuato.

Church

Writing in 1571, the bishop of Michoacán stated that Juan Sánchez de Alanís had for many years been vicar in charge of the Indians of Sichú. Sometime between 1583 and 1586 this doctrina, known as S Juan Bautista Sichú de los Indios,

was given to the Franciscans of the province of
S Pedro y S Pablo de Michoacán, although
at the same time (1586) it was transferred from the
diocese of Michoacán to the archdiocese of
Mexico (Bravo Ugarte, 1963, p. 65. Miranda
Godínez, 9/41. Muñoz, p. 17). Four years later
S Luis de la Paz was founded as a Jesuit mission
(diocese of Michoacán), and not long afterward
a secular priest was assigned to the mining camp
of S Francisco Sichú de los Amues (in the archbishopric) (Powell, p. 209. Jiménez Moreno,
1958, p. 91). By 1639 the real of S Pedro de los
Pozos (Palmar de Vega) had its own parish priest,
subordinate to Michoacán. A Dominican mission
seems to have existed at Sta Rosa, quite close to
Sichú de los Amues, by 1683, but it was abandoned sometime before 1743 (Espinosa, 1964,
pp. 228–9). The Jesuits were replaced by secular
clergy in 1767 and the Franciscans two years
later, at which time a separate priest (from the
archdiocese of Mexico) was assigned to S José
Casas Viejas.

Population and settlements

The original Chichimec population was gradually
replaced by other Indians, principally Otomíes
and Mexicans with a few Tarascans, beginning
in the 1540s. In 1571 there were 585 tributaries
at Sichú and its dependencies (Miranda Godínez,
9/41). The 1743 report shows 2,343 Indian families
in the jurisdiction, including a few Chichimecs
in the east around Sichú. By 1803 there were
3,762 Indian tributaries.[6]

Spaniards, mestizos, and Negroes moved into
the area and settled at the various mining camps
and haciendas after 1590. In 1743 there were 190
families of Spaniards, 263 of mestizos, and 310
of Negroes and mulattoes. 375 mulatto tributaries
were registered in 1803.

Sichú and Puxinguía between them had ten
subject estancias in 1552–71, although most of
them were in what became the jurisdiction of
Cadereyta. By 1743 the Indians in the east were
concentrated in three settlements, S Juan Bautista
Sichú with its dependency Sto Tomás Tierra
Blanca (apparently a sixteenth-century Otomí
foundation), and another cabecera, Sta Catarina

Mártir; there was also in that year a barrio of
Chichimecs, subject to Sichú, called La Siene-
guilla, or Nuestra Señora de Guadalupe (Velázquez,
1946–8, I, pp. 370–2).

The real de minas of S Francisco Sichú de los
Amues (Suchi, Sinchue; 1950: Xichú, pueblo),
founded towards 1590, was still functioning on a
modest scale in 1743, together with a smaller
mining camp, La Tarjea.

The Jesuit mission of S Luis de la Paz (1950:
ciudad) in 1649 had four or five Spaniards and
50 or 60 Indian families, in addition to the tiny
presidio with a captain-magistrate and four Spanish
soldiers. A century later it was a thriving agricultural and wine-producing center with four Indian
barrios. The nearby mining camp of Los Pozos or
Palmar de Vega (1950: Pozos, ciudad), founded
soon after S Luis in the early 1590s, had seven
Spanish vecinos and 90 'personas de servicio' in
1649; by 1743 the mines were no longer worked, but
there were a number of haciendas in the vicinity.

S José (S Juan) de los Llanos, or Casas Viejas
(1950: S. José Iturbide, ciudad), a parochial center
founded in 1769 on lands belonging to a powerful
mayorazgo, did not thrive. In 1777 it had only two
families, and it is not mentioned as a pueblo in 1792.

Sources

A document of 1552 tells of the foundation of
Sichú and lists its estancias (L de T, pp. 296–7),
while the 1571 report of the bishop of Michoacán
describes the doctrina as it was two decades
later (Miranda Godínez, 9/41). There was a
relación geográfica in the 1580 series, but it has
been lost. Ponce (I, pp. 222–3) gives a brief
account of the mission as it was in 1586.

The western part of the jurisdiction is covered
in two reports dated 1639[7] and 1649.[8]

There are two copies of the 1743 padrón, one
accompanied by a long *expediente* answering the
questions posed in the cédula of 1741.[9] Two
parishes, Casas Viejas and Palmar de Vega, are
described in the 1777–8 series of 'topographic'
reports.[10] We have also seen a list of placenames
dated 1792.[11]

Monographic treatment of the area includes
Soustelle (1937) and Velázquez (1946–8).

74 *San Luis Potosí*

The colonial jurisdiction of this name occupied the central portion of what is now the state of S Luis Potosí (the rest of the modern state was divided between Valles, El Venado y la Hedionda, and Nueva Galicia). This is in general a high (800–2,800 m) plateau sloping gently towards the Gulf but with areas of internal drainage. The higher, western part is quite dry and cool, with eroded mountain ranges and xerophytic grasslands. The Río Verde area, to the east, is lower, warmer and rainier.

There were three groups of hunters and gatherers here, the Guamares occupying the southwest corner, the Pames south and east of Río Verde, and the Guachichiles to the north. A sub-group of the Guamares known as the Guaxabanes lived in the vicinity of Sta María del Río. The population was thinly distributed in rancherías with a primitive political organization.[1]

First Spanish contact was probably in the early 1550s, when the Franciscan Cossin went from S Miguel to the vicinity of Sta María del Río. In the following decade, Augustinians and others from S Felipe entered the valley of S Francisco, where a presidio was established perhaps as early as 1573. A military expedition led by the mestizo Miguel Caldera resulted in the founding of a Franciscan mission among the Guachichiles at Mezquitic in 1583, but it was not until 1592 that a real de minas was settled at S Luis Potosí; in the same year, Caldera explored the Río Verde area, which began to be invaded by cattle-raisers from Querétaro towards the end of the century. Sedentary Indians (Tlaxcalans, Otomies, Tarascans) immigrated from the south to work in mines and haciendas and gradually replaced the Chichimecs, although the latter continued to raid Spanish settlements into the eighteenth century. The eastern and northern parts of the jurisdiction came more or less under Spanish control in 1616–17, with the establishment of Franciscan missions around Río Verde and the opening of the Guadalcázar mines (Borah, 1964, p. 540. García Pimentel, 1904, pp. 122–4. Jiménez Moreno, 1958, pp. 36, 79–80, 84, 86. Powell, p. 147. Velázquez, 1946–8, I, pp. 357–9, 409, 416–18, 434–5, 510; II, pp. 94, 98–105).

There were no encomiendas here.

Government

Before the appointment of an AM at Minas de S Luis in 1592, the area or parts of it were claimed by the *justicias* of Xilotepec, S Miguel el Grande, Minas de Sichú, Querétaro, Pánuco, Valles, Nuevo León, and Nueva Galicia (Charcas). Further to complicate matters, Miguel Caldera and his successors in the office of *justicia mayor de chichimecas y tlaxcaltecas* were supposed to handle Indian affairs until late in the seventeenth century, frequently colliding in jurisdictional disputes with the AM, who held the additional military title of *teniente de capitán general*. The valley of S Francisco was contested between S Luis Potosí and S Miguel until it was assigned to the former in 1605. A similar dispute over Sierra de Pinos was resolved in favor of Nueva Galicia, which had an AM there by 1605. The Río Verde area, claimed by S Luis, Querétaro, Sichú, and Valles, was administered from S Luis from 1618 (Velázquez, 1946–8, I, pp. 393, 508; II, pp. 28, 45–8, 90, 99, 107, 167, 243). Venado y la Hedionda (q.v.), throughout the seventeenth century and later, were the object of a four-sided jurisdictional struggle between the AM of S Luis, the justicia mayor of Chichimecas, the administrator of the Peñol Blanco saltworks, and the AM of Charcas, until a separate AM was appointed *c.* 1770. The Tula–Palmillas–Jaumave area, claimed by both Valles and S Luis, seems to have been assigned to the gobierno of Nuevo Santander in the 1770s.

When mines were opened at S Pedro Guadalcázar, a separate AM resided there from 1618

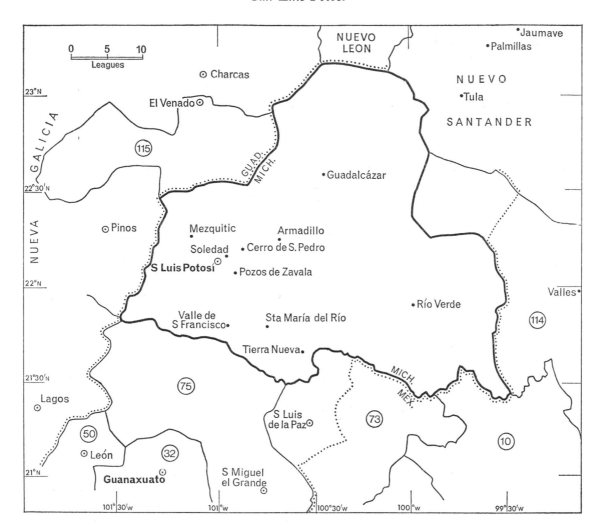

until 1743, when the area was returned to S Luis. During this period, the Río Verde missions remained in the jurisdiction of S Luis Potosí with the exception of those from Tula to Jaumave, which belonged to Guadalcázar.

In the eighteenth century tenientes of the AM were posted at Armadillo, Guadalcázar, Pozos, Río Verde, S Pedro, Sta María del Río, and Valle de S Francisco. From 1787 S Luis Potosí was the residence of an intendente, with subdelegados at Guadalcázar, Río Verde, Sta María del Río, and Valle de S Francisco (annexed to Sta María in 1792). The intendencia also included the former alcaldías mayores of Valles and Venado y la

Hedionda in Nueva España, and Charcas in Nueva Galicia, together with the northern gobiernos of Coahuila, Nuevo León, Nuevo Santander, and Texas.

Church

While Franciscan and Augustinian missionaries visited here in the 1550s and 1560s, the first permanent mission was more than likely that of S Miguel Mezquitic, a Franciscan hospice from 1583 and a monastery–parish from 1590. This and other Franciscan establishments in the jurisdiction first came under the province of S Pedro y S Pablo de Michoacán, although in the following century they (with the exception of the Río Verde missions) were transferred to the Colegio of Guadalupe de Zacatecas.

The second Franciscan mission, Sta María (Asunción) Atotonilco or Sta María del Río, may date from 1589, while a Franciscan monastery was opened at S Luis Potosí in 1591 (Jiménez Moreno, 1958, pp. 145–6. Powell, p. 147). The regulars at S Luis were joined in 1593 by a secular priest from the diocese of Guadalaxara, soon replaced by an appointee of the bishop of Michoacán. When the Augustinians arrived at the real in 1603, parochial duties were divided between the two regular orders and the secular curates. A Franciscan visita, Asunción Tlaxcalilla, soon become a separate parish, as did (some time later) the Augustinian visita of S Sebastián (Velázquez, 1946–8, II, pp. 10–11, 36, 57, 314–15).

By 1639 secular parishes had been organized at Sta Isabel (S Nicolás) Armadillo, Cerro de S Pedro, S Pedro Guadalcázar, S Francisco de los Pozos, and Valle de S Francisco.

In 1597 the Río Verde area was claimed for the archdiocese of Mexico, and a priest from Querétaro resided there briefly, but in 1607 the Franciscan Mollinedo arrived to choose mission sites, and the region was set aside for the province of Michoacán of his order. Ten years later Franciscan mission-parishes were established at Sta Catarina del Río Verde, S Felipe de los Gamotes, S Antonio Lagunillas, and Presentación Pinihuán. In 1621 the Custodia of Río Verde was organized to minister these and other parishes in the adjoining jurisdictions of Valles (q.v.) and Escanela (cf. Cadereyta). S José de los Montes de Alaquines was a separate mission from *c.* 1680, and Divina Pastora de Piedras Negras from 1753 (Borah, 1964, pp. 544–5. Espinosa, 1964, p. 298. Velázquez, 1946–8, II, pp. 28, 94–5, 297–9).

The parishes of Mezquitic, S Sebastián, and Sta María del Río were secularized sometime after 1744. Tlaxcalilla and the Río Verde missions remained Franciscan doctrinas until after Independence. All parishes, after the early claims of Guadalaxara and Mexico were set aside, belonged to the diocese of Michoacán.

Population and settlements

The Indians here were long exempt from tribute payment, and there is little information on the native population. The Pames are reported to have had large rancherías while those of the Guachichiles were somewhat smaller. Beginning in 1591, with the arrival of Tlaxcalan immigrants at Mezquitic and S Luis (moved the following year to Tlaxcalilla), the Guachichiles declined. Forced from their lands, some went to work for Spaniards in the mines and haciendas, but many died from disease and other causes, and others moved on to the wilder areas. By 1614 the Indians around S Luis were predominantly Tlaxcalans, Mexicans, Otomies, and Tarascans. The Chichimecs of the Río Verde survived longer, protected by the missionaries and joined by Guachichiles fleeing from the mining camps in the west, but here also haciendas and missions attracted Otomies and other *advenedizos* better suited to sedentary life. Epidemics in 1738–9 and 1762–3 caused much mortality (Velázquez, 1946–8, II, pp. 88, 489). In 1743–4 there were 4,955 Indian families in the jurisdiction. The 1800 census shows 9,389 Indian tributaries.[2]

Even for the non-Indian population there is an annoying paucity of data. We know that Spaniards, mestizos, mulattoes, and Negroes formed a large proportion of the total in mining camps and haciendas beginning in the 1590s, that the population fell off during the mining depression of the mid-1600s and recovered towards the end of that century. In 1649 there were perhaps 800 non-Indian families in the jurisdiction, 500 of them at S Luis. The 1743–4 census shows 4,560 families of Spaniards, mestizos, and mulattoes. In 1800 there were 4,817 free Negro and mulatto tributaries.

S Luis Potosí (1950: ciudad) was founded in 1592 and became a ciudad in 1656. The mines at Cerro de S Pedro were discovered in 1592, and those of Guadalcázar in 1615. Mezquitic (1950: Mexquitic, villa) and Atotonilco were settlements of Christianized Indians established in 1589–91; the latter was moved to its final site at Sta María del Río (1950: ciudad) in 1610. Armadillo (1950:

Villa Morelos), Monte de Caldera (1950: congregación), Pozos de Zavala (1950: Pozos, congregación), and Valle de S Francisco (1950: Villa de Reyes) were all at first dispersed congregations, largely of non-Indians living in haciendas with a parish church at the center; all existed by 1639. Other pueblos in the west were Tierra Nueva (founded in 1712) and Soledad (by 1793) (Borah, 1964, p. 540. Powell, pp. 213–15. Velázquez, 1946–8, I, pp. 438–46; II, pp. 194, 315–20).

The mission foundations grouped around Río Verde are mentioned above. A non-Indian settlement, Villa del Dulce Nombre de Jesús, was begun in 1694 just west of Sta Catarina Río Verde and became the cabecera (1950: Ríoverde, ciudad).

In 1793 there were fifty-eight haciendas and a great many ranchos in the jurisdiction.

Sources

Few parts of New Spain have been the object of such scholarly attention as that devoted to S Luis Potosí in the eight thick volumes compiled by Primo Feliciano Velázquez (1897–9, 1946–8); numerous documents are given in excerpt or summary in these two works. Woodrow Borah (1964) used a private collection in his admirable study of a seventeenth-century provincial administration at S Luis.

We have little to add. There are valuable if brief descriptions of the area dated 1639[3] and 1649,[4] relaciones for both S Luis and Guadalcázar in 1743–4,[5] and a 'topographic' report from Guadalcázar in 1778.[6] We have seen lists of placenames dated 1792 and 1793,[7] and a detailed report on the Río Verde missions of 1800.[8]

75 *San Miguel el Grande*

The territory assigned to the twin *villas* of S Miguel and S Felipe, now in north central Guanajuato, is a bleak country of broad plains and eroded hills on the Meseta Central (1,800–2,900 m), draining into the Lerma or Santiago system. The climate is cool and excessively dry.

While there is some evidence that the Tarascans had outposts in this area at one time, on the arrival of the Spaniards it was mostly occupied by Guamare-speaking Chichimecs (Jiménez Moreno, 1958, pp. 63–4). We assume that the situation at contact was similar to that of the 1570s, when the 'principal habitation' of the Guamares was in the vicinity of S Miguel el Grande; they then extended from Chamacuero to Guanajuato and S Felipe. Beyond S Felipe was another Chichimec group, the Guachichiles. Tribes within the Guamare area included the Copuces and the Guaxabanes in the north. These Indians were hunters and gatherers and lived in dispersed rancherías.[1]

First contact may have occurred in the late 1520s, but no settlement was effected until 1542–5, when Franciscans with Otomí and Tarascan colonists from Acámbaro established a mission near the future site of S Miguel. Later in that decade and in the early 1550s, despite unsettled conditions related to the Mixton war and subsequent disturbances, the Franciscans extended their sphere of influence, and Spaniards began grazing cattle near S Miguel. Augustinians may have entered the S Felipe region at this time. In 1549–50 a cart-road leading from Mexico to the Zacatecas mines was opened through here. To protect this vital artery from Indian attacks, Spanish settlements were founded at S Miguel (1555) and S Felipe (1561–2), but Chichimec raids continued into the 1580s (Jiménez Moreno, 1958, pp. 54–6, 80, 84. Powell, pp. 5, 67–9).

The Indians here were not granted in encomienda.

Government

In the late 1540s this region was placed within the jurisdiction of the justicia mayor of Chichimecas y Provincia de Xilotepec. The founder of S Miguel el Grande, Angel de Villafañe, was made AM of the new *villa* at the end of 1555, but this

long endure, and the AM of Xilo-
~imecas continued in charge at
~la of S Felipe was settled in 1562.
~ortly afterwards the two settlements
~re combined in one large jurisdiction under
an AM resident at S Miguel. Each *villa*, of course,
had its ayuntamiento for local administration.[2]

The territorial aspirations of this alcaldía
mayor were much curtailed with the appointment
of an AM at S Luis Potosí (q.v.) in 1592; the
valley of S Francisco, which had been settled from
S Felipe, was claimed by both magistrates but
was assigned to S Luis in 1605. Meanwhile, the
mines of Palmar de Vega were attached to the
jurisdiction of S Miguel in 1595 and remained
in it until they, together with S Luis de la Paz
(q.v.), were transferred to the AM of Sichú
early in the seventeenth century.[3]

The AM of S Miguel generally kept a deputy
at S Felipe. After 1787 S Miguel and Dolores each
had a subdelegado subordinate to the intendente
of Guanaxuato.

Church

A Franciscan mission subordinate to the doctrina
of Acámbaro began at the original site of S Miguel

towards 1542. It was raided by the Chichimecs
in 1551, and when the Spanish settlement four
years later was founded nearby at a site until then
known as Izcuinapan, parochial duties were
assumed by a secular priest of the diocese of
Michoacán: however, the place had a Franciscan
cloister throughout the colonial period.

In the first decade or so after its founding, the
villa of S Felipe had a small Augustinian monastery with parochial functions. Subsequently (by
1583) the doctrina seems to have been turned over
to Franciscans who ministered there until they
were replaced by secular clergy sometime between
1743 and 1770. Los Dolores, midway between the
two *villas*, had a secular priest from 1717–20.
This, as well as the other parishes, was in the
bishopric of Michoacán.

Population and settlements

Beginning in the 1550s, the Chichimecs were
gradually displaced by Tarascans and Otomies
and, to a lesser extent, Mexicans, who came to
form Indian congregations near the *villas* and to
work on the Spaniards' cattle estancias and
haciendas. There were 100 Christianized Indian
families at S Miguel in 1571, and a small colony
of Tarascans at S Felipe; by 1649 there were
Mexicans and Otomies as well as Tarascans
throughout the jurisdiction. We have no numeri-
cal data before 1800, when there were 6,423
Indian tributaries altogether.[4]

S Miguel and S Felipe each had some 20 Spanish
vecinos in 1571. By 1649 the number had increased to 62 vecinos at S Miguel and had dropped
to 12 or 14 at S Felipe, but there were other
Spaniards, together with a growing mestizo
population and a good number of mulattoes
and Negro slaves, living on eighty-two haciendas.
The 1743 report gives the non-Indian population
as 3,000 families at S Miguel, 500 at S Felipe, and
200 at Los Dolores. In 1800 there were 1,591 free
Negro and mulatto tributaries.

Both S Miguel el Grande, as it came to be
called (1950: S Miguel de Allende, ciudad), and
S Felipe (1950: ciudad) were established on sites
previously occupied by Spanish cattle haciendas,
from which land was taken to form the two

settlements and their ejidos. A presidio at Portezuelos (1950: Ocampo, pueblo?), founded *c.* 1570, was probably abandoned in the 1590s. Around the two central settlements, from their inception, the Spanish vecinos were given grants of land to develop new haciendas, principally devoted to cattle breeding. S Miguel, in the eighteenth century, became a thriving center for the manufacture of sarapes, leather, and iron goods (Chevalier, p. 62. Wolf, p. 184). Towards 1717 a congregación known as Pueblo Nuevo de los Dolores (1950: Dolores Hidalgo, ciudad) became a new parochial center and settlement.

Sources

There is a report of *c.* 1570 describing the Augustinian doctrina of S Felipe,[5] and another, quite brief, concerning the secular parish of S Miguel in 1571 (Miranda Godínez, 9/41). A relación of *c.* 1580 has been lost, but the map which went with it has survived.[6]

Reports drawn up in 1639[7] and 1649[8] are followed by a brief summary in Villaseñor y Sánchez (II, pp. 35–8) of the missing relación of *c.* 1743. There is an excellent description of S Miguel parish, with colored sketches of the Indians, prepared by a friar in 1777.[9] We have seen two lists of placenames, accompanied by padrones, made in 1792.[10]

Ajofrín (I, pp. 291–6) visited S Miguel in 1764 and has a little map of the *villa* in his journal. Both Lafora (pp. 212–13) and Morfi (pp. 9–11) have interesting things to say about this area, which they traversed in 1768 and 1777 respectively.

The monograph of Maza (1939) should be consulted.

76 *Sayula*

Also known as the province of Avalos (after its sixteenth-century encomendero), this region in what is now south central Jalisco extends from the Sierra de Tapalpa (2,800 m) to the shores of Lake Chapala (1,500 m), and includes the interior drainage basins of Atotonilco and Sayula, as well as headwaters of the Armería and Ameca systems flowing towards the Pacific (minimum elevation, 1,300 m). The climate is mostly dry and temperate with sparse vegetation, but the higher parts are cold and forested.

Not long before the Spaniards arrived, the Tarascans seem to have invaded this area inhabited by people speaking at least four languages (*Relación de...Michoacán*). The southernmost political division with its center at Zayolla extended southward across the mountains to Atlaco; the language here was Sayultecan, probably in the Nahua group. Between Zayolla and Lake Chapala were six states where 'Pinome' was spoken, Tépec, Amacueca, Atoyac, Tachalotlan, Tzacualco, and Teocitatlan or Teocuitlatlan. Off to the northwest were a people speaking Coca or Tachtoque (related to Pinome) with their center at Cocolla. Another language of Nahua affiliation prevailed along the shore of Lake Chapala, at Xocotépec, Cuetzala, and Chapalla (cf. Santoscoy).

The western part of this area from Zayolla to Cocolla was reduced to Spanish rule towards 1524, presumably by an expedition originating in Michoacán. By 1530 control had been extended to the western end of Lake Chapala.

Encomiendas

Atoyac, Cocula, Chulitla, Tusitatan, Çaqualco, and Çayula appear in a tribute assessment of May 1528, as an encomienda held jointly by Alonso de Avalos (Dávalos) and his brother, Fernando de Saavedra.[1] In September of that year Saavedra, a resident of Tenochtitlan, commissioned Francisco de Mendoza as resident administrator 'in the Indian villages of the province of Tevquitatlen' which he held in encomienda (Millares Carlo and Mantecón, I, no. 1470). This grant perhaps originated with governor Estrada, one of whose daughters married Alonso de Avalos, although the brothers were cousins of Cortés and may have received their encomienda from him. It seems to

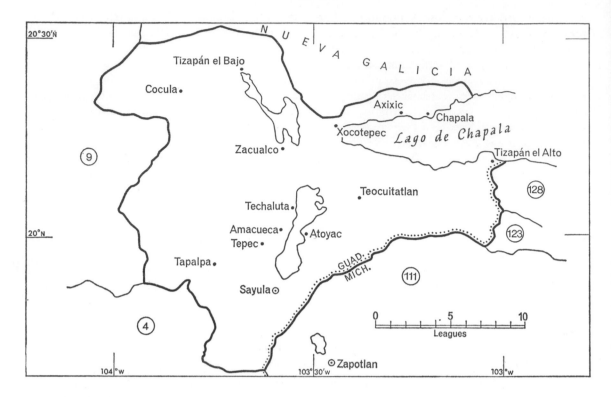

have been re-assigned by the first audiencia, perhaps to Alonso de Vargas or Manuel de Guzmán, and returned to the Avalos-Saavedra brothers under the second (Dorantes de Carranza, pp. 264, 270–1. Icaza, II, p. 65. Sauer, 1948, pp. 26–32. Simpson, 1950, p. 167. Velázquez, 1968, p. 178). Sometime between 1536 and 1545 Fernando de Saavedra's half escheated (*see below*).

Alonso de Avalos Saavedra, who in 1528 appears as a resident of both Mexico and Michoacán, was still alive in Guadalaxara 40 years later. On his death not long thereafter he was succeeded by a son, Fernando (Gonzalo?) de Avalos, who married Mariana Infante Samaniego; the latter appears as holder in 1597–1604, by which time she had remarried to Rodrigo de Villegas. There were no further heirs, and in 1606 the tributes were re-assigned to Sebastián Vizcaíno; the descendants of the latter continued as encomenderos of the former Avalos share after Vizcaíno's death in the early 1620s. A tenth of the tributes were still privately assigned as late as 1801

(Scholes and Adams, 1959, p. 68. Velázquez, 1968, p. 173).

Government

We have mentioned the acquisition by the crown of half of this vast encomienda shortly before 1545, in which year 'Atoyaque' appears in a list of corregimientos in Nueva España. There had been a dispute over jurisdiction here beginning in 1530, when Nuño de Guzmán claimed the area for Nueva Galicia, but a cédula of 1533 assigned it to Mexico. By 1552 the magistrate was referred to as AM of Pueblos de Avalos and C of the crown half.[2] In the 1570s and 1580s this official resided at Zacualco.[3]

Late in 1578 a cédula arrived placing this and neighboring jurisdictions within the judicial limits of the audiencia of Guadalaxara, although matters of gobierno were still to be handled from Mexico city.[4] This order caused much confusion in later years and was not always obeyed. By 1615 the AM had moved to Sayula, and although the Avalos encomienda had passed into other hands (*see above*) the old designation, Provincia de Avalos, was still used occasionally. In 1787 the magistrate became a subdelegado under the intendente of Guadalaxara, with *tenientes* at Atoyac, Cocula, Tapalpa, Tizapán el Alto, Xocotepec, and Zacualco.

Church

The Franciscans arrived *c.* 1530 and founded a monastery at S Andrés Axixic the following year (Ricard, p. 83. Torres, p. 35). Subsequent regular parochial foundations, all in the province of Santiago de Xalisco (from 1606), occurred at S Francisco Amacueca in 1547, S Francisco Chapala in 1548, and S Francisco Zacualco in 1550 (Ricard, p. 86). By 1569 the parish seat of Amacueca had been moved to S Francisco Sayula and there were additional Franciscan doctrinas at S Juan Bautista Atoyac and S Miguel Cocula. In a list of 1583 we find Amacueca again a parish center and two more Franciscan residences, S Sebastián Techalutla, and S Miguel Teocuitatlan; within a few years Amacueca, Chapala, and Teocuitatlan were reduced to the status of visitas or vicarías subject to neighboring parishes, but they were separate doctrinas again by 1743 (Muñoz, p. 18). Tizapán el Alto and S Antonio Tapalpa also appear as Franciscan parishes in the 1743 report (the minister of Tapalpa was living at S Gaspar Ataco in that year).

Secularization of Chapala, Sayula, Techalutla, Teocuitatlan, Tizapán el Alto, and Zacualco parishes had occurred by 1760. In 1791 Axixic was in charge of a secular priest living at S Francisco Xocotepec, and Tapalpa had also been secularized. Only Cocula survived as a Franciscan doctrina until after Independence. The area was in the diocese of Michoacán until 1548, after which ecclesiastical jurisdiction was claimed and eventually secured by the bishopric of Nueva Galicia or Guadalaxara.

Population and settlements

The *Suma de visitas* (*c.* 1548) gives a total of 10,920 tributaries. Later counts show 5,800 tributaries in 1569, 3,500 in 1597, 1,625 in 1605, and 1,372 in 1657, after which there was a recovery to 1,656 tributaries in 1698, 3,072 Indian families in 1743, 5,626 (families) in 1760, 7,290 (tributaries) in 1788, and 7,433 Indian tributaries in 1801.[5]

Ponce found 'many Spaniards' at Sayula in 1587, and others arrived later to found haciendas and live in the towns. The 1743 census has 1,371 families of Spaniards and castas in the jurisdiction, while a 1760 report gives 4,228 such families. Sayula and Cocula were predominantly non-Indian settlements by 1743, soon to be joined by Amacueca and Atoyac. That there was a large Negroid element can be seen from the 1801 tributary count, which has 1,498 free Negro and mulatto tributaries (excluding slaves).

The Franciscans moved some cabeceras about and may have reduced the Indians to fewer settlements. The cacique of Cuetzala changed his court to Axixic, and that of Cocula moved from a hill-site to the plains below, both at Franciscan urging in the 1530s; we assume that similar changes of site occurred elsewhere. An attempt at congregation proposed in 1598 seems to have had little effect.[6] The listing of 1548 shows eleven cabeceras with twenty-one subordinate settlements; of the latter, five had disappeared by the eighteenth century, but nine 'new' settlements (some actually founded before 1600) had achieved pueblo status. One place, Tepec, was claimed as a *sujeto* by Amacueca in 1576 and lost its former cabecera category.[7] On the other hand, certain sujetos later became cabeceras (there were eighteen altogether in 1801).

Amacueca (1950: pueblo) had four estancias in 1548. Two of them (Atlimaxac or Atemaxac, Xalpa) were subject pueblos in the eighteenth century, Tapalpa became a cabecera, and a barrio of Atemaxac called Xonacatlan or Juanacatlan had been transferred as a subject pueblo to Zacualco by 1743.

Atoyac (1950: *villa*) had two estancias in 1548; only one, Cuyacapan, survived as a pueblo.

S Andrés Axixique (Axixic; 1950: Ajijic, pueblo) had three dependencies, Cuezala (Cosalá, the original cabecera), S Buenaventura Tomatlan, and S Cristóbal Zapotitlan de la Laguna. Tomatlan seems to have disappeared *c.* 1600, the other places continuing as pueblos.

Cocula (1950: ciudad) in the 1580s had three sujetos. Acatlan (S Martín de la Cal), Sta Cruz, and Tizapán el Bajo (Tizapanito) all survived as pueblos.[8]

Only four estancias appear under Chapala (1950: *villa*) in 1548, but there were two more in 1585, and five were pueblos in 1743–92. Atecontitlan can perhaps be identified with Sta Cruz Soledad, Coacan became Istlahuacan, while the others were S Luis Soyatlan, Tlayacapan, and Tuscueca (S Bartolomé disappeared *c.* 1600).

Taxelutla (1548) became Tlachelutla and eventually Techaluta (1950: pueblo), it had no estancias.

The 'Tusitatan' mentioned as a cabecera in 1528 was most likely the same as Çitatlan, one of three sujetos of Teucuitlatlan (Teocuitatlan; 1950: Teocuitatlán de Corona, pueblo) in 1548. It was abandoned, together with Toluco (Toluquilla), in the sixteenth century, while Tizapán el Alto, far to the east on the lake shore, became a cabecera.

Xucutepeque (Xocotepec, Jocotepec; 1950: *villa*), another lakeside cabecera, had three nearby dependencies in 1585, one of which, S Martín Techistlan, was a pueblo in 1791–2.

Under Zacualco (Zacoalco; 1950: *villa*) there was only one estancia, Sta Ana Acatlan, in the late sixteenth century. By 1648 there were two more, S Marcos and Atotonilco (all were some distance north of the cabecera, along the boundary with Nueva Galicia), and all three survived.[9]

Zayula (Sayula; 1950: ciudad) also grew, from three estancias in 1548 to five in 1792. The original settlements were Atlaco (Ataco), Huxumachaque (Axomaxac, Osmaxac, Uxmajac), and Xequilistla (Chiquilistlan). Apango is mentioned as early as 1648, while Ameca was perhaps an eighteenth-century foundation.

In addition to these pueblos, there were in 1792 twenty-nine haciendas and 133 ranchos in the jurisdiction.

Sources

The eleven original Avalos cabeceras are briefly described in the *Suma* of *c.* 1548 (PNE, I, nos. 3–5, 102–5, 535–7, 796). A 1569 report is much abbreviated (Códice Franciscano, pp. 152–3) and a relación drawn up *c.* 1580 has disappeared, but there is a most useful description of the region in the journal of Father Ponce (I, pp. 43–4, 49–51; II, pp. 16–22, 43–5, 116–24), who visited most of the Franciscan missions in 1585–7.

The work of Mota y Escobar (pp. 59–62) on his diocese, written *c.* 1605, is of interest. For the rest of the seventeenth century, we have seen only an extract from a missing report of 1648 (Santoscoy) and a few tributary counts (Miranda, 1962a, p. 189. Scholes and Adams, 1959, p. 68).

There is an excellent report drawn up by the AM in 1743,[10] followed by a condensed census of all parishes dated 1760.[11] The curates of Amacueca, Cocula, and Atoyac submitted descriptions of their doctrinas in 1778.[12] Towards 1788 the subdelegado sent in census data for each settlement in his jurisdiction,[13] and three years later he wrote a general description of considerable interest.[14] For 1792 there is a complete list of placenames down to the category of rancho.[15] An undated document describing the area probably belongs to the end of the eighteenth century (*Noticias varias...*, pp. 53–61).

A 1563 map of the Chiquilistlan area is reproduced by Ramírez Flores (1959). Sauer (1948, pp. 26–32) discusses the Avalos encomienda in the sixteenth century.

77 *Sochicoatlan*

This is rugged, mountainous country, much of it forested, on the northeast slope of the Sierra Madre Oriental in Hidalgo state, draining into several affluents of the Tempoal, a major branch of the Pánuco system. Elevations range from less than 200 m near Huautla to 2,000 m above Xochicoatlán, with the expected variation in temperature. Precipitation is heavy and almost continuous.

At contact most if not all of this area was under

the hegemony of Metztitlan. Cuezalinco, Xochi-cuauhtlan, and Yahualiuhcan seem to have been autonomous states tributary to (or allies of) Metztitlan, while the status of Cuauhtlan is obscure. To the north was the hostile Huaxteca, to the east the Aztec tributary province of Xiuh-coac, and south of Yahualiuhcan was enemy territory belonging to Hueyacocotlan. A 'corrupt'

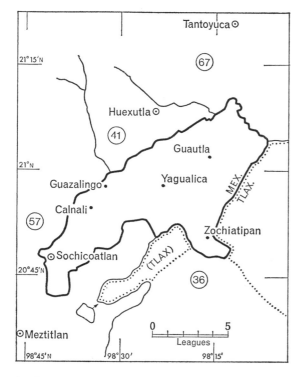

(archaic?) Náhuatl was spoken throughout, again with the possible exception of Cuauhtlan where there may have been an intrusion of Huaxtecan.

Spaniards perhaps first visited the region in 1522 and reduced it to submission soon afterwards.

Encomiendas

The right to assign encomiendas here was claimed by both Pánuco and New Spain in the late 1520s and early 1530s. Sochicoatlan was held by Gerónimo de Aguilar from *c.* 1526 until its escheat-ment in November 1531.[1]

Guzmán, as governor of Pánuco, assigned Guautla to two encomenderos, Juan de Cervantes and Andrés de Inero, who still held it at the

beginning of 1533. By the late 1540s they had been replaced by Cristóbal Bezos, followed *c.* 1550 by Isabel de Frías (Bezo's widow?) and her son, Cristóbal de Frías. The latter still appears in 1597, but soon afterward the tributes were re-assigned to the Moctezuma heirs. Partial escheatment occurred after 1643.

Guazalingo, held by Diego González in 1532–3, was later acquired by a Juan Rodríguez who in turn sold his rights to Gabriel de Aguilera, listed in 1548–69. Diego de Aguilera was encomendero in 1579, and Luis Hurtado de Mendoza in the 1590s. Tributes escheated between 1643 and 1688.[2]

Domingo Martín claimed Yagualica was granted him by Marcos de Aguilar in 1526, but it was re-assigned by Guzmán the following year to his secretary, Juan de Torquemada. Gómez Nieto appears as the holder in 1531–3, and Yagualica escheated sometime before 1545 (Chipman, pp. 160–1, 292).

Government

Soon after Guzmán arrived as governor of Pánuco in 1527 a boundary dispute developed between him and governor Estrada of Nueva España involving this region. After some rather bloody skirmishes, the cabildo of Tenochtitlan decided in February, 1528, to relinquish Guautla and Yagualica to Pánuco, retaining jurisdiction in Guazalingo and Sochicoatlan (*Actas de cabildo...*, I, p. 160. Chipman, pp. 153–7). The matter lost its signifi-cance after 1533, when Pánuco was re-united with Nueva España.

A C was first appointed to Sochicoatlan in late 1531, and another went to Yagualica sometime between 1536 and 1545. In the provincial division of the 1560s, Sochicoatlan was suffragan to Meztitlan and Yagualica to Pánuco. A decade later Yagualica was without a resident C, and its Indians were being visited by four neighboring justices (the AM of Meztitlan, the Cs of Huexutla and Tancuilave, and a magistrate from Tampico); the viceroy in 1576 ordered that only the AM of Meztitlan should enter the village.[3]

Towards the beginning of the seventeenth century both Yagualica (with Guautla and

Guazalingo) and Sochicoatlan became independent corregimientos, although the latter was annexed to Meztitlan briefly in 1603.[4] The two jurisdictions, their magistrates re-designated AMs, continued to exist side by side until they were combined, first in 1713 and again *c.* 1750.[5] From 1786 Yagualica, as it was now generally called, was a subdelegación in the intendencia of Mexico.

Church

The area was visited in the 1530s and later by Augustinians working out of Molango and Huexutla (*Diccionario Porrúa...*, p. 1585). In 1569 Sochicoatlan was in the parish of Molango and Guautla was a visita of Huexutla, while S Juan Bautista Yagualica had a secular curate also in charge of Guazalingo. S Nicolás Sochicoatlan was an Augustinian monastery–doctrina from 1572.

Sometime between 1684 and 1743 S José (S Pablo) Guazalingo was made a secular parish, and by 1771 S Marcos Calnali and Sta Catarina Zochiatipan had resident priests. Sochicoatlan was secularized in 1753. The area was on the borderline with the diocese of Tlaxcala (in 1684 a priest from Puebla was actually in charge of Yagualica), but all five parishes belonged to the archdiocese of Mexico.

Population and settlements

The number of tributaries dropped from 3,110 in 1548 to 2,613 in 1570, *c.* 1,700 in 1600, and 873 in 1643 (L de T, p. 303). In the 1590s the jurisdiction was a refuge for Indians fleeing from Spanish control, so there were some camping about who did not pay tribute.[6] Later counts show 1,245 tributaries in 1688, 2,268 Indian families in 1743, and 3,352 Indian tributaries in 1803.[7] Náhuatl continued (and continues) to be spoken.

There was little to attract non-Indians here. Sochicoatlan and Yagualica each had *c.* 60 families of Spaniards and castas in 1743. 33½ mulatto tributaries are reported in 1803.

S Juan Bautista Guautla (Cuautlan, etc.; 1950: Huautla pueblo) in 1548 had four sujetos within an area of three by four leagues. A congregation was proposed here in 1600.[8] In 1794 the cabecera had eight dependent rancherías.

Guazalingo (Cuetzalingo, Huatzalinco, etc.; 1950: Huazalingo, pueblo) had seven estancias in 1548 and nine in 1569. Only two of these places are recognizable among the pueblos which existed in 1794: Atotomoc, S Francisco and Sto Tomás Cuazahual, Chalchocotla, Chiatipan (Chiaticpac), S Pedro Huazalingo, and Tlamamala.

A 1570 report names thirty-seven places within ten leagues of Sochicoatlan (Suchiguautla, Xuchicuautlan, Zochicoatla, etc.; 1950: Xochicoatlán, pueblo). There was a congregation here in *c.* 1600, but in 1684 there were still fifteen pueblos and sixteen rancherías visited from the monastery, although there were only 433 tributaries altogether.[9] The congregation center for the northern estancias (in the tierra caliente) was Calnali (= Chinantlatoque in 1579?), which eventually became a separate cabecera. A surprisingly large number, twenty-one of the sixteenth-century communities survived as pueblos in the eighteenth century (these are indicated below with an asterisk), together with ten places not mentioned in 1548–70: Acomulco*, Aguacatlan*, Atempan*, Calnali, Conchitlan, Coyula*, Cuatlamayan*, Chalco (Papatlachalco*), Chichilchayotla (Chichiuhayotla*), Guacintlan (Cuamintlan*), Guatencalco (Cuentencalco*), Istaco, Mazalhuacan, Mecapala*, Michatla*, Papastla (Papachtlan*), Pauchula (Pazocholan*), Pesmatlan*, S Juan Evangelista, Santos Reyes, Tecpaco (Tepanco*), Tenexco*, Tescaco, Tlacuechac, Tochintlan, Tostlamantlan*, Tuzancoac*, Xacalco, Xalamelco*, Zacatipan*, Zapocuatlan (Tzapocuauhtla*).

The 1569 description of Yagualica (Ayagualican, Yahualiuhca; 1950: Yahualica, pueblo) mentions thirteen sujetos and five *hermitas*. An attempt at congregation began in the 1590s, and by 1603 the cabecera had been moved to a new site some distance away.[10] We guess that the old site was re-occupied at a later date and called Zochiatipan (Xochiatipan), which eventually became a cabecera also. Yagualica and Zochiatipan in 1794 had the following dependant pueblos: Achiocuatlan, Atotomoc, Cruzican, Cuahuecahuasco, Guazahual, Nanayatla, Pachiquitla, Pocantlan, Tecacahuasco, Tenexhueyac, Tlaltecatlan, Xoxolpan, Zacatlan, and Zoquitipan. Within Yagualica's limits there were in 1794 three haciendas and six ranchos.

Sources

The area, excluding Sochicoatlan, is covered in the *visita* of 1532–3 (cf. Chipman, pp. 292–3). Brief articles of *c.* 1548 in the *Suma* (PNE, I, nos. 26, 266–7, 488) are followed by reports dating from 1569–71 (García Pimentel, 1904, pp. 135, 143–4. PNE, III, pp. 120–3, 126–9). The 1579 relación of Meztitlan gives additional information.[11]

There are tributary data for 1643–88.[12] The journal of an archbishop's visit here in 1684 lists estancias at Guazalingo and Yagualica, but is of less value for Sochicoatlan.[13] There is a good report sent in by the AM of Sochicoatlan in 1743,[14] supplemented by the résumés of the twin jurisdictions in Villaseñor y Sánchez (I, pp. 128–9, 234–6). We have a complete list of toponyms and a report dated 1794.[15]

Further details are found in Fernández (1940–2).

78 *Sochimilco*

Sochimilco's pre-Conquest and colonial territory lay between the fresh-water lake of that name and the summit of the mountains which form the

south edge of the basin or valley of Mexico (this is now the southeast quadrant of the Distrito Federal). Elevations are 2,200–3,400 m, the climate cool with moderate seasonal rainfall.

The Xochimilca, once a powerful tribe whose domain extended far to the southeast (cf. Cuautla Amilpas), were dominated in the fifteenth century by the Mexica and Acolhuaque. Tribute, probably in the form of flowers and other produce of the chinampas (marshy garden plots along the lake shore), was taken by canoe to Tenochtitlan. The government of Xochimilco was shared between three tlatoque, the rulers of Olac, Tepetenchi, and Tecpan (Gibson, 1964, pp. 41–2). Settlements were considerably dispersed, but the principal community center on the lake-side was of urban proportions (Cortés, p. 143. Díaz del Castillo, I, pp. 481–2). Náhuatl was the language spoken, with an Otomí minority (Ponce, I, p. 173).

First contact with the Spaniards was in late 1519. The city of Xochimilco, after a spirited resistance in late April 1521, was razed by order of Cortés.

Encomienda

Sochimilco, assigned to Pedro de Alvarado, was briefly held in the 1530s by Alvarado's brother, Jorge (Sherman, p. 205). Escheatment occurred after the death of Pedro de Alvarado and his widow, on 10 September 1541 (ENE, I, p. 146. Icaza, I, p. 103. L de T, p. 304).

Government

A corregimiento from 1541, Sochimilco was suffragan to Tezcuco in the provincial division of the 1560s, but in the following decade and subsequently it was considered a quite independent jurisdiction whose magistrate was often referred to as AM. Tlalpan, originally part of Sochimilco, was transferred to Cuyoacán in the 1540s. From 1787 Sochimilco was a subdelegación in the intendencia of Mexico.

Church

The usual date given for the foundation of a Franciscan monastery at S Bernardino Sochimilco is 1535, but it may have been a decade earlier. The doctrina was divided, perhaps in the 1560s, with the establishment of another Franciscan house at Asunción Milpa Alta. While these two were the only parishes that survived as such, there were Franciscan *asistencias* or *vicarías* at S Antonio Tecómitl (by 1581), S Gregorio Atlapulco (by 1600), S Pedro Atocpan (by 1603), and Visitación (Sta María) Tepepan (by 1646).[1] Milpa Alta was secularized in 1772–4, and Sochimilco in 1786.

Population and settlements

After four decades of decline, there were still 10,583 native tributaries in Sochimilco in 1564 (there had been considerable loss during an epidemic the previous year) (L de T, p. 306). The number fell to 8,577 in 1570, and only 2,686 tributaries are reported in 1643. Later counts show 2,734 tributaries in 1688, and 3,440 Indian families in 1743. The 1778 census, after mentioning that over 2,000 Indians had died in a recent epidemic (probably that of 1772–3), gives a total of 18,049 persons, representing perhaps 4,000 tributaries. There were 4,282 Indian tributaries in 1801.[2]

'Many' Spaniards resided in Sochimilco in 1586, but only 300 non-Indians are reported in 1697. The following data are available for the late colonial period:

	Spaniards	Mestizos	Mulattoes	Total
1778	1,306	482	75	1,863
c. 1791	1,329	578	204	2,111

There was probably an early congregation of settlements at Sochimilco (Xochimilco, Suchi-milco; 1950: Xochimilco, ciudad), carried out by the Franciscans, but the Indians were still dispersed in thirty-odd sujetos in 1570. There was a good deal of shifting about, temporary abandonment of sites and re-location of the population, in 1600–4; here as elsewhere, these forced reductions were broken up and the natives gradually moved back to their ancestral homes.[3] By 1643 Asunción Milpa (Milpa Alta) was a separate cabecera, and one of its sujetos, S Pedro Atocpan, was given cabecera status before 1688. Twenty-nine subject pueblos are named in 1697, and twenty-six existed in 1791–4 (by 1801 there were four more cabeceras).[4]

Sources

There is a great deal of unexploited source material on Sochimilco. Gibson (1964, *passim*) has much to say about this jurisdiction and cites many documents.

Cortés (pp. 143–4) and Díaz del Castillo (I, pp. 481–2) describe Sochimilco as they saw it in 1521. The *Suma* article (c. 1548) is disappointingly brief (PNE, I, no. 500). Most of the jurisdiction appears on the unique Santa Cruz map of c. 1555 (Linné, 1948). Reports of 1558–64 describe the tribute system (Scholes and Adams, 1958, pp. 102–16, 122–5). Another document of c. 1570 lists estancias and contains population data.[5] Father Ponce (I, pp. 20–21, 77, 171–4, 196) visited this area on several occasions in 1585–6. The *Anales de San Gregorio Acapulco* (Tlalocan, III, pp. 103–41) contain information about land disputes here in the sixteenth century, and the congregations of c. 1603.

For the seventeenth century, we have tributary data for 1623–88,[6] the account of an archbishop's visit in 1646,[7] and a description of the Franciscan doctrinas c. 1697 (Vetancurt, 4a parte, pp. 56–7, 75, 84, 86, 88–9).

A lost report of c. 1743 is summarized in Villaseñor y Sánchez (I, 164–6). There is a general census of 1778,[8] an incomplete one made in 1783,[9] and a padrón of non-Indians, accompanied by an excellent map of the jurisdiction, of c. 1791.[10] For 1794 we have a complete list of placenames.[11]

79 Tacuba

Tacuba has now quite lost its identity, engulfed by the city of Mexico (Distrito Federal), but its colonial jurisdiction based on the late pre-Conquest limits extended from the lake shore to the summit of Sierra de las Cruces on the western edge of the valley or rather basin of Mexico (2,250–3,900 m); thus most of it is in what is now the state of

Mexico. The climate is cool to frigid depending on the altitude, with adequate seasonal rains.

The Tepaneca, a Náhuatl-speaking people, entered a period of military expansion towards the middle of the fourteenth century in which they became the dominant power in central Mexico, with their center at Azcaputzalco. In the 1430s they were defeated by the Mexica and the Acolhuaque, and their chief settlement became Tlacopan, recognized as one of the partners in the Triple Alliance. In 1519 there were Tepaneca tlatoque at Tlacopan, Tenayocan, Toltitlan, and other places beyond these limits. Azcaputzalco was shared between two rulers, one Tepaneca and the other Mexica. The principal settlements were quite large, although there was a dense rural population as well. Alongside the Náhuatl-speakers was a large Otomí minority.

The Spaniards first saw this area in 1519, and occupied it in the spring of 1521.

Encomiendas

Cortés assigned Tacuba to himself, but it was seized by the acting governors in 1525.[1] The following year Cortés set aside Tacuba as a permanent grant to Isabel Moctezuma (the emperor's daughter) and her descendants. This encomendera outlived her first two Spanish husbands, Alonso de Grado (dead by 1527) and Pedro Gallego (died c. 1531), and married a third, Juan Cano, before her own death c. 1550. At this time the tributes were divided among four claimants, the widower Cano (who died in 1572), his two sons by Isabel, Gonzalo and Pedro, and the eldest son of Isabel by Pedro Gallego, Juan de Andrade (Gallego) Moctezuma. After Andrade's death towards 1577 the mestizo encomenderos were confined to the Cano branch of the family. Further intricacies of this perpetual encomienda (tributes were privately assigned to the end of the colonial period) are traced by Gibson (1964, pp. 423–6).

Teocalhueyacan (Tlalnepantla) was separated from its original cabecera, Tacuba, and was assigned by Cortés to Alonso de Estrada c. 1528. Two years later it was inherited by Estrada's widow, María de la Caballería and on her death in 1551 it passed to her daughter, Luisa de Estrada, widow of Jorge de Alvarado. In the 1570s and later Juan de Villafañe appears as encomendero, while in 1597–1629 the holder was Angel de Villafañe (a great-grandson of Alonso de Estrada). The tributes escheated and were reassigned in part in the seventeenth century (Gibson, 1964, pp. 427–8).

Tacuba

The first holder of Azcapotzalco was the con- quistador Francisco de Montejo, followed in 1553 by a daughter, Catalina, married to Alonso Maldonado. The latter died in the 1560s, and his widow, Catalina, sometime after 1582. In the early 1600s the tributes were assigned to viceroy Luis de Velasco and continued to be paid to his heirs for a century, after which they were re-assigned to the Moctezuma descendants (Gibson, 1964, p. 414).

Tenayuca, first held by Cristóbal Flores or Juan de la Torre, escheated in 1532, was re-assigned to the treasurer Juan Alonso de Sosa in 1537, and again became a crown possession in 1544.

Tultitlan was granted by Cortés to Bartolomé de Perales, who died c. 1540 (Juan de la Torre was also an early claimant). Perales's widow, Antonia Hernández, then married Juan de Moscoso, who was the holder until c. 1567 when the tributes escheated.[2] Almost immediately they were re- assigned to Luis de Velasco the younger, whose heirs continued here as encomenderos until c. 1700 when final escheatment occurred.[3]

Government

Tenayuca had a C in 1532–7 and again after 1544, but his jurisdiction was first confined to this crown village; from the 1550s he was supposed to look after Azcapotzalco, Tacuba, and Teocalhueyacan as well. For several decades the corregimiento was considered suffragan to the AM of Guautitlan. In 1573 the viceroy combined the jurisdictions of Tenayuca–Tacuba and recently-sequestered Cuyo- acán under a single magistrate, generally referred to as AM, a post which came under direct crown control ten years later. This arrangement lasted until 1595 when the marquis del Valle regained the right to appoint his magistrate in Cuyoacán, but the council of the Indies continued to appoint AMs in Tacuba, as the jurisdiction was now more often called.[4]

There were minor adjustments of boundaries through the years. Certain distant sujetos of Tacuba were attached for convenience to Tenango del Valle (q.v.). Tultitlan, although assigned to the AM of Tacuba in 1583, was more often adminis- tered from Guautitlan until it was annexed to Tacuba's jurisdiction in the mid-seventeenth

century. Popotla was transferred from Tacuba to Mexico city in the 1600s. After 1786 the magistrate here was a subdelegado under the intendente of Mexico.[5]

Church

First visited by Franciscans and Dominicans from Mexico city, this area had four monastery- parishes in the 1560s, Santiago y S Felipe Azcapot- zalco (Dominican), S Gabriel Tacuba, Corpus Christi Tlalnepantla, and S Lorenzo Tultitlan (the last three Franciscan). S Antonio Huizquilucan had a secular priest in 1575; subsequently it was ministered by Jesuits, but returned to the secular clergy early in the seventeenth century.[6] S Bartolomé Naucalpan was briefly a separate Franciscan doctrina towards 1600; it was soon re-incorporated in the parish of Tacuba and con- tinued as a visita until it became a secular parish towards 1768. Meanwhile, Tacuba, Tultitlan, and Tlalnepantla were secularized in 1754, while Azcapotzalco remained Dominican until after Independence. All parishes belonged to the arch- diocese of Mexico.

Population and settlements

The number of tributaries in the jurisdiction fell from about 10,000 in 1570 to only 2,473 in 1643, much of this loss occurring in the epidemics of 1576–81 and 1629–31. Recovery was at first slow, to 2,918 tributaries in 1688, 3,965 Indian families in 1743, and 6,562 Indian tributaries in 1799.[7]

Spaniards and other non-Indians settled both at Tacuba and elsewhere in the jurisdiction. Tacuba itself is described as a town of Spaniards and Indians in 1646. Fifty years later there were 1,375 non-Indians at Tacuba, Tlalnepantla, and Tultitlan, and others (including a good number of Negro slaves) living at Azcapotzalco, Huizquilucan, and numerous haciendas and *obrajes*. The 1792 census shows 1,826 Spaniards (individuals), 3,523 mesti- zos, and 309 mulattoes.

We have a complete list (native toponyms) of the sujetos originally claimed by Tacuba (Tlaco- pan; ciudad from 1564, later *villa*; 1950: part of México, D.F.), but it is not easy to identify many of them nor to determine which fell within

248

the final limits of the jurisdiction.[8] Many of the places listed were in fact quite independent native states at contact, while others were soon separated from their cabecera and were given to various encomenderos. There remained a small enclave (Cepayautla, Ciutepec) far to the southwest, still considered subject to Tacuba in the eighteenth century (cf. Tenango del Valle). While there was probably an early attempt at congregation in the 1550s, there were still perhaps fifty estancias or pueblos within the jurisdiction directly subject to Tacuba in 1593, when a new program of reduction began. A number of these settlements were uprooted at this time and were moved to various congregation centers, among them Azcapotzaltongo, Chimalpa, Huizquilucan (S Antonio de los Otomíes), Natívitas (=Tepantitlan?), Naucalpan, Tecpan-Xilocingo, and Tacuba itself. By 1793 Huizquilucan and Naucalpan had become cabeceras, and there were twenty-three subject pueblos altogether.[9]

Azcapotzalco (Escapuzalco, etc.; 1950: Azcapotzalco, *villa*, D.F.) had seven estancias in 1570, together with a great many barrios near and within the cabecera; the most distant sujeto was a league away. A congregation seems to have occurred here *c.* 1600.[10] The 1793 report names twenty-five barrios, most adjoining the cabecera but others up to two leagues distant.

Tenayuca (1950: S Bartolo Tenayuca, pueblo, Mex.) and nearby Teocalhueyacan (1950: S Lorenzo, rancho) both were considered cabeceras by the Spaniards, although the latter had been subject to Tacuba (Gibson, 1964, pp. 56–7). Tenayuca was a Náhuatl-speaking community, while Teocalhueyacan was Otomí. Some decades after the conquest the Franciscans chose a site between the two cabeceras for their monastery, which became known as Tlalnepantla (1950: ciudad, Mex.), meaning literally 'a place in between'. The site was actually within the limits of Teocalhueyacan, so that cabecera became known as Tlalnepantla. Tenayuca remained separate in the tribute lists as a crown community, but it was gradually engulfed by Tlalnepantla; it had a number of barrios or estancias which were ordered congregated in 1593. Also during the 1590s, con-

gregation centers were formed at Tlalnepantla and certain of its sujetos, resulting in the disappearance of a number of estancias. By 1793 Tenayuca was considered one of fifteen pueblos subject to Tlalnepantla. Certain villages in this area which before the Conquest were directly subject to Tenochtitlan and Tlatelolco were absorbed in the same way.[11]

Tultitlan (Toltitlan; 1950: Tultitlán de Mariano Escobedo, pueblo, Mex.) had four or five sujetos which may have been moved about in a congregation of 1604, although it appears in 1793 with five dependent pueblos up to two leagues distant.

Altogether, nineteen places in the jurisdiction had cabecera status by 1799. Many of the old communal lands had been acquired through the years by haciendas.

Sources

There are early tribute assessments for Azcapotzalco (1547–60), Tenayuca (1537–66), and Tultitlan (1544–69) (L de T, pp. 57–8, 390–3, 539–43). Tenayuca, Tacuba, and Tultitlan are most summarily described in the *c.* 1548 *Suma de visitas* (PNE, I, nos. 777–9). The earliest report covering the whole jurisdiction that we have seen is that in the Ovando series of *c.* 1570.[12] Ponce went through here twice, in 1585 and 1587, but has little to add to our information (Ponce, I, pp. 27–8; II, pp. 154–5). There are a good many scattered references to congregations in 1593–1604.[13]

A few data for the seventeenth century are found in the journals of two archbishops' visits in 1646[14] and 1685,[15] tributary counts of 1623 (Scholes and Adams, 1959, p. 51) and 1643–88,[16] and the work of Vetancurt (4a parte, pp. 70, 72, 80) corresponding to *c.* 1697.

A missing relación of *c.* 1743 is condensed in Villaseñor y Sánchez (I, pp. 74–7). Ajofrín passed through a corner of the jurisdiction in 1764 (I, p. 181). We have seen a padrón of the parish of Naucalpan dated 1775,[17] and another of non-Indians covering the whole jurisdiction in 1792, accompanied by a brief description and a map.[18] There is a complete list of placenames, submitted in 1793.[19]

A great many more documents are cited by Gibson (1964) and in the archival guides of Colín (1966, 1967).

80 *Tancítaro*

Today in westernmost Michoacán, this is mainly an arid and very hot region on both sides of the Tepalcatepec, an important affluent of the Balsas, which flows from west to east (320–200 m). However, the jurisdiction extended northward to the volcano of Tancítaro (3,845 m) and south to the Sierra Madre del Sur (1,700 m), falling in greatly eroded plains to the river basin. Tancítaro, at 2,000 m, is quite cool and relatively humid.

The Tarascans controlled most if not all of this area. A paragraph in the *Relación de...Michoacán* lists 'cuaquaran / charapichu / paraǭro / paǭhoato euaquaran / tiristaran / pucohoato / tanzitaro / eruzio / ziramaritio' as Tarascan conquests of the fifteenth century, and in the following paragraph appears 'hapazingani'. Tlapalcatépec was the Náhuatl name for Eruzio. Arimao, the mountainous region south of the river, may have been independent. In general, there seems to have been an older Náhua-speaking population here (Xilotlantzinca was the language around Tlapalcatépec) alongside the Tarascan colonists, who were dominant around Tancítaro.

Part of the Olid military force may have entered this region before the end of 1522, and certainly Rodríguez de Villafuerte passed through early in 1523. Spaniards looking for gold explored the area thoroughly and had established control by 1528.

Encomiendas

Arimao-Pinzándaro was held by Juan de Jaso and Juan Jiménez in the spring of 1528.[1] It was re-assigned in equal parts, probably by the second audiencia, to Pedro Ruiz de Requena and Juan Gómez de Herrera. Ruiz died without issue towards 1536 and his half was taken for the crown (Millares Carlo and Mantecón, II, no. 2162). Gómez de Herrera was succeeded in the 1540s by a son, Francisco, although for a time the encomienda was held by Juan de San Juan, who had married Gómez's widow (L de T, p. 53). Escheat-ment of the private half occurred in the 1570s (Icaza, I, p. 116).

Pedro (de la) Isla and Domingo de Medina were joint encomenderos of Tancítaro early in 1528.[2] Isla's share escheated in 1531, but the other half still belonged to Medina as late as 1569, and he was followed by Diego Enríquez de Medina (listed in 1580–97). By 1623 the Medina portion had escheated, but later it was re-assigned, and half of the tributes were privately held in 1657–98 (Icaza, I, p. 214. Scholes and Adams, 1959, p. 52).

Three encomenderos, Pedro Sánchez (Farfán?), Alonso de Avila (Dávila), and Hernando de Ergüeta (Elgueta), seem to have shared Tlapalcatepec (including Cecasta) in 1528.[3] It escheated, along with half of Tancítaro, in August, 1531 (L de T, p. 343). Half the tributes were re-assigned privately before 1657.

Government

Tancítaro y Tlapalcatepec were jointly ruled by a C from late 1531. Arimao y Borona also had a C, suffragan to the AM of Zacatula, in the 1540s and later, but the Arimao region was apparently annexed to that of Tancítaro towards 1560 (L de T, pp. 51, 54). In the 1580s the C of Tancítaro unsuccessfully claimed jurisdiction in neighboring Periban (cf. Xiquilpa).[4]

In the seventeenth century the magistrate of Tancítaro, now more often referred to as AM, also collected tributes from the corregimiento of Xilotlan (cf. Colima). Shortly before 1743 the adjacent jurisdiction of Cinagua y la Guacana (q.v.) was annexed to that of Tancítaro, and Motines was absorbed in the same way *c.* 1780. Each of these former alcaldías mayores became a subdelegación in the intendencia of Valladolid after 1787, and they have been considered separately here. By 1787 the residence of the magistrate had been moved from Tancítaro to Apazingán, which became the new name of the jurisdiction.

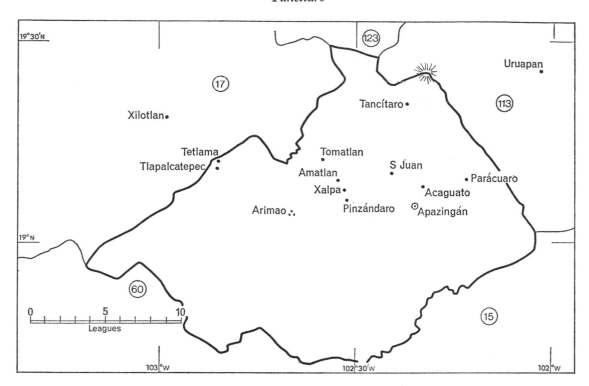

Church

While there must have been earlier missionary activity here, the first parochial foundation was that of S Francisco (Sta Cruz) Tancítaro, a Franciscan doctrina from 1552 (Romero, IX, p. 32). A secular priest was living at Xilotlan (cf. Colima) in the late 1560s and visited Tlapalcatepec and Arimao. By 1623 both S Francisco Tlapalcatepec and S Juan Pinzándaro Arimao were separate parishes. A year or so later two Franciscan visitas, Sta Ana Amatlan and Asunción Apazingán, became *guardianías* (Bravo Ugarte, 1963, p. 51).

All of these parishes were in the diocese of Michoacán. The Franciscan doctrinas were secularized *c.* 1775 (León y Gama, p. 98. Romero, IX, p. 32). Apó, in the jurisdiction of Valladolid, was visited by the curate of Tancítaro, while the parish of Tlapalcatepec included Xilotlan until 1803.

Population and settlements

Disease and mistreatment took an early toll of the Indians here, especially in the hot country. By 1565 only 1,200 tributaries survived, almost half

of them in the relatively small highland portion. Their number dropped to *c.* 1,000 in 1600, 700 in 1623, 493 in 1657, 368 in 1698, 395 in 1743, and 393 in 1804 (the 1743 figure refers to Indian families, the others to tributaries). The Arimao–Pinzándaro area had no Indians at all by 1743.

Thus vast parts of the tierra caliente were deserted, and although the climate was oppressive, in 1649 there were over 100 non-Indian families in the jurisdiction, together with a large retinue of Negro slaves and servants living on cattle haciendas, sugar plantations, and cacao estates. Pinzándaro, Tomatlan, and Xalpa became exclusively mestizo and mulatto communities. By 1743 there were 78 Spanish and 276 mestizo and mulatto families, and in 1804 the jurisdiction had 661 free negro and mulatto tributaries, far out-numbering the Indians.[5]

Tancítaro (Tanxitaro; 1950: Tancítaro, *villa*) probably had an early congregation under the aegis of the Franciscans. It still had fourteen sujetos in 1580, six in the highlands and eight in the hot country. Only the latter survived a second reduction in 1598–1604; of these, Apazingán (1950: Apatzingán de la Constitución ciudad) became a separate cabecera, Puco (Tuco) last appears in 1639, and Acaguato, Amatlan, S Juan Andacutiro (Tendechutiro) de los Plátanos, Parácuaro, Tomatlan, and Xalpa were pueblos in 1639–1793. Another pueblo, S Gregorio Taciran, was annexed from Uruapan shortly before 1789.[6]

The cabecera of Arimao, originally on the Tepalcatepec river, was moved in the 1570s to its final site, Pinzándaro (1950: rancho), two leagues away. In 1580 there were four sujetos mostly south of the river in the mountains up to 15 leagues from the cabecera. Three subject pueblos are reported in 1649, and none in 1743. In the latter year Pinzándaro was a *villa* of cattle-raisers, but by 1789 it had fallen to the category of congregación.

Tlapalcatepec (later, Tepalcatepec; 1950: pueblo) had only three dependencies in 1570–80. Chilatlan perhaps survived as Alima, which became an hacienda after 1743. Tamazulapa was deserted by its Indians after the epidemic of the late 1730s, while Sta Ana Tetlama survived as a pueblo just north of the cabecera.

In 1789 there were sixteen haciendas and nine ranchos in the jurisdiction.

Sources

Only Tancítaro is described, quite briefly, in the *Suma* of c. 1548 (PNE, 1, no. 669), but we have tribute records of all three cabeceras in 1546–68 (L de T, pp. 51–6, 343–50). There are two reports in the Ovando (1569–71) series.[7] The relación geográfica of 1580 for this area is of more than usual interest.[8]

Reports of 1639[9] and 1649,[10] and tributary data for 1623 (Scholes and Adams, 1959, pp. 52–3) and 1657–98[11] give a sketchy idea of what this jurisdiction was like in the seventeenth century.

There is a useful report from the AM dated 1743,[12] followed by a detailed study of Indian community properties drawn up c. 1789.[13] For the last years of the colonial period, we have a brief report of 1793[14] and the Martínez Lejarza compilation of 1822 (Martínez de Lejarza, pp. 135–43).

Aguirre Beltrán (1952) gives a valuable analysis of many of these documents.

81 *Tasco*

This is an area of barren hills and low mountains, forested in the higher parts, with elevations of 1,000–2,200 m, draining southward towards the Balsas. It is now in northern Guerrero. The climate is cool, with adequate seasonal rains, in the north, and dryer and warmer in the south.

There were several native states here which, together with neighboring Tzicaputzalco (cf. Iscateupa) and Tepexahualco (cf. Temazcaltepec), formed a tributary province of the Aztec empire. Tlachco itself had a military governor. Acamilixtlahuacan, Chontalcoatlan, Nochtépec, Teotliztacan, Tepexahualco, Tetenanco, Teticpac, and Tlamacazapan were old Chontal kingdoms which had been subdued by the Triple Alliance; we do not know whether they still had Chontal rulers or Mexica governors appointed from Tenochtitlan. Acuitlapan, Atzalan, and Pilcayan may have had

a certain amount of autonomy. The conquered and the conquerors, Chontal and Mexica, lived in separate settlements and spoke their own languages; there may have been some Mazatecan-speakers in the northwest.

The area was probably first visited by Spaniards in late 1519, and surrendered to them in 1521 or 1522.

Encomiendas

Tasco may have been claimed by Cortés, at whose order tin deposits were being worked there in 1524, but it seems likely that, as a mining center, it was soon set aside for the crown; this had occurred at the latest by 1534 (Cortés, p. 232).

Other places which escheated at an early date were Tenango (by 1536) and Teulistaca (by 1545).

Acamistlaguaca was held by the conquistador

Bachiller Alonso Pérez, succeeded in the 1550s by a son of the same name; the latter was followed by Alonso Pérez de Bocanegra, grandson of the first holder (listed in 1597–1604). The place escheated before 1643.

Coatlan and Acuitlapan were given to another conquistador, Juan Cermeño, and were inherited *c.* 1550 by his widow, who married Diego Pérez de Zamora. The latter was still alive in 1597,

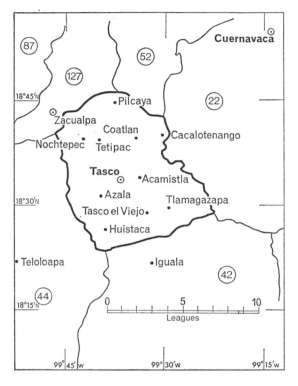

but part of the tributes were going to the crown in 1643–88.

Nochtepec and Pilcaya were held as early as 1526, by Juan de Cabra, a conquistador (Millares Carlo and Mantecón, I, no. 1058). Cabra died *c.* 1551 and was followed by his widow, María de Herrera, who then married Francisco Ramírez Bravo (listed in 1564–70). The encomienda seems to have escheated before 1597, but tributes were privately assigned in 1643–88.

Teticpac, first held by Francisco Quintero (de Zamora?), was purchased probably in the late 1530s by Juan de la Peña Vallejo, a miner at Tasco

(ENE, III, p. 255. Icaza, I, p. 202). De la Peña died soon after 1560 and was followed briefly by a son, Juan de Vallejo, and towards 1566 by the latter's widow, Bernardina de Rivera. By 1586 tributes had been re-assigned to Luis de Velasco, and were collected by his heirs throughout the seventeenth century.

Government

Nuño de Guzmán appointed an AM at Tasco, presumably before he left Mexico at the end of 1529 (ENE, XIV, p. 179). There was a C of Tasco in 1534, and the title AM was again in use by 1538 (BAGN, X, p. 251). Meanwhile, Tenango appears together with Capulalcolulco (cf. Tetela del Río) as a corregimiento in 1534–6, but in 1542 'Tasco e Tenango' are linked in the title of the AM.[1] In the 1550s the surrounding encomiendas were added to the jurisdiction. Teulistaca had its own C in 1545–76, but by 1581 it was being administered by the AM of Tasco and was annexed to his jurisdiction soon afterward.[2]

Towards 1780 the alcaldía mayor of Iguala (q.v.) was joined with that of Tasco, both being governed from 1787 as a single subdelegación in the intendencia of Mexico. Iguala has been dealt with separately here.

Church

There may have been some early activity here by Franciscans working out of Cuernavaca, and the real de minas surely had a secular priest from the 1530s. In 1569 there were secular parishes at S Sebastián (much later, Sta Prisca) Tasco and Santiago Nochtepec. Five years later priests were also living at S Francisco Tasco el Viejo and Sta Cruz Teticpac.[3] We have no further information until 1794, when secular parishes existed at S Martín Acamistla, Asunción Cacalotenango, Concepción Pilcaya, Sta Prisca Tasco, and Sta Cruz Tetipac. All were in the archbishopric of Mexico.

Population and settlements

There was much loss in the native population during the epidemics of 1545–8, 1576–81, and later, periodically offset by the arrival of Indian miners from other regions. The fluctuations in the mining population are perhaps only vaguely reflected in the tributary data available. There were 4,570 native tributaries in 1570, 4,050 in 1581, and 1,012 in 1643. In 1688 there were 765 tributaries, while the 1743 census has 1,047 Indian families. By arbitrarily dividing the 1799–1804 count for Tasco–Iguala, we guess that there were 3,200 Indian tributaries at that time in the original jurisdiction of Tasco.[4] The miner immigrants on occasion came from considerable distances (Tarascans are mentioned in 1581).

While tin and gold placer mining began here very soon after the Conquest, exploitation of the silver ores seems to have started in the early 1530s (Mecham, 1927a. Wagner, 1942, p. 53). The mines, which were in full production in 1552, attracted considerable numbers of Spaniards and castas as well as Indians (ENE, VI, p. 149). Towards 1570 there were 100 Spanish vecinos, 900 Indian miners, and 700 Negro slaves living at the various reales. Soon afterwards mining activity began to fall off, and while there were occasional spurts of relative prosperity there was no real recovery until the bonanza of 1748–57 (*Diccionario Porrúa...*, p. 203). 260 non-Indian families are reported in 1743, at which time the real was in a depression; by 1794, when the mines were again in a state of decline, there were 892 free Negro and mulatto tributaries in the jurisdiction, most of them no doubt at Tasco (cf. Humboldt, p. 383, N.Y. ed. vol. 3, pp. 284–5).

The original cabecera of Tasco (Tlaxco, Tlachco el viejo; 1950: Taxco el Viejo, pueblo), some two leagues south of the real de minas (1950: Taxco de Alarcón, ciudad), had two subject cabeceras, Azala (Atzalan) and Tlamagazapa, with a total of twenty-four or twenty-five lesser estancias, in 1570–81. Most of the latter were eliminated in congregations of 1595–1603, leaving only the places mentioned together with Cozcatlan (Cuscatlan) and Tecalpulco as pueblos. Tetelcingo, listed as a cabecera in the seventeenth century, was a former estancia which became the principal real of Tasco, and residence of the AM.

Tenango (Cacalotenango by 1794; 1950: pueblo) had fifteen estancias within two leagues of the cabecera in 1548–81 (the cabecera itself or a place nearby was a subordinate mining camp in 1581). These all seem to have been reduced to a single settlement in the late 1590s.

Nochtepec (Noxtepec, Nuchitepec; 1950: Noxtepec, pueblo) and Pilcaya (1950: pueblo) were twin cabeceras with ten nearby estancias between them in 1569–81. The Indians were to have been gathered in the cabeceras and one estancia, S Marcos Tecozauhyan, in 1594; Xocotitlan seems to have taken the place of Tecozauhyan as a pueblo.

Teticpac (Tetipac; 1950: pueblo), with ten estancias in a radius of two leagues, was consolidated at the cabecera c. 1600; the latter was moved at an early date from its original hill-top site.

Of ten estancias belonging to Coatlan (Chontalguatlan in 1794; 1950: Chontalcuatlán, pueblo) and Acuitlapan (Cuitlapa; 1950: Acuitlapan, pueblo), only one, Cacaguamilpa, survived the congregation of c. 1600 as a pueblo, in addition to the cabeceras.

According to one report, Acamistlaguaca (Acamixtlahuacan; Acamistla in later years; 1950: Acamixtla, pueblo) had eighteen estancias in 1569, although another document of about the same date names only ten, and the 1581 relación lists but five. All were congregated at the cabecera in the 1590s.

S Andrés Teulistaca (Talistaca, etc.) had an alternate name, Hueystaca (Veiiztaca, etc.; Huistaca in 1794; 1950: Huixtac, pueblo), which eventually prevailed. It had nine or ten estancias within two leagues, all moved to the cabecera c. 1600.

Sources

A fragment of the lost 'description' of 1531 indicates that the silver mines of Tasco were being worked at that early date (Herrera, 4a década, p. 231). The various cabeceras as they were c. 1548 are succinctly described (PNE, I, nos. 37, 163, 273, 410, 670–2). The Ovando series (1569) report which we have seen[5] seems to be a summary of a more detailed lost document (cf. Vera, p. 140). There is a good relación submitted by the AM in 1581 (PNE, VI, pp. 263–82).

We have scattered details concerning congregations here in the 1590s and early 1600s,[6] and tributary data for 1643–88,[7] together with the journal of an archiepiscopal visit in 1685 which we have not examined.[8] A missing document of *c.* 1743 is condensed in Villaseñor y Sánchez (I, pp. 237–9). There is a curious but useful description of the jurisdiction as it was in 1794.[9]

The monograph of Toussaint (1931) should be consulted.

82 *Tecali*

Tecali is in central Puebla state, along the great bend in the Atoyac (Balsas) river where it changes course and heads westward towards the Pacific. It is a bleak region, quite dry and cold, at 1,800–2,400 m. There is little surface water except in the river, which flows in the bottom of a deep canyon.

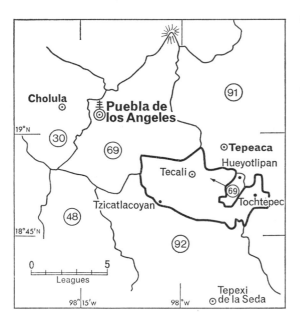

The Tecalca delivered their tribute to the Aztec garrison at nearby Tepeyacac. The ruler and most of his subjects were Náhuatl-speakers, but there were Popolocan and Otomí minorities.

In the summer of 1520 a force of Spaniards and Indian allies defeated the combined armies of Tecalco and Tepeyacac.

Encomienda

Francisco Montaño was perhaps the first encomendero here (Icaza, I, p. 53), followed in the 1520s by Juan Pérez de Arteaga and another holder who shared the tributes. The other holder may well have been Francisco de Orduña (Loyando, Orduña y Mota), who, after acquiring Pérez's share, appears as sole encomendero in 1531 (Icaza, I, p. 19. L de T, p. 365). When Orduña died in 1550 he was succeeded by his son, José (Jusepe) de Orduña, still holder in 1580 (ENE, xv, p. 216. L de T, p. 366). In 1597 the encomendera was María del Castillo, presumably a granddaughter of Francisco de Orduña and a niece of José; soon afterward the tributes escheated and were subsequently re-assigned. Tecali was still a private encomienda in 1696, and part of the tributes were privately collected in 1803.[1]

Government

In early years the administration of justice in Tecalco, or Tecali as it came to be called, seems to have been left to the encomendero and his agents, with the occasional intervention of a neighboring magistrate (Gibson, 1952, p. 73). The Franciscans probably had some temporal influence during this period. From 1555 Tecali was attached to the newly-created alcaldía mayor of Tepeaca (q.v.), and in later years a teniente resided there.[2] This arrangement was still in effect in 1643, but in documents of 1664 and later Santiago Tecali appears with its own AM.[3] From 1787 the magistrate was a subdelegado under the intendente of Puebla.

Church

First visited from Tepeaca, Santiago Tecali had a Franciscan monastery from *c.* 1540 until the parish was secularized *c.* 1641 (Ricard, p. 84). In 1643 there were two doctrinas, Tecali and S Pedro (Apaxtlaguaca), but the latter did not long survive.

Sometime between 1697 and 1743 a curate began living at Sta María Tochtepec, with a vicar at Sta Clara Huichitepec. By 1777 there was a third parish, S Juan Tzicatlacoyan, for the villages on the right bank of the Atoyac. The area belonged to the bishopric of Tlaxcala. As elsewhere, political and parochial boundaries did not always coincide.

Population and settlements

There is a good deal of confusion in the various counts of the native population here, but any calculation shows an unusual density at contact. After two serious epidemics, the *Suma* of *c.* 1548 gives a total of 3,314 married men and 1,035 bachelors, roughly the equivalent of 3,830 tributaries. In 1564 there were 5,463 tributaries, and two estimates of *c.* 1570 give 5,000 and 6,000 respectively (L de T, pp. 366–7). The relación of 1580, after stating that nine tenths of the population at contact had disappeared and that there was great mortality in the epidemic of 1576–7, claims that there were still 5,000 vecinos at Tecali. In 1595 we are told that a new count showed 600 tributaries more than had appeared in a previous census; the new count is most likely that given in 1597, 4,042 tributaries.[4] Then there was a severe dip, to 'more than 3,000' vecinos in 1610, and 1,518 tributaries in 1626. Later counts show 2,287 Indian tributaries in 1651, 2,589 in 1696, 1,517 families in 1743 (loss in the epidemic of 1737–9?), and 2,136 tributaries in 1803.[5]

The non-Indian population was insignificant, mostly confined to the few haciendas. There were no Spaniards according to the 1643 report, and only forty non-Indian families in 1743.

Náhuatl was the language of the cabecera in 1585, with Popolocan and Otomí spoken in certain estancias. Asunción (Tochtepec?), S Lorenzo (Ometepec), and Sta Clara (Huichitepec) are identified as Popolocan settlements in 1643, Náhuatl being spoken elsewhere.

The Franciscans must have eliminated a good many minor settlements here, perhaps in the 1550s. In 1548 there were seventy-two estancias and six barrios divided in four unequal 'partes', Vtlimaya, Tepetiquipaque, Atiçapan, and Tezcacingo. Only ten '*aldeas*' are mentioned in 1570, but ten years later there were nineteen estancias; three of the latter seem to have disappeared in another congregation *c.* 1600. The surviving settlements can be traced through various lists (1643, 1697, 1743, 1777, 1792) and roughly identified with Indian pueblos in the eighteenth century, although sites were probably abandoned and re-occupied during this period. The pueblos were Santiago Tecali (1950: Tecali de Herrera, *villa*), Sta María Aguatepec, S Pedro Apaxtlaguaca, S Salvador Atoyatempan, S Luis Axaxalpan, S Buenaventura (Caltenpan), S Martín (Caltenco), Sta Clara Huichitepec, S Miguel Huizcolotla or Acuexomac, S Francisco Mixtla, S Lorenzo (Ometepec), S Gerónimo, Sta Isabel, S Bartolomé (Tepetlacaltechco), Tepeyagualco (Asunción?), Sta María Natívitas Tochtepec, Trinidad, and S Juan Tzicatlacoyan. Three of these places had acquired cabecera status by 1803. Twenty-odd barrios which appear in the 1777 padrón of Tecali may correspond to some of the old estancias, moved in in the congregations.

Besides the pueblos listed, there were in 1792 five haciendas and twenty ranchos in the jurisdiction.

Sources

The description of Tecali in the *Suma de visitas* (*c.* 1548) is unusually informative (PNE, I, no. 543). Little can be gleaned from known documents of the Ovando (*c.* 1570) series (*Códice franciscano*, pp. 24–5. García Pimentel, 1904, p. 17. López de Velasco, p. 223). The area is covered in the 1580 relación of Tepeaca (PNE, V, pp. 12–45). Ponce (I, pp. 139–40, 508) passed through here in 1585 and again the following year.

The journal of bishop Mota y Escobar describes Tecali as he saw it in 1610, 1617, and 1623.[6] Father Cobo (p. 203) went through in 1630 and makes a brief mention of the place. Bishop Palafox's account of his visit here in 1643 is of special interest.[7] Vetancurt (4a parte, pp. 69–70) gives a list of barrios and visitas as they were perhaps *c.* 1697.

For the eighteenth century, we have a good report drawn up by the AM in 1743,[8] censuses of the three parishes dated 1777,[9] and a complete list of placenames in 1792.[10]

83 *Teciutlan y Atempa*

Now in the northeast corner of Puebla, adjoining Veracruz, this jurisdiction lay on the seaward slope of the Sierra Madre Oriental draining into the Tecolutla and Nautla rivers. There is a good deal of rain most of the year. There is a wide range of temperatures depending on the altitude (180–2,500 m; Teciutlán itself is just under 2,000 m).

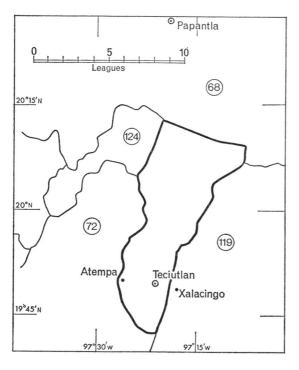

Tequeciuhtlan and Atenpan or Atenco, together with Hueytlamalco and Chiconauhtlan, delivered tribute to the Triple Alliance at Tlatlauhquitépec. The people here spoke Náhuatl.

The area was probably traversed by Cortés and his party in August 1519, coming under Spanish rule in 1521 or 1522.

Encomienda

This whole region was assigned to the conquistador Bernardino de Santa Clara, escheating on his death in December 1537 (Icaza, no. 263. Millares Carlo and Mantecón, I, no. 267; II, nos. 2440, 2456).

Government

These villages were ruled by the C of Tlatlauquitepec from 1538 until a separate C was appointed here *c.* 1553.[1] The magistrate was suffragan to the AM of Xalapa in the late sixteenth century, and became an AM after *c.* 1640. From 1787 the jurisdiction was a subdelegación in the intendencia of Puebla.

Church

Franciscans were active here in early years and had a small monastery at S Juan (later, Sta María) Teciutlan, but relinquished it to secular clergy towards 1567 (*Alegaciones...*, fol. 23. L de T, p. 446). S Francisco Atempa was visited from Tlatlauquitepec, while Xiutetelco belonged to the parish of Xalacingo. The area was in the diocese of Puebla.

Population and settlements

The earliest useable data are those of 1564, when there were 1,829 tributaries here (1,570 at Teciutlan, 259 at Atempa); probably by this time there were few Indians left in the hot country. The tributary total dropped to 1,700 in 1569 and only 347 in 1626, after which there was a recovery to 843 tributaries in 1696, 911 Indian families in 1743, and 1,978 tributaries in 1800.[2] The 1743 census shows 150 families of Spaniards, 96 of mestizos, and 25 of mulattoes (1,340 people altogether).

Chiconautla and Hueytlamalco, originally cabeceras, were soon absorbed by Teciutlan (Tecistlan, Teusitlan, Toziutlan, etc.; 1950: Teziutlán, ciudad). There were a dozen or more estancias in 1548–70. A number of these sites were deserted in a congregation of *c.* 1600.[3] Of the old settlements, Chicnautla, Mexcalcuautla, Tzinpaco (Sinpaco), and Xiutetelco were pueblos in the eighteenth century, together with Acateno, Atoluca, and Tletapani (S Sebastián).

Atempa (Atenpa; 1950: Atempan, pueblo) had only two small estancias in 1548, and none are reported thereafter, although the 1743 report shows four barrios here.

In 1792 there were five sugarcane haciendas and ten ranchos in the jurisdiction.

Sources

Brief articles in the *Suma de visitas* of *c.* 1548 (PNE, I, nos. 13, 520) are supplemented by tribute assessments of 1548–64 (ENE, VIII, p. 152. L de T, pp. 444–9), and clerical reports of *c.* 1569 (García Pimentel, 1904, pp. 9–10. PNE, V, pp. 208, 244). Episcopal visits in 1609[4] and 1646[5] add a few details, as do tributary counts of 1629–96.[6]

A relación sent in by the AM in 1743 includes a complete census list.[7] There is a non-Indian padrón of 1791, accompanied by a map of the jurisdiction,[8] and a list of toponyms dated 1792.[9]

84 *Tecuicuilco*

On the north slope of the Sierra de Juárez in central Oaxaca, this area contains much of the upper drainage basin ('la Cañada') of the Río Grande, a principal source of the Papaloapan. The climate is semi-arid and temperate, elevations ranging from 1,300 to 2,300 m.

Tecuicuilco (Quiaguie, or Yaxía, in Zapotecan) and Macuiltianguizco, together with Atépec (Quieniza) and Zoquiapan (Quiagona), were probably all autonomous Zapotec communities in the Aztec tributary province of Coyolapan. To the north was Yoloxonecuillan (Noó in Chinantecan), a Chinantecan state which had also been conquered by the Mexicans.

Perhaps first seen by Spaniards in 1520, the region was not secured by them until several years later.

Encomiendas

Tecuicuilco, with Atepec, Zoquiapa, and Xaltianguizco, were held by Martín de la Mezquita (Montesinos), a conquistador, from the early 1520s. They escheated on 30 July 1531 (Boyd-Bowman, I, no. 3755. Icaza, I, p. 56. L de T, p. 428).

Both Macuiltianguis and Yoloxinecuila were assigned before 1527 to another conquistador, Juan Rodríguez de Salas. He was succeeded towards 1550 by a son, Sebastián de Salas, still listed in 1597. A grandson of the first holder, Cristóbal de Salas, was encomendero by 1599. When escheatment occurred (before 1647) tributes were re-assigned to the Moctezuma heirs.[1]

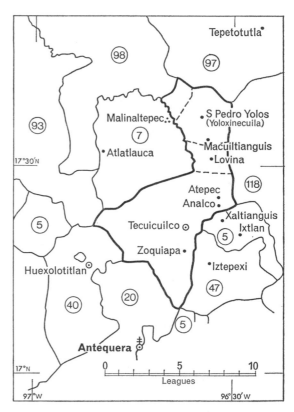

Government

Tecuicuilco y Atepec (and presumably Xaltianguizco and Zoquiapa as well) were put in a single corregimiento in the summer of 1531. Macuiltianguis and Yoloxinecuila seem to have been administered from Teutila in early years; in 1580 we find Yoloxinecuila attached to the short-lived corregimiento of Tepetotutla.[2] In the late sixteenth century Tepetotutla was suffragan to Teutila, and Tecuicuilco to Antequera.

Possibly a result of the 1599–1603 congregations, the Chinantec Indians of Malinaltepec (cf. Atlatlauca) when they moved from the left to the right bank of the Río Grande came under the jurisdiction of Tecuicuilco, which by 1630 apparently included the Yolos area.[3] It was perhaps about the same time that Xaltianguis (until then a sujeto of Tecuicuilco) was transferred to the alcaldía mayor of Antequera.

Soon after 1676, Tecuicuilco and Teozacualco, the latter far to the southwest, were put under a single AM who sometimes lived in one part of his awkward jurisdiction and sometimes in the other. Here the two partidos are considered separately. After 1787 Teococuilco (as it was now called) y Teozacualco constituted a subdelegación in the intendencia of Oaxaca.

Church

There was probably some early Dominican activity here, but by 1570 secular clergy were in charge. In that year there was a curate at S Juan Bautista Atepec who visited the Yolos villages, while Tecuicuilco was visited by a priest from Iztepexi. Within the next decade the curate of Atepec moved to S Pedro Tecuicuilco, and a new secular parish was founded at S Pablo Macuiltianguis (including Yoloxinecuila).

After the congregations in the early seventeenth century S Pedro Yolos became the center of Macuiltianguis parish, to which Malinaltepec was added. Parochial boundaries were re-drawn *c.* 1700, when Atepec and Analco were shifted from Tecuicuilco to the northern doctrina, its seat once again at S Pablo Macuiltianguis; for some years S Pedro Yolos had a vicar subordinate to this curacy. Then the priest of Macuiltianguis moved his headquarters first to Atepec and shortly afterwards (by 1745) to S Juan Analco; it was probably at this time that Yolos again became a separate benefice. The area fell within the diocese of Antequera (Berlin, pp. 74–5).

Population and settlements

There were perhaps 2,000 Indian tributaries here towards 1550, more or less evenly divided between the Zapotecs of Tecuicuilco and the Chinantecs and Zapotecs of Yoloxinecuila–Macuiltianguis. By 1565 the number had dropped to 1,315, only 500 of whom were in the encomienda villages. We are told that a third to half the population of Tecuicuilco died in the epidemic of 1577. The few surviving Chinantecs in the adjoining jurisdiction of Atlatlauca, 40½ tributaries altogether, were moved to Yolos *c.* 1600. At mid-seventeenth century there were probably no more than 500 tributaries in the area under consideration, after which there was a gradual recovery to 1,115 in 1745 and *c.* 1,500 in 1795.[4] The non-Indian population was negligible.

Tecuicuilco (Tecoquilco, etc.; Teococuilco by 1699; 1950: Teococuilco de Marcos Pérez, pueblo) in the sixteenth century had three subject cabeceras, Atepec (Atepéquez), Zoquiapa, and Xaltianguis(co); under Tecuicuilco was the estancia of Sta Ana Yeztepec (=Yareni?), while Atepec had three sujetos, Aluapa (Oluapam), Tanatepec (=Analco?), and Zozotla (Abejones). All these communities seem to have survived as pueblos (the eighteenth-century forms are given in parentheses), although the sites were moved about some. Xaltianguis, as we have mentioned, was transferred to the partido of Ixtlan (cf. Antequera).

The other Zapotec cabecera, Macuiltianguis, seems to have had two sujetos. S Pedro, a nearby barrio, was annexed to the cabecera, while S Juan Duevina (Lovina, Lubina) may correspond to Huitziltengo (Huiziziltengo), originally subject to Atlatlauca.

There is a confused history of shifting settlement sites in the dispersed Chinantecan community of Yoloxinecuila (Yolos Sinequila, Ginecuila, etc.; pueblos de los Yolos; 1950: S Pedro Yolox, pueblo). In the 1599–1603 congregation the cabecera itself was to be moved 1½ leagues south to Santiago Chinantepec (Sinantepec), together with three other estancias of Yolos, the cabecera and two estancias of Malinaltepec, and S Juan Quiotepec, a sujeto of Atlatlauca. Thus all the Chinantecs of the Río Grande were to be reduced to a single settlement. While we have no further record of Chinantecs on the left bank of the river, some of the old estancia sites were re-occupied and new settlements were made. By 1699 we find the cabecera of Yolos surrounded by the pueblos of Comaltepec, Malinaltepec, S Francisco (de las Llagas), S Juan (Quiotepec?), S Martín, Sta María de las Nieves, Tectitlan, and Totomostla. All these places except Malinaltepec and S Martín survived as pueblos in 1804.

Sources

Tecuicuilco as it was *c.* 1548 is briefly described in the *Suma* (PNE, I, no. 646) and in a series of tribute assessments of 1549–65 (L de T, pp. 428–31). A report of *c.* 1570 in the Ovando series (García Pimentel, 1904, pp. 65, 67, 92–3) is followed by a relación geográfica of the corregimiento (minus the Yolos area), accompanied by a map, dated 1580.[5] Various documents on the Yolos congregation of 1599–1603[6] are summarized with valuable notes by Howard Cline (1955). Berlin (1947, pp. 74–5) reproduces an interesting item on parochial changes in 1699.

A brief report from the AM dated 1745[7] was apparently not used by Villaseñor y Sánchez (II, pp. 175–6), who had access to other material. There is a padrón of Yolos parish in 1777,[8] and a good report from the curate of Tecuicuilco in 1778.[9] The jurisdiction is well described in the report of Bergosa y Jordan's visit of 1804,[10] and again in the statistical summary of *c.* 1821.[11]

The abovementioned monograph by Cline (1955), as well as the work of Bevan (1938) and Spores (1965) should be consulted.

85 *Teguacán*

The upper part of the broad valley of Tehuacán lies at 1,000–1,800 m and drains southeasterly into the Papaloapan system. The colonial jurisdiction, now the southeastern extremity of Puebla state, straddles the continental divide (2,700 m) above Zapotitlan on the western edge of the valley, while in the east it crosses an even higher (3,000 m) range, dropping precipitously in the headwaters of the Tonto river to 175 m. The low, eastern section is hot with abundant rainfall much of the year, but the rest of the jurisdiction is very dry and generally warm.

In 1520 there were four principal political units with their centers in the valley, which lay astride an important route of trade and conquest. The largest was Teohuacan, a predominantly Náhuatl-speaking community with a Popolocan (Chocho) minority in the west. Above Teohuacan was a Popolocan state, Chiapolco. Some Náhuatl may have been spoken at Tzapotitlan, but most of the people there were Popolocans; the ruler of this state seems to have controlled the vast salt deposits, and his realm extended southward across the mountains to include a corner of the Mixteca.

Acatépec, Atzompan, Caltzintenco (=Ecatitlan?), Itztépec, and Metzontlan were perhaps semi-autonomous communities in this area, under the hegemony of Tzapotitlan. In the valley below Teohuacan was the chief settlement of a Náhuatl kingdom, Cozcatlan, with a Popolocan minority in the west and a pocket of Mazatecan-speakers forming an enclave far to the east in the hot country; under Cozcatlan were the semi-autonomous regions of Teteltitlan (Otontépec), in Popoloca country, and Mazateopan and Petlaapan, the latter a Mazatec settlement. On the eastern slope of the Sierra Madre and in the wet jungles below were Eloxochitlan (Axalyahualco) and Tzoquitlan, mainly inhabited by the descendants of Nonoalca Chichimecs speaking Nahua, although there was a Mazatecan minority at Tzoquitlan. The Triple Alliance probably controlled the valley states, but those east of the Sierra Madre may well have been independent.

The valley of Teohuacan was traversed by Spanish explorers early in 1520, and Teohuacan, Tzapotitlan, and Cozcatlan sent representatives who surrendered to Cortés at Tepeyacac later in that year (Vázquez de Tapia, pp. 46, 114). The Eloxochitlan–Tzoquitlan region perhaps came under Spanish control somewhat later.

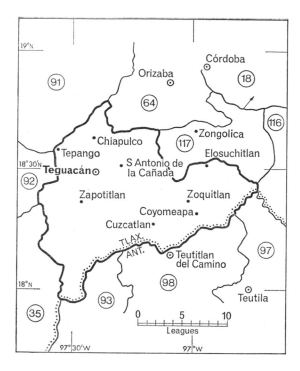

Encomiendas

We do not know to whom Cuzcatlan was assigned; it escheated on 24 May 1534 (L de T, p. 163).

Chiapulco was held by a conquistador called Barrera, perhaps Cristóbal Barrera, who died sometime between 1536 and 1548 (Millares Carlo and Mantecón, II, no. 2012). Barrera was succeeded by a daughter who married Esteban de Carvajal, still listed (perhaps a son?) in 1603. Escheatment occurred shortly after 1610, but part of the tributes were privately assigned late in the seventeenth century (cf. Icaza, II, pp. 14–15).

Elosuchitlan–Axalyagualco was held by Juan Durán until his death *c.* 1551, when the enco- mienda was inherited by Durán's widow, and soon after by a daughter, Luisa de Frías. The latter was married first to Bernardino de Sala and later to Diego de Cisneros (listed in 1604). Tributes escheated sometime between 1629 and 1664.[1]

Teguacán was shared between several en- comenderos. One part had escheated by 1534. A share was held by Antonio Caicedo (d. 1536), and a quarter was assigned to Alonso Castillo Mal- donado (d. *c.* 1546). At some point half the tributes were granted to the conquistador Juan Ruiz de Alanís, followed (before 1550) by a son, Antonio Ruiz de Castañeda. Final escheatment occurred on the latter's death shortly before 1578.[2]

Another divided encomienda was Zapotitlan (see below for the various sub-cabeceras here). The original holders (from 1522) were perhaps Rodrigo de Segura and García Vélez (ENE, III, p. 129). Vélez died *c.* 1525, and his share seems to have been inherited by Catalina Vélez (a daughter?), who married first Bartolomé Her- nández de Nava (d. *c.* 1540) and subsequently Francisco de Orduña; this half was disputed, however, with Francisco Montaño, who appears as encomendero in 1548–97. Segura's share was taken from him by the audiencia *c.* 1530 and was apparently assigned to Gaspar de Garnica, followed in the 1540s by his widow, and somewhat later by a son of the same name; towards 1600 a grandson, Antonio de Garnica, was encomendero. A Montaño (perhaps by this time Pedro, the con- quistador's son) and a Garnica were still joint holders of Zapotitlan in 1610, but escheatment of both halves occurred sometime between 1629 and 1664. Subsequently part of the tributes were re- assigned (Dorantes de Carranza, pp. 181, 200. Icaza, I, p. 116; II, p. 15. L de T, pp. 611–12).

Zoquitlan, with neighboring Aculcingo (cf. Orizaba), was held in part by the conquistador Francisco de Montalvo, the other half escheating before 1545. Montalvo was succeeded *c.* 1550 by a son, Diego, followed by his widow and another Diego de Montalvo who was still alive in 1597. The private half of this encomienda escheated before 1664, and was later re-assigned (Icaza, I, p. 217).

Government

In the early 1520s this area was within the limits claimed by Villa Segura de la Frontera (cf. Tepeaca). In 1534 a C was first appointed to Cuzcatlan; in the same year we find a single magistrate administering Teguacán and Teutitlan del Camino, but two years later Teguacán was a separate corregimiento, and by 1545 the crown half of Zoquitlan had its own C. In 1554-5 the C of Teguacán was re-designated AM and was put in charge of nearby encomiendas, for some years exercising suffragan jurisdiction in Cuzcatlan, Teutitlan del Camino, Tequila y Chichiquila, Tuxtepec y Quimistlan, and Tecomavaca y Quiotepec.[3] The C of Zoquitlan at this time was made subordinate to Teutila (q.v.). Towards the end of the century Zoquitlan was attached to the corregimiento of Cuzcatlan, which in turn was annexed to Teguacán shortly before 1643.[4]

The AM of Teguacán became a crown appointee in 1646, although later appointments were occasionally made by the viceroy. Deputies resided at Cuzcatlan and Zapotitlan most of the time.[5] After 1787 the magistrate was a subdelegado in the intendencia of Puebla.

Church

The Franciscans were the first missionaries here, founding a monastery at Concepción Teguacán in the 1530s. This doctrina was secularized towards 1567 but returned to Franciscan control a year or so later, by which time secular parishes had been established at two old Franciscan visitas, S Juan Evangelista Cuzcatlan and S Martín Zapotitlan (*Alegaciones...*, fol. 23). While Teguacán was again secularized in 1641 (the new patron was S Nicolás Tolentino), the regular clergy seem to have retained some parochial duties there.

By 1777 additional secular curates were living at S Pedro Chiapulco, S Miguel Elosuchitlan, S Antonio de la Cañada, and S Juan Tepango, and still another parish, Sta María Coyomeapa, existed by 1791. All these doctrinas belonged to the diocese of Tlaxcala.

Population and settlements

After much early loss, in 1570 there were some 6,430 native tributaries (3,000 at Teguacán, 2,000 at Zapotitlan, 500 at Cuzcatlan, 400 at Chiapulco, 280 at Zoquitlan, 250 at Elosuchitlan). The linguistic situation was roughly that reported above. Epidemic and endemic disease and other factors reduced the total to 4,400 tributaries in 1600, and only 1,670 in 1629. Later counts show a strong recovery, perhaps aided by immigration, to 4,380 tributaries in 1696, 4,832 Indian families in 1743 (just after another epidemic), 36,301 Indians (individuals) in 1791, and 8,152 Indian tributaries in 1804.[6]

Beginning in the sixteenth century, Spaniards carved wheat farms and haciendas from lands which were vacated by the Indian communities, especially in those parts of the valley which could be irrigated. By 1643 there were 100 Spanish vecinos at Teguacán and 30 at Cuzcatlan, with twenty-three wheat farms and a number of sugar haciendas. In 1743 some 500 non-Indian families are reported, while in 1791 there were 1,821 Spaniards (individuals), 2,209 mestizos, and 1,436 mulattoes in the jurisdiction. Late eighteenth-century reports name seventeen haciendas, twenty-three ranchos, and three *trapiches*.

We have no complete sixteenth-century listing of settlements subordinate to Teguacán (later, Tehuacán de las Granadas; 1950: Tehuacán, ciudad), which had some thirty-eight 'barrios' in 1548. The site of the cabecera was changed at least once (*c.* 1567, from Calcahualco to the final location), and there may have been an earlier move (in the 1530s, from Cerro Colorado to Calcahualco). The cabecera seems to have acquired the title of ciudad in the seventeenth century. There was probably a congregation carried out by the Franciscans towards 1540, and a further reduction of estancias was proposed in 1598.[7] Reports of 1643 and 1697 name the pueblos de visita here, but we cannot be certain which belonged to Teguacán and which to Chiapulco. Some seventeen early estancias probably subject to Teguacán can be identified with pueblos surviving in the late eighteenth century (Acapan, Altepexi, Axalpa, Cuauhtla, Chalma, Chilac, Necochtla, Sta María del Monte [de las Nieves] Nonoalco, Oxpanco [=Miaguatlan?], Teutipilco [=Teloxco, Teloxtoc?], Tepetzinco, S Lorenzo, S Esteban del Monte Tlalquexcalco, S Juan de los Chochos Tlaltepanco, Tlaltizapan [=Teontepec?], Tzinacantepec, and S Antonio de la Cañada Xitehuacan). A dozen places named in 1697 no longer existed as pueblos a century later, while Atzingo, Coapa, and Sta Catarina seem to have been founded after 1697. There were apparently a good many abandonments, re-occupations, and changes of site through the years.

Chiapulco (Chapolco, etc.; 1950: Chapulco, pueblo), according to the visita of *c.* 1548, had only six barrios, while a congregation document of 1603 names seven subject estancias. Six places perhaps subject to Chiapulco, some of them probably in new sites, existed as pueblos in the eighteenth century. These were Cuayocan (Coayucatepec), Miaguatlan, Sta Catalina del Monte Ocelotepec, S Bernardino Ocelotepec, Tepango, and Tepetiopan (= Temimiloc?).

S Martín Zapotitlan (Tzapotitlan; 1950: Zapotitlán Salinas, *villa*) was originally on a hill, Cuta, a league northeast of its final site; this cabecera was moved down by the Franciscans, perhaps in the 1540s. There is a good deal of confusion about the toponymy of this area. The 1570 report names ten subject estancias, one of which was Santiago Acatepec. A document of 1603 lists eleven places to be congregated at Acatepec, but only two or three of them can be remotely identified with those in the 1570 list. The distant Mixtecan estancia of Xuquila, mentioned in 1570, was disputed between Zapotitlan and Cuestlaguaca in 1576.[8] Several places (among them Acatepec, Acatitlan, Coatepec, and Iztepec) claimed cabecera status in the sixteenth century.[9] Eight settlements which survived as pueblos (some of them cabeceras) in the late eighteenth century were most likely early sujetos of Zapotitlan. They were Acatepec, Acatitlan (Acatitemoapa, Acatlixtinuapa, Calticlan, Ecatitlan, etc.), Azumba (Chiatzumba, Ozumba), Caltepec, Coatepec, Mezontla, S Francisco Rinconada (Xochiltepec), and Sta Catalina. Here, as elsewhere, townsites were moved about a good deal. S Antonio de la Sal seems to be a relatively late foundation.

Cuzcatlan (Coscatlan, Cuexcatlan; 1950: Coxcatlán, *villa*), which was at first a short distance east of its final cabecera site, had twenty-two barrios in 1548, but only eleven are mentioned in 1570–80, from which we guess that there was a Franciscan congregation here in the 1550s. Two sujetos,

Mazateopan and Petlapa, were far to the east in tierra caliente beyond Zoquitlan, while the rest were within three leagues of the cabecera. Some disappeared, swallowed up by sugar haciendas, but Asuchitlan, Mazateopan, Otontepec (Tetitlan), Tlacuchcalco (Tlacoxcalco), Xitlama (Jitlaman), and Xuxutla (Chimalguacan, Xocotla) survived as pueblos, some perhaps in different sites.

S Pablo Zoquitlan (Zuquitlan; 1950: Zoquitlán, pueblo) had five visitas within six leagues in 1570. Atzala and Matzatzongo were abandoned, but Coyomeapa, S Juan Cuautla, and S Sebastián Tlacotepec (Guacapa in 1570) were pueblos in 1791–2.

'Axalyaualco y Elosuchitlan' appear as a single encomienda with nine barrios in 1548. Towards 1570, S Miguel Elosuchitlan (Elojuchitlan, etc.; 1950: Eloxuchitlan, pueblo) had two sujetos, Axalyagualco and Alcomunga; both were still pueblos in 1791, although Alcomunga was also claimed as a sujeto by Zongolica (cf. Vera Cruz Vieja). The cabecera of Elosuchitlan was moved from an early site nearby on the south.

Sources

The region as it was *c.* 1548 is described in the *Suma de Visitas* (PNE, I, nos. 18, 127–30, 510). In the Ovando series of *c.* 1570 there are useful reports from the curates of Cuzcatlan and Zapotitlan (PNE, v, pp. 205–7, 223–4), but only a truncated synthesis from the Franciscans at Teguacán (*Códice franciscano*, p. 26. Cf. García Pimentel, 1904, p. 14). We have a most interesting relación geográfica sent in, with a map, by the C of Cuzcatlan in 1580.[10] Ponce's (I, pp. 261–7, 503–7) journal tells of his visits here in 1586.

Congregation documents from Acatepec[11] and Chiapulco (Paredes Colín, pp. 56–7) have been found. Bishop Mota y Escobar was here in 1610,[12] and Palafox's report of his 1643 visit is of special interest.[13] Tributary data for the seventeenth century are derived from two documents.[14] A report on the doctrine of Teguacán of *c.* 1697 contains a list of visitas (Vetancurt, 4a parte, p. 66). There is a curious map of S Juan Cuautla dated 1690.[15]

The description of this area given by Villaseñor y Sánchez (I, pp. 349–52), corresponding to *c.* 1743, is supplemented by the journal of P. Ajofrín (II, pp. 42–7), who went through here in 1766. For 1777, we have found padrones from most of the parishes,[16] together with 'topographic' reports from the curates of Cuzcatlan, Chiapulco, and Elosuchitlan.[17] There is a good description and map of the jurisdiction in 1791,

submitted with the non-Indian padrón,[18] as well as a list of toponyms dated 1792.[19]

The valley of Tehuacán has been the object of an intensive inter-disciplinary study in recent years (MacNeish, 1964. MacNeish *et al.*, 1967). The little monograph of Paredes Colín (1960) contains material not found elsewhere.

86 *Teguantepec*

The province of Teguantepec, in southeasternmost Oaxaca, comprised the Pacific side of the isthmus together with headwaters of the Coatzacoalcos river. Here the continental divide sinks to a low pass (200+ m) where there is a sharp climatic boundary, humid and forested to the north, dry treeless savannas to the south. Most of the area is a low, featureless plain with extensive salt-water lagoons along the coast, but elevations reach 2,400 m above Chimalapa in the Sierra Madre de Chiapas. The western part is drained by the Tehuantepec river and its affluents, while to the east numerous short watercourses flow into the coastal estuaries. Lowland temperatures are high except in the winter months, when a cold north wind frequently blows across the isthmus.

Tecuantépec (Zapotecan, Guixegui) was ruled by a powerful Zapotecan king related to Moctezuma. His political influence probably extended westward to Nexapa and along the coast from Mazatlan to Tlapanatépec.[1] Tequixixtlan and Xallapan either had subordinate rulers or governors sent by the lord of Tecuantépec. Zapotecan was predominant in the area from Tecuantépec to Xallapan, Chontal at Mazatlan and Tequixixtlan, and Mixe–Zoquean in the mountains, while along the coast east of Tecuantépec lived a primitive fisher folk, the Huaves. The mountain Mixes, with their center at Utlatépec or Anepaan, and the coastal Huaves to a lesser extent, probably had some autonomy. Tecuantépec was an important trade and religious center, and while it seems to have paid no tribute to the Aztecs it allowed them the right of passage to their province of Xoconochco.

First contact with Spaniards was in late 1521, when the ruler of Tecuantépec submitted to Spanish control (Bancroft, II, p. 40. Cervantes de Salazar, p. 807). There were perhaps two Spanish entries the following year, an expedition led by Pedro de Alvarado from the west, and a smaller group of explorers through the Mixe country to Utlatépec and Xoconochco (Díaz del Castillo, II, pp. 101–2. Herrera, 3a década, p. 133). Alvarado and his army passed through again in January, 1524, on their way to Guatemala, and it was perhaps at this time that native resistance at Tequixixtlan and Xallapan was quelled and Spanish control firmly established (Díaz del Castillo, II, p. 122). The mountain Indians remained belligerent for another decade (Icaza, nos. 9, 24, 38).

Encomiendas

Teguantepec and neighboring states were set aside for himself by Hernán Cortés by 1524 at the latest. The vast encomienda was re-assigned by the acting governors, recovered by Cortés in 1526, seized for the crown by the first audiencia in July 1529, and reoccupied by Cortés as Marqués del Valle in 1530. During his absence in Spain (1528–30) Cortés seems to have 'deposited' the area with his *mayordomo*, Pedro de Carranza. The grant of the Marquesado specifically mentioned Teguantepec, Xalapa, and Utlatepec.[2]

According to Cortés's petition of 1532, Teguantepec had a common boundary on the west with his valley of Guaxaca possessions, but the second

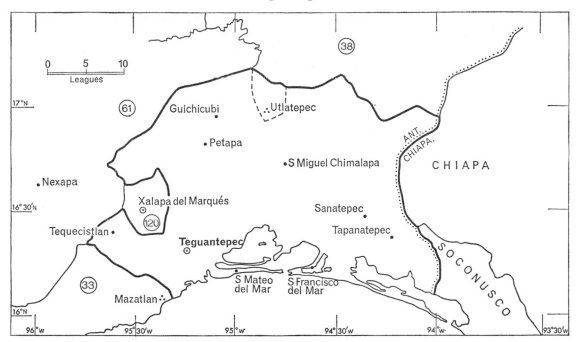

audiencia soon separated them. Nexapa, Maxaltepec, and Xilotepec were annexed to the crown province of Zapotecas (cf. Villa Alta, Nexapa), Tequecistlan was given to another encomendero, and Ecatepec and Mazatlan were assigned to the corregimiento of Guamelula.[3]

The shipyard at Teguantepec (*see below*) from the late 1520s was the key to Cortés's maritime projects in the Pacific, but subsequently there was much discussion of the propriety of allowing a 'port' to remain in private hands, and in 1560 an agreement was reached with the second marquis by which the encomienda escheated. This went into effect three years later, at which time the Marquesado was left with the *villa* of Xalapa (q.v.) and a number of cattle estancias.

Tequecistlan was perhaps first assigned to Luis de la Cueva, who sold his rights to Tomás de Lamadriz. The latter was succeeded sometime before 1548 first by his widow, María Ramírez, and then by a daughter, Juana de Castañeda, married to Diego de Alavés. A son, Melchor de Alavés, inherited sometime between 1583 and 1597. After escheatment the tributes were re-assigned and were still privately held in 1797 (Dorantes de Carranza, p. 314).

Government

Teguantepec had a justice appointed by Cortés in 1526, briefly replaced by a crown AM in 1529 (Gardiner, 1955; 1958, p. 84). Thereafter the magistrate, variously called C or AM, was an appointee of the Marqués del Valle until 1563, when he again became a crown official. The jurisdiction's boundaries remained unchanged from the 1530s, with the addition of Tequecistlan. Xalapa del Marqués (q.v.) was administered separately after 1563, although it was attached to Teguantepec during the various periods of sequestration, notably in 1570–95.[4] From 1787 Teguantepec was a subdelegación in the intendencia of Oaxaca.

Church

A clergyman (perhaps a Franciscan) retained by Cortés was replaced towards 1540 by Dominicans, who founded the doctrina of Sto Domingo (S Pedro) Teguantepec. A monastery was built in 1544–55 (McAndrew, p. 556). Sta María (Asunción) Xalapa became a Dominican parish *c.* 1565, and Magdalena Tequecistlan before 1571. Other doctrinas (Dominican), probably organized as a result of the congregations of *c.* 1600, were Sto Domingo Sanatepec and S Francisco Istactepec del Mar.[5] S Juan Bautista Guichicubi and Asunción Petapa were later (after 1646) Dominican foundations. Tequecistlan was secularized early in the eighteenth century, but most if not all of the remaining parishes continued under Dominican control until after Independence. The priest of Sanatepec moved to S Miguel Chimalapa sometime between 1802 and 1820.

Teguantepec was briefly (1551–5) in the Dominican province of S Vicente de Guatemala before it was transferred to that of Santiago de México, and finally (from 1592) S Hipólito Mártir de Oaxaca. The area fell within the diocese of Antequera.

Population and settlements

The 1580 relación says that Teguantepec once had 20,000 native tributaries, and Tequecistlan more than 4,000; considering the area, the estimate for Teguantepec is probably too low, and may not include the mountain Mixes. There were perhaps 6,250 tributaries in the two encomiendas in 1550 (5,258 at Teguantepec alone), and 5,500 in 1563 (L de T, p. 376). A plague in 1567–8 reduced the number to 3,800 in 1570, while the 1580 count has 3,850 tributaries (3,200 at Teguantepec, 650 at Tequecistlan). In 1623 there were 2,437 tributaries at Teguantepec, perhaps 2,800 altogether. Burgoa has 1,500 families at Teguantepec towards 1670, but it is not clear whether the other parishes are included in this figure. Later counts give 3,831 tributaries in 1743 and 4,407 in 1797.[6]

Spaniards and Negroes began arriving in the 1520s. The number of Spanish vecinos was reported as 15 or 20 in 1571, 25 in 1580, and 50 (including mestizos) in 1743. Sanatepec was a predominantly Negroid settlement by 1670. The 1797 census has 506 free Negro and mulatto tributaries.

Teguantepec (Tecoantepeque, etc.; 1950: Sto Domingo Tehuantepec, ciudad) at contact probably had its ceremonial and political center on the slopes of the mountain now called Guiengola, where there are extensive ruins (Covarrubias, pp. 196–9). There was an early congregation, most

likely in the 1540s, when many estancias were collected around the final site on either side of the river and became barrios of the cabecera. The latter was re-baptized Villa de Guadalcázar towards 1620, but the new name did not long endure.

Cortés, in his petition of 1532, names five places as sujetos of Teguantepec, in addition to those which were removed from his encomienda (*see above*). These were Guaçontlan, Ocotepeque ('q̄ despues se llamo Chimalapa y despues Guavtlinchan y agora Talotaquepeque', i.e. 'first called Chimalapa, then Guavtlinchan, and now Talotaquepeque), Tlapanatepeque, Ystactepeque, and Çuatlan. Since Teguantepec had many other dependencies, we assume that the places mentioned by Cortés had a special status from pre-Conquest times. Guazontlan (S Mateo del Mar) and Istactepec (S Francisco del Mar) were Huave settlements, while Tlapanatepec (Tapanatepec) and Izguatlan were Mixe-Zoque communities. The much re-named Ocotepeque was also in Zoque country, and can probably be identified in its last designation with S Bernardo Utlatepec or Puerto Viejo, the head of canoe navigation on the upper Coatzacoalcos. This place was important to Cortés, who had equipment and supplies brought across the isthmus for his shipyard of Santiago, located first on the Laguna Superior and later (from *c.* 1535) at El Carbón, at the mouth of the Teguantepec river (Borah, 1954, p. 23. Brand, 1956, p. 588. Moorhead, 1949). Utlatepec was claimed for the Marquesado as a dependency of Xalapa as late as 1618.[7]

The places in Cortés's 1532 list soon lost their cabecera status. In 1550 the *villa* of Teguantepec had twenty-seven pueblos and estancias and forty-nine barrios subject to it. The abovementioned places and others, thirty-two in all, were directly subject to Teguantepec in 1580. A congregation of *c.* 1600 further reduced the number of estancias while creating a few new communities. By the late eighteenth century there were twenty-four pueblos within the old subject territory of Teguantepec, all of which had somehow acquired the category of cabecera. In the following list, sixteenth-century variant spellings are indicated with an asterisk. Chihuitan, S Miguel Chimalapa

(Anepaan in Zoque), Sta María Chimalapa, Espinal, Guevea, Guichicubi (Pueblo Nuevo), Guienagati, Huilotepec, Iztaltepec (Iztactepec de la Sierra★), Iztepec, Juchitán (Suchitlan★), Lachiguiri (S Martín de la Sierra★?), Laullaga, Magdalena (Amatitlan de la Sierra★?), Mixtequilla, Neutepec (Nectepec★), Petapa (Zapotec, Guegodáha), Sanatepec (Zanatepec★), S Dionisio (Huaxtiaca, Hualixtiaca; Tepeguazontlan★, in a different site), S Francisco del Mar (Iztactepec de la mar★, Istaquetepeque de la costa★), S Mateo del Mar (Guazontlan★), Sta María del Mar (Ocelotlan★), Tapanatepec (Tepanatepec, Tlapanatepec★), and Tlacotepec.

Magdalena Tequecistlan (Tequixistlan, etc.; Chontal, Maadú; 1950: Magdalena Tequisistlán, pueblo) in 1550 had fifteen subject estancias, three of them deserted. Six sujetos are named in 1580, but only one, S Miguel Tenango, appears as a pueblo in 1802–20.

Much of Teguantepec's territory was taken up by cattle estancias belonging to the Marquesado del Valle. They are listed here under Xalapa del Marqués (*see below*).

Sources

Besides the usual brief cabecera descriptions in the *Suma de visitas*, there is a detailed report on Teguantepec dated 1550 (PNE, I, nos. 748, 780; pp. 312–14); we also have tribute records of 1542, 1553, and 1563 (L de T, pp. 372–7). The area is summarily described in reports of *c.* 1570 (García Pimentel, 1904, pp. 65, 71–2. López de Velasco, pp. 235–6. In 1580 the AM submitted a valuable relación geográfica with two maps, one showing the entire jurisdiction with all its sujetos, the other a chart of the coast.[8] The road crossing from Tequecistlan to Soconusco was traveled and described by Ponce (I, pp. 287–91, 488–92) in 1586, and again by Gage (pp. 115–21) in 1627 and by Cobo (pp. 197–8) in 1630. There are some few data on congregations in 1598–1604.[9]

We have not looked into the details of an Indian uprising at Teguantepec in 1660–1 (cf. Cook and Borah, 1968, pp. 34–5; Gay, II, pp. 308–14). Burgoa (1934a, II, pp. 284, 313–411) describes the various parishes as they were a few years later and adds historical information.

A lost document of *c.* 1743 is abbreviated in Villaseñor y Sánchez (II, pp. 184–6). For the year 1777, we have a padrón of Sanatepec parish,[10] a 'topographic' report on Guichicubi,[11] and both for S Francisco del Mar;[12] the relación of S Francisco, in particular, gives a wealth of information. Four of the six parishes (Guichicubi, Petapa, Sanatepec, S Francisco del Mar) are described in the admirable *visita* of 1802.[13] For the final years of the colonial period there is a lengthy description and statistical summary of the area, accompanied by a fine map in colors.[14]

Colonial Teguantepec has been the object of much scholarly attention. The work of Covarrubias (1946) is of special interest. The situation at contact is examined by Spores (1965). Cortés's activities here are studied by Cadenhead (1960), García Martínez (1969), and Gardiner (1955). A local historian's monograph (Cajigas Langner, 1954) should be approached with caution but gives worthwhile leads.

87 *Temazcaltepec y Zultepec*

Today forming the southwest corner of the state of Mexico, this jurisdiction extended from the Nevado de Toluca (4,558 m) to a minimum elevation of *c.* 500 m. Drainage is southwestward into the Balsas system. It is a well-watered region, with wide temperature variation according to altitude. Parts are heavily forested.

Apparently there were two chief political divisions here, Texcaltitlan (which included Temazcaltépec and Texopilco) and Amatépec (including Atlamoloyan, Tlatlayan, and Zoltépec). Metlatépec and Tepexahualco (Teoxahualco, Hueyxahualco) were perhaps minor autonomous regions. Only Tepexahualco appears (in the tributary region of Tlachco) on the Codex Mendoza; Atlamoloyan and Teoxahualco are listed as tributaries of Tlacopan, while Tlatlayan and Zoltépec are said to have been conquered by Moctezuma II. Much of the area was probably called upon for service in warfare against the

neighboring Tarascans, and thus fell under Triple Alliance hegemony. Náhuatl was the dominant language, but Matlatzincan was also spoken (in 1569) at Texcaltitlan, as was Mazahuan at Atlamoloyan.

Spaniards were here in 1520 and probably controlled the area within the next year or so.

Encomiendas

Amatepec, Metlatepec, and Hueyxagualco were seemingly combined in a single encomienda which was given to the conquistador Juan de Salcedo, escheating on his death in the fall of 1536 (L de T, p. 37).

Texcaltitlan and its sujetos were held by the conquistador Antón Caicedo, who died in 1535 or 1536. At first the encomienda escheated, but it was soon re-assigned to Caicedo's widow, Marina

de Montes de Oca. The second husband of Doña Marina, Francisco de Chávez, appears as encomendero until his death at the beginning of 1561, when the viceroy ruled that his daughter, Catalina de Chávez, should succeed. Three years later, when Catalina died, there was a suit between Caicedo's widow, Doña Marina, and Catalina's widower, Pedro Lorenzo de Castilla. The latter appears as encomendero in 1569, but soon thereafter tributes escheated. In the seventeenth century Texcaltitlan's tributes were set aside in part for the Moctezuma heirs, and were still being paid to them as late as 1801.[1]

Government

While both Amatepec and Texcaltitlan became corregimientos in 1536, the latter soon reverted to private encomienda. At the same time, the silver deposits of Zultepec attracted miners (they were discovered before 1532), and the C of Amatepec became AM of Minas de Zultepec towards 1540.[2] The mines of Temazcaltepec were opened some five years later and had a separate AM for a while, although in the 1560s Zultepec and Temazcaltepec were combined under a single magistrate.[3] In the following decade they were again split into two alcaldías mayores, the AM of Temazcaltepec doubling as C of Texcaltitlan and Tuzantla (cf. Maravatío), the latter in adjoining Michoacán. For some reason the villages of Coatepec and Cuitlapilco, although subject to Zacualpa (q.v.), were administered by the AM of Zultepec until 1575.[4] Tuzantla was transferred from Temazcaltepec to Maravatío perhaps in the 1680s.

Towards 1715 the two jurisdictions were once more placed under a single AM, with residence at Temazcaltepec (actually, tributes from Amatepec were collected by the AM of Zacualpa during much of the seventeenth century). From 1787 Temazcaltepec y Zultepec was a subdelegación in the intendencia of Mexico.

Church

There was probably a secular priest at the mining camp of S Miguel (later, S Juan Bautista) Zultepec from the mid-1530s; Zumárraga is said to have dedicated the church there (Vera, p. 55). In 1569 we find secular clergy assigned to S Pedro Almoloya and Santiago Texcaltitlan, but they were living at the reales de minas of Zultepec and Temazcaltepec, respectively. In connection with the congregations of *c.* 1600, priests took up residence at S Gaspar Amatepec, S Francisco Temazcaltepec del Valle, and S Pedro Texupilco, and there may have been a curate at Santiago Tlatlaya for a time.[5] S Martín Ozoloapan was separated from the parish of S Francisco Temazcaltepec towards 1690.[6] All these parishes were in the archdiocese.

The doctrina of Texupilco seems to have been ministered for some years by regular clergy (Vera, p. 143). In the eighteenth century Zultepec, in addition to two secular priests who shared the benefice, had a monastery of Dieguinos helping with parochial matters.

Population and settlements

There must have been a notable drop in the native population before 1569, when there were 2,872 Indian tributaries (1,333 at Amatepec, 1,539 at Texcaltitlan), in addition to 1,335 Indian miners (individuals), or a total of perhaps 3,500 families. By this time the old cabeceras of Hueyxagualco and Metlatepec had only 69 tributaries each. Further loss in the epidemic of 1576–81 and later brought the total down to 1,011 tributaries in 1643, without counting tribute-exempt miners. Subsequent counts show 2,193 tributaries in 1688, 3,163 Indian families in 1743 (much mortality is reported during the plague of 1737–9), and 8,090 Indian tributaries in 1801 (by this time miners had been added to the tribute rolls).[7]

Silver mining began at Amatepec perhaps in 1531, and within a few years there was a growing colony of Spanish miners and both Indian and Negro slaves (ENE, xv, p. 154. Herrera, 4a década, p. 231. Millares Carlo and Mantecón, II, nos. 1890, 1956, 2051–4, 2064, 2066, 2202, 2355–6). In 1569 there were 211 Spaniards, probably vecinos, and 692 Negroes (individuals) at Temazcaltepec and Zultepec. The mining zone in general is often referred to in colonial documents as Provincia de la Plata. During the mining slump of the seventeenth century some left, but a number of erstwhile miners acquired cattle and sugar

haciendas. In 1743 there were 695 families of Spaniards, 404 of mestizos, and 206 of mulattoes; the number of slaves is not recorded. The census of 1801 shows 386 free Negro and mulatto tributaries in the jurisdiction.

The various reales de minas seem to have moved about as the old deposits were exhausted and new ones discovered. A map accompanying the 1580 relación shows, in addition to the principal real of Temazcaltepec (1950: Real de Arriba, pueblo?), those of S Andrés, los Ríos, and Real Viejo. By 1743 Temazcaltepec's miners were dispersed in three settlements all within a half league, the reales de Carnicería, Arriba, and Temazcaltepec proper. The original real in the Amatepec area was perhaps S Miguel Zultepec (1950: Sultepequito, pueblo), but by 1569 it was four leagues north, at S Juan Bautista Zultepec (1950: Sultepec de Pedro Ascencio, villa). Here also there were a number of lesser reales and cuadrillas. In 1754 almost half the total mining population of Zultepec lived at the cuadrilla of Coyametitlan, one league from the principal settlement.

According to the *Suma* (*c.* 1548), Amatepec (1950: pueblo) had five estancias, Almoloya, Aquiapa, Gueyxaualco, Tletlayan, and Çultepeque. The 1569 report recognizes Almoloya, Tlatlayan, and Çultepec as sub-cabeceras under Amatepec, Aquiapa as simply an estancia of Almoloya, and Hueyxahualco (Uhuixavalco, etc.; 1950: S Pedro Hueyahualco, pueblo) and Metlatepec (1950: pueblo) as 'pueblos por sí', i.e., cabeceras independent of Amatepec; in addition, some thirty lesser estancias in this area are named (saints' names only) in 1569. Thirteen years later the relación geográfica lists Hueyxagualco and Metlatepec as dependencies of Almoloya, and mentions only twenty-five lesser estancias. Congregations were attempted here *c.* 1600 without great success.[8] In addition to the places mentioned, fifteen of the old estancias are recognizable as pueblos in 1743–54: Santiago Aguacatitlan, Sta Cruz Capula, S Felipe Coatepec, S Francisco Coaxusco, S Francisco (Atiquisca), S Juan (Tepetlatlaya), S Mateo (Tototepec), S Miguel (Aguayutla), S Pedro (Mecatepec), S Simón (Chaneca), Sta Ana (Cicatacoya), Sta Cruz (Huetititlan), Sta

María la Goleta (Cacaguatlan), Sto Tomás (Copaltitlan), and S Andrés Tepexititlan. Six eighteenth-century pueblos of Indians (Asuchitlancillo, S Felipe Atenco, Asunción Pozoltepec (Pozontepec), Santiago, Tehuilotépetl, Totolmaloya) seem to have been later foundations. The Indian cabecera of S Miguel Zultepec appears as Sultepeque (Zoltepec) Mazehualpa in 1743–54.

In the late sixteenth century, Texcaltitlan (Tescaltitlan; 1950: Santiago Texcaltitlán) had the sub-cabeceras of S Francisco Temazcaltepec (Temascaltepec del Valle; 1950: Temascaltepec de González, *villa*) and S Pedro Texupilco (=Talistaca in 1548?; 1950: Tejupilco de Hidalgo, *villa*). Thirty subject estancias altogether are listed (saints' names in most cases) in 1569, and fifty-one in 1580 (Náhuatl toponyms). Sixteen pueblos (besides the three old cabeceras) survived in the eighteenth century, some identifiable with those listed 200 years earlier: Acamuchitlan, S Mateo Acatitlan, Almomoloya (Mazamamaloya, S Mateo de los Ranchos), S Juan Atescapa, S Gabriel Cuentla, S Miguel Ixtapa, S Martín Ocosuchitepec, S Miguel Oxtotipac de los Ranchos, S Martín Ozoloapan, Sta María Pipioltepec, S Andrés de los Gamas, S Francisco de los Ranchos, S Lucas del Valle, S Simón Ciutepec de los Barreteros, Sto Tomás (de los Plátanos?), and S Martín Tequixquiapan. Certain other places, such as Sta Cruz Miaguatlan (Ixtapan del Oro), were perhaps later foundations.

In 1801 there were fifty-four cabeceras in the jurisdiction, an extreme example of how subordinate Indian communities obtained from the Spaniards a political autonomy which they did not have before the Conquest.[9] A good many haciendas and minor settlements (estancias, cuadrillas, ranchos, trapiches, etc.) are named in the 1743–4 report.

Sources

Amatepec and Texcaltitlan with their subjects are described as they were at mid-sixteenth century (PNE, I, nos. 38, 673) and in 1569.[10] Relaciones submitted by the AMs of Temazcaltepec (in 1580) and Zultepec (1582) have been published, together with four maps which accompanied the first of these reports (PNE, VII, pp. 8–28).

For the seventeenth century, there are tributary data for 1643–88,[11] and a description of the area as it was in 1685, part of the journal of an archbishop's visit, which we have not examined.[12]

An excellent report and census dated 1743–4[13] is inadequately summarized in Villaseñor y Sánchez (I, pp. 207–16). Further data on the parish of Zultepec are given in an Inquisition document of 1754.[14]

Many documents at AGN are listed in the works of Colín (1966, 1967).

88 *Tenango del Valle*

This is a cold, dry region astride the watershed which separates the Lerma and Balsas systems, at 2,500–3,000 m (a corner goes up to the Nevado de Toluca), including the principal source of the Lerma. Today it is in the state of Mexico.

At contact there were a great many small native states here, all tributary to the Aztecs directly or indirectly. Calimayan, Teotenanco, and Tepemaxalco took their tributes to Calixtlahuacan, and may have been politically subordinate to that center. Cepayauhtla and Ciuhtépec were outlying dependencies of Tlacopan. Most or all of the remaining communities (Atlapulco, Capoloac, Cuauhpanoayan, Chichicuauhtla, Huitzitzilapan, Maxtécatl, Ocoyacac, Ocelotépec, Tepehuexoyucan, Texcalyacac, Xallatlauhco, Xochiyocan) were old Tepaneca conquests which paid tribute to the Aztec garrison at Cuahuacan (Cuyoacan?). Some of these places were probably ruled by calpixque rather than tlatoque. Languages spoken were Matlatzincan, Otomí, and Náhuatl, frequently all three in a single village.

The region came under Spanish control in 1521.

Encomiendas

With the possible exception of Atlatlauca, the entire area was considered by Hernando Cortés to form part of his holdings as subject either to Cuyoacan, Toluca, or Tacuba. During his absences from Mexico and later most of the places mentioned were re-assigned at least once.[1]

Atlapulco was given in January, 1528, to the *comendador* Leonel de Cervantes, who some few years later had it transferred to his son, Juan (Alonso) de Cervantes. The latter was succeeded towards 1550 by his widow, Catalina de Zárate, who then married Juan Gaitán. Doña Catalina alone appears as encomendera in 1560–97. Escheatment occurred between 1643 and 1688.[2]

The two cabeceras of Atlatlauca and Suchiaca were held by the conquistador Hernando (Gómez?) de Xerez until his death in 1537. The encomienda was claimed by Xérez's widow, Ana Rodríguez, but the viceroy assigned it to the royal mint; it was a crown possession from 1544 (ENE, xv, p. 95. Icaza, I, p. 110; II, p. 8. L de T, p. 81).

Calimaya and Tepemaxalco had the same encomienda history as Metepec (q.v.), tributes going to the counts of Santiago de Calimaya into the eighteenth century. The succession of encomenderos at Chichicuautla was identical to that at Chilacachapa and Cuezala (cf. Iscateupa), final escheatment occurring between 1643 and 1688. Ocelotepec and its dependencies were held by Alonso de Villanueva and his descendants (cf. Guachinango) until tributes were re-assigned to the Moctezuma heirs in the seventeenth century; it was a crown village by 1688.

A group of cabeceras subject in a sense to Tacuba had parallel encomienda histories. Ocoyoacac was included in the 1526 Tacuba grant, but was soon re-assigned to Antonio de Villagómez. It was recovered in the 1540s by Isabel Moctezuma, encomendera of Tacuba, who also held Capuluac, Cuapanoaya, and Tepexoyuca. All of these places were parcelled out to Isabel Moctezuma's heirs after her death *c.* 1551, and their tributes were assigned in perpetuity.

Half of Teutenango was assigned to the crown *c.* 1535 (the encomendero may have been Diego Rodríguez). The other half was held by the conquistador Juan de Burgos, who in 1538 sold his share to Francisco Vázquez de Coronado. Vázquez was followed in 1554 by a daughter, Isabel de Luján, married to Bernardino Pacheco de Bocanegra. The latter died soon after 1570 and was perhaps succeeded by his brother, Nuño de Chávez Pacheco de Bocanegra (he was married to another daughter of Vázquez de Coronado); at any rate, tributes were still going to that family in 1597. Final escheatment occurred by 1688.[3]

Another Cervantes encomienda (cf. Atlapulco, *above*), Xalatlaco, was inherited in 1550 by Leonor de Andrada, Cervantes's widow, followed in the 1560s by their daughter, Isabel de Lara, married to Alonso de Aguilar. When both were dead, in the 1570s, tributes escheated and were re-assigned to Don Luis de Velasco; Velasco's descendants continued receiving them throughout the seventeenth century.[4]

Three other places in the jurisdiction had a rather peculiar status. An island in the upper Lerma originally belonging to Capulhuac was purchased sometime before 1536 by Don Vasco de Quiroga and became the village of S Pedro y S Pablo Tultepec, a dependency of Quiroga's hospital of Santa Fé (cf. Cuyoacan) (Warren, 1963*b*, pp. 46, 60). The tributes of Cepayautla and Ciutepec, two estancias south of Teutenango, went to the encomenderos of Tacuba (q.v.), of which cabecera they were distant subjects.

Government

The early political history of this jurisdiction is closely related to that of the valley of Matalcingo (cf. Metepec, Toluca). While Cortés was struggling for control of the area, Cs were sent to Metepec y Tepemachalco (*c.* 1533), Teutenango (*c.* 1535), and Atlatlauca y Suchiaca (1537). From the early 1550s, Huicicilapa and Teutenango were suffragan corregimientos in the province of Valle de Matalcingo, while Atlatlauca y Suchiaca was subordinate to the AM of Malinalco. Huicicilapa and a large number of private encomiendas were administered directly by the AM of Valle de Matalcingo from 1569.

By the end of the sixteenth century, the Cs of Atlatlauca y Suchiaca and Teutenango had shed their suffragan status, and towards 1645 they were re-designated AMs, the jurisdictions now being referred to as Atlatlauca del Valle and Tenango del Valle, respectively.[5] In the 1670s the two were combined in one alcaldía mayor, Tenango del Valle. The size of the jurisdiction was more than doubled in 1762, with the transfer of Atlapulco, Calimaya, Capuluac, Cuapanoaya, Chichicuautla, Huicicilapa, Ocelotepec, Ocoyoacac, Tepexoyuca, Tepemaxalco, Tultepec, and Xalatlaco, from Metepec to Tenango.[6] Huicicilapa and Ocelotepec formed an enclave to the north, separated from the rest of the partido by the corregimiento of Lerma. After 1787 Tenango del Valle was a subdelegación in the intendencia of Mexico.

Church

The area was visited from Toluca until a separate Franciscan parish was founded at S Pedro y S Pablo Calimaya in 1557 (McAndrew, p. 574). By 1569 there were secular priests at S Pedro Atlapulco (visitas: Capuluac, Ocoyoacac, Cuapanoaya, Tepexoyuca), Teutenango (visitas: Atlatlauca, Suchi-

aca), Asunción Xalatlaco (visita: Tescaliacac), and S Lorenzo Huicicilapa (visitas: Chichicuautla, Ocelotepec, Talasco). Soon afterward (by 1573) the Augustinians established a monastery at S Bartolomé Capuluac.[7] S Bartolomé Ocelotepec was a secular parish by 1575, and somewhat later Huicicilapa was attached to it as a visita.[8] Meanwhile, probably as a result of the congregations of *c.* 1600, the curate of Atlapulco moved to S Martín Ocoyoacac, and a new secular doctrina was founded at S Mateo Tescaliacac.

A report of *c.* 1743 shows Asunción (S Gerónimo) Tepexoyuca as a Franciscan parish, but if this was the case it was soon secularized, as were the regular doctrines of Calimaya (by 1754) and Capuluac.[9] All parishes were in the archdiocese.

Population and settlements

Epidemics in 1576–81 and 1595–7 caused the number of native tributaries to drop from 10,620 in 1569 to 5,300 in 1597. Later counts show 2,447 tributaries in 1643, 3,376 in 1688, and 5,650 Indian families in 1743. There were 10,751 Indian tributaries in 1802.[10] Non-Indians, mostly living on the haciendas, were few. One hundred-and ninety-four mulatto tributaries were reported in 1802.

Altogether the 1569 report lists fourteen cabeceras and sixty-six subject estancias here. The absence of any later complete list of settlements allows only a few generalizations about their development. Congregations were planned throughout the area in the 1590s and early 1600s, and while many estancias were no doubt abandoned or moved closer to their cabeceras at this time, a large number of the old sites were subsequently re-occupied. There was less hacienda encroachment on communal lands here than elsewhere, and the region was dominated by Indian settlements. After the congregations, subordinate native communities began a long struggle for independence which was crowned with success in the eighteenth century. By 1688 nineteen places were recognized as cabeceras; there were three more in 1743, while the tributary census of 1802 shows a total of fifty-one cabeceras in the jurisdiction!

The sixteenth-century cabeceras were S Pedro

Atlapulco (1950: pueblo), S Bartolomé Atlatlauca (1950: Atlatlahuca, pueblo), Santiago Calimaya (1950: Calimaya de Díaz González, *villa*), S Bartolomé Capuluac (1950: Capulhuac de Mirafuentes, *villa*), Cuapanoaya (Cuauhpanoayan, Guapanoaya; 1950: S Juan Coapanoaya, pueblo), Chichicuautla (later, Xochicuautla; 1950: S Francisco Xochicuautla, pueblo), Huicicilapa (Uitzitzilapa, etc.; 1950: S Lorenzo Huitzitzilapan, pueblo), S Bartolomé Ocelotepec (Otzolotepec; 1950: Villa Cuauhtémoc), Ocoyoacac (Coyoacaque, Ocuyacac, etc.; S Martín; 1950: Ocoyoacac, pueblo), Suchiaca (S Juan Xuchiacan; 1950: Xochiaca, pueblo), Tepemaxalco (Tepemachalco; 1950: S Lucas Tepemajalco, pueblo), S Gerónimo Tepexoyuca (Tepehuexoyucan; 1950: Asunción Tepezoyuca), Teutenango (later, Tenango del Valle; 1950: Tenango de Arista, *villa*), and Asunción Xalatlaco (1950: Jalatlaco, pueblo). By 1643 S Miguel Mimiapan (1950: pueblo) had broken away from Ocelotepec, and two former sujetos of Xalatlaco, S Mateo Tescalyacac (1950: pueblo) and Santiago Capuluac del Tianguis (Tianguistengo; 1950: Tianguistenco de Galeana, *villa*) had acquired cabecera status. S Miguel Chapultepec (formerly subject to Calimaya) and S Francisco Xonacatlan (a sub-cabecera of Ocelo-tepec) had their own gobiernos by 1688, while S Mateo Mexicalcingo, S Pedro Tultepec, and Sta Ana Xilocingo were recognized as cabeceras by 1743.[11]

Sources

Incompletely covered in the 1548 *Suma de visitas* (PNE, I, nos. 113, 418, 445, 782), the numerous cabeceras here are described in detail in reports of the Ovando series, all apparently drawn up by curates in 1569.[12] The Cs of Atlatlauca y Suchiaca[13] and Teutenango (PNE, VII, pp. 1–7) each submitted a relación accompanied by a map, in 1580 and 1582 respectively. There is quite a lot of dispersed information on the congregations of 1593–1604.[14]

Two archbishops left accounts of their visits here in 1646[15] and 1685.[16] Population data for 1643–88 are derived from various tribute records.[17] Vetancurt (4a parte, p. 71) has a brief description of Calimaya *c.* 1697.

Lost relaciones of *c.* 1743 are summarized in Villaseñor y Sánchez (I, pp. 231–2). There is a good description of Capuluac parish, undated but made *c.* 1789,[18] and a map showing the southern part of the jurisdiction in 1791.[19]

The documentary guides of Colín (1966, 1967) are most useful.

89 *Teotiguacán*

Extending northeast from the shore of Lake Texcoco to the valley of Mexico's rim (2,200–2,700 m), this is a cold, rather bleak area with slight seasonal precipitation, now in the state of Mexico.

Teotihuacan and Tepechpan were ruled in 1519 by tlatoque of Acolhua lineage, subordinate in a sense to Texcoco but politically quite autonomous. Only Tepechpan appears in the Codex Mendoza as a tributary state. Tequixixtlan, probably a dependency of Tepechpan, may have had some autonomy. The language was Náhuatl, with Otomí and Popolocan minorities.

First visited by Spaniards in 1519, these places came under Spanish control early in 1521.

Encomiendas

Teotiguacan was assigned to the conquistador Francisco de Verdugo, followed on his death in the 1540s by a daughter, Francisca, who married Alonso de Bazán. Their son, Andrés de Bazán, received tributes for a few years before he died *c.* 1568. Then they were re-assigned to Don Luis de Velasco, but soon thereafter another son of Alonso de Bazán, Antonio Velázquez de Bazán, was installed as encomendero. The latter, still mentioned in 1597, was succeeded by a son, Rodrigo Velázquez de Castro y Bazán, from *c.* 1603 to 1620 or later. The last encomendera, Josefa Bazán y Castro, died between 1643 and 1658, when Teotiguacan escheated.

A poblador, Gerónimo de Medina, held Tepexpan from the 1520s until 1538 when he gave it in dowry to his daughter, Inés de Vargas, wife of Juan Baeza de Herrera. Baeza died *c.* 1552, and his widow and later their son, Gerónimo Baeza de Herrera, are listed to 1597. Tributes were reassigned before 1643 to the Moctezuma heirs. Partial escheatment occurred by 1688.

Originally there were two encomenderos at Tequecistlan (recognized as a separate cabecera by the Spaniards). One half escheated in 1534, the other share being held by the conquistador Juan de Tovar. Towards 1555 Tovar's half was inherited by a son, Juan Hipólito de Tovar, who died in 1600. Four years later the Tovar tributes were reassigned to Juan Cano Moctezuma, who with his heirs continued to receive them for many years.

Government

Early in the 1530s a single C was appointed to administer the crown portions of Tequecistlan and neighboring Cempoala. Towards 1557 this corregimiento was divided, and the magistrate of Tequecistlan was given charge of nearby encomiendas (Acolman, Teotiguacan, Tepexpan); he was suffragan to the AM of Tezcuco until the end of the sixteenth century.[1]

Towards 1640 the jurisdiction, by then called S Juan Teotiguacan, became an alcaldía mayor. A significant change in boundaries occurred perhaps late in the seventeenth century when Acolman and its sujetos were transferred from this jurisdiction to that of Tezcuco. From 1786 Teotiguacan was a subdelegación in the intendencia of Mexico.

Church

First entered by Franciscans from Tezcuco, the area was visited after 1540 from the Augustinian center of Acolman. In 1559, after two years of controversy over the proposed construction of an Augustinian monastery, S Juan Evangelista Teotiguacan became a Franciscan parish (Ricard, p. 84). S Bartolomé Tequecistlan and Magdalena Tepexpan long remained visitas of Acolman; they are listed as Augustinian parishes in 1743, but only Tepexpan survived as a separate doctrina after the secularization in 1754. Teotiguacan was secularized in 1771–2. All parishes were in the archdiocese of Mexico.

Population and settlements

After great early loss, the native population stood at about 4,000 tributaries in 1570, further reduced to 2,500 by 1580, 2,000 in 1600, and only 305 in 1643 (there was a serious epidemic in 1629–31). Later counts give 414 tributaries in 1688, 1,036 Indian families in 1743, and 1,814 Indian tributaries in 1804.[2] There were somewhat over 300 non-Indian communicants at Teotiguacan in 1697. The 1743 census shows 257 non-Indian (mostly Spanish) families in the jurisdiction, while that of *c.* 1791 has 895 Spaniards (individuals), 388 mestizos, and 266 mulattoes.

There must have been an early effort at congregation here in the 1550s or 1560s. In 1580 Teotiguacan still had eighteen sujetos, Tepexpan thirteen, and Tequecistlan two; these were scattered about in a complicated pattern (cf. Gibson, 1964, p. 46, and the map accompanying the relación), some close to the cabeceras and others up to five leagues distant.

A further concentration occurred in 1599–1604 in which many minor settlements disappeared, either abandoned or moved into congregations where they became barrios. At Teotiguacan (1950: S Juan Teotihuacán, *villa*), seven of the old estancia names are recognizable as pueblos in the eighteenth century: S Lorenzo (Atezcapan), Sta María Coatlan, S Sebastián (Chimalpa), S Francisco Mazapa (Mazatlan), S Martín (Teyacac), Santiago Tolman, and S Luis Xiuhquemecan (Tecuautitlan). Sta María Maquixco Bajo and Purificación Tilhuacan had become pueblos by the late seventeenth century.

Only three of Tepexpan's (1950: pueblo) 1580 estancias seem to have been permanently obliterated in the congregation of 1603–4. The others either survived or were later resurrected as pueblos with some changes in nomenclature: S Bartolomé Actopan (Atocpan), Sta María Aticpac (Actipac, = Suchitepec?), S Miguel Atlamaxac, S Cristóbal Culhuacan (Culhuacatzinco), Sta María Maquixco Alto, S Juan Teacalco, S Francisco Temazcalapa, S Mateo Teopancala (Teopalcanco), Sta Ana Tlachagualco, and Santiago Zagualuca.

Of the two estancias of Tequecistlan (1950: Tequisistlán, pueblo), one, S Miguel Totolcingo, survived as a pueblo.

In the late eighteenth century there were three haciendas and five ranchos, plus a considerable number of barrios, in the jurisdiction.

Sources

The early (*c.* 1548) reports in the *Suma de visitas* (PNE, I, nos. 263, 512, 514), and those in the Ovando series of *c.* 1570,[3] are quite succinct, but the jurisdiction is described in detail, with a map, in the 1580 relación (PNE, VI, pp. 209–36). Data on congregations in 1599–1604 can be gleaned from various fragments.[4]

The journal of an archiepiscopal visit in 1683[5] gives useful information, as does the report of *c.* 1697 on the Franciscan monastery (Vetancurt, 4a parte, pp. 73–4).

There is a lengthy relación submitted by the AM in 1743,[6] followed by a general description, map, and non-Indian census made *c.* 1791.[7] The jurisdiction is briefly described in another document dated 1792.[8]

The massive work of Gamio (1922) is basic to any study of this area. Sanders (1967, 1968) summarizes his observations on settlements at Teotihuacán. Many documents not seen by this writer are cited in Gibson (1964), and in the archival guides of Colín (1966, 1967). Fernández de Recas (1961, pp. 113–25) reproduces several interesting items concerning Teotiguacan and its caciques.

90 *Teozacualco*

The Sierra Madre del Sur runs from east to west through this wild and remote region in central Oaxaca, draining into the deep canyon of the Cuanana river, an affluent of the Río Verde. Because of the broad range (400–2,500 m) of altitudes here, the climate varies from very hot with little rain and xerophytic flora in the lower parts to cold with pine–oak forests on the higher mountain slopes. The northern half is in the Mixteca Alta, while the south more properly belongs to the Mixteca de la Costa.

Teotzacualco (Chiocano in Mixtecan) was a large Mixtec kingdom whose ruler was related to the dynasty of Tilantongo (cf. Nochistlan). Off to the southwest were two smaller Mixtec states, Amoltépec (Yucunama or Yucumama in Mixtecan), and Iztayutla (Yutañuhu). East of these places, occupying the region between the Río Verde and the Sierra Madre, was Zentzontépec (Yucueetuvui), where the people spoke Chatino. This was frontier country between the rival powers of Tototépec and the Triple Alliance. Shortly before the Spaniards arrived, Moctezuma II invaded the area and apparently gained control of Teotzacualco. Zentzontépec and Iztactlallocan (= Iztayutla?) are listed among his conquests, but it seems more likely that they were under the influence of Tototépec, as was Amoltépec.

We do not know when Spaniards were first seen here. The region came under their control in the early 1520s, when Guaxaca and Tototépec were subdued.

Encomiendas

Teozacualco was perhaps first held by Antón de Arriaga and Juan Ochoa de Lexalde. Arriaga's half was taken for the crown in May 1532. On Ochoa's death towards 1555 his share was inherited

by a son of the same name, and escheated on the latter's death *c.* 1563.[1]

Amoltepec, whose encomendero is not known to us, escheated sometime between 1536 and 1545.

Cortés gave Istayutla to a conquistador, Román López, followed in the mid-1560s by a son, Cristóbal López de Solís. The latter, still alive in 1597, may have been succeeded *c.* 1600 by a third holder, Juan de Guzmán Sotomayor (grandson of Román López).[2]

Cenzontepec was held in the 1520s by Alonso Zimbrón de Vitoria, but it was re-assigned by the second audiencia to Juan de Valdivieso and Alonso de Contreras. Valdivieso's share was inherited *c.* 1540 by a son of the same name (he appears as Juan Vázquez de Valdivieso in one document). By 1604 the holder in the third generation was another Juan de Valdivieso. The half belonging to Contreras, who died in 1559, passed to his son, García de Contreras, still listed in 1604 (Dorantes de Car-

ranza, pp. 164, 210. Gardiner, 1958, p. 155. Icaza, I, p. 27. L de T, pp. 323, 329).

Government

Cs were appointed to Teozacualco (from May, 1532) and Amoltepec (by 1545), and in the early 1550s both of these were placed within the jurisdiction of the AM of Teposcolula, along with the encomienda of Cenzontepec.[3] Istayutla was probably administered from Cuahuitlan or Xicayan in early years. In the 1570s there was a single corregimiento, Teozacualco y Amoltepec, suffragan to the AM of Antequera, but Istayutla and Cenzontepec were not at first included in this jurisdiction. When mineral deposits were discovered at Teoxomulco (a subject of Cenzontepec), that area was assigned to the C of Teozacualco. Towards 1680 Teozacualco and Tecuicuilco (q.v.) were combined under a single AM (they are dealt with separately here).[4] The divided jurisdiction formed a subdelegación within the intendencia of Oaxaca after 1786. Santiago Minas seems to have been transferred from the jurisdiction of Cimatlan to that of Teozacualco sometime after 1745.

Church

A secular curate lived at S Pedro Teozacualco from *c.* 1550. His parish in the 1570s included Amoltepec, while Istayutla was visited at that time from Zacatepec (cf. Xicayan), and Cenzontepec from Zola (cf. Cimatlan y Chichicapa).

Sometime in the late sixteenth or early seventeenth century a priest was assigned to the real de minas of Sto Domingo Teoxomulco, a parish which in 1699 extended westward to Cenzontepec and Amoltepec. Very soon afterward, Amoltepec, Istayutla, and Yutanino were transferred to the new doctrina of Cuanana (cf. Teposcolula). In the eighteenth century Teozacualco parish included Yuta and Tamazola (cf. Nochistlan), and Santiago Minas was visited from Teoxomulco. All parishes were in the diocese of Antequera.

Population and settlements

Spores (1967, p. 54) thinks that this was a relatively sparsely settled region at contact. In 1548 there were perhaps a total of 700 native tributaries at Amoltepec, Istayutla, and Cenzontepec, while 1,982 are listed at Teozacualco, or 2,682 altogether. Within the following decades the decline was remarkable, particularly in the higher country of Teozacualco. An assessment of the latter place in 1565 states that $451\frac{1}{2}$ tributaries 'seem to have died and gone away' since the previous census, some having emigrated to Zola (L de T, pp. 463-4). By 1571 only 960 tributaries are reported, 600 of them at Teozacualco (L de T, pp. 323-9). Mining activity at Teoxomulco and resulting immigration may have been responsible for an increase at Cenzontepec from 200 tributaries in 1570 to 533 in 1597; there were perhaps 1,000 tributaries at that time in the jurisdiction (Cook and Borah, 1968, p. 72). After this there was a decline and gradual recovery. In 1745 there were 759 Indian families representing perhaps 900 tributaries, a third of them at Teozacualco and the rest in the south (the mines were no longer being worked in that year). The number of Spaniards and mulattoes was relatively insignificant except during periods of mining activity, although there were a few cattle ranches.

The *Suma* of *c.* 1548 gives Náhuatl names of twenty-three estancias subject to S Pedro Teozacualco (1950: pueblo). By 1580 their number had been reduced to fourteen, the most distant being 16 leagues southwest of the cabecera. Nearby Elotepec (cf. Nochistlan), one of the Peñoles villages, appears on the 1580 map as a former estancia of Teozacualco. In 1575-6 the encomendero of Cenzontepec was attempting to annex an almost deserted estancia of Teozacualco called Quiausosola.[5] A further reduction in settlements took place *c.* 1600.[6] Six of the old sujetos either survived this congregation or were re-occupied at a later date, and were pueblos in the eighteenth century: S Francisco Caguacuaha, S Miguel de las Piedras (Cunama, Ñuyuhu), S Mateo Sandihui (Indigüi), S Felipe Zapotitlan (Nundaya, Ñuundela), Sta María Yutanduchi (Yutacagua), and Sto Tomás (S Sebastián) Yutanino.

Santiago Amoltepec (1950: pueblo) was almost de-populated by 1555 (L de T, p. 39). In 1580

it had only 50 tributaries, all living at the cabecera.

The Indians of Santiago Istayutla (Iztlayutla, etc.; 1950: Santiago Ixtayutla, pueblo) were distributed in 1548 between the cabecera and five estancias, the latter disappearing soon afterwards.

Cenzontepec (Zesontepeque, etc.; 1950: Sta Cruz Zenzontepec, pueblo) had a very large area in 1548, 11 by 13 leagues, containing eleven small estancias. These were probably congregated at the cabecera *c.* 1600 or earlier, with the exception of Teoxomulco, which became a mining camp perhaps late in the sixteenth century.[7] S Jacinto, S Lorenzo, and Santiaguito were eighteenth-century pueblos in this area. Another pueblo within the jurisdiction but south of the Río Verde, Sta María Tlapanaquiahui, may have been an old estancia of Cenzontepec.

Sources

The cabeceras (excepting Amoltepec) as they were *c.* 1548 are described in the *Suma de visitas*. There is summary treatment of the area in a report of 1571 (García Pimentel, 1904, pp. 64, 85-6). A brief but important relación geográfica submitted by the C in 1580 covers the two cabeceras of Teozacualco and Amoltepec;[8] of special interest are two accompanying maps, one of which (that of Teozacualco) contains genealogical data which provided the key to Alfonso Caso's reconstruction of Mixtec dynastic history (Caso, 1949).

Berlín (1947, pp. 74-6) reproduces an interesting document of 1699 concerning the southern half of this jurisdiction.

In 1745 the AM sent in a brief report,[9] extracted by Villaseñor y Sánchez (II, pp. 173-4). For the year 1777, there is a valuable description of the parish of Teozacualco,[10] as well as a padrón from the curate of Teoxomulco.[11] Reports made in connection with the visit of a bishop in 1803-4 describe the doctrinas of Cuanana and Teozacualco.[12] Finally, there is the statistical summary of *c.* 1821.[13]

Dahlgren (1954) and Spores (1965) provide useful summaries of much sixteenth-century material.

91 *Tepeaca*

This large and important jurisdiction, now in central Puebla, straddles the volcanic divide running from the isolated peak of Matlacuéyatl (Malinche) to snow-capped Citlaltépetl (Pico de Orizaba). The land to the south drains into the Atoyac (Pacific) system except for a small portion which runs into the valley of Tehuacán (Atlantic drainage), while on the north are the barren Llanos de San Juan, a basin with no outlet. Most of the area is at 2,000–2,500 m (extremes of 1,900–5,700 m), and the climate is generally very dry and cold.

The dominant state here was Tepeyacac, its government shared between three related tlatoque. This was a mountain-top fortress and a center of tribute collection for the Triple Alliance in an area stretching from Popocatépetl to Citlaltépetl. Acatzinco seems to have had a governor subordinate to the rulers of Tepeyacac, perhaps a calpixqui, while Quechulac and Tecamachalco together were ruled by a single tlatoani, also dominated by (or related to) those of Tepeyacac. To the north was a frontier with hostile Tlaxcallan. Nopallocan appears to have been an enclave between the two powers, although its ruler may have been an ally of Tlaxcallan.

People speaking three languages lived here in interspersed settlements. Náhuatl was perhaps dominant at Tepeyacac, Popolocan to the east and south, and Otomí in the north. There was a dense rural population outside the principal political and religious centers.

While it had been visited previously by Spaniards, the area was reduced by them in a campaign which lasted several months in the summer of 1520. In July of that year, Cortés established his headquarters at Tepeyacac, which he called Villa Segura de la Frontera (Cervantes de Salazar, p. 547. Cortés, pp. 103–6).

Encomiendas

Cortés assigned Tepeaca to Pedro Almíndez Chirinos. In 1526 the acting governor Alonso de Estrada took the encomienda for himself, but later in the same year Almíndez regained possession, and held it until the grant escheated under the New Laws in 1544.[1]

Quechula, detached from Tecamachalco at an early date, was given to two brothers, the conquistadors Fernando and Pedro de Villanueva. Fernando's share, on his death, was re-assigned to Gonzalo Rodríguez de la Magdalena. Both encomenderos died in the 1560s and were succeeded by their sons, Diego de Villanueva and Alonso Coronado (Rodríguez). By 1580 the Villanueva half had been inherited by Nicolás de Villanueva, grandson of the first holder, and towards 1600 Gonzalo Coronado succeeded to the Rodríguez share. Both halves escheated between 1633 and 1664 (Dorantes de Carranza, p. 197. Icaza, I, p. 137).

Cortés assigned Tecamachalco to his secretary, Alonso Valiente, in later years a resident of Puebla (Nobiliario..., p. 124). In the 1550s tributes were shared between Valiente and Diego de Ocampo and his heir Ramiro de Arellano. Valiente was followed soon after 1560 by his widow, Melchora Pellicel Aberrucia, who very shortly married a nephew of the viceroy, Rodrigo de Vivero. The latter, still alive in 1597, was followed by a son, Rodrigo de Vivero y Aberrucia, who in 1627 became Conde del Valle de Orizaba. Tributes may have escheated towards the end of the seventeenth century (Icaza, I, p. 191. Scholes and Adams, 1961, p. 230).

We have no information about the encomenderos of Nopaluca. It seems to have been crown property in 1537, but may have been re-assigned in private encomienda as it does not appear in lists of crown pueblos in 1545–50. It was again a crown village in 1552 and later (ENE, VIII, p. 151).

Government

Tepeaca had a C from 1544, and eleven years later this magistrate was re-designated AM and was given charge of nearby encomiendas (Quechula, Tecali, Tecamachalco), with suffragan jurisdiction in the corregimientos of Guatlatlauca, Nopaluca, and Tepexi de la Seda.[2] Towards 1600 Nopaluca was annexed to Tepeaca.[3]

Shortly before 1664 Santiago Tecali was made

cisco Tepeaca in 1530 (Historia Tolteca–Chichimeca, par. 429). A decade later, Franciscan doctrinas were founded at Magdalena Quechula and Asunción Tecamachalco, while that of S Juan Evangelista Acacingo dates from *c.* 1558. By 1570 certain former Franciscan visitas had become

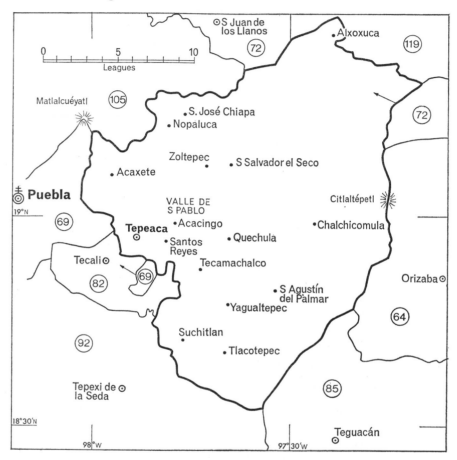

a separate alcaldía mayor. A cedula of 1706, which took effect in 1709–10, gave the Dukes of Atlixco the right to name AMs at Tepeaca (Títulos de Indias, p. 217). After 1787 the jurisdiction was, in effect, part of the intendencia of Puebla. Deputy magistrates lived at Acacingo, Acaxete, Chalchicomula, Nopaluca, Quechula, S Agustín del Palmar, S Salvador el Seco, Tecamachalco, and Tlacotepec.

Church

Franciscans began working here in the late 1520s and established the monastery-parish of S Fran-

secular parishes: Santiago Nopaluca, S Salvador el Seco (Cuauyagualulco), and Sta Cruz Tlacotepec. S Andrés Chalchicomula acquired a secular priest when it was congregated *c.* 1600.

In 1640 the Franciscan doctrines were secularized (the cloisters remained occupied by regulars). In the eighteenth century, additional parishes were founded at Asunción Acaxete and S Agustín del Palmar (by 1743), and at S José Chiapa, Stos Reyes, Todos Santos Suchitlan, S Simón Yagualtepec, and S Hipólito Zoltepec (all by 1777). S Gerónimo Alxoxuca was perhaps a later foundation. The region was in the diocese of Tlaxcala.

Population and settlements

Sixteenth-century estimates give a contact population here of *c.* 100,000 tributary families (ENE, XVI, p. 9. Herrera, 1a década, p. 360). The number dropped to 25,300 in 1570, 11,500 in 1600, and 4,138 in 1626 (ENE, VIII, p. 155. L de T, pp. 371, 399). Subsequent figures show 5,045 tributaries in 1651, 7,189 in 1696, and 5,133 Indian families in 1743 (the last census was probably incomplete). In 1800 there were 11,432 Indian tributaries.[4]

Spaniards and others moved in here at an early date, although the Villa Segura de la Frontera at Tepeaca had an ephemeral (late 1520 to 1522) existence (Gardiner, 1961, p. 56). By 1580 there were perhaps 200 Spanish vecinos, most of them operating wheat farms in the fertile S Pablo valley between Acacingo and Quechula. The 1743 count shows 820 families of Spaniards, 581 of mestizos, and 154 of mulattoes, not including a large number of Negro slaves. The 1791 padrón has 8,691 Spaniards (individuals), 13,199 mestizos, and 1,245 mulattoes in the jurisdiction.

Tepeaca (Tepeyacac; 1950: Tepeaca, ciudad) was originally on a hill some distance west of its present site; in later years the old site was occupied by a barrio called Tlaytec.[5] The Franciscans effected the move to the flat country below, in 1543 (ENE, VII, p. 109). In the following two decades a great many outlying settlements were abandoned, Acacingo was congregated, and Tepeaca itself became a ciudad in 1559; three estancias were transferred to Nopaluca in 1563 (L de T, p. 399). There were still seventy-three subject estancias in 1580 (their Christian names only are given in the relación). Another congregation effort towards 1600 reduced their number considerably, many village sites being absorbed by haciendas.[6] In succeeding years other settlements were deserted and old sites were re-occupied. Some twenty-seven places survived as pueblos subject to Tepeaca in the eighteenth century, although several acquired cabecera status: S Juan Acacingo (Acatzinco), Asunción Acaxete, Acatlan, Acozaque, Actipan, Coatepec (Tepalcatepec), Chisco el Chico, Chisco

el Grande, Huiscolotla, S Bartolomé and Sta María Asunción Nenetzintla, Ocopetlayuca (Tlacomilco, Tetopizco), Ocotitlan (Hueyotlipan), Ostoticpac (Atlaquiyucan?), S José de los Carpinteros, Sta Catarina, Sta Margarita, Sta María Candelaria, Stos Reyes, Tepetlachco (Tepetlacingo), Tepulco, Tetela, Tlachco (Tzompantitlan), Xaltelolco, Zacaula, Zoltepec, and Zoyapetlayucan.

Nopaluca (Napalucan; Santiago; 1950: Nopalucan de la Granja, pueblo) seems to have had a reduced territory, most of it in the bogs of S Juan. Of the three estancias acquired from Tepeaca (*supra*), only two are mentioned in 1570, S Pedro and Sta Cruz, each two leagues from the cabecera. In the late eighteenth century, S Pedro had disappeared, Sta Cruz had become an hacienda, and S José Chiapa was a *santuario* or parish church surrounded by haciendas. Near Nopaluca was Sta María Ixtayucan, a pueblo in 1792.

Quechula (Cachulac, Quecholan, etc.; 1950: Quecholac, *villa*) and Tecamachalco (1950: ciudad) at contact are said to have formed a single state under one ruler, although they appear separately in Aztec conquest and tribute lists, and the Spaniards treated them as separate encomiendas (Quechula, in turn, was split between two encomenderos). Thus each place was recognized as a cabecera with dependent settlements, but many of these sujetos were shared between Quechula and Tecamachalco, with the tributaries living in separate barrios. S Salvador el Seco (Cuauyagualulco) and S Andrés Chalchicomula (1950: Ciudad Serdán), with numerous barrios and estancias, were jointly held in this way, while other places belonged exclusively to either Quechula or Tecamachalco (e.g., Alxoxuca was subject to Quechula, Tlacotepec to Tecamachalco). Here, as at Tepeaca, the Franciscans combined many estancias in the 1540s, and the cabecera of Tecamachalco was moved from a hilltop to its final site a league away. In the 1580 relación, twenty-nine places are listed under Tecamachalco, and thirty-four under Quechula. There was a general consolidation towards 1600, and subsequently sites were re-occupied and changed about. The following places, originally subject to one or the other or to both cabeceras, were pueblos in the eighteenth century: Acicintla, Alcececa, Alxoxuca, Cacaloapan, Cuachnopalan, S Salvador el Seco (Cuauyahualulco), Chalchicomula, Sta María la Alta (Huexoapa?), Ixtapa, S Agustín del Palmar, S Marcos, S Pablo, S Simón, Sta Ursula, Todos Santos Suchitlan, Techachalco, S Luis Temalacayucan (Tlacotepec) de los Chochos, Tenango, S Gabriel Tesayucan (Ixtepec), Tlacomulco, Sta Cruz Tlacotepec, Tlaixpa, Xaltepec, Yahualtepec (Igualtepec), S Miguel Zozutla (el Viborero).

In 1792 there were 202 haciendas (mostly cattle and wheat), and sixty-one ranchos in the jurisdiction.

Sources

Articles in the *Suma* of *c.* 1548 give Náhuatl toponyms and other information not found in later reports (PNE, I, nos. 118, 519, 532). There is an interesting document on the Indian government of Tepeaca in 1552.[7] The secular parishes are relatively well described in the Ovando (*c.* 1570) series (PNE, V, pp. 234, 246, 261–2), while the Franciscan

reports are much less useful (Códice Franciscano, pp. 25–6). There is a well executed *relación geográfica* of 1580 (PNE, V, pp. 12–45). Father Ponce (I, pp. 140–6, 260–1, 507) visited the monasteries here in 1585–6.

Two bishops, Mota y Escobar (1609–17)[8] and Palafox (1643–6),[9] left valuable journals of their visits. Seventeenth-century tributary counts are found in several places.[10] There are brief reports on the former Franciscan doctrinas *c.* 1697 (Vetancurt, 4a parte, pp. 60, 65, 71, 74).

We have an excellent description of the jurisdiction drawn up by the AM in 1743,[11] and the account by Ajofrín (I, p. 42; II, pp. 20–1, 41, 137–9) of his several visits there in 1763–6. Census lists have been found from all parishes except S Salvador el Seco, dated 1777,[12] as well as a topographic description of Acacingo in the same year.[13] The 1791 padrón of non-Indians contains a brief description and list of toponyms,[14] the latter supplemented by a more complete list dated 1792.[15]

92 *Tepexi de la Seda*

Tepexi is in the center of a severely eroded, hilly region in southern Puebla state, 1,200–2,000 m above sea level, draining into the Atoyac river. Vegetation is sparse, and there is little surface water except in canyon bottoms.

Most of this area was occupied by a Popolocan-speaking people with their political center at Tepexic (Tja'nja', in Popolocan). North of the Atoyac were two states, Cuatlatlauhcan and Huehuetlan, predominantly Náhuatl in speech; however, there were minorities of Otomies at Cuatlatlauhcan and Mixtecans at Huehuetlan, and perhaps there were Náhuatl and Mixtecan settlements subject to Tepexic.

In 1502, when the ruler of Tepexic attacked that of Cuatlatlauhcan, the latter appealed to his allies the Mexica who in turn 'destroyed' the warriors of Tepexic. Presumably from that date the entire area paid tribute to the empire center of Tepeyacac.

The area was reduced by the Spaniards in the summer of 1520.

Encomiendas

The first holder of Tepexi was perhaps Pedro de Carranza, Cortés's mayordomo (Icaza, I, p. 142). The encomienda was vacant in 1537 when it was given to Martín Cortés, a poblador, in a special contract whereby he was to receive full tribute during five years, and half during the next fifteen, after which all would go to the crown. This was to assist Cortés in the development of a silkworm culture at Tepexi and elsewhere, the European mulberry having been imported. By 1550 Cortés was dead, and his widow, Teresa Jiménez de Arreola, was collecting part of the tributes, although her right to do so was disputed by the crown, which won the suit soon after (Icaza, I, p. 224. L de T, pp. 410–11).

Guatlatlauca was divided between two encomenderos, one share escheating by 1534. The other half was perhaps held by Bernardino de Santa Clara, escheating on his death in 1537 (Icaza, I, p. 143. Millares Carlo and Mantecón, II, no. 2440).

The conquistador Cristóbal de Soto held Huehuetlan until his death in the 1540s. He was

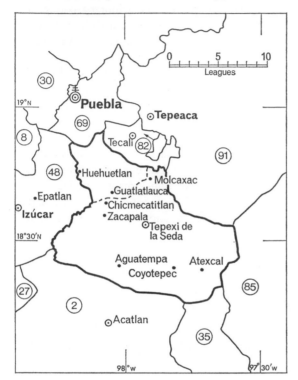

followed by a son, Luis, and then in 1553 by a daughter, María de Soto, married to Juan de Carvajal, who appears as encomendero in 1553–64; María de Soto was sole encomendera in 1568–97. Huehuetlan escheated, in part, between 1665 and 1696.

Government

The crown half of Guatlatlauca was included in the corregimiento of Epatlan (cf. Izúcar) in 1534, and had its own C by 1536. Tepexi is listed as a crown village in 1550, and may have had a C for the king's half from 1542. Each continued as a separate jurisdiction, suffragan to Tepeaca in the 1560s and 70s, re-designated AMs towards 1665. Guatlatlauca included the encomienda of Huehuetlan. Sometime between 1743 and 1770 Guatlatlauca and

Huehuetlan were annexed to the alcaldía mayor of Tepexi de la Seda, which from 1787 was a subdelegación in the intendencia of Puebla.

Church

We are told that the Dominicans entered the Tepexi region towards 1534, but it was the Franciscans who founded a small monastery at Tepexi towards 1550; it was transferred to the Dominicans in 1567–8, after which the patron was Sto Domingo (Cook de Leonard, 1961, p. 95. ENE, IX, p. 45. Vetancurt, 4a parte, p. 29). There may have been another Franciscan mission at Los Reyes Guatlatlauca, which became an Augustinian doctrina in 1567. By 1569 the Dominicans had a parish at Sto Domingo Huehuetlan.

These were apparently among the few doctrinas in the diocese of Tlaxcala which were not secularized in 1640–1. According to Villaseñor, all three were administered by Dominicans in 1743, but Guatlatlauca at least had been secularized by 1777. Sometime after 1646 secular parishes were established in Sta Inés Aguatempa, S Martín Atexcal, S Vicente Coyotepec, Sta María Chicmecatitlan, Asunción (Sta María) Molcaxac, and S Juan Zacapala, all erstwhile visitas of Tepexi.

Population and settlements

Towards 1570 there were perhaps 3,800 tributaries in the area (2,500 at Tepexi, 800 at Guatlatlauca, and 500 at Huehuetlan). Subsequent counts and estimates give 2,400 tributaries in 1600, 1,118 in 1626, 1,932 in 1696, 2,440 Indian families in 1743, and 5,146 native tributaries in 1804.[1] The non-Indian population was small. Villaseñor has 130+ families in 1743, most living on haciendas. At Guatlatlauca in 1777 there were 842 families of Indians, 28 of Spaniards, 75 of mestizos, and four of mulattoes.

We have no list of sixteenth-century dependent settlements at Tepexi (Tepexe de la Seda, Tepexic; 1950: Tepexi de Rodríguez, *villa*).[2] The cabecera may have been moved at an early date.[3] A congregation proposed here in 1598 had been carried out five years later, but we have no details.[4] Twenty-nine places, in addition to the cabecera, survived in 1792 as Indian pueblos; several had shed sujeto status and had their own gobiernos. They were Aguanapa, Aguatempan, Atexcal, Coayuca, Coyotepec, Cuautempan, Chapultepec, Chicmecatitlan, Huitziltepec, S Juan Ixtacuistla (Ichcaquiztlan), Magdalena, S Andrés (Mimiaguapan?), Mimiapan, Molcaxac, Nopala, Sto Tomás (Otlaltepec?), S Felipe Quitlaxcoltepec, S José de Gracia, S Lucas, S Nicolás, S Pablo (Ameyaltepec?), S Luis (Tehuizotla?), Teneyuca, Sta Catalina (Tlaltempan?), Tonahuistla (Tehuixtla), Sta María del Rosario (Xochiteopan?), Todos Santos Xuchitepec, Zacapala(n), and Zoyamayalco.

Los Reyes Guatlatlauca (Quauhtlatlauca, Coatlatlaucan, etc.; 1950: Huatlatlauca, pueblo) had one estancia and five barrios in 1548. The saints' names of four sujetos, up to two leagues from the cabecera, are given in the 1579 relación. Three places survived as pueblos in 1792, besides the cabecera: Sto Tomás (=Cocuacán?), S Miguel Cuausautla, and Sta María Cuausautla.

According to the *Suma*, Huehuetlan (Ahuehuetlan, Gueguetlan; 1950: Sto Domingo Huehuetlán, *villa*) in 1548 had seven barrios and fifteen unnamed estancias. The 1579 relación gives the Christian names of seventeen estancias within $2\frac{1}{2}$ leagues of the cabecera which are roughly located on the accompanying map. In the same year there was a proposal to congregate these estancias.[5] In 1792 Huehuetlan had seven subject pueblos: S Agustín Ahuehuetlan, Atzompa, Cuatetelco, Osolotepec, Tlachichilco, Tlatlauquitepec, and Yanhuitlalpan.

Sources

There is an interesting pictorial document showing pre-Columbian tribute items at Tepexi, published by Cook de Leonard (1961). Records of the Cortés silk contract at Tepexi in 1537 have also been found (CDI, XII, p. 197). Guatlatlauca and Huehuetlan as they were *c.* 1548 are described in the *Suma de visitas* (PNE, I, nos. 259, 261). In the Ovando series, there is a brief report from the Augustinian prior of Guatlatlauca,[6] as well as the Diocesan report covering all three parishes (García Pimentel, 1904, pp. 17–18, 21), both dated *c.* 1570. Sixteenth-century relaciones geográficas were made for both Tepexi and Guatlatlauca, but only the latter (with a map of Huehuetlan and its estancias) has been found (1579).[7]

The bishop of Tlaxcala visited Tepexi twice, in 1613 and 1623, and left a valuable account.[8] Population data for 1623–96 are derived from two sources.[9]

Another missing relación of *c.* 1743 is summarized in Villaseñor y Sánchez (I, pp. 323–5, 342–3). Ajofrín (II, pp. 136–7) traveled through a corner of the jurisdiction in 1766. There are censuses of Guatlatlauca and Zacapala parishes in 1777.[10] The only complete list of placenames we have seen is that of 1792.[11]

Borah (1943) concentrates on the colonial silk industry. Carmen Cook de Leonard (1952–3) describes the area from personal observation.

93 *Teposcolula*

Most of the Ñuñuma, or Mixteca Alta, falls within this large and complex jurisdiction in northwestern Oaxaca state. The climate is generally dry and cool, with most of the settlements at 1,800–2,500 m, although extremes range from 800 to 3,400 m. The higher mountains are forested, while elsewhere there is severe erosion and scant vegetation. Drainage is northwest to the Balsas system, southward to the Río Verde, and northeast into the Papaloapan.

The three largest native states here were Coaixtlahuacan (Mixtec, Yodocoo; Popolocan, Yuguinche), Tlachquiauhco (Mixtec, Naísinu), and Yancuitlan (Mixtec, Yodzocahi). In the first, Chocho (Popolocan) was the language spoken. Mixtecan kings ruled a predominantly Mixtec-speaking population in the other two, although Tlachquiauhco had a Trique minority at Chicahuaztla, and the borders of Yancuitlan extended into the Cuicatec country at Almoloyan. There was a bewildering number of smaller Mixtec communities, most or all of them politically auto-

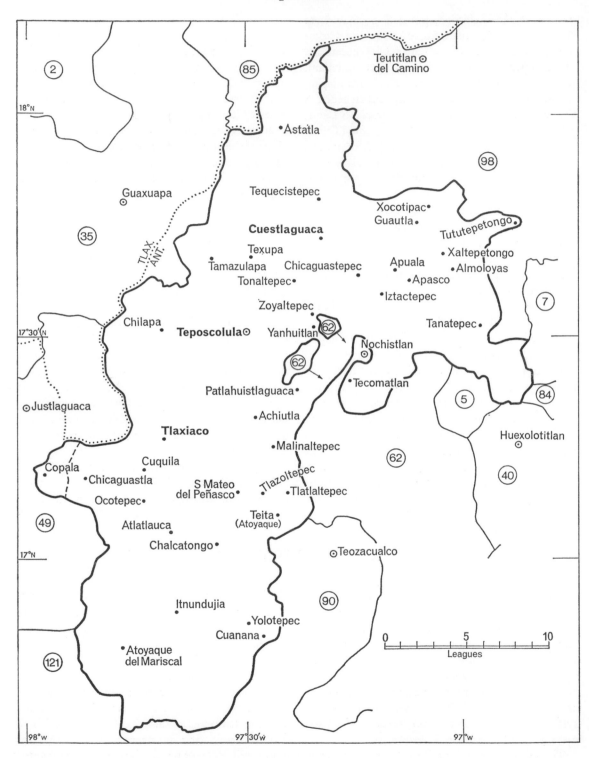

② 85 Teutitlan ⊙
del Camino

18°N

98

•Astatla

•Tequecistepec

Guaxuapa
⊙ Xocotipac•
Guautla •

Cuestlaguaca Tututepetongo•

35 •Texupa •Xaltepetongo

Tamazulapa• Chicaguastepec• Apuala• •Almoloyas
Tonaltepec• •Apasco

Zoyaltepec •Iztactepec

Chilapa• 62 Tanatepec•

Teposcolula⊙ 7
Yanhuitlan 62

17°30'N Nochistlan
⊙
62 •Tecomatlan

Patlahuistlaguaca• 5

⊙Justlaguaca
Huexolotitlan
•Achiutla ⊙
84

Tlaxiaco •Malinaltepec 62

Cuquila• 40
•Chicaguastla Tlazoltepec
Copala• S Mateo• •Tlatlaltepec
Ocotepec• del Peñasco

49 Teita•
Atlatlauca• (Atoyaque)

17°N Chalcatongo• ⊙Teozacualco

Itnundujia• 90

•Yolotepec
Cuanana•
0 5 10
121 •Atoyaque
del Mariscal Leagues

98°w 97°30'w 97°w

nomous. These were Achiotlan (Mixtec, Ñundico, an important religious center), Apouallan (Yutatnuhu), Atlatlahucan (Nuucuaha), Atoyaque (Yutacanu), Atoyaque (another, Ayuta or Teita), Cuicuila (Nuucuiñc), Chalcatonco (Ñundeya), Chicahuastépec or Iztactépec (Yucucuisi), Huautla (Yucundeq), Malinaltépec (Yucuañe), Ocotépec (Yucuite), Patlahuixtlahuacan (Yodzocono), Tepozcolotlan (Yucundaá), Texupa (Ñundaá, Mixtec with a Popolocan minority), Tlatlaltépec (Yucuquesi), Tlazoltépec (Yucucuy), Xaltepetonco (Papalotlayahua; Itunnuti), Yolotépec (Inicuan), and Zoyatépec (Añuu)–Tonaltépec (Yucunchi). We are not sure that all of the states just listed were independently ruled, and there may have been others that were. Tequixistépec, Xocotlícpac, and perhaps Tamazollapan seem to have been subordinate to Coaixtlahuacan. There were two small Cuicatec states to the east, Tanatépec (whose lord 'lived at Tilantonco') and Tototepetonco (Yada in Cuicatec), the latter ruled by a military governor.

Probably all this area had been conquered by the Aztecs, who had garrisons and tribute-collecting centers at Coaixtlahuacan and Tlachquiauhco. Somewhere to the south was a military frontier between the Mexica and Tototépec.

Gonzalo de Umbría and his party traversed this region early in 1520, and envoys from Coaixtlahuacan surrendered to Cortés in September of that year (Cortés, p. 111). Orozco's army went through in 1521, and Alvarado's in 1522, but there was some resistance before Spanish control was established in the 1520s (Vázquez de Tapia, p. 52).

Encomiendas

Nine cabeceras in this jurisdiction (Achiutla, Atlatlauca, Atoyac–Yutacanu, Cuicuila, Chalcatongo, Mitla, Ocotepec, Tlatlaltepec, and Yucucuy–Tlazoltepec) were granted by Cortés to the conquistador Francisco Maldonado. Maldonado's widow, Isabel de Rojas, in 1548 married Tristán de Luna y Arellano who succeeded in the multiple encomienda, followed in 1573 by a son, Carlos; the latter was still alive in 1597.[1]

Apuala and Xocoticpac were given to Gonzalo de Robles, succeeded on his death in the 1540s by a son, García de Robles. In 1597 the encomienda was shared between García (Apuala) and Juan de Robles (Xocoticpac).

Atoyaquillo was held by a Greek conquistador, Juan Gricgo, succcccdcd shortly aftcr 1560 by a son, perhaps the Pedro Sánchez who appears as encomendero in 1597.

Cuestlaguaca escheated by 1534, but three years later it had been re-assigned to Francisco de Verdugo and Pedro Díaz de Sotomayor, both of whom died in the 1540s (BAGN, x, p. 229). Verdugo's half went to his daughter, Francisca, and her husband, Alonso de Bazán, followed in turn by their son, Andrés de Bazán, *c.* 1564. On the latter's death a few years later the Bazán half was briefly held by Luis de Velasco; then it escheated (1569–70), and by 1571 it had been recovered by Antonio Velázquez de Bazán, who still held it in 1597. This share remained in the Bazán family well into the seventeenth century. The other half was inherited in 1544 by a son of the first holder, Gaspar de Sotomayor, who seems to have died *c.* 1579 when his share escheated.[2]

Chicaguastepec and Iztactepec were assigned to Alonso de Morcillo, followed shortly before 1553 by his widow, Catalina García (L de T, pp. 592–3). Escheatment occurred *c.* 1568.

Guautla, Tanatepec, and Tututepetongo were all held by Juan Ochoa de Lexalde, succeeded towards 1555 by a son of the same name. When the latter died *c.* 1563 the encomienda escheated.[3]

Hernán Martín held Malinaltepec until his death (before 1543), soon after which his widow married Bartolomé Tofiño, listed as encomendero in 1548–64. By 1568 Tofiño was dead, and the widow was replaced by D. Luis de Velasco as encomendero in the 1570s.[4] Velasco's heirs continued to receive the tributes in the seventeenth century.

Patlahuistlaguaca, assigned to Melchor de Alavés, was inherited between 1564 and 1571 by a son, Francisco de Alavés Avendaño. Tributes were still privately held in 1623 (Icaza, I, p. 54. Scholes and Adams, 1959, p. 34).

Tamazulapa was acquired by a poblador, Juan Suárez (Xuarez), succeeded in the late 1550s by a son, Luis Suárez de Peralta; the latter still appears as holder in 1597.

Teposcolula in 1527 was held by Gonzalo de Alvarado, and two years later by Juan Peláez de Berrio, AM of Antequera. The second audiencia exiled Peláez and seized Teposcolula for the crown in March, 1531 (Gay, I, p. 446. L de T, p. 354. Millares Carlo and Mantecón, I, no. 721).

A conquistador, Melchor de San Miguel, was encomendero of Tequecistepec until his death in the early 1560s. His widow, María de Godoy, was holder in 1567–76, but escheatment occurred by 1597.[5]

We do not know who was encomendero of Texupa, a crown property by 1534.

Tlaxiaco and its dependencies were first assigned by Cortés to Juan Núñez Sedeño, but by 1528 Martín Vázquez was encomendero. Vázquez died in the late 1540s, and his mestizo son, Francisco Vázquez Lainez, was followed in the 1550s by a third generation holder, Matías Vázquez Lainez. Escheatment occurred on the latter's death towards 1600 (Gibson, 1964, p. 433. Icaza, I, no. 29).

A conquistador and vecino of Antequera named Astorga was holder of Tonaltepec and Zoyaltepec until 1540, when he died and the grant escheated (Díaz del Castillo, II, p. 349. L de T, p. 526).

Xaltepetongo and other places in adjoining jurisdictions were held by Gerónimo de Salinas, followed soon after 1560 by a son, Agustín. Tributes escheated between 1597 and 1623.

According to Burgoa (1934a, I, p. 290), the first encomendero of Yanhuitlan died without heirs. Tributes went to the crown in 1534–6, but soon afterward they were re-assigned to Francisco de las Casas, a cousin of Cortés, followed in 1546 by a son, Gonzalo. Another Francisco de las Casas succeeded in 1591 and was still encomendero in 1622 (Jiménez Moreno and Mateos Higuera, pp. 13–15).

Yolotepec and Ixcatlan were held by a poblador, Alonso de Castellanos, succeeded in the early 1560s by a son of the same name who was alive in 1597.

Government

Cs were appointed first to the crown villages of Teposcolula (from 20 March 1531), Cuestlaguaca, Texupa, and Yanhuitlan (all appear in the 1534 list). Cuestlaguaca and Yanhuitlan soon reverted to private encomienda, while Tonaltepec y Zoyaltepec became a corregimiento on 13 September 1540.

In 1552 the C of Teposcolula was elevated to the rank of AM in charge of a large province which included the crown and private encomiendas of Amoltepec, Atoyaquillo, Cenzontepec, Malinaltepec, Mitlantongo, Mistepec, Patlahuistlaguaca, Tamazola, Tamazulapa, Teozacualco, Teposcolula, Texupa, Tezuatlan, Tilantongo, Tlaxiaco, Tuctla, Yolotepec, and all the villages (Achiutla, etc.) belonging to Tristán de Luna y Arellano.[6] Other nearby places, among them Cuestlaguaca, Chicaguastepec, Iztactepec, Guautla, Tequecistepec, Xaltepetongo, Xocoticpac, and Yanhuitlan, were at the same time assigned to the jurisdiction of the C of Tonaltepec y Zoyaltepec, who soon became known as AM of Yanhuitlan.[7] From *c.* 1563 Guautla was a corregimiento suffragan to Yanhuitlan, and after 1566 Tilantongo (with Mitlantongo and Tamazola) had its own C suffragan to the AM of Teposcolula, as were the Cs of Justlaguaca and Texupa. When Cuestlaguaca became a corregimiento towards 1579, it was made suffragan to Yanhuitlan.[8] Teozacualco and Amoltepec were placed under the AM of Antequera at this time. Towards 1600, Cuestlaguaca and Guautla were annexed to the jurisdiction of Yanhuitlan, and the other corregimientos became independent, until Texupa was absorbed by Teposcolula sometime between 1640 and 1676.

Thus for over a century the area under consideration was divided politically between the AMs of Teposcolula and Yanhuitlan. In 1688–9 the province of Yanhuitlan was abolished, the northern part (including Yanhuitlan itself) being annexed to Teposcolula, while the Nochistlan-Tilantongo region was made into a new jurisdiction under the AM of Nochistlan (q.v.).[9]

After 1787 Teposcolula was a subdelegación in the intendencia of Oaxaca.

Church

The Dominicans began their work at Sto Domingo Yanhuitlan in 1529, but they soon abandoned the area. Secular curates are recorded at Tlaxiaco in the 1540s, at Yanhuitlan in 1541–6, and at Achiutla in the early 1550s, by which time the Dominicans had returned to found the doctrinas of S Pedro Teposcolula (*c.* 1538), S Juan Cuestlaguaca (1544), Asunción Tlaxiaco (1548), and once again Yanhuitlan (1547). In 1556–7 monastery-parishes were begun at S Miguel Achiutla, Sta María (Natividad) Tamazulapa, and perhaps Magdalena Patlahuist-laguaca ('Petlaostoco' appears in a list of Dominican houses dated 1562, but it was being visited from Tilantongo in 1571).[10] In the same period (by 1571) secular priests settled at Apuala and Nativi-dad Chalcatongo, and Dominicans at Texupa. The parish of Sta María Yolotepec, first Dominican but soon secularized, is said to have been founded in 1576, while a Dominican doctrina at Natividad Almoloyas (until then visited from Yanhuitlan) dates from 1587.[11]

We have no record of further parochial changes until Sta Catalina Cuanana was separated from Chalcatongo in 1699–1700 (Berlín, p. 76). Two visitas of Tlaxiaco became parishes in 1710 (S Mateo del Peñasco, Dominican) and 1713 (S Andrés Chicaguastla, secular). Sta Cruz Itnundujia (secular) was separated from Chalcatongo in 1715. By 1745, Sta María (Presentación) Chilapa and S Miguel Tecomatlan had become Dominican doctrinas, and Almoloyas had been secularized. Peñasco, Tamazulapa, and Texupa were turned over to secular clergy between 1745 and 1766, and Chilapa before 1777. Cuestlaguaca, Teposcolula, Tlaxiaco, and Yanhuitlan continued to be ministered by Dominicans until after Independence, but Achiutla and Tecomatlan were secularized.

All parishes were in the diocese of Antequera. The Dominican doctrinas were in the province of Santiago de México until 1596; after that the provincial boundary bisected the jurisdiction, with Cuestlaguaca, Tamazulapa, Teposcolula, and Texupa remaining in the province of Santiago (= Santos Angeles de Puebla after 1656), and the other parishes attached to S Hipólito de Oaxaca. Parochial boundaries, here as else-where, crossed into adjoining political juris-dictions.

Population and settlements

If we interpret Cook and Borah (1968) correctly, the area under consideration here had seven times as many people in 1520 as it had in 1570, after a half century of decline from disease and lesser causes. In 1570 there were some 26,500 Indian tributaries here. Thirty years later, after further loss in the plagues of 1576–81, 1591–2, and 1599, the number had been reduced to 14,100 tribu-taries.[12] A nadir (perhaps 5,000 tributaries) was reached in mid-seventeenth century, after which there was a slow recovery to 7,570 tributaries (8,160 Indian families) in 1745, and 11,623 in 1797. Non-Indians were largely confined to a few towns (Astatla, Cuestlaguaca, Teposcolula, Texupa, Tlaxiaco, Yanhuitlan). Three hundred families of Spaniards and castas are reported in 1745. The 1797 census shows only 58 free Negro and mulatto tributaries.[13]

The complex pre-Conquest political situation is reflected in the large number of separate cabeceras during the colonial period. Many erstwhile sujetos sought and achieved cabecera status under the Spaniards (there were sixty-four separate Indian gobiernos by 1797); here we will consider the sixteenth-century cabeceras individually.

Achiutla (Achutla, Chiautla; Iñudico, Ñundico; 1950: S Miguel Achiutla, pueblo) in 1548 had four barrios within an area of 3½ by 4 leagues. In the eighteenth century there were three pueblos besides the original cabecera (S Juan Achiutla Nudzeñu, Sto Domingo Huendio, Sta Catarina Tayata Itnuyete), all within 1½ leagues.

Apuala (Apoala; Yutatnuhu; 1950: Santiago Apoala, pueblo) towards 1548 had two subordinate cabeceras (Apazco, Xocoticpac) and ten estancias distributed among them. Both Apasco and Xoco-tipac survived as pueblos in the eighteenth century, as did an estancia of Xocotipac, Texcatitlan. S Pedro Nodón, which may also have been a de-pendency of Xocotipac, is said to have moved from a mountain to its final site *c.* 1700.

Atlatlauca (Quatlatlauca, etc.; Nuucuaha; 1950: S Esteban Atatlahuca, pueblo) may have had some estancias which were congregated in 1603 at the cabecera.

There were two cabeceras in this jurisdiction called Atoyaque in the sixteenth century. Efforts to distinguish them by applying the diminutive Atoyaquillo to one or the other were unsuccessful. The first (Sta María Asunción Atoyaque del Mariscal; Yutacanu; 1950: Asunción Atoyaquillo, ranchería) was part of the Luna y Arellano (Mariscal de Castilla) encomienda, and was far to the south in tierra caliente. The other (S Juan Atoyaque; Ayuta, Teita; more often Atoyaquillo; 1950: S Juan Teita, pueblo), whose early encomendero was Juan Griego, was near Achiutla. We have no record of estancias in either place.

Sta María Cuicuila (later, Cuquila; Nuucuiñe; 1950: Sta María Cupila, ranchería) was another small Luna y Arellano cabecera, without estancias as far as we know. It had an early boundary dispute with Chicaguastla.[14]

Cuestlaguaca (Cuextlauaca, Cueztlahuac, Quistlabaca, Cohixtlahuaca, etc.; Mixtec, Yod[z]ocoo; Popolocan, Yuguinche [Inguiche?]; 1950: S Juan Bautista Coixtlahuaca, *villa*) had a great many dependent settlements within a territory extending six leagues or more northwest of the cabecera. There was probably an early (1550s?) congregation here, and another *c.* 1600. We have no complete list of sixteenth-century estancias, and several of those mentioned in the 1570s and 1580s (Aguatongo, Atitlique, Icpala or Ispala, Malinalcingo, Malinaltepec, Miltongo, Xocotepec) remain unidentified.[15] Other sites were deserted in the seventeenth century (some, no doubt, were reoccupied), leaving thirteen old sujetos which survived as pueblos in 1745–1803. Cook and Borah (1968, p. 12) have pointed out the pattern of sub-cabeceras here, notably S Miguel Astatla (Tepito). The others were Sta Cruz Calpulalpan, Concepción (Tonalá), Santiago de las Plumas Ihuitlan (Popolocan, Nguixinga), Natívitas (Tixaltepec), S Gerónimo Otla, S Antonio (Cuautoco; Popolocan, Nguicutnaá), Sta Catarina (Ocotlan; Mixtecan, Yucundacua), S Cristóbal Suchixtlaguaca (Xochicoixtlahuac), S Francisco Teopan, Sto Domingo Tepenene (Tepetlmeme), S Mateo Tlapiltepec (Tlaltiztépetl), and Magdalena Xicotlan.

Sta María (Natividad) Chalcatongo (Chacaltongo; Ñundeya; 1950: Chalcatongo de Hidalgo, *villa*) in the late sixteenth century had eight estancias, half of them near the cabecera in high country and half in tierra caliente off to the south. In 1603 they were all supposed to be reduced to two sites, the cabecera and Sta Cruz Itnundujia; all but one, however, survived or were resurrected as pueblos in the eighteenth century. Those near the principal cabecera were Santiago Yosondúa (Mizteguaca), S Miguel el Grande (Ñucaño), Sta Catarina Yosonotnu, and S Andrés Tiza (not mentioned after 1603). Around Itnundujia (Itunduxia; Pozoltitlan; 1950: Sta Cruz Itundujia, pueblo) were Los Reyes, Sta Lucía Nutneñu (Monteverde), and S Andrés Doyoñana (Xacala; =Cabecera Nueva?). Off to the southeast were two other places, both pueblos in 1745–1803, which seem to have been detached sujetos of Chalcatongo, Sta Catarina Cuanana (Guanana) and S Mateo Yucutindoó.

Chicaguastepec (Tzicahuastepeque; 1950: S Miguel Chicahua, pueblo) and Iztactepec (Istaltepec, etc.; Yucucuisi, Yucuyachi; 1950: S Juan and Santiago Ixtaltepec) were twin cabeceras with no known estancias.

S Miguel Guautla (1950: S Miguel Huautla Nochixtlán) had already been congregated in 1580 and then had no sujetos.

Two barrios, Azala and Zapotitlan, are listed in 1548 under Malinaltepec (Marinaltepec; Yucuañe; 1950: S Bartolomé Yucuañe, pueblo), but they disappeared, probably towards 1600.[16]

Two neighboring places called Ocotepec (Yucuite; 1950: Sta María Yucuhiti, pueblo. Yutesuya; 1950: Sto Tomás Ocotepec, pueblo) probably both came within the Luna y Arellano encomienda of that name. We know of no estancias.[17]

Perhaps holding a record for variant spellings, Patlahuistlaguaca (Patlahua-ixtlahuacan, Patla-iztlaguacan, Petlahuayxtlauaca, Petlastlahuac, Magdalena Tepetlastlaguacas, etc.; Yodzocono; 1950: Yodocono de Porfirio Díaz, *villa*) had several estancias, some of which were pueblos in the eighteenth century. S Pedro Tototitlan Tidzaá (Tidaá) was one of them, and S Francisco Patlahuistlaguaca (Nusuhañuhu; Chindúa) was another.[18]

The cabecera site of Natividad Tamazulapa

(1950: Tamazulapan del Progreso, *villa*) seems to have been moved at some point (Spores, 1967, p. 38). Of six sujetos in 1548, four (Acutla, Nopala, Teotongo, Tulancingo) survived the congregation of *c.* 1600.[19]

S Juan Bautista Tanatepec (Tonatepec; 1950: S Juan Tonaltepec, rancho) had two sujetos in 1580 which disappeared, probably *c.* 1600.[20]

The old ceremonial site of Teposcolula, and perhaps the chief settlement at contact, is on a hill-top nearby to the southwest of the final cabecera site (cf. Spores, 1967, pp. 40–1). The latter (Tepuzculula, etc.; Yucundaá; 1950: S Pedro y S Pablo Teposcolula, *villa*) had six barrios in 1548, and thirteen estancias in the late sixteenth century. In 1603 it was proposed to congregate them in seven places, but the same names appear as pueblos in the eighteenth century. These were Sta María Dayaco (Nduayaco, Yedoayaco), S Juan Dique (Itnuyaya, Teposcolula), Santiago Inibo (Yolomecal), S Miguel Lucane (Nucani, Tixaa; Alipizagual), S José Nihcho (Nichio, Nuhuchiyo), S Vicente Nonoho (Yucunuhu), S Felipe Numihaha (Ixtapa, Salinas), S Pedro Yucunama (Amoltepec), Sta Catarina Yutacuiñi, Magdalena Duayi (Nduahayihí; Cañadaltepec), Sto Tomás Yodotiñi (Guajolotitlan, Tecolotitlan), Sto Domingo Ticuhu (Ticuú, Itnuquhuu), and S Andrés de la Laguna Yocotno (Yodiotnoho).[21]

Tequecistepec (later, Tequistepeque; Mixtec, Yucuñuni; 1950: S Miguel Tequixtepec) is easily confused with nearby S Pedro Tequecistepec (cf. Guaxuapa). This was a Popolocan community which formed a wedge through the middle of Cuestlaguaca's territory. In 1548 it had two barrios and three estancias, most of which were eliminated in a congregation towards 1600. Only one subject pueblo remained in the eighteenth century, Santiago Tepetlapa (Mixtec, Toyunyada; Popolocan, Catundarja or Gataundarja).[22]

Texupa (Mixtec, Ñundaá or Ñundzaá; 1950: Santiago Tejupan, pueblo) had six barrios whose Náhuatl names are given in the 1548 report. One was perhaps the 'Sta Catarina Texupan' of the Códice Sierra (Léon, 1933). The 1579 relación declares there were no sujetos, but in 1582 eighty Indians from Texupa wanted to move to 'Gue-guetlan' (Ahuehuetlan), and the following year they received permission to do so.[23]

Tlatlaltepec (Yucuquesi, Nocuiñe; 1950: Sta María Tataltepec, pueblo), southeast of Achiutla, had no known estancias.

We have no complete list of estancias belonging to Tlaxiaco (Taxiaco; Naísinu; 1950: Sta María Asunción Tlaxiaco, ciudad). Towards 1548 the population was dispersed in eight subject cabeceras which we can only partly identify, with a total of a hundred estancias, not counting Tlacotepec (which is listed as a separate cabecera of the same encomendero). In 1553 the Indians were ordered to cooperate with the Dominican friars in reducing these settlements in a number of congregations.[24] Another series of congregations was proposed in 1598.[25] Somewhat more than thirty places that were probably once subject to Tlaxiaco survived as pueblos in the eighteenth century, including the cabeceras of Chicaguastla (Mixtec, Itnutno; 1950: S Andrés Chicahuaxtla, ranchería), Presentación Chilapa (1950: Sta María Chilapa de Díaz, *villa*), and S Mateo del Peñasco (Yuunuu; 1950: S Mateo Peñasco, pueblo). S Juan Copala seems to have been disputed between Chicaguastla and Puctla (cf. Justlaguaca).[26]

Tlazoltepec (later, S Pedro el Alto; Yucucuy; 1950: S Pedro el Alto, pueblo) had no estancias that we know of.

Tonaltepec (Yucunchi; 1950: Sto Domingo Tonaltepec, pueblo) and Zoyaltepec (S Bartolomé Soyaltepeque; Añuu; 1950: S Bartolo Soyaltepec, pueblo) were cabeceras in the same encomienda, between Yanhuitlan and Texupa. Zoyaltepec had six barrios in 1548, absorbed in a congregation towards 1600.[27]

Tututepetongo (later, Tutepetongo; Cuicatec, Yada; 1950: S Francisco Tutepetongo, ranchería) had five estancias in 1548, but only one (Copalticpac) is mentioned in 1580, and it no longer existed in the eighteenth century.[28]

Xaltepetongo (Xaltepequetongo; Itunnuti; Papalotlayagua; 1950: S Pedro Jaltepetongo, pueblo) apparently had no sujetos.

Yanhuitlan (Anguitlan, etc.; Yodzocahi or Yodzoquehe in Mixtecan; 1950: Sto Domingo Yanhuitlán, pueblo) had a great many dependent settlements on all sides, particularly to the east and south, but we have no complete sixteenth-century listing. Náhuatl names of sixteen sujetos are given in 1548, while twenty-six places are listed in 1565.[29] Certain places (Coyotepec Yucuñana, Mascaltepec, Suchitepec Yucuita, Iquisuchitlan Chioyu) were trying to acquire separate cabecera status in 1552.[30] Sta María Natividad Almoloyas became a cabecera de doctrina in 1587, as did S Miguel Tecomatlan Nutiaa somewhat later.[31] At least one congregation was proposed here, but there were perhaps thirty-four pueblos in the eighteenth century which had once been sujetos of Yanhuitlan.[32]

Yolotepec (1950: Sto Domingo Yolotepec, pueblo) had what may have been a subordinate cabecera, Sto Domingo Ixcatlan, in the sixteenth century, together with a number of estancias. S Miguel Ixcatlan Ituyucu and Sta Cruz Tacahua (Noditacahua) were perhaps sujetos.

In the eighteenth century, Popolocan or Chocho was spoken at Cuestlaguaca, Tamazulapa, and Tequecistepec, in other words throughout the northern part of the jurisdiction. There was a Popolocan minority at Texupa in 1579 (no longer reported in 1777), but there and elsewhere Mixtecan was the predominant language, with two further exceptions. Both Mixtecan and Trique were spoken at Copala and Chicaguastla, and south and east of Almoloyas the people spoke Cuicatecan.

Sources

Several early pictorial manuscripts from this region have been discovered. The *lienzos* of Coixtlahuaca and Santiago Ihuitlan (Glass, 1964, pp. 169–70. Caso, 1961) contain toponymic details of the Cuestlaguaca region. The Codex of Yanhuitlán has been published with useful commentary by Jiménez Moreno and Mateos Higuera (1940). *Códice Sierra* (MS at Academia de Bellas Artes, Puebla) is concerned with community expenses at Texupa in 1550–64.

Most of the cabeceras here are described in the 1548 *Suma de visitas* (PNE, I, nos. 33, 86, 88, 152, 228, 308, 364, 654–8, 751–2, 754–5). The Ovando report of 1571 is brief (García Pimentel, 1904, pp. 64–8, 74–6, 84–5). Reports of *c.* 1580 from the AMs of Teposcolula and Yanhuitlan reached Spain but have either been lost or destroyed (Gerhard, 1968, p. 621); other documents in this series from the Cs of Guautla (Tlalocan, I, pp. 3–16) and Texupa (PNE, IV, pp. 53–7) are dated 1580 and 1579, respectively. The Texupa relación has an interesting map.

Data on congregations in 1598–1604 include detailed reports from Chalcatongo[33] and Teposcolula,[34] while elsewhere only scattered information is given.[35] Burgoa (1934*a*, I, pp. 285 ff.) has much to say about the history of the Dominican doctrinas and their condition *c.* 1670.

Villaseñor y Sánchez (II, pp. 128–36, 171–3) describes the jurisdiction as it was *c.* 1743, apparently using a source other than the brief report submitted by the AM in 1745.[36] Ajofrín (II, pp. 128–32) went through here in 1766 and left a succinct account. For the year 1777, we have 'topographical' reports from the parishes of Apuala,[37] Cuestlaguaca,[38] Chicaguastla (with a map),[39] Chilapa,[40] and Texupa,[41] as well as padrones from those of Achiutla, Almoloyas, Apuala, Chicaguastla, Chilapa, Itnundujia, and Yolotepec.[42] There is another relación sent in by the priest of Tlaxiaco in 1791.[43] All but three parishes (Apuala, Chalcatongo, Chilapa) are represented in the 1802–3 Bergosa y Jordán *visita* reports.[44] For 1822, we have both a lengthy statistical summary[45] and a testimony gathered in 147 pueblos of the jurisdiction.[46]

There is a good deal of monographic material on the Mixteca Alta in pre-Conquest and colonial times. In addition to the works already cited, we might mention Cook (1949*b*, pp. 2–22), who discusses the relationship of soil erosion to population in the Tamazulapa–Yanhuitlán area, and Dahlgren de Jordán (1954) and Spores (1965, 1967), both of whom attempt to re-construct the situation at contact. A perceptive analysis of population changes in 1520–1960 (Cook and Borah, 1968) could serve as a model for the better sort of regional study, ranging far beyond its immediate theme. A new edition of the Mixtecan dictionary of Fray Alvarado (1962) contains pertinent comments by Jiménez Moreno on the Dominican missions, toponymy, etc. Studies concentrating on the actual ethnography and ecology of this area (Peña, 1950; Marroquín, 1957) should be consulted.

94 *Tetela del Río*

The Balsas (Mexcala) river flows from east to west through this large jurisdiction, now in Guerrero, receiving the waters of the Alahuixtlán and the Cutzamala from the north and the Truchas and Tehuehuetla on the south. These southern affluents rise in the Sierra Madre del Sur, which here reaches

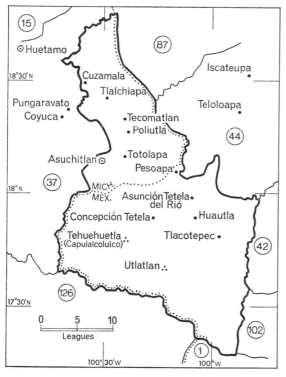

tis highest point at 3,700 m, but most of the area is very hot and dry, at 250–1,000 m.

The Tarascan-Aztec frontier ran through here, Axochitlan (Titichucumo in Cuitlatec) and Cusamala (Apazingani in Tarascan) being tributary to the cazonci, while Calpulalcolulco (Xanimeo), Otlatlan, Tlacotépec, and Tetellan were in the service of Moctezuma. The chief settlements were probably all garrison towns with military governors. The confused linguistic pattern at contact can be conjectured from the 1570 reports. Tarascan was spoken in the garrisons of Axochitlan

and Cusamala, but the first was essentially a Cuitlatec community, while both seem to have had an old residue of Náhuatl-speakers. Cuitlatecan extended up the Balsas along the left bank past Tetellan, where Chontal was spoken on the right bank. The mountain people of Calpulalcolulco were Cuitlatec, while those of Otlatlan and Tlacotépec spoke Tepuztec. Coixca (Nahua) was the language in the easternmost estancias of Tlacotépec.

We do not know when the Spaniards entered here, but we assume that the Mexica-dominated states were visited first, perhaps as early as 1519, by gold prospectors, and the Tarascan area a few years later, probably in 1523–4.

Encomiendas

Of the six native states here, two were taken for the crown at an early date. Asuchitlan was held by Cristóbal Martín de Gamboa in early 1528, and became a corregimiento in July 1533.[1] Capulalcolulco, whose encomendero we do not know, is listed with Tenango (cf. Tasco) as a crown possession as early as 1534.

Cuzamala had two encomenderos in 1528, Diego Rodríguez and Juan de Burgos.[2] By 1533 Burgos was the only holder, and five years later he was replaced by Francisco Vázquez de Coronado (AMM, 6, p. 45. BAGN, VI, p. 364). Vázquez was succeeded in 1554 by a daughter, Isabel de Luján, who married Bernardino Pacheco de Bocanegra. Both were dead by 1597, when Cuzamala appears as a crown possession, but tributes were reassigned privately in the seventeenth century.[3]

The conquistador Juan de Mancilla received title from Cortés to Tetela, and seems to have sold his interests there to Francisco Rodríguez (Odrero) de Guadalcanal in 1538. By 1594 Rodríguez had been replaced by Juan de Silva (a son?). Escheatment occurred between 1643 and 1688.[4]

Tlacotepec was held from the 1520s by Francisco Rodríguez Magariño. By 1548 the encomienda had been inherited by a son, Juan Rodríguez (Enríquez) Magariño, who towards 1565 was followed by his widow, Polonia de la Serna (still alive in 1597). Tlacotepec escheated after 1643.

The encomendero of Utlatlan, Isidro Moreno, was succeeded in the 1550s by a son, Bernardino (Moreno) de Casasola, still alive in 1597. Tributes were still privately assigned in 1643.

Government

Cs were appointed to nearby Teloloapa y Totoltepec in 1531, to Asuchitlan in 1533, and to Capulalcolulco by 1534. The encomenderos in this region were little interfered with until the 1550s, when the various magistrates were ordered to handle Indian complaints and other matters in private encomiendas. Thus in 1551–3 the C of Capulalcolulco went on a commission to Asuchitlan, and in 1554 the C of distant Tiripitio was given jurisdiction in both Asuchitlan and Cuzamala because there was no resident magistrate there.[5] Then or soon afterwards, Tetela, Tlacotepec, and Utlatlan were assigned to the corregimiento of Iscateupa (q.v.). In the 1560s a resident C at Asuchitlan was in charge of neighboring Coyuca, Cuzamala, and Pungaravato; in the provincial division of that decade and later, Asuchitlan was considered suffragan to Michoacan, while Capulalcolulco and Iscateupa appear in the 'province' of Chiautla.[6]

Mines were discovered near Capulalcolulco in 1599, as a result of which the C became AM of Minas de Tetela, with an enlarged jurisdiction including Asuchitlan, Coyuca, and Cuzamala, as well as Tetela, Tlacotepec, and Utlatlan.[7] Pungaravato, and eventually Coyuca, were put under the AM of Guaymeo y Sirándaro. By 1743 the AM of Tetela del Río, as the jurisdiction was now called, had moved his headquarters to Asuchitlan. From 1786 he was a subdelegado under the intendente of Mexico.

Church

In the 1540s and later the Asuchitlan–Cuzamala region was visited by Augustinians from Tiripitio, although a curate lived at Asuchitlan in 1548–50; there was another secular priest at this time assigned to Capulalcolulco, but actually resident at Sta María Asunción Tetela.[8] By 1568 both Asuchitlan (Asunción) and Cuzamala (S Cristóbal) had become secular parishes; Tlacotepec at this time was visited from Cuezala, but later was transferred to the doctrina of Tetela. The Indians of Capulalcolulco complained in 1582 that they had to walk three days to participate in religious fiestas at Tetela and asked to be put in a closer parish (presumably Asuchitlan).[9] However, they remained in the archbishopric, while Asuchitlan and Cuzamala were in the diocese of Michoacán.

Population and settlements

Perhaps two thirds of the Indians who survived in 1550 disappeared between then and 1570, the greatest loss occurring in the mountain villages of Capulalcolulco and Utlatlan which were left almost deserted. Many Indians fled from Utlatlan because of excessive tributes levied by the encomendero (PNE, VI, p. 127). In 1570 there were some 3,800 tributaries (2,100 in Asuchitlan–Cuzamala, 1,375 at Tetela–Tlacotepec, 325 at Capulalcolulco–Utlatlan). 3,130 are reported in 1579–80, and only 525 towards 1650, and 275 tributaries in 1690. By the latter date, Capulalcolulco and Utlatlan no longer appear in the tribute lists. Immigration, perhaps due to the opening of new mines, may account for a total of 1,195 Indian families in 1743. There were 3,110 native tributaries in 1801.[10] Cuitlatecan was still spoken at Asuchitlan, and Tarascan at Cuzamala, in 1743, but elsewhere Náhuatl had become the chief language.

Mining activity brought Spaniards and mulattoes to this area beginning in the late sixteenth century. In 1649 the real de minas of Nuestra Señora de la Concepción (near Asuchitlan) and another center near Tlalchiapa (Cuzamala) were busy producing mercury and silver. A bonanza began shortly before 1743 when rich ores were found at Coronilla, above Tetela; in that year the jurisdiction had 65 families of Spaniards, 110 of mestizos, and 220 of mulattoes. In 1792 there were five mining camps (Alba de Liste, Coronilla or Concepción Tetela, Paguaro, S Vicente, Tepantitlan), twenty-nine haciendas (mostly cattle, some sugar), and 114 ranchos. The 1801 census shows 1,086 free Negro and mulatto tributaries.

Asuchitlan (Axuchitlan, etc.; 1950: Ajuchitlán del Progreso, pueblo) had thirty-one sujetos in 1579, of which only two (Poliutla and Totolapa) survived the congregation of 1594–1604. A barrio, S Cristóbal, was considered a separate pueblo in 1792.

Cuzamala (Cutzamala, Cosamala, etc.; Apatzingan; 1950: Cutzamala de Pinzón, pueblo) had twenty-two sujetos within four leagues of the cabecera in 1570. In 1598–1604 these were reduced to five pueblos, Sacapuato, Tecomatlan, Tlalchiapa, Tupátaro, and Zacango; only Tecomatlan and Tlalchiapa were pueblos (Zacapuato was a barrio) in 1743–92.

Capulalcolulco, which by 1743 had been renamed Tehuehuetla (also called Xanimeo in 1548; 1950: Tehuehuetla, cuadrilla) had seven estancias within twelve leagues in 1570, all of which were probably moved to the cabecera in 1594–1604.

Ten estancias are named at Utlatlan (Utatlan; 1950: Otatlán, cuadrilla) in the 1570 report, but only six in 1579. The entire area including the cabecera may have been abandoned in the 1598–1604 congregation. 'Otlatlan' last appears in a tributary list in 1643, by which time the Indians were probably living at Tetela.

Tetela (1950: Tetela del Río, pueblo) in 1570 had some twenty-four estancias up to nine leagues from the cabecera (the latter had been moved from

a hilltop nearby); four languages (Náhuatl, Cuitlatec, Chontal, Tepuztec) were spoken in them. There was a congregation here in 1595–1604, after which only Huautla and Pesoapa continue to appear as pueblos.

The cabecera of Tlacotepec (1950: pueblo) also had a change of site. There were thirteen sujetos in 1579, all congregated *c.* 1600.

Sources

The area, with the exclusion of Tlacotepec and Utlatlan, is described briefly in the 1548 *Suma de visitas* (PNE, I, nos. 39, 166, 675, 814). Several reports in the Ovando series (*c.* 1570) are extant, two short ones for the Michoacán parishes (García Pimentel, 1904, pp. 46–7. Miranda Godínez, 9/37), and a valuable detailed document for those in the archbishopric.[11] For 1579, we have most interesting relaciones geográficas submitted by the Cs of Asuchitlan[12] and Iscateupa (PNE, VI, pp. 87–152), but none from Capulalcolulco.

Congregation data of 1591–1604 are found in several places.[13] Two reports of the diocese of Michoacán dated 1639[14] and 1649[15] describe that part of the jurisdiction, while tributary information exists for both Mexico (1643–88)[16] and Michoacán (1657–98).[17]

There is a good relación with a complete *matrícula* dated 1743,[18] followed by an excellent description sent in by the subdelegado in 1792.[19]

95 *Tetela del Volcán*

Now in the northeast corner of the state of Morelos, this small, wedge-shaped jurisdiction stretches southward from the peak of Popocatépetl (5,450 m) to a minimum elevation of 1,650 m. It is a cold and misty region most of the year, much of it forested.

Tetellan belonged to the realm of Ocuiltuco (cf. Cuautla Amilpas) until that little kingdom was broken up into four parts; it is not entirely clear whether this occurred shortly before or after the Conquest (cf. Gerhard, 1970, p. 100). Both

Tetellan and Hueyapan (which was probably an autonomous state) were colonies of Náhuatl-speaking Xochimilca and as such were indirect tributaries of the Aztecs. Nepopoalco, although subject to Tetellan, may have had a semi-autonomous status.

The area was traversed by Alvarado and Vázquez de Tapia in September, 1519, and must have submitted to the Spaniards in 1521 (Vázquez de Tapia, p. 36).

Encomienda

Tetela, Hueyapa, and Nepopoalco perhaps from the beginning were made a single encomienda which Cortés gave to the conquistador Pedro Sánchez Farfán. Towards 1536 Sánchez was succeeded by his widow, María de Estrada, who then

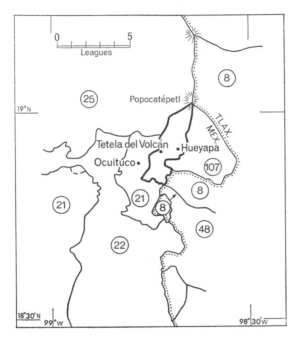

married Alonso Martín Partidor. On the latter's death, 8 August 1558, succession was disputed among various heirs; the suit was taken to the council of the Indies where it was decided that none of the pretenders had a valid case, and the encomienda was taken for the crown towards 1561.[1]

Government

A corregimiento from 1561 at the latest, Tetela was first made suffragan to the province of Chalco, although by 1643 tributes were being sent to Cuautla Amilpas. The post of C or AM (both terms were used in later years) was little coveted as it produced scant revenue, but Tetela del Volcán still appears as a separate jurisdiction as late as 1777. By 1784 it had been annexed to Cuautla Amilpas.

Church

First visited by Augustinians from Ocuituco, Tetela had a secular priest from 1553.[2] Towards 1561 the priest was replaced by Dominicans who founded two monasteries, first at S Juan Bautista Tetela, and c. 1575 at Sto Domingo Hueyapa. Included in the latter parish was a village, Alpanoca, belonging politically to Tochimilco. Tetela was secularized in 1751, and Hueyapa somewhat later. Both parishes were in the archdiocese of Mexico.

Population and settlements

The number of tributaries fell from 2,000 in 1548 to 1,800 in 1557, 1,500 in 1570, 562 in 1588, 327 in 1623, and only 165 in 1643 and 135 in 1688. The 1743 census shows 205 Indian families. In 1801 there were perhaps 260 tributaries.[3] The non-Indian population grew to 15 families in 1743, and perhaps three times that number by the end of the colonial period.

Tetela (1950: Tetela del Volcán, pueblo) in 1531 had seven estancias, not counting Hueyapa (Gueiapan, Ueyapa, etc.; 1950: Hueyapan, pueblo) and Nepopoalco. In 1548 Tetela appears with two sujetos, 'Nepopoçalco' (with two small estancias) and Hueyapa. The first of these was adjacent to Tetela and was eventually absorbed as a barrio, while Hueyapa, considered a separate cabecera in 1570–81, was off to the east, separated from Tetela by a deep barranca; in this last decade, Tetela–Nepopoalco had six dependent settlements altogether, while three are reported at Hueyapa. Most of the outlying places disappeared in a congregation towards 1600. In addition to the cabeceras of Tetela and Hueyapa, two of the old estancias (Metepec, Suchicalco) survived as barrios in the eighteenth century.

Sources

For Tetela and its estancias, we have a most rare copy of the 1531 *visita* made in connection with the lost 'description de la tierra' submitted by the second audiencia.[4] There are tribute assessments for 1545–65 (L de T, pp. 436–42), together with a brief report in the 1548 *Suma* (PNE, I, no. 505).

The Dominican monastery-parish of Tetela-Hueyapa as it was *c.* 1570 is described in an unpublished document,[5] followed by an interesting relación geográfica submitted by the C in 1581 (PNE, VI, pp. 283–90). There is also a curious map of Hueyapa which formed part of a lawsuit in 1574.[6]

Tributary data for 1588–1623 (Scholes and Adams, 1959, p. 30) and 1643–88[7] are found in two documents.

There are two reports sent in by the AM in 1743.[8] The Tetela region is included in a non-Indian padrón of Cuautla Amilpas, accompanied by an excellent map, of *c.* 1791.[9]

Tetela del Volcán is the subject of a scholarly local history (Martínez Marín, 1968) which reproduces several seventeenth-century documents concerning land disputes, and other material on the monastery.

96 *Tetepango Hueypustla*

An arid plateau occasionally broken by low mountain ranges, this jurisdiction occupies portions of the upper Tula and Amajac basins (northward-flowing tributaries of the Pánuco, now in the state of Hidalgo), although the southernmost part extends into the valley of Mexico (state of Mexico). The climate is dry and cold, with elevations of 1,800–3,000 m. The area includes most of what was called in the sixteenth century the Teotlalpan, and in later years Valle del Mezquital.

There was an extraordinarily dense population at contact in this bleak countryside; settlements were practically contiguous, with houses everywhere. Otomí was the predominant language, but many places had Náhuatl-speaking minorities. There were perhaps twenty or more native states, shared between three tributary provinces of the Triple Alliance. All were within the historical zone of influence of the Tepaneca, and several still had Tepanec tlatoque. Atotonilco was governed by a calpixqui, and received tribute from Apazco and Atlitlalaquian. Quetzalmacan, Tehuehuec, and Xalac may have been in this area. Axocopan was another tribute-collecting center, to which Atenco, Mizquiyahuallan, Tzayulan, Tecpatépec, Tetepanco, Tezcatépec, Tlaahuililpan, and Xochichiuhcan delivered goods and services. Atenco, Mizquiyahuallan, and Tzayulan seem to have been politically dependencies of Tollan (cf. Tula). Within the valley of Mexico, Hueypochtlan received tribute from Tetlapanaloyan and Xomeyocan. Tezontépec, Tlacaxique, Tolnacochtlan,

and Yeitecómatl may have had some political autonomy.

The region was perhaps first seen by Spaniards in late 1519, and came under their control in 1521.

Encomiendas

Apazco was assigned to Cristóbal Hernández (Mosquera), followed in the 1530s by a son, Gonzalo (Cristóbal, Francisco?) Hernández de Figueroa, still alive in 1604 (Dorantes de Carranza, p. 230. ENE, XIV, p. 149). Part of the tributes were still privately held as late as 1688.

Diego Ramírez was an early encomendero of Atengo (Icaza, I, p. 143). He held the place until he died *c.* 1550, being succeeded briefly by his widow, Ana de Acosta; when she died without issue the encomienda escheated, in January 1556 (L de T, pp. 65–6).

Cortés divided Atitalaquia between two 'foreign' conquistadors, Juan Catalán and Juan Siciliano. The former died in the 1520s, and his share was further divided between his widow (cf. Tlamaco, below) and a daughter. Siciliano's share was re-assigned by the first audiencia, and the whole encomienda escheated in March 1531 (Icaza, I, pp. 23, 108–9. L de T, p. 69).

Atotonilco, with its dependency of Zacamulpa, was held by the conquistador-surgeon Maese Diego de Pedraza until his death in the 1550s. A son, Melchor, inherited and was still alive in 1597. Escheatment occurred between 1643 and 1688 (Icaza, I, p. 206. Millares Carlo and Mantecón, I, p. 591).

Held for some years by Benito de Vejer (Bejer), Axacuba was taken for the crown in the early 1530s (L de T, p. 96). In 1543 it was re-assigned to Gerónimo López, followed towards 1550 by a son of the same name (ENE, IV, p. 75); the latter died in 1608, and the encomienda escheated between 1643 and 1688.

Mizquiaguala was another double encomienda, divided between Antonio Gutiérrez de Almodóvar and Pablo de Retamales (Millares Carlo and Mantecón, 1, p. 225). When Gutiérrez died, his half was split between his mother (whose share escheated before 1545) and his widow, María Corral or Carral, who then married Juan de

Hueypustla and its dependencies were shared by two conquistadors, Antón Bravo and Pedro de Valencia (Valenciano) (Icaza, 1, p. 158). Towards 1548 Bravo's half had been inherited by a son, Antonio Bravo de la Laguna (still alive in 1604), while the Valencia portion passed to a daughter, María Garao (Guercio?), married successively to Juan de Manzanares, Dr Frías de Albornoz (died towards 1569), and Dr Ambrosio de Bustamante (listed in 1604) (Dorantes de Carranza, p. 225). Tributes were re-assigned to the Moctezuma heirs and partly escheated by 1688 (Gibson, 1964, p. 420).

Vargas (Icaza, 1, p. 184). This remaining Gutiérrez portion escheated in the 1550s. Meanwhile, the Retamales half was inherited shortly before 1550 by a son, Melchor de Contreras, still alive in 1597. In the early 1600s the crown portion was re-assigned to D. Juan Andrade Moctezuma. Mizquiaguala was still part private encomienda in 1688.

Tecaxique and Chicaguasco, perhaps originally part of another encomienda, were assigned to the conquistador Diego de Olvera, followed towards 1545 by his widow, Juana Ruiz, and then by a son,

Juan de Olvera (Icaza, I, p. 128). When the latter died without issue in the mid-1560s, tributes were re-assigned to D. Luis de Velasco, whose heirs continued to receive them in the seventeenth century.

Tetepango, whose encomendero is not known, escheated in March 1531 (L de T, p. 432).

Tezcatepec and Tuzantlalpa were divided, half held by Francisco de Estrada and half by Alonso Martín Jara. In the 1540s Martín sold his share to Cristóbal Cabezón, and Estrada was succeeded by a son, Juan (Andrés) de Estrada. The latter was still alive in 1604, but Cabezón had been replaced by a son, Gregorio (Gerónimo?) de Soto. Both halves escheated between 1643 and 1688.

Bachiller Alonso Pérez was encomendero of Tezontepec, followed in the 1550s by a son of the same name, and somewhat later by a grandson, Alonso Pérez de Bocanegra, listed in 1597–1604. Escheatment occurred before 1643, but some of the tributes were subsequently re-assigned.

Tlagualilpa (like Atitalaquia, to which it was perhaps once joined) was given by Cortés to Juan Catalán; we are not sure whether Juan Siciliano shared in the encomienda. On Catalán's death in the 1520s his family claimed inheritance, entering into a prolonged dispute with other claimants and the crown (Icaza, I, pp. 23, 108–9). In 1534–6 half of Tlagualilpa had escheated, but soon afterwards tributes were being shared between Rodrigo de Albornoz and Juan de Rodríguez Bejarano. The half belonging to Albornoz escheated under the New Laws in April 1544, while Rodríguez's share was taken for the crown after his death, in January 1546 (L de T, p. 359).

Tlamaco, once an estancia of Atitalaquia, was assigned to the widow of Juan Catalán, Ana de Segura, who subsequently married Gerónimo Trías. By 1564 a son, also called Gerónimo Trías, had inherited, and he still appears as encomendero in 1597 (Icaza, I, pp. 108–9). By 1643 Tlamaco had escheated.

The encomienda variously listed as Tlanocopan, Talguacpa, and Tecpatepec, was held first by Lorenzo Suárez (Xuárez), a Portuguese conquistador (Greenleaf, 1961, p. 51). It was taken from him 'por cierto delito' (he seems to have murdered his wife) and appears as a crown pos-session in the 1540s, but within the next decade tributes were restored to Gaspar Suárez, son of the first holder, who towards 1565 was followed by his son, Andrés. Part of Tecpatepec was still privately held in 1688.

Tlapanaloya was assigned to a poblador, Juan Díaz del Real. When he died in the 1540s, his widow inherited (she seems to have married Lope Vázquez de Acuña); a son of the first holder, Melchor de Chávez, appears as encomendero in 1564–97. Escheatment occurred after 1643.

The conquistador Gonzalo Hernández de Mosquera (brother of the encomendero of Apazco) held Tornacustla, followed late in the sixteenth century by a son, Gonzalo Hernández de Figueroa, and still later (1599) by a grandson, Juan Pacheco (Simpson, 1934, p. 59). In 1643 tributes were going to the crown.

Yetecomac seems to have been held by Francisco Quintero de Zamora, who in 1537 gave it in exchange for another encomienda to Francisco Rodríguez (Millares Carlo and Mantecón, II, p. 279). On the latter's death in the 1540s his widow and children claimed the tributes, but they escheated towards 1550.

Sayula was taken from an unknown encomendero and became a crown village perhaps as early as 1531 (L de T, p. 239).

Government

Within a year or two of its arrival, the second audiencia appointed Cs to Tetepango, Atitalaquia, Sayula (with Mexicalcingo), Axacuba, and the crown half of Tlagualilpa. As we have seen, Axacuba reverted to private encomienda in 1543, while Tlanocopan was a corregimiento from c. 1540 into the next decade. Additional Cs were named on the escheatment of part of Mizquiaguala and Yetecomac in the 1540s. Thus at mid-century this area was divided between seven crown magistrates and sixteen private encomenderos. When Atengo escheated in 1556 it was put in the jurisdiction of Mizquiaguala.[1]

Shortly before 1560 the corregimientos of Tetepango and Yetecomac were being administered by a justice called AM of Minas de Tornacustla.[2] This official had charge of those crown villages together with Axacuba, Hueypustla, Tecaxique y Chicaguasco, Tecpatepec–Tlanocopan, Tezcatepec, and Tornacustla.[3] Suffragan to him were the Cs of Atengo y Mizquiaguala, Atitalaquia, Tlagualilpa, Tula and Sayula, although by 1563 Tula (q.v.) had its own AM with suffragan powers in Tlagualilpa and Sayula. The C of Atengo y Mizquiaguala had Tezontepec in his jurisdiction, and that of Atitalaquia administered Apazco, Atotonilco, Tlamaco, and Tlapanaloya. This division prevailed, with minor adjustments, for a century. The AM lived at Hueypustla by 1569, and towards 1600 he lost his suffragan prerogatives in the corregimientos of Atengo y Mizquiaguala (to which Sayula was annexed) and Atitalaquia. Tlagualilpa was absorbed by Tula about 1600, but later it was transferred to Atengo y Mizquiaguala.[4]

In a list of 1676 we find Tetepango attached to the alcaldía mayor of Ixmiquilpan, but for most of that century the three jurisdictions here were maintained. Towards 1690 Atengo y Mizquiaguala and Tetepango were combined under a single magistrate, and about 1720 Atitalaquia was also annexed to the alcaldía mayor. From 1787 the magistrate was a subdelegado in the intendencia of Mexico, and lived at Atitalaquia.

Sayula was separated from the rest of this jurisdiction by an intrusion of Tula (see map). There was another enclave off to the east, consisting of Tecaxique–Chicaguasco, Tornacustla, and Tilcuautla (a subject of Tezcatepec); these places were provisionally placed under the AM of Actopan in 1595, but in later years continued to be administered by that of Tetepango Hueypustla.[5]

Church

This area was visited in early years by regular clergy, Franciscans from Tula and Augustinians from Actopan and elsewhere. S Bartolomé Hueypustla was perhaps the oldest secular doctrina. Beneficiaries began living at S Miguel Atitalaquia in 1563 and at S Nicolás (S Andrés, S Antonio) Mizquiaguala in 1568, while Sta María Axacuba was a secular parish before it was transferred to Augustinians in 1569. Tezcatepec, at its old site in the south (see below), had a resident curate in

1569–75, but it, as well as S Lorenzo Tlacotlapilco (curacy in the 1580s), ceased to exist as separate parishes after the congregations of *c.* 1600.[6]

The Augustinian monastery-parish of Axacuba had its center in Asunción Tetepango in 1623 and was secularized sometime before the end of that century (Scholes and Adams, 1959, p. 58). All of the parishes were in the archbishopric of Mexico. Some places were visited from parish centers outside the jurisdiction.

Population and settlements

There were still, in 1570, some 21,450 native tributaries in the places which composed the final jurisdiction here (4,300 at Axacuba, 3,070 at Hueypustla, 2,815 at Atitalaquia, 2,150 at Tezcatepec, 1,810 at Atotonilco, 1,210 at Apazco, and the rest spread out among the other units). Almost half died in the plague of 1576–81, and an equal portion disappeared between 1580 and 1600, when there were perhaps 5,270 tributaries. Later censuses show 1,236 tributaries in 1643, 1,421 in 1688, 2,378 Indian families in 1743, and 4,540 Indian tributaries in 1803.[7] The non-Indian population was of little consequence until the eighteenth century. The 1791 padrón has 1,762 Spaniards (persons), 2,460 mestizos, and 297 mulattoes, most of them living on haciendas (there were twenty in that year). $111\frac{1}{2}$ mulatto tributaries are reported in 1803.

S Francisco Apazco (Apasco; 1950: Apaxco de Ocampo, pueblo, Mex.) had three nearby estancias in 1569 and two in 1580 which were moved to the cabecera in 1592–3. The same occurred with the single sujeto of Sta María Natividad Atengo (Otomí, Andehee, Dexó; 1950: Atengo, pueblo, Hgo.).

S Miguel Atitalaquia (Atlitalaque; 1950: Atitalaquia, pueblo, Hgo.) had four dependencies within a half league in 1569. One of them, Acagualco or Açagualco, can perhaps be identified with Acocolco (Açocolco?) in the Codex Mendoza. Only two sujetos are mentioned in 1580, and none after a congregation proposed in 1598.

Santiago Atotonilco (1950: Atotonilco Tula, Hgo.), according to the 1548 visita, had two 'estancias sujetas' (Jomiltongo, Tepetitlan) and another (Çacamilpa) 'no sujeta', the latter indicating pretensions to cabecera status. The 1569 report has Xumiltongo and Tepetitlan three leagues north of the cabecera, Çacamulpa one league west, and three other estancias nearby. Efforts at congregation occurred here in the 1570s and again in the 1590s. Of the sujetos, only Zacamulpa (Zaguamulpa, etc.; Otomí, Mapuhi) survived as a pueblo in the eighteenth century.

Sta María Axacuba (Axocopan, Xacuba; 1950: Ajacuba, pueblo, Hgo.) in 1548–71 had six estancias, the most distant of which was Santiago Tulancalco, 2½ leagues away. These were apparently reduced to two congregation centers *c.* 1600, both of which (Axacuba, Santiaguito) survived as pueblos. Tulancalco became an hacienda.

Many alternate spellings were used for S Bartolomé Hueypustla (Gueypuchtla, Huipuztla, Veipochtlan, Teupuztla, etc.; 1950: Hueypoxtla, *villa*, Mex.). In 1548–80 it had three sujetos, Tianguistongo (two leagues north of the cabecera), Tezcatepec, and Tlacuitlapilco (Tlalcotlapilco), the last two far off to the north. In another article of the *Suma* (*c.* 1548), Tlalcuitlapilco (with five barrios) and Tezcatepec appear separately, as crown possessions. Xomeyucan (Xumeiuca) was a distant subject of Tlapanaloya (*below*) in 1548–69, but is shown as a dependency of Hueypustla in 1579. A congregation was proposed in 1592. Two centuries later, we find Hueypustla, Tianguistengo, and Zacacalco (= Xomeyuca?) in a southern group of pueblos, while Tezcatepec and Tlacotlapilco survived as pueblos in the north. The sixteenth-century cabecera of Tezcatepec (*see below*) seems to have been a homonym in an entirely different site.

S Nicolás Mizquiaguala (Misqueahuala, etc.; 1950: Mixquiahuala, pueblo, Hgo.) had but one estancia in 1569–79, Sta María Huilotepec, a league north of its cabecera across the Tula river. It seems to have disappeared in a congregation of the 1590s. Off to the west was the cabecera of S Francisco Sayula (Zayula; Otomí, Michuc; 1950: Sayula, pueblo, Hgo.); it also had a nearby sujeto in 1580, abandoned soon thereafter.

S Francisco Tecaxique (Teguaxeque, Tlacachique; 1950: Tecajique, pueblo, Hgo.) towards 1548 had two sujetos, Atleuçian and Chicaguasco (Chicoavasco, Chicabasco). Atleuçian disappeared, but the other two settlements were pueblos in 1743–92. In the same area, 'Talguacpa' appears as a cabecera *c.* 1548 and can probably be identified with 'Tlanocopan' (1545–65). In the earlier report it had three dependencies, Teapa, Tecpatepec, and Teticpan. By 1569 Tecpatepec (1950: Tepatepec, pueblo, Hgo.) had become the cabecera and no estancias are mentioned, but two pueblos existed here in the 1790s, Tepa and S Juan Tepatepec.

Asunción Tetepango (Tetabanco, etc.; 1950: Tetepango, pueblo, Hgo.) in 1548 had three barrios and two estancias, all nearby. The 1571–9 reports mention none of these but name instead a single estancia, Uluapan (Vlapa). Its residents were to move to their cabecera in 1598; later reports show an hacienda, S Nicolás Vlapa, about where the old estancia must have been.

Tezcatepec and Tuzantlalpa were twin cabeceras a quarter of a league apart in the sixteenth century, on the slope of Cerro Temoaya, southeast of Axacuba. The 1569 report names eleven dependencies all within a league except Tlilcuautla, which was three leagues off to the north. A congregation in the 1590s apparently caused the abandonment of the old cabecera sites, although their names continued to be used in the tribute lists. Two of the estancias, Axuluapa (Axoloapan; 1950: Sta María Ajoloapan, pueblo, Mex.) and Tlilcuautla (1950: Tilcuautla, pueblo, Hgo.), were pueblos in the late eighteenth century, while Tuzantlalpa became an hacienda. The later pueblo of Tezcatepec was an old estancia of Hueypustla (*see above*).

S Juan Bautista Tezontepec (Otomí, Teantexeh; 1950: Tezontepec de Aldama, *villa*, Hgo.), although no estancias are mentioned in the sixteenth century, may have included within its limits the pueblo of S Gabriel (1791).

Tabaliloca (1534–6) became Tabalilpa (1545–80), and eventually S Francisco Tlagualilpa (Tlahuililpan, etc.; Otomí, Huantex; 1950: Tlahuelilpa de Ocampo, pueblo, Hgo.). It had a nearby estancia, S Pedro Tlachcoapan (Tlascoapan), which became a congregation center in 1594 and survived as a pueblo (it was the cabecera in 1792).

Tlamaco (1950: Tlemaco, pueblo, Hgo.) in 1569 was divided in two adjacent barrios (S

Gerónimo, S Martín) which became a single community.

Asunción Tlapanaloya (Tetlapanaloya; 1950: Tlapanaloya, pueblo, Mex.) in 1548–69 had Xomeyucan as a subject (*see above*); both names appear in the Codex Mendoza. By 1579 Xomeyucan was considered a subject of Hueypustla.

Tornacustla (Tulnacuchtla; 1950: Tornacuxtla, pueblo, Hgo.) had three estancias, Capula, S Francisco, and Sta María. The first of these places became the mining camp of S Bartolomé Capula in the 1550s and may well have been the residence of the AM in early years, but it was practically abandoned in 1570. The Indian pueblo of Tornacustla existed in 1792, as did the reales of Capula and Sta Rosa.

Yetecomac (S Nicolás Yeitecomatl), which had no known sujetos, can probably be identified with the eighteenth-century pueblo of Tecomate (1950: Tecomatlán, Hgo.).

Sources

Most of the cabeceras as they were *c.* 1548 are briefly described in the *Suma de visitas* (PNE, I, nos. 1–2, 8–10, 235, 258, 347, 534, 546–50), and there are a number of reports in the Ovando series of 1569–71.[8] Relaciones geográficas dated 1579–80 have been found from the alcaldía mayor of Minas de Tornacustla (PNE, VI, pp. 12–38), and the corregimientos of Atengo y Mizquiaguala (with a map),[9] Atitalaquia (PNE, VI, pp. 199–208), and Sayula (PNE, VI, pp. 178–82). There are a number of congregation documents from the 1590s.[10]

Seventeenth-century material is largely confined to tributary counts of 1643–88.[11] Places visited from Tula and Tepetitlan are mentioned in the 1697 work of Vetancurt (4a parte, pp. 64, 86).

A missing report of *c.* 1743 is condensed in Villaseñor y Sánchez (I, pp. 138–41). A padrón of *c.* 1791 is accompanied by a useful description and map of the jurisdiction.[12] Finally, there is a list of placenames dated 1792.[13]

Both Cook (1949) and Mendizábal (1947) have published monographs on the Teotlalpan from which additional information can be gleaned. For further documentary citation on the Hueypustla area, Gibson (1964) and Colín (1966, 1967) should be consulted, and for places in the state of Hidalgo, Fernández (1940–2) is useful.

97 *Teutila*

This is very rugged country in what is now north central Oaxaca, dropping from the summit (2,600 m) of the Sierra Juárez to the Gulf coastal plain (less than 100 m). Drainage is easterly into the Papaloapan system, the principal branch of which (Quiotepec–Santo Domingo) cuts through the mountains here and is joined by the Tonto river on the north and the Valle Nacional from the south (much of the Tonto's lower basin is now flooded by the Miguel Alemán reservoir). Heavy rains much of the year, increasing from west to east, produce a dense forest growth in the eastern part. Temperatures vary according to altitude.

Teuhtillan (Cuicatec, Coeteyaco) was an important and populous Cuicatecan state, mostly in high country south of the Papaloapan. On the eastern slope of the mountains and in the river plain below were seven Chinantecan communities, Tecomaltépec, Tlacuatzintépec (Chinantec, Maxaá), Huitzilla (Geugeín), Tepetototla (Yoojuíi), Chinantla (Jungiá), Xicaltépec, and Oxitlan (Cooguum). In a similar situation north of the river were the Mazatec-speaking states of Izoatlan, Micaoztoc, Tenanco (Mazatec, Gatiaá), Ayauhtla (Giiyufii), and Tepeapa, all of which may have been politically subordinate to Teotitlan. Farther down in the hot country were other Mazatec communities, Aticpac, Ichcatlan (Ningutxié), Tecpantzacualco, Tlecuauhtlan, Tzinacanoztoc with Puctlantzinco, Xallapan (Ndaxoó), Zoyatépec, and Zoyatlan. Below these places, on the south bank of the river, was Tochtépec, with an Aztec garrison and military governor in charge of collecting tribute from the abovementioned states

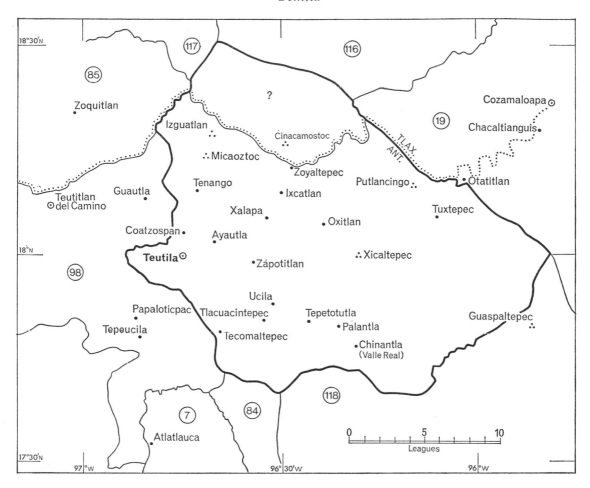

and others in the lower Papaloapan. It seems likely that Tochtépec was an old Popolucan settlement which had been taken over by Nahua-speakers; in 1743 the language there was 'a crude Mexican which they call Olmec, which has always been spoken here' (cf. Cozamaloapan).

There may have been minorities speaking still other languages. In the eighteenth century, Chinantec, Mazatec, and Mixtec were all spoken at Chiquihuitlan (a subject of Teutila), while a dialect known as 'Misteco Nudeñu' was used at Coatzospan.

In 1520 a Spanish gold-hunting expedition visited Tochtépec and continued on to the Chinantec country, where two Spaniards remained for several months. At this time the Aztec forces seem to have lost control of the Chinantla (perhaps

a recent development), and when a Spanish force was destroyed at Tochtépec the Chinantec remained loyal to the Spaniards. A punitive force led by Diego de Ordaz and Alonso de Avila seized Tochtépec late in 1520, but hostilities continued into the following year and perhaps until 1522 (Bancroft, I, pp. 321–3. Cortés, pp. 64–5, 147–8. Herrera, 2a década, pp. 276–7, 356–8. Oviedo, III, pp. 376–7). An uprising of the Chinantec at Tepetotutla was quelled in the early 1530s (Icaza, nos. 94, 845, 1163, 1345).

Encomiendas

Aticpac and Tenango were assigned to a resident of Vera Cruz, Francisco de Rosales, escheating on his death *c.* 1560 (L de T, pp. 71–3).

We do not know the encomendero of Ayautla

and Tepeapa, which were taken for the crown *c.* 1535. By 1546 Cinacamostoc and Putlancingo had been added to this corregimiento (L de T, p. 109).

Hernán Cortés claimed Chinantla for himself and attempted to transfer it to his daughter's dowry (Cortés, pp. 396, 564). It was not included in the Marquesado grant and was under crown control by 1534, although part of the tribute was set aside for Cortés in early years.[1]

Ixcatlan was held by Juan López de Ximena, a vecino of Vera Cruz, succeeded *c.* 1540 by his widow, Francisca de Nava, and then by a son, Pedro de Nava. By 1566 the latter had died and his son, Diego de Nava, was encomendero. A Diego de Nava still appears as holder in 1630 (Dorantes de Carranza, p. 204. Icaza, I, p. 104. L de T, p. 596).

Micaoztoc belonged to Antón Martín Brena, followed in the 1550s by his widow. Juan de Vivanco (a son?) inherited between 1570 and 1597 (Icaza, II, p. 14).

Francisco Daza de Alconchel was the holder of Oxitlan, which escheated on his death towards 1535.

Bartolomé Román, a conquistador and an early settler of Medellín, held Tepetotutla. By 1551 his widow had married Francisco de Reinoso, who appears as encomendero in the 1560s. Escheatment occurred by 1580.[2]

Teutila was assigned to Diego de Ordaz until his death, and was placed in corregimiento in March, 1533 (Dorantes de Carranza, p. 170. ENE, IV, p. 174. L de T, p. 458).

Tlacuacintepec and Tecomaltepec had several early claimants, including Juan López de Ximena, Gonzalo Jiménez, and Diego de Leiva (Icaza, I, pp. 104, 255). Leiva won possession and was followed in the 1550s by a son of the same name, although his rights were contested by his mother, Francisca de la Cueva. The younger Leiva died *c.* 1565, and his widow, Juana de Cabrera, was soon re-married to Alonso de Olivares. Escheatment occurred before 1597.

The first holder of Ucila was perhaps the conquistador Rodrigo de la Peña (Icaza, II, p. 158). Nuño de Guzmán re-assigned it to Ginés de Cárdenas, a resident of Vera Cruz, but it escheated under the second audiencia before 1534 (Icaza, II, p. 171).

Xalapa was held by Juan Coronel, succeeded by a son, Matías, who appears as encomendero in 1560–1604. Tributes were still privately assigned in 1630.[3]

Xicaltepec belonged first to Pedro Castellar, a conquistador and an early resident of Guazacualco. The encomienda was inherited sometime before 1548 by Castellar's widow, María de León, but by 1560 the holder was Diego Núñez de Guzmán (Diego de Esquivel), who had married Castellar's daughter, Antonia de León. Esquivel was still receiving tributes in 1597 (ENE, XIV, p. 150. Icaza, I, p. 111).

We do not know the original holder of Zoyaltepec which may have included Zoyatlan (Coyatlan?). In 1548 it was a crown possession, but four years later it had been awarded after a lawsuit to Bartolomé Sánchez, a resident of Antequera (L de T, p. 381). In the 1560s it seems to have been divided between the crown and a son of Sánchez, total escheatment occurring by 1567.[4]

The encomenderos of Izguatlan (a crown holding by 1544), Tecpanzacualco, Telcuautla, and Tuxtepec (in the crown by 1560) are unknown.

Government

This area was disputed in the 1520s between the ayuntamientos of Vera Cruz, Segura de la Frontera (Antequera), and Espíritu Santo (Guazacualco). The first corregimiento was probably that of Teutila (1 March 1533), but within a year or so Cs were appointed to Ayautla y Tepeapa, Chinantla, Oxitlan, and Ucila.

In May, 1554, the C of Teutila received a commission to administer justice in the entire basin of the Alvarado (Papaloapan) from Teutila to Tlacotalpa.[5] A year later the viceroy assigned the corregimientos of Chinantla, 'Cucatlan' (Zoquitlan?), Oxitlan, Ucila, Papaloticpac, and Ayautla–Tepeapa to the jurisdiction of the C of Teutila, after noting that the magistrates appointed to these places did not reside in them.[6] From 1556 the justice was referred to as AM of Teutila y Río de Alvarado, and in the following decades he had suffragan powers in Ayautla y Tepeapa, Zoyaltepec y Zoyatlan, Zoquitlan, Guaspaltepec, Tlacotalpa, Chinantla, Papaloticpac y Tepeucila,

Ucila, and Oxitlan.[7] Perhaps to avoid overlapping jurisdictions, the Cs of Ayautla y Tepeapa and Zoyaltepec were sent to administer the Guatusco and Cozamaloapa regions, respectively, in 1560.[8] Meanwhile, the AM of Teutila took charge of the various private encomiendas mentioned above.[9]

Towards the end of the sixteenth century, Ayautla–Tepeapa and Zoyaltepec y Zoyatlan were absorbed by the alcaldía mayor of Teutila, and about the same time Zoquitlan was combined with Cuzcatlan (cf. Teguacan), Guaspaltepec with Oxitlan, and Chinantla with Ucila; these corregimientos shed their suffragan status under Teutila, as did Papaloticpac y Tepeucila (cf. Teutitlan del Camino). Not long afterwards the Oxitlan–Tuxtepec region was annexed to the corregimiento of Chinantla y Ucila, which in turn was absorbed by the alcaldía mayor of Teutila in the jurisdictional reforms of the 1670s. In 1692 Chinantla–Ucila–Tuxtepec were transferred to Cozamaloapa, but this area was returned to Teutila towards 1770. We know of no boundary changes after this.[10]

From 1787 Teutila was a subdelegación in the intendencia of Oaxaca.

Church

We have no record of parochial foundations before 1560, by which time there was a Dominican monastery at S Pedro Teutila.[11] Ten years later there were secular priests living at Chinantla (S. Juan Bautista?), S Felipe Ucila (the parish included Oxitlan and Xicaltepec), and S Pedro Ixcatlan (with Izguatlan, Micaoztoc, Putlancingo, Tenango, Xalapa, and Zoyaltepec), while Tuxtepec was in the parish of Guaspaltepec. In 1572 the doctrina of Teutila was secularized, and in 1582 we find a secular priest at S Juan Bautista Tlacuacintepec.[12] Towards the end of the sixteenth century the parish of Chinantla was turned over to the Dominicans, but a century later they had abandoned their house there and it was being visited from Ucila.[13]

In 1743 the abovementioned parishes still existed, although the curate of Ixcatlan had moved his seat to S Felipe y Santiago Xalapa, and that of Tlacuacintepec was perhaps living at Sta Cruz Tepetotutla. By 1777 Tepetotutla and Tlacuacin-

tepec were separate doctrinas, while the Chinantla area again had a priest, living at S Juan Bautista Valle Real. The latest parochial erection was that of S Pedro Ixcatlan, separated from Xalapa in 1780. In the late eighteenth century, Ayautla, Coatzospan, and Tenango belonged to the parish of Guautla (cf. Teutitlan del Camino), while Tuxtepec was visited from Chacaltianguis (cf. Cozamaloapa).

The area north of the Alvarado was theoretically in the diocese of Tlaxcala, and its encomiendas appear in that bishopric in some sixteenth-century documents, but by 1570 the bishop of Antequera had extended his control to those places, and thus the whole political jurisdiction of Teutila came to belong ecclesiastically to Antequera. There was, however, a parish of Guadalupe de Amapa founded in 1767 under the auspices of the bishop of Puebla (Taylor, 1970).

Population and settlements

The tierra caliente of this jurisdiction was struck by the same scourge which decimated the natives of the whole Gulf coastal plain within a decade of the Conquest. Thus the Chinantec and Mazatec in the lowlands declined by perhaps 90 per cent in those first years, while the mountain Chinantec and Cuicatec were relatively unaffected; the latter, however, were hit by later plagues. The 1570 report shows 4,640 tributaries (1,400 Cuicatec, 2,390 Chinantec, 850 Mazatec). By 1630 only half as many Mazatec survived, the Chinantec had lost 30 per cent, and the Cuicatec registered a slight gain; in that year there were 3,963 tributaries. In 1743 we find a remarkable recovery among the Mazatec but further loss in the other two groups, perhaps due to the plague of 1737–9; there were 3,290 tributaries in that year. Counts of 1785–98 give a total of 5,710 Indian tributaries. There were very few non-Indians here, mostly living on vast cattle haciendas in the deserted lowlands. Only $17\frac{1}{2}$ mulatto tributaries are reported in 1798.[14]

While there may have been some urban concentration at Tuxtepec at contact, the overall settlement pattern was dispersed until depopulation made it convenient to gather the survivors into a few congregations. The cabeceras of Tecpanzacualco and Tlecuautla are no longer mentioned in 1570. Other places (Cinacamostoc–Putlancingo, Izguatlan, Micaoztoc, Xicaltepec) had so few inhabitants by the century's end that they disappeared in congregations and lost their cabecera status.

Aticpac and Tenango were combined in a single Mazatec community (Tenango; 1950: S José Tenango, pueblo) towards 1600. Ayautla and Tepeapa were perhaps joined together at the same time; S Bartolomé Ayautla (1950: pueblo) in the eighteenth century had a sujeto, S Juanico Coatzospan (Cuajospan).

According to the 1579 relación, Chinantla had four barrios and twenty-four sujetos. One of the latter, 'Caltepeque', perhaps can be identified with Xicaltepec, whose encomendero happened to be C of Chinantla at that time. A congregation was proposed here in the 1590s, and there was an epidemic in 1609 (Espinosa, 1961, p. 82). Of the 1,000 tributaries mentioned in 1579, only 97 remained in 1743, distributed in four diminutive pueblos (some had moved to the Ucila area, *see below*). The cabecera of Chinantla, which had already had several changes of site in 1579, by 1743 was at S Juan Palantla (1950: ranchería); the other pueblos were Asunción Acatepec (Xacatepec), S Pedro Usumacín, and S Mateo Yetla. Sometime before 1766 Palantla was replaced as cabecera by Valle Real (1950: S Juan Bautista Valle Nacional, pueblo), probably at or near the site occupied by 'Chinantla' in 1579 (Bevan, p. 9). Another pueblo mentioned in 1766 was Chiltepec.

The cabecera and perhaps the only settlement of Ixcatlan (Ichcatlan; 1950: S Pedro Ixcatlán, pueblo) is said to have been moved after a flood, in 1592 (Espinosa, 1961, p. 99).

Oxitlan (1950: S Lucas Ojitlán, *villa*) is reported to have had a congregation of various sujetos following an epidemic and flood, in 1571 (Espinosa, 1961, p. 89). Cocahuatlan and S Juan were barrios in 1777.

We do not know how many estancias Tepetotutla (1950: pueblo) had, but one of them, distant S Juan Zapotitlan, was a pueblo in 1766–1820.

Teutila (Teotila; 1950: S Pedro Teutila, pueblo) was perhaps moved from its old ceremonial site when the Dominicans founded a mission there in the 1550s. In 1548 it had five sujetos and an undisclosed number of minor estancias. A congregation proposed here in 1598 reduced their number. There were nine subject pueblos in 1766 whose Cuicatec names are found in the 1803 report: Chijuine or Chivini (Chiquihuitlan), Chyuna (Sta Ana), Diñuhne (Sta Cruz Teutila), Diyaca (S Francisco Chapulapa), Jalitatuane (not mentioned after 1766), Naico (S Andrés Teitilalpan), Nayco (Sto Domingo del Río), Nanduia (Cuyomecalco), and Tayco or Téico (Sta María Talixtaca).

Tlacuacintepec (Tlacoazintepec; 1950: S Juan Bautista Tlacoatzintepec, pueblo) and Sta Ana Tecomaltepec (Comaltepec) are listed as separate cabeceras, although they belonged to the same encomendero and adjoined each other. Each had four estancias in 1548, which were supposed to be congregated in 1599. Four of them (S Antonio Analco, Santiago Quezalapa, S Antonio del Barrio, S Esteban Tetitlan) seem either to have survived or were later re-occupied, while the affiliation of two more eighteenth-century pueblos (S Juan Zautla, S Pedro Zochiapa) is uncertain.[15] Both of the original cabeceras apparently had changes of site.

The old Tuxtepec was probably a league or so south of its final site (Tochtepec; 1950: S Juan Bautista Tuxtepec, ciudad), at a place where extensive stone ruins are mentioned in 1777. It is said to have once had nine sujetos (Espinosa, 1961, p. 113). In 1600, when only 23 tributaries remained, the settlement was ordered to be moved far downstream to Cacaguaxuchitlan (cf. Cozamaloapa). We are told that 80 years later Tuxtepec was re-populated at its final site (Espinosa, 1961, p. 114).

Ucila (Vzila; 1950: S Felipe Usila, pueblo), a Chinantec community, had only two estancias in 1548, but there were five in 1579, all within two leagues of the cabecera. One of them, Santiago (de Arriba) Mayoltianguis, survived in the eighteenth century as a pueblo. Two other places, S Pedro and Santiago Tlatepuscos, can perhaps be identified with Ayotustla la Grande and Ayotustla la Chica, listed as sujetos of Chinantla in 1579 but subject to Ucila in 1610 (Espinosa, 1961, pp. 90–1).

We know little about Xalapa (1950: S Felipe Jalapa de Díaz, pueblo), which at some point was moved from a hillside to the river bank where it is today.

Zoyaltepec (Suyatepec; 1950: S Miguel Soyaltepec, *villa*), a Mazatec community, was perhaps united with a companion village, Zoyatlan (Coyatlan?), towards 1600. A congregation of Negroes was founded at Amapa in 1769 (Taylor, 1970).

Sources

All the cabeceras here are mentioned in the *Suma* of *c.* 1548 (PNE, I, nos. 15–16, 124–5, 297–8, 349, 422, 450, 506, 509, 768–70, 793, 802, 837). There is a brief report of *c.* 1570 in the Ovando series (García Pimentel, 1904, pp. 81–3). We have two valuable relaciones of 1579 submitted by the Cs of Chinantla and Ucila (PNE, IV, pp. 45–52, 58–68), but others received from the AM of Teutila and the C of Oxitlan y Guaspaltepec have disappeared. The congregation of Tuxtepec is described in an interesting document,[16] and there are scattered data on other congregations.[17]

Tributary information for 1630 and 1644–92 is given in two places.[18] The Chinantla–Ucila region is described in a most useful document of 1743,[19] while a lost report on the rest of the jurisdiction is summarized in Villaseñor y Sánchez (I, pp. 376–8; II, pp. 187–9). Ajofrín (II, pp. 51–80) left an unusually detailed account of his trip here in 1766. A report from the curate of Chacaltianguis dated 1777 describes Tuxtepec.[20] For the same year, we have padrones from the parishes of Tepetotutla, Tlacuacintepec, and Xalapa.[21] Reports made in connection with an episcopal visit in 1803–4 cover the doctrinas of Guautla, Ixcatlan, Teutila, and Xalapa.[22] The jurisdiction as it was *c.* 1821 is described in detail.[23]

A reconstruction of this region at contact is found in Scholes and Warren (1965). Monographic treatment of the Chinantec area is voluminous (Bevan, 1938. Cline, 1961. Weitlaner and Castro, 1954). Cline's (1966) work on Mazatec pictorial documents includes useful maps of this area north of the Papaloapan. The pioneer study of Mariano Espinosa (1910, re-published 1961) contains material not found elsewhere.

98 *Teutitlan del Camino*

Most of this region, now in north central Oaxaca, consists of a hot, arid basin drained by the Grande and Salado rivers at an elevation of 200–1,000 m, closed in on the west and east by high (2,500–3,000 m) mountains. The two watercourses mentioned meet at Quiotepec to form the Santo Domingo or Papaloapan (Río Alvarado) which then flows eastward, piercing the Poblano–Oaxaqueño section of the Sierra Madre, to continue its way to the Gulf. At the summit of these mountains the climate changes abruptly with almost year-round precipitation producing a dense tropical growth below, with cloud forest in the vicinity of Huautla and Pápalo.

While the elders of Teotitlan in 1581 claimed that they had always been independent of the Aztecs, other perhaps more reliable sources indicate that the entire region including Teotitlan had been conquered by the Triple Alliance and paid tribute in one form or another (Byam Davies, pp. 14–16). Teotitlan itself seems to have been a Náhuatl-speaking community, a religious center of importance, whose political influence extended to a number of Náhuatl and Mazatec states both in the valley and in the mountains to the east; among these autonomous or semi-autonomous communities were Ohuatlan or Huauhtlan (Mazatec, Tejoó), Matzatlan, Nanahuaticpac, Nextépec, and Tecolotlan, and perhaps Ayauhtla, Izoatlan, Micaoztoc, and Tenanco as well (cf. Teutila). South of Teotitlan and following the chief artery of trade and conquest from central Mexico to Oaxaca were several lesser states, including the Mazatec communities of Tecomahuacan and Quiyotépec (*cf. below*), and the Cuicatec kingdoms of Cuicatlan, Atlipitzahuayan, Cuetlahuiztlan, and Nanalcatépec. In the mountains east of Cuicatlan were two more Cuicatec states, Papaloticpac and Tepehuitzillan, and off to the west was Ichcatlan, where the language was a Popolocan dialect, Ixcatecan.

In addition to the abovementioned places, other toponyms in this area appear in the 'Memorial de

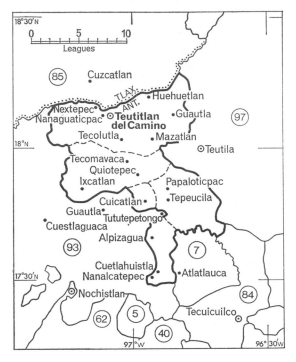

los pueblos...', which may mean that they enjoyed a certain political autonomy before the Spaniards came.[1] Coyollan, Tehuasco, and Tequecistépec by 1548 were considered subjects of Quiyotépec, while Cozollan, Nacaztlan, and Pochotépec were dependencies of Tecomahuacan.

Spaniards went through here in 1520, and subdued the area late in the next year.

Encomiendas

A conquistador, Juan Moreno, held Alpizagua until it was re-assigned to Gerónimo de Salinas in 1527. It escheated in April, 1544 (Icaza, II, p. 72. L de T, p. 381).

Cuetlahuistla was assigned to Gonzalo de Robles, followed in the 1540s by a son, García de Robles (still listed in 1580). Juan de Robles was the holder in 1597–1604.

Cortés assigned Cuicatlan first to Juan Tirado and then (by 1524) to Juan de Jaso. It was re-assigned by the first audiencia, perhaps to Tirado, who held it in the 1530s, followed by a son. Escheatment occurred between 1545 and 1548.[2]

Both Guautla and Nanaguaticpac were given to the conquistador Juan Navarro, succeeded in the early 1550s by a daughter married to Melchor de Castañón. The latter, a resident of Puebla, died shortly before 1580. In 1597 another Melchor Castañón appears as encomendero of Guautla, while Nanaguaticpac was held by Juan Pacheco (Icaza, I, p. 13. L de T, p. 208).

Ixcatlan was at first shared between Rodrigo de Segura and García Vélez, but Vélez's share was given to Segura *c.* 1525. After some difficulties with the crown, Segura retained possession until his death towards 1565, when his widow inherited. Tributes escheated in the 1570s, but were re-assigned after 1580 to D. Luis de Velasco (ENE, III, p. 129. Icaza, I, p. 53).

The conquistador Melchor de San Miguel held Nanalcatepec, to be followed soon after 1560 first by a son and then by his widow, María de Godoy. Escheatment occurred after Doña María's death early in 1587.[3]

Papaloticpac was perhaps first held by Francisco de Ribadeo, and then (in the 1530s) by Francisco Casco, escheating *c.* 1541 (Icaza, I, p. 141. L de T, p. 285).

Tecomavaca belonged to Juan Núñez Mercado, as probably did neighboring Quiotepec, both places escheating in November 1531 (L de T, p. 380).

Tepeucila was held by Luis de Cárdenas and escheated when he left New Spain, in April 1544.[4]

Juan Jiménez de Rivera was perhaps encomendero of Teutitlan, a crown possession since 10 March 1531 (L de T, p. 460).

Government

Cs were appointed in 1531 to Teutitlan and to Tecomavaca y Quiotepec (Tepetotutla [cf. Teutila] was included in the latter corregimiento in 1534–6). Papaloticpac had a crown justice from *c.* 1541, and Tepeucila was added to his jurisdiction three years later. Cuicatlan had a C by 1548.

In 1555 Cuicatlan and Papaloticpac were temporarily placed under the C of Teutila, since their magistrates were absent. In the provincial division of the 1560s and 1570s, we find Teutitlan (with the encomiendas of Guautla and Nanaguaticpac) and Tecomavaca y Quiotepec (with Ixcatlan) assigned as suffragan corregimientos under the AM of Teguacan; Papaloticpac and Tepeucila formed a corregimiento suffragan to Teutila, while Cuicatlan was subordinate to Antequera. Alpizagua, Cuetlahuistla, and Nanalcatepec formed a little group off to the south administered directly by the AM of Antequera, although the C of Cuicatlan was given jurisdiction in Nanalcatepec in 1579.[5]

In 1583 the corregimientos of Cuicatlan and Tecomavaca were united under a single magistrate, and while they are listed separately in later years the union seems to have become permanent by 1640.[6] The three jurisdictions went their separate ways in the seventeenth century until the administrative reforms of the 1680s, at which time they were combined under a single AM with residence first at Cuicatlan and later at Teutitlan del Camino. From 1787 this magistrate was a sub-delegado in the intendencia of Oaxaca.

Among minor boundary disputes through the years was one with the AM of Teguacan over jurisdiction in the salt mines of Nextepec (Casa Blanca), resolved in favor of Teutitlan,[7] and controversies with neighboring jurisdictions over the limits of Ixcatlan (*see below*).

Church

Franciscans from Teguacan were visiting the Teutitlan area in the 1540s and began construction of a monastery there in late 1559.[8] Eight years later this doctrina, S Miguel Teutitlan, was turned over to a secular priest who also had charge of the valley settlements as far as Quiotepec and the mountain villages around Guautla.[9] Meanwhile, a curate had been living at Sta María (Concepción) Papaloticpac from the 1550s, visiting Cuicatlan, Tepeucila, and Tututepetongo (cf. Teposcolula). S Juan Bautista Cuicatlan, S Juan Evangelista Guautla, and Sta María Ixcatlan all became secular parishes in the 1570s. S Francisco Huehuetlan seems to have been a separate doctrina from *c.* 1600

to 1635 when it was annexed to Teutitlan; it again had a resident priest from *c.* 1700.

By the eighteenth century Ixcatlan had become a visita of the Dominicans at Cuestlaguaca (cf. Teposcolula), while Alpizagua, Cuetlahuistla, and Nanalcatepec were visited by the curate of Atlatlauca (q.v.). All parishes were in the diocese of Antequera.

Population and settlements

There was a dense rural population at contact of which only a fraction survived at mid-century. Teutitlan is said to have been struck by the first great epidemic (1520–1), which must also have affected the other communities along the road to Oaxaca. At Ixcatlan, where 8,000 tributaries are reported at contact, the Indians were sent off as slaves to the encomendero's mines at the rate of 200 monthly; only 300 tributaries survived in 1579, many having fled to other parts. Of 3,200 tributaries which Tecomavaca and Quiotepec are reputed to have had in 1521, there were only 400 in 1570. In the latter year, the whole jurisdiction as finally constituted had 1,780 Cuicatec tributaries, 1,450 Mazatec, 600 Popoloca, and 400 Náhuatl-speaking tributaries, or a total of 4,230. The mountain communities were reduced by about half in the epidemic of 1576–80, leaving some 2,500 tributaries in 1600. After further loss there was a recovery to 3,729 tributaries in 1743, and 4,633 in 1801.[10]

The non-Indian population was mostly confined to a few Spanish and mestizo merchants in the principal towns and some mulatto workers and slaves on sugar haciendas. One hundred and eighteen non-Indian families are mentioned in 1743, and 163 mulatto tributaries in 1801.

The distribution of languages is mentioned above, but there is some confusion about the Tecomavaca–Quiotepec area, listed as Mazatec-speaking in 1570. The 1579 report states that Quiotecan, 'a tongue somewhat similar to but quite different from Mixtecan', was used at Quiotepec, while at Tecomavaca 'the language of los Pinoles' was spoken. In the eighteenth century Mazatec is reported at Tecomavaca, and both Cuicatec and Mazatec at Quiotepec.

For Alpizagua (Alpitzahuac, etc.; Don Dominguillo was an alternate name by 1586; 1950: Santiago Dominguillo, ranchería), Cuetlahuistla (Cuitlahuiztlan; Cotahuistla in the eighteenth century; 1950: S Francisco Cotahuixtla, ranchería), and Nanalcatepec (Nanacaltepec; 1950: Santiago Nacaltepec, pueblo), the dependent settlements, if there were any, seem to have been congregated before 1548. Nanalcatepec included within its limits the *venta* of S Miguel. All survived as small pueblos in the eighteenth century.[11]

Cuicatlan (Cuicatec, Guetrabaco; 1950: S Juan Bautista Cuicatlan, *villa*) in 1548 had four barrios and three estancias. The 1580 relación mentions no sujetos and states that the cabecera, then on the west bank of the Río Grande, had been moved down from a nearby hill-site; in that year a new settlement was being made at Xocoyoltepec, on somewhat higher ground. A congregation planned here in 1598 was probably carried out the following year. It was perhaps at this time that the cabecera was again moved, to the east side of the river, and the residents of Xocoyoltepec and a ranchería called Cocohuapa were collected at the central settlement.

Guautla (Huauhtla, etc.; 1950: Huautla de Jiménez, ciudad) in 1581 had five sujetos within four leagues. Only two of these, S Miguel Tamaltepec and Sta María Asunción Tepexititlan (Mazatec, Guinaxii; 1950: Sta María Jiotes), survived the congregations; another eighteenth-century pueblo, S Mateo, was perhaps a later foundation. Although Guautla was a Mazatec community, it had a barrio of Mexicans in 1803.

Ixcatlan (Izcatlan; 1950: Sta María Ixcatlán, pueblo) in 1543 had three sujetos and one estancia (L de T, p. 599). By 1579 the cabecera had been moved to Temazcalapa from its old site, Tecopango or Teopatongo. In 1580 we hear of a recently occupied estancia, Axumulco, whose site was disputed between Ixcatlan and Guautla (cf. Teposcolula). The dependent settlements probably disappeared in a congregation towards 1600. Cook (1958, pp. 12–13) mentions seven deserted sites to the north of Ixcatlan. Among these were S Antonio Nopala and S Gerónimo Xuquila, definitely sixteenth-century estancias, the latter caught up in a three-way dispute between Ixcatlan, Cuestlaguaca, and Zapotitlan in 1576.[12]

Nanaguaticpac (Nanaotiquipa, Nanaguatipa, etc.; S Antonio de las Salinas, Los Cués; 1950: S Antonio Nanahuatipan, pueblo) had a single sujeto, S Francisco Coyolapa, in 1581; it is not heard from thereafter.

The 1579 relación gives both Náhuatl and Cuicatec names of seven estancias subject to Papaloticpac, the most distant being seven leagues from the cabecera. It is not clear where the cabecera was originally. A nineteenth-century source states that Los Reyes and Sta María were 'old' settlements, while Concepción (1950: Concepción Pápalo, pueblo) and S Lorenzo were founded in 1600 (*Colección de 'Cuadros Sinópticos'* ...). In addition to the places mentioned, S Andrés and S Pedro were pueblos in 1743–1821.

Santiago Quiotepec (1950: ranchería) once had its cabecera on the west side of the Río Grande, but by 1579 it had moved a half league to the right bank. Of five sixteenth-century estancias (*cf. above*), only Coyula (which also seems to have had a change of site) survived the congregations.

Tecomavaca (Tecomabaca, Tecomahuaca; 1950: Sta María Tecomavaca, pueblo) had six estancias in 1548, three in 1579, and none after the congregation of *c.* 1600.

The Indians of Tepeucila (Cuicatec, Cocaá or Hicocucan; 1950: S Juan Tepeuxila, pueblo) received permission to move their cabecera in 1552.[13] There were nine estancias in 1548, eight within seven leagues of the cabecera in 1579, and two subject pueblos (Teponastla, Tlacolula) in 1777–1821.

S Miguel Teutitlan del Camino Real (1950: Teotitlán del Camino, *villa*) at contact had its ceremonial center on a hill-site from which it was moved at an early date, presumably by the Franciscans, to the final site nearby. According to the *Suma* (*c.* 1548), it had six barrios, five sujetos (Elosuchitlan, Huehuetlan, Mazatlan, Tecolutla, Tehuaque or Tecoac), and an estancia (Nextepec); this last place, however, appears in the same document as a separate cabecera. By 1581, Mazatlan (with two estancias), Nextepec (one estancia), and Tecolutla were recognized as sub-cabeceras, while the other old sujetos were included among fifteen villages directly subordinate to the principal cabecera of Teutitlan. Eleven of the latter survived the reductions of *c.* 1600 and were pueblos in 1699–1821: Sta Ana Ateticpac (Mazatec, Dasulajoó), Magdalena Chilchoc (Chilchotla), S Antonio Elosuchitlan (Mazatec, Guitxoó), S Francisco Huehuetlan, Santiago Mexcala (= Texcalcingo?), S Pedro Ocopetlatlan (Mazatec, Nanguinaja), S Lucas Tetjapocan (= Zoquiapan?), S Gerónimo Tecoac (Mazatec, Natzhií), Sta María Teopochco, Sta Cruz Teutlilhuacan (Mazatec, Datzundá), and S Martín Toxpalac or Toxpalan. S Cristóbal Mazatlan (Mazatec, Chintií), S Gabriel Nextepec Casablanca, and S Juan Tecolutla (Los Cúes) absorbed their dependencies. One other eighteenth-century pueblo, S Lorenzo Guichnituc, we do not find mentioned before 1699.

Sources

All cabeceras but Cuetlahuistla and Ixcatlan are described as they were *c.* 1548 in the *Suma de visitas* (PNE, I, nos. 89, 227, 400–1, 475, 478, 486, 507, 760–1, 785). The Ovando report of *c.* 1570 is of limited value (García Pimentel, 1904, pp. 67–8, 83, 93–4). There is extraordinarily good and thorough coverage of the region in the relaciones geográficas of 1579–81. Four of these reports have been found, from the C of Cuicatlan in 1580 (PNE, IV, pp. 183–9), the C of Papaloticpac y Tepeucila in 1579 (PNE, IV, pp. 88–93), the C of Tecomavaca y Quiotepec in 1579 (with two nearly identical maps),[14] and the C of Teutitlan in 1581 (PNE, IV, pp. 213–31, with map). For 1580 there is also an interesting pictorial representation of Ixcatlan with a text in Spanish concerning the boundaries of that community.[15] Father Ponce went through here in 1586 and left a succinct account of his visit (Ponce, I, pp. 267–9, 497–8).

We have seen only a brief reference to congregations, dated 1598.[16]

Aside from the few references cited above, we have almost nothing from this area in the seventeenth century except a useful document concerning the division of Teutitlan into two parishes, dated 1699 (Berlín, 1947, pp. 72–4).

Villaseñor y Sánchez (II, pp. 136–41) summarizes a lost description sent in by the AM towards 1743. Ajofrín (II, pp. 46–50, 81–5) went through along the highway in 1766. There is a census of the parish of Teutitlan dated 1777.[17] 'Topographic' reports of uneven value describing places within this jurisdiction were submitted in 1777–8 by the curates of Atlatlauca,[18] Cuicatlan,[19] Cuestlaguaca,[20] and Papaloticpac.[21] There is a brief description of the parish of Teutitlan, written *c.* 1789.[22]

Of particular interest is a series of cleric's reports (1803–4) covering the whole jurisdiction except the southernmost tip.[23] The area is well described in another document of *c.* 1821.[24]

The massive work of MacNeish *et al.* (1967), a model of interdisciplinary cooperation, is mainly concerned with the archaeology of the Tehuacán valley from Teutitlan north; it has much to add to these notes. The work of Cook (1958) on Sta María Ixcatlan is an adept blend of field work and documentary investigation. Cline (1966) publishes several pictorial manuscripts from the Mazatec area, with valuable comments. Sixteenth-century documents in the native tradition from the Cuicatlan region, which include place glyphs and historical information, deserve careful study (Chavero, 1892. Peñafiel, 1895). MacNeish *et al.* (1967, I, pp. 114–30) present convincing evidence that the pre-Conquest ritual-calendrical manuscripts known as the Borgia Group are related to the Teutitlan area (cf. Nowotny, 1961).

99 Teutlalco

This is an excessively hot, dry country of barren hills and few water sources, now in southwestern Puebla, draining into the Balsas (Mexcala) river from the north. Elevations range from 900 to 1,800 m.

Teotlalco and Centeopan or Cuitlatenamic,

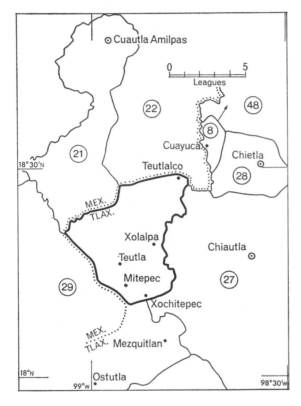

both Náhuatl-speaking communities, seem to have been the political units here at contact. They do not appear in any lists that we have seen of Aztec conquests or tributary states; there may, however, have been some pre-Conquest connection between this region and Chiyauhtla (cf. Chiautla), which most likely was under Triple Alliance hegemony.

Presumably the area came under Spanish control in the early 1520s.

Encomienda

Nicolás López de Palacios claimed to be the first holder of Teutlalco with a grant from Cortés which was cancelled after 1528 and re-assigned to the conquistador Ruy González. The second audiencia took half the encomienda for the crown in 1531. González died towards 1559, and while his half of the tributes were claimed by a mestiza daughter married to Francisco de Nava, they soon escheated.[1]

Government

On 14 June 1531, one half of Teutlalco y Centeupa became a corregimiento. In early years the jurisdiction included neighboring Ostutla (cf. Chilapa), and in the 1560s it was suffragan to Chalco.[2]

We first hear of the silver mines at Tlaucingo in 1576, from which date the magistrate here is usually called AM of Minas de Teutlalco or Tlaucingo.[3] Sometime between 1743 and 1770 the jurisdiction was annexed to the alcaldía mayor of Chiautla (q.v.), but we choose to consider it separately here.[4]

Church

Franciscans working out of Chietla began construction of a monastery at Teutlalco in 1552, but eight years later the parish had been secularized.[5] By 1569 there were two secular parishes, S Juan Teutlalco and Cuitlatenamic, both in the diocese of Tlaxcala. In the 1580s a priest was living at the Mines of Tlaucingo, but he was removed.[6]

In 1593–8 the parish center of Cuitlatenamic moved to Concepción Xolalpa. By 1754 the curate of Teutlalco was resident at S Antonio Cuayuca, in the adjoining jurisdiction of Atrisco, but there was still a priest at Xolalpa.

Population and settlements

This small, arid region had at first an extraordinarily dense population. In 1555, after two epidemics and much loss from 'famine, drought, excessive tributes and bad treatment', there were still 5,060 native tributaries.[7] Part of the subsequent drop in population (2,500 tributaries in 1569, 1,000 in 1595) was due to emigration, some of it in the direction of the Tlalnaguas and other villages in the adjoining Marquesado.[8] Only 186½ tributaries are reported in 1626, and 67½ in 1696, although the 1743 census shows 227 Indian tributaries.

The Spaniards attracted to the mines of Tlaucingo went away when they found them no longer profitable. In 1743 the old real de minas was abandoned, and the jurisdiction contained but one family of Spaniards, 18 of mestizos, and two of mulattoes, most of them living at a sugar hacienda and two cattle ranches.

Before the congregations of 1593–1603, there were a great many dispersed settlements subject to two principal cabeceras. In the earlier documents (1531–60) these are referred to as Tcutalco and Centeupa. After 1560, Centeupa's place is taken by Cuitlatenamic.

Teutlalco (Teutalco, Teotlalco, etc.; Ayacaxocuichco in 1611; 1950: Teotlalco, pueblo) in 1569 had fifty estancias within four leagues of the cabecera. One of them was Tlatzinco (Tlaucingo; 1950: ranchería), presumably where the mines were. Another was Aguacayuca, which survived as a separate cabecera in the seventeenth century, but no longer is mentioned in 1743. The remaining

estancias seem to have disappeared in a congregation towards 1600.[9]

The twenty estancias which Cuitlatenamic (Tecuistlatenamique; = Centeupa?) had in 1569, all within a radius of four leagues, seem to have been gathered together towards 1600 at Xolalpa (1950: Jolalpan, pueblo), although the old cabecera continues to be mentioned until 1665. Two former estancias, Mitepec and Teutla, were pueblos of Indians in the eighteenth century. Another, Sta Ana, was moved in a quarter of a league and became a barrio of Xolalpa. Santiago Xochitepec seems to be a later foundation.[10]

Sources

There is a brief report of an official visit here in 1555.[11] The myriad estancias of 1569–70 are named and approximately located (PNE, v, pp. 202–3, 266–9). References to congregations in 1593–8 are found in several places.[12]

The journal of an episcopal visit in 1611 is of interest.[13] Tributary data for 1626–96 are derived from other documents.[14]

There is a valuable relación submitted by the AM in 1743,[15] followed by a report made for the Inquisition in 1754.[16] We have a 1777 census of Teutlalco parish,[17] and a short description drawn up by the curate of Xolalpa in 1778.[18] For 1792, there is a complete list of placenames.[19]

100 *Tezcuco*

This region, now shared between the states of Mexico and Tlaxcala, rises from the eastern shore of Lake Texcoco (2,200 m) to the divide (2,700–4,150 m) separating the valley of Mexico from headwaters of the Atoyac river, and in fact crosses this divide to emerge on the plains of Apan. The climate is cold with moderate seasonal rains.

Texcoco was the home territory of the Acolhuaque, one of the three components (with the Mexica and the Tepaneca) of the aggressive Triple Alliance. It was bounded on the east by the frontier

with hostile Tlaxcallan, but its political influence at contact extended some distance north and south of the colonial limits. In 1519 the area here considered was ruled by seven tlatoque, among whom the tlatoani of Texcoco was pre-eminent; the others were the lords of Acolma, Coatlinchan, Chiauhtla, Huexotla, Tepetlaoztoc, and Tezoyucan. The population was dense and scattered in a great many small, generally contiguous settlements, although Texcoco and Acolma were impressive urban centers. While Náhuatl was the predominant language, there was a minority of Otomí-speakers.

First seen by Spaniards in October, 1519, Texcoco and its satellites first submitted to their rule, later rebelled, and were finally controlled by the Spaniards at the end of 1520.

Encomiendas

It seems likely that the whole area of Tezcuco with its subordinate states was assigned to himself

by Hernán Cortés towards 1522. Subsequently, several places within the province were given to other encomenderos (*see below*), leaving Tezcuco with the sub-cabeceras of Coatlinchan, Chiautla, Huexutla, and Tezoyuca. This encomienda was taken from Cortés in 1525, regained by him the following year, seized by the first audiencia in 1529, and finally escheated in March 1531. However, some of the tributes continued to be paid to Cortés in the 1530s, and they were all assigned to the Augustinians of Mexico city in 1541–4 (Gibson, 1964, p. 431. Chauvet, p. 221).

Acolman was granted to Pedro Núñez (Maese de Roa), and re-assigned by 1528 to Pedro de Solís Barrasa, a conquistador. The latter was followed *c.* 1565 by a son, Francisco de Solís Orduña, and towards 1610 by a grandson, Francisco de Solís y

Barrasa. Escheatment probably occurred in the 1680s (Gibson, 1964, p. 413).

Tepetlaostoc, first held by Cortés, was seized by the acting governors in 1525 and subsequently was assigned to Diego de Ocampo. Miguel Díaz de Aux was the holder from mid-1527 to 1528, when governor Estrada transferred the encomienda to Gonzalo de Salazar, succeeded *c.* 1553 by a son, Juan Velázquez de Salazar. After the latter's death, in 1612 tributes were re-assigned to the Moctezuma heirs (Gibson, 1964, p. 429).

Far to the east in the vicinity of Calpulalpa, Tequepilpa (Actipa) and Zultepec probably had some autonomy under calpixque rule before the Conquest and were made separate encomiendas by the Spaniards (García Granados, II, p. 45). Tequepilpa, first held by Francisco Ramírez, was sold *c.* 1540 to Pedro de Meneses. When the latter died *c.* 1566 the encomienda was divided between a son, Germán, and a daughter, Agustina. The latter married Andrés de Loya, but she survived both her husband and brother and was still encomendera in 1597 (L de T, pp. 420–1).

The first holder of Zultepec was Diego Motrico, followed after 1535 by his widow, Isabel Muñoz, who then married another conquistador, Gonzalo Hernández Calvo. Isabel died, and there was a dispute over succession in the 1540s, at which time half of the encomienda seems to have been purchased by Pedro de Meneses, who also held neighboring Tequepilpa. Meanwhile Hernández Calvo remarried and in turn was succeeded *c.* 1552 by his widow and children. In the 1560s the joint encomenderos were Meneses and Francisco Calvo, a son of Hernández. In 1597 Zultepec and Tequepilpa are listed together, with Calvo and Agustina de Meneses as holders. Both places had escheated by 1688 (Dorantes de Carranza, pp. 198, 222. Icaza, I, pp. 41, 71. L de T, pp. 651–2).

Government

Tezcuco and its subjects were ruled by a C from 1531. After 1550 this magistrate was given charge of nearby encomiendas, and towards 1552 he was re-designated AM. In the sixteenth century Tezcuco had a number of suffragan corregimientos (Coatepec, Chiconautla, Mexicalcingo y Sayula,

Sochimilco, Tequecistlan). The jurisdiction's limits underwent little change until the late seventeenth century, when Acolman and its subjects were transferred from Teotiguacán to Tezcuco. After 1786 the AM was a subdelegado in the intendencia of Mexico.[1]

Church

The Franciscans probably had a mission at S Antonio Tezcuco by 1525, and were followed soon afterwards by the Dominicans at Magdalena Tepetlaostoc; the Augustinians took charge of S Agustín Acolman towards 1540. Each became a doctrina which survived to Independence. While Acolman was secularized in 1754, and Tepetlaostoc in 1777, Tezcuco remained in Franciscan hands.

Additional Franciscan monasteries were built in the sixteenth century, first as visitas of Tezcuco and eventually as separate parishes. These were S Miguel Coatlinchan and S Luis Huexutla (visitas from c. 1528), S Simón y Judas Calpulalpa (by 1569), and S Andrés Chiautla (by 1585). With the exception of Calpulalpa, which remained a Franciscan dependency of Tezcuco, these doctrinas were secularized in 1753–77. All were in the archdiocese of Mexico.

Population and settlements

There were probably 100,000 tributaries here in early years. The first useable estimate after the great epidemic of 1545–8, that of c. 1570, gives a total of 18,851 tributaries (12,787 at Tezcuco, 3,500 at Tepetlaostoc, 2,564 at Acolman). In this reckoning, the encomiendas of Tequepilpa and Zultepec are included under Tezcuco. The 1582 relación states that ⅔ of the population died in the epidemic of 1576–80. However, an interpolation of data available for the encomiendas in 1597 shows a loss of 53 per cent since 1570, leaving 8,860 tributaries in the jurisdiction at the century's end. Later censuses and estimates give 4,000 tributaries in 1623, 1,565 in 1643, 2,295 in 1688, 5,913 in 1744, 7,540 in 1782, and 7,546 in 1802.[2]

The non-Indian population grew from 60 families in 1570 to 505 in 1744. In 1792 there were 5,720 non-Indian persons, mostly Spaniards and mestizos with a few mulattoes, representing 15 per cent of the total. In the latter year, the jurisdiction had thirty-six haciendas and fifteen ranchos.

There was a prolonged dispute between the principal cabecera of Tezcuco and certain places which it held subject, and which in turn claimed cabecera status. The encomiendas of Acolman, Tepetlaostoc, Tequepilpa, and Zultepec were first given cabecera rank by the Spaniards, although the last two often appear in the records under Calpulalpa, a subject of Tezcuco. Coatlinchan, Chiautla, Huexutla, and Tezoyuca were recognized as crown cabeceras each with its own Indian government by 1580 at latest. Seven other former sujetos had broken off by 1688, and in 1802 there were a total of twenty-five cabeceras here.

While we have no complete sixteenth-century listing of dependent settlements at Tezcuco (Tescoco, etc.; ciudad from 1543; 1950: Texcoco de Mora, ciudad, Mex.), it seems probable that there was a concentration around the monasteries in the 1550s resulting in the disappearance of many small settlements. Another such consolidation occurred in 1603–4.[3] A report of 1697 names forty-nine pueblos de visita around the monasteries of Tezcuco, Coatlinchan, Chiautla, and Huexutla (Calpulalpa will be considered separately below). The same document lists nineteen hermitas or barrios within the city of Tezcuco, and nine more among the visitas (we assume that most of these barrios had been moved from more distant sites in the congregations). Only twenty-nine places here survived as pueblos in the late eighteenth century, of which twelve had acquired cabecera status by 1792: S Salvador (Transfiguración) Atengo (Atenco), S Miguel Coatlinchan (Coatlichan, Coatinchan), Sta María Asunción Cuanalá, Santiago Cuautlalpa (Cuauhtlalpan), S Andrés Chiautla, S Miguel Chiconcoac, S Luis Huexutla (Guaxutla, Huexotla), S Cristóbal Nexquipayac, Sto Toribio Papalotla, La Purificación Tenochco, S Buenaventura Tezoyuca (Tesoyucan), and Sta María Tlailotlacan.[4]

The sub-cabecera (subject to Tezcuco) of Calpulalpa (S Simón y Judas; 1950: Calpulalpan, ciudad, Tlax.) in 1570 was the center of a group of eighteen settlements in the easternmost part of the jurisdiction. Four of these, we do not know which, belonged to the encomiendas of Tequepilpa and Zultepec (*see above*). Only five places survived as pueblos after the 1599–1604 congregation: S Mateo Actipa (=Tequepilpa, Tecpilpa?), Santiago Cuaula, S Marcos Guaquilpa, Santorum (Todos Santos), and S Felipe Zultepec (Soltepec).

S Agustín Acolman (Aculma; 1950: El Calvario Acolman, pueblo, Mex.) in 1580 still had twenty-seven sujetos which are named and approximately located in the relación and map. Some of these were nearby while others formed an enclave off to the north, separated from their cabecera (the latter were in the parish of Tezontepec, cf. Pachuca). These were all reduced to four subject pueblos in the congregation of 1603–4. Santiago Atla (Atlatongo) and S Miguel Xometla (Xomitla, Sometla) were near the cabecera. The northern estancias were collected at S Mateo Ixtlaguacan (=Tochatlauco?) and S Felipe Zacatepec. Two other places, S Agustín Atipac and Sta Catalina, appear as pueblos in the late eighteenth century.

According to a 1570 report, Tepetlaostoc (Magdalena Tepetlaoztoc, Tepetlaxtoc; 1950: Tepetlaoxtoc de Hidalgo, *villa*) had twenty-three estancias within five leagues of the cabecera. Some of these were eliminated in 1603–4, when the more remote settlements seem to have been reduced to one, Sto Tomás Acuautenco (Apipilguasco). In 1683 there were still twelve visitas, all except Sto Tomás quite close to the cabecera. In the late eighteenth century, Tepetlaostoc and Apipil-guasco were both cabeceras, and S Pedro Chaucingo and Concepción Tepetitlan were subject pueblos.[5]

Sources

The *Suma de visitas* (*c.* 1548) has little to say about Tezcuco (PNE, I, nos. 19, 776). A lawsuit between the Indians of Tepetlaostoc and their encomendero in the 1550s is accompanied by maps (Paso y Troncoso, 1912). There are several reports of *c.* 1570, only partially published.[6] The relación drawn up in 1582 by Juan Bautista Pomar survives in two MSS copies and has been published several times.[7] Ponce (I, pp. 68, 72, 76–7, 109–11, 193–4) describes the area as it was in 1585.

There are some data on the congregations of the northern Acolman estancias in 1603–4.[8] Gage (pp. 52–6) left a brief but interesting description of Tezcuco in 1625. The number of tributaries in 1643–88 is derived from another document.[9] For the late seventeenth century, we have seen a report of the archbishop's visit in 1683[10] and descriptions of the Franciscan doctrinas in 1697 (Vetancurt, 4a parte, pp. 51–2, 74, 82–3, 85, 87, 89).

A valuable report by the AM in 1744[11] is inadequately summarized in Villaseñor y Sánchez (I, 155–63). There are two censuses with lists of placenames, dated 1786[12] and 1792.[13]

Many other documents are cited in Colín (1966, 1967) and Gibson (1964).

101 *Tinhuindín*

The western half of this jurisdiction occupies a basin of interior drainage near the summit of the main volcanic divide in western Michoacán, the rest of it draining southward into the Tepalcatepec (Balsas) system. Elevations range from 1,500 to 3,750 m at Cerro Patamban. The climate is temperate with moderate rainfall; the higher slopes are covered with pine–oak forest. There are several fresh-water lakes.

There is some reason to believe that this region formed part of a rather large Tarascan state, called Tepehuacan in Náhuatl, which included Periban, Tacáscuaro, Tarecuato, and Tinhuindín. Its ruler was subordinate to the cazonci to whom the people paid tribute, also serving in wars against the Chichimecs on the north and in other places.

While Spaniards perhaps penetrated this area in late 1522, the ruler of Tepehuacan was proving intractable in the spring of 1528, and at least some of his subjects had fled to the mountains.[1]

Encomienda

Antón Caicedo held Tarecuato and Tepeguacan (which we assume included the Tinhuindín area) in April 1528. Periban and Tinhuindín escheated on Caicedo's death in 1535 or 1536, and while the widow sued for possession and was allowed to keep Periban and Tarecuato (cf. Xiquilpa), Tinhuindín and Tacáscuaro were made a separate corregimiento in July 1540.[2]

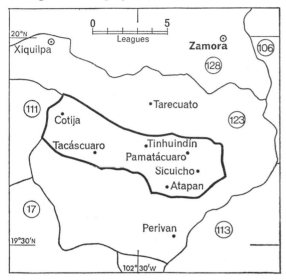

Government

A C was appointed to Periban y Tinhuindín in 1536. From 1540 the jurisdiction was called Tinhuindín y Tacáscaro, or sometimes Chocandiran in reference to the new cabecera site (*see below*). While a separate magistrate seems to have been appointed here as late as 1770, for much of the colonial period tributes were collected and justice was administered by the Cs and AMs of Xiquilpa or Zamora y Xacona. Thus in 1579 the C of Xiquilpa listed Chocandiran among the cabeceras in his jurisdiction, while two years later the C of Tinhuindín submitted a report on the same place. Both Cs were supervised by the AM of Michoacán in the late sixteenth century. In 1657–98, although a C resided at Tinhuindín, tributes are recorded under Xacona. In the 1750s we find a single AM governing Tinhuindín, Xiquilpa, and Periban. After 1787 the combined area formed a

subdelegación in the intendencia of Valladolid (Títulos de Indias, pp. 220–1).

Several estancias were disputed between Tinhuindín and Tarecuato (Xiquilpa) in 1576.[3]

Church

Sta María Asunción Tinhuindín, first a Franciscan visita, was a secular parish from the 1560s. In the eighteenth century the curate maintained vicars in several outlying villages. The doctrina belonged to the bishopric of Michoacán.

Population and settlements

The number of native tributaries, estimated at 3,000 in 1522, dropped to 608 in 1566, 480 in 1579, 220 in 1649, and 150 in 1657 (L de T, p. 389). Later counts show 392 tributaries in 1698 and 451 in 1743. The language spoken was Tarascan.

The cabecera of Tinhuindín was moved at an early date from a hill-top site to its final location, often called Chocandiran in sixteenth-century documents. Fourteen sujetos within 5 leagues, including the former cabeceras of Tacáscuaro and Tocumbo (=Tepeguacan?), are listed in the relación of 1581. Most of these disappeared in a congregation carried out in 1593–1604. Three places which survived, Charat, Querandan, and Xandumban, were abandoned soon afterwards. Besides the cabecera (1950: Tingüindín, *villa*), four places appear as Indian pueblos in the mid-seventeenth century: Atapan, Pamatácuaro, Sicuicho, and Tacáscuaro. Atapan seems to have been annexed from neighboring Periban.

In 1649 there were 4 Spanish vecinos and 224 communicants living on cattle and sugar haciendas in the jurisdiction. By 1743 the non-Indian population (306 families plus Negro slaves) rivalled that of the Indians. A village of Spanish *arrieros*, Valle de Cotija (1950: Cotija de la Paz, ciudad), was founded shortly before 1743 in the mountains northwest of Tinhuindín.

Sources

The area is summarily described in reports of *c.* 1546 (PNE, I, no. 668) and *c.* 1570 (García Pimentel, 1904, p. 43. Miranda Godínez, 9/40).

Reports concerning Tinhuindín were next received both from the C of Xiquilpa[4] and the C of Tinhuindín,[5] dated 1579 and 1581, respectively. Congregation history is found in several places.[6]

The parish of Tinhuindín is mentioned in reports of 1639[7] and 1649,[8] and there are tributary data for 1657–98.[9] We have a good description submitted in 1743 by the AM,[10] a list of settlements with population data for 1778,[11] a fine description of 1789[12] and a shorter one of 1793.[13] The jurisdiction as it was *c.* 1821 is treated in the work of Martínez de Lejarza (pp. 214–17).

102 *Tistla*

The Sierra Madre del Sur traverses this region (now in central Guerrero state) east–west, but is interrupted by a relatively low pass between affluents of the Balsas or Mexcala and the Papagayo rivers, forming a natural corridor between Mexico city and Acapulco. While elevations range from 350 to 3,000 m, the inhabited portion is mostly 500–1,500 m. The climate is hot and dry except in the higher sierra where there is a pine–oak forest cover.

This was a frontier area, the northern part belonging to the Triple Alliance province of Tepecuacuilco and the south inhabited by unreduced Tlapanecans (Yopes). The people in the north were known as Coixca and spoke a rustic Náhuatl, although there were small groups of Tuxtecan- and Matlatzincan-speakers around Tixtlan, perhaps remnants of an older population. The realm of the tlatoani of Ouapan lay on either side of the Balsas and perhaps included the semi-autonomous states of Huitzitziltépec, Muchitlan, and Tixtlan. Tzompanco, also tributary to the Mexica, had its own ruler. While early documents show that the lands of Muchitlan, Tixtlan, and Tzompanco reached southward to the Papagayo and Omitlan rivers, this was likely a post-Conquest extension after the defeat of the Yopes.

The Coixca surrendered to Cortés in the summer of 1521, but the Yopes remained unconquered for another decade.

Encomiendas

The conquistador Martín de Ircio (Dircio) held the multiple encomienda of Huitziltepec, Muchitlan, Oapa, and Tistla until his death *c.* 1566. Ircio married a sister of viceroy Mendoza, and was succeeded by a daughter, María, married to the future viceroy D. Luis de Velasco the younger. After the latter's death in 1617 tributes went to his heirs, the marquises of Salinas.[1]

Zumpango was given to another conquistador, Diego García Xaramillo, followed before 1548 by his widow, Cecilia Lucero. The encomienda was claimed by the crown in the 1550s and definitely escheated in September 1562, although part of the tributes were assigned to Cristóbal de Vargas, a grandson of the first holder.[2]

Totolcintla belonged to the encomienda of Tlalcozautitlan (cf. Chilapa).

Government

The mines of Zumpango must have had an AM at an early date, although we have no record of such an appointment before the late 1540s; in 1558 this magistrate's jurisdiction included the Zumpango area, Chilapa, and Tlapa. When production at the mines fell off, the AM moved to nearby Chilapa, and in 1579 Tlapa was made a separate jurisdiction.[3] Oapa was transferred from Iguala to Zumpango sometime between 1582 and 1593,[4] and about the same time certain estancias south of the Balsas belonging to Tepecuacuilco were shifted from Zumpango to Iguala. Towards 1600 the alcaldía mayor of Minas de Zumpango was split in two, Chilapa becoming a separate partido with its own AM, while Tistla (together with Zumpango, Muchitlan, Huitziltepec, and Oapa) was attached as an agregado to the jurisdiction of Acapulco.[5] Thereafter Tistla was the residence of a teniente, and often during the rainy season the AM (later, gobernador) of Acapulco stayed there. After 1787 the magistrate was a subdelegado, subordinate to the intendente of Mexico.

Church

Secular priests probably lived at the mining camp of S Martín Zumpango from the 1530s. In 1570 there were two secular parishes, one at Zumpango

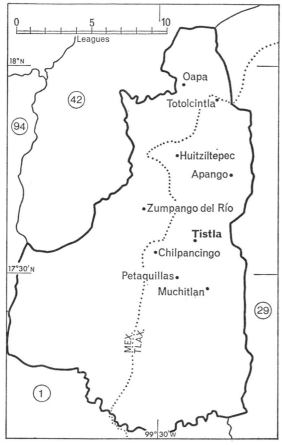

(including Huitziltepec and Oapa) belonging to the archbishopric of Mexico, the other at S Martín Tistla (with Muchitlan) in the diocese of Tlaxcala. New doctrinas were erected *c.* 1605 in connection with the congregations, at S Francisco Apango (Tlaxcala) and S Agustín Oapa (Mexico); the parishes of Sta María Chilpancingo (Mexico) and S Juan Bautista Totolcintla (Tlaxcala) were founded considerably later.[6] Chilpancingo seems to have been transferred to the diocese of Tlaxcala in the eighteenth century.

Population and settlements

The 'muchos y muy buenos pueblos' mentioned here in 1531 were much reduced a few decades later. The tributary population stood at 3,300 in 1566, 2,950 in 1570, 2,725 in 1582, and 2,930 at the century's end (L de T, pp. 209, 655). Thereafter there was a swift decline to *c.* 1,350 in 1626, and a gradual recovery to 1,760 in 1696. The census of 1743 gives 2,838 families of Indians, all Náhuatl-speakers. In 1797 there were 4,589 Indian tributaries.[7]

Silver deposits (they seem to have been in the mountains five leagues southwest of the village of Zumpango) were discovered *c.* 1531, attracting 'many' Spaniards, but they were almost abandoned fifty years later (ENE, xv, p. 155; L de T, p. 490). There were 30 Spanish vecinos in 1662, and 348 families (mostly mestizos and mulattoes) in 1743.[8] The 1792 padrón shows 1,471 Spanish individuals, 1,475 mestizos, and 1,701 mulattoes in the jurisdiction. In 1743 no mines were being worked, but there were sizeable non-Indian settlements at Chilpancingo, Zumpango del Río, and especially Tistla. In 1792–3 the jurisdiction had four sugar haciendas, four ranchos, and four ventas (inns); the latter, from north to south along the Acapulco road, were at El Zopilote, Acahuizotla, Cuaxinecuilapan, and Tierra Colorada.

Oapa (Huapan, Vapa, etc.; 1950: S Agustín Oapan, pueblo) had six subject estancias in 1570, most of them on the banks of the Balsas. All were ordered moved to the cabecera *c.* 1603, but the congregation was called off when it was argued that Indians were needed at different places to ferry passengers and goods across the river (the principal crossings of alternate Mexico-Acapulco roads were at Mexcala, Totolcintla, and Tlalcozautitlan).[9] Surviving as pueblos in 1743 were Ahuelican, Amayotepec, Guacacingo, Oapa, Osomatlan, Tecuisiapan, and Tetelcingo. S Juan Totolcintla, originally belonging to Tlalcozautitlan, seems to have been annexed to Oapa in the seventeenth century.

Huitziltepec (Uiziltepec, Huiciltepec; 1950: Huitziltepec, pueblo) had only three estancias within two leagues in 1570. Two of them were congregated at Zumpango in 1603, while a third,

S Agustín Ostotipan, was apparently shifted to Oapa. The cabecera itself was ordered moved to Apango in 1603 but actually remained *in situ*.

Zumpango (Tzonpango, Sumpango del Río in the eighteenth century; 1950: Zumpango del Río, pueblo) had ten estancias which are located on the map of the 1582 relación, some close by, others far to the southwest along the Papagayo; five others had been transferred to one of the Ircio cabeceras in 1561 (L de T, pp. 656–7). Only one, Chilpancingo (1950: Chilpanzingo de los Bravos, ciudad) survived the congregation of *c.* 1600. Another place, Petaquillas, became a pueblo in the seventeenth century.

The 1570 report names twenty-eight estancias under Tistla (Tixtlan; 1950: Tixtla de Guerrero, ciudad), some nearby and the rest forming a pocket off to the south, separated from their cabecera by an intrusion of Muchitlan. By 1582 these had been reduced to eighteen. All of their inhabitants were supposed to move to Tistla in 1603, but those of two estancias, Apango and Atliaca, were allowed to return to their primitive sites. Another sujeto, Yacapitzatlan, received permission to be re-established in 1625, but is not heard of thereafter. Indians surviving in the southernmost estancias were gathered at Dos Caminos.

Muchitlan (Sta Ana Mochitlan; 1950: Mochitlan, pueblo) had eighteen estancias in 1570 and twelve in 1582, the most distant being eight leagues south of the cabecera. All were apparently congregated at Muchitlan in 1598–1604.

Sources

There is brief mention of the area in the 1531 'Description de la Tierra' (Herrera, 4a década, p. 231), followed by unusually good early (1531–50) tribute data for the Ircio encomiendas (L de T, pp. 489–93). Only Oapa, Tistla, and Zumpango are succinctly covered in the *Suma* of *c.* 1548 (PNE, I, nos. 237, 773, 794). We have excellent reports of *c.* 1570.[10] All five cabeceras are described in detail in relaciones dated 1579[11] and 1582,[12] but only Muchitlan and Zumpango and their dependencies are shown on two most interesting maps accompanying them.

Valuable data on the congregations of 1598–1604[13] are followed by tributary information from 1626 to 1696.[14] There is a good report from the teniente dated 1743,[15] together with padrones from the three Tlaxcala parishes drawn up in 1777,[16] a non-Indian census of 1792,[17] and a brief description dated 1793.[18]

103 *Tlalpuxagua*

Lying on the northern slope of the Sierra Volcánica Transversal, this jurisdiction was divided into two parts, both now in northeasternmost Michoacán. The western portion drains mostly into the enclosed Cuitzeo basin, but part of it is traversed by the Lerma river; all of the eastern portion falls within the Lerma drainage. It is a mountainous region (1,880–3,600 m), the higher parts covered with pine–oak forest. The climate is cold with moderate seasonal rains.

Most if not all of this area was held by the Tarascans, although the predominant language was Mazahuan. The cazonci appointed rulers and kept garrisons at Araró, Sinapécuaro, Ucario, and Taimeo. Facing them on the east were hostile Mexica-dominated states, while to the north were Pame-speaking Chichimecs. The Mazahuan (Otomí) population, with minorities speaking Pame and Náhuatl, lived in many dispersed rancherías.

While the area presumably submitted to the Spaniards in 1522, first contact may well have been the visit of Caravajal in 1523 or 1524.

Encomiendas

Of the encomenderos favored in the first distribution by Cortés towards 1524, only Gonzalo Rioboz de Sotomayor appears to have survived the scrutiny of the first and second audiencias. He held Araro and Cinapécuaro until his death in 1538, when they escheated.[1]

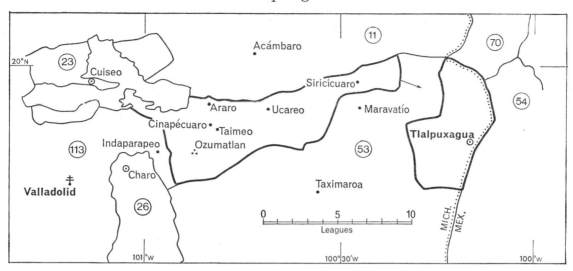

Ucareo was first held by Gonzalo Holguín, replaced in 1529 by Juan Bezos. The latter assignment was annulled, perhaps in 1531 and certainly by 1536, although Bezos was still fighting his case in the courts as late as 1542.[2]

Only Taimeo remained in private encomienda for some time. Diego Hurtado was encomendero in 1528, to be replaced the following year by the conquistador Gaspar de Avila Quiñones. Soon afterwards half of this encomienda was acquired by Francisco Quintero, who in 1537 gave it, in exchange for another pueblo, to Francisco Rodríguez. When Rodríguez died, his half was claimed by his widow, but it escheated before 1550. Avila's share was inherited towards 1550 by a son, Pedro de Avila Quiñones, who still held it in 1579; escheatment occurred before 1597, but later the tributes were re-assigned.[3]

Government

Ucareo became a crown possession probably in 1535 or 1536, and a single C was put in charge of Ucareo–Cinapécuaro–Araro, together with Maravatío and Taximaroa, on 10 August 1538. Taimeo was added to the jurisdiction sometime before 1550, while Maravatío became a separate corregimiento in that year. These jurisdictions were suffragan to the AM of Michoacán in the 1560s.[4]

The silver mines of Tlalpuxagua were discovered within the limits of Taimeo in 1558, and in June of that year the C of Ucareo y Cinapécuaro was ordered to proceed to the new real de minas as juez visitador and justicia.[5] Soon he was given the additional title of AM of Minas de Tlalpuxagua, with a jurisdiction which included neighboring Taximaroa. However, for some years a separate C was appointed to Taimeo, and this magistrate in turn was made AM of the mines of Ozumatlan (a subject of Taimeo) in the 1590s.[6] The inevitable jurisdictional conflict was resolved towards 1600 by abolishing the alcaldía mayor of Ozumatlan, returning Taimeo to the AM of Tlalpuxagua, and transferring Taximaroa to the C of Maravatío. Henceforth Tlalpuxagua was split into two parts by the intrusion of Maravatío, and it was not until 1787–8 that this anomaly ended, when separate subdelegados were appointed by the intendente of Valladolid to reside at Tlalpuxagua and Cinapécuaro.[7]

Church

A Franciscan monastery-parish seems to have been founded at S Pedro y S Pablo Cinapécuaro somewhat after 1538 (Kubler, 1948, II, p. 493. L de T, p. 49). The doctrina was secularized by 1764 (Ajofrín, I, p. 203).

Work on an Augustinian house at S Agustín Ucareo began in the early 1550s (Kubler, 1948, II, p. 521). Sometime between 1743 and 1770 the parish was taken over by a secular priest who lived at Asunción Siricícuaro (León y Gama, p. 98).

S Miguel Taimeo was a secular curacy in the 1570s and later, but by 1639 it had become a visita of neighboring Indaparapeo. In the eighteenth century it belonged to the parish of Cinapécuaro.

There was a secular curate at S Pedro y S Pablo Tlalpuxagua by 1565. The place also had a small Franciscan hospice in the seventeenth and eighteenth centuries.

The abovementioned parishes were in the diocese of Michoacán.

Population and settlements

Towards 1555 there were some 2,900 Indian tributaries in the four cabeceras and their sujetos (slightly more than half were at Ucareo). There seems to have been little subsequent loss until the epidemic of 1576–81, which carried off about half the population. The number of tributaries dropped to 1,260 in the late 1590s, 600 in 1623, 415 in 1657, then rose to 1,158 in 1698. Towards 1743 there were 1,445 Indian families (half of them in Taimeo). Later counts show 1,510 Indian tributaries in 1789, and 2,556 in 1804.[8] Not included in these figures is the non-tributary mining population of Tlalpuxagua and Ozumatlan.

Reports of 1570–1 indicate that there were then thirty houses of miners and merchants at the real de minas of Tlalpuxagua, or *c.* 100 'Spanish' vecinos, plus an undisclosed number of workers, Negro and Indian. In 1649 the mines had forty Spanish vecinos and over 1,000 Indians, Negroes, and mestizos, while the census of *c.* 1743 gives 500 non-Indian families. In 1804 there were 535 mulatto tributaries in the jurisdiction.

Cinapécuaro (Sinapecora, Tzinapequaro, etc.; 1950: Zinapécuaro de Figueroa) and Araro (1950: pueblo) between them had seven subject barrios according to the *Suma* of *c.* 1548, but there were others. Besides the two cabeceras, Coro (Corao, Coraro) and Queréndaro survived as pueblos after the congregations of 1593–1604. Lands from the abandoned settlements were taken to form haciendas, notably the large Jesuit establishment at Queréndaro.

Ucareo (Huquario, etc.; 1950: Ucareo, pueblo) towards 1548 had two sub-cabeceras, Yrechoato (= Yurécuaro?) and Aguandero, with a total of twenty-four barrios; some of these seem to have been far to the east of the main cabecera in the vicinity of Tlalpuxagua, with lands of Maravatío in between. An early congregation may have been carried out by the Augustinians *c.* 1560, and we know of later consolidations in 1593–1604. In addition to Ucareo, seven pueblos existed in the eighteenth century: Curinguato, Geráhuaro, Guaraqueo (abandoned in 1737), Puriacícuaro, Siricícuaro (which became the cabecera de doctrina), Uripitío, and Yurécuaro.

The lands of Taimeo (1950: pueblo) were divided into two parts quite distant from each other, with both Ucareo and Maravatío intervening. Ten estancias are named in 1558, and there were probably others; a number of these were congregated near the mines of Tlalpuxagua in 1593–1601.[9] By 1649 much land had been taken for haciendas in the valleys of Tepetongo and Tepustepec. Eight places in addition to the cabecera (Bocaneo, Pío, Los Remedios, S Francisco de los Reyes, S Lorenzo, Sta María Asunción, Tlacotepec, and Tlalpuxahuilla) survived as Indian pueblos in the eighteenth century. S Agustín Ozumatlan, an Indian estancia as late as 1601, seems to have been absorbed by the small mining camp of that name. Tlalpuxagua (1950: Tlalpujahua, pueblo) had four barrios and a subordinate mining camp (Real de Arriba) in 1789.

Sources

The area is summarily described in the *Suma* of *c.* 1548 (PNE, I, nos. 35, 158, 664, 787), and in two Ovando series reports of 1570–1 (García Pimentel, 1904, pp. 44–5. Miranda Godínez, 1967, 9/35, 9/41). There is an interesting relación from the C of Taimeo dated 1579.[10] Congregation data for 1593–1604 appear in several scattered documents.[11] For the seventeenth century, we have reports dated 1639[12] and 1649,[13] and tributary counts of 1657–98.[14]

A missing report of *c.* 1743 is summarized in Villaseñor y Sánchez (II, pp. 67–9). Later documents include a detailed account by the AM concerning Indian towns and *cofradías* dated 1789,[15] a brief summary of 1793,[16] and a valuable description of *c.* 1821 (Martínez de Lejarza, pp. 42–66).

104 *Tlapa*

Straddling the Sierra Madre del Sur in eastern Guerrero, this is a most rugged country of forested mountains and barren hills with an occasional fertile valley. Drainage is both northward to the Mexcala and south into the Pacific coastal plain. The climate is dry and hot except in the higher parts, elevations ranging from 150 to 3,000 m.

In the north were two rather large kingdoms of Náhuatl-speakers, Cuauhmochititlan and Olinallan, controlled by a Mexican garrison at Quiauhteopan. The latter place, with Ahuacatlan and Cualac, seem to have belonged to the lord of Olinallan, while Cuauhtecomatlan may have been a small state subordinate to Cuauhmochititlan. Tlapan was an Aztec garrison settlement and tribute-collecting center probably ruled by a military governor appointed from Tenochtitlan. Tlanchinollan and Caltitlan, near Tlapan, had a semi-autonomous status; we guess that they had their own rulers, perhaps the original kings of the region who had become subordinate to the Aztecs. Both Mixtecan and Náhuatl were spoken there, and there may well have been a minority of Tlapanecan-speakers, the unruly people who gave the area its name and who had been driven southward by the Triple Alliance armies. In the vicinity were a number of states which may once have been tributary to the kings of Tlapan but at contact had their own rulers: Acocozpan, Acuitlapan, Atlimaxac, Atlixtacan, Chipetlan, Huitzannollan, Ichcateopan, Ihuallan, Malinaltépec, Ocoapan, Petlacallan, Tetenanco, Totomixtlahuacan, and Xocotlan. Some of these kings were Mixtecans, while others were Náhuatl-speakers, such as the tlatoque of Chipetlan and Tetenanco who founded colonies here toward the end of the fifteenth century; Malinaltépec and Totomixtlahuacan were Tlapanecan communities, although they were under Aztec hegemony. Off to the south was the frontier with the unreduced Tlapanecans; Atzoyuc seems to have been a center of Tlapanecan power. The contact situation here should become better known when certain pictorial manuscripts (*see below*) are deciphered and published.

Presumably, the Aztec garrisons submitted to the Spaniards in 1521 or 1522, and Tlapan was controlled by Cortés in 1524; the Tlapanecans, however, rebelled several times between 1523 and 1535. A Spanish settlement at S Luis, near Atzoyuc, maintained a precarious existence in the 1520s.

Encomiendas

Hernando Cortés set aside Tlapa and its dependencies for himself, in view of their wealth in gold and produce.[1] It was seized in 1525 by the acting governors, and it was probably at this time that Francisco de Ribadeo became encomendero (Icaza, I, p. 141). Ribadeo soon died, and Governor Estrada in 1527 split up the encomienda; all that we know of this division is that Bernardino Vázquez de Tapia was assigned a quarter of the tributes (ENE, III, p. 91; IV, p. 19). In 1529 or 1530 the first audiencia gave Vázquez another quarter and granted the remaining half to Alonso de Estrada himself, but these grants were annulled by the second audiencia which took three quarters for the crown, probably in 1532 (Cortés, p. 509. ENE, III, pp. 28–9. Vázquez de Tapia, p. 54). The Estrada half was returned by royal order and was held by the widow, Marina de la Caballería, from 1533 until 1537, when she gave her share to a daughter, Beatriz de Estrada, the wife of Francisco Vázquez de Coronado (CDI, II, p. 194. L de T, p. 511). Doña Beatriz survived her husband and still appears as encomendera in 1597, although for a brief period in the 1560s she renounced her rights in favor of her daughter and son-in-law, Luis Ponce de León. By 1604 the encomienda had been acquired by a great-grandson of Estrada, Francisco Pacheco de Córdoba Bocanegra. Meanwhile, the Vázquez de Tapia quarter was inherited on the death of the conquistador (1559) by a son of the same name who was still alive in 1604, and later by a grandson also called Bernardino Vázquez de Tapia. As late as 1696 Tlapa was still three quarters private encomienda.

Guamuchtitlan was given by Cortés to the same Vázquez de Tapia who later acquired a share of Tlapa, and the encomienda history was repeated (ENE, IV, p. 19).

Olinalá was assigned to a poblador, Alonso de Aguilar, followed in the late 1550s by a son, Baltasar. It escheated *c.* 1567 when the latter was implicated in the 'conspiracy' of the Marqués del Valle.[2]

Government

There are vague references to a Spanish settlement or *villa* called S Luis (at or near present S Luis

Acatlán), founded *c.* 1522 and abandoned during the Yope rebellion of 1530–1 (ENE, II, pp. 31–3. PNE, IV, pp. 263–4). Tlapa became a corregimiento when part of it was taken for the crown *c.* 1532. In the provincial division of the 1550s, Guamuchtitlan and Olinalá were attached to the alcaldía mayor of Minas de Ayoteco (cf. Chiautla), while the AM of Minas de Zumpango (cf. Tistla) assumed the duties of C of Tlapa.[3] For the next few decades, Tlapa and its subjects were administered by a teniente of this magistrate, while distant Azoyú (including S Luis) was temporarily annexed to the province of Xalapa, Cintla y Acatlan (cf. Igualapa). This situation prevailed until 1579, when a separate AM was appointed to Tlapa and Azoyú was returned to his jurisdiction.[4] It was probably in the 1670s that Olinalá and Guamuchtitlan were shifted from Chiautla to Tlapa, and the distant sujeto of Cuitlapa was annexed to Igualapa.[5] This left the small enclave of Totolapa, belonging to Chiautla, surrounded by the alcaldía mayor of Tlapa (see map).

From 1787 Tlapa was a subdelegación, first in the intendencia of Mexico and after 1792 in that of Puebla.[6] Tenientes lived at Olinalá and S Luis de la Costa.

Church

Secular priests resided at Tlapa and S Luis in the early 1530s and probably before.[7] When S Luis was abandoned, the curate moved to Acatlan (then in the neighboring jurisdiction of Igualapa) and continued to visit the Azoyú region. Meanwhile, the Augustinians entered the area and founded doctrinas at Olinalá (1533), Guamuchtitlan (1534), and Tlapa (1535). By 1570 Sta María Guamuchtitlan had been turned over to a secular priest who visited Olinalá. In 1574 Sta Mónica Alcozauca, until then visited from Tlapa, became a separate Augustinian parish.[8]

As a result of the congregations, towards 1605 another priest was appointed to Olinalá and additional Augustinian curates were sent to S Juan Bautista Atlistaca and Totomistlaguaca. Sometime before 1743 the list of parishes was expanded to include S Luis de la Costa (Acatlan), S Miguel Cualac, and Santiago Sochiuehuetlan (all secular), and S Juan Bautista Atlamaxacingo del Monte (Augustinian). Most if not all of the Augustinian doctrinas were secularized before 1777, in which year we find additional parishes at S Miguel Chipetlan, S Lucas Ixcateopan, S Miguel Metlatono, and S Nicolás Soyatlan. Still another parish, Azoyú, is listed in 1791. All were in the diocese of Tlaxcala.

Population and settlements

The native population here was much diminished by mid-sixteenth century, the area being described as 'despoblado' in 1555 (ENE, VIII, pp. 120–1). The *Suma* of *c.* 1548 shows 10,718 tributaries (6,802 at Tlapa, 2,247 at Guamuchtitlan, 1,669 at Olinalá). The total continued to drop, to 8,231 in 1570, 5,500 in 1600, and only 1,600 in 1626 (we question the last figure). Later censuses show 4,180 tributaries in 1696, 8,053 Indian families in 1743, and 7,649 Indian tributaries in 1799.[9] A visitor in 1653 claimed that there were still 1,500 Tlapanecan-speakers in the mountains above Tlapa, despite the Augustinians' attempts to 'extinguish' that language. In 1743 Náhuatl was still predominant in the northern part of the jurisdiction, Mixtecan in the east, and Tlapanecan to the southwest.

We have mentioned the early (1522–31) Spanish settlement at S Luis, perhaps related in some way to Villa Segura de la Frontera (cf. Xicayán). With the exception of a few ephemeral mining camps (El Cairo and Sta Ursula were abandoned early in the seventeenth century) and a fair number of haciendas, there were no other predominantly non-Indian settlements. In 1662 there were 50 or 60 Spanish vecinos at Tlapa.[10] The 1743 census has 19 families of Spaniards and 374 of mestizos, mulattoes, *coyotes* (in eighteenth-century usage the offspring of a mestizo and an Indian woman), and chinos (Filipinos?), while the 1791 padrón lists 859 Spaniards (individuals), 1,284 mestizos, and 1,962 mulattoes.

Many Indian settlements were deserted and consolidated in early years. Seemingly there were two periods of congregation, the first perhaps in the 1550s and 1560s and another in 1598–1605.[11] Tlapa (1950: ciudad) in 1573 had over 130 subject villages, including the sub-cabeceras. According

to the 1548 report, these were divided between the two *partes* of Tlapa (Atlimaxac, Atlistaca, Caltitlan, Cuitlapa, Ichcateupa, Igualan, Petlacala, Totomistlauaca) and Tlachinola (Azuyuc, Chipetlan, Tenango). A good many sites which were to have been abandoned towards 1600 either survived or were later re-occupied, and new sites were chosen for settlements. Of 122 places named in 1571, fifty-eight appear as pueblos in the eighteenth century, together with twenty-six places not mentioned in 1571. By 1791 the following pueblos, once subject to Tlapa, had acquired cabecera status: Alcozauca(n), Atlamaxa(l)cingo del Monte, Atlistaca, Azoyú, Chipetlan, Ixcateopan, Metlatono, S Luis de la Costa, Soyatlan, and Totomistlaguaca. The former sub-cabeceras of Caltitlan and Tlachinola had been absorbed as barrios of Tlapa, while Atlamaxac, Iguala, Petlacala, and Tenango had become simply pueblos sujetos, and Cuitlapa had been transferred to neighboring Igualapa. Tlapa itself became a *villa* by 1777.[12]

Guamuchtitlan (Huamustitlan, etc.; 1950: Huamuxtitlán, ciudad), according to the 1570 report, had sixteen estancias, but still others are named in contemporary documents.[13] Eleven subject settlements survived as pueblos in the eighteenth century, including the parish seat of Sochihuehuetlan (Xuchihuehuetlan).

Olinalá (1950: pueblo) had eighteen estancias in 1570, of which eleven were pueblos in 1743. Among them was the parish center and cabecera of Cualac (Qualaque, Gualac; 1950: Cualac, pueblo).

Sources

The area is described in a fragment of the 1532 'Description de la Tierra' (Herrera, 4a década, p. 231), and each cabecera has an article in the *Suma de Visitas* of *c.* 1548 (PNE, I, nos. 29–30, 82–4, 216–18, 322–3, 437, 471, 485, 725–7). Reports of 1570–1 describe the two parishes in detail,[14] but only Azoyú is covered in a relación of 1582 (PNE, IV, p. 257). We have not seen certain sixteenth-century pictorial manuscripts from this area, said to contain important historical and cartographical details.[15]

Bishop Mota y Escobar went through here in 1610–11 and left a valuable journal.[16] Tributary figures for 1623–96 are from several sources,[17] and the report of an official clerical visit here in 1653 is of special interest.[18]

There is an excellent description submitted by the AM in 1743.[19] For 1777, we have complete census reports from the parishes of Alcozauca, Atlamaxacingo, Atlistaca, Guamuchtitlan, Ixcateopan, Metlatono, Sochihuehuetlan, and Soyatlan,[20] and a most illuminating 'topographic' report by the curate of Chipetlan, describing some early codices.[21] A non-Indian padrón dated 1791 contains a complete list of toponyms.[22]

105 *Tlaxcala*

This cold, bleak country is composed of several broad valleys and plains straddling the continental divide at an elevation of 2,100–2,600 m, with the volcano of La Malinche (Matlalcuéyatl) on the southeast border reaching 4,460 m. Drainage is mostly southward into the Atoyac system, although a small portion flows into the Tecolutla (Gulf) and the eastern part belongs to the Llanos de S Juan, an interior drainage basin. Rainfall is seasonal and moderate. Severe erosion has removed most of the soil and natural vegetation. The area occupies nearly all the modern state of Tlaxcala except the westernmost part.

At contact, Tlaxcallan was densely populated with a Náhuatl-speaking majority dominating a sizeable minority of Otomies and a smaller group speaking 'Pinome' (=Popolocan?). The territory was divided among a number of autonomous states, most if not all of which were loosely united in a military federation hostile to the Triple Alliance. The lord of Ocotelulco occupied a special position as military leader on the Spaniards' arrival, while both he and the lord of Tizatlan seem to have exercised a sort of political hegemony over the tlatoque of surrounding states, but this may have been a transitory situation. Atlihuetzian, Quiahuixtlan, Tecoac, Tepetícpac, Topoyanco, and Tzompantzinco were each ruled separately, as were other places, perhaps as many as sixty political entities altogether (Gibson, 1952, pp. 9, 11, 13. Herrera, 2a década, p. 360). Chiauhtempan was an important religious center.

Cortés and his army, on their march inland, entered Tlaxcallan at the beginning of September 1519, reaching Ocotelulco on the 23rd of that month. After several skirmishes, the native military leaders headed by Maxixcatzin, lord of Ocotelulco, joined the Spaniards to oppose the Mexica early in October. The alliance survived the disastrous retreat from Tenochtitlan in July of the following year, when the Spaniards were given refuge in Tlaxcallan and used it as a base for future military activity.

Government

Because of their loyalty in the Conquest, the Tlaxcalans for years enjoyed a special status and were not given in private encomienda, being considered wards of the king of Spain. Crown rule was informally exercised until 1531, when a C was appointed to Tlaxcala and Cholula. This magistrate lived at the recently founded city of Puebla (q.v.), but in 1545 a separate C began to reside at Tlaxcala. From 1555 he was re-designated AM and supervised the suffragan Cs of Cholula, Guatinchan, and Huexocingo (this relationship came to an end in the 1570s). In 1587 the AM's title was changed to gobernador; while this magistrate continued to report to the viceroy, appointment was controlled by the crown from 1609.[1]

A teniente de gobernador was stationed at Guamantla in the late sixteenth century.[2] Two hundred years later, six places had tenientes: Apizaco, Chiautempan, Guamantla, Ixtacuixtla, Natívitas, and Tlaxco. From 1787 to 1793 Tlaxcala was included in the intendencia of Puebla, after which it formed a separate military government directly under the viceroy.[3]

Alongside the Spanish government was that of

324

the Indians, headed by a gobernador at first elected and later appointed by the viceroy. Details of the native political structure are discussed by Gibson (1952, chapter IV).

The boundaries of this jurisdiction were more or less finally determined in the late 1550s, with the

annexation of various buffer zones and lands disputed with surrounding communities.

Church

A Franciscan monastery-doctrina was established in 1524 in the palace of Maxixcatzin at Ocotelulco. It was moved to the barrio of S Francisco Cuitlixco in 1527–8, and to the new city of Asunción Tlaxcala towards 1539 (Gibson, 1952, pp. 43–5. Kubler, 1948, II, pp. 481–2). The diocese of Tlaxcala had its seat here from the arrival of the first bishop in 1527 until that prelate began to reside in Puebla (by 1539), the move receiving royal sanction in 1543.

By 1540 the Franciscans had fifty or sixty visitas in the province (Gibson, 1952, p. 42). Towards 1554 separate regular doctrinas were founded at Sta María (Concepción) Atlihuecian, and S Francisco Topoyanco, and fifteen years later there were additional Franciscan parishes at Sta Ana Chiautempan, S Luis Guamantla, S Ildefonso Hueyotlipan, and S Felipe Cuixtlan (Ixtacuixtla). A

monastery was established at S Juan Totolac, a suburb of Tlaxcala, in 1575, but it did not endure as a parish. Sta María Natívitas parish may date from 1570, and S Juan Bautista Atlangatepec from 1573–80. The last Franciscan parochial foundation was that of Sta María Texcalac, towards 1600.

In 1640 the ten Franciscan parishes mentioned were secularized by Bishop Palafox, although a few monasteries were allowed to continue as cloisters (*Alegaciones...*, fol. 90v). At this time Palafox's priests assumed parochial duties, the curate of Atlangatepec moved to S Agustín Tlaxco, and a new parish was created in a visita of Topoyanco, Sta Inés Zacatelco.

By 1777 there were additional secular doctrinas at S Lorenzo Cuapiastla, S Juan Bautista Ixtenco, S Pablo del Monte, Sta Cruz Tlaxcala, and S Salvador Zompaxtepec. Six others may have existed at this time, and are listed in 1791: S Pablo Apetatitlan, S Pablo Citlaltepec, S Nicolás Panotla, S Luis Teolocholco, Sta Isabel Tetlatlauca, and S Andrés Xaltocan. Meanwhile, the parish centers of Texcalac and Atlihuecian had moved to Santiago Tetla (later, to S Luis Apizaco) and S Dionisio Yauquemecan, respectively. All were in the diocese of Tlaxcala with its see at Puebla.

Population and settlements

The native tributaries of Tlaxcala, which is said to have had 120,000 vecinos in 1519, dropped in number to perhaps 60,000 in 1538, 50,000 in 1563, 40,000 in 1569, 24,000 in 1583, 16,000 in 1593, and 8,954 in 1626. Recovery was slow, to 10,972 tributaries in 1696 and 11,000 in 1743; later censuses show 51,471 Indians (individuals) in 1777, and 62,173 in 1810. Some fluctuation was caused by migration to and from the province (thus heavy loss in the epidemic of 1545–8 was partly compensated by the arrival of many Indians from other jurisdictions). Especially severe were the plagues of 1576–81 and 1587–8 in which 60 per cent of the Indians died (Scholes and Adams, 1961, p. 164).

In the sixteenth and seventeenth centuries Náhuatl was predominant in the center and Otomí on the borders, especially near Guamantla,

Atlangatepec, Hueyotlipan, and Ixtacuixtla. The Pinome-speakers soon disappeared.

The number of Spanish vecinos increased from 50 in 1570 to 700 in 1662, the greatest concentrations being at the city of Tlaxcala and Guamantla. By the late eighteenth century the mixed population formed a quarter of the total. The figures for 1777 are (individuals): 8,235 Spaniards, 9,405 mestizos, and 1,535 mulattoes and Negroes (excluding slaves). Many of the non-Indians lived on haciendas and wheat farms (there were 243 in 1791), and others owned and administered textile factories (*obrajes*).

The Spaniards found the Indians here, as elsewhere on the central plateau, dispersed in numerous settlements grouped politically in a number of native states. We may guess that there were in 1519 two hundred such settlements and forty or fifty *señoríos*, each of the latter with a politico-religious center. Whereas elsewhere in New Spain each of these centers was considered by the Spaniards a cabecera, and each native state was assigned in encomienda to an individual Spaniard, this did not occur in Tlaxcala where the entire area from the beginning was treated as a unit under the protection of the crown. There may have been some primitive allotment by local cabecera in the collection of the royal tribute during the first years after the Conquest, but we have no record of this, and in later years a fixed amount was assigned to the whole 'province' of Tlaxcala, supposedly a reduced figure in recognition of the Tlaxcalans' services and loyalty during the Conquest. For purposes of Spanish administration and Indian government, towards 1540 the region was apportioned among four main cabeceras, Ocotelulco, Tizatlan, Quiahuixtlan, and Tepetícpac, all within a short distance just north of the city of Tlaxcala. The southern quadrant was assigned to Ocotelulco, the east to Tizatlan, the north to Tepetícpac, and the west to Quiahuixtlan. It is not clear whether this division had its roots in the political supremacy of these places before the Conquest or whether it was a conception introduced by the Spaniards (Gibson inclines to the latter view).

The new ciudad of Tlaxcala (1950: Tlaxcala de Xicoténcatl, ciudad) began to be built *c.* 1536 just south of the four cabeceras (Gibson, 1952, p. 125). Other settlements were formed and sites were changed at the instigation of religious and political authorities in the sixteenth century and later, but we have few details. The general plan to congregate the Indians in fewer centers, perhaps first proposed here in 1560 and again in 1598, met with vigorous and seemingly effective opposition.[4] Of 129 pueblos which existed in 1570, 112 either survived or had been founded anew by 1697. In 1791 there were still 111 Indian pueblos in the jurisdiction.

Late in the colonial period the four Indian cabeceras, in effect suburbs or barrios of the city of Tlaxcala, were still recognized as such, but the political division of the province had been redrawn in seven *tenientazgos* or *cuarteles* with their centers at Tlaxcala itself and the six pueblos (Apizaco, Chiautempan, Guamantla, Ixtacuixtla, Natívitas, Tlaxco) where tenientes of the governor resided.

Sources

Because of the prominent role Tlaxcala played in the Conquest, there is unusually good documentation for the contact period, synthesized in the work of Gibson (1952). The omission of this area in the Suma de Visitas is in part compensated by an incomplete and as yet unpublished census of 1556–7.[5] There are two brief documents in the Ovando series of *c.* 1570 (*Códice Franciscano*, pp. 20–2. López de Velasco, pp. 208–23). The Franciscan Ponce (I, pp. 17–19, 69–70, 114–21, 128–35, 146–50, 163–8, 205–8) describes the region as it was in 1584–7.

The journals of two bishops who each visited Tlaxcala several times (1610, 1614, 1622;[6] 1644, 1646)[7] are of considerable interest. Tributary data for 1626–96[8] are followed by a report on the secularized parishes listing visitas, published in 1697 but probably compiled somewhat earlier (Vetancurt, 4a parte, pp. 52–4, 69, 75, 80–1, 83–4, 86, 87).

For the eighteenth century, we have first a much abbreviated description of *c.* 1743 (Villaseñor y Sánchez, I, pp. 306–10); another, with a crude map of the city as it was in 1766 (Ajofrín, II, pp. 139–45); and census reports submitted in 1777 by the curates of Cuapiastla, Ixtenco, S Pablo del Monte, Sta Cruz Tlaxcala, Tetla, Yauquemecan, and Zompaxtepec.[9] There are padrones with lists of toponyms dated 1778 and 1791,[10] the latter accompanied by an interesting descriptive commentary. We have seen another list of placenames, dated 1792.[11]

Many additional documents are cited in Gibson's work (1952), which has an exhaustive bibliography on sixteenth-century Tlaxcala. The standard early history is that of Muñoz Camargo. A Náhuatl MS of the seventeenth century, when it is translated and published, should add much to our knowledge.[12] Recent monographs include Anaya Monroy (1965) and González Sánchez (1969).

106 *Tlazazalca*

Today in northwestern Michoacán, this region descends from the summit (3,000 m) of the Sierra Volcánica Transversal northward to the Lerma river (1,530 m), although it contains a basin of interior drainage. The climate is generally cool and dry.

Cirapo (Chilchota) and Uralca (Tlazazalca) were probably both Tarascan outposts on the Chichimec frontier. The area to the north seems to have been a meeting place of several tribes, Guamares, Guachichiles, and perhaps Tecuexes. The lord of Cirapo was subject to the cazonci and supplied warriors in the campaigns to extend Tarascan hegemony in the west; that of Uralca probably had the same function. The population was scattered in numerous settlements.

This area may have been visited by part of the Olid expedition in 1522 and was certainly under Spanish control by 1524, at least in the south. A subsequent rebellion at Chilchota in which several Spaniards were killed was put down with harshness. Chichimec raids were still occurring in the mid-1570s.[1]

Encomiendas

In the spring of 1528, Chilchota was in encomienda to Juan de Sámano and Tlazazalca to Antón de Arriaga, both residents of Michoacán in 1533. Tlazazalca became a crown possession after Arriaga's death in October 1534. Chilchota escheated sometime between 1536 and 1542.[2]

Government

Chilchota and Tlazazalca were governed by separate Cs for many years. They were suffragan to the AM of Michoacán in the 1560s, and to the AM of Zamora from 1574 to 1588.[3] In the seventeenth century both magistrates were re-designated AM, and by 1713 the two jurisdictions were joined under a single AM living at La Piedad.[4] Tributes were often collected by the AM of Zamora y Xacona in the seventeenth and eighteenth centuries. From 1787 Tlazazalca y Chilchota were a subdelegación in the intendencia of Valladolid.

Church

Vasco de Quiroga, who died in 1565, is said to have founded secular parishes at both Sta María Chilchota and Tlazazalca, which may well be the case, although the Augustinians were granted a license to build monasteries in both towns as early as January 1553.[5] The report of 1639 mentions an Augustinian 'priorato y doctrina' at S Francisco Acachuen Ichan, actually two separate subjects of Chilchota. In any event, both Chilchota and Tlazazalca were ministered by secular priests in 1570 and later.

S Sebastián (Nuestra Señora) de la Piedad was detached from Tlazazalca and made a separate secular parish in 1707 (Romero, p. 49). The three parishes belonged to the diocese of Michoacán.

Population and settlements

In 1561, after much early loss from epidemic disease, Chilchota had 800 tributaries, while in 1565 Tlazazalca had 857 (including 220 Chichimecs) (L de T, p. 363. Cf. Powell, p. 87). Tarascan was the predominant language throughout in

1571, although some spoke 'Mexicano' at Tlazazalca. Towards 1570 the number of tributaries is recorded as 849 (593 at Chilchota, 256 at Tlazazalca). Later counts show 547 tributaries in 1600, 350 in 1649, 292 in 1657, 498 in 1698, 875 Indian families in 1743, and 2,040 Indian tributaries in 1802.[6] The Chichimecs of Tlazazalca practically disappeared in the seventeenth century.

Numerous Spanish cattle haciendas and farms (twenty in 1649; twenty-two haciendas and twenty-five 'puestos' in 1743), especially in the north along the Lerma, attracted a large mixed population. There were over 1,600 non-Indian families in the jurisdiction in 1743, mostly in the La Piedad region. In 1802 901 free Negro and mulatto tributaries are recorded.

The 1579 relación of Chilchota (1950: pueblo) says that originally the Indians were dispersed in groups of three or four houses each and that they had been reduced to sixteen pueblos. Further efforts at congregation were made in 1594 and 1603. Ten places formerly subject to Chilchota survived as pueblos in the eighteenth century.

Tlazazalca (1950: pueblo), which probably also had an early congregation, had twelve Indian sujetos in 1570. Some of these survived another reduction in 1592–1602. In the late eighteenth century there were seven pueblos here, one of which, Ayaramutaro (Aramutaro, Amutarillo), had become the cabecera of Nuestra Señora de la Piedad (1950: La Piedad Cabadas, ciudad).

Sources

Brief articles describing both cabeceras towards 1548 (PNE, I, nos. 159, 666) are followed by equally succinct reports of 1570–1 (García Pimentel, 1904, pp. 43–4. Miranda Godínez, 9/35–6), and a most interesting relación geográfica from the C of Chilchota dated 1579.[7] Congregation data for 1592–1603 are found in several documents.[8]

The area is described in two general reports of Michoacán dated 1639[9] and 1649.[10] A 1743 relación by the AM includes a complete padrón.[11] The parishes of La Piedad and Tlazazalca are covered in an Inquisition report of 1754.[12] Finally, there is a list of towns with population data for 1793,[13] and a valuable description of c. 1821 (Martínez de Lejarza, pp. 235–54).

107 *Tochimilco*

Tochimilco is on the southern slope of Popocatépetl in the present-day state of Puebla. The pre-Columbian state, the colonial jurisdiction, and the modern municipality seem to be conterminous, stretching from the peak of the volcano (5,450 m) to less than 2,000 m, with the expected variation in precipitation and temperature (the inhabited part is cool with moderate rains).

Perhaps originally called Ocopetlayocan or Acapetlayocan, this was an outpost of Xochimilca governed by two related tlatoque subordinate to the Triple Alliance and on bad terms with neighboring Calpan and Huexotzinco. Náhuatl was the language.

The rulers of Ocopetlayocan, after being visited by Pedro de Alvarado and Bernardino Vázquez de Tapia in September, 1519, submitted to the Spaniards. One of the tlatoque later rebelled, but the other sent envoys to Cortés in the fall of 1520 promising allegiance (Cortés, p. 109. Vázquez de Tapia, p. 36).

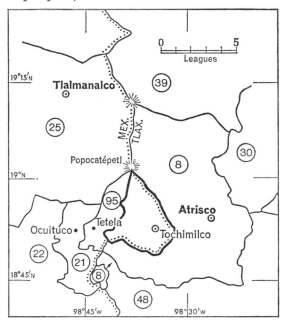

Encomienda

Cristóbal Pacheco seems to have been encomendero here until his death *c.* 1525. Two years later the holder was Gonzalo Rodríguez de Ocaño, a servant of Cortés. Escheatment occurred when Rodríguez died without issue, in February 1546.[1]

Government

Ocopetlayuca was a corregimiento from 1546, suffragan to Chalco in the 1560s and occasionally dependent on neighboring jurisdictions (Atrisco, Cuautla Amilpas) for tribute collection, but surviving as an alcaldía mayor in the eighteenth century.[2] In later years the jurisdiction was more often referred to as Tochimilco. From 1786 it was a subdelegación in the intendencia of Puebla.

Church

First visited by Augustinians from Ocuituco, Sta María Asunción Ocopetlayuca (later, Tochimilco) became a Franciscan parish with the construction of a monastery there in 1552.[3] It is not clear whether the original monastery or a later structure was built at the present site of Tochimilco (*see below*). The parish and the corregimiento had the same boundaries with two exceptions. Texupa, in the jurisdiction of Atrisco, was for some years visited from Tochimilco before being transferred to the doctrina of Guaquechula. Alpanocan and Cuautomatitla, visitas of the Dominicans at Hueyapan (cf. Tetela del Volcán), belonged politically to Tochimilco. Secularized in 1767, the parish of Tochimilco belonged to the archdiocese of Mexico.

Population and settlements

In 1570 there were perhaps 3,000 Indian tributaries here. Over a thousand died in the epidemic of 1576–81, later counts showing 1,206 tributaries in 1588, 474 in 1623, 342 in 1643, 554 in 1688, 891 in 1743, 1,030 in 1755, 1,672 Indian families in 1789, and 1,215 Indian tributaries in 1801. Non-Indians comprised $16\frac{1}{2}$ per cent of the total population in 1789; there were $48\frac{1}{2}$ mulatto tributaries in 1801.[4]

The cabecera is variously referred to as Ocopetlayuca(n) and Tochimilco (Tuchimilco).[5] Perhaps the original site was not approved of by the Franciscans, and one of the estancias (1950: Tochimilco, pueblo) was chosen for the monastery. At any rate, Santiago Tochimilco appears as an estancia subject to Asunción Ocopetlayuca in 1570–80. There was probably a congregation of outlying estancias in the 1550s. Nine estancias are named in 1570–80, and if any were eliminated in the proposed congregation of 1598–1604 they seem to have been replaced by others or reappeared in the same or new sites.[6] In the late eighteenth century the jurisdiction had nine pueblos (five of them cabeceras), two haciendas, and three ranchos.

Sources

There are two descriptions of the monastery-parish in 1569–71,[7] and a good relación sent in by the C in 1580 (PNE, VI, pp. 251–62). The Franciscan Ponce (I, pp. 156–9; 509–10) went through here in 1585. Population data for 1588–1688 are derived from several sources,[8] and there is a valuable description of *c.* 1697 (Vetancurt, 4a parte, pp. 65–6). For the eighteenth century, we have a report compiled by the AM in 1743,[9] another drawn up for the Inquisition in 1755,[10] an accounting of community property in 1770,[11] and two relaciones topográficas dated 1789.[12] In addition, there is a non-Indian padrón of 1791 accompanied by a good map,[13] and a list of placenames dated 1792.[14]

108 *Toluca*

This cold, dry country begins at the Nevado de Toluca or Chiuhnautzin (also called Xinantécatl) at 4,560 m and drops off in a northeasterly direction to the Lerma river at 2,500 m. It was inhabited at contact by people speaking four languages. Perhaps the Mazahuans and Otomies had been there longest, followed by the Matlatzincans, all linguistically related. Náhuatl-speaking immigrants were brought in by Axayácatl, the Mexica ruler who conquered the Matlatzincans, until then the dominant group, in 1474. The surviving Matlatzincans paid tribute and aided the Triple Alliance in its wars with the Tarascans to the west. Calixtlahuacan, with an Aztec garrison, was the religious and political center, while the province seems to have been called Tolocan. The population was dispersed in many small settlements.

Most likely visited by Spaniards in late 1519, the area was subdued in the summer of 1521 when Sandoval and a large army of Otomies overcame the Mexican garrison in a bloody engagement (Cortés, pp. 174–5).

Encomienda

Hernando Cortés assigned to himself the valley of Matalcingo, as this area was long called, using it as a cattle raising center (CDI, XII, p. 279. Cortés, p. 471). According to the Aztec tribute records, the province extended beyond the headwaters of the Lerma to Zoquitzingo and included all the land west of the river to the borders of Michoacán; all this was claimed by Cortés, although a great many autonomous states were involved. The encomienda was seized by the acting governors during Cortés's first absence (1524–6) but was recovered by him on his return.[1] In November,

1528, after Cortés had gone to Spain, Alonso de Estrada assigned Calimaya, Metepec, and Tepemachalco to another encomendero (cf. Metepec), and in the following year Nuño de Guzmán took the whole valley for himself and his friends; Toluca was given at this time to García del Pilar.[2]

Cortés returned at the beginning of 1531 with his grant of the Marquesado, in which Matalcingo, Toluca, and Calimaya were all named. However, the second audiencia retained most of this area for the crown, leaving only the *villa* of Toluca with a few immediate sujetos within the Marquesado. A long process of litigation ensued, but Cortés was unable to recover the places claimed by him (Calimaya, Cinacantepec, Metepec, Tepemachalco, Tlacotepec, Tlalchichilpa).[3] The second marquis renewed the suit in 1563 without success (cf. Charo), and the jurisdiction of Toluca was further reduced when S Mateo Atengo was taken for the crown in 1575. Fifteen years later the royal prosecutor sought to have Toluca's limits confined to a league or so around the *villa*, but on this occasion the matter was resolved in favor of the Marquesado.[4]

Government

Except during the various periods of sequestration, magistrates here were controlled by the Marqués del Valle. In the provincial division of the 1550s the whole valley of Matalcingo seems to have been assigned to the AM of Toluca.[5] An appointee of the viceroy governed Toluca y Valle de Matalcingo in 1570–83, to be replaced by a C sent out from Spain who ruled the area until civil jurisdiction of Toluca alone was returned to the third marquis towards 1595.[6] The corregimiento was attached informally to the intendencia of Mexico from 1787.

Church

Asunción (later, S. José) Toluca was a Franciscan parish, founded perhaps in the late 1520s and not

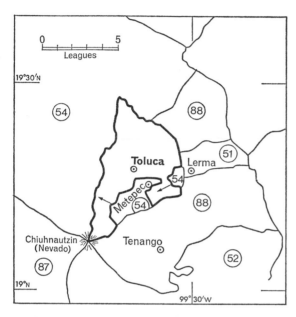

secularized until 1859 (McAndrew, p. 33. Salinas, pp. 6, 31).

Population and settlements

A parochial census of 1569 shows 5,207 tributaries, but some of these may have been outside the final political jurisdiction of Toluca. There was great loss in the epidemic of 1576–81. Later tributary figures are 2,208 in 1597, 1,491 in 1636, 2,368 in 1684, 2,200 in 1743, 3,806 in 1785, and 4,599 in 1800 (García Martínez, pp. 166–7).[7]

A number of Spaniards, cattle-raisers and others, began to move to the *villa* of Toluca c. 1550 (ENE, VI, p. 141). By 1585 there was a large non-Indian community there (Ponce, I, pp. 31–2). There were said to be 1,300 families of Spaniards, mestizos, and mulattoes in 1697, but the 1743 report shows only 618. According to a padrón of 1791, over half were considered Spaniards, a very few were mulattoes, and the rest mestizos.

There was probably an early congregation here carried out by the Franciscans. However, there were still thirty-two subject estancias in 1580–90, eleven of which seem to have disappeared in the congregation of 1598–1604. Twenty settlements in addition to the *villa* survived as pueblos, and all of them had acquired cabecera status in the late eighteenth century. The villa of Toluca (1950: Toluca de Lerdo, ciudad, Mex.) became a ciudad c. 1675. There were thirty-seven haciendas and ranchos in the jurisdiction in 1697, and seventy-three in 1791.[8]

Sources

Zorita (pp. 263–70) makes some interesting comments on the pre-Conquest tribute and political situation here. A brief article in the *Suma* of c. 1548 (PNE, I, no. 561) is followed by a detailed report of 1569,[9] and lists of estancias in 1580–1.[10] Father Ponce (I, pp. 31–2, 56) describes Toluca as he saw it in 1585.

For the seventeenth century, we have records of tributaries in 1643–88,[11] and of two archbishops' visits in 1646[12] and 1685.[13] Vetancurt (4a parte, pp. 61–2, 89) gives details of the parish as it was c. 1697.

There is a lengthy deposition concerning Toluca in 1743,[14] followed by a report dated 1754,[15] and a non-Indian census of 1791.[16]

Monographic treatment with further citation includes García Martínez (1969), Romero Quiroz (1963), and Salinas (1965). Many documents at AGN are listed in Colín (1966, 1967).

109 *Tula*

At the headwaters of the northward-flowing Tula river (an affluent of the Pánuco), this is a broad valley surrounded by low, barren mountains. Elevations are 1,950–2,600 m, and the climate is cold and dry. The region is now in southern Hidalgo.

The ancient Toltec center of Tollan, destroyed and abandoned after a Chichimec invasion in A.D. 1156, was inhabited by an Otomí-speaking people in 1519. At contact, Tollan's hegemony may have extended to nearby Atenco, Mizquiahuallan, and Tzayulan, together with Acocolco and Huapalcalco, most likely all autonomous states with related dynasties. These communities, as well as Otlazpan (the latter belonging to the Tepanec lord of Cuauhtitlan), delivered their tribute to Triple Alliance collectors at Atotonilco; Otomí was the chief language in them all. Tepexic and Xipacoyan, Náhuatl-speaking states, each had its own tlatoani. Farther north were four more Otomí communities, Michmaloyan, Nextlalpan, Tepetitlan, and Xochitlan, which sent tribute to Xilotépec.

The area, first visited by Spaniards late in 1519, came under their control in 1521.

Encomiendas

Tula and its dependencies, while they probably had earlier encomenderos, were held in the late 1530s by the royal accountant, Rodrigo de Albornoz (Gibson, 1964, p. 590. L de T, p. 535). This grant escheated under the New Laws in 1544, but tributes from certain estancias were assigned twenty years later to Pedro Moctezuma, son of the emperor (L de T, pp. 537–8. Scholes and Adams, 1961, p. 133). In the seventeenth century the estancias of Tepeitic and Tultengo were still held in private encomienda by the descendants of D. Pedro.

Michimaloya was given to the conquistador Juan de Zamudio. When he died in the 1540s Zamudio was succeeded by his widow, who then married Alonso Velázquez. The latter was followed by his widow, Isabel de Olmos, in the 1570s. Escheatment occurred between 1597 and 1643 (Dorantes de Carranza, p. 204. Icaza, II, p. 12).

Nextlalpa in early years was shared between two conquistadors, Pedro Moreno Cendejas and Juan (Sánchez) Galindo. Moreno was followed c. 1565 by a son of the same name; in 1597 a Sebastián Moreno was encomendero. The half belonging to Galindo, who died before 1550, was inherited by a daughter married to Pedro Valdovinos; in 1597–1604 the holder was Luis de Valdovinos, grandson of Galindo. Part of the tributes were still privately held in 1688.

Another conquistador, Bartolomé Gómez, held Tepetitlan until his death in the 1560s. He was succeeded by a daughter married to Juan (Diego) de Azpeitia. By 1597 the heir of Azpeitia had inherited, perhaps the Juan Jiménez de Riancho listed as encomendero in 1623 (Scholes and Adams, 1959, p. 51). Escheatment occurred before 1643.

Both Tepexi and Otlazpa were assigned by Cortés to Sebastián de Moscoso, followed in 1551 by a son, Juan.[1] Another Sebastián de Moscoso is listed in 1593–7.[2] The encomiendas escheated between 1643 and 1688.

The conquistador who held Xipacoya, Lorenzo Payo, gave his rights in dowry to a daughter, Isabel, who in the 1540s was married to Juan de Jaso the younger; the latter had been succeeded by his widow in 1597 (Dorantes de Carranza, p. 214. Icaza, I, p. 197; II, p. 21). Half of Xipacoya was still in private encomienda as late as 1688.

Suchitlan may have been first held by Rodrigo de Salvatierra, but in the 1540s the conquistador Andrés Rozas was considered the original holder. Rozas was succeeded c. 1565 by a son of the same name, still alive in 1604 (Dorantes de Carranza, p. 160. Icaza, I, p. 93).

Government

Tula was a corregimiento from its escheatment in 1544. Eight years later the C's jurisdiction extended to Tepexi–Otlazpa and probably other nearby encomiendas, although in 1555 the C of

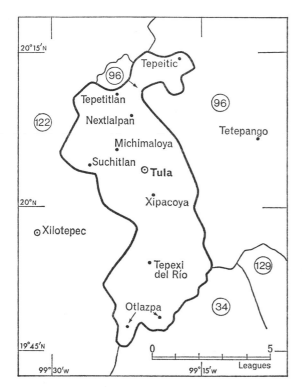

Sayula was given temporary charge of Otlazpa, Tepexi, and Suchitlan.[3] Towards 1560 the magistrate of Tula was subordinate to the AM of Minas de Tornacustla, but by 1563 Tula itself had become an alcaldía mayor with suffragan jurisdiction in Tlagualilpa and Sayula (both later absorbed by Tetepango Hueypustla).[4] After 1707 the dukes of Atlixco had the privilege of appointing the AM of Tula, who was in a sense subordinate to the intendente of Mexico from 1787.

Church

In 1529 Franciscans founded the parish of S José Tula, subsequently split into three doctrinas, Tula, S Francisco Tepexi del Río (1552–8), and

S Bartolomé Tepetitlan (1571) (Kubler, 1948, II, pp. 476, 484. McAndrew, p. 469). A number of villages in Tetepango Hueypustla (q.v.) were visited from the monasteries of Tula and Tepetitlan; others belonging politically to Xilotepec were visited from Tepexi, while the estancia of Tepeitic belonged to the parish of Mizquiaguala. Secularization began at Tepetitlan (1754) and extended to Tula (1763) and Tepexi (1768). The area fell within the archdiocese of Mexico.

Population and settlements

The number of Indian tributaries, after much early loss, was c. 11,000 in 1570. Great toll was taken in the 1576–81, 1604–7, and later epidemics, reducing the total to 3,485 tributaries in 1600 and only 706 in 1643. Later counts show 1,368 tributaries in 1688, 1,266 families in 1743, and 2,134 Indian tributaries in 1801.[5]

Spaniards, beginning in the sixteenth century, acquired the vacated Indian lands for their haciendas. The padrón of c. 1790 has 2,003 Spaniards (individuals), 1,843 mestizos, and 227 pardos.

S Juan Bautista Michimaloya (Michmaloyan; 1950: Michimaloya, pueblo) had four visitas in 1570. These were to have been congregated at their cabecera c. 1600.[6] Two pueblos mentioned in 1794, S Miguel Texaquique and Sta María del Pino (Tehcli), were perhaps old estancias.

S Pedro Nextlalpan (Nestalpa; Otomí, Quiquihu; 1950: S Pedro Nextlalpan, pueblo) had two unnamed visitas in 1570. One of these was probably Natividad Atenco (Otomí, Dexó), which became Sta María Tlachinoltepec by 1794 (1950: Sta María Daxthó). The other may have survived in the 1794 pueblo of S Mateo Ixtlahuaca L de T, pp. 267–70).

Otlazpa (Utlaspa, Vtlaxpan, etc.; 1950: S José Piedra Gorda, pueblo?), where both Otomí and Náhuatl were spoken, had four subjects in 1570; their unglossed glyphs appear in the *Códice de Otlazpan*. A document of 1552 mentions a dispute between Otlazpa and Guautitlan concerning the estancia of Tetitlan.[7] The natives here were congregated in the late 1550s when a monastery was placed at the limits of Otlazpa and Tepexi, and again in 1594, but each time the old sites were re-occupied.[8] Three pueblos with the cognomen Otlaxpa (S Buenaventura, S Francisco, S José) existed in 1794, as well as two ranchos called S Bernardino and S Miguel Otlaxpa.

Sta María (Asunción) Suchitlan (Xochitlan, Asuchitlan; Otomí, Nic; 1950: Xochitlán, pueblo) had five visitas in 1570. The 1794 pueblo of S Andrés was perhaps an old estancia.[9]

S Bartolomé Tepetitlan (Otomí, Madietezc; 1950: Tepetitlán, pueblo) was divided into ten barrios, quite close together, in 1548; three of these, all within the cabecera, existed in 1697.

The original cabecera of Tepexi (Tepexe, Tepexic) was probably some two kilometers northwest of the site chosen in the 1550s for the monastery of S Francisco del Río (1950: Tepeji del Río, pueblo), actually on the boundary between Tepexi and Otlazpa. The Christian names of ten visitas within 1½ leagues of the cabecera appear in the 1570 report, but we do not know that all of these belonged politically to Tepexi. Two further attempts at congregation were made here, in 1594 and 1598–9, while a document of 1608 states that many Indians had returned to their old homesites.[10] One sixteenth-century estancia, Nochistongo, ended up in the jurisdiction of Guautitlan.[11] Three places which survived as pueblos in 1794 may have belonged to Tepexi: S Ignacio Nopala, S Ildefonso, and Santiago Zacualoya.

The cabecera of S José Tula (Tollan; 1950: Tula de Allende, *villa*) was originally on the east side of the Tula river at or near the site of the ruined Toltec capital on a hilltop. When a more permanent monastery was to be built, perhaps in the 1540s, a site on the west bank of the river was chosen, although the town plaza in 1603 was still on the east bank below the barrio of Tultengo. Tula had twelve outlying estancias in 1548, and the same number are mentioned and located in the 1603 congregation report, half of them tributary to D. Diego Luis de Moctezuma and half to the crown. Some were close to the cabecera, while the most distant, Los Reyes Tepeitic, was four leagues north. Those which existed in 1603

may have occupied somewhat different sites than earlier, as there were two attempts at congregation, *c.* 1550 and in 1593–4.[12] In the late eighteenth century, four of the old estancias survived as pueblos: Sta Ana Ahuehuepan, Sta María Natívitas Ilucan, Reyes Tepeitic, and Santiago Tultengo.

A kind of dispersal, as opposed to congregation, seems to have occurred at Xipacoya. Only two estancias are mentioned in 1548. Later in the sixteenth century there were twin cabeceras here, S Lorenzo Xipacoya (1697: Quapachtli, Manzindo; 1950: S Lorenzo, pueblo) and S Marcos Tlaliztacapa (1697: Iztlatlali, Tazai; 1794: S Marcos Xipacoya; 1950: S Marcos, pueblo). A congregation padrón of 1603 mentions three estancias under Tlaliztacapa, Cuaxochpan, S Miguel Ilucan, and Teacalco (S Lucas), which can perhaps be equated with the eighteenth-century pueblos of Guaxuspa, Noxtitlan (Vindhó), and S Lucas (Huantela). The 1794 pueblo of S Pedro Alpuyeca may also be a former estancia.[13]

In 1794 the jurisdiction had a total of twenty-eight pueblos (nine cabeceras), twelve haciendas, five barrios, and fourteen ranchos.

Sources

A document of 1541 is concerned with land disputes at Tula.[14] The *Códice de Otlazpan* (1549) has been published in a handsome edition with scholarly apparatus (Leander, 1967). Each cabecera is summarily described in the *Suma de Visitas* of about the same date (PNE, 1, nos. 397, 417, 498, 538, 560, 771, 781, 838). There are several reports of 1569–71, only partly published.[15] An interesting document concerning Otlazpa in 1580 is accompanied by a map.[16] Ponce (1, pp. 224–7) left a brief account of Tula as he found it in 1586.

For the period of congregations in the 1590s and early 1600s, in addition to scattered references, two valuable documents have appeared: a report on the Moctezuma estancias at Tula (with a good map)[17] and a padrón of Tlaliztacapa and its dependencies.[18] We have tributary data for 1623–88,[19] and a description of the Franciscan doctrinas of *c.* 1697 (Vetancurt, 4a parte, pp. 64–5, 69, 86).

A missing relación of *c.* 1743 is condensed in Villaseñor y Sánchez (I, pp. 86–9). Late eighteenth-century material includes a non-Indian padrón (with a good map) of *c.* 1791,[20] and a list of toponyms dated 1794.[21]

A few details are found in the work of Fernández (1940–2).

110 *Tulancingo*

This large territory, now in southeast Hidalgo, has a most varied topography and climate, extending from the north rim of the Apan basin and the lofty (3,000 m) range above Acatlán to the hot country of Tutotepec and beyond (200 m). Drainage is in a northerly direction into the Pánuco and Tuxpan systems. Rainfall is minimal south of Tulancingo, moderate towards Atotonilco, and torrential in the Tutotepec area.

Tototépec was an independent region, perhaps allied with Metztitlan, almost surrounded by tributaries of the Triple Alliance (cf. Byam Davies, pp. 29–61). To the west were the states of Atotonilco (a center of tribute collection) and Cuachquetzaloyan (perhaps a dependency of Atotonilco), on unfriendly terms with neighboring Metztitlan, Tollantzinco was an important political center which normally housed an Aztec garrison, but in 1519 it was controlled by the rebel Acolhua ruler, Ixtlilxóchitl (cf. Otumba), whose influence may have extended to the states of Tzihuinquillocan and Acaxochitlan; all three, in former times, had sent tribute to Atotonilco. There was a disputed area between Tototépec and Pahuatlan on the south, and perhaps a permanent state of hostility occurred between Tototépec and the Aztec garrisons at Xiuhcoac and Atlan on the north and east (Scholes and Adams, 1961, p. 390). The population was predominantly Otomí with Náhuatl-speaking minorities in the principal centers and rancherías of Tepehuas at Acaxochitlan and on the edges of Tototépec. The settlement pattern was greatly dispersed.

This region was traversed by the Cintos party in late 1519 or early 1520 and submitted to the Spaniards in 1521. Tototépec subsequently rebelled on two occasions, the second time being joined by Atotonilco; the latter revolt was put down by an army under Vázquez de Tapia in 1523–4 (Oviedo y Valdés, III, pp. 439–40. Vázquez de Tapia, p. 50).

Encomiendas

Cortés is said to have assigned Tulancingo to Francisco de Vargas and then to have taken it from him. Perhaps the next encomendero was Francisco de Terrazas, a conquistador, who at first held the place alone and later shared it with a poblador, Francisco de Avila (Icaza, I, pp. 22, 201). Avila died before 1541, his half being inherited by a son, Hernando, while the Terrazas share passed *c.* 1548 to a son of the same name (*Actas de cabildo*, IV, p. 248). Sometime between 1597 and 1604 both encomenderos died and were succeeded respectively in the third 'life' by a daughter (María de Avila) and a son (Francisco de Terrazas). The husband of Doña María was Angel de Villafaña y Alvarado, still alive in 1629. Tributes from both halves were still privately assigned in 1643, but they had escheated by 1688 (Dorantes de Carranza, pp. 178, 280. ENE, XV, p. 212).

Acasuchitlan was assigned to Luis de la Torre, a poblador who also held neighboring Paguatlan; when he died *c.* 1550 he was followed by his widow, Luisa de Acuña, who died shortly before 1610. Subsequently tributes were assigned to the Moctezuma heirs (ENE, VIII, p. 24; XV, p. 212).

Atotonilco, first held by Cortés, was then assigned to a poblador, Pedro de Paz. Just before Paz died at the beginning of 1565 he married a servant of the marchioness del Valle, Francisca Ferrer, and soon after his death Doña Francisca married Pedro Gómez de Cáceres, a son of Andrés de

Tapia. Between 1573 and 1597 the encomienda was inherited by Andrés Ferrer de Tapia, son of this last union. By 1643 Atotonilco was crown property.[1]

Tututepec was assigned at an early date to Alonso Giraldo, a trumpeter in the Conquest, and then re-assigned to Maese Manuel Tomás

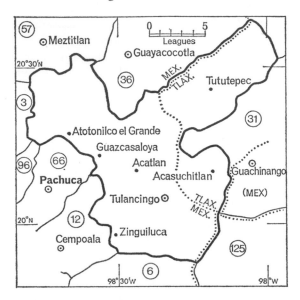

(Icaza, II, p. 64). Sometime before 1548 Tomás had his rights transferred to a son, Diego Rodríguez de Orozco, still alive in 1597. Part of the tributes were privately assigned as late as 1696.[2]

We do not know who was encomendero of Cinguiluca. It was claimed as a distant sujeto of Texcoco in the mid-sixteenth century and seems to have escheated shortly before 1545 (ENE, XVI, p. 75).

Government

The encomiendas listed above were among the largest and most remunerative in New Spain, and crown control in this area was successfully excluded for some decades. The C of Cinguiluca seems to have had jurisdiction at Tulancingo as early as 1557.[3] In the following decade he was considered suffragan to the AM of Meztitlan and was executing commissions at both Atotonilco and Tulancingo.[4] By 1575 he was re-designated AM, with residence at Tulancingo.

In October of that year Tututepec was transferred from the jurisdiction of Metateyuca (cf. Guachinango) to that of Tulancingo, although the order was not carried out for a year or so.[5] By 1583 both Tututepec and Acasuchitlan were being administered from Tulancingo, which thus acquired its final boundaries with only a few minor subsequent adjustments.[6] From 1787 the AM became subdelegado in the intendencia of Mexico, maintaining deputies at Acasuchitlan, Atotonilco, Guascazaloya, Tenango, Tututepec, and Zinguiluca.

Church

Both Franciscans and Augustinians arrived at an early date, the first founding a doctrina at S Juan Bautista Tulancingo (c. 1528), the second at S Agustín Atotonilco el Grande (c. 1536). Towards 1557 additional Augustinian parishes were created at S Miguel Acatlan and Stos Reyes (later, Magdalena) Tututepec. Sometime before 1570 the bishop of Tlaxcala assigned a secular priest to Asunción Acasuchitlan. S Antonio Zinguiluca was visited from Cempoala and Epazoyuca before becoming an Augustinian parish c. 1572.[7]

By 1743 (perhaps long before) there were additional Augustinian doctrinas at S Juan Bautista Guascazaloya and S Agustín Tenango, previously visited from Atotonilco and Tututepec respectively. Towards 1754 the parishes of Acatlan, Atotonilco, Cinguiluca, Guascazaloya, and Tulancingo were secularized, the same process occurring in the other regular doctrinas soon thereafter. The last parishes to be founded here (by 1777) were S Lorenzo Achiotepec and S Benito Huehuetla, both old visitas of Tututepec. These three, together with Acasuchitlan and Tenango, belonged to the diocese of Tlaxcala, while the others were in the archbishopric of Mexico.

Population and settlements

The number of Indian tributaries here dropped from somewhat over 15,000 in 1570 to c. 6,700 in 1597, 1,950 in 1626, and c. 1,700 towards 1690, much of the loss occurring in the epidemics of 1576–81 and 1604–7. Actually there was some recovery in the Indian population in the seventeenth century except at Tututepec, where we are told that 1,000 families 'fled' from the Augustinian doctrinas and emigrated to Chicontepec shortly before 1646 (*Alegaciones*..., p. 160v). Later estimates show 3,106 Indian families in 1743, and 6,707 Indian tributaries in 1804.[8] In 1646 Náhuatl, 'Otomí cerrado', Tepehuan, and some Totonac were spoken at Tututepec, while eighteenth-century reports indicate a gain of Náhuatl over Otomí in the rest of the jurisdiction.

Spaniards and other non-Indians began moving into the area in the sixteenth century, settling at Tulancingo and Atotonilco and founding vast cattle and wheat haciendas on lands vacated by the declining Indian communities, a process which accelerated in the seventeenth century. The 1792 census shows 7,263 'Spaniards' (individuals), 7,830 mestizos, and 1,161 mulattoes in the jurisdiction. By that time the cabecera of Tulancingo had become an urban center with twice as many gente de razón (4,000) as Indians (2,000).

Acasuchitlan (Acaxochitlan, Caxochitla; 1950: Acaxochitlán, pueblo) in 1570 had 15 estancias within two leagues of the cabecera. Mexicans and Otomies lived together in the cabecera, while the dependent settlements had Otomies, Totonacs, and Mexicans. A congregation was proposed here in 1598 and carried out soon after.[9] Certain estancias were absorbed by the haciendas of Apapaxtla, S Antonio, and Zacatepec. S Pedro (Amaxac), Asunción (Atlan), S Miguel (Cuacuacala), Los Reyes (Cuatlan), and Santiago (Tepepa), which either survived or were reoccupied, appear as Indian pueblos in 1792.[10]

Atotonilco el Grande (Hueyatotonilco; 1950: *villa*) in the sixteenth century had two sub-cabeceras, Acatlan and Cuachquetzaloya (Coauquezaloya, Guetzquetzaloya, etc.; Guazcasaloya or Guazca in 1743–92; 1950: Huasca de Ocampo, pueblo), with a total of twenty-two estancias listed in 1571. There were Náhuatl-speakers in the cabeceras but only Otomies in the estancias, which were considerably spread out. About half of these satellite communities disappeared in the congregations of *c.* 1600, their lands being taken by numerous haciendas. In addition to the three cabeceras, eleven places were pueblos in 1792: Amaxac, Clasocoyuca (Tlaxocoyucan), Los Reyes (two places), S Bartolomé, S Martín, S Sebastián, Sta Catarina, Santiago (=Quauhtla in 1571?), Santorum (=Yautengo in 1571?), and Sto Tomás.[11]

Tulancingo (Tulanzinco, etc.; 1950: Tulancingo, ciudad) had thirteen estancias within three leagues in the late sixteenth century. These were to be reduced to three congregation centers in 1602, but seven of them are recognizable as pueblos de visita in 1697, and six survived in 1792: Sta Ana Hueitlalpan, Magdalena Metepec, Natívitas, Santiago, S Antonio (Tlatoca), and S Francisco Xaltepec. Haciendas occupied the deserted sites and encroached on still existing pueblos.[12]

In 1548 Tututepec (Tototepec, etc.; 1950: the original cabecera of Magdalena should perhaps be identified with modern Sta María Temaxcalapa) had eighty-five 'estancias y barrios' divided between Tututepec itself and three sub-cabeceras, Cayucan, Chiconcoac, and Xucuaycapan (Xococapan). Many of these settlements were congregated by the Augustinians towards 1560; the 1570 report names twenty-seven estancias up to eleven leagues from the principal cabecera. Another congregation proposed in 1594 was less successful, as there were still twenty-three pueblos in addition to the principal cabecera in 1792.[13] Several had achieved cabecera status in the eighteenth century. They were S Lorenzo Achiotepec, S Benito Huehuetla, S Agustín, S Ambrosio, S Andrés, S Antonio, S Bartolomé, S Esteban, S Gerónimo, S Gregorio, S Guillermo, S Juan, S Mateo, S Martín, S Pedro, S Sebastián, Sta Cruz, Sta Inés y S Clemente, Sta María, Sta Mónica, Sta Ursula, Santiago, and S Agustín Tenango (few can be identified with the Náhuatl names in the 1570 list). There were no haciendas in this area.

Zinguiluca (Cinguilucan, Yçinguiluca, Zonguiluca, Xinguilucan, etc.; 1950: Singuilucan, pueblo) had two or three sujetos near the cabecera before a congregation of *c.* 1600. One of them, Santiago, is mentioned as a visita in 1683, but it was only a rancho in 1792. Another 1570 estancia, Xalapan, perhaps corresponds to the 1792 rancho of Xalapilla, quite close to Epazoyucan.[14]

In addition to the places mentioned, in 1792 the jurisdiction had forty-four haciendas, twenty-two ranchos, two molinos, and a venta (inn).

Sources

Acatlan, Atotonilco, Cuachquetzaloya, and Tututepec are briefly described in the *Suma* of *c.* 1548 (PNE, I, nos. 21–2, 133, 759). There are reports of *c.* 1570 from all parishes, with lists of estancias and other details.[15] Ponce (I, pp. 210–11) visited Tulancingo in 1586.

A document concerning the congregation of Tulancingo in 1602[16] is followed by Bishop Mota y Escobar's brief description of Acaxuchitlan in 1610.[17] We have tributary data for Cinguiluca in 1588–1623 (Scholes and Adams, 1959, p. 61), from the Tlaxcalan parishes in 1626–96,[18] and those in the archbishopric in 1643–88.[19] Bishop Palafox went through here in 1646,[20] as did an archbishop of Mexico in 1683–4.[21] Vetancurt (4a parte, p. 63) describes the monastery-parish of Tulancingo as it was *c.* 1697.

A lost *relación* of *c.* 1743 is summarized by Villaseñor y Sánchez (I, pp. 134–6). Of limited value is a report of 1754 with a crude map.[22] There are parochial censuses from Huehuetlan and Tenango dated 1777.[23] The non-Indian *padrón* of 1792 includes a brief description and map, with a list of toponyms.[24]

Fernández (1940–2) should be consulted for additional details.

III *Tuspa*

This region includes the headwaters of the Tepalcatepec and Tuxpan river systems at the western end of the Sierra de Michoacán, and the eastern side of the volcanoes of Colima, with extreme elevations of 700–4,300 m, but mostly within the 1,500–2,000 m range. The Laguna de Zapotlán is a basin of interior drainage. In the higher mountains, which are forested, rainfall is considerable, but much of the area is semi-arid. It is now in southern Jalisco state.

The Tarascans invaded this region a generation or two before the Spaniards arrived and found it inhabited by people speaking a variety of languages, few of which can be satisfactorily identified. Cochin, Chichimeca, Nahua, Piñol or Pino, Tiam, Xilotlantzinco, Zapotlanejo, and Zayulteco (some of these are surely synonyms) are mentioned in sixteenth-century documents. By 1570 Nahua was predominant in the north and what was perhaps a related tongue, Xilotlantzinca, from Tamazula south, while Tarascan prevailed around Mazamitla; however, by this time only a small part of the contact population survived, and there are indications of Nahua immigration from Colima after the Conquest.

At any rate, the Tarascans conquered a non-Tarascan population here, and perhaps were in the process of expanding their borders to the north, west, and south when the Spaniards appeared. The lord of Tamazollan was subordinate to the cazonci and in turn had primacy over the rulers of Masamitlan, Tochpan, Tzapotlan, and possibly Amole (cf. Amula).

An offshoot of Olid's expedition passed through here late in 1522 and met no resistance. Actual Spanish control may date from 1524.

Encomiendas

The whole area was assigned to himself by Hernán Cortés, probably in 1523. It was re-assigned by the acting governors in 1525 and seems to have been held for a while by Rodrigo de Albornoz; in November of that year the ayuntamiento of Colima asked to have Tuspa assigned to it, and it was likely at this time that the *villa* was moved to the original site of Tuspa (ENE, I, p. 84. Sauer, 1948, p. 64). Cortés re-asserted his claim when he returned to Mexico in 1526. Two years later we find him in control of 'Amula y Tamaçula y Tuspa y Çapotlan', together with

'Masanytra'.[1] The encomienda was seized by Nuño de Guzmán in 1529, and probably became a crown possession in 1531.

An area to the south of Tuspa called Miaguatlan, all or part of which eventually belonged to this jurisdiction, was held first by Alonso de Arévalo,

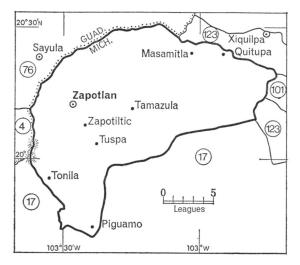

succeeded towards 1550 by his widow, Beatriz López, and somewhat later by a son, Pedro de Arévalo. Escheatment occurred when the last encomendero died between 1573 and 1578.[2]

Government

Tuspa, Tamazula, y Zapotlan most likely had a C from 1531.[3] At first the jurisdiction was considered subordinate to the AM of Colima, but sometime between 1556 and 1562 it became an alcaldía mayor.[4] In the 1580s the C of Xilotlan was suffragan to Tuspa, a temporary arrangement as eventually it was annexed to Colima.[5] The residence of the AM moved from Tuspa to Zapotlan sometime before 1639. In later years the jurisdiction came to be called Zapotlan el Grande, and from 1787 it was a subdelegación in the intendencia of Guadalaxara.

Church

Franciscan monastery-parishes were founded perhaps in the early 1530s at Asunción Zapotlan and S Juan Bautista Tuspa. Another convent was built at S Francisco Tamazula before 1551,

but it was subordinate to Tuspa for many years, and in 1571 we find Tamazula being ministered by a secular priest; by 1587 it had been returned to the Franciscans.[6] In 1623 it was decided that no more than a single friar should live at each of the three parish seats, and yet in 1649 there is mention of a fourth monastery, at Zapotiltic. The area was in the province of Santiago de Xalisco until secularization, which occurred at Tamazula and Zapotlan in the 1760s and at Tuspa shortly after 1774. It belonged to the diocese of Michoacán until 1795, and to Guadalaxara thereafter (Brambila, 1964, pp. 62, 281).

Masamitla and Quitupa were visited from Tamazula in 1571 and from Xiquilpa later, until S Cristóbal Masamitla became a secular parish sometime after 1789.[7] Perhaps at the same time (at latest by 1803), two erstwhile visitas of Tuspa, Santiago Piguamo and S Marcos Tonila, became independent parishes.

Population and settlements

Tamazula alone is said to have had '20,000 Indians and more' at contact, but by 1580 the number of tributaries in the jurisdiction was reduced to 1,700. Later counts show 685 tributaries in 1623, 829 in 1698, 2,000 towards 1743, and 2,459 in 1800.[8]

There were only a few Spaniards in the sixteenth century, officials, priests, cattle raisers and miners, but the non-Indian element became important later with the development of haciendas (there were twenty-six in 1792, together with fifty-five ranchos and one real de minas called Plomosas). Most of the silver mines for which the area was famous in the 1520s were apparently in the mountainous region southeast of Tamazula which became attached to Colima. The 1800 census shows 788 free Negro and mulatto tributaries.

There must have been an extensive program of congregation carried out here by the Franciscans before 1552, in which many native settlements disappeared. Another reduction occurred in the 1590s.[9]

Tuspa (1950: Tuxpan, pueblo), according to Lebrón, was moved from its first site at or near Colima when the Spanish *villa* was transferred there c. 1525. It had only two sujetos in 1580, one of which, Tonantla (=Tonitlan, Tonila), survived as a pueblo in the eighteenth century. Piguamo seems to be a more recent settlement.

The original site of Zapotlan (Villa de Alburquerque in the mid-seventeenth century; later, Zapotlan el Grande; 1950: Ciudad Guzmán) was three leagues west of its final location. S Andrés Istlan and S Sebastián Teponaguastlan (Ponahuastitlan, Cuautepunahuaztla) were nearby subjects in 1580, and pueblos in 1792.

Tamazula (1950: Tamazula de Gordiano, *villa*) had nine sujetos in 1580, six of which disappeared in a congregation towards 1600. The natives of Masamitla and Quitupa were ordered to move to Xiquilpa in 1604, but subsequently these sites re-appear as pueblos, still in the jurisdiction of Tuspa.[10] Zapotiltic also survived as a pueblo.

Sources

Conditions here towards the middle of the sixteenth century are reported briefly in the *Suma de Visitas* (PNE, I, nos. 115, 371, 551–2), and extensively in the visit of Lebrón de Quiñones (1952). There is a curt description of Tamazula–Masamitla in 1571 (Miranda Godínez, 9/39). The relación geográfica of 1580 is of special interest.[11] Father Ponce visited the area in 1585–7, and described it in his journal (Ponce, I, p. 51; II, pp. 109–16).

A short description of the Franciscan parishes in 1623 (Scholes and Adams, 1959, p. 67) is followed by an equally brief report of 1639,[12] and tributary data for 1698.[13]

A lost document of *c.* 1743 is summarized in Villaseñor y Sánchez (II, pp. 241–2). The parish of Zapotlan is described in a valuable report of 1778.[14] Lists of placenames and other information are given in two documents dated 1788[15] and 1792.[16]

Monographs include those of Sauer (1948) and Brambila (1964).

112 *Tuxtla y Cotaxtla*

As finally constituted, this jurisdiction (now in central Veracruz state) was split into three unconnected parts, Tuxtla, Cotaxtla, and La Rinconada. The part corresponding to Tuxtla extends from the mouth of the Alvarado (Papaloapan) to Lake Catemaco and from the Gulf coast inland as far as the S Juan river, with elevations from sea level to 1,738 m at the volcano of S Martín. Cotaxtla and La Rinconada occupy broad river valleys in the lowlands behind Veracruz. Precipitation is slight around La Rinconada and Cotaxtla and much more abundant in the mountains around Tuxtla, which have a thick rain forest on the windward slopes.

At contact the area was tributary to the Mexica, having been conquered during the reign of Axayácatl. Most of the people spoke an archaic Nahua, but there were probably some Popolucans at Toztla. There were three principal native states, Ixcalpan, Cuetlaxtlan, and Toztla, governed by calpixque. Ixcalpan sent its tribute to Cuauhtochco. Cuetlaxtlan had both an important ceremonial center and a Mexican garrison where tribute from numerous communities was collected. Toztla was controlled from the Aztec garrison of Tochtépec and had a frontier on the east with hostile Coatzacualco.

Grijalva's expedition sailed along the coast here in 1518, and one of its ships commanded by Pedro de Alvarado explored the mouth of the river later named for him. Indians from Cuetlaxtlan visited the Spaniards when they landed near Veracruz on this occasion, and both Cuetlaxtlan and Ixcalpan submitted to Cortés and his men in the spring of 1519. Toztla, while perhaps visited by Spaniards at an early date, was not subdued until early 1522 (Díaz del Castillo, I, p. 142. Melgarejo Vivanco, pp. 48–51, 60).

Encomienda

Cortés considered the Indians of the entire Gulf coastal area his personal vassals and assigned them

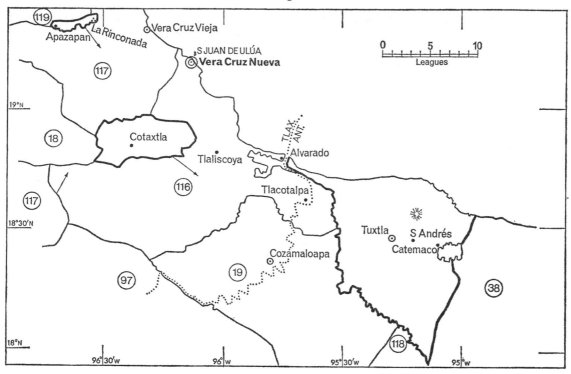

to himself in the first distribution of encomiendas. Cotaxtla, which then comprised the coast and hinterland north of the Alvarado river, Tuxtla, and the basin of the Alvarado as far as Chinantla, all were included (CDI, XII, p. 279. Cortés, p. 396). During Cortés's absence in Honduras these places were seized by the acting governors, and in 1525 the ayuntamiento of Vera Cruz asked the king to grant it the Indian labor of Ixcalpan (La Rinconada), but Cortés regained and held possession until he sailed for Spain in 1528.[1] On his return in the summer of 1530, the new Marqués del Valle took formal possession of his estate in Ixcalpan.[2] Other *villas* mentioned in the grant of the Marquesado were Atroyatan (= Otatitlán?), Quetasta (=Cotaxtla), Tustla, and Tepeca(Tepeaca, etc.). The last-named place was the sugar hacienda near Tuxtla that Cortés had installed in 1525 (Cuevas, 1915, p. 43. L de T, p. 582).

Here as elsewhere the marquis was soon embroiled in litigation with the audiencia over the extent of his possessions. Cortés claimed eleven sujetos of Cotaxtla, but those on the sea were taken for the crown and the rest were assigned to other encomenderos, leaving the cabecera alone within the marquisate. Tuxtla and Tepeca, as well as Ixcalpan, remained in the Cortés estate.[3]

Government

From 1530 magistrates were appointed here in the name of Cortés and successive Marqueses del Valle, except during the periods of sequestration (1570–93, 1710–25, 1810––) when they were named by the viceroy or king (cf. ENE, XI, pp. 31–3). At first there was a C or AM in each *villa*, but later they were combined under a single magistrate, generally resident at Tuxtla. In the 1570s and 1580s Tuxtla and Cotaxtla were attached to the alcaldía mayor of Tlacotalpa, and Ixcalpan–Rinconada to that of Vera Cruz.[4] In the eighteenth century there was an AM at Tuxtla with deputies at nearby S Andrés, Cotaxtla, and perhaps at Rinconada. After 1787 the jurisdiction was *de facto* attached to the intendencia of Vera Cruz.

Church

There was probably a curate in each *villa* in early years, although we do not hear about this until 1556, when a vicar is reported at Santiago Tuxtla.[5] In 1570 this priest, subordinate to the bishop of Antequera, was also in charge of the marquis's sugar hacienda, while S Pedro Cotaxtla had been annexed to the parish of S Juan de Ulúa and La Rinconada was a visita of Vera Cruz. Some years later, in 1609, Cotaxtla was being visited from Tlalixcoya, and by 1743 it had become a separate parish. In 1754 and later there was a curate in the Rinconada area with his headquarters at Apazapan. The doctrina of Tuxtla was divided, perhaps in 1718, with another secular priest at S Andrés. Tuxtla and S Andrés belonged to the bishopric of Antequera, and the remaining parishes to that of Tlaxcala.

Population and settlements

The native population here at contact was quite dense and spread out in many settlements; Cotaxtla alone is said to have had over 40,000 families (Aguilar, pp. 88, 138. Sanders, 1952, pp. 71–3). Only a small fraction survived the first great mysterious plague of the 1520s and 1530s. Still, Cotaxtla was described as a 'población recia' in 1544 (ENE, IV, p. 140), and there were probably over 2,000 tributaries towards 1560, 1,200 in Tuxtla and 800–900 at Cotaxtla and Ixcalpan. The decade of the 1560s was disastrous, some 643 tributaries of Tuxtla being reported as 'muertos y guidos' in 1564–72, while Cotaxtla was left with only 24 tributaries, and Ixcalpan with 100, in 1569.[6] There was further loss in the seventeenth century, and while Tuxtla had a remarkable recovery for which immigration must have been largely responsible, the northern enclaves remained practically depopulated. Later counts show 742 tributaries in 1597, 629 in 1620, 735 in 1682, 1,046 in 1706, 2,080 in 1743, and 2,468 in 1793.[7]

Negro slaves were introduced early in the sixteenth century to work on Cortés's sugar estate and on several cattle haciendas. However, we have no information on the number of Negroes and mulattoes here; there were very few Spaniards and mestizos.

Soon after the Conquest the cabecera of Tuxtla was moved from its original fortress site on a spur of the volcano to the valley below (1950: Santiago Tuxtla, *villa*); this may have occurred after an eruption c. 1530 (Medel y Alvarado, I, pp. 29–30). Tuxtla had six sujetos in 1580, two of which (Catemaco and S Andrés Zacualco or S Andrés Tuxtla) seem to have survived as pueblos after the congregation of 1598–1604.[8] In 1777 there was another settlement near S Andrés, at Rivera de Totoltepec.

In a petition of 1532, Cortés listed eleven places subject to Cotaxtla (Quetastla, Cotlachtla, etc.; 1950: Pueblo viejo, ranchería? Later moved to what is now Cotaxtla, *villa*); these places seem to have been removed from the marquisate before October, 1532, leaving Cotaxtla with approximately the same limits as the modern municipio.[9]

We know nothing about the dependencies, if any, of La Rinconada (Ixcalpan, Izcalpa; 1950: Rinconada Antigua, congregación). It was one league east of a venta of the same name, established in 1567 on the highway from Vera Cruz to Mexico (ENE, XI, p. 33. Gage, pp. 45–6. Ponce, II, p. 315). The Indian village perhaps corresponds to the pueblo of Apazapan, listed in this jurisdiction in 1743.[10]

Sources

Several early documents give information about tributes here (ENE, IX, p. 5. L de T, pp. 580–6. Scholes and Adams, 1957, p. 55). There is an inventory of Marquesado property, together with brief reports in the Ovando series, dated 1569–71 (ENE, XI, pp. 29–33. García Pimentel, 1904, pp. 12, 80–1. PNE, V, p. 196). The relación sent in by the AM of Tlacotalpa in 1580 describes Tuxtla and Cotaxtla and is accompanied by a chart of the coast (PNE, V, pp. 1–11); the area also appears on another map of the same date.[11] Congregations at Rinconada and Tuxtla are discussed in a document of 1598.[12]

For the seventeenth century, we have reports of episcopal visits in 1609[13] and 1646,[14] together with tributary information for 1626–96,[15] covering the parishes in the diocese of Tlaxcala, but nothing special for Antequera.

A missing report of c. 1743 is condensed by

Villaseñor y Sánchez (I, pp. 269–70). We have not seen another report, presumably from the eighteenth century, mentioned by García Martínez.[16] Complete censuses of Apazapan and S Andrés Tuxtla parishes dated 1777 have been found,[17] and there is brief mention of both Tuxtla curacies in a report of 1802 (Pérez, 1888, table at end).

A careful perusal of the immense ramo of Hospital de Jesús at AGN could change the above picture considerably. García Martínez (1969) adds many details taken from the archive. The Tuxtla area is covered in the monographs of Medel y Alvarado (1963) and Scholes and Warren (1965).

113 *Valladolid*

Now in the north central portion of the state of Michoacán, the colonial jurisdiction of Valladolid was the heart of the Purépecha or Tarascan empire. Like the 'valley' of Mexico, most of this area is a series of high basins or *cuencas* of volcanic origin, draining into the lakes of Pátzcuaro, Cuitzeo, Zacapu, and Zirahuén. Elevations here range from 1,880 to 3,000 m, and the climate is cool with moderate rainfall. Outside this basin, west of Pátzcuaro is a rugged country known as the Sierra de Michoacán, dominated by the great isolated volcano of Tancítaro (3,845 m); this is a region of much precipitation and vast pine–oak forests. The northern part of the jurisdiction drains into the Lerma river. On the south, the slopes of the Sierra Volcánica drop off into the dry, hot basin of the Mexcala or Balsas river, the tierra caliente, descending to 400 m.

Much of this area was within the original Tarascan kingdom directly subject to the cazonci, whose court was at Tzintzuntzan, but it also included the vassal states of Aran, Capula (Xeréngaro), Comanja (Espopuyuta), Cheran, Chocándiro, Etúcuaro, Huaniqueo, Indaparapco, Jaso, Paracho, Puruándiro, Sacapo, Sansani, Sihuinan, Tacámbaro, Tarímbaro, Teremendo, Tiripitio, Urapan, Urecho, and Uruapan, and probably others. Most of these were semi-autonomous communities governed by tribute-collectors (Tarascan, *ocámbecha*) or hereditary rulers (*carachacapacha*) controlled by the cazonci. Tarascan was the principal language (Swadesh hesitatingly places it in the Quechuan family, supposing a distant connexion with Perú), but there were pockets of an older population speaking Nahua. Undameo and Guayangareo (cf. Charo) were inhabited by recent Otomí immigrants, allies of the Tarascans, who spoke Matlatzinca (Pirinda). The region north of Puruándiro and Sacapo was occupied by Guamare-speaking Chichimecs against whom the Tarascans waged intermittent warfare. On the east, south, and west were other states tributary to the Tarascans.

First visited by Montaño and his party in 1521, the cazonci received peaceably a force led by Cristóbal de Olid in July, 1522. Two years later, after having a survey made of Michoacán, Cortés distributed the villages to his captains, reserving to himself the 'city' of Tzintzuntzan with its immediate dependencies, in other words, the kingdom of Michoacán less the vassal states. Conversion was begun by the Franciscans probably in 1525. The decade of the 1520s was a period of confusion and violence, the result of a double conflict between native rulers and Spanish encomenderos and between rival groups of Spaniards. During these years many Indians were sent off to slavery and death in the gold placers and silver mines of the Pacific slope. Others died from disease, and still others were impressed into service outside the area by Nuño de Guzmán, who executed the cazonci in 1530, after which there was continued native resistance for some few years (Icaza nos. 387, 1188).

Encomiendas

Tzintzuntzan (Huichichila, Mechuacan), which included the Tarascan capital and a good many dependent settlements around Lake Pátzcuaro (*cf. below*), was taken from Cortés by the acting

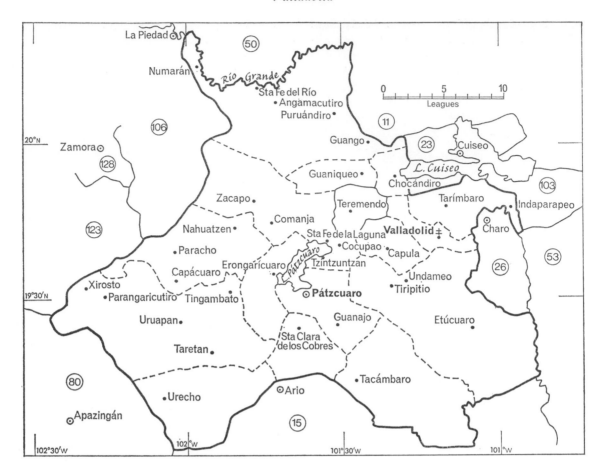

governors in 1525 and recovered by him after his return in 1526.[1] Part or all of this important encomienda was claimed by Juan Infante in accordance with a grant made by governor Estrada in 1528, but in the following year the whole area was seized by the first audiencia ostensibly for the crown. Tzintzuntzan was not included in the Marquesado grant, but Cortés's former rights were recognized by setting aside for him certain 'residual' tributes.[2] Meanwhile, the C of Michoacán in November, 1531, complying with orders of the audiencia, relinquished to Infante possession of Tzintzuntzan's dependencies. Four years later, Infante's encomienda again escheated, but in 1540 it was returned to him (Warren, 1963b, pp. 90–101). At this time three places claimed by Infante, Pátzcuaro, Tzintzuntzan, and Guayameo (Sta Fé de la Laguna), were *de facto* retained by the

crown authorities. It was not until 1554 that the council of the Indies ruled against Infante and re-united the Pueblos de la Laguna, as they had come to be called, with their original cabecera of Michoacan, a crown possession (ENE, xv, pp. 95–6).

Capula (Xenguaro) was perhaps first held by Pedro Núñez, Maese de Roa, although the physician Pedro López is also mentioned as encomendero.[3] It was re-assigned, seemingly in 1528, to Dr. Cristóbal de Ojeda, who may have shared the tributes with Luis de Berrio (Bravo Ugarte, 1963, II, p. 90. Millares Carlo and Mantecón, I, no. 1341). Both Berrio and Ojeda had their property confiscated early in 1533, at which time presumably Capula escheated.

Comanja and Naranja were divided between two encomenderos early in 1528, Juan de Solís and Hernán Cortés, respectively.[4] In the following year Juan Infante acquired both places and held them, except for a period of escheatment in the 1530s, until his death in 1574. He was followed by a son, Juan Infante Samaniego, and later by Francisca de Estrada Infante Samaniego (listed in 1592–1604), a daughter, who married Diego Fernández de Velasco (Dorantes de Carranza, pp. 293–4). In the seventeenth century this encomienda was re-assigned to the Moctezuma heirs.

Chocándiro was held in the late 1520s by Alvaro Gallego, whose widow, Leonor de la Peña, inherited and held the encomienda with her second and third husbands, Antón de Silva (1530s and 1540s) and Gonzalo Galván (by 1560). Escheatment occurred between 1571 and 1597.[5]

In November, 1527, Guaniqueo was held jointly by Fernando Alonso and Marcos Ruiz (Rodríguez). Alonso was arrested and subsequently executed as a relapsed Jew in 1528 (Millares Carlo and Mantecón, I, nos. 870, 894, 1695). By April of that year Guaniqueo had been re-assigned to Hernán Cortés, who claimed that he had held it at an earlier date.[6] It was seized with the rest of Cortés's properties in 1529 and became a corregimiento.[7] Towards 1538 this encomienda was re-assigned to Bishop Vasco de Quiroga and was held by him until its final escheatment under the New Laws in April, 1544 (L de T, pp. 196–7).

Francisco Morcillo, who was granted Indaparapeo by Cortés, was succeeded in the 1550s by a son, Gaspar.[8] The latter is still listed in 1597, but by 1604 his son, Alonso de Vargas Morcillo, was encomendero (Dorantes de Carranza, pp. 280–1). Escheatment occurred late in the seventeenth century.

A poblador, Gonzalo Gómez, held a title from Estrada to Istapa (Etúcuaro) (Icaza, I, p. 201). Gómez was followed in the early 1560s by a son, Amador. Francisca López de Herrera was encomendera in 1597, but tributes escheated before 1657.

Jaso and Teremendo together were held early in 1528 by Andrés de Monjarraz. Escheatment took place in 1532.[9]

Necotlan (Undameo) formed part of the encomienda of Matalcingo (cf. Charo), escheating between 1536 and 1545.

Purúandiro and Guango formed a very large encomienda, mostly in Chichimec country, extending northward to the Río Grande and beyond (cf. León). Cortés granted it to a poblador, Juan de Villaseñor, who seems to have survived into the 1570s. A son, Juan de Villaseñor Cervantes, inherited (he is still listed in 1604), and tributes were still privately assigned in 1698.[10]

A group of mountain villages known collectively as Los Pueblos de la Sierra (often listed under the name of one of the cabeceras, Pamacoran, Paracho, Sevina, etc.), while they seem to have been at contact political dependencies of Tzintzuntzan and Uruapan, were placed in a single encomienda held towards 1528 by Juan de Solís. On his deathbed, Solís transferred his rights to Hernán Cortés, but almost immediately the encomienda was claimed by a certain Ruiz and Juan Infante. Sevina, at least, was in Infante's control by 1531.[11] The subsequent encomienda history is similar to that of Comanja–Naranja (*see above*).

Tacámbaro was perhaps first held by Alonso de Avalos.[12] By 1528 Cristóbal de Oñate was encomendero, and he was succeeded after his death in 1568 by a son, Hernando. The latter was alive in 1604, and his son and perhaps a grandson held the encomienda until escheatment occurred in the 1650s.[13]

Cristóbal de Valderrama, a poblador, held Tarímbaro from 1528 at the latest until his death in 1537.[14] He was followed by a mestiza daughter, Leonor de Valderrama y Moctezuma (granddaughter of the emperor), who later married Diego Arias de Sotelo. The latter retained the encomienda after his wife's death until he was exiled c. 1568, at which time his son, Fernando de Sotelo Moctezuma, inherited in the third 'life'. Fernando was alive in 1604, but Tarímbaro had escheated by 1657.

Tiripitio, held by Hernán Cortés in April, 1528, was soon thereafter re-assigned to Juan de Alvarado. When the latter, a bachelor, died in 1550 the place became a crown possession.[15]

The holder of Urapa and Guanaxo in 1528–33

was Diego Rodríguez de Valladolid. In the latter year Rodríguez left for Spain, the encomienda being re-assigned to the royal treasurer, Juan Alonso de Sosa. Escheatment presumably occurred in 1544.[16]

The conquistador Francisco de Villegas was assigned the large encomienda of Uruapan in 1524. On his death towards 1550 tributes were split between two sons, Pedro and Francisco, the first being given Uruapan and Xicalan and Francisco getting Xirosto and its dependencies. Pedro de Villegas died in 1585 and was followed by a son, Martín, still listed in 1597. The second Francisco de Villegas continued to hold Xirosto in 1599–1604. Both parts of the encomienda were still in private hands in 1698 (ENE, XII, p. 162. L de T, p. 212. Warren, 1963b, p. 409).

Zacapo, and perhaps somewhat later Tescalco, were granted in 1524 to the conquistador Hernando (Gómez?) de Xerez, succeeded in 1537 by his widow, Ana Rodríguez; she relinquished her rights in dowry to their daughter, Juana de Xerez, on the occasion of her marriage to Gonzalo de Avalos. The latter was still encomendero in 1568, but by the end of the century Zacapo seems to have escheated.[17]

Jaime Trías is mentioned as encomendero of Zanzan in 1528.[18] This can perhaps be identified with a place north of Zacapo, in Chichimec country, which re-appears in the eighteenth century as a pueblo subject to Puruándiro (*see below*).

Government

A magistrate appointed by the first audiencia arrived at Tzintzuntzan early in 1529. At the end of that year the audiencia's president, Nuño de Guzmán, left Mexico city and went to Michoacán where he spent a month, leaving the province in chaos when he continued on to the conquest of Nueva Galicia. For the next few years jurisdiction here was disputed between Guzmán, who claimed Michoacán for Nueva Galicia, and the audiencia of Mexico, which defended it as part of Nueva España. The latter sent a C to Tzintzuntzan in 1531 and gave him authority as justicia mayor over the entire province of Michoacán and sub-ordinate areas from Zacatula and Colima on the south to the Lerma and beyond into the Chichimec country in the north. A royal cédula of 1533 definitely assigned the area with which we are concerned here to Nueva España. Vasco de Quiroga, then an oidor of the audiencia, first visited the province in 1533 at which time he established a protected Indian hospital-settlement at Sta Fé de la Laguna as well as the first Spanish ciudad with its ayuntamiento, called Granada, both in the vicinity of the Tarascan capital (Warren, 1963a, pp. 78–81). When Pátzcuaro, a barrio of Tzintzuntzan, was selected as the seat of government in 1538, both Spaniards and Indians with their respective ayuntamientos moved there. In 1541 viceroy Mendoza, annoyed because Quiroga had not consulted him in the selection of a capital, ordered the 'çibdad de Mechuacan' moved again, to Guayangareo (Valladolid, *see below*), several leagues to the east. In subsequent years, Quiroga continued to call Pátzcuaro the city of Michoacán, while Mendoza and later viceroys when they used that title meant Guayangareo–Valladolid.

Meanwhile, within the two decades between 1531 and 1551, the C of Tzintzuntzan–Huichichila had pre-eminence among his colleagues in Michoacán, the magistrates who were appointed to rule the escheated encomiendas surrounding the old Tarascan state. Tancítaro y Tapalcatepec became a corregimiento in 1531, Jaso y Teremendo in 1532, Asuchitlan, Capula, Cinagua, Cuiseo de la Laguna, Guaniqueo, and Tlazazalca in 1533–4, Tinhuindín y Perivan and Ucareo in 1536, Cinapécuaro in 1538. By 1545 Chilchota had a C, as did Guanaxo y Urapa, Guaniqueo (for the second time), Matalcingo, Necotlan, Xacona, Xiquilpa, and Yurirapúndaro; Tuzantla followed in 1546, and Maravatío, Taimeo, and Tiripitio in 1550–1. From 1550 the chief magistrate here was called AM of Michoacán, and in 1553 he received license to administer justice throughout the province in both crown and private encomienda villages.[19] His residence was first at Tzintzuntzan, then (1539) Pátzcuaro, and then (1576) Valladolid; in the latter year the ayuntamiento of the ciudad of Michoacán moved from Pátzcuaro to Valladolid, and in theory Pátzcuaro became a *tenencia*, although in fact the AM soon returned to live there.

The C of Tiripitio in 1554 was given charge of all the tierra caliente, including Asuchitlan, Tuzantla, and Cinagua, as these distant places were rarely visited by their justices.[20] In 1566 Cs were sent to Cuiseo (near Huetamo) and Guaymeo y Sirándaro as they became crown possessions. Meanwhile, Matalcingo (cf. Charo) was turned over to the Marquesado del Valle towards 1564. The last corregimientos to be organized in this area were Tzintzuntzan (recognized as yet another ciudad of Michoacán in 1595) and Chocándiro (by 1597).[21]

It would seem that Guaniqueo and adjoining encomiendas were for a time in the 1560s administered by the AM of Guanaxuato. During the same decade the Cs of Ucareo y Cinapécuaro and Guaymeo y Sirándaro became AMs of two new mining centers, Tlalpuxagua and Espíritu Santo. Spanish towns were founded at Celaya and Zamora, within the boundaries of Yurirapúndaro and Xacona respectively, and each of these corregimientos became an alcaldía mayor, the first *c.* 1571 and the second in 1574. Tuzantla in the 1570s was attached for administration to the alcaldía mayor of Temazcaltepec, while Taimeo was annexed to Minas de Tlalpuxagua.

Towards 1600 most of the Cs in Michoacán (Asuchitlan, Cinagua, Cuiseo de la Laguna, Chilchota, Jaso y Teremendo, Maravatío, Sichu, Tancítaro, Tinhuindín, Tlazazalca, Xiquilpa) which were formerly suffragan to the AM became accountable only to the viceroy. On the other hand, Capula, Chocándiro, Guaniqueo, Necotlan, Tiripitio, and Tzintzuntzan were eliminated as separate corregimientos and were absorbed by the jurisdiction of Michoacán, or Valladolid as it came to be called. The corregimiento of Guanaxo y Urapa seems to have been divided between Cinagua y la Guacana (with Ario) and Valladolid (Guanaxo), although this may have been a change of settlement site rather than a shift in boundaries.[22]

Thus by the early years of the seventeenth century the area administered by the AM of Valladolid (=Pátzcuaro=Michoacán) acquired approximately its final limits, extending from the Río Grande south to Urecho and Tacámbaro, and from the westernmost dependencies of Uruapan to Indaparapeo and Etúcuaro in the east (see map). The corregimiento of Jaso y Teremendo (to which Capula and Guaniqueo were occasionally attached) remained an enclave within the province at this time.[23] During the seventeenth century the jurisdiction was divided into tenencias governed by deputies (*tenientes*) of the AM. The boundaries of these administrative divisions in most cases coincided with those of the old corregimientos and encomiendas (Chocándiro, Etúcuaro, Guango, Guaniqueo, Indaparapeo, Puruándiro, Sevina, Tacámbaro, Tiripitio, Uruapan). Erongarícuaro and its dependencies became a tenencia, and the C of Tzintzuntzan became teniente of Cocupao, with jurisdiction in Comanja and Zacapo. Sta Clara de los Cobres and Urecho, which perhaps formed part of the former corregimiento of Guanaxo y Urapa, were both made tenencias.

From *c.* 1690 the corregimiento of Jaso y Teremendo was administered as an isolated dependency first of Zamora y Xacona and somewhat later from Maravatio. Towards 1770 it was absorbed by Valladolid and placed, together with Capula, in the tenencia of Guaniqueo. In the eighteenth century we find Etúcuaro and Necotlan administered by the teniente of Tiripitio, and Tarímbaro by that of Indaparapeo. Angamacutiro and Taretan were separated from Puruándiro and Uruapan, respectively, and became tenencias, while the teniente of Sevina moved his headquarters to Paracho.

Meanwhile the entire province was governed by the AM resident at Pátzcuaro, although his functions during occasional interregna were assumed by the alcaldes ordinarios of Valladolid. From 1775 to 1787 the magistrate's title was again C, and from 1787 be became *intendente corregidor* with residence at Valladolid. The intendencia included roughly the same area that had been suffragan to the AM in the late sixteenth century, with the addition of Colima and Motines (Colima was transferred to the intendencia of Guadalaxara in 1795). The country north of the Río Grande formed a separate intendencia, that of Guanaxuato. The old tenencias of Valladolid, together with neighboring alcaldías mayores, were re-designated subdelegaciones, an arrangement which continued until Independence.

Church

Parochial duties (until secularization occurred in the late eighteenth century) were shared here between the Franciscans (from 1526), the secular clergy (before 1530), and the Augustinians (from 1537) (Chauvet, p. 38). The Franciscans seem to have founded a doctrina at S Francisco Tzintzuntzan in 1526, and while they abandoned Michoacán twice in early years, they soon returned to establish houses at Sta Ana Zacapo (1530?) and S Francisco Uruapan (*c.* 1533) from which they visited much of central and southern Michoacán. Their church at Tzintzuntzan served as a provisional cathedral in 1538 when the first bishop of Michoacán, Vasco de Quiroga, arrived to set up his diocese, but it was soon a regular doctrina again. Franciscan monasteries were established at Pátzcuaro soon after 1540, and at S Buenaventura Valladolid in 1546; the latter was headquarters of the province of S Pedro y S Pablo de Michoacán from 1565. Later sixteenth-century Franciscan establishments were Asunción Erongarícuaro (between 1563 and 1570), S Miguel Tarímbaro (by 1570), S Gerónimo Purenchécuaro (by 1583), and S Francisco (Sto Tomás) Pichátaro (by 1585).

Before Michoacán became a diocese, Bishop Zumárraga of Mexico sent at least one secular priest to the province, perhaps the same one who was living at Tarímbaro (later a Franciscan parish) in 1533. In the same year, the hospital and secular curacy of Sta Fé de la Laguna came into being. Quiroga returned as bishop in 1538, but very soon moved his cathedral from Tzintzuntzan to Pátzcuaro, where it remained until a royal command caused its removal to Valladolid in 1580. There were undoubtedly priests of whom there is little record in these early years, paid by conscientious encomenderos (a curate is mentioned at S Nicolás Guango from 1536), but most of the secular parishes in the diocese were founded by Quiroga (1539–65) and his successors. In addition to those mentioned, by 1571 secular doctrinas existed at S Gerónimo Aranza, S Juan Comanja, Santiago Capula, S Nicolás Chocándiro, Sta Marta Guaniqueo, Asunción Indaparapeo, Istapa (Etúcuaro), Santos Reyes Teremendo, S Juan Bautista Puruándiro, Sta María Sevina, and Sta Ana Xirosto. Before the century's end, a priest was assigned to Natividad Zirahuén (Asunción Huiramángaro was another center for this parish).

Meanwhile, the Augustinians began with doctrinas at S Juan Bautista Tiripitio (1537) and S Gerónimo Tacámbaro (1538). In 1550 they were given the parish of S Nicolás Guango, and about the same time they began to build a monastery at Valladolid. Another secular curacy, Xirosto, was turned over to the Augustinians in 1575; the following year the order assumed parochial functions at Chocándiro and Pátzcuaro. Santiago Tingambato was an Augustinian parish from 1581, while S Juan Parangaricutiro, S Felipe de los Herreros, and Santiago Necotlan were organized in 1595.

A number of new parishes were created as a result of the congregations at the beginning of the seventeenth century. S Juan Bautista Capácuaro was separated from Sevina in 1603. By 1639 we find additional secular doctrinas at Sta Clara de los Cobres and S Juan Urecho, Franciscan parishes at S Diego Cocupao and S Andrés Ziróndaro, and an Augustinian monastery at S Pedro Sacán. Sta Fé de Río, on the south bank of the Lerma in Chichimec country, may have been founded by Quiroga; it was long a dependency of Sta Fé de la Laguna and, like Puruándiro, a center of conversion and assimilation of Chichimecs; by 1743 it was a separate parish. With the great decline in the native population, some of these foundations did not endure. Cocupao, S Felipe, Zacán, and Ziróndaro were all reduced to the status of visitas (only Cocupao was revived as a secular doctrina at the end of the colonial period). Etúcuaro was administered by Augustinians from 1623–6.

Valladolid

In mid-eighteenth century the parish seats of Aranza and Sevina were moved to S Pedro Paracho and S Luis Nahuatzen, respectively, and an Augustinian house was founded at S Ildefonso Taretan. The regular doctrinas were secularized between 1754 and 1771 with the exception of Tiripitio and Necotlan (Undameo), ministered by Augustinians until 1787. The priest of Comanja moved to Rosario Cueneo, and finally to Los Reyes Tiríndaro. Shortly before 1771 the vast parish of Puruándiro was divided, when a priest went to live at S Francisco Angamacutiro. Numarán was first visited by the curate of Tlazazalca, but from 1589 it belonged to the parish of Pénjamo (cf. León).

The entire region fell within the bishopric of Michoacán.

Population and settlements

The number of Indian tributaries here fell from 37,100 in 1554 to 25,385 in 1570, 12,770 in 1600, and 4,406 in 1657. Later estimates show 5,143 tributaries in 1698, 8,008 in 1745, and 12,863 Indian tributaries in 1798-9.[24] Towards 1550 the greatest density was in the Sierra de Michoacán and the lake basins, with a relatively sparse population in the hot country to the south, and a scattering of Chichimecs in the Lerma valley. There was much mortality from epidemic disease in the sixteenth century and later. The plague of 1545-8 was especially felt in the tierra caliente, while that of 1576-81 caused greater loss in the highlands. By 1649 very few Indians survived in the south (there were perhaps 175 Indian families altogether in Urecho, Sta Clara, and Tacámbaro). In the late seventeenth and eighteenth centuries the native population recovered and increased, and there was a noticeable tide of immigration into the Lerma valley (Puruándiro, Angamacutiro); this gain was interrupted by the epidemic of 1736-9.

There were few non-Indians here before the seventeenth century, the period of greatest expansion of the haciendas, principally concerned with cattle raising and wheat farming in the north and sugar production in the south. There were c. 220 families of Spaniards and other non-Indians in 1570, most of them living at Pátzcuaro and Valladolid. In spite of depressed economic conditions, the number had risen to c. 820 in 1649; many sugar haciendas had been abandoned at that time because of the scarcity of labor, and destitute Spaniards who could no longer maintain houses in Valladolid had retired to their cattle estates in the Chocándiro–Puruándiro region. With the subsequent revival of prosperity the non-Indian population grew spectacularly to c. 5,800 families in 1745, more than half of them at Valladolid. In 1798-9 there were 4,037 free Negro and mulatto tributaries in the jurisdiction, plus a large number of slaves; the greatest concentration of Negroes was in the hot country, on the northern haciendas, and at Valladolid, although mulattoes and mestizos had spread over the entire area – only the Sierra de Michoacán and the villages around Lake Pátzcuaro had insignificant numbers of non-Indians.

In theory, the ciudad de Mechuacan, as the Spaniards called it, was the area directly subject to the cazonci as distinguished from those communities which, while tributary to the cazonci, had their own rulers and a certain amount of political autonomy. Just how far this original Tarascan kingdom extended is not an easy matter to determine and must await a careful study of the documents and testimony put forth in law suits between the Spanish crown and rival encomenderos, particularly Juan Infante. There can be no doubt that there were significant changes in the 'city's' boundaries after the Spanish Conquest. The original political center when the Spaniards arrived was Tzintzuntzan (Zinzonza, Cinsunsa, etc.; Náhuatl, Huichichila, Uitzitzila, etc.; 1950: Tzintzuntzan, ciudad), although both Pátzcuaro and Ihuatzio had been court residences, and Pátzcuaro was still the most important religious center (cf. *Relación de... Michoacán*, introduction by Paul Kirchhoff). In 1533 Quiroga founded the Spanish 'city' of Granada at or near Tzintzuntzan, and at the same time collected Indians from a number of the lakeside villages at the sujeto of Guayameo, which he baptized Sta Fé de la Laguna. Five years later the new bishop chose Pátzcuaro

(Pasquaro, etc.; 1950: Pátzcuaro, ciudad), another sujeto, as the site both for the cathedral and the principal Spanish and Indian settlement and political center of the ciudad of Michoacán. Within a few years we are told that 14,000 tributaries moved from subordinate settlements to Pátzcuaro. Thus Quiroga, aided by the Franciscans, effected a massive congregation here in the 1530s and again after the epidemic of 1545–8 in which many sujetos must have been deserted. Yet the relación of 1581 states that Pátzcuaro still had seventy-three 'barrios', fifteen within the city and the remainder from one to ten leagues distant. Most of these were on or near Lake Pátzcuaro, but others formed isolated enclaves far from their cabecera. Among the latter, listed in 1571, were Aguanuato, Ario, Istaro, Chiquimitío, and Urecho. A number of the dependencies listed under Erongarícuaro in 1524 seem to have been transferred at a later date to the Infante encomienda (*see below*), while Aguanuato and Chiquimitío came to belong to other cabeceras. On the other hand, there is some reason to believe that Ario, Istaro, and Urecho fell within the encomienda of Urapa y Guanaxo (*see below*) and were annexed to Pátzcuaro as an administrative measure after escheatment.

There were three subsequent congregations here. In 1595 the newly resurrected city of Tzintzuntzan still had eighteen outlying villages subject in both government and doctrine which the viceroy agreed should be moved to that cabecera. Azinvo, Pacanda, Serandangacho, Sinsícuaro, Arameo, Siparamuco, Tacupan, and Ucasangatucu seem to have been abandoned at this time.[25] Three years later a juez de congregación was sent to Pátzcuaro to examine all the lake villages and decide which could be eliminated.[26] Finally, after the epidemic of 1737, at least four places (Zanambo, S Juan Evangelista, Urumbécuaro, Yaguaro) were deserted.[27] Twenty-seven of the old subject pueblos of Tzintzuntzan-Pátzcuaro survived as Indian communities in the late eighteenth century, although by this time they were divided between three subdelegaciones (Cocupao, Erongarícuaro, Pátzcuaro) and several had acquired cabecera status. They were Arúcutin, Axuno, Cocupao, Cucuchuchao, Chapítiro, Erongarícuaro, Guanajo, Huecorio, Huiramángaro, Iguatzio, Janicho, Nocutzepo, S Bartolomé and S Pedro Pareo, Pichátaro, Poácuaro, Purenchécuaro, Sta Fé de la Laguna, Tócuaro, Tumbio, Tupátaro, Uricho, Xarácuaro, Tzentzénguaro, Zirahuén, Ziróndaro, and Zurumútaro.

Within the city of Pátzcuaro or very close to it there were, a few years after its foundation in 1538, some fifty or sixty barrios, reduced to fifteen in 1581 and eleven or twelve in 1649. These were divided into three parishes attended by a secular curate and regulars from the Augustinian and Franciscan monasteries. By 1754 Pátzcuaro, a predominantly mestizo city, still had nine barrios, two of them reserved to Indians, four exclusively non-Indian, and three with mixed races. At one point in the seventeenth century Pátzcuaro was re-baptized Carpio de Haro, but the new name did not thrive.[28]

Off to the south of Pátzcuaro were two distant dependencies, Opopeo and Ario, and far to the southwest was Urecho. Near Opopeo Quiroga founded a community of copper artisans which came to be known as Sta Clara de los Cobres. The source of the metal was the ancient mine of Inguarán (cf. Cinagua y la Guacana). The area was almost abandoned in 1649, at which time there were many ruined villages nearby, but somewhat later Sta Clara was considered important enough to station a teniente there; at one point the settlement was re-named Villa de Portugal, and it is now officially Villa Escalante. Ario was annexed to Cinagua y la Guacana towards 1600. S Juan Urecho was moved to a new site, S Antonio, sometime between 1639 and 1745, and had a teniente. Somewhere in the vicinity of Ario and Urecho we may place the mysterious encomienda (*see above*) of Urapa y Guanaxo. Guanaxo is identified with Ario *c.* 1548, but later appears as a pueblo, Natividad Guanajo or Cuanaxo, just southeast of Pátzcuaro.[29] Urecho became the center of a number of cattle and sugar haciendas and had a small mining camp, Apupato, in 1788.

Capula (1950: pueblo), also known as Xeréngaro or Xénguaro, in 1571 had twelve estancias within 2 leagues of the cabecera, but these were concentrated in two settlements, Capula and Tacícuaro, in the decade following 1594. One of the estancias managed to survive as another pueblo, S Nicolás Obispo, although the Indian population almost disappeared, reduced to 45–50 tributaries in 1649–98. The vacated lands of former barrios were incorporated into a vast hacienda owned by the Augustinians.

The names of thirty-eight places subject to Espopuyuta, later known as Comanjá (1950: pueblo) are given in the 1523 report. Some of these (Apúndaro, Tescalco) were annexed to neighboring Zacapo, while others either disappeared in an early congregation or moved to new sites. Six villages were abandoned in 1600–4, and eight others at a later date, some of them deserted after the epidemic of 1737. Santiago Asajo, Cipiajo, Cueneo, Naranja, and Tiríndaro were pueblos here in the late eighteenth century.

S Nicolás Chocándiro (1950: Chucándiro, pueblo), at the west end of Lake Cuitzeo, had nine estancias which were concentrated at the cabecera in 1603.

The twin cabeceras of Guango (Huango; 1950: Villa Morelos) and Puruándiro (Pururandiro; 1950: Puruándiro, ciudad) had nineteen dependencies between them in 1548. Other sixteenth-century sources list a number of places which apparently disappeared in a congregation in 1599–1604, at which time the Chichimecs were to be concentrated at the north (Sta Fé del Río, Pénjamo) while Tarascan settlements were founded in the vacated lands. The original Villaseñor encomienda here included only Puruándiro and Guango, but it seems to have spread out to the northwest into lands of other encomenderos, if we can equate Zansan (Sansan) with the Trías grant (*see above*). Aguanuato (Aguanato), a 'barrio' of Pátzcuaro in 1571, perhaps included the site of Sta Fé del Río. Zanzan, Carupo, and Caurio were abandoned after the epidemic of 1737. Aguanato, Angamacutiro, Conguripo, Epejan, Guango, Numarán, Panindícuaro, Puruándiro, and Sta Fé del Río all are listed as pueblos in 1649–1792.

Guaniqueo (1950: Huaniqueo de Morales, *villa*) in 1524 had forty-four estancias, most quite

near the cabecera but some as far as 3½ leagues away. Some of these were abandoned at an early date, and others seem to have been annexed to Comanja, leaving only fourteen barrios in 1548 and seven, all nearby, in 1571. These were moved to the cabecera in 1601–4, with the exception of S Miguel, still a pueblo in 1649 but not mentioned thereafter.

Indaparapeo (1950: pueblo) had three sujetos in 1548–71. Only the cabecera and Santiago Singuio (Cingeo, Tzindo, Santiago de los Pescadores) survived a congregation of *c.* 1600.

Istapa (later, Etúcuaro; 1950: pueblo) in mid-sixteenth century had four estancias, Copoyo, S Gerónimo Atécuaro (Atequao), S Juan, and S Miguel Tziquí. Atécuaro and Tziquí were ordered to be moved to Necotlan in 1603, while Copuyo survived as a pueblo subject to Etúcuaro.

Generally considered together, Jaso and Teremendo had a total of twenty-four subordinate estancias in 1548; only nine are mentioned in 1602, at which time it was decided to leave both Jaso and Teremendo *in situ*, moving in the Indians from the sujetos. Only Teremendo (1950: pueblo) survived in the late eighteenth century.

Necotlan, or Undameo in Tarascan (1950: Santiago Undameo, pueblo) became a separate cabecera towards 1544, having previously been subject to Matalcingo (Charo). In 1548 it had six barrios, one of which perhaps was the site of Valladolid (Guayangareo).[30] Necotlantongo, a visita in 1570, is identified as the cabecera in 1579. In the congregation of 1603 it was first proposed to move all the Indians to one of the barrios, Jesús del Monte, but in the end Necotlan–Undameo remained *in situ*, with the addition of two estancias, Atécuaro and Tziquí, until then subject to Istapa.

The place called Guayangareo, selected by the viceroy in 1541 to be the third 'city of Mechuacan', while within the limits of the Pirinda community of Matalcingo–Necotlan (*see above*), seems to have been owned as a cattle estancia by Gonzalo Gómez, the encomendero of Istapa.[31] The first residents, who were Spaniards generally without encomiendas, moved from Pátzcuaro in the early 1540s (ENE, v, pp. 205–7), and the site became known as Valladolid in accordance with a cedula of 1537. The ayuntamiento of Michoacán moved here in 1576, and the bishop's seat in 1580. In 1826 the city's name was changed to Morelia. The immediate political jurisdiction of the city was not extensive, hemmed in by encomiendas and corregimientos; it comprised a narrow strip extending from Chiquimitío (originally a 'barrio' of Tzintzuntzan) to the hills on the south. Some few places which in the sixteenth century appear in other jurisdictions are subsequently listed as barrios of Valladolid, but it is difficult to determine from available documents whether they were moved, or the political boundaries of the city were enlarged, or a change in ecclesiastical jurisdiction occurred. From the 1550s Valladolid was divided into two parishes ministered from the Franciscan and Augustinian monasteries, and a third parish was assigned to a secular curate of the cathedral after 1580. In 1649 the cathedral doctrina included all Spanish residents and six Indian barrios, while the Franciscans had five barrios and the Augustinians four, all of Indians. Here as elsewhere the regular orders were deprived of parochial functions in the late eighteenth century.

The Solís–Infante encomienda in the Sierra de Michoacán, often referred to as Pueblos de la Sierra, was made up of several individual native communities together with certain estancias usurped from Tzintzuntzan and Uruapan. In the *Suma* (*c.* 1548), 'Pamacoran' (Pomacoran, Punguacuaran, Pomacuaran; 1950: Pomacuarán, pueblo) is identified as the principal cabecera, and Aran, Aranza, and Cheran as subject cabeceras, with a total of fifteen 'barrios' between them; 'Sabiñan' (Sevina, Sabina, Siguinan, etc.; 1950: Sevina, pueblo) was subject to Cheran at that time. In 1571 there were 18 pueblos here, with priests living at Aranza and Sevina.[32] A juez congregador was appointed in 1593 to examine the area. By 1603 Indians had been moved into Capácuaro, Nahuatzen, and Sevina, but many had fled the congregations and were hiding in the mountains. Forced reductions continued in 1604 and then were given up as impossible. The old

cabecera of Aran (Arancaracua, Arancipacua) was deserted after 1639, but seventeen Indian pueblos survived until Independence. S Pedro Paracho (1950: Paracho de Verduzco, *villa*) became the chief cabecera and the residence of a teniente. The other pueblos were Ahuiran, Arantepacua, Aranza, Capácuaro, Comachuen, Cocucho, Cheran el Grande, Cheran Atzicurin, Nahuatzen (Naguatzin, Naguasi, etc.), Nurio Tepacua, Pomacuaran, Quinzio, Sevina, Tanaco, Turícuaro, and Urapicho.

Tacámbaro (1950: Tacámbaro de Codallos, ciudad) towards 1548 had a sub-cabecera, 'Cozaronde' (=Cutzaro?). Reports of 1570–1 name eighteen visitas of the monastery, some adjacent to the monastery and others as much as 10 leagues away. All were probably congregated at or near the main cabecera soon after 1600.[33]

Tarímbaro (also called Istapa in early years, and thus frequently confused with a nearby homonym, Istapa–Etúcuaro; 1950: Tarímbaro, pueblo) had at least a dozen estancias in the sixteenth century which seem to have been moved into the cabecera in 1604. Lands vacated by a distant sujeto, Santiago Irapeo, with its barrios of Acerumbenio, Cherepario, Tzitzio, and Ucareo, apparently were acquired by the Marquesado del Valle, as certain of these toponyms appear in later reports of Charo (q.v.).

A congregation of the eleven or twelve dependencies of Tiripitio (1950: Tiripetio, pueblo) proposed in 1594 was carried out in 1603, when all the Indians were ordered to move to Tiripitio and Acuitzio (Aquiceo). Another village, Huiramba (Uranbani, Huiciramban), survived as a pueblo, while the estancia of Ichaqueo re-appears as a barrio of Valladolid in 1649.

Towards 1548, Uruapan (Huruapa, etc.; easily confused with nearby Urapa, cf. *above*) had seven 'barrios', while the subject cabecera of Xirosto (Zirosto) had fourteen, and that of Xicalan had one barrio. An early congregation was made at Uruapan towards 1540. Reports of the late sixteenth century name twenty-four dependent settlements, to which we must add ten more that were abandoned in the 1600s.[34] At least eight pueblos disappeared in the congregation of 1599–

1604, and eleven others were de-populated in the seventeenth century;[35] some of the latter re-appear in later years as haciendas and ranchos. Seventeen Indian pueblos (eight of them cabeceras) survived in the late eighteenth century: Angaguan, Apó, Corupo, Jucutacato, Parangaricutiro, Paricutín (a new town?), S Felipe de los Herreros, S Lorenzo, Taciran, Taretan, Tingambato, Uruapan (1950: Uruapan del Progreso, ciudad), Xicalan, Xirosto, Zacán, Ziracuaretiro, and Zurumucapio.

Sta Ana Zacapo (1950: Zacapu, *villa*) in the 1540s had nine barrios. Two of them, Apúndaro and Guapaxécuaro, are mentioned in a document of 1575,[36] and seven others are named in a source of uncertain date (AMM, VI, p. 165). There was a congregation here from which many had fled in 1603. Of the barrios, only Tarejero survived as a pueblo.

Sources

Fragments have been found of the report submitted by Antonio de Caravajal, who made an official inspection of Michoacán in 1523-4; the areas described are Comanja, Erongarícuaro, Guaniqueo, and Uruapan.[37] A valuable document of 1533 concerning copper mining has been published (AMM, VI, pp. 35–52). The *Suma de Visitas* (*c.* 1548) gives succinct descriptions of the various encomiendas (PNE, I, nos. 155–7, 160–1, 270–1, 287–8, 310–12, 409, 459–60, 660–3, 813). In the Ovando series (1570–1), we have a general report on part of the bishopric,[38] another on secular curacies,[39] and detailed descriptions of the Augustinian doctrinas of Guango and Valladolid–Necotlan,[40] and Tacámbaro and Tiripitio.[41] The region is only partly covered in the 1579–81 series of relaciones geográficas. The report on Pátzcuaro (1581) is brief, describing the city and immediate environs,[42] while that from Necotlan (1579) is even briefer;[43] an interesting description of Tiripitio (1580) remains unpublished.[44] The baptism register of Aranza parish (1574–99) is at NYPL. The relación of Ponce (*passim*) describes Michoacán as it was during his several visits in 1585–7. There is abundant but uneven documentation concerning the congregations of 1592–1604.[45]

For the first half of the seventeenth century, we have three interesting descriptions of the diocese dated 1619,[46] 1639,[47] and 1649;[48] citations for tributary data in 1623 and 1657–98 are given above.

The alcaldía mayor as it was in 1743–5 is described in detail, with complete padrones of some places, in an unpublished report accompanied by a map.[49] The western part of the jurisdiction is covered in another series drawn up for the Inquisition in 1754.[50] There is an interesting MS map of the diocese dated 1762.[51] Ajofrín (I, pp. 207–47) visited parts of this area in 1764. Only one parish, Puruándiro, is represented in the 1777–8 series of 'topographic' reports.[52]

For the last years of the viceroyalty, we have a valuable discussion of Indian community properties and settlements in the southwestern part of the jurisdiction,[53] a report on the parish of Urecho in 1789,[54] and a list of settlements with population data for 1793.[55] The work of Martínez de Lejarza (1824) gives valuable details for the period of Independence.

The Tarascan area has attracted the attention of many scholars and others, from early colonial times to the present. The *Relación de...Michoacán*, written by an unknown Franciscan drawing on native informants towards 1540, is the chief source for the history of Michoacán from the Tarascan to the Spanish Conquest, and a mine of ethnohistorical data. The monographs of Brand (1944), Stanislawski (1947), West (1948), and Beals (1969) provide further details and analysis of early sources. Fintan Warren (1963b) concentrates on the early colonial period, as does Miranda Godínez (1967). The standard authorities on the missionary orders in Michoacán are Beaumont, Muñoz (1950), and Larrea (1643) for the Franciscan province, and González de la Puente and Basalenque for the Augustinians. The work of López Sarrelangue (1965) traces native dynasties under Spanish rule. The perceptive studies of Justino Fernández (1936a, b and c) contain material not found elsewhere. Romero (1860–1), Pérez Hernández (1872), and Bravo Ugarte (1963) should also be consulted.

114 *Valles*

This large jurisdiction occupies the eastern part of what is now San Luis Potosí state, with perhaps a bit of northeasternmost Querétaro. Above Xilitla, elevations of over 2,000 m are reached, but for the most part this is low (50–500 m), hot country draining into the Pánuco system. There is a good deal of rain.

'Oxitipan' appears in the Codex Mendoza as a distant tributary of the Aztecs, but it is not mentioned in any of the lists of Triple Alliance conquests, nor have we seen any other evidence linking this area to the Aztec empire. At least four different languages were spoken. The eastern part, low and fertile, was inhabited by the Huaxtecans (cf. Pánuco), divided into many autonomous communities. Perhaps among the more important political units here were Chalchicuauhtlan, Nexpan, Oxitipan, Tamintlan, Tantalan, Tauzan, and Tlapacuauhtlan, but there were others. To the south were several Náhuatl-speaking states, including Chalchitlan, Huexco, Tamazunchale, Topla, and perhaps Tlanchinamol. West of these was Xilitlan, a rather extensive realm with both Náhuatl and Otomí subjects,

perhaps allied with Metztitlan. The country beyond Xilitlan and Oxitipan to the west and north was the home of Pame-speaking Chichimecs, hunters and gatherers. Other Chichimec groups lived along the northern fringe.

While there may have been some previous contact with Spaniards, it was probably not until the mid-1520s that the Huaxtecans and Mexicans here came under encomienda rule, at first mostly a pretext for taking slaves. There was a good deal of resistance in the Coxcatlan–Xilitlan region. A Spanish outpost was established at Santiago de Valles in 1533. West of Valles, the Pame area remained uncontrolled until early in the seventeenth century when the Franciscans began reducing those Indians to mission settlements. Chichimecs from Tamaulipas and the Sierra Gorda continued to raid Spanish settlements until mid-eighteenth century.

Encomiendas

We may assume that there, as elsewhere, each relatively civilized native state was given in encomienda to a conquistador, poblador, or favorite of the governor. Cortés himself claimed Oxitipa and Tamoín, but reassignments of these and other places were made in 1527 by Nuño de Guzmán (many of these grants are listed in the Gómez Nieto report of 1532–3). Beginning in 1534, the audiencia cancelled most of Guzmán's grants, took some for the crown, and made fresh assignments for the most part to residents of Santiago de Valles.

Oxitipa was held first by Hernán Cortés and then (from 1527) by Nuño de Guzmán, who turned it over to a kinsman, Pedro de Guzmán.[1] Somewhat later, this encomienda was acquired by a poblador, Francisco Barrón, followed before 1550 by a son of the same name. Other Huaxtecan cabeceras (Amatlan, Tambolon, Tancaxen, Tancolon, Tancoxol, Tantoyn, etc.) were added to the Barrón holdings, which were later concentrated at Huehuetlan and persisted as a private encomienda at least until 1688.

Tanchinamol, Mecatlan, and Huesco were held by Francisco Bernal in 1532–3; the following year Mecatlan was acquired by Gregorio de Saldaña (*see below*), while Tanchinamol seems to have been assigned to Juan de Busto. In 1537 Saldaña gave a third of Mecatlan (perhaps all he owned) in dowry to a daughter, María, married to Bartolomé de Perales; part of Mecatlan's tributes were still going to Saldaña's heirs in 1548, but they escheated soon after, as did all of Tanchinamol's (Icaza, I, pp. 172, 190. Millares Carlo and Mantecón, II, no. 2452).

Juan de Carrascosa held several encomiendas which were taken from him by Guzmán, but still had Tamalol in 1532–3. His widow, Beatriz Ruiz, married Rodrigo de Orduña (listed in 1548), and was followed towards 1565 by a daughter married to Juan de Navarrete. By 1597 Rodrigo de Navarrete was encomendero. Escheatment occurred before 1643 (Icaza, I, p. 203).

Diego de Castañeda held several small villages (Tamacuiche, Tampasquín, Tamunal, Tanchava) near Valles towards 1550. His widow married Gerónimo de Mercado, listed in 1569.

Juan de Cervantes had a number of encomiendas in 1532–3, including Tamasunchale. He was succeeded *c.* 1564 by a son, Leonel de Cervantes, still alive in 1597. The place escheated after 1643.

Diego Cortés held Tampaca in 1532–48.

Juan de Gallegos had an encomienda taken from him by Guzmán (Chipman, p. 302). In 1548 he held Tampucho, perhaps the same as Tampuxeque, held in 1569–84 by Diego de Salas (Velázquez, I, p. 314 n.).

Cuzcatlan, a crown village in the 1530s, was later assigned to Diego Gutiérrez (Lavado), who before 1560 was succeeded by a daughter married to Juan Sánchez Bermejo (Icaza, I, p. 238). From *c.* 1567 to 1604 the holder was Alonso Montaño, a grandson of Gutiérrez, although a Francisco Tello is mentioned in 1597 (Dorantes de Carranza, p. 174). Cuzcatlan was still privately held in 1688.

Tamoín was at first shared between Hernán Cortés and his lieutenant-governor in Pánuco, Alonso de Mendoza. When Guzmán took Tamoín for himself in 1527, another encomienda, Tamistla or Tancuilave, was assigned to Mendoza. Tamoín was later acquired by Francisco de Villegas, followed by his widow, Catalina de Castro; on her death in 1543 it escheated. Meanwhile, Tancuilave was taken from Mendoza in 1527 and assigned first to Juan de Guzmán and then (1533–7) to the crown. Shortly before he died in 1537 Mendoza recovered the encomienda, to be succeeded by his widow, who then married Lic. Alemán (listed in 1548–73). Tancuilave escheated on Alemán's death, before 1576.[2]

Tantala (Tampacayal) and Topla were shared in 1532–3 between Cristóbal de Ortega and Alonso Romero (Icaza, I, p. 237). Romero's part seems to have been acquired by Ortega, who was succeeded by his widow, Catalina Maldonado, subsequently married to Diego de Torres. Torres is listed in 1548–53, and his son, Diego (Pedro) de Torres Maldonado, was holder in 1560–97. Escheatment occurred after 1643.

Alvaro de Rivera was encomendero of Tamalacuaco and Tanlocuc (Talecuen, Tealoquen?), near Valles, and was followed by a son of the same name (listed *c.* 1567), and a grandson, Diego de Rivera (listed in 1597) (Velázquez, 1946–8, I, p. 248).

Nespa in 1532–3 was held by Diego de las Roelas, while Tauzan was shared between him and Alonso de Navarrete; some four years later Navarrete purchased las Roelas's share of Tauzan and all of Nespa. This encomienda, which perhaps fell in part within the neighboring jurisdiction of Huexutla, escheated when Navarrete became an Augustinian in October 1555 (L de T, p. 264).

Cristóbal de Scpúlveda held several villages, including Chalchitlan and Tlapaguautla, in the early 1530s (Icaza, I, p. 241). His widow inherited the encomiendas and married Francisco de Torres (listed in 1548–73); escheatment occurred by 1597.

Tanzuy (Tanhuicin) was held by a Negro, Juan de Villanueva or Juan el Negro, *c.* 1550. By 1567 his widow, Ana (Antonia) Vázquez, had inherited (she is still listed in 1597).

There were other small encomiendas here (they are listed in the *Suma de Visitas*), most of which disappeared through de-population or in the sixteenth-century congregations.

Government

In early years this area was part of Pánuco province, although when Guzmán in 1533 founded the *villa* of Santiago de los Valles de Oxitipa he declared that it belonged to his gobierno of Nueva Galicia. This stratagem to give Guzmán an 'empire' stretching from sea to sea was foiled by the cedula of 19 March 1533, which returned Pánuco to the jurisdiction of the audiencia of Mexico. The order probably reached Pánuco toward the end of 1533. Guzmán went from Valles to Nueva Galicia in the spring of 1534, and soon thereafter the audiencia ruled that the Valles region belonged to the revived alcaldía mayor of Pánuco (Chipman, pp. 247–9), although the *villa* of Santiago continued to be governed by its ayuntamiento. Cs were assigned to various places as they escheated. Corregimientos of Cuzcatlan and Xilitla appear in a list of 1536, although the former was soon re-assigned to a private encomendero. El Tamohi (Tamoin) became a corregimiento in 1543, while Chachapala y Tanquian, Nanaguautla, Tamahol y Tamatlan, Tancuiname, Tlacolula, and Tanchinamol (with Huesco and Mecatlan) are listed in 1545. From 1555 Nespa y Tauzan had a C, as did Tancuilave (Tancuayalab) from *c.* 1575. These were all considered suffragan jurisdictions within the alcaldía mayor of Pánuco until *c.* 1579, when a separate AM was assigned to Valles.[3]

In 1575–7 the C of Tancuilave was Luis de Carvajal y de la Cueva, an ambitious magistrate who either was given or usurped jurisdiction in a number of other villages. Carvajal went to Spain in 1578 and the following year obtained a royal commission to colonize the country north and west of the Pánuco, with the title of governor and captain-general of Nuevo León. He returned, probably in early 1581, with a party of Jewish colonists to engage in a five-year jurisdictional conflict with the AMs of Pánuco and Valles. Soon thereafter the controversy ended with the arrest of Carvajal by the Inquisition.[4]

Towards 1600 the suffragan corregimientos were absorbed into the alcaldía mayor of Valles, and the final boundaries of the jurisdiction were roughly set, with the exception of the unreduced northern portion. Xilitla was annexed from Meztitlan in the seventeenth century, and Xaltocan (=Nespa y Tauzan?) was transferred to Huexutla somewhat later. The AM was re-designated C *c.* 1695, and his residence was moved from Valles to Tamaquichmon (Aquismon) towards 1728. At the beginning of 1749 a new gobierno was organized north of the Pánuco with the name of Nuevo Santander. Until the early 1770s the Canoas–La Laxa area belonged to Valles, but at that time it was transferred to Nuevo Santander, leaving a boundary coinciding with the present state line between San Luis Potosí and Tamaulipas.

In 1770 the C of Valles, living at Aquismon, kept deputies at Cuzcatlan, Tamazunchale, Tampamolon, and Valles.[5] From 1787 he was a sub-delegado subordinate to the intendente of S Luis Potosí.

Church

We know nothing of the early parochial history here, although there was surely a curate at Santiago de Valles from the 1530s. Both Augustinians and Franciscans worked here from the 1540s, the former establishing a mission at S Nicolás (Asunción) Xilitla *c.* 1550. Twenty years later there were also secular priests at Valles and Tampacayal (with residence at S Juan Bautista Cuzcatlan).

The Franciscans founded several mission-parishes here beginning in the 1570s. By 1586 their custodia of Tampico had seven houses shared between the jurisdictions of Valles and Pánuco; a Franciscan monastery was being built at the *villa* of Valles early in 1593.[6] Somewhat later, probably in the 1620s, Franciscans from the province of Michoacán began a mission among the Pames at Concepción del Valle del Maiz; henceforth this northwestern corner of the jurisdiction was claimed by the diocese of Michoacán.

By 1684 the secular priest of Tampacayal (Cuzcatlan) had moved to Santiago Tampamolón, and there was another secular parish at S Juan Tamazunchale. In that year the Franciscans of Tampico had houses at S Miguel Aquismon,

Sta María (S Antonio) de los Guayabos, S Diego Huehuetlan, S Francisco de la Palma, Concepción Tamitas (founded in 1647), Santiago Tamoin, Santiago Tampasquín, S Francisco Tancuayalab, S Pedro y S Pablo Tanlacum, and Santiago de Valles; within a decade, S Miguel Tamapache was added to this list. Another Franciscan mission, Sta María Acapulco, was abandoned in 1663, but again had a resident minister from *c.* 1749. The old doctrinas of Valle del Maiz (Michoacán Franciscans of the custodia of Río Verde) and Xilitla (Augustinian) continued to exist.

Towards 1740 the priest of Tampamolón moved to S Miguel Tancanhuitz, and a new secular parish had been established nearby at S Juan Cuzcatlan. The Franciscans of Tampico added to their chain of missions the doctrinas of Sta Ana Tanlaxas (*c.* 1700), Sta María Tampalatín (*c.* 1750), and S Francisco del Sauz (by 1790). Both Tancanhuitz and Tampamolón had curates towards the end of the colonial period, and Xilitla was secularized, but the parishes of the Tampico custodia remained in Franciscan hands with the possible exception of La Palma, listed as a Dominican doctrina in 1813.

Population and settlements

There must have been a rather dense Huaxtecan and Náhuatl-speaking population here at contact, with relatively few Chichimecs in the northwest. By 1533 a good many Indians had died or had been shipped off as slaves, and disease caused further subsequent loss. Here more than elsewhere, tributary figures give an incomplete picture, since the Pames and others on the Chichimec frontier were often exempt from tribute payment (cf. Scholes and Adams, 1959, p. 62). Reports of 1569–71 give a total of 4,238 tributaries (2,255 Huaxtecans, 1,632 Mexicans, 351 Otomies). Only 1,342 tributaries are registered in 1643, and 1,286 in 1688. On the other hand, the census of 1743 has 11,494 Indian families (3,456 Huaxtecans, 3,522 Mexicans, 900 Otomies, 3,516 Pames, and *c.* 100 'Mecos'). In 1803 there were 6,932 Indian tributaries.[7]

The Spanish and mestizo population was very small (12 families in 1569, 35 in 1743), but Negroes and mulattoes came to form a sizeable element (692 families in 1743, with the largest concentrations at Valles, Valle del Maiz, Tancuayalab, Tampamolón, and Tanlacum). Free Negro and mulatto tributaries numbered 1,369 in 1803.

In the sixteenth century there was a bewildering number of Indian settlements. Many of them disappeared before 1570, and many more were eliminated in the congregations of the 1590s; only sixteen Indian cabeceras are mentioned in the tribute lists of 1643–88, compared with well over a hundred in 1550. The process of consolidation continued in the seventeenth century and later, with frequent changes of site for one reason or another. We know very little, really, about the Spanish *villa* of Santiago de los Valles (1950: Ciudad de Valles, S. L. P.), which may have been moved about in early years. S Miguel Tamaquichmon (Aquismon; 1950: *villa*, S. L. P.) was perhaps founded in the 1570s (Velázquez, 1946–8, I, pp. 316–17, 319). The mission settlement of Valle del Maiz (1950: Ciudad del Maiz, S. L. P.) was destroyed by floods in the 1750s, after which it was moved from the river bank to a hillsite.

A number of places which survived as pueblos in the eighteenth century can be recognized in the reports of two centuries earlier. Among these are Valles, Aquismon, Cuzcatlan, Chalchicuautla, Chapulguacan, Huesco, Mecatlan, Picula, Tamazunchale, Tamoín, Tampacan, Tampamolón, Tampasquín, Tancuayalab, Tilaco (also claimed by Cadereyta), and Xilitla (Xalitla; Tlaziol in Otomí?). Other eighteenth-century pueblos seem to be later foundations, such as Acapulco, Astla, Chalco, Guayabos, Huehuetlan, Huichihuayan, Matlapan, La Palma, Puxantla, S Francisco, S Miguel de los Cántaros, S Nicolás de los Montes, El Sauz, Tamapache, Tamasopo, Tamitas, Tancanhuitz, Tanlacum, Tanlaxas, Tanquián, Tansosob, Tansuio, Valle del Maiz, and S Antonio Zayultepec. Altogether, in the 1790s the jurisdiction contained twenty-three cabeceras, fifteen haciendas, and many ranchos.

Sources

Chipman, in his admirable work on the years of Guzmán's rule at Pánuco, cites a unique *visita* report of 1532–3.[8] Descriptions of a great many places in the Valles area are found in the *c.* 1548 *Suma de Visitas* (PNE, I, *passim*). There are several reports in the Ovando series (1569–71).[9] The Ortelius map of *c.* 1584, of which there are many editions and plagiarisms, roughly locates most of the settlements mentioned in sixteenth-century reports (Cline, 1962, p. 104). Data on the congregations of the 1590s are scattered.[10]

We have tributary information for 1643–88,[11] as well as an informative journal of an archbishop's visit here in the spring of 1684.[12] Vetancurt (4a parte, pp. 92–4) adds details on the custodia of Tampico as it was *c.* 1697.

The C's report of 1743[13] gives much information not found in the summary of Villaseñor y Sánchez (I, pp. 98–120). We have noticed statistical tables concerning the Franciscan missions dated 1744,[14] 1753,[15] 1793 (Revilla Gigedo, pp. 94–7), and 1798.[16] A document submitted by the sub-delegado in 1792 contains historical data on settlements,[17] while another of 1793 lists toponyms.[18]

Complementing the work of Chipman (*see above*), Meade (1939, 1962) and Velázquez (1897–9, 1946–8) have written histories covering the Valles area, with useful citations and much information partly used above.

115 *Venado y la Hedionda*

This is a very dry, rolling country, now in western-most San Luis Potosí, most of it draining into a series of salt flats, with elevations of 1,650–2,500 m.

At contact the area was occupied by Guachichil-speaking Chichimecs, hunters and gatherers. They lived in rancherías of about one hundred persons each, and may have paid tribute to a chief at Mazapil (Powell, 1952, pp. 37, 235 n.).

Spaniards discovered the salt deposits of Peñol Blanco and Sta María *c.* 1562, but it was some years before they could exploit them.[1] Intermittent warfare was carried on with the Indians until the end of the century. By perhaps 1580 there was a seasonal Spanish occupation of the saltworks, conveniently close to the great mines of Zacatecas. In 1591 a group of Tlaxcalan colonists arrived at Agua del Venado, followed within a few years by a second Tlaxcalan colony at Agua Hedionda. Both became frontier posts from which food and clothing was distributed to the Chichimecs, and soon each had a sizeable sedentary population of converted Guachichiles, who with the Tlaxcalans aided the Spaniards in subduing still unreduced tribes in the vicinity.

No encomiendas were granted here.

Government

Until the late eighteenth century this area was shared between two and sometimes three juris-

dictions. The saltworks, Salinas de Sta María and Peñol Blanco, each had an AM appointed by the audiencia of Guadalaxara from 1582 at the latest.[2] The viceroy protested that these offices were superfluous, but ceased to object when he was given the right of appointment.[3] In later years the two *salinas* were governed by a single *administrador*, sometimes referred to as AM, generally the same individual who had contracted to operate the salt-works.

Meanwhile, the audiencia of Guadalaxara claimed control over Minas de las Charcas in 1573, and while the mines were abandoned on several occasions because of Indian hostility, an AM resided there more or less permanently from 1584. When El Venado and La Hedionda were settled in the 1590s, jurisdiction was disputed between Nueva España and Nueva Galicia, but by 1605 both places were within the alcaldía mayor of Charcas, the boundary between the two gobiernos passing between La Hedionda and S Luis Potosí; a deputy of the AM of Charcas resided at El Venado. As late as 1640 the viceroy of Nueva España appointed the AM of the Reales Salinas del Peñol Blanco, but by 1674 this magistrate seems to have become subordinate once again to Nueva Galicia, and had extended his jurisdiction to El Venado, where he kept a teniente; this so annoyed the AM of S Luis Potosí that he went to El Venado with a large entourage and arrested the AM of Peñol Blanco (Vclázquez, 1946–8, II, pp. 236 f.). The conflict continued in the late seventeenth and early eighteenth centuries, during most of which time the disputed villages were *de facto* ruled from Peñol Blanco.[4]

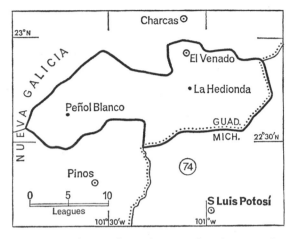

In 1767 El Venado and La Hedionda were the scene of an Indian uprising sparked by the general unrest due to the expulsion of the Jesuits. The rebellion was put down with great severity by the visitador general, José de Gálvez. Twelve Indians were executed, 72 were exiled, and the privileges of all (principally exemption from tribute payment) were cancelled; the erstwhile rebels were put to work in the salt mines. Subsequently the jurisdiction was governed by the AM–administrador of Peñol Blanco, who from 1786 was a sub-delegado under the intendente of S Luis Potosí.

Church

A Franciscan doctrina was founded at S Sebastián Agua del Venado very soon after its settling, probably in 1592 (Jiménez Moreno, 1958, p. 144). This parish, which included La Hedionda, fell within the diocese of Guadalaxara and belonged to the Franciscan province of Zacatecas until it was secularized shortly before 1760.[5] The saltworks of Peñol Blanco had no permanent curate; in 1603 they were visited by Augustinians from Zacatecas (province of S Nicolás de Michoacán).[6]

Population and settlements

The original Guachichil population here, perhaps a thousand families, did not thrive in the mission settlements. A count of 1674 shows 110 families of Tlaxcalans, 41 of Tarascans, and 40 of Guachichiles in the two settlements of El Venado and La Hedionda. Each year from December to May a large number of Indians from surrounding jurisdictions was transported to work at the salinas, but these transients did not figure in the permanent population (Humboldt, p. 375, N.Y. ed. vol. 3, pp. 259–60). A census of 1760 gives a total of 1,217 families representing 6,493 persons, mostly Indians; there were still some Guachichiles at this time, together with a growing number of Negroes. In 1799 there were 972 Indian and 367 free Negro and mulatto tributaries.[7]

Venado (1950: pueblo) and S Gerónimo de la Hedionda (1950: Moctezuma, ciudad) were both cabeceras in the late eighteenth century. In addition to these two pueblos, in 1793 there were eight haciendas, a number of ranchos, and a congregación of the Reales Salinas at Peñol Blanco.

Sources

The basic work on the Chichimecs is the MS attributed to Gonzalo de las Casas.[8] The history of the Tlaxcalan colonies is briefly treated in Gibson (1952, pp. 185 f.) and Powell (1952, pp. 195–220). Seventeenth-century descriptions of this region are found in documents of *c.* 1605 (Mota y Escobar, pp. 159–60), *c.* 1620 (Arregui, p. 124), and 1674 (Velázquez, 1946–8, II, pp. 236–45).

Villaseñor y Sánchez (II, p. 267) has a succinct notice of El Venado as it was *c.* 1743. Population data for 1760 are found in a diocesan report.[9] Much has been written about the rebellion of 1767 and its aftermath (Priestley, 1916, pp. 219–20. Velázquez, 1946–8, II, pp. 521–58). Finally, we have a complete list of placenames compiled in 1793.[10]

More details are found in the works of Velázquez (1897–9, 1946–8).

116 *Vera Cruz Nueva*

Now in central Veracruz state, this is a hot, low region (less than 100 m above sea level) with numerous rivers draining into the Gulf. It includes the delta of the Papaloapan (Alvarado) with an intricate system of lagoons and marshes. A rather heavy, year-round precipitation produces rain

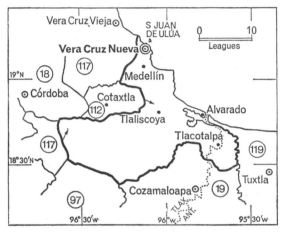

forest over much of the area. Settlements, today as in pre-Columbian times, are on natural levees.

Acozpan, Mictlancuauhtla, Oxpichan, Teociocan, and Tlapanicxitlan were the political divisions in the north; all delivered tribute to the Aztec garrison at Cuetlaxtlan. Near the mouth of the Papaloapan was Tlacotlalpan, ruled by a calpixqui appointed from Tenochtitlan and tributary to Tochtépec. Náhuatl was the language spoken.

According to the 'Description' of 1532, the coastal area near Vera Cruz was unhealthy long before the Spaniards arrived, ravaged by epidemics which left it de-populated on several occasions, after which the Mexica emperor would send thousands of colonists from the central plateau and give them lands and temporary freedom from tribute payment. Another source indicates that immigration to this hot and fertile country occurred in times of famine in central Mexico (Durán, I, pp. 248–9). Mictlancuauhtla is listed among the conquests of Ahuítzotl, and it

may be that most or all of this region had recently been settled in this way when the Spaniards arrived.

Grijalva's expedition reached this coast in June 1518, visiting both Tlacotlalpan and Tlapanicxitlan. Cortés and his men landed at Chalchicueyecan (near modern Veracruz) in April of the following year before continuing up the coast to Quiahuahuixtlan, which had been chosen as the site of Villa Rica. Within the next year most of the area came under Spanish control, although Tlacotlalpan may not have been reduced until after Sandoval's capture of Tochtépec at the end of 1521.

Encomiendas

Cortés considered all of the native states here subject to Cotaxtla, which he took for himself.[1] The *villa* of Medellín (*see below*) was moved from its first inland site in 1523 to the vicinity of Mitlancuautla, and two years later its ayuntamiento petitioned to have 'Ospacha' (Oxpichan) and Teziuca (Tlaliscoya) assigned to it as *propios* (ENE, I, p. 84. Herrera, 1a década, p. 24. Oviedo, III, pp. 427, 524). However, Tlaliscoya seems to have been assigned to Alvaro Maldonado ('el fiero'), a conquistador and resident of Medellín (Icaza, I, p. 130). Maldonado was succeeded in 1527 by his widow, María del Rincón, but Governor Estrada gave his encomienda to Gil de Molina (Icaza, II, p. 313). Escheatment of Tlaliscoya occurred by 1534.

We know nothing of encomenderos in the remaining places nearby (Acozpan or Alcozagua, Mitlancuautla, Ospicha, Tlapaniquita); they were still claimed by Cortés in 1532, but they were probably taken for the crown then or soon after.

Tlacotalpa was assigned to another conquistador and resident of Vera Cruz, Alonso Romero, followed by his widow, Isabel Vélez. It escheated on the latter's death, in September, 1541 (L de T, p. 312).

Government

In the 1520s jurisdiction here was exercised by the ayuntamientos of Villa Rica and Medellín. When

360

Villa Rica was moved from distant Quiahuiztlan to a more southerly site in 1525, the acting governors ordered the abandonment of Medellín, and by 1528 the few Spaniards who remained at the latter *villa* had moved to Vera Cruz (La Antigua). In 1529 the entire coastal area was being exploited ('se sirve dello') by the AM of Villa Rica (ENE, I, p. 141).

Tezayuca (Tlaliscoya) became a corregimiento by 1534, and Tlacotalpa seven years later. In the 1550s and later we find Tezayuca annexed to the jurisdiction of Vera Cruz (Villa Rica), and Tlacotalpa administered from Teutila, the latter a temporary situation.[2] Towards 1570 the C of Tlacotalpa was re-designated AM, and the sequestered Marquesado holdings (Tuxtla y Cotaxtla, q.v.) were attached to his jurisdiction until 1595.[3]

Until the end of the sixteenth century the port of S Juan de Ulúa and nearby crown villages were thus controlled by the AM of Vera Cruz (cf. Vera Cruz Vieja), whose jurisdiction also included Cempoala, Mizantla, and Zongolica. In 1599–1600 the city of Vera Cruz was moved to the mainland opposite S Juan de Ulúa, at which time the castellan of that fortress was made *justicia mayor de la tierra firme* and thus became chief magistrate in the new city (Calderón Quijano, p. 22). At first the AM of Vera Cruz Vieja continued to administer justice as far south as Tlacotalpa (which was eliminated as a separate alcaldía mayor), but within a few years the jurisdiction was divided and a C was appointed to Vera Cruz Nueva and Tlacotalpa.[4] From 1629 appointment to the latter office was made in Spain, and towards the end of that century the magistrate began to be referred to as gobernador (Díez de la Calle, fol. 60v. Títulos de Indias, p. 233). After 1786 the governor of Vera Cruz Nueva received the additional title of intendente, with a much enlarged supervisory jurisdiction outside his immediate gobierno (Beleña, II, p. vi. Navarro García, pp. 60, 71).

Church

In early years the northern part of this area was visited by a curate from Vera Cruz (Vieja); there was probably also a priest at Medellín in the 1520s.

By 1570 we find a chaplain–curate at the castle of S Juan de Ulúa, while the Tlaliscoya–Tlacotalpa region belonged to the parish of Cozamaloapa. Towards 1600 new parishes were founded at Vera Cruz Nueva (the parish church was first in the Augustinian monastery; later, the patron was S Sebastián), Sta María Tlaliscoya, and S Cristóbal Tlacotalpa. The last-named place was reduced to the category of visita after 1618 and did not again become a separate parish until mid-eighteenth century. By 1743 there were resident curates at S Cristóbal Alvarado and S Miguel Medellín, while the priest of Tlaliscoya had moved to Cotaxtla, but in 1777 both Tlaliscoya and Tlacotalpa were parish seats. All were in the diocese of Tlaxcala. The principal regular orders maintained monasteries at Vera Cruz Nueva.

Population and settlements

By 1532 the native population here was already much reduced, and it was still dwindling in 1570 when there were but 443 Náhuatl-speaking tributaries. Later counts give 134 tributaries in 1626, 189 in 1696, 347 Indian families in 1743, and 434 in 1777 (419 at Tlacotalpa, 15 at Tlaliscoya). By 1799 there were 545 Indian tributaries in the jurisdiction.[5] The empty lands were taken up by cattle ranches.

Reports of 1570–1 show 600 Negro slaves (individuals) together with some mulattoes and a few Spaniards living at the fortress of S Juan de Ulúa, and six or eight Spanish vecinos at Tlacotalpa. Some 200 Spanish and mestizo residents moved to Vera Cruz Nueva in 1599–1600, but the overall population remained predominantly Negroid throughout the later colonial period. In 1609–18 Bishop Mota y Escobar found small settlements of Spaniards and Negroes at Tlaliscoya, Tlacotalpa, and Alvarado, and a colony of Greek fishermen intermarried with Negroes at the mouth of the Jamapa river (Boca del Río). A census of 1754 shows 2,751 'Spaniards' and 3,065 persons of 'color' at Vera Cruz Nueva, divided into 1,645 families; in the same year there were 325 individuals in the castle of S Juan de Ulúa, and 918 persons (75 Spaniards, 65 Indians, the rest mostly mulattoes) scattered along the Jamapa. Humboldt

(p. 181, N.Y. ed., vol. 2, pp. 250 ff.) indicates that the city had 16,000 inhabitants, excluding the military, towards 1800.

Mitlancuautla (Mitangutlan, etc.), Oxpichan (Espiche, Uzpicha), Alcozagua (Alcuzuacan, Acozpan?), and Tlapaniquita, all Indian communities in the lower reaches of the Jamapa (Xamapa) river, together with the former *villa* of Medellín, had a congregation *c.* 1600. Medellín (1950: Medellín de Bravo and Boca del Río, pueblos) survived with the title of *villa* in the eighteenth century. In 1777 there were three haciendas, five ranchos, two inns, and a ranchería (Xamapa) in this area.

Tlaliscoya (Teziuca, Tezayuca, etc.; Tlalixcoyan; 1950: *villa*) had two estancias (Amayaca, Cavtla) within two leagues in 1571. Cuauhtla survived a congregation proposed in 1598 but is not mentioned after 1618.[6]

Tlacotalpa (Tacotlalpan; 1950: Tlacotalpan, ciudad) had five dependencies on both sides of the Alvarado up to five leagues from the cabecera in 1570–1600. Only one of them, Atlacintla, continued as a pueblo, Alvarado, after a congregation of *c.* 1600.[7] Both were predominantly mulatto settlements in the eighteenth century.

A fortress on the island of S Juan de Ulúa was begun during the reign of viceroy Mendoza and was much modified in later years, with additional constructions on the mainland opposite. This was the only recognized port on the Gulf coast of New Spain, the terminus of the annual *flotas* which maintained communication with Spain, bringing European goods to Mexico and returning with American and Asiatic merchandise and silver. It was also the base for the Armada de Barlovento, maintained to protect the fleets and the port from raids by foreign privateers and pirates. In the sixteenth century goods were transferred in launches between this port and the old city of Vera Cruz, five leagues up the coast, while passengers went ashore opposite Ulúa, where there were three inns (Ventas de Buitrón) in 1588. The city was moved here (1950: Veracruz Llave, ciudad) in 1599–1600, and was subsequently protected by a wall and additional batteries and fortifications.

Sources

There are eyewitness accounts of the coast and its people as they appeared to the Spaniards in 1518–19 (Cortés, pp. 19–20. Díaz del Castillo, I, pp. 68–73, 125. Mártir de Anglería, I, pp. 405–10, 415–16, 419–23; II, p. 440). We have what seems to be a fragment of the lost 'Description de la Tierra' of 1531–2 commenting on the near disappearance of the native population (Herrera, 4a década, p. 236). A letter from the AM describing port facilities (ENE, VI, pp. 154–5) is followed by testimony of the damage done there by a hurricane (*ibid.*, pp. 180–206), both dated 1552. Tribute records for Tlacotalpa and Tlaliscoya run from 1541 to 1565 (L de T, pp. 312–15, 470–1). The area is described in some detail in two reports by clerics written in 1570–1 (PNE, V, pp. 189–201, 235–7). The AMs of Tlacotalpa (PNE, V, pp. 1–11) and Vera Cruz[8] both submitted relaciones, accompanied by maps, in 1580 (cf. Cline, 1959).

There is an interesting congregation report from Tlacotalpa, dated 1600.[9] Mota y Escobar passed through here twice, in 1609 and 1618,[10] and Palafox in 1646,[11] both leaving valuable accounts. Tributary data for 1626–96 are gleaned from several documents.[12]

The governor's report of 1743–4[13] contains much information omitted in the summary of Villaseñor y Sánchez (I, pp. 271–8) and is accompanied by a complete matrícula. The Vera Cruz–Medellín region is described in a good report made for the Inquisition in 1754.[14] Ajofrín (I, pp. 33–40) was here in 1763, and made a map of the city. For 1777, there are padrones submitted by the curates of Alvarado, Medellín, Tlacotalpa, and Tlaliscoya.[15]

Many travelers other than those mentioned visited Vera Cruz and left descriptions of the port and city, including González de Mendoza (pp. 349–50) in 1581, Ponce (I, pp. 14–15; II, p. 315) in 1584–8, Gage (pp. 32–9) in 1625, Navarrete (I, p. 24) in 1646, Gemelli Carreri (II, pp. 244–9) in 1697 and López Matoso in 1816–17. There is a good monographic history of the port and its fortifications, well illustrated (Calderón Quijano, 1953). Further data on the Tlacotalpa area are found in Scholes and Warren (1965).

117 *Vera Cruz Vieja*

As finally limited, this jurisdiction contained three more or less disconnected areas. The first extends from below Vera Cruz Vieja (La Antigua) north along the coast to Barra de las Palmas and some distance inland; it is hot, dry country (0–1,000 m) with numerous short watercourses draining into the Gulf. West of Vera Cruz Vieja is another group of villages (Tenampa, etc.) in the foothills of Pico de Orizaba (500–1,100 m) with somewhat more rainfall. Far off to the southwest is the enclave of Zongolica, in the upper reaches of the Tonto river (150–2,500 m), most of it cool with heavy precipitation. All three sections are in central Veracruz state.

There were several Totonac states here, the most important being Cempoallan, with a large population clustered around a ceremonial center. Inland from Cempoallan were Atocpan and Tizapantzinco, each with an Aztec garrison, and Chicoacentépec; there may have been other autonomous communities in this vicinity. Farther up the coast, the political divisions included Quiahuahuixtlan (a hilltop fortress) and Colipan (Colícpac?). Beyond these places were other Totonac communities (Mazantle, Cipactlan, Pilopan, Paxil–Tlalocan, Tochpan, etc.) dominated by a Mexican garrison at Nauhtlan. Tribute from these places was probably sent directly to Tenochtitlan.

Ozomatzintlan and Tlatictlan, together with Tenampa, were Náhuatl-speaking communities, all perhaps under a single ruler. Tlatictlan is listed as a conquest of Moctezuma the elder, but none of these names appears in the Matrícula de Tributos.

Tzoncoliuhcan was an old colony of Nahua-speaking people called Nonoalcas, who were perhaps allies of the Aztecs, most likely ruled by a single tlatoani (cf. *Historia Tolteca–Chichimeca*).

Juan de Grijalva's fleet was on this coast in June, 1518, and left behind a Spaniard, Miguel de Zaragoza, who lived here among the Indians until the arrival of Cortés's expedition in April of the following year when he rejoined his countrymen (Dorantes de Carranza, pp. 217–18). The Totonac lords, weary of Aztec oppression, received the Spaniards amicably. Cortés founded Villa Rica de la Vera Cruz first near Ulúa and then (18 May 1519) at Quiahuahuixtlan, setting forth for Tenochtitlan in August. Before the end of 1519 a joint expedition of Spaniards from Villa Rica and Indians from Cempoallan attacked and overcame the Aztec garrison at Nauhtlan (ENE, I, p. 76).

Encomiendas

Cempoala was held first by Cortés and then assigned to Alvaro de Saavedra, escheating under the first audiencia. Later it was given to the contador, Rodrigo de Albornoz. Final escheatment occurred in April, 1544.[1]

Mizantla, held by Luis de Saavedra in 1527–8, was a crown possession by 1534.[2]

Ozumacintla and Tlatectla, which may have included Tenampa and Tlacotepec, were given by Cortés to the conquistador Diego Marmolejo, succeeded on his death (after 1533) by his widow, who then married Juan de Miranda. The encomienda escheated when the latter died in March, 1564 (ENE, III, pp. 35–7; XV, p. 8. L de T, p. 277. Millares Carlo and Mantecón, I, no. 392).

Pilopan was held by Miguel de Zaragoza until his death in 1527; it was taken for the crown soon thereafter (Icaza, I, p. 107). Other nearby villages, including Colipa and Papalo(te), may have been assigned to Hernando de Padilla; they had escheated by 1534.[3]

Zongolica was divided between two encomenderos, one half escheating before 1534. The other share was held by Pedro de Sepúlveda, a resident of Vera Cruz, followed after 1537 by a daughter; it went to the crown sometime between 1550 and 1560.

Probably there were other early encomiendas here about which we know nothing. The few surviving Indian communities were all under crown control by 1564.

Government

La Villa Rica de la Vera Cruz, the first Spanish settlement in Mexico, was moved from Quiahuizt-

In the early 1530s the second audiencia appointed Cs to 'Miçante' (Mizantla), 'Pueblos de tapacoya e de los pueblos de padilla e nautla e colipa e papalo' (Papalote de la Sierra, 'por otro nombre Tizapancingo y Atlaliloya y Cicaquautla' in 1545), and the crown's half of Zongolica. Cotaxtla and

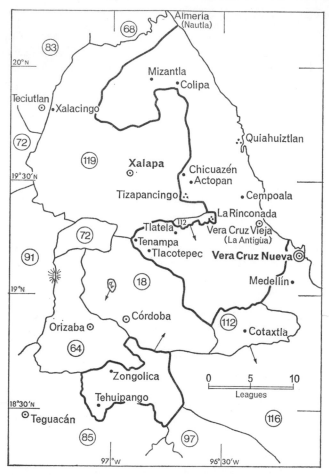

lan to a new site eight leagues south (La Antigua) in 1525 (Oviedo y Valdés, III, p. 529). Its jurisdiction was gradually circumscribed with the creation of other ayuntamientos. In the mid-1520s it extended westward to meet the limits of Mexico–Tenochtitlan near Perote, north along the coast to Huaxteca, and south to join Guazacualco (*Actas de Cabildo*, II, p. 34). In 1529 the AM of Vera Cruz controlled Guaspaltepec (cf. Cozamaloapa), Tataltetelco (cf. Córdoba), Cotaxtla and Rinconada (cf. Tuxtla y Cotaxtla), and Cempoala (ENE, I, p. 141).

La Rinconada, meanwhile, belonged to the Marquesado del Valle from 1530. Two more corregimientos, Cempoala and Chicuacentepec, appear in the 1545 list; by 1566 they had been combined under a single C whose jurisdiction included Atocpa and Tenampa. The AM of Vera Cruz doubled as C of Cempoala and supervised the other corregimientos together with that of Guatusco (cf. Córdoba).[4]

A major jurisdictional change occurred after 1599–1600, when the inhabitants of Vera Cruz moved from the site occupied since 1525 (thereafter referred to as Vera Cruz Vieja, or Antigua) to the final site (Vera Cruz Nueva) on the mainland opposite S Juan de Ulúa. At this time a separate C was appointed to Vera Cruz Nueva (q.v.). The AM of Vera Cruz Vieja continued to administer the hinterland and was given jurisdiction in Tlacotalpa, but within a few years the southern part of this vast province was transferred to Vera Cruz Nueva.[5] Simultaneously, in the first years of the seventeenth century the old corregimientos of Cempoala, Mizantla, and Zongolica were absorbed by the alcaldía mayor of Vera Cruz Vieja. Colipa seems to have been acquired from Xalapa about the same time, while Guatusco became an independent jurisdiction.[6]

In the seventeenth century Indian tributes here seem to have been collected by the AM of Xalapa. The magistrate of Vera Cruz Vieja occasionally lived at Mizantla, by which name the jurisdiction is referred to in some documents. In 1770 it was recommended that distant Zongolica be administered from Orizaba, but we do not know whether such a transfer was made.[7] The AM was redesignated subdelegado under the gobernador-intendente of Vera Cruz (Nueva) from 1787.

Church

From its foundation, Villa Rica de la Vera Cruz had a chaplain who became parish curate. It also had a Franciscan monastery, perhaps as early as 1529, although no such establishment is recorded in 1571 (Kubler, 1948, p. 485). Mizantla was visited in the 1550s by Franciscans working out of Xalapa, while Zongolica had a small Franciscan monastery, secularized *c.* 1567 (*Alegaciones...*, fol. 23). Two years later, we find secular priests in charge of Vera Cruz, Asunción Mizantla, and S Francisco Zongolica.

When Vera Cruz was moved to its final site in 1600, its parish was divided, a priest remaining at Vera Cruz Vieja to attend to the few Spanish and Negro residents and a handful of Indians at Cempoala. The Franciscan cloister was moved to Vera Cruz Nueva before 1609. In 1754 Vera Cruz Vieja was being visited from Apazapan (cf. Tuxtla y Cotaxtla), but nine years later it again had a

resident curate. New parishes were founded at S Francisco Actopan and Santiago Tehuipango before 1777. All were in the diocese of Tlaxcala.

Various places other than those mentioned were visited at times by priests from adjoining jurisdictions. Actopan and Chicuacentepec belonged to the parish of Tlacolula in 1569–1643, while the villages of Tenampa, Tlatela, and Tlacotepec had their parish seat at Quimixtlan in 1569, at S Antonio Guatusco in 1609–43, and at Totutla in 1777.

Population and settlements

The native population at contact was estimated at 20–30,000 tributaries in Cempoala, and 6,000 at Colipa. Totonac was spoken from Cempoala north and Náhuatl to the south; the Ozumacintla-Tlatectla region may have been settled by recent Náhuatl immigrants (cf. Vera Cruz Nueva).

In May or June 1520, smallpox (introduced by a Negro slave) broke out at Cempoala. A decade later there were only twenty tributaries there and the whole coast was reported to be 'despoblada' (ENE, I, p. 141). In 1570 Mizantla and Colipa together had 705 tributaries, Cempoala-Actopan-Chicuacentepec had 176, and the Tlacotepec area had perhaps 50. Zongolica in that year had 770 tributaries, making a total of 1,701 tributary families in the jurisdiction in 1570. Later counts show 380 tributaries in 1626, 820 in 1696, 1,326 Indian families in 1743, and 902 tributaries in 1796.[8]

In early years, many Spaniards who appeared as vecinos of Villa Rica actually lived in healthier places in the interior. In 1571 the city is said to have had 200 vecinos and 600 Negro slaves. Ten years later only 140 vecinos are reported, while an estimate of 1590 gives 200 (Calderón Quijano, 1953). Nearly all moved to Vera Cruz Nueva in 1599–1600. Mota y Escobar in 1609 found only eight Spaniards and some free Negroes at Vera Cruz Vieja (Antigua), but by this time there were 30 Spanish families and a good number of Negroes and mulattoes living on cattle haciendas along the coast between Cempoala and Nautla. Travelers passing through the old 'city' in 1697 and 1763 describe it as a fishing village with only a few inhabitants, while a count of *c.* 1743 gives 230 non-Indian families in the jurisdiction. The 1754 report mentions seven families of Spaniards and 70 of pardos, a total of 300 individuals, at Antigua Veracruz (1950: congregación).

Cortés (p. 34) noted that there were fifty '*villas y fortalezas*' near Cempoala in 1519. Several places in that vicinity which may once have been populous settlements (Quiahuiztlan, Papalote, Tizapancingo, etc.) disappeared soon after the Conquest. Cempoala itself (Cenpuala, etc.; briefly baptized Sevilla in 1519–20; 1950: Zempoala, congregación), Atocpa (Actopan in the eighteenth century; 1950: pueblo), and Chicuacentepec (Santiago Chicuazén in 1777; 1950: Chicuasén, congregación), were congregated with their estancias at the respective cabeceras, surviving as small Indian pueblos, by 1569. The natives of Cempoala were to have moved to Xalapa towards 1600, but either this did not happen or they soon returned. In 1765 twenty-two families of Indians from Pensacola (Florida) were settled near Cempoala in a colony called S Carlos (1950: Ursulo Galván, *villa*) (Gold, 1965).

Both Colipa (1950: pueblo) and Mizantla (Mizante or Mizantle in early years; 1950: Misantla, ciudad) originally had numerous dependent settlements extending to the Gulf coast. The cabecera of Mizantla was moved several leagues north to its final site in 1564, but there had been an earlier congregation here in the 1550s, at which time the old señoríos of Cipactlan, Paxil-Tlalocan, Pilopan, and Tochpan apparently lost their cabecera status.[9] Mizantla itself was congregated at the former site of Tochpan, and in 1569 retained five subject estancias up to eight leagues distant (their inhabitants were moved to the cabecera in still another congregation *c.* 1603) (Ramírez Lavoignet, 1959, pp. 138–9). The estancias of Colipa were gathered at their cabecera towards 1558, after which the abandoned coastal plains were taken over by Spanish cattlemen; the cabecera was moved to a new site before 1588 (*ibid.*, p. 124). Colipa appears as 'Macuimanalco' in a document of 1696.[10]

We hesitatingly identify the encomienda of Ozumacintla y Tlatectla, as it appears in documents of 1552–64, with a group of villages which subsequently appear in the jurisdiction of Vera Cruz Vieja.[11] These were S Francisco Tenampa (1950: pueblo), S Martín Tlacotepec (1950: Tlacotepec de Mejía, pueblo), and Sta María Tlatela.

Zongolica (Zonguiluca in 1548; Tzoncoliuhcan in 1610–43; Songolica, etc.; 1950: Zongolica, ciudad) had thirteen estancias in 1569, five in the mountains and eight in the lowlands up to seven leagues from the cabecera. A congregation proposed in 1598 seems to have had little effect.[12] While there was considerable change in toponymy through the years, ten places besides the cabecera survived as pueblos in the 1770s: S Sebastián Alcomunga (also claimed as subject to Elosuchitlan, cf. Teguacán), Astasinga, Coezala, Mistla or Mixtlan, Los Reyes, S Gerónimo (Atzingo), Tehuipango, Tenexapa, Teoixhuacan, and Tlaquilpa.[13]

Sources

As the first part of Mexico explored by Cortés and his party in 1519, the Cempoala area was described by the conquistadors in several firsthand accounts (Aguilar, pp. 88–9. Cortés, pp. 19–25, 34–6. Díaz del Castillo, I, pp. 72–3, 125–7, 132–80). Only Zongolica is represented by an article of *c.* 1548 in the *Suma de Visitas* (PNE, I, no. 843). There are reports of 1569–71 from the various parish priests (García Pimentel, 1904, pp. 12, 15. PNE, V, pp. 189–201, 204–5, 230–1, 244). A short but useful relación was submitted by the C of Mizantla in 1579,[14] and a more detailed but confused report from the AM of Vera Cruz in 1580,[15] each accompanied by a map.

The area was visited by Bishop Mota y Escobar in 1609–10,[16] and by Bishop Palafox in 1643–6,[17] both leaving valuable journals. Tributary data for 1626–96 are derived from several documents.[18]

A lost report of *c.* 1743 is summarized in Villaseñor y Sánchez (I, pp. 279–80). For the second half of the eighteenth century, we have a brief report dated 1754 describing the vicinity of Vera Cruz,[19] a succinct description of the old city in 1763 (Ajofrín, I, p. 40), and padrones sent in by the curates of Actopan, Mizantla, and Tehuipango in 1777.[20]

Ramírez Lavoignet (1959) cites many documents having to do with the Mizantla region. Clinc (1959) reproduces various sixteenth-century maps and identifies placenames. The little guide of

Gurría Lacroix (1960) about Cempoala is useful. Other monographic treatment of this area includes Bernal and Dávalos Hurtado (1952–3) and Kelly and Palerm (1952).

118 *Villa Alta*

Villa Alta de San Ildefonso de los Zapotecas was a very large and important jurisdiction extending from the top of the Sierra Madre down into the Gulf coastal plains, in what is now northeastern Oaxaca with a slice of Veracruz. West of the great peak of Zempoaltépetl (3,396 m) lies the valley of Cajonos or Villa Alta (400–2,000 m) draining into the Tesechoacán river, an affluent of the Papaloapan. To the east of that mountain are the headwaters of other streams flowing northeastward into the Coatzacoalcos system. There is rain much of the year, and great temperature variation depending on elevation. Much of the area is forested.

In 1520 this was the home of Indians speaking four distinct languages. The mountain Zapotec (there were two dialects, Cajono and Netzicho) filled the Cajonos valley and crossed the mountains to the east where their settlements extended far down onto the coastal plain. Political divisions here included Cacalotépec, Camotlan, Comaltépec (Zapotec, Guiac-laxun), Cuexcomaltépec, Choapan (Guinvetzi), Hueyacatépec, Ixcuintépec, Lachichina, Lalopa, Lazagaya, Malinaltépec, Tabaá, Taguí, Tecomatlan, Tehuilotépec, Temaxcalapa, Teotlaxco, Tepecpanzacoalco, Tiltépec, Tizatépec, Totolinca, Yabago, Yachave, Yagavila, Yagayó, Yatobi, Yaxila, and Zultépec.

Below the Zapotec country to the north was a pocket of Chinantec-speakers known as Guatinicamane, perhaps divided into several communities: Lalana, Petlapa, Teotaltzinco, Tlapanala, and Toavela (cf. Weitlaner, 1961). Beyond these people and still further down in the hot country were the headquarters of a Popolucan state, Cuauhcuetzpaltépec.

On the slopes of Zempoaltépetl, in well-defended settlements on mountain ridges, lived the wild Mixes. Mixitlan or Mixistlan (Mixe, Tepchquiushmj) was their capital, and may have exercised some political control over the states of Amaltépec, Ayacaxtépec (Uach-quiatezm), Ayacaxtla, Chichicaxtépec (Pushyom), Huehuetépec, Maxihuixi, Metépec, Ocotépec (Tshll-qm – the Mixe were not strong on vowels), Tlahuiltoltépec (Saam-deshm), Tonaguía, Totontépec, Xareta, Xochitépec, and Yacoche (Yucmedej).

In the tropical rain forest off to the northeast was a populous Zapotecan kingdom, Xaltépec (Zapotec, Yiacvetze), which had a common boundary with Coatzacualco.

Although the Aztec histories claim that Moctezuma II won a campaign against Xaltépec, other sources indicate that both the Mixe and the mountain Zapotec, while they fought each other, were unsubjugated by the Triple Alliance (Herrera, 4a década, pp. 234–5). Both Xaltépec and Cuauhcuetzpaltépec, however, may have had some military agreement with the Aztecs.

Gonzalo de Sandoval's army in 1522 entered the northern part of this region, and after some opposition brought Tiltépec and Xaltépec under Spanish control (Díaz del Castillo, II, pp. 93f.). A small party of Spaniards in that year explored the northern slope of the Sierra Madre perhaps as far as Utlatépec (cf. Teguantepec), while Sandoval assigned several encomiendas (Guaspaltepec, Tiltepec, Xaltepec) (Herrera, 3a década, p. 133). Rodrigo de Rangel led two campaigns against the mountain Zapotec and the Mixe in 1523–4 and made some headway, at least with the Zapotec, but they soon rebelled (Herrera, 3a década, p. 213. Oviedo y Valdés, III, p. 461). The acting governors in 1526 sent out another expedition under Gaspar Pacheco and Diego de Figueroa, who hunted down the Indians with dogs and established Villa

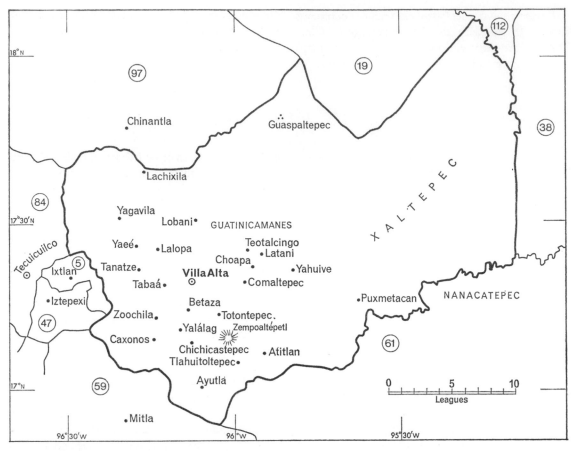

Alta de S Ildefonso in 1527, after which they distributed the various Indian states in encomienda to the settlers of that fortress settlement. It was perhaps at this time that a garrison of Mexican soldiers was stationed at Analco, near Villa Alta. The Spaniards dedicated themselves to enslaving the Indians and forcing them to work the gold placers, which brought on another rebellion at Tiltépec (1531) and another 'pacifying' foray under Francisco Maldonado (1533) (ENE, III, p. 111). There were subsequent troubles, including a general uprising in 1550, another at Choapan in 1552, and the Mixe rebellion of 1570.[1]

Encomiendas and government

Perhaps the first AM of the province of Zapotecas was Luis de Berrio, sent by the audiencia in 1529.[2] Berrio and the ayuntamiento of Villa Alta engaged in an acrimonious territorial dispute with the rival municipal governments of Vera Cruz, Guazacualco, and Antequera concerning which had the right to exploit the human and natural resources of a vast area (BAGN, x, p. 283. Díaz del Castillo, II, p. 97). In 1529–30 Guaspaltepec was included within the limits of Vera Cruz, while Nexapa and the Chontal country were contested in a three-way conflict between Villa Alta, Antequera, and Hernán Cortés (who insisted they belonged to his encomienda of Teguantepec). This left Villa Alta in possession of the mountain Zapotec, part of the Mixe, and the Guatinicamanes. The old kingdom of Xaltepec was contested at this time between Villa Alta and Guazacualco.

After the second audiencia convened in 1531, certain encomiendas here were taken for the crown. These were grouped in nine corregimientos: Guatinicamanes (half remained in private encomienda); Hueyacatepec y la Hoya; Iscuintepec y

368

Xuquila; Lalana 'e otros pueblezuelos'; Metepec y Alotepec; Nestepec ($\frac{1}{3}$) y Teotalcingo ($\frac{1}{2}$); Quezalapa, Nanacatepec, Xaltepec ($\frac{1}{2}$), y Yacoche; Tiltepec y Yagavila; and Tlahuitoltepec y Huitepec.[3] From the beginning, the corregimiento here was an institution for the support of the vecinos of Villa Alta; the Cs apparently had little real political power and were rotated annually, appointments being made by the AM who handled matters of justice. Whatever crown tributes could be collected were kept by the Cs.[4] By 1545 there were twenty-one corregimientos in the area under consideration here, and in 1560–70 the number had levelled off at twenty-five (there were others outside this area in what was to become the jurisdiction of Nexapa). Towards 1600 the suffragan corregimientos were abolished. The progress of encomienda succession and escheatment will be traced below, under 'Population and settlements'.

We have mentioned (cf. Nexapa) how the Nexapa-Chontal area, for a time governed from Villa Alta, became an independent alcaldía mayor towards 1570, and how Tlahuitoltepec was transferred from Nexapa to Villa Alta a decade later.[5] The next boundary change of significance occurred *c.* 1740 when Guaspaltepec and Tesechoacan (until then in the jurisdiction of Cozamaloapa) were annexed to Villa Alta; somewhat later, Tesechoacan was returned to Cozamaloapa.[6] From 1787 Villa Alta was a subdelegación in the intendencia of Oaxaca.

Church

There was a secular priest resident at S Ildefonso Villa Alta as early as 1528 (ENE, III, p. 72). Dominicans from Antequera began to visit the region in the 1530s, at which time two secular clergy based at Villa Alta had the entire province as their parish. A Dominican establishment in 1548 was abandoned five years later, but in 1558 the area was transferred from secular to regular control, with the exception of Guaspaltepec and Guatinicamanes (S Juan Teotalcingo), which had secular priests. In the 1570s additional Dominican doctrinas were founded at Santiago Zoochila and Asunción Totontepec.[7] S Juan Tanetze (El Rincón) began as a secular parish but in 1592 had been

assigned to Dominicans (Dávila Padilla, pp. 64, 634).

As a result of the congregations of *c.* 1600, the parish seat of Guaspaltepec was moved to Chacaltianguisco, and a secular priest went to live at Santiago Lalopa (the parish seat was later moved to S Juan Yaeé), while the Dominicans opened a new doctrina at Santiago Choapa. S Francisco Caxonos had a Dominican monastery from 1623.

Eleven more parishes were created here in 1706–7, one of them (S Pedro Ayutla) ministered by Dominicans and the rest by seculars. The latter had their headquarters at Santiago Atitlan, S Melchor Betaza, S Juan Comaltepec, S Cristóbal Chichicastepec, Asunción Lachixila, Sto Domingo Latani, Sta María Puxmetacan, S Juan Tabaá, Sta María Yahuive, and S Juan Yalálag. Zoochila parish was secularized at this time. By 1743 secularization had occurred at Caxonos, Choapa, Totontepec, and Villa Alta, and additional parishes (secular) existed at Sta María Ocotepec (soon afterward re-annexed to Totontepec) and Sta Cruz Yagavila. S Juan Tanetze, which had been attached to Yaeé parish, was separated from it before 1777. Ayutla was the last parish to be secularized (after 1743). Sta María Lobani was separated from Teotalcingo parish early in the nineteenth century.

The jurisdiction was in the diocese of Antequera.

Population and settlements

We have discussed elsewhere the great drop in the native population of the Gulf coastal plains in the first decade of the colony. Burgoa (1934a, II, pp. 165–6) describes the populous settlement of Xaltepec, which by mid-century was reduced to 303 tributaries (it is not even mentioned in the 1570 report). The mountain people were not affected by this early scourge, and even in later years their isolated settlement pattern seems to have protected them to some extent from epidemic disease. In 1570 there were 4,500 Zapotec tributaries, 1,500 Mixes, and 1,500 Chinantecs. To the latter, we might add 350 'Chinantec'-speakers at Guaspaltepec, although the few survivors there in 1600 were Popolucans. This gives a total of 7,850 Indian tributaries in the jurisdiction towards 1570. There was considerable loss in the epidemic of

1576–7,[8] followed by an apparent recovery between 1588 and 1623 (Scholes and Adams, 1959, pp. 41–2); thus there were perhaps 6,000 tributaries in 1600. Later counts show *c.* 11,000 tributaries in 1743, and 10,676 in 1801.[9]

Aside from the clergy and a handful of ranchowners and attendants in the almost deserted plains of Guaspaltepec–Xaltepec, the non-Indian population resident at Villa Alta remained fairly steady at 20 to 30 vecinos in 1530–1743. The *villa* (1950: S Ildefonso Villa Alta) had a change of site within a few years of its foundation, and was destroyed by fire in 1580.[10] Rebuilt, it remained the residence of the AM and subdelegado, although in 1820 it was entirely an Indian village.

We have seen no complete sixteenth-century list of pueblos, nor do we have details of the several attempts at congregation and the no doubt frequent changes of settlement site. The evidence at hand suggests that at contact settlements were dispersed and occupied defensible sites, generally mountain ridges. The Spaniards tried to force the Indians to move into the valleys in more compact settlements, and while they had a limited success with the Zapotecs, Mixe resistance was too strong to overcome.[11] The only urban concentration we know of was on the edge of the hot country, at Xaltepec; there Burgoa (1934*a*), speaking in 1670 of the ruins, states that 'the lines of streets and traces of buildings extend for more than a league', but this could have been a deserted Spanish congregation.

Santiago Amaltepec, a Mixe village, was held by Juan de Bonilla, followed *c.* 1565 by a daughter; it was still a pueblo in 1743–1820.

Juan Becerra, a resident of Villa Alta in the 1530s, held S Pedro Ayacastepec with its sujetos, Catoan (= Cotzocón?) and Metlaltepec (Mecaltepec), until his death. His widow, Inés Corneja, married Francisco de Salazar before 1550 and was sole encomendera in the 1560s. A Martín Méndez is listed in 1597 as holder.

Also in the Mixe country was Ayacastla, which had seventeen estancias in 1548, although each paid tribute separately; these included Alotepec (= Madobac?), Nobá (= Atitlan), and Guiazona (= Huiscoyan?). Gonzalo Jiménez, a resident of

Villa Alta in 1533, first held them, followed towards 1565 by his widow who married Gaspar de Vargas (listed in 1570–97). Only Alotepec and Atitlan seem to have survived the congregation of *c.* 1600.

Cacalotepec, a Zapotec mountain community, was given to a vecino of Villa Alta, Antón Miguel, replaced before 1550 by a son, Diego Miguel Negrete, who was still encomendero in 1597. There was another Cacalotepec which was made a corregimiento before 1548, together with Tonaguía and Tututepitongo (later, Tonaguía appears with a separate C). One of these Cacalotepecs survived as a pueblo in the eighteenth century, as did Tonaguía.

Santiago Camotlan, held by Pedro de Molina, escheated before 1545, as did S Juan Comaltepec a year or so later; both were Zapotec villages.

Cuescomaltepec (Guazcomaltepec), a mountain Zapotec community, was held by Juan de Aracena in the 1540s but had escheated by 1560; it apparently disappeared in the congregations.

S Cristóbal Chichicastepec (Mixe) was held by Hernando Alonso as late as 1560; in 1597 Pedro Gómez Quintero was encomendero.

Choapa (Chuapan) was a large Zapotec encomienda which escheated shortly before 1545. Zapotequillas (two barrios) belonged to this corregimiento in 1550 but were later (1567–70) annexed to that of Mazuich (Macihuixi). The last two places were perhaps moved to Choapa in a congregation of *c.* 1600.

Guaquilpa, or Guaxilpa, is listed as a corregimiento in 1545 but is not heard from thereafter.

The encomienda history of Guaspaltepec, together with details of its congregation, are given above (cf. Cozamaloapa).

The Chinantec villages known collectively as the Guatinicamanes were at first divided between Juan Antonio de Acevedo and Juan de Bonilla, but Bonilla's half escheated by 1534. In the 1540s the crown portion was included in the corregimiento of Yagavila, while later a separate C was appointed (Gay, I, p. 345. Icaza, I, pp. 228, 255). According to the 1570 report, the Acevedo encomienda consisted of half of two pueblos, Petlapa and Toabela (Tuavela), while the crown held the other half;

other places nearby, while within the parish of Guatinicamanes, were held by the crown and other encomenderos. Various settlements were moved down from hilltop sites to valleys in 1574.[12] Petlapa and Toabela still appear with the same division (Acevedo and the crown) in the 1597 list, and were pueblos in the eighteenth century.

Huehuetepec (Gueytepec, etc.), a corregimiento in the 1540s, is linked with Pazoltepec in 1550; they appear separately in 1560, while a few years later a C of 'Metepec y Gueytepec' (*see below*) is mentioned. Huehuetepec perhaps survived as Sta María Huitepec, an eighteenth-century Mixe pueblo.

Hueyacatepec (Guayaquetepec, etc.) was held by the conquistador Diego de Figueroa from 1527, but he sold his rights to Alonso de la Fuente (Millares Carlo and Mantecón, I, no. 828). By 1534 the encomienda had escheated and was joined in a corregimiento with La Hoya; only the latter seems to have survived.

Iscuintepec, a Zapotec settlement with several dependencies (Xuquila, Yachas), was a crown possession in 1534–45, but a year or so later it had been assigned to Juan García de Lemos, succeeded shortly by a daughter married to Juan de Aldaz. Somewhat later the old Mixe capital of Mixistlan (Mixitlan) was added to this encomienda, together with Talea and Sayultepec. Escheatment occurred towards 1578, when both Aldaz and his widow, Juana Verdugo, were dead.[13] Mixistlan, Talea, and Xuquila survived as pueblos.

Sta María Lachichina (Zapotec) was held by Francisco de Tarifa as late as 1567, and then (1597–1604) by a son of the same name.

S Juan Lalana, a Chinantec village in the Guatinicamanes area, as early as 1534 was a corregimiento which perhaps included Lacoba and Yaci; the last-named place disappeared towards 1600.

Lalopa escheated by 1545 and appears then and later as a corregimiento.

Lazagaya (there was a homonym, Taguí, *see below*) was held by Francisco Franco Estrada, followed by a son of the same name (1597). It disappeared in the congregations.

Francisco del Aguila was encomendero of Malinaltepec (S Juan Marinaltepec), a Zapotec community in the hot country which had five barrios in 1548. Aguila was followed by a son of the same name *c.* 1560, but Diego Núñez Pinto is listed in 1597. The place is not mentioned after 1743.

Metepec and Alotepec, Mixe villages belonging to the crown in 1534, were soon afterwards joined in corregimiento with a Zapotec pueblo, Yabago (Yavago); the last-named place disappeared.

Ocotepec, a large Mixe community, had eleven estancias in 1548, among them Ayutustepec, Moctum (Moheton), and Xayacastepec. It was held by Francisco Gutiérrez, succeeded in the 1550s by a son, Diego; in 1570–97 a Juan Gutiérrez is listed. All these places survived except Ayutustepec.

Suchitepec was a crown possession seven leagues from Villa Alta in 1548, while Tlazoltepec in that year was 17 leagues from the *villa* in hot country, and was held by Alonso Díaz 'Caruallar Portugues'; the latter place had six estancias which delivered their tribute to Xaltepec. In 1560 'Caruallar' (Alonso Díaz de Carvajal) appears as encomendero of Meyana (Mayana), and six years later we find him in possession of 'Andaama y Suchitepeque...y Guayatepeque'. None of these places can be located very precisely, and all had ceased to exist in the eighteenth century, but a document of 1592 identifies Suchitepec with Candayoc, a place whose location corresponds roughly to the 1548 description of Tlazoltepec.[14] Díaz de Carvajal died *c.* 1565 and was followed by a son, Juan de Espinosa, still encomendero in 1597.

Tabaá (Taua, etc.) was quite close to Villa Alta, but in 1548 it had a dependency, Miaguatlan, in the hot country; both places had recently escheated in that year. S Juan Tabaá survived as a pueblo.

In the sixteenth century there were two Zapotec communities called Taguí, or El Tagui, one linked with Lazagaya and the other with Yalahuí; both were crown possessions by 1548. Lazagaya disappeared, while Taguí and Yalahuí survived the congregations.

Tecomatlan was a corregimiento in 1545 but is not mentioned thereafter; perhaps it had another name.

Tehuilotepec (Teolotepec), in the Caxonos district, belonged to León Sánchez in 1548–60. Within a few years, Sánchez's widow had inherited, followed by Francisco Sánchez Jara (1570–97), presumably a son. This place may have survived as S Francisco Caxonos (Cajones).

Alonso Cano, one of the first settlers of Villa Alta, held Temascalapa, a league north of the *villa*.[15] He was succeeded by a son, towards 1564, and escheatment occurred by 1597.

The Chinantec village of Teotalcingo, which had five estancias, was joined in corregimiento with Nestepec as early as 1534, but half of it was held by Francisco Franco Estrada. In 1570 a Francisco Flores was encomendero.

S Juan Teotlasco (Teutlaxco) was a crown village by 1545 and survived the congregations.

Tepecpanzacualco (S Juan Tepanzacoalco) belonged to Alvaro Manzano, followed *c.* 1560 by a son; Juan Manzano de Chávez appears as holder in 1597.

Tiltepec was shared in early years between Alonso de Ojeda and Rodrigo de Segura, until Segura's half escheated in 1532 (ENE, III, pp. 53, 129). The original Ojeda was still encomendero in 1567, and perhaps in 1597.

Pedro Durán, an early resident of Villa Alta, held Tizatepec (Quelabichi) until his death in the 1550s, when escheatment occurred. The place seems to have disappeared *c.* 1600.

Tlahuitoltepec, an important Mixe community with eight sujetos, was a crown possession in 1534–45, but was briefly held thereafter by Juan Gómez; it escheated again before 1560. In 1572 the cabecera was moved from a mountaintop to a valley, but four years later it returned to the original site.[16] It became a congregation center towards 1600.

Tlapanalá, or Lachixila, a Chinantec settlement, had four barrios in 1548 when it was held by Bartolomé Alcántara, followed in the 1560s by a son, Daniel. It was still a private encomienda in 1597. By the eighteenth century the Chinantec here had been replaced by Zapotec.

Francisco de Saldaña was encomendero of Totolinga until his death shortly after 1560. His widow, Isabel de Carvajal, still held the place in

1597. It no longer existed in the eighteenth century.

Totontepec, a Mixe community with three barrios, escheated before 1548. It became a parish center in the 1570s, and the nucleus of a congregation *c.* 1600 (Burgoa, 1934*a*, II, pp. 188–203).

Valachita is mentioned as a corregimiento in 1545.

Venchinaguía, or Vichinaguia, a crown village in 1545, can perhaps be equated with Yatobi, a Zapotec settlement quite close to Villa Alta; it may have survived as S Bartolomé Yatoni.

Xaltepec was assigned in 1522 to Luis Marín. By 1534 half of this large encomienda had escheated and was administered by the C of Nanacatepec (cf. Nexapa). Twelve years later Xaltepec was entirely a crown possession, with a much-reduced population scattered in ten barrios. The place appears as a corregimiento (with Lalana) in the 1560s. There was a pueblo of S Juan Xaltepec in the parish of Yahuive in the eighteenth century, but it seems to have had a different site from the old cabecera.

Xareta and certain other Mixe villages were assigned to Gaspar Pacheco, who sold his rights to Hernando de Lorita in 1536 (Millares Carlo and Mantecón, II, no. 1831). Lorita's widow inherited in the 1550s. In 1597 Diego Dávila was encomendero.

Yacoche, a Mixe town, was a crown possession as early as 1534 and survived the congregations.

Yachave and other Zapotec villages were held by Juan Martín (Martínez) de Viloria in 1567 and later. There was a congregation here in 1579–80.[17] In 1604 the encomendero was Juan de Viloria, son of the first holder. Eighteenth-century survivals of this encomienda included Yagzachi, Yalálag, Yaveo, Zogocho, and Zoochila.

Yagavila, a Zapotec community, was crown property by 1534, linked first with Tiltepec and later (1545) with the Guatinicamanes. It survived as a parish and congregation center.[18]

'Chichitepeque e Aguayo', a corregimiento in 1534, can be identified with Yagayó, a place with three barrios in 1548 and a pueblo in the eighteenth century.

Yalaxi (Yagila, Yacila, S Juan Yaguila) had escheated by 1545 and survived as a pueblo.

Zultepec, eight leagues from the *villa*, seems to have included Tultitlan and Zoquio. It was held by Marcos de Paredes in the 1540s, followed by his widow, Francisca de Grijalva, last mentioned in 1567; the name does not appear thereafter.

Altogether there were 110 places in the jurisdiction which had the category of pueblo in the eighteenth century. Sixty of them were cabeceras in 1801, some still in private encomienda.[19]

Sources

A testimony drawn up by the vecinos of Villa Alta in 1533 contains valuable details (ENE, III, pp. 48–78). The *Suma de Visitas* (PNE, I, *passim*) briefly describes most of the cabeceras here as they were towards 1548, and a report of *c.* 1570 supplements this information (García Pimentel, 1904, pp. 61, 65–7, 69, 72–3). Most unfortunately, the AM's relación of *c.* 1580 has been lost. Burgoa (1934a, II, pp. 128–203, 219–31) tells of the Dominicans' activities here. Details of the congregations carried out in the 1590s and early 1600s are few and far between,[20] although there is a good report from the Guaspaltepec area.[21]

We have a most interesting document dated 1706–7 about parochial divisions, with maps.[22] The jurisdictional dispute over the Guaspaltepec region is covered in an expediente of *c.* 1740.[23] A brief report from the AM sent in *c.* 1743[24] is copied with omissions by Villaseñor y Sánchez (II, pp. 190–202). There are complete padrones from six parishes (Betaza, Chichicastepec, Tanetze, Totontepec, Yaeé, Yalálag),[25] and topographic descriptions of one of these and five others (Comaltepec, Puxmetacan, Tabaá, Tanetze, Yagavila, Yahuive),[26] dated 1777. The relación of Tanetze is accompanied by a schematic drawing. The various parish visitas are listed, with indications of the languages spoken in each, in a report of 1802 (Pérez, 1888, table at end). There is an excellent description of this area as it was in 1821.[27]

Lemoine (1966) is worth consulting for further details.

119 *Xalapa de la Feria*

Dominated by the towering Nauhcampatépetl (Cofre de Perote, 4,280 m), most of this area lies on the Gulf slope of the Sierra Volcánica Transversal, with drainage northeast to the sea in numerous short watercourses (a small portion is in the Llanos of S Juan). There is year-round precipitation, while temperatures vary considerably according to altitude. Today the region is in central Veracruz state.

An older Totonac-speaking population by 1519 had been replaced by Mexicans in the south, while Totonac was predominant in the north. The chief Náhuatl state was perhaps the fortress settlement of Xicochimalco, on a steep hillside. Teoixhuacan, Xalapan, Coatépec, Atexcac, and Xalcomolco were probably dependencies of Xicochimalco, although each may have had a local ruler. North of Xalapan were the Totonac communities of Tlacuilollan or Hueycalli, Xilotépec, Cuacuauhtzintlan, Chapultépec, Naolinco, Acatlan, Miahuatlan, Chiconquiauhco, Cihuacoatlan, Tepetlan, Almolonca, Maxtlatlan, Pangolutla, and Chiltoyac; these autonomous states were kept in submission by a Mexican garrison at Acatlan, which had a military governor appointed by Moctezuma. Off to the northwest was Mexcaltzinco, a large state running from the mountains down to the coast at Nauhtla; the latter was another Mexican strongpoint which dominated a Totonac majority, although there was a significant number of Náhuatl-speakers here. The proportions were reversed at Xalatzinco, still another Aztec fortress settlement where people speaking an archaic Nahua dominated a Totonac minority.[1] Thus the whole region was tributary to the Triple Alliance.

Miguel de Zaragoza, a member of the Grijalva expedition who was left on the coast in 1518, may well have been the first Spaniard to see this area (Dorantes de Carranza, p. 217). The Cortés party traversed the southern part in August of the

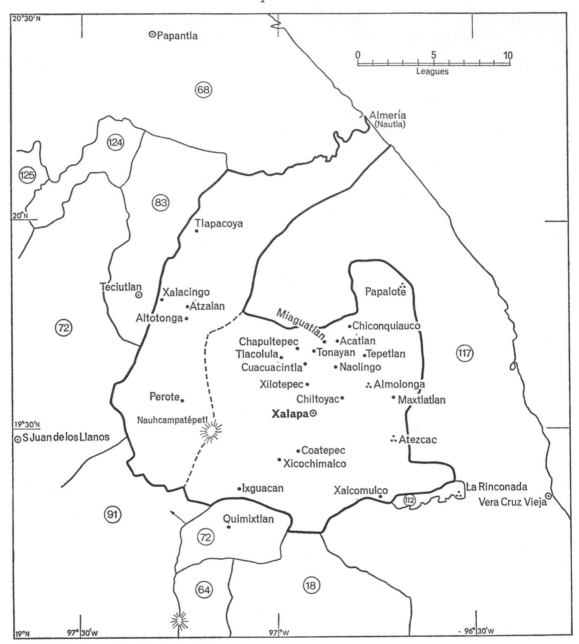

following year, passing through Xicochimalco, where they were received amicably. The Totonacs joined the Spaniards in a successful campaign against the hostile Mexican garrison at Nauhtla in late 1519, and an army under Gonzalo de Sandoval overwhelmed the defenders of Xalatzinco in 1520. Almolonca is said to have been 'destroyed' after

a revolt, while there was a serious Totonac uprising in the late 1520s (Icaza, nos. 945, 1012, 1287).

Encomiendas

A number of places here were assigned to Miguel de Zaragoza, including Coatepec, Chiltoyac, and

Pilopan (cf. Vera Cruz Vieja). Zaragoza died in 1527, and Chiltoyac at least was acquired by the conquistador Pedro Maldonado, who also held Almolonga, Atezcac, Ocuequila, Pangololutla, Mazatlaxoya (= Maxtlatlan?), and Xalcomulco. Maldonado by 1544 had been succeeded by his widow, María del Rincón, who then married Gonzalo Rodríguez de Villafuerte. Escheatment occurred when the latter died, between 1573 and 1578.[2]

Acatlan may have been held by Pedro Moreno Cendejas, whose son, Martín de Mafra, was encomendero in 1569–97; it was a crown possession by 1626 (Icaza, I, p. 128).

Cuacuacintla was given to the conquistador Lucas Gallego, followed before 1551 by a son, Miguel Arias, and in the 1570s by Domingo Gallego, presumably a grandson of the conquistador. It escheated between 1597 and 1626 (ENE, XV, p. 216. Millares Carlo and Mantecón, II, no. 2605).

A conquistador and resident of Medellín, Bartolomé Román, held Ixguacan. His widow inherited, and by 1551 had married Francisco de Reinoso. The encomienda escheated in the 1580s (ENE, XV, p. 217. Icaza, I, p. 114. Millares Carlo and Mantecón, II, no. 2599).

Chiconquiauco and Miaguatlan were assigned to Melchor de Arévalo, whose widow by 1553 had been succeeded by her second husband, Juan Valiente. The latter died without heirs in the 1580s.

Xalapa may have been held briefly in the 1520s by Diego de Salamanca and then re-assigned. Towards 1537 this encomienda was set apart as a royal monopoly for the production of a blue dye (*pastel, glastum*), an experiment which was abandoned in the 1550s. Henceforth Xalapa appears as a crown possession except for a brief period when it was held by Alonso Hidalgo (1562–3) (ENE, IV, pp. 77–8, 81; VIII, p. 151; IX, pp. 151, 216, 240. Icaza, I, p. 66).

Atzalan-Mexcalcingo belonged to Alonso de Benavides, followed c. 1540 by his widow, María de la Torre, who then married Andrés Dorantes de Carranza; when Dorantes died in the 1550s Doña María became sole encomendera. She was followed by a daughter, Antonia de Benavides, married to Antonio Ruiz de Castañeda (listed in 1580). By 1609 Atzalan had escheated, but later part of the tribute went to the Moctezuma heirs (Dorantes de Carranza, pp. 265, 267. Icaza, I, pp. 151, 195).

The conquistador Martín Pérez held Xalacingo until it escheated between 1533 and 1536. Tlapacoya was seemingly held by another encomendero and became crown property by 1534; shortly afterward it was annexed to Xalacingo, and, still later, transferred to Atzalan (Icaza, II, p. 96. L de T, p. 258).

We know nothing about the encomienda history of Cihuacoatlan, Chapultepec, Naolingo, Tepetlan, or Tlacolula, all of which were crown cabeceras in 1569. Some of these places may have been held by Hernando de Padilla (*see below*). Xilotepec was granted to Juan Sedeño, but was taken for the dye industry on his death in the 1530s (Icaza, nos. 897, 915).

Government

In a list of c. 1534 we find a C assigned to 'Pueblos de Tapacoya e de los pueblos de Padilla e Nautla e Colipa e Papalo'.[3] This may be the magistrate who by 1545 had become C of Papalote de la Sierra,[4] identified elsewhere as 'por otro nombre... Tizapancingo y Atlaliloya y Cicaquautla' (L de T, p. 497). Meanwhile, separate Cs were appointed to Xalacingo (c. 1535) and Chapultepec y Maltrata (also in the 1530s) (L de T, p. 222). The latter by 1551 held the additional title of justicia mayor in Xalapa, and soon afterward he was put in charge of all the nearby encomienda and crown villages.[5] In 1553 Xalacingo and Atzalan–Mexcalcingo were placed in the jurisdiction of Tlatlauquitepec, but soon they were returned to their own magistrate.[6] Towards 1558 the justice of Xalapa was made an AM and was given powers of suffragan supervision over the Cs of Teciutlan y Atempa, Tlatlauquitepec, and Xalacingo. In the sixteenth century the jurisdictions of both Xalapa and Xalacingo extended to the Gulf, but Xalapa lost its seacoast when Colipa was transferred to Vera Cruz Vieja towards 1600.[7]

The alcaldía mayor of Xalapa and the corregimiento (later alcaldía mayor) of Xalacingo were combined under a single magistrate in the jurisdictional reforms of *c.* 1680.[8] In 1787 the AM became a subdelegado under the intendente of Vera Cruz; by the century's end Xalacingo was considered a separate subdelegación.

Church

First visited by secular clergy from Vera Cruz, the area came under regular control in the 1530s when Natividad Xalapa was chosen as the site of a Franciscan doctrinal center (Melgarejo Vivanco, p. 131. Ramírez Lavoignet, 1959, p. 167). S Bartolomé Xalacingo (from 1548) and Sta María Tlapacoya also had small monasteries which were turned over to secular priests in 1567 (*Alegaciones...*, p. 23). Two years later, the area from Xalapa to the south and east was being visited by Franciscans, while secular parishes existed at Xalacingo, S Andrés Atzalan (a new center for Tlapacoya parish), and Concepción Tlacolula (originally a Franciscan visita). In 1592 the Franciscans received permission to found another doctrina at Santos Reyes Ixguacan, but in 1640 both Xalapa and Ixguacan were secularized.

Atzalan and Xalacingo were combined in a single parish by 1609 and separated again sometime before 1743. Additional curacies are recorded by 1646 at S Mateo Naolingo and Sta María Tlapacoya. S Gerónimo Coatepec had its own priest from 1702, and Magdalena Xicochimalco from 1754; the latter was the approximate foundation date of S Miguel Perote, S Pedro Tonayan, and Asunción Xilotepec parishes.

All these doctrinas were in the diocese of Tlaxcala.

Population and settlements

There was great loss in the native population from smallpox and other causes in the first decade after the Conquest (cf. Herrera, 4a década, p. 236. L de T, pp. 205, 222–5, 277–8, 309–10, 497, 559). By 1569 there were only 7,270 tributaries, 3,000 in the corregimiento of Xalacingo and the remainder in Xalapa. Later tributary counts show 5,589 in 1580, 1,434 in 1626, and 3,008 in 1696 (Scholes and Adams, 1959, p. 49). By 1743 there were 4,275 Indian families, in 1777 there were 25,631 Indians

(persons), and in 1802–4 Xalacingo had 2,352½ Indian tributaries and Xalapa 4,508½, a total of 6,861.[9]

The non-Indian population (20 Spaniards in the town of Xalapa in 1580 and none elsewhere; perhaps 70 vecinos in 1609) increased considerably after the sixteenth century, with notable concentrations at Xalapa and nearby haciendas. In 1743 there were 767 families of Spaniards and 455 of mestizos and mulattoes. The 1777 padrón gives 5,943 Spaniards (individuals), 6,095 mestizos, and 3,032 mulattoes, excluding Negro slaves.

Xalapa (Xalapa de la Feria after 1720; 1950: Jalapa Enríquez, ciudad), which once had 30,000 tributaries according to the relación of 1580, had in that year only 639 tributaries in the cabecera (which had been moved from a higher site), two small estancias a league to the south, and nearby sugar haciendas. The estancias were moved in *c.* 1600.[10] Xalapa became a flourishing commercial center during the years (1720–77) when the annual trade fairs of European goods were held there (cf. Real Díaz, 1959).

Acatlan (1950: pueblo) had no recorded estancias, and disappeared from the tribute rolls in the seventeenth century, but survived as a pueblo.

Almolonga (Atlmoloncan, etc.; 1950: Almolonga, congregación) was down to 4½ tributaries in 1626, and is not heard from thereafter.

Atezcac (1950: Atexca, ranchería), a cabecera with 50 tributaries in 1580, disappeared in the congregations *c.* 1600.

Atzalan (Azala; known in early years as Mexcalcingo or Mascalçingo, or Azala-Mexcalcingo; 1950: Atzalan, *villa*) must have had a large population scattered in many settlements. In 1569 there were still 1,600 tributaries (a third Náhuatl-speakers, the rest Totonacs) in the cabecera and six estancias, the most distant on the sea at or near ancient Nauhtla (called Almería by the Spaniards); all were apparently congregated at the cabecera towards 1600.[11] Tlapacoya was transferred from Xalacingo to Atzalan sometime before 1696.

A number of places on the coastal plain (Atlaliloya, Papalote, Tizapancingo, etc.) seem to have been congregated towards 1554 at Cihuacoatlan (Ciguacoatla), which was a cabecera in 1569–80 and still existed in 1626 as Papalote de la Sierra, with only 10 tributaries.[12] We have found no later mention of this place, which was in the vicinity of Juchique de Ferrer (1950: pueblo).

Coatepec (Guatepec, etc.; 1950: Coatepec, ciudad), which was moved before 1560 from its original site to a lower location two leagues away, by 1580 had been reduced to the cabecera and a single nearby estancia which disappeared *c.* 1600.

Cuacuacintla (Huehuecintla, Quaquauhtzintlan, etc.; 1950: Coacoatzintla, pueblo) had a congregation *c.* 1550, after which a single estancia, Zonalcuatlan, survived for a few years.[13] There was a protracted boundary dispute between Cuacuacintla and neighboring Chapultepec (1950: congregación), complicated by the establishment of other villages in this area during the sixteenth century and later.[14] S Pedro Tonayan, said to have been founded by settlers from Mizantla in 1555, may correspond to S Pedro Tziuayan, the sole estancia of Chapultepec in 1580; it became a parish center and was recognized as a cabecera by 1665 (Ramírez Lavoignet, 1959, pp. 132–3). Other places classified as pueblos in 1743–91 are S Pablo Coapan, Magdalena, S José Pastepec (Apaxtepec, founded *c.* 1683), and S Marcos.

Chiconquiauco (Xiconquiaco, etc.; 1950: Chiconquiaco, pueblo) and Miaguatlan (1950: Miahuatlán, pueblo), although separate cabeceras, belonged to the same encomendero and generally appear together in the records. The only sujeto shown in the 1569–80 reports is Asunción Yeicoatlan (Yecuatla), an estancia of Chiconquiauco five leagues north of its cabecera, which survived as a pueblo in the eighteenth century.[15] Towards 1600 Miaguatlan was divided in two parts, S Juan and S José, both eventually becoming cabeceras. Shortly before 1743 another pueblo, S Miguel de las Aguasuelas (Aquazuelas), was founded within the limits of S Juan.

Sta María (Asunción) Chiltoyac, which had no sujetos in 1580, survived as a small cabecera in 1743–91.

Ixguacan (Teoizhuacan, Ixoacan, etc.; 1950: Ixhuacán de los Reyes, pueblo) had twelve estancias located on the 1580 map, most of which disappeared in a congregation of *c.* 1600. Asunción (Tecomalticpac or Tecucingo) is last heard of in 1697, while Santiago Ayagualulco survived as a pueblo.

Maxtlatlan (near modern Alto Lucero), a much-reduced cabecera in 1569–80, had only 7½ tributaries in 1626 and is last mentioned in 1643.

Naolingo (Naulinco; 1950: Naolinco de Victoria, pueblo) had a single nearby estancia in 1580.

The cabecera of Tepetlan (1950: pueblo) was moved sometime before 1569 from its first site at S Lorenzo to S Antonio; four estancias were eliminated at this time (Kutscher, 1964).

Tlacolula (Tecolula, Tlacuilollan, etc.; 1950: Tlacolulan, *villa*) and Xilotepec (1950: Jilotepec, pueblo) had the same Indian governor in 1551, but they were separate cabeceras in 1569 and later. After an early congregation in the 1540s, Tlacolula had six estancias within four leagues; these were congregated *c.* 1600, but S Pedro Tlatatila (re-settled in the 1670s) and S Salvador were pueblos in 1743–91, together with S Miguel de las Vigas, an old inn on the Vera Cruz–Mexico highway. Xilotepec in 1569 had two sujetos which, after the congregation of *c.* 1600, were re-occupied and became the pueblos of S Miguel del Soldado and Tlalnehuayocan.[16]

Xalacingo (Xalatzinco; 1950: Jalacingo, ciudad) at first extended from Perote in the south to Tlapacoya in the north. The original venta (inn) of Perote was built in the 1520s in the valley of Temazcalapa, and later acquired a hospital operated by the order of S Hipólito.[17] In the eighteenth century it became a cabecera, S Miguel Perote, where the fortress of S Carlos was built in 1770–7. The former sujetos of Altotonga and Tlapacoya (*see above*) were also late colonial cabeceras.

S Juan Xalcomulco (1950: Jalcomulco, pueblo) adjoined lands of the Marquesado del Valle on the Vera Cruz road.[18] In 1580 it had one sujeto, S Miguel, two leagues west of the cabecera. Venta del Río was within its limits.

Xicochimalco was moved down from the mountainside (1950: Jico Viejo, ranchería) to its final site (1950: Jico, *villa*) by the Franciscans, probably in the 1540s. It had three estancias within a league, above the cabecera, in 1580. S Juan Teocelo, a pueblo in 1643–1791, was perhaps an old sujeto.

There are firsthand descriptions of Xicochimalco as it was when the Spaniards saw it in 1519 (Cortés, pp. 37–8. Díaz del Castillo, I, p. 181. Mártir de Anglería, II, p. 444). Only Atzalan is described briefly c. 1548 in the *Suma* (PNE, I, no. 351). The notarial records of Xalapa covering part of 1551–2 contain some interesting items, including a boundary delineation between Atzalan and Xalacingo in 1531–43 (Millares Carlo and Mantecón, II, nos. 2543–646 and pp. 286–302). There are unusually useful reports of 1569–70 from the curates of Atzalan, Tlacolula, and Xalacingo (PNE, V, pp. 204, 239–43, 247–9, 264–5), supplemented by a brief mention of the Franciscan doctrina of Xalapa (*Códice Franciscano*, p. 27). A lengthy *relación geográfica* submitted by the AM in 1580 is accompanied by a fine map (PNE, V, pp. 99–123); it does not include the corregimiento of Xalacingo. Father Ponce (I, pp. 15–16; II, pp. 311–15) went through Xalapa in 1584 and 1588.

Seventeenth-century visitors include Mota y Escobar in 1609,[19] Gage (pp. 43–5) in 1625, and Palafox in 1643 and 1646.[20] We have tributary data and lists of cabeceras for the period 1626–96.[21]

There is a most interesting report from the AM dated 1743,[22] followed by a brief item on Xalapa (parish) in 1754,[23] and the description left by Ajofrín (II, pp. 21–4), who was there in 1765–6. For the year 1777 there is a complete census of the jurisdiction,[24] as well as individual padrones from the parishes of Atzalan, Ixguacan, Perote, Tonayan, Xalapa, and Xilotepec.[25] A census of non-Indians dated 1791 is accompanied by a valuable description.[26]

Monographs on this area include Bernal and Dávalos Hurtado (1952–3), Cline (1959), Kelly and Palerm (1952), Pasquel (1959), and Ramírez Lavoignet (1959, 1965).

120 *Xalapa del Marqués*

This small jurisdiction, now in southeastern Oaxaca, consisted only of the *villa* of Xalapa, on the river of Tehuantepec, with a few leagues around it. It is a region of barren hills (much of it is today covered by an artificial lake) at 100–800 m, with a hot, dry climate.

Xallapan was a Zapotec community (there may have been a Mixe minority) with a ruler or governor subordinate to the lord of Tecuantépec. The Zapotec name for this state was Yuuchi.

While Tecuantépec surrendered to the Spaniards at the end of 1521, we are told that Pedro de Alvarado encountered some resistance at Xallapan which was quelled with the death of 20,000 Indians (Vázquez de Tapia, pp. 114–15); this presumably occurred at the beginning of 1524. Other sources indicate that this massacre took place somewhere else (cf. Díaz del Castillo, II, p. 122).

Encomienda

Although it was considered a separate if subordinate cabecera, Xalapa's encomienda history coincides with that of Teguantepec (q.v.) until the latter became a crown possession in 1563. Thereafter, Xalapa remained in the Marquesado del Valle.

Government

Governed at first from Teguantepec, Xalapa in 1563 became a corregimiento whose magistrate was to be appointed in perpetuity by the Marquéses del Valle. In 1570–95 and during subsequent sequestrations of the marquisate Xalapa was attached to Teguantepec. In later years the office of C here was given customarily to the lessee of the marquisate's cattle haciendas (*see below*), and there was some question whether these vast estates belonged in a jurisdictional sense to Xalapa or Teguantepec. Furthermore, the marquis's agents claimed that a place mentioned in Cortés's original grant, Utlatepec, was not included in the escheated area and should be administered from Xalapa (cf. Teguantepec). This suit was still unsettled as late as 1618, but eventually the jurisdiction of Xalapa del Marqués was confined to the *villa* and a single hacienda, that of Lachitova.[1] For all practical purposes, Xalapa del Marqués fell within the intendencia of Oaxaca after 1787.

Church

First visited from Teguantepec, Sta María Asunción Xalapa had resident Dominican priests as

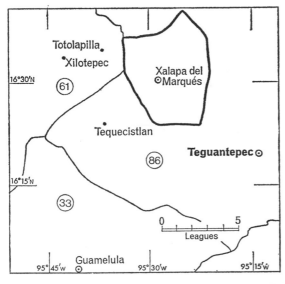

early as 1558.[2] The parish included a number of places which belonged politically to Nexapa and Teguantepec. It was in the diocese of Antequera, and was secularized in 1707, but later was re-assigned to the Dominicans.[3]

Population and settlements

According to the 1580 relación, Xalapa once had 4,000 tributaries, reduced to 1,238 in 1564, 1,000 in 1571, and 770 in 1580; in the latter year all the natives spoke Zapotecan except those of two barrios who were Mixes. Later censuses show 740 tributaries in 1597, 394 in 1620, 417 in 1670, 453 in 1706, 225 in 1745, 175 in 1756, 92 in 1777, and only 45 Indian tributaries in 1797.[4] Free Negro and mulatto tributaries numbered 38½ in 1797.

Apparently there was an early congregation here, carried out by the Dominicans, as by 1580 Xalapa (1950: Sta María Jalapa del Marqués, pueblo) had no outlying sujetos. It did, however, have thirteen barrios in and near the cabecera (Burgoa, 1934a, II, pp. 328–9).

There are several lists and descriptions of the Marquesado's cattle haciendas and ranches in the Teguantepec area. Some of the earlier properties (Almoloya, Las Cruces, Las Minas, La Ventosa) either were relinquished by the marquisate or changed their names. There were ten such properties in 1670: Aguas Frías, Buena Vista, Guazontlan, La Isla, Lachitova, Lachivela, Las Lomas, Las Salinas, S Miguel, and La Tarifa.[5]

Sources

Xalapa is summarily described as it was *c.* 1570 (ENE, XI, pp. 41–4. García Pimentel, 1904, pp. 65, 72) and in 1580.[6] The latter report is accompanied by a map. Father Ponce (I, p. 492) went through here in 1586.

Burgoa (1934a, II, pp. 326–38) has a good deal to say about the monastery here from its foundation to 1670. There is a good topographic report from the curate, dated 1777.[7] We have a brief description of 1802 (Pérez, 1888, table at end), and a more extensive one of *c.* 1820.[8] Additional details are found in García Martínez (1969).

121 *Xicayan*

This area in southwestern Oaxaca includes the lower valley and delta of the Atoyac (Verde) river, the Pacific coastal plain, and a rugged, mountainous area (Sierre Madre del Sur, 3,000+ m) inland. Rainfall is much heavier in the mountains than on the coast, causing seasonal floods.

At contact, most if not all of this region was controlled by the ruler of Tototépec (Mixtec, Yucudzaa), a powerful state which not only resisted the hegemony of the Aztecs but was in the process of extending its frontiers on the east and north. There were a number of communities which, while directly subject and tributary to Tototépec, seem to have retained a certain degree of political autonomy, with hereditary rulers, governors, or tax collectors. Among these were Comaltépec (Mixtec, Yucusiyo), Cuetzpaltépec (Sinititi), Chahayucu, Ixtapan, Malinaltépec, Mixtépec (Yodzonuuhuico), Nopalla, Pinoltecpan (Dooyú), Temazcaltépec, Tuxtla, Xamiltépec

Encomiendas

Alvarado was given a Tututepec in encomienda in 1522, but the reference is clearly to another place of that name some distance to the west (cf. Igualapa). It is equally clear that in 1524, when

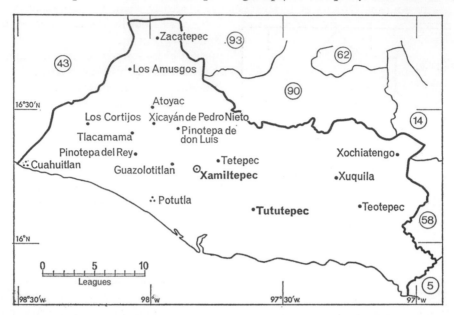

(Casandó), and Xochiatenco. Off to the west were other states most likely dominated by Tototépec: Xicayan (Ñuusijcuaha), Pinoltecpan (Nocoo, west of the above homonym), Atoyac, Ayotla, Tetépec, Potuctla, Tlacamama (Ñuchicnaa), Coahuitlan (Yonoyuto), Amuchco (Ñuñama), and Zacatépec (Yucuchatuta); the last-named place was a border settlement facing the Aztec garrison at Poctla. The language spoken from Tototépec east was Chatino; Mixtecan was spoken in the west, and Amuzgan (a Mixtec dialect) at Amuchco and Zacatépec.[1]

The Spaniards found a state of war existing between Tototépec and the Zapotec kingdom of Tecuantépec. Having received the allegiance of the latter, Cortés sent Pedro de Alvarado with a large force to subdue Tototépec, which was accomplished in the spring of 1522. A subsequent uprising of the Tototepecanos was put down with great severity by another expedition under Alvarado in 1523.

Cortés left Mexico, the Tututepec with which we are here concerned formed part of his own holdings. It was then seized by the acting governor, Salazar, was recovered by Cortés on his return in 1526, and was probably held by him until it was taken for the crown in 1531 or 1532.[2] Tututepec with its many dependencies was re-assigned to a kinsman of Cortés, D. Luis de Castilla, at the end of 1534. D. Luis was succeeded by his eldest son, D. Pedro Lorenzo de Castilla, in 1587; the latter still appears as encomendero in 1597, but had died by 1604.[3] Part of the tributes were still privately assigned as late as 1801.

The encomendero of Los Amusgos, Francisco de Avila, was succeeded by a son, Hernando, sometime before 1541. The latter was followed *c.* 1600 by his daughter, María de Avila, whose husband, Angel de Villafaña y Alvarado, was still alive in 1629 (Dorantes de Carranza, p. 280. L de T, p. 40).

Cuahuitlan, whose encomendero we do not know (it may have been a dependency of Tututepec), had escheated by 1536. Pinotepa del Rey and Potutla were soon annexed to this corregimiento.

Tlacamama was assigned to the conquistador Francisco de Sta Cruz, and by 1560 had passed to his son, Alvaro; it escheated on the latter's death in 1569.[4]

Xicayan, together with Ayutla (Atoyac) and Tetepec, were shared between two conquistadors, Pedro Nieto and Cristóbal de Mafra (Millares Carlo and Mantecón, I, nos. 1301–2. Miranda, 1965, p. 27). Mafra's half escheated *c.* 1544, while Nieto was succeeded after 1570 by Francisco Nieto Maldonado (listed in 1597).

Zacatepec was given to the conquistador Rafael de Trejo, and was inherited (before 1548) by a son, Rafael de Trejo Carvajal, still alive in 1604 (Dorantes de Carranza, p. 229).

Government

The second Spanish municipality in Mexico, Villa Segura de la Frontera, occupied a site somewhere near Tututepec for a brief period in 1522 before its vecinos moved to Antequera (Oaxaca). The first royal magistrate to arrive subsequently was the C of Tututepec, who was relieved of his office on 1 December 1534, when D. Luis de Castilla took possession of the encomienda.[5] It was perhaps at this time that a C was appointed to Cuahuitlan. From *c.* 1544 there was another C who administered the crown's half of Xicayan. These magistrates seem to have alternated in governing the area during the next few decades, although Zacatepec was assigned to the C of Justlaguaca. In 1560 we find the C of Cuahuitlan exercising the duties of justice in the province of Tututepec; in the 1570s it was the C of Xicayan who ruled the entire coast, while the magistrate of Cuahuitlan resided far inland at Icpatepec (cf. Justlaguaca) until his jurisdiction was abolished in 1582.[6] Thereafter, Cuahuitlan and nearby cabeceras were administered by the C of Xicayan, who had the additional title of AM of Tututepec. During the seventeenth century this official changed his residence to Xamiltepec, and his realm was enlarged by the acquisition of Zacatepec from Justlaguaca. From 1787 the alcaldía mayor of Xicayan was a subdelegación in the intendencia of Oaxaca.

Church

Reportedly first evangelized by Dominicans, Tututepec nevertheless appears as a secular doctrina, subsidized by its encomendero, from the 1530s; the original patron was no doubt S Luis, later changed to S Pedro. Another priest had established residence at S Pedro Xicayan by 1563 (Scholes and Adams, 1961, p. 299).

During the seventeenth century, secular parishes were founded at Sta María (Asunción) Guazolotitlan, Asunción Pinotepa de Don Luis, Santiago Pinotepa del Rey, and Santiago Xamiltepec. Meanwhile, the priest of Xicayan had moved to S Pedro Atoyac, and another curate who had been living at Sta María Zacatepec (already a parish in 1570) moved to S Pedro de los Amusgos. Sta Catalina Xuquila was separated from Tututepec and made a parish before 1742. Sometime between 1742 and 1777 a resident priest was appointed to Sta María de los Cortijos, a parish which extended into the neighboring alcaldía mayor of Igualapa. The doctrina of Sta Lucía Teotepec was founded about the same time or soon after. All parishes were in the diocese of Antequera.

Population and settlements

According to the 1580 relación of Cuahuitlan, a contact population of 180,000 men at Cuahuitlan–Pinotepa–Potutla was reduced to 400 tributaries after two epidemics, smallpox in 1534 and measles in 1544. Later counts and interpolation give a total tributary number for the final jurisdiction as 7,000 in 1550, 4,900 in 1570, 3,775 in 1597, 2,500 in 1650, 3,447 Indian families in 1743, and 5,272 Indian tributaries in 1801.[7] By far the largest proportion of these was at Tututepec. Negroes, some freedmen and others fleeing from their masters, began to arrive on the coast in the sixteenth century, and their descendants came to form a majority of the total population in some places, although the Indians predominated inland. The padrón of 1777 shows a total of 28,384 individuals here, divided among 20,834 Indians, 6,276 mulattoes, 635 mestizos, 481 Spaniards, and 158 Negroes.

Los Amusgos (Amozcos, etc.; Ñuñama; 1950: S Pedro Amusgos, pueblo) in the sixteenth century consisted of two cabeceras, Amusgo el Grande and Amusgo el Pequeño, with four estancias. While there may have been a congregation towards 1600, there were still five pueblos in the vicinity in 1743–77.[8]

Of the villages centering around Pinotepa del Rey (Pinoteca, Pinotecpa; Nocoo; 1950: Santiago Pinotepa Nacional, *villa*), only Pinotepa itself and Xicaltepec survived as pueblos. Cuahuitlan and Potutla disappeared in the eighteenth century. Tlacamama was added to this group when it escheated in 1569.

Tututepec (1950: S Pedro Tututepec, *villa*) had a large area with many settlements. We have mentioned (*see above*) twelve places which are identified as immediate dependencies of Tututepec towards 1550 and yet which seem to have had a special status as sub-cabeceras. Other places listed as sujetos in 1580–1620 include Acatepec, Cuistla, Chicometepec, Chila, Guasintepec, Guazolotitlan, Jutecato, Mechuacan, Palanistlaguaca, Tepenistlaguaca, Tlatlaltepec, Xocotepec, and Yolotepec; but there were still others, more than seventy altogether in 1575.[9] Many of these dependant settlements disappeared in congregations in 1602–4, but some of the abandoned sites were re-occupied.[10] About thirty places within the original limits of Tututepec survived as pueblos, many of them with cabecera status, in the late eighteenth century.

Xicayan (1950: S Pedro Jicayán, pueblo), Ayutla (later, Atoyac; 1950: S Pedro Atoyac, pueblo), and Tetepec (1950: Santiago Tetepec) between them had ten estancias in 1548; the cabeceras and several of the sujetos survived as pueblos.

Sta María Zacatepec (1950: pueblo) had twelve estancias in 1548, reduced to half that number in 1580. They seem to have been collected at the cabecera towards 1600.[11]

Sources

Leaving aside for the moment published monographs and interpretations of codices, we have what appears to be a much truncated fragment of the 1531 'Description de la Tierra' in which Tututepec is briefly mentioned (Herrera, 4a década, p. 230), together with Bartolomé de Zárate's report of 1544 (ENE, IV, pp. 143–4). The area as it was *c.* 1548 is covered in 22 articles in the *Suma de Visitas* (PNE, I, nos. 31–2, 99–100, 306, 362–3, 407, 454–6, 480–1, 491, 648–53, 808–9). The Ovando series reports of *c.* 1570 give few details (García Pimentel, 1904, pp. 64–5, 86–8. López de Velasco, pp. 229, 232–4). The C of Cuahuitlan submitted a rather unsatisfactory report and map of his jurisdiction in 1580 (PNE, IV, pp. 155–62); for the same year, there is a relación from Justlaguaca which describes Zacatepec.[12]

We have seen little of interest from the seventeenth century other than a list of Tututepec's subject villages, dated 1620.[13]

A series of parochial reports made in 1706[14] is followed by a tabular report sent in by the AM *c.* 1743[15] and enlarged on by Villaseñor y Sánchez (II, pp. 159–65). There is a general census of the jurisdiction in 1777,[16] together with individual padrones from the curates of Los Amusgos, Atoyac, Los Cortijos, the two Pinotepas, Tututepec, and Xuquila, also dated 1777.[17] Topographical descriptions of the parishes of Amusgos,[18] Atoyac,[19] Guazolotitlan,[20] and Xamiltepec[21] have been found, drawn up in 1777–8. There are subsequent reports for 1802 (Pérez, 1888, table at end) and *c.* 1820.[22]

Berlin (1947), Peñafiel (1900), and Smith (1963) have published and analyzed several sixteenth-century documents concerning this area and their works should be consulted for further details. Byam Davies's (1968) reconstruction of the pre-Conquest political geography of Tututepec is a commendable effort. The monographs of Dahlgren de Jordán (1954) and Spores (1965) are of limited value in this instance.

122 *Xilotepec*

Extending from the lofty (3,800 m) Sierra de las Cruces in the south across a series of eroded hills and plains draining northward into affluents of the Pánuco system (1,600 m), this is a cold, dry, barren country. It now comprises the northwest corner of Mexico state and southwestern Hidalgo, with a bit of Querétaro.

Xilotépec (Otomí, Madenxi) was an ancient Otomí kingdom whose ruler was related to Moctezuma. It may have included a distant dependency, Tecozauhtla, on the Chichimec frontier (both places appear as tributaries of the Triple Alliance in the Codex Mendoza). Otomí was the predominant language, but there were groups of Mazahuas in the south and Chichimecs (Pames) in the north, as well as a Náhuatl-speaking minority. There were several smaller states here, also tributary to the Aztecs, including Tzayanalquilpan and Tlachco (= Chiapantonco or Querétaro?). Acaxochitlan and Michmaloyan were perhaps ruled by the tlatoani of Chiapan, or they may have been autonomous states.

Probably first seen by Spaniards late in 1519, the southern part of this area was under Spanish control in the mid-1520s. Soon after the Conquest, the northern part was occupied by Chichimecs (it is not clear whether this was the situation at contact or whether the Chichimecs moved southward with the collapse of Otomí power at this time). A Spanish expedition explored the north in 1526 and an outpost was founded at Hueychiapan in 1531. Warfare between the Spaniards with their Otomí allies and the Chichimecs lasted for many years, reaching a climax in the 1570s and 1580s.[1]

Encomiendas

By far the most populous private encomienda in New Spain in the late sixteenth century, Xilotepec as a tribute-paying entity extended beyond the political jurisdiction of that name to include provinces (cf. Cimapan, Querétaro) occupied by Otomí colonists after the Conquest. At first the encomienda seems to have been divided into quarters, one of which was held by Hernando de Cantillana; other early claimants were Francisco de Quevedo and Juan Núñez Sedeño (Icaza, I, pp. 145, 166; II, pp. 160, 167). By 1533 the whole province was assigned to the conquistador Juan Jaramillo de Salvatierra, who was married to Malinche (Malintzin, Marina), the interpreter and early companion of Cortés (ENE, III, pp. 31–2). Jaramillo had a daughter by Malinche, Doña María (Marina) Jaramillo, then became a widower and was re-married to Beatriz de Andrada. On Jaramillo's death c. 1550 Doña Beatriz inherited the encomienda and soon took another husband, Francisco de Velasco, brother of the viceroy. However, the mestiza Doña María claimed part of the inheritance, and by 1555 half of Xilotepec was held by her and her husband, Luis de Quesada (ENE, VIII, p. 28. PNE, VI, p. 5). Quesada and Velasco shared the tributes in the 1560s and later, but before the century's end the Velasco half had escheated. In 1592–1604 the Quesada half was held by a grandson of Jaramillo, Pedro de Quesada.[2] By 1623 the private portion, claimed by Luis de Quesada's widow, had been reduced to a third (Scholes and Adams, 1959, p. 50); sixty-five years later the recipient was Pedro de la Cadena.

Chiapa was assigned to a conquistador, Gerónimo Ruiz de la Mota, followed in the 1560s by a son, Antonio, and still later by a grandson of the same name (Dorantes de Carranza, p. 195).[3] Escheatment occurred between 1604 and 1643, but part of the tributes were subsequently re-assigned.

Hernán Sánchez de Hortigosa held Chiapantongo until he died in the 1550s, to be followed by his widow, Leonor Vázquez de Vivanco. The place escheated in June 1562.[4]

Zayanaquilpa was assigned to Juan (Antonio) Navarro, succeeded c. 1545 by his widow, who then married Juan Bautista Marín (Icaza, I, p. 185. L de T, pp. 618–19). The latter, widowed and re-married, was followed towards 1565 by his widow, Leonor

Marín. There was a dispute over this inheritance and the place escheated shortly before 1571.[5]

Government

A magistrate known as Justicia mayor de Chichimecas was first appointed *c.* 1548 and charged

with the government of the frontier colonies and their defense against Chichimec raids (Powell, p. 9). His jurisdiction extended from Xilotepec north and west into the unsettled lands, reaching for a time the borders of Nueva Galicia and San Luis Potosí. In the 1550s and early 1560s this AM, as he came to be designated, spent most of his time on the frontier, while the powerful encomenderos of Xilotepec were left without interference.[6] During these years occasional visits to the Xilotepec–Chiapantongo area were made by Diego Ramírez (1551, 1555) and by the neighboring Cs of Otumba (1551), Zayula (1555), and Iscuincuitla-pilco (1560).[7] Meanwhile, the territory administered by the AM of Xilotepec–Chichimecas was diminished as separate AMs were appointed to Guanaxuato (1559) and S Miguel el Grande (*c.* 1562). In the latter year, Chiapantongo escheated, followed shortly by Zayanaquilpa; the AM of

Xilotepec doubled as C of these places. In 1567 a new AM reported that he was attending to the correction of encomenderos' abuses, a problem which his predecessors had not dared to concern themselves with (ENE, x, p. 202). Querétaro had its own magistrate from *c.* 1577, and Sichú and Cimapan from *c.* 1590. This left the province of Xilotepec, once the largest in New Spain, with more or less its final boundaries. It remained an unwieldy jurisdiction, and in the 1640s separate magistrates are reported for Xilotepec and its northern dependency, Hueychiapa, but they were soon united again under a single AM with residence at Hueychiapa.[8] From 1787 the AM was a subdelegado in the intendencia of Mexico.

Church

The Franciscans established a doctrina in 1529 at S Pedro y S Pablo Xilotepec, and another two years later at S Mateo Hueychiapa. A third Franciscan parish, S Martín Alfaxayuca, dates from *c.* 1559. Seven years later Augustinians from Actopan founded a vicaría at Santiago Chiapantongo which became a priorate in 1569. By this time a secular priest was resident at S Miguel Chiapa. Seventeenth-century foundations were the Franciscan parishes of Santiago Tecozautla and S Gerónimo Aculco and an asistencia at S Miguel Acambay, later raised to parochial status. The secular curacy of Nuestra Señora de la Peña de Francia (Villa del Carbón) was created from a visita of Chiapa probably late in the seventeenth century. All the regular doctrinas were secularized between 1754 and 1768 (Vera, pp. 5, 12, 35, 97, 110, 142).

By 1794 there was a parish at S Bernardino Taxquillo, and somewhat later Magdalena Nopala acquired a resident priest; they had been visited from Alfaxayuca and Hueychiapa, respectively. Three villages, Atzcapozaltongo, Calpulalpan, and Tlautla, belonged to the parish of Tepexi (cf. Tula), while S Ildefonso was visited from Amealco (cf. Querétaro). All parishes were in the archbishopric of Mexico.

Population and settlements

Tributary counts here must be used with care, since the principal encomienda (Xilotepec) extended into adjoining jurisdictions; furthermore, a large part of the population was at times exempt from tribute payment. The earliest figure we have for Xilotepec is 18,335 tributaries in *c.* 1565. Five years later the three Franciscan monasteries had 12,900 tributaries, from which we gather that some 5,000 tributaries lived in what later became the jurisdictions of Querétaro, S Miguel, S Luis de la Paz, and Cimapan. In the area with which we are concerned here (the final jurisdiction of the AM of Xilotepec) we must add 3,300 tributaries at Chiapa, 1,580 at Chiapantongo, and 680 at Zayanaquilpa, making a total of 18,460 tributaries towards 1570. In addition, there may have been 500 families of Chichimecs at that time. The tributaries were almost all Otomíes, but there were Náhuatl-speakers at the cabeceras of Xilotepec and Chiapa, and at Alfaxayuca. The native population fell drastically after 1570, owing partly to continued emigration but far more to death from epidemic disease, especially in 1576–81 and 1604–7. An interpolation of various data gives estimates of 9,100 tributaries in 1588, 6,130 in 1597, 3,490 in 1623, and only 1,470 in 1643. By the latter date there were very few unassimilated Chichimecs. Then there was a remarkable increase, apparently helped by immigration. 6,530 tributaries are recorded in 1688, 7,179 Indian families in 1743, and 15,851 Indian tributaries in 1799.[9] Non-Indians were insignificant in number at first, but by 1580 there were many cattle and sheep haciendas worked by a growing number of Spaniards and mulattoes (*Actas de cabildo...*, IV, pp. 86–8. Chevalier, pp. 121, 155). After 1600 more Indian lands were taken for this purpose, and with the disappearance of the Chichimec menace the area became a huge grazing tract, especially in the north. By the end of the seventeenth century, non-Indians formed almost a fourth of the population at Hueychiapa, and a lesser proportion elsewhere.

In the sixteenth century, Chiapa (S Miguel Chapa de Mota; Te[pe]ticpac; 1950: Chapa de Mota, pueblo, Mex.) had twenty-two or more estancias within 3½ leagues (the Náhuatl names are given in the 1570 report). There was a congregation here in 1592–3 with two centers, S Luis and S Félix, and while some settlements were aban-

doned at this time, others remained *in situ* and still other sites were later re-occupied.[10] Among the 1570 sujetos were Acaxuchitla and Michemaloya, one and two leagues respectively from the cabecera, both mentioned in the Codex Mendoza. In the eighteenth century the surviving settlements were grouped around two cabeceras de doctrina. Chiapa itself had six satellite pueblos, S Felipe Cuamango, S Gregorio Mascapesco, S Bartolomé de las Tunas, S Francisco, S Marcos (Tlazalpan), and S Juan Bautista Tuxtepec. The other center, a seventeenth-century creation, had the interminable name of Villa Nueva del Carbón de Nuestra Señora (Sta María) de la Peña de Francia (1950: Villa del Carbón, Mex.). About it were the pueblos of S Martín (Cachihuapan), S Francisco Magú, S Lorenzo Malacota, S Lorenzo Pueblo Nuevo, S Sebastián, S Luis de las Peras (Taxhimay), and S Gerónimo Zacapexco. There were sixteen haciendas and an equal number of ranchos here in 1794.

Santiago Chiapantongo (1950: Chapantongo, pueblo, Hgo.) had three estancias with fifteen barrios in 1548, reduced to two nearby settlements, S Juan and S Pedro, in 1571. Only S Juan, in addition to the cabecera, survived as a pueblo in 1794; in that year there were three haciendas and five ranchos in this area.

There were a great many scattered settlements subject to Xilotepec (1950: Jilotepec de Abasolo, ciudad, Mex.), at least a hundred in the sixteenth century. We have mentioned that Querétaro, Cimapan, and other places on the Chichimec frontier were colonized by Otomíes from Xilotepec and thus were considered sujetos of that encomienda. Acahualtzinco, Tecozauhtla, Tlachco, and Tlauhtla may originally have been considered sub-cabeceras here. In 1570 there were sixty-six estancias visited from the Franciscan monasteries of Xilotepec, Hueychiapa, and Alfaxayuca, but only their Christian names are given in the report. Many of these disappeared in the congregations of 1593–4 and 1598–1601 (there must have also been an earlier reduction, perhaps in the 1540s).[11] S Gerónimo Acahualtzinco (Acagualcingo) seems to have been moved to S José Atlan in 1601, while other places (e.g., Sta María

Amealco, S Bartolomé Ozocalapan) were abandoned later. Some forty-seven pueblos listed in 1794 can probably be identified with old estancia sites of Xilotepec: S Miguel Acambay, S Juan Acaxuchitlan, S Gerónimo Aculco, S Martín Alfaxayuca (Alhuexuyuca; Otomí, Audaxitso), S José Atlan, Sta Ana (Azcapozaltongo), Magdalena Calpulalpan, S Juan Caltimacan, Concepción, S Miguel Chipaté (Caltepantla; Domni), S Sebastián (Dacpani), S Pedro Denxí, S Pedro Donicá, S Pablo Guantepec, S Sebastián Huauquilpa, S Mateo Huichapan (Hueixoapan, Hueychiapa, etc.), S Buenaventura Juanacapa, Sta María Macua, Sta Ana (Matlabat), Santiago Maxdá, Natívitas, Magdalena Nopala, S Lorenzo Oteyuco, Santiago Oxthó (Ostoc), S Pablo (Oxtotipan), Sta María de la Palma, Sta Cruz del Portezuelo, Los Angeles Pueblo Nuevo, S Francisco Sacachichilco, S Antonio, S Francisquito, S Ildefonso (1950: pueblo, Qro.), S Lucas, S Miguelito, S Francisco Saxní, S Bernardino Taxquillo, Santiago Tecozautla, S Antonio Tesoquipan, S Andrés Timilpan, Sta María Tixmadegé, S Agustín Tlalistacapa, Santiago Tlautla, S Bartolomé Tlaxcalilla, Santiago Toxié, Guadalupe Xigui, Santiago Xomtaá, and S Pedro Xotho. The 1794 report names twenty-five haciendas and ninety-five ranchos within the limits of Xilotepec (excluding those outside the political jurisdiction).

S Francisco Zayanaquilpa (Sayanalquilpa; 1950: S Francisco Soyaniquilpan, pueblo, Mex.) in 1548 had an area 2 by 2½ leagues, but no estancias are named in the report. The eighteenth-century pueblo of S Agustín Buenavista was probably within its limits, together with two haciendas and three ranchos.[12]

Sources

The three smaller encomiendas here (but not Xilotepec) are briefly mentioned in the *Suma* of *c.* 1548 (PNE, I, nos. 106, 110–11). Somewhere there should be a report, which we have not found, on the Ramírez visita of 1551 (cf. ENE, VI, pp. 50–1). Information of *c.* 1570 is voluminous.[13] Ponce, while he did not visit the area, left an account of the Franciscan doctrinas as they were *c.* 1586 (Ponce, I, pp. 220–2).

There is a congregation report from Hueychiapa dated 1601.[14] We have found tributary data for 1623 (Scholes and Adams, 1959, pp. 50, 62) and 1643–88.[15] The journal of an archbishop's visit here in 1685 should be consulted,[16] while Vetancurt (4a parte, pp. 63–4, 71, 80, 84, 87, 88) describes the Franciscan doctrinas as they were *c.* 1697.

Villaseñor y Sánchez (I, pp. 137–8) summarizes a lost document of *c.* 1743. There is a complete list of toponyms submitted by the subdelegado in 1794.[17]

The *Códice de Huichapan* (which we have not seen) is said to contain place glyphs and historical data to 1632.[18] Colín (1966, 1967) gives further citations for the southern part of this area, while Fernández (1940–2) is useful for the Hidalgo portion.

123 *Xiquilpa*

Xiquilpa's colonial jurisdiction straddles the main volcanic divide in western Michoacán, with elevations from 800 to over 3,500 m (at Cerro Patamban); thus drainage is both northward towards the Lerma and Lake Chapala and southward into the Tepalcatepec basin, with a few mountain lakes. The higher mountains are forested with pine and oak. There are moderate seasonal rains, temperature varying with elevation.

Guanimba (the Tarascan equivalent of Xiquilpa), according to the relación of 1579, was settled by a Nahua- (Sayultecan?) speaking people from Amula only nine years before the arrival of the Spaniards; they were allied with the cazonci and fought in his wars of expansion in the west. The eastern portion of this area, together with Tinhuindín, probably formed a single state, Tarecuato or Tepehuacan, inhabited by Tarascans with a ruler controlled by the cazonci (Kelly, 1945–9, II, p. 30. Stanislawski, p. 50).

Some of Olid's men may have passed through here late in 1522, but the region was not subjugated for some years. In 1528 the natives of Tepehuacan were proving rather uncooperative, and those of Guanimba had fled westward into the mountains.[1]

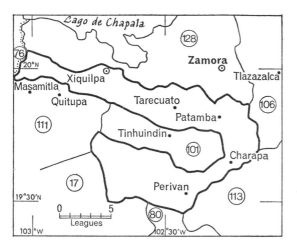

Encomienda

In the spring of 1528, Xiquilpa belonged to someone called Leonardo, while Tarecuato–Tepeguacan were held by the conquistador Antón Caicedo.[2] Xiquilpa escheated sometime between 1536 and 1545. Caicedo's title was disputed after his death c. 1535, at which time his encomienda was divided, Perivan and Tinhuindín being taken for the crown and Tarecuato going to the widow, Marina Montes de Oca or Montesdoca (one source shows Alonso Izquierdo as the former encomendero of Perivan and Tinhuindín). Within a year or so, Perivan was assigned to the Montesdoca encomienda, generally referred to in contemporary documents as Perivan y Tarecuato (Tepeguacan). Doña Marina soon re-married, to Francisco de Chávez. When the latter died in 1561, he was succeeded briefly by a daughter, Catalina de Chávez, and within three years by Doña Marina again. Sometime between 1570 and 1579 the encomienda passed to Antonio de Luna, who had married a daughter of Caicedo. Luna was followed towards 1600 by a son, Rodrigo. Escheatment occurred before 1657, but the

tributes were soon re-assigned (Icaza, I, p. 227. Scholes and Adams, 1961, pp. 134–6).

Government

The C of Xiquilpa during the sixteenth century was considered suffragan to the AM of Michoacán, and for most of that period administered justice in the neighboring encomienda of Perivan y Tarecuato. When, in 1583, jurisdiction in Perivan was disputed between the Cs of Xiquilpa and Tancítaro and the AM of Michoacán, that area was awarded to Xiquilpa.[3] This left Xiquilpa's territory almost split in two by the intrusion of Tinhuindín, a situation which prevailed until Tinhuindín was definitely attached to Xiquilpa in the eighteenth century.

In 1604 the Mazamitla–Quitupa area was briefly annexed to Xiquilpa, but it soon returned to the jurisdiction of Tuspa.[4] After 1650 the magistrate of Xiquilpa was generally called AM, and from 1787 he was a subdelegado in the intendencia of Valladolid, with deputies at Cotija, Patamba, Periban, and Tinhuindín.

Church

The Franciscans entered this area in the 1520s and eventually founded six monasteries, five of which survived as parishes. S Juan Perivan, Sta María de Jesús Tarecuato, and S Francisco Xiquilpa probably date as doctrinas from the 1540s. S Antonio Charapa was detached from Perivan c. 1585, while two parishes were created from visitas of Tarecuato, Asunción Patamba (by 1626) and Santo Angel (by 1649); the last-mentioned was reduced to a visita in the late eighteenth century. These parishes were secularized in the 1770s, and all belonged to the diocese of Michoacán.

The doctrina of Xiquilpa included Mazamitla and Quitupa (cf. Tuspa) until they were made a separate parish after 1789, while Charapa in the eighteenth century was the parish seat for Corupo and S Felipe de los Herreros (cf. Valladolid).

Population and settlements

Throughout the colonial period, the Indians of Xiquilpa are said to have spoken 'Sayulteca', apparently a Nahua dialect, while Tarascan prevailed in the rest of the jurisdiction. Various censuses and estimates show the number of native tributaries as 1,700 in 1579 (after a serious epidemic), 1,435 towards 1600, 1,010 in 1657, and 763 in 1698 (cf. Scholes and Adams, 1959, p. 52). By 1743 there were 1,383 Indian families, and in 1804 there were *c.* 2,370 native tributaries.[5]

After the congregations, much of the land was taken up by cattle haciendas and (in the low country) sugar plantations operated by Spaniards with a work force of Indians and Negroes. In 1743 there were 355 non-Indian families in the jurisdiction, free mulattoes being in the majority, plus an undisclosed number of Negro slaves. The 1804 census shows 950 free Negro and mulatto tributaries, but Tinhuindín is included in this figure.

S Francisco Xiquilpa (Huanimba; 1950: Jiquilpan de Juárez, ciudad) had only four estancias in 1579 (there was probably an earlier Franciscan congregation here). They were in two groups, separated by the intrusion of Tarecuato. A congregation proposed in 1604 in which Masamitla and Quitupa were to be moved to Xiquilpa met with little success. In the eighteenth century the western section was composed of the cabecera and the pueblos of S Francisco and S Martín Tototlan (this last place can perhaps be identified with the barrio of Tzipin or Los Sepines, claimed by Zamora y Xacona in the sixteenth century). In the east were the pueblos of Ocumicho, Patamba, and S José Changaxo.[6]

Five estancias of S Francisco Tarecuato (1950: pueblo) were to have been collected at the cabecera in 1594.[7] Only the latter and S Angel survived as pueblos.

Perivan (Perihuan, Periban; 1950: Peribán de Ramos, *villa*) in the sixteenth century had a dozen or more subordinate settlements within four leagues of the cabecera. Atapa, Charapa, and Xaratango were sub-cabeceras in 1548. All were to have been reduced to five congregation centers in 1594.[8] Santiago Atapan was transferred to Tinhuindín before 1639, leaving S Juan Periban, S Francisco Periban Pequeño, Charapa, Los Reyes, and S Gabriel as pueblos.

Sources

Brief articles in the *Suma* of *c.* 1548 (PNE, I, nos. 458, 667, 812) are followed by an Ovando report of *c.* 1570 (García Pimentel, 1904, p. 48), and a good relación drawn up by the AM in 1579.[9] For the seventeenth century, we have a description of 1639[10] and tributary data for 1657–98.[11]

There is a most interesting report from the AM in 1743,[12] followed by a census dated 1778,[13] a long description of the area in 1789,[14] a shorter one for 1793,[15] and the work of Martínez de Lejarza (pp. 209–22) corresponding to 1822.

The interesting book of Luis González (1968) cites many other documents concerning haciendas in this area.

124 *Xonotla y Tetela*

This jurisdiction was divided into two distinct parts, both on the Gulf slope of the Sierra Madre Oriental in what is now northern Puebla. Xonotla–Tenampulco lies at elevations of 100–1,200 m, while Tetela is in cooler country, at 1,400–3,000 m. Drainage is to the northeast into the Tecolutla river. There is abundant rainfall much of the year.

Ayutuchco and Xonoctla are shown in the *Matrícula de Tributos*, in the tributary province of Tlatlauhquitépec. Other places listed as Aztec conquests are Quetzalcouac and Tenampolco. These were all Totonac communities rather close

to each other. Off to the southwest was Tetella, a Náhuatl-speaking colony which had absorbed the older Totonac population. The tlatoani of Tetella dominated lesser rulers at Calpulalpan, Tzanacuauhtlan, and Tzotzompan; none of these places appears in the Aztec tribute lists, but since they fought the Tlaxcalans we assume they were at least allies of the Mexica (they also had wars with neighboring Zacatlan).

The rulers of Tetella are said to have sent a delegation which submitted to Cortés at Tzaoctlan in August, 1519, but the area probably did not come under Spanish control for another year or so.

Encomiendas

Tetela, held by Pedro de Escobar, seems to have escheated towards 1535.

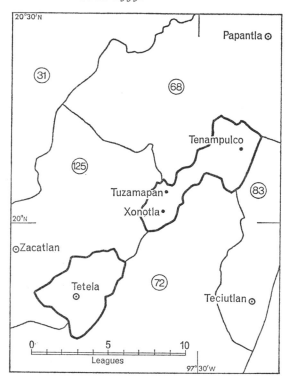

Diego Valadés held Tenampulco until his death sometime between 1568 and 1581, when he was succeeded by a son, Alonso. Escheatment occurred after 1626 (Dorantes de Carranza, p. 173. Icaza, I, p. 54).

Xonotla and its dependencies formed part of the joint encomienda of Pedro Cindos de Portillo and Hernando de Salazar. The Cindos share was relinquished when the holder became a Franciscan *c.* 1528; both halves apparently went to the crown in 1533 (*Códice Franciscano*, p. 219. Icaza, II, p. 292. L de T, p. 217. Mendieta, IV, pp. 127–8).

Government

The corregimiento of 'Yztepeque y Juanotla y Queçalcoal e Citusco' was organized in May, 1533, to administer those recently escheated places, and

Tetela was added to the jurisdiction by 1536. Zetusco was joined in corregimiento with nearby Tonatico in 1544, while Iztepec was absorbed by Hueytlalpa. In the early 1550s the C of Xonotla y Tetela did not live in his jurisdiction, for which reason commissions were given first to the C of Tlatlauquitepec and then to the C of Hueytlalpa to administer justice there, a situation which prevailed for several decades.[1] Tenampulco at this time belonged to the jurisdiction of Huey-tlalpa, whose magistrate kept a deputy there. By 1629 the C of Xonotla y Tetela was collecting tribute at Tenampulco and his jurisdiction thus assumed its final boundaries. In the 1660s and later this magistrate was called AM of Minas de Tetela, because of the silver mines being worked there.[2] He was re-designated subdelegado, subordinate to the intendente of Puebla, from 1787.

Church

We are told that Fray Andrés de Olmos preached here, and the Franciscans visited both Tetela and Xonotla, erecting a monastery at Xonotla which was relinquished to secular clergy *c.* 1567 (*Alegaciones...*, fol. 23). Two years later, Sta María (Asunción) Tetela and S Juan Xonotla appear as secular parishes, each with visitas in adjoining jurisdictions. These parishes survived, with the addition in the late eighteenth century of S Martín Tuzamapan. Tenampulco in the late colonial period was visited from Espinal (cf. Papantla). The area was in the diocese of Tlaxcala.

Population and settlements

Originally there was a dense native population, but many died from disease in the 1540s, and others were taken off as slaves (ENE, VIII, p. 154). The number of tributaries is recorded as 1,436 in 1569, 1,350 in 1581, 231 in 1626, 323 in 1696, 718 (families) in 1743, 1,751 in 1791, and 1,877 in 1804.[3] Totonac continued to be spoken at Xonotla and Tenampulco, and Náhuatl at Tetela. There were few non-Indians until silver was discovered near Tetela in the mid-seventeenth century. The 1743 census shows 76 families of Spaniards and 165 of mestizos and mulattoes at the mines. In 1791 there were 533 families of gente de razón living at Tetela and six nearby mining camps, and only one Spanish family in the Xonotla area.

Reports of 1548–1569 state that Tetela (1950: Tetela de Ocampo, *villa*) had four subject estancias, the most distant of which, Tututla, was five leagues north of the cabecera. These places (Capulapa, Tututla, Tzanacuauhtla or Cuautenco, Tzotzonpan) are named in the 1581 relación, together with two villages (Hueytlentla, Tonalapa) which were founded in the early 1570s to protect the communal lands from invasion. A congregation was proposed here *c.* 1600.[4] Three places besides the cabecera were pueblos in the eighteenth century: S Esteban Cuautempan, S Pedro Hueytentan, and S Cristóbal Iztulco. The chief mining camps in 1791 were La Cañada and Tonalapan.

Before the congregation of *c.* 1600, Xonotla (1950: Jonotla, pueblo) had three 'old' estancias (Ayotuchco, Ecatlan, Tutzamapa) within a league of the cabecera, and seven 'pueblos nuevos' (Asunción, S Pedro Cocoyola, Concepción Cuauhtla, S Bartolomé, S Andrés Tetela, Tres Reyes Xalcuauhtla, S Miguel Zoquiapa) spread out along the community boundaries, as at Tetela. Ayotuchco and Ecatlan (= Quetzalcouac or Quetzalcóatl?) may well have been the pre-Columbian cabeceras, absorbed by Xonotla after

the Conquest (*see above*). Santiago Ecatlan, S Martín Tuzamapan, S Andrés Tetelilla, Santos Reyes, and Zoquiapan survived as pueblos in 1743–92.

Tenampulco (Tenanpulco; 1950: Tenampulco, pueblo, or perhaps Tenampulco Viejo, ranchería) had eight estancias in 1548, four in 1569, and two in 1581, but only the cabecera is mentioned later.[5]

Sources

There are short descriptions of *c.* 1548 in the *Suma de Visitas* (PNE, I, nos. 294, 527, 557), several reports from clergy of 1569–70 (PNE, V, pp. 210–13, 265), and an unusually detailed relación (with two fine maps) submitted by the C of Xonotla y Tetela in 1581 (PNE, V, pp. 124–73). Tenampulco is briefly described (also with a map) in the report from the AM of Hueytlalpa, also dated 1581.[6]

Bishop Mota y Escobar was in Xonotla in 1610 and left a short description of the place,[7] as did Bishop Palafox, who visited both Tetela and Xonotla in 1646.[8]

There is a report from the AM dated 1743,[9] with additional details in Villaseñor y Sánchez (I, pp. 315–17). A useful description was compiled in 1791 by the subdelegado,[10] who sent in a list of placenames the following year.[11]

125 *Zacatlan de las Manzanas*

Just west of the last jurisdiction, and also draining northeastward into the Tecolutla system on the Gulf-facing side of the Sierra Madre in northern Puebla state, this is a region of widely varying climate. Above Chicnahuapan is a cold, dry, barren country where elevations reach 3,400 m. Descending towards Zacatlan, one enters a region of almost constant mist and considerable rain, while in the canyons below Zacatlan (to 200 m) it is hot, with rain much of the year; this is a deeply eroded, mountainous area, much of it forested.

Zacatlan (perhaps the Acazacatlan of the Matrícula de Tributos), or Tenamitic, was dominated by a Náhuatl-speaking majority, with a sizeable

minority of Totonacs in the low country on the north; there may well have been some Otomies in the south. The ruler was probably a military governor, either subject to or allied with the Triple Alliance. Zacatlan was on bad terms with Tlaxcallan, and between the two was a community called Chicnahuapan which can perhaps be identified with the pre-Conquest state of Tliliuhquitépec; the affiliation of the latter in 1519 is not clear, although after the Conquest the Spaniards considered Chicnahuapan to be a dependency of Zacatlan. Xiloxochitlan seems to have been a Totonac state dependent on Zacatlan. Farther down in the hot country were three small but populous Totonac communities, Chapolicxihtla

(=Chila?), Xochicuauhtitlan (Xuxupango), and Tlapacoyan (Matlactlan), the latter a center of tribute collection for the Aztecs with a military governor appointed from Tenochtitlan. Off to the east and also in the lowlands were three more Totonac chiefdoms, Itztépec, Ixcoyamec, and

Teotlalpan (Hueytlalpan), which delivered their tribute to the Aztec garrison at Tlatlauhquitépec. Other states in this general area which are mentioned in the Matrícula de Tributos were Aztaapan, Caltépec, Coapan, and Tuchtlan. The population was scattered in many settlements (Byam Davies, pp. 73–4, 79. Torquemada, I, p. 280).

A group of eight Spaniards explored the region in late 1519 and early 1520 (*Códice Franciscano*, pp. 217–18). Hernán López de Avila is said to be the discoverer of Zacatlan, and Pedro Cindos de Portillo and Hernando de Salazar of Teotlalpan. Gonzalo Portero is credited with exploring Xuxupango, and Francisco de Montejo the Chila–Matlactlan area.

The Indians of Zacatlan revolted towards 1525 (Icaza, nos. 796, 955, 1203).

Encomiendas

Zacatlan, with Chicnahuapan and Xiloxochitlan, were held by the conquistador Antonio de Cara-

vajal (Carvajal) until his death *c.* 1565. He was succeeded by a son, and later (by 1604) by a grandson, both of the same name. In 1646 an Antonio de Caravajal was living at Zacatlan, and a century later Esteban de Carvajal was receiving the tribute (Dorantes de Carranza, p. 159).

The conqueror of Chila and Matlactlan, Francisco de Montejo, was given those places in encomienda. He was followed on his death in 1553 by a daughter, Catalina, married to Lic. Alonso Maldonado. The latter died in the 1560s, and tributes escheated on the death of Doña Catalina (after 1582), but they were re-assigned in the seventeenth century (Dorantes de Carranza, p. 184. ENE, xv, p. 212. Gibson, 1964, p. 414).

Cortés gave Xuxupango to Luis de Avila, after which Governor Estrada assigned it to Alonso de Avila and Diego de Villapadierna (Icaza, I, pp. 68, 194). Alonso de Avila was followed *c.* 1540 by a daughter, Antonia, married to Gonzalo de Salazar. The latter appears in 1548–81, to be replaced by Hernando de Salazar in 1597. Villapadierna's share was inherited towards 1565 by a son of the same name who is still listed in 1597. Half (we do not know which) of this encomienda escheated between 1626 and 1664, and the rest by 1696.

Hueytlalpa, Ixtepec, and Ixcoyamec, with other nearby places, were given to Pedro Cindos de Portillo and Hernando de Salazar. Cindos renounced his half when he became a Franciscan (*c.* 1528), and the remaining share escheated in March, 1531 (*Códice Franciscano*, pp. 217–20. L de T, p. 454).

Government

A C of 'Teutalpa e Iztepec' was appointed from 11 March 1531. This officer had little to do with the encomiendas, and Teutalpa (Hueytlalpa) was being visited by the C of Tlatlauquitepec in the early 1550s.[1] In 1554 Ixcoyamec and Zoncozcatlan were annexed to Hueytlalpa, having until then been attached to Tlatlauquitepec (L de T, p. 454). In September, 1556, the C of Hueytlalpa was given jurisdiction in all the neighboring crown and encomienda villages, and soon after he was made AM in charge of a large province extending from

Zacatlan to the Gulf.[2] Towards 1600 this jurisdiction was reduced to more or less its final limits, with the separation of Papantla (q.v.). By 1620 the AM had established residence at Zacatlan; in the eighteenth century he was re-designated C, and from 1787 he was a subdelegado, subordinate to the intendente of Puebla.

Church

Franciscans working out of Tlaxcala founded monastery-parishes at S Andrés Hueytlalpa (by 1546) and S Pedro y S Pablo Zacatlan (by 1555) (Kubler, 1948, II, pp. 461, 487). Both Hueytlalpa and S Miguel Xuxupango were given to secular clergy towards 1567 (*Alegaciones...*, fol. 23). In the congregations of *c.* 1600 additional secular priests were assigned to S José Olintla, Sta María Xopala, and Sta María (Natívitas) Zapotitlan. In 1646 we find Zacatlan secularized, and a priest living at S Juan Aguacatlan. By 1743 the curate of Xuxupango had moved to S José Amixtlan, while that of Hueytlalpa was temporarily at Sta María (Asunción) Ixtepec. Sometime between 1743 and 1777 new doctrinas were created at S Miguel Atliquizayan, S Pedro Camoguautla, Santiago Chignahuapan, and Sta María Tepecintla. All parishes here were in the diocese of Puebla or Tlaxcala.

Population and settlements

After much early loss, the native population was reduced to 6,050 tributaries in 1570, 3,980 in 1581, and 1,656 in 1626. Later counts show 2,926 tributaries in 1696, 4,079 in 1743, and 8,228 in 1803.[3] Mestizos, with a few Spaniards and mulattoes, were mostly confined to the Zacatlan area where there were haciendas and ranchos. There were a few Spaniards in Zacatlan in 1580, fifty or sixty vecinos in 1662, and 570 non-Indian families in 1743.[4]

The cabecera of Zacatlan (1950: ciudad), known in later years as Zacatlan de las Manzanas, had fourteen sujetos in 1570 and thirteen (only the saints' names are given) in 1581.[5] Chicnahuapan (Chiconaupa, Chignahuapan, etc.) and Xiloxochitlan, perhaps originally considered subcabeceras, were soon included in the overall tribute assessment of Zacatlan, although we are told that the Totonac minority here was given a separate government in the sixteenth century (Torquemada, I, p. 280). There was probably an early Franciscan congregation, reducing the number of estancias, in the 1550s. A further reduction proposed in 1598 seems to have met with little success.[6] All but two of the 1581 sujetos are recognizable as pueblos in the eighteenth century, together with seven others: Aguacatlan, Aquixtla, Chicuasentépetl, Chignahuapan, Misquiahuacan, Omitlan, Siloxochitlan, Tenango or Tanaco, Tepango, Tepeixco, Tepecintla, Tlacotepec, Tlaquilpan, Tlayohualacingo, Tomalixco, Tonalan, Xuchimilco, and Zoquitlaxco. There were abandoned silver mines near Tanaco in 1743.

Hueytlalpa (Ueitlalpan, etc.; Teutlalpa; 1950: Hueytlalpan, pueblo) had an early congregation, with much opposition from the natives, in 1553.[7] In 1570–80 there were twenty-one subject settlements up to six leagues from the cabecera. A number of these places were abandoned in the congregation of *c.* 1600 (Comapa, Chilchotla, Chimalco, Ixcoyamec, and Zapotlan are among the names which disappear), but again there was resistance and re-occupation of old sites.[8] The old estancia of Zoncozcatlan (*see above*) survived as the pueblo of Zongozotla and still maintained its independence in 1743. Eighteen places in addition to the cabecera were considered pueblos in the late eighteenth century, some having achieved separate cabecera status: Atliquizayan, Camoguautla, Caxhuacan (Cachuacan), Coatepec, Concepción, Chichipahuatlan, Huehuetlan, Huitzilan (Uitzila), Ixtepec, Nanacatlan, Nexquitilan (Nestequilan), Ocelonacastla, Olintla, Sta Catarina, Tapayula, Tuxtla (Tuchtlan), Zapotitlan, Zitlala (L de T, pp. 454, 521).

The names of four estancias are given in the 1548 visita of Chila (1950: pueblo): Xupala, Panatlan, Cutlaxtepeque, and Xicalango. We guess that 'Xupala–Chila' was originally Chapolicxihtla, which appears in this general area in a list of conquests of Moctezuma I. In 1569 the natives were scattered in twenty estancias up to 5 leagues from the cabecera; the 1581 map shows only eight sujetos, which seem to have been congregated at Xopala *c.* 1600. In 1646 Chicontla is mentioned as a second cabecera here, while in 1696 we find Chila, Chicontla, and Xopala together in a tribute assessment. These and two other places, Patla and Tlaolan(tongo), survived as eighteenth-century pueblos.

Matlactlan (Matlatlan) last appears in the records we have seen in 1665. It had eight estancias in 1570, and seven in 1581. Sixteenth-century references place it between Xuxupango and Chila, and this leads us to equate it with pre-Columbian Tlapacoyan (1950: pueblo), today a Náhuatl-speaking community more or less where Matlactlan must have been.

Xuxupango (Jujupanco; 1950: Jojupango, pueblo) had eight sujetos within $3\frac{1}{2}$ leagues in 1569, reduced to four by 1580.[9] These four estancias (Amixtlan, Coyayango, Cuautotola, Tecpatlan) together with the cabecera, were still pueblos in 1743–92.

Sources

Only Chila and Xuxupango are represented with articles in the *Suma de Visitas* of *c.* 1548 (PNE, I,

nos. 136, 798). We have seen tribute assessments of Hueytlalpa covering the period 1547–56 (L de T, pp. 454–5), Matlactlan in 1537–54 (*ibid.*, pp. 226–7), and Zacatlan-Chicnahuapan in 1543–66 (ENE, VIII, pp. 4–8. L de T, pp. 607–9). The area is described in varying detail in reports of 1569–70 (*Códice Franciscano*, p. 26. López de Velasco, p. 223. PNE, V, pp. 213–19). There is an excellent relación geográfica with four maps, submitted by the AM in 1581.[10] Fray Ponce (I, pp. 208–9) made a brief visit to Zacatlan in 1586.

Two seventeenth-century bishops inspected this area, Mota y Escobar in 1610, 1615, and 1623,[11] and Palafox in 1646.[12] The brief description of *c.* 1697 in Vetancurt (4a parte, p. 66) is of little interest.

There is a useful report from the AM dated 1743,[13] followed by parish censuses of Aguacatlan, Atliquizayan, Camoguautla, Chicnahuapan, Tepecintla, and Zapotitlan, all made in 1777.[14] A complete list of toponyms was sent in in 1792.[15]

126 *Zacatula*

This vast province extends from the Sierra Madre del Sur (3,000+ m) to the sea, and from the vicinity of Acapulco to the Balsas river and beyond. Foothills of the Sierra Madre, which occasionally reach the shore to intersect a restricted coastal plain, form parallel ranges separated by short, precipitous watercourses most of which empty into extensive litoral lagoons. The coast is hot with slight seasonal precipitation, but heavy summer rains in the mountains flood the lowlands. This area is now in southwestern Guerrero state, with a slice of the Michoacán coast.

There were a great many independent or autonomous native states here peopled by farmers and fishermen speaking a variety of languages. From west to east, the languages reported in mid-sixteenth century were Chumbian, Tolimecan, Pantecan, and Cuitlatecan, and there were probably

others. Most of the area was outside the tributary hegemonies of the Tarascans and the Triple Alliance. There may have been Tarascan outposts, most likely trading stations, among the Tolimecans and the Pantecans. The Mexica invaded the region from the east during the reign of Ahuítzotl (1486–1502) and established control as far as Xuluchuca. This section was given the name of Cihuatlan in the tributary lists, and probably included the populous Cuitlatecan kingdom of Mexcaltépec. The population was considerable, and dispersed in numerous settlements. Mexcaltépec alone is said to have had over 150,000 families (Torquemada, I, p. 287). Names of the principal native communities are given below, under 'Encomiendas'.

An expedition led by Alvarez Chico explored the coast from Acapulco to Zacatula in the winter of 1521–2. Sometime before May 1522 a shipyard was established near the mouth of the Balsas, and early the following year a Spanish settlement called Villa de la Concepción de Zacatula was founded nearby. Later in 1523 the rebellious natives of the coast were subdued by an army

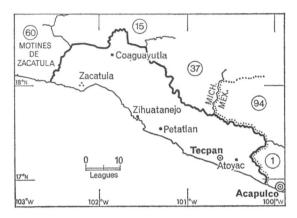

led by Gonzalo de Sandoval. There were further uprisings into the 1540s (Brand, 1960, pp. 54–8. Herrera, 3a década, pp. 132, 137. Icaza, nos. 336, 523, 1337. Sauer, 1948, pp. 2–17).

Encomiendas

Cortés at first set aside the province of Zacatula for the crown, but in 1524, after receiving the report of Antonio de Caravajal who had examined the region, he assigned the various native communities to private encomenderos, most of them residents of the *villa* (Cortés, pp. 447–8. Warren, 1963*a*, p. 407). Many of these grants were reassigned by the acting governors, the whole province was appropriated by Cortés for himself on his return from Honduras in 1526, and other changes occurred under the first audiencia in 1529–30 (Cortés, p. 470). In 1531 certain encomiendas escheated and others were re-assigned. We know practically nothing about these early encomenderos, having no complete list before 1550 by which time many communities had disappeared. Subsequent documents show the following private encomenderos (their villages are given in parentheses.)

Diego Correa (Mitla), in 1550, succeeded by his widow who married Hernán Martín (1560–8).

Sebastián de Ebora (Axapoteca), in 1550–60, followed by a son Alonso (1564–8).

Juan Flores (half of Echancaleca and Zapotitlan), 1550–64, having inherited from Lic. Alemán.

Francisco Gutiérrez (Pochutla and half of Chipila), in 1550–60, succeeded by a son (?), escheated *c.* 1564.

Francisco Rodríguez (half of Petatlan and Xalxucatitan), traded to Francisco Quintero in 1537; escheated by 1545.

Juan Rodríguez de Villafuerte (Mexcaltepec), followed in the 1550s by a daughter, Aldonza, who married García de Albornoz and survived as sole encomendera (1587–97); escheated before 1643.

Diego Ruiz (half of Huitaluta, Coyuca), in 1550–64, succeeded by a son, Juan Ruiz de Mendoza (1568–97).

Pedro Ruiz de Guadalcanal (La Guagua, Coyuca), from 1520s; inherited in 1553 by his son-in-law, Francisco de Castrejón, and later by Castrejón's widow.[1]

Antón Sánchez (Cacaopisca, Istapa, Tlaula), succeeded by a son of the same name (1550–97).

Francisco de Saucedo (Ciguatlan, Tamaloacan), in 1550–8; escheated by 1560.

Gonzalo Varela (Gallego) (Huiztla), in 1550, followed by a daughter, Ana de Porras (by 1560), who married Andrés Hurtado, still listed in 1597.

Juan Alonso de Vargas (Cigua, Tecpan), in 1550–5 (Dorantes de Carranza, p. 166).

Alonso Verdejo (Mechia), in 1550, succeeded by a daughter who married Juan de Castañeda (1560–4); escheated soon afterwards.

With the decline in population, most of these grants had become worthless by the late sixteenth century.

Government

The crown was represented in the *villa* of Zacatula, perhaps as early as 1524, by an AM who had jurisdiction over the entire coast from the Cachan river in the west almost to the mouth of the Coyuca river in the east. The province was divided into two parts by the Balsas river, the western portion being known as Motines de Zacatula (much

394

reduced sometime after 1649, when the boundary with Motines was shifted from the Cachan to the Carrizal river). The crown villages were grouped in corregimientos with constantly changing boundaries, whose Cs were residents of the *villa*, generally Spaniards without encomiendas who held their posts as a means of subsistence. These magistrates collected the tribute from which they derived their salaries, but the business of governing the province was generally left to the AM. We have several lists of these sinecure-corregimientos, drawn up at different dates.

c. 1534	1545	1580
Cacaluta	Ceutla	Axalo
Cuyuca, Pustla y Ciutla	Ciguatanejo	Ayutla
Pantla y Yautepec	Coyuca	Cayaco
Cigualpan, Camotla, Mitla y Citlaltomagua	Cuacuatlan	Cuacuactlan
Cinagua, Ayutla, Atlan y Coatlan	Nexpa	Mechia
	Pantla	Pantla
Texupan y Topetina	Petatlan	Petatlan
	Tecomatlan	Pochutla
	Texupa	Tecomatlan
	Xiguacan y Pichique	Texupan
	Zacatula	Zoyatlan

Several of these suffragan corregimientos were subsequently transferred to the jurisdictions of Acapulco (Citlaltomagua) and Motines (Cuacuatlan, Nexpa, Texupa y Topetina). Cinagua became a separate corregimiento. Towards 1600 the remaining Cs were eliminated.

The AM, at first resident at Zacatula, by 1575 had left the almost abandoned *villa* and was living far down the coast at Tecpan.[2] In 1649 he had acquired the additional title of *capitán a guerra* and maintained residences at both Tecpan and Petatlan. Tecpan remained the administrative center of the jurisdiction to the end of the colonial period; when the coast was held by insurgents in 1810–14, Tecpan was their headquarters and the center of a vast province.[3]

Sometime between 1669 and 1676, for reasons unknown to us, the jurisdiction of Zacatula was combined with that of León, far to the north.[4] In a report of 1676, while 'Leon y su agregado de Zacatula' appear together, there is a puzzling reference to a separate magistrate at 'Ciutla

prouᵃ de Çacatula', perhaps a C or a teniente subordinate to the AM of León.[5] In the mid-eighteenth century Zacatula occasionally had its own AM, and after 1786 it became a subdelegación in the intendencia of Mexico.[6]

Church

We hear of a secular curate at the villa of Concepción Zacatula as early as 1525 (Millares Carlo and Mantecón, 1, nos. 212, 1701). There are vague references to the presence of Franciscans and Augustinians on the coast, and Brand (1960, pp. 131–2) suggests that certain encomenderos may have subsidized priests. In the Motines area, there was a curate at Texupa as early as 1547; he had moved to Laguagua (cf. Motines) by 1571.[7] In the latter year there were secular parishes at Concepción Zacatula, S Pedro Petatlan, and Asunción Tecpan. By 1639 the curate of Zacatula was living most of the time at S Agustín Coaguayutla, which thus became the new parochial center; in the same year there was a priest at S Miguel Apuzagualcos, an hacienda near Atoyac, but ten years later he had retired. Asunción Atoyac, long visited from Tecpan, was a separate parish by 1743. All parishes were in the diocese of Michoacán.

Population and settlements

De-population of this area began in the 1520s and accelerated in the 1530s. Disease and forced emigration to work in the gold placers both undoubtedly had a part in this. 5,500 tributaries are reported in 1550, reduced to 1,812 in 1571. At least some of the subsequent decline can be ascribed to emigration by viceregal command (Gerhard, 1960, pp. 79–80, 95). The English corsair Cavendish was off Zacatula in 1587, in which year the viceroy reported that the entire coast was deserted by his order, leaving nothing for the enemy to rob.[8] Later, the Dutch 'Pechelingues' of Speilbergen (1615) and the Nassau fleet (1624) put in here. The 1639 report states that the Indians had greatly diminished within the previous twenty years 'from the bad treatment that the Spaniards give them'. In 1649, when there were only 230 Indian families in the jurisdiction, the 'total destruction of this province' is blamed on 'a ship from Peru which maliciously landed two leagues from the *villa* [Zacatula], and there were many robberies, and many judges came to investigate, so that the people fled and the entire region was ruined'. Thus contraband activity played a role in keeping this jurisdiction sparsely inhabited. Only 356 Indian families are reported in 1743. By 1803 there were 680 Indian tributaries; eleven years later the subdelegado, reporting the victory of royalist forces over the insurgents, wrote that 'more than two thirds of the Indians went off with the scoundrels' (i.e., the insurgents, who had taken to the hills).[9]

There must have been a great many settlements scattered everywhere, perhaps several hundred, of which ninety-odd survived in 1550 and sixty-nine in 1580. The province was examined by a *juez de congregación* in 1598–9, and the AM was ordered to carry out his recommendations in October, 1603.[10] West of the Balsas, the surviving natives in the Motines of Zacatula were reduced to one congregation at Laguagua, later transferred to the jurisdiction of Motines (q.v.). Those in the Balsas valley were collected at Coaguayutla (1950: Coahuayutla de Guerrero, pueblo). To the east there were at first two congregations, at Petatlán (1950: pueblo) and Tecpan (1813: Ciudad de Nuestra Señora de Guadalupe; 1950: Tecpan de Galeana, ciudad), but in 1614 the Indians of the old Villafuerte encomienda of Mexcaltepec (already moved two leagues below its original site, then reduced to Tecpan) were given permission to settle at one of the former sujetos, Atoyac (1950: Atoyac de Alvarez, ciudad). Thus the native population of the entire jurisdiction was concentrated in four settlements which survived as pueblos in the eighteenth century.

In 1571 Cuitlatecan was still spoken in the east and various other languages survived in the west, but a form of Náhuatl ('mexicano tosco') had been imposed as a lingua franca all along the coast.

While the non-Indian population of Zacatula was never numerous, in time it surpassed the native element. When recently founded, the *villa* of La Concepción had 122 Spanish vecinos. Most of these went elsewhere when the gold placers were exhausted, but there was another period of prosperity with the development of cacao plantations towards 1550 (ENE, VI, p. 149). In 1571 the *villa* had only seven or eight Spanish residents, and it was entirely deserted in 1649, when the white population consisted of ten or twelve families of cacao planters with houses at Petatlán, and thirty harquebusiers stationed at the port of Zihuatanejo (only occasionally inhabited, but listed as a pueblo in 1794). Negro slaves were introduced before 1550 and spread along the coast; by 1583 many of them had escaped from bondage and were annoying Spaniards and Indians.[11] By the mid-seventeenth century there was a fair number of mestizos, mulattoes, and 'chinos' (Filipinos) working on cacao and coco plantations and cattle ranches. Only about 150 non-Indian families are reported in 1743, but there were 572 free Negro and mulatto tributaries in 1803. In 1794, besides the five pueblos mentioned, there were thirty haciendas and twenty-four ranchos in the jurisdiction.

Sources

We know of two early *visitas* of Zacatula province, the first by Antonio de Caravajal in 1523–4 and another by Gaspar Xuárez *c.* 1550, and while Caravajal's report has yet to be found, that of Xuárez is preserved as an appendix to the *Suma de Visitas* and is of great value (PNE, I, pp. 318–32). There is a brief but valuable report of 1571 (Miranda Godínez, 9/38. Cf. López de Velasco, pp. 243–4), and a most useful *relación* by the AM dated 1580.[12] Lemoine (1960b) has published some interesting documents from AGN, namely a map of the Tecpan area dated 1579 and testimony about the congregation of Atoyac in 1614. Reports of 1639[13] and 1649[14] give rare details. Villaseñor y Sánchez (II, pp. 107–9) summarizes a missing document of *c.* 1743. There is a complete list of toponyms sent in by the subdelegado in 1794.[15]

The shoreline of Zacatula is described in several coast pilots or waggoners. There is one such document compiled in 1602 by Gerónimo Martín Palacios,[16] and another probably made *c.* 1675, the latter accompanied by 'charts' which must have caused many a shipwreck.[17] Dampier (1927) and Funnell (1707) have much to say about this coast as it was in the 1680s. The chronicle of Anson's expedition (Walter, 1748) tells of an English squadron's stay in 1742 at Zihuatanejo (or rather Ixtapa, nearby) and provides a map of the anchorage.

127 *Zacualpa*

Zacualpa and its territory, now in southwestern Mexico state, is on the south slope of the Nevado de Toluca (Chiuhnautzin), at 1,500–2,800 m, with deep barrancas draining southeastward towards the Amacuzac (Balsas) river. The higher parts are forested. Rainfall is moderate and seasonal.

'Mazatec' or Mazahuan, Matlatzincan, and Chontal were all spoken at Tzacualpan in the sixteenth century, but this multi-lingual situation perhaps came about with immigration to the mines (*see below*). Tzacualpan's ruler seems to have dominated several lesser states, Coatépec, Cuitlapilco, and Xahualtzinco (Yahualtzinco?). Nearby were two autonomous communities, Iztapan and Tonatiuhco, where Matlatzincan was spoken. Tzacualpan was an early conquest of the Mexica, while Cuitlapilco and Tonatiuhco were also Aztec tributaries.

Spaniards probably explored here in 1520 and controlled the area by the following year or 1522.

Encomiendas

Zacualpa and its dependencies formed part of the holdings of Juan de Salcedo, escheating on his death in 1536. Pedro de Salcedo, the conquistador's son, sued for possession and was assigned the encomienda at the beginning of 1547 (L de T, pp. 37, 615). On Pedro's death (between 1570 and 1591), his son, Ruiz López de Salcedo, inherited.[1] Tributes again escheated in the seventeenth century, and were re-assigned to the Conde de Moctezuma.[2]

We know nothing about the encomenderos of Iztapan and Tonatico, which were crown possessions by 1545.

Government

Zacualpa had a C in 1536–47, as did Iztapan from its escheatment sometime before 1545. Within the next decade the C of Iztapan was given jurisdiction in Tonatico and Zacualpa, and by 1563 he was being addressed as AM of Minas de Zacualpa.[3] Two sujetos of Zacualpa, Coatepec and Cuitlapilco, were visited by the AM of Zultepec until the mid-1570s, when they were transferred to the jurisdiction of Zacualpa.[4]

Towards 1680 the corregimiento of Iscateupa (q.v.) was eliminated and attached to the alcaldía mayor of Zacualpa. From 1787 the magistrate was a subdelegado in the intendencia of Mexico.

Church

In 1569 two secular priests were living at the real de minas of Concepción Zacualpa and visiting nearby Indian villages; Iztapan and Tonatico in that year were in the parish of Zumpaguacan (cf. Malinalco). Six years later a separate priest had been assigned to S Juan Bautista Zacualpa, the

Indian cabecera.[5] Parochial duties at the mining camp were assumed by Augustinians either in 1593 or 1602, but the doctrina was returned to secular clergy c. 1611 (Kubler, 1948, II, p. 524. Vera, p. 83).

S Lorenzo Tecicapan became a separate parish in the seventeenth century, while Asunción (S Miguel) Iztapan and Santiago (Natividad) Malinaltenango achieved that status after 1744. By this time the two Zacualpas were re-united under a single curate. The four parishes were in the archdiocese of Mexico.

Population and settlements

In 1569 there were 1,267 Indian tributaries, plus 224 tribute-exempt Indian families working in the mines (see below). Later counts and estimates give c. 700 tributaries in 1600, 269 in 1643, 426 in 1688, 775 Indian families in 1743, and c. 3,000 native tributaries in 1800.[6] The non-Indian population fluctuated considerably with the ups and downs of mining activity. In 1569 the mines had 25 married Spaniards and 134 Negro slaves. The 1743 report shows 100 non-Indian families. Not all lived at the mines, as six sugar haciendas and thirteen ranchos are named in 1794.

Although earlier dates have been suggested for their discovery, the mines of Zacualpa are not mentioned in the records we have seen before 1552, when the AM of Zultepec reported that he had found rich silver deposits there.[7] The real de minas of La Concepción (1950: Zacualpan, pueblo) was established some two leagues southwest of the Indian village of S Juan Zacualpa (1950: Zacualpilla, pueblo).[8]

Zacualpa(n) had under it the three sub-cabeceras of Coatepec (Guastepec, etc.; Cuatepec Harinas by 1764; 1950: Coatepec Harinas, pueblo), Cuitlapilco (1950: Acuitlapilco, pueblo), and Xahualcingo (Jahualcingo). In the late sixteenth century these places had twelve or thirteen outlying estancias between them. In 1593 it was proposed to reduce the surviving Indians to three congregations, Zacualpa, Capula, and Tecomatepec. Xahualcingo and certain estancias disappeared soon thereafter, but the other places mentioned survived as eighteenth-century pueblos, together with the old estancias of Huizoltepec, Malinaltenango, Mamatlac, Tecicapan, and Teocalcingo.[9] Coloxtitlan we do not find mentioned before 1794.

Iztapan (Ystapa, etc.; 1950: Ixtapan de la Sal, pueblo) in 1569 had five nearby estancias, but the congregation order of 1593 lists six. In the latter year the cabecera with its adjacent estancia of S Gaspar were to receive the inhabitants of the other five settlements. Sta Ana Sochuca (Xochiuhcan) either refused to move or was later re-occupied and appears as an eighteenth-century pueblo.[10]

Only two estancias are mentioned in 1569 at Tonatico (Tonaltiuhco), but six are named in 1593, at which time they were all to be congregated at the cabecera and nearby S Francisco. Concepción (Asunción) Tonatico was the only pueblo here in 1743–94; at some later date the cabecera itself was apparently moved to the old estancia of S Gaspar (1950: S Gaspar Tonatico, pueblo).[11]

Sources

Zacualpa alone is described in the Suma of c. 1548 (PNE, I, no. 109), while the whole area is covered in the archdiocesan report of 1569.[12] A relación of c. 1580 has been lost. A congregation document of 1593 has the most complete list of settlements we have seen.[13] For the seventeenth century, we have tributary data for 1643–88[14] and the journal of an archbishop's visit in 1685.[15]

A missing report of c. 1743 is summarized in Villaseñor y Sánchez (I, pp. 229–31). There is a brief topographical description of Iztapan parish dated 1777.[16] Late colonial documents include a series of reports on cajas de comunidad in 1785–1809,[17] and an excellent report of 1794.[18]

Additional citations are found in Colín (1966, 1967).

128 *Zamora y Xacona*

This rather dry region in northwest Michoacán extends from the north slope of the Sierra Volcánica to the shores of Lake Chapala in a series of broad valleys drained by the Duero and other rivers, with the Lerma as its northern boundary. In colonial times the lake waters covered much land since reclaimed for agriculture. Temperatures vary slightly according to elevation (1,400–2,000 m).

Xacona seems to have been a Tarascan outpost on the Chichimec frontier, with a military governor under the cazonci. To the west, beginning at Tamandagapeo, were a series of settlements (Cahao, Cuarachan, Chaparaco, Pajacoran, Sanguayo, Xuruneo) of Nahua-speaking people (Sayultecans, Tamazultecans) who served the cazonci in his border wars. From Xacona to the Lerma and beyond were Chichimecs of unknown affiliation.[1]

First contact may have occurred in 1522, with part of the Olid expedition (Sauer, 1948, pp. 12–16). The Nahua-speakers were proving uncooperative in 1528. Chichimecs continued to raid here into the 1570s.[2]

Encomiendas

Cortés assigned Xacona to Juan de Albornoz in August 1524 (Warren, 1963a, p. 409). It was probably in 1525 that Pedro Almíndez Chirinos took this encomienda for himself, and in 1527 that Gonzalo de Sandoval acquired it.[3] Both Xacona and Pajacoran–Sanguayo were held by Sandoval in the spring of 1528 (in later documents they appear as a single encomienda). After Sandoval went to Spain in 1528 Xacona was disputed between Albornoz and Almíndez, but the latter retained it until it was taken under the New Laws and became a crown possession, in April 1544 (L de T, p. 214. Warren, 1963a, p. 409).

Government

Xacona was a corregimiento, generally considered suffragan to the AM of Michoacán, from 1544. The C of Xacona held the additional title of AM of Zamora after 1574, although he did not move to the new *villa* (*see below*) until 1581.[4]

There was a confusing overlapping of administrative functions here, with the AM of Zamora y Xacona collecting tributes from several other jurisdictions in the sixteenth and seventeenth centuries. From about 1692, for some obscure reason, Zamora y Xacona was joined to the alcaldía mayor of Maravatío (q.v.), far to the east; at times the AM of this awkward province lived at Zamora, but more often he left a deputy here and stayed in the east.[5] From 1787 Zamora was a subdelegación in the intendencia of Valladolid.

Church

We are told that Xacona was first visited by Franciscans and then had a secular priest for a while before an Augustinian doctrina was established at S Agustín Xacona (la Vieja) in 1551 (Basalenque, p. 172. Rodríguez Zetina, pp. 13, 17, 120). Two years later a license was issued for another Augustinian monastery to be erected at S Francisco Ixtlan, but a secular priest took charge there in the 1560s.[6] S Martín Zamora was a secular parish from its foundation in 1574.[7] Two visitas of Xacona, Santiago Tangamandapio and Asunción Tangancícuaro, became Augustinian priorates c. 1622 and c. 1649, respectively, but they were subordinate to the monastery at Xacona (Basalenque, pp. 331, 426–7). Santiago Saguayo was separated from Ixtlan and was made a secular parish sometime before 1743, while Xacona and its dependencies were secularized by 1770 (León y Gama, p. 98). Only the Franciscan hospice at Zamora remained in the hands of regulars until after Independence. All parishes were in the diocese of Michoacán.

Population and settlements

In the early 1540s, when Xacona was still a private encomienda, the Mixton war against the Chichi-

mecs was fought nearby in Nueva Galicia. Indians of many nations were recruited to form armies which passed through Xacona on their way to and from the battles, and there are hints that some of them remained and settled in this frontier area after the war, which perhaps explains why five native languages were spoken at Xacona in 1573.[8]

Towards 1546 there were 4,361 Indian tributaries at Xacona and its six subject cabeceras (*see above*), divided between Tarascans and 'Chichimecs' (some of the latter were undoubtedly Nahua-speakers). The number of tributaries dropped to 1,185 in 1566, from which we gather that there was considerable mortality in the epidemic of 1545–8. It continued to decline (1,000 tributaries in 1571, 935 in 1588, 672 in 1600, 436 in 1623, 278 in 1657), and then gradually recovered, to 536 in 1698. There was further loss in the plagues of 1736–7 and 1767. The census of 1743 shows 496 Indian families, and later counts give 968 in 1789 and 1,247 Indian tributaries in 1804.[9] In the mid-seventeenth century, Tarascan was spoken at Xacona and a 'corrupt' Mexican elsewhere; there were still a few Chichimecs.

There was a general congregation carried out by the Augustinians when Xacona was moved from its old site, Xacona la Vieja (near Tangamandapio) to the final one in 1555 (Basalenque, p. 173). The Spanish *villa* of Zamora was founded at the beginning of 1574, and moved to its final site (1950: Zamora, ciudad) the following year.[10] As early as the 1540s Spaniards acquired extensive portions of land for vast cattle haciendas and wheat farms. Another Indian congregation in 1594–1603 swallowed up more pueblos and made more land available to the Spaniards.[11] In 1649 there were twelve cattle haciendas and twenty-two wheat farms, and by 1789 these had increased to twenty haciendas together with forty-nine ranchos and farms (one hacienda, S Juan Guaracha, had 55 square leagues). Ten places in addition to the cabecera of Xacona survived as Indian pueblos (each had achieved cabecera status) in the late eighteenth century: Ario, Caro, Coxumatlan, Guarachita, Ixtlan, Paxacuaran, Saguayo, Tangamandapio, Tangancícuaro, and Xaripo.

Non-Indians gradually came to outnumber Indians. Zamora had somewhat more than 100 'Spanish' vecinos in 1649. In 1743 there were 1,181 non-Indian families. By 1789 the number had risen to 1,545, of whom 179 were recognized as Spaniards. There were 1,789 free Negro and mulatto tributaries in 1804.

Sources

Early descriptions and tribute counts of Xacona are found in the *Suma de Visitas* of *c.* 1546–8 (PNE, I, nos. 457, 811), the *Libro de las Tasaciones* covering the years 1537–66 (L de T, pp. 213–17), and elsewhere.[12] There are several brief reports in the Ovando series of 1569–71.[13] Population data for 1588–1623 (Scholes and Adams, 1959, p. 55) and 1657–98[14] are available, and the area is described in documents of 1639[15] and 1649.[16]

A relación submitted by the teniente de AM in 1743 contains a partial matrícula of both Spaniards and Indians.[17] There is a long and interesting report

on cofradías, community property, and other matters dated 1789,[18] followed by a list of settlements in 1793,[19] and a description of 1822 (Martínez de Lejarza, pp. 223–34).

The work of Luis González (1968) is, among other things, a well-documented study of hacienda history here. One of the better local histories is that of Rodríguez Zetina (1956).

129 *Zumpango de la Laguna*

In the lake district on the north edge of the basin of Mexico, at an elevation of 2,200–2,600 m, this bleak little territory has a cold climate with moderate seasonal rains. It is now in northern Mexico state.

Citlaltépec, Tequixquiac, Tzompanco, and Xilotzinco were ruled by tlatoque of Tepaneca lineage in 1519. They were tributary to the Aztecs, and subordinate in a sense to Tlacopan. This was the beginning of the area known as Teotlalpan, which extended further north. Náhuatl was spoken by most at Tzompanco and Xaltocan, while Otomíes were a majority at Tequixquiac and Xilotzinco.

The region came under Spanish control in 1521.

Encomiendas

Tequixquiac was shared at first by two encomenderos, Andrés Núñez and Martín López. Núñez was succeeded before 1543 by a daughter and her husband, Gonzalo Portillo, who were still alive in 1568; by 1597 the Núñez half had been re-assigned to Francisco Tello de Orozco. Martín López died c. 1575, his share being inherited by a son, Martín López Osorio, who was in turn followed in 1591 by his widow and a son of the same name; the latter was still alive in 1604. Escheatment occurred after 1666, but part of the tributes were subsequently re-assigned (Gibson, 1964, pp. 430–1).

Although Juan de Nájera claimed to be an early holder, Xilocingo was acquired at an early date by Martín Vázquez, succeeded towards 1548 by a

mestizo son, Francisco Vázquez Lainez (Icaza, 1, p. 92). When Francisco died in the 1550s the encomienda went to his widow and a son, Matías Vázquez Lainez. Tributes escheated on the latter's death c. 1600, but were re-assigned to the Moctezuma heirs (Gibson, 1964, p. 433).

Zumpango and Xaltocan were included in the encomienda of Guautitlan (q.v.), which escheated in 1566.

Government

For some years Citlaltepec and its Indian labor were assigned to Mexico city and provided much of the limestone used in building there. It had a C from the 1560s, at first suffragan to the AM of Guautitlan but later independent.[1] This magistrate from the beginning administered the encomiendas of Tequixquiac and Xilocingo, but Xaltocan and Zumpango were disputed with Guautitlan before they were finally assigned to Citlaltepec. The C (an AM from the late seventeenth century) moved first to Xilocingo and later to Zumpango.[2] The jurisdiction was a subdelegación in the intendencia of Mexico after 1787.

Church

Santiago Tequixquiac and Concepción Zumpango each had a resident secular priest before 1569. Another curate set up a parish at S Miguel Xaltocan in the seventeenth century, but his successors usually lived at S Andrés Xaltenco. Xilocingo was visited from Hueypustla. All parishes were in the archdiocese of Mexico.

Zumpango de la Laguna

Population and settlements

The reports of *c.* 1570 give a total of 6,600 native tributaries, many of whom died in the epidemic of 1576–81. There was further loss in 1604–7 and 1629–31, and the records show only 662 tributaries in 1643. According to later counts, there were 781 tributaries in 1688, 1,206 Indian families in 1743,

902 tributaries in 1782, and 1,363 in 1801.[3] The 1791 census shows 500 'Spaniards' and 1,292 mestizos (individuals) here, while 72 mulatto tributaries were counted in 1801.

Congregations took place in the 1590s and early 1600s. Citlaltepec (1950: S Juan Zitlaltepec, pueblo) in 1579 had six estancias, all within a league of the cabecera, which disappeared in 1592. At Tequixquiac (Tequisquiaque; 1950: Tequix-

quiac, pueblo) three barrios within a quarter of a league seem to have been congregated at the same time. Xaltocan (1950: S Miguel Jaltocan, pueblo) had nineteen barrios, some nearby and others spread out to the north and west, in 1580. Two of these, together with a 'new' settlement, Tonanitla, appear as pueblos in the eighteenth century (the others were Nextlalpan and Xaltenco). Xilocingo (Xilotzingo; 1950: Jilotzingo, pueblo) had three estancias in 1550–79 which may have been abandoned in the early 1600s; they were within a league of the cabecera. Only four estancias of Zumpango (Zumpango de la Laguna in the eighteenth century; 1950: Zumpango de Ocampo, ciudad) are named in the 1569 report, but ten barrios were moved in to the cabecera in 1594.[4]

There were two haciendas, a ranchería, and three ranchos in the jurisdiction in 1791–2.

Sources

Tequixquiac, Xaltocan, and Xilocingo are summarily described as they were *c.* 1548 (PNE, I, nos. 502, 533, 795). Various reports of 1569–71 cover the jurisdiction (PNE, III, pp. 33–5, 49–52. Cf. Vera, p. 150). For 1579–80, there is a relación describing Citlaltepec, Tequixquiac, and Xilocingo,[5] and another concerning Xaltocan (PNE, VI, pp. 169–70). A few details of the 1592–1603 congregations have been found.[6] Tributary data for 1643 and 1688 are given in two documents.[7]

There is a good report drawn up by the AM in 1743.[8] For the late eighteenth century, there is a non-Indian padrón of 1791, with a description and a map of the jurisdiction,[9] followed by a brief relación dated 1792.[10]

Much further material concerning this area is cited in Colín (1966, 1967) and Gibson (1964).

Appendices
Glossary
Bibliography
Index

Kings and Viceroys of New Spain

HABSBURGS

Carlos I
(1517–56)

	1535–50	Antonio de Mendoza, conde de Tendilla

Felipe II
(1556–98)

	1550–64	Luis de Velasco (the elder)
	1564–6	(Audiencia)
	1566–7	Gastón de Peralta, marqués de Falces
	1567–8	(Judges, Audiencia)
	1568–80	Martín Enríquez de Almansa
	1580–3	Lorenzo Suárez de Mendoza, conde de la Coruña
	1583–4	(Audiencia)
	1584–5	Pedro Moya de Contreras, archbishop of Mexico
	1585–90	Alvaro Manrique de Zúñiga, marqués de Villamanrique
	1590–5	Luis de Velasco (the younger)

Felipe III
(1598–1621)

	1595–1603	Gaspar de Zúñiga y Acevedo, conde de Monterrey
	1603–7	Juan de Mendoza y Luna, marqués de Montesclaros
	1607–11	Luis de Velasco (the younger)
	1611–12	García Guerra, archbishop of Mexico
	1612	(Audiencia)
	1612–21	Diego Fernández de Córdoba, marqués de Guadalcázar

Felipe IV
(1621–65)

	1621	(Audiencia)
	1621–4	Diego Carrillo de Mendoza y Pimentel, marqués de Gelves
	1624	(Audiencia)
	1624–35	Rodrigo Pacheco de Osorio, marqués de Cerralvo
	1635–40	Lope Díaz de Armendáriz, marqués de Cadereyta
	1640–2	Diego López Pacheco Cabrera y Bobadilla, duque de Escalona y marqués de Villena
	1642	Juan de Palafox y Mendoza, bishop of Puebla
	1642–8	García Sarmiento de Sotomayor, conde de Salvatierra
	1648–9	Marcos de Torres y Rueda, bishop of Yucatán
	1649–50	(Audiencia)
	1650–3	Luis Enríquez de Guzmán, conde de Alba de Liste, marqués de Villaflor
	1653–60	Francisco Fernández de la Cueva, duque de Alburquerque
	1660–4	Juan de Leyva y de la Cerda, marqués de Leyva y conde de Baños
	1664	Diego Osorio de Escobar y Llamas, bishop of Puebla

Carlos II
(1665–1700)

	1664–73	Antonio Sebastián de Toledo, marqués de Mancera
	1673	Pedro Nuño Colón de Portugal, duque de Veragua
	1673–80	Payo Enríquez de Rivera, archbishop of Mexico
	1680–6	Tomás Antonio de la Cerda y Aragón, marqués de la Laguna, conde de Paredes
	1686–8	Melchor Portocarrero Lasso de la Vega, conde de la Monclova
	1688–96	Gaspar de la Cerda Sandoval, Silva y Mendoza, conde de Galve
	1696	Juan de Ortega y Montañés, bishop of Michoacán

BOURBONS

Felipe V
(1700–46)

	1696–1701	José Sarmiento y Valladares, conde de Moctezuma y de Tula
	1701–2	Juan de Ortega y Montañés, archbishop of Mexico
	1702–11	Francisco Fernández de la Cueva Enríquez, duque de Alburquerque
	1711–16	Fernando de Alencastre Noroña y Silva, duque de Linares
	1716–22	Baltasar de Zúñiga y Guzmán Sotomayor y Mendoza, marqués de Valero
	1722–34	Juan de Acuña, marqués de Casafuerte
	1734–40	Juan Antonio de Vizarrón y Eguiarreta, archbishop of Mexico
	1740–1	Pedro de Castro y Figueroa, duque de la Conquista
	1741–2	(Audiencia)
	1742–6	Pedro Cebrián y Agustín, conde de Fuenclara

Fernando VI
(1746–59)

	1746–55	Juan Francisco de Güemes y Horcasitas, conde de Revillagigedo
	1755–60	Agustín de Ahumada y Villalón, marqués de las Amarillas

Carlos III
(1759–88)

	1760	(Audiencia)
	1760	Francisco Cagigal de la Vega
	1760–6	Joaquín de Monserrat, marqués de Cruillas
	1766–71	Carlos Francisco de Croix, marqués de Croix
	1771–9	Antonio María de Bucareli y Ursúa
	1779	(Audiencia)
	1779–83	Martín de Mayorga
	1783–4	Matías de Gálvez
	1784–5	(Audiencia)
	1785–6	Bernardo de Gálvez, conde de Gálvez
	1786–7	(Audiencia)

Carlos IV (1788–1808)	1787	Alonso Núñez de Haro y Peralta, archbishop of Mexico	Fernando VII (1808)	1808–9	Pedro de Garibay
	1787–9	Manuel Antonio Flores	[Joseph	1809–10	Francisco Javier Lizana y Beaumont, archbishop of Mexico
	1789–94	Juan Vicente de Güemes Pacheco y Padilla, conde de Revillagigedo	Bonaparte (1808–13)]	1810	(Audiencia)
	1794–8	Miguel de la Grúa Talamanca y Branciforte, marqués de Branciforte		1810–13	Francisco Javier Venegas de Saavedra
			Fernando VII (1814–33)	1813–16	Félix María Calleja del Rey
	1798–1800	Miguel José de Azanza		1816–21	Juan Ruiz de Apodaca, conde del Venadito
	1800–3	Félix Berenguer de Marquina		1821	Francisco Novella
	1803–8	José de Iturrigaray		1821	Juan O'Donojú

APPENDIX B

Modern states and colonial divisions

STATE OF COLIMA (Col.)

Colima	Motines

DISTRITO FEDERAL (D.F.)

Cuyoacán	México
Chalco	Sochimilco
Mexicalcingo	Tacuba

DURANGO (Dgo.)

Nombre de Dios

GUANAJUATO (Gto.)

Celaya	León
Guanaxuato	S Luis de la Paz
	S Miguel el Grande

GUERRERO (Gro.)

Acapulco	Igualapa
Cuernavaca	Iscateupa
Chiautla	Tasco
Chilapa	Tetela del Río
Guaymeo y Sirándaro	Tistla
Iguala	Tlapa
	Zacatula

HIDALGO (Hgo.)

Actopan	Ixmiquilpan
Apa y Tepeapulco	Meztitlan
Cadereyta	Pachuca
Cempoala	Sochicoatlan
Cimapan	Tetepango Hueypustla
Guayacocotla	Tula
Huexutla	Tulancingo
	Xilotepec

JALISCO (Jal.)

Amula	Izatlan
Autlan	Sayula
Colima	Tuspa

MEXICO (Mex.)

Coatepec	Tacuba
Chalco	Temazcaltepec y Zultepec
Guautitlan	Tenango del Valle
Lerma	Teotiguacán
Malinalco	Tetepango Hueypustla
Metepec	Tezcuco
Mexicalcingo	Toluca
Otumba	Xilotepec
S Cristóbal Ecatepec	Zacualpa
	Zumpango de la Laguna

MICHOACÁN (Mich.)

Cinagua y la Guacana	Tinhuindín
Cuiseo de la Laguna	Tlalpuxagua
Charo	Tlazazalca
Guaymeo y Sirándaro	Valladolid
Maravatío	Xiquilpa
Motines	Zacatula
Tancítaro	Zamora y Xacona

MORELOS (Mor.)

Cuautla Amilpas	Chalco
Cuernavaca	Tetela del Volcán

OAXACA (Oax.)

Antequera	Nexapa
Atlatlauca	Nochistlan
Cimatlan y Chichicapa	Tecuicuilco
Cuatro Villas	Teguantepec
Guatulco y Guamelula	Teozacualco
Guaxuapa	Teposcolula
Huexolotitlan	Teutila
Iztepexi	Teutitlan del Camino
Justlaguaca	Villa Alta
Miaguatlan	Xalapa del Marqués
Mitla y Tlacolula	Xicayán

PUEBLA (Pue.)

Acatlan y Piastla	Chiautla
Atrisco	Chietla

Cholula
Guachinango
Huexocingo
Izúcar
Puebla
S Juan de los Llanos
Tecali

Teciutlan y Atempa
Teguacán
Tepeaca
Tepexi de la Seda
Teutlalco
Tochimilco
Xonotla y Tetela
Zacatlan de las Manzanas

TABASCO (Tab.)

Guazacualco

TLAXCALA (Tlax.)

Tezcuco

Tlaxcala

VERACRUZ (Ver.)

Córdoba
Cozamaloapa
Guachinango
Guayacocotla
Guazacualco
Orizaba
Pánuco

Papantla
S Juan de los Llanos
Tuxtla y Cotaxtla
Vera Cruz Nueva
Vera Cruz Vieja
Villa Alta
Xalapa de la Feria

QUERÉTARO (Qro.)

Cadereyta

Querétaro
  Xilotepec

SAN LUIS POTOSÍ (S.L.P.)

S Luis Potosí

Valles
Venado y la Hedionda

Glossary

agregado: a district attached to another for administrative convenience.

alcalde mayor: (1) deputy governor. (2) local magistrate and judge, governor of an *alcaldía mayor*.

alcalde ordinario: municipal magistrate and presiding officer of an ayuntamiento (there were two in each cabildo).

aldea: small village, hamlet.

alguacil: constable.

alguacil mayor: chief constable.

arriero: muleteer.

arroyo: watercourse, often dry much of the year.

audiencia: supreme tribunal.

ayuntamiento: municipal council.

bachiller: holder of a university degree.

barrio: settlement subordinate to a pueblo, usually a lesser division within or contiguous to the main settlement but sometimes synonymous with *estancia*.

cabildo: (1) same as ayuntamiento. (2) governing body of a diocese.

cacique: hereditary ruler of an Indian state. This is an Arawakian word brought by the Spaniards from the Antilles, roughly equivalent to tlatoani (q.v.).

caja de comunidad: community treasury in an Indian pueblo.

calpixqui (plur. calpixque): tribute collector.

calpulli (plur. calpultin): group of families (Indian) living in one vicinity, either in an *estancia* or a *barrio*.

capitán a guerra: magistrate invested with military duties.

castellan: governor of a fort or castle.

cazonci: the supreme ruler of the Tarascan empire in Michoacán.

cédula: written communication from the king (more correctly, cédula real).

ciudad: settlement with royally-granted privileges superior to those of a *villa*; it was always a *cabecera*.

cofradía: religious confraternity.

congregación: nuclear Indian settlement into which a dispersed population was moved, often forcibly, to facilitate administrative and religious control; also a small community of mixed races.

conquistador: Spaniard (rarely of other nationality) who participated in the Conquest before the fall of Tenochtitlan.

contador: royal accountant, comptroller (one of the four *oficiales reales*).

corregidor: local magistrate and judge, governor of a *corregimiento*.

cuadrilla: small settlement (a modern and localized term).

chinampa: artificially built piece of land irrigated by capillarity in swampy areas or along lake-shores (often anchored to solid ground but sometimes afloat), used for intensive agriculture.

doctrina: parish, generally an Indian congregation.

ermita: a chapel.

escribano de minas: clerk of a mining tribunal.

estancia: (1) outlying settlement subordinate to a pueblo. (2) —— de ganado: cattle ranch.

factor: royal factor (one of the *oficiales reales*).

flota: the annual fleet from Vera Cruz to Spain and return.

ganado mayor: neat cattle and horses.

ganado menor: sheep and goats.

gañán: privately employed Indian worker.

gente de razón: non-Indians.

guardianía: Franciscan monastery ruled by a *guardián*, and its parochial jurisdiction.

hacienda: (1) royal treasury department. (2) private landed estate.

huerta: small agricultural plot or orchard.

intendente: intendant, an official with administrative, judicial, financial, and military functions who governed an intendancy (*intendencia*).

juez congregador: judge in charge of establishing a congregación.

justicia: judge (includes corregidor, alcalde mayor, alcalde ordinario, alguacil, etc.).

labor: cultivated area.

licenciado: lawyer.

lienzo: pictorial or other document painted on cloth.

llano: a plain or level area.

macehuales: Indian commoners, below the *pipiltin* on the social scale, and above the slaves and *mayeques*.

matrícula: census or tribute list (=*padrón*).

mayeques: Indian serfs subject to private tribute and service.

mayorazgo: entailed estate.

meco: =*chichimeco* (Chichimec). Hunters and gatherers who lived beyond the agricultural zone of Mexico, to the north.

merced: a royal grant (of land, office, or anything else).

obraje: textile workshop.

oficiales reales: royal treasury officials (tesorero, contador, factor, veedor).

oidor: judge of an *audiencia*.

pipiltin: Indian nobles (Spanish, *principales*).

poblador: Spanish settler who arrived after the Conquest.

presidio: a frontier military post or fortress.

propios: community property, common lands, etc.

protomédico: king's physician.

pueblo: settlement with lesser or no privileges; it could be either a *cabecera* (center of Indian government and tribute-collection), or a *sujeto* (dependency of a *cabecera*). It could also be a small non-Indian settlement.

ramo: section of an archive.

ranchería: small Indian settlement, usually of Chichimecs.

rancho: (1) small Indian settlement. (2) ranch, generally a small settlement subordinate to an hacienda.

real de minas: settlement in a mining area; it could be a *ciudad, villa,* or *pueblo*; it was usually the residence of an alcalde mayor, but might have a corregidor, or neither.

regidor: municipal councillor.

señorío: native state.

teniente: lieutenant, deputy of a governor, alcalde mayor, corregidor, etc., in charge of a *tenientazgo*.

tesorero: royal treasurer (one of the *oficiales reales*).

tlatoani (plur. tlatoque): hereditary ruler of a native state (cf. cacique).

trapiche: sugar-mill.

vecino: inhabitant of a pueblo, villa, ciudad, etc., usually a householder or property owner.

veedor: royal overseer (one of the *oficiales reales*).

venta: inn.

vicaría: (1) monastery ruled by a *vicario*, and its parochial jurisdiction, if any. (2) parish in charge of a secular *vicario*, subordinate to a *curato*.

villa: settlement with royally-granted privileges inferior to those of a *ciudad* but superior to those of a *pueblo*; it was always a *cabecera*.

visita: (1) an official visit or inspection trip made by a *visitador* (a royal or ecclesiastical official designated for this purpose). (2) a visiting station or settlement (*pueblo, estancia,* etc.) on the circuit of a parish priest, regular or secular.

Bibliography

ABBREVIATIONS

AA	Archivo Arquiepiscopal, Mexico City
AGI	Archivo General de Indias, Seville
AGN	Archivo General de la Nación, Mexico City
AHH	Archivo Histórico de Hacienda, Mexico City
AHN	Archivo Histórico Nacional, Madrid
AMM	Anales del Museo Michoacano
BAGN	Boletín del Archivo General de la Nación (Mexico)
BE	Real Biblioteca de San Lorenzo del Escorial
BNE	Biblioteca Nacional, Madrid
BNM	Biblioteca Nacional, Mexico City
BNP	Bibliothèque Nationale, Paris
CDI	Colección de documentos inéditos relativos al descubrimiento, conquista y organización de las antiguas posesiones españolas de América y Oceanía...
DA	Department Agrario, Mexico City
ENE	Epistolario de Nueva España
HAHR	The Hispanic American Historical Review
HS	Hispanic Society of America, New York
INAH	Instituto Nacional de Antropología e Historia, Mexico City
LdeT	El libro de las tasaciones de pueblos de la Nueva España...
MNA	Museo Nacional de Antropología e Historia, Mexico City
NL	Newberry Library, Chicago
NYPL	New York Public Library
PNE	Papeles de Nueva España
RAH	Real Academia de Historia, Madrid
SMGE	Sociedad Mexicana de Geografía y Estadística, Mexico City
UT	University of Texas

MANUSCRIPT SOURCES

Archivo Arquiepiscopal (Mexico City)

Archivo General de Indias (Seville)
  Audiencia de Guadalajara
  Audiencia de México
  Contaduría
  Escribanía de Cámara
  Indiferente General
  Justicia
  Mapas y Planos
  Patronato Real
Archivo General de la Nación (Mexico City)
  Alcaldes Mayores
  Civil
  Clero Secular y Regular
  Congregaciones
  General de Parte
  Historia
  Hospital de Jesús
  Indios
  Inquisición
  Intendentes e Intendencias
  Mercedes
  Padrones
  Reales Cédulas (duplicados)
  Tierras
  Tributos
  Vínculos
Archivo General de Simancas (Valladolid)
Archivo Histórico de Hacienda (Mexico City)
Archivo Histórico Nacional (Madrid)
  Documentos de Indias
Bancroft Library (Berkeley)
  Mexican manuscripts
Biblioteca del Palacio Real (Madrid)
Biblioteca Nacional (Madrid)
Biblioteca Nacional (Mexico City)
Biblioteca Publica del Estado de Jalisco (Guadalajara)
Bibliothèque Nationale (Paris)
  Fonds Mexicains
Colección Castañeda Guzman (Oaxaca)
Departmento Agrario (Mexico City)
  Archivo Histórico

409

Hispanic Society of America (New York)
Library of Congress (Washington)
  Harkness Collection
Museo Michoacano (Morelia)
Museo Nacional de Antropología e Historia
  (Mexico City)
Newberry Library (Chicago)
  Ayer Collection
New York Public Library
  Rich Collection
  Phillips Collection
Parroquia de Tepoztlán (Tepoztlán)
  Parochial registers
Real Academia de Historia (Madrid)
Real Biblioteca de San Lorenzo del Escorial
Sociedad Mexicana de Geografía y Estadística
  (Mexico City)
University of Texas (Austin)
  Latin American Collection

PRINTED SOURCES

Actas de cabildo de la ciudad de México. 54 vols.
  México, 1889–1916.

Aguiar y Acuña, Rodrigo. *Svmarios de la reco-
  pilacion general de las leyes...* Mexico,
  1677.

Aguilar, Francisco de. *Relacion breve de la conquista
  de la Nueva España...* México, 1954.

Aguirre Beltrán, Gonzalo. *El señorío de Cuauhtochco – luchas agrarias en México durante el
  virreinato.* México, 1940.

  *La población negra de México 1519–1810. Estudio
  Etnohistórico.* México, 1946.

  *Problemas de la población indígena de la cuenca del
  Tepalcatepec.* México, 1952.

Ajofrín, Francisco. *Diario del viaje que...hizo a la
  América Septentrional en el siglo xviii el P. Fray
  Francisco Ajofrín Capuchino.* 2 vols. Madrid,
  1959.

Alcocer, José Antonio. *Bosquejo de la historia del
  colegio de Nuestra Señora de Guadalupe y sus
  misiones. Año de 1788.* México, 1958.

*Alegaciones en favor del clero, estado, eclesiastico, i
  secular, españoles, e indios del obispado de la
  Puebla de los Angeles...* [1646].

Alessio Robles, Vito. *Acapulco en la historia y en la
  leyenda.* México, 1948.

Alvarado, Francisco de. *Vocabulario en lengua
  mixteca.* México, 1962.

Amaya, Jesús. *Ameca, protofundación mexicana...*
  México, 1951.

Anales del Museo Michoacano. Morelia.

Anales del Museo Nacional de México (later, *Anales
  del Instituto Nacional de Antropología e Historia*).

Anaya Monroy, Fernando. *La toponomía indígena en
  la historia y la cultura de Tlaxcala.* México,
  1965.

Anonymous. 'Lista de los pueblos que pertenecen
  a Tezcoco', *Anales del Museo Nacional de
  México*, 1ª serie, IV (1897), pp. 51–6.

Arregui, Domingo Lázaro de. *Descripción de la
  Nueva Galicia.* Seville, 1946.

Arteaga Garza, Beatriz. 'Documentos sobre don
  Diego Luis Moctezuma', *Homenaje a Rafael
  García Granados*, pp. 73–81. México, 1960.

Bancroft, Hubert H. *History of Mexico.* 6 vols. San
  Francisco, 1883–6.

Bargalló, Modesto. *La minería y la metalurgía en la
  América española durante le época colonial...*
  México and Buenos Aires, 1955.

Barlow, Robert H. *The extent of the empire of the
  Culhua Mexica.* Berkeley and Los Angeles,
  1949. Ibero-Americana: 28.

  'El palimsesto de Veinte Mazorcas', *Revista
  Mexicana de Estudios Antropológicos*, XVII (1961),
  pp. 97–110.

  'Tres pueblos del valle de Atlixco', *Tlalocan*,
  IV (1963), pp. 274–6.

Barlow, Robert H, and George T. Smisor. *Nombre
  de Dios, Durango: Two documents in Náhuatl
  concerning its foundation...* Sacramento, Calif.,
  1943.

Basalenque, Diego. *Historia de la provincia de San
  Nicolás de Tolentino de Michoacán del orden de
  N. P. S. Agustín.* México, 1963.

Beals, Ralph L. 'The Tarascans', *Handbook of
  Middle American Indians*, VIII (1969), pp. 725–73.

Beleña, Eusebio Bentura. *Recopilación sumaria de
  todos los autos acordados de la real audiencia y
  sala del crimen de esta Nueva España...* 2
  vols. México, 1787.

Berlin, Heinrich. *Fragmentos desconocidos del códice
  de Yanhuitlan y otras investigaciones mixtecas.*
  México, 1947.

Bernal, Ignacio, and E. Dávalos Hurtado, ed. 'Huastecos, totonacos y sus vecinos', *Revista Mexicana de Estudios Antropológicos*, XIII (1952–3).

Berthe, Jean-Pierre. 'Xochimancas – les travaux et les jours dans une *hacienda* sucrière de Nouvelle-Espagne au XVIIᵉ Siècle', *Jahrbuch für Geschichte von Staat, Wirtschaft und Gesellschaft Lateinamerikas*, Bd III (Köln, 1966), pp. 88–117.

Bethencourt Massieu, Antonio. 'El real astillero de Coatzacoalcos (1720–1735)', *Anuario de Estudios Americanos*, XV (Seville, 1958), pp. 371–428.

Bevan, Bernard. *The Chinantec – report on the central and south-eastern Chinantec region*. Vol. I. – *The Chinantec and their habitat*. México, 1938. Instituto Panamericano de Geografía e Historia, Pub. No. 24.

Boas, Franz. 'El dialecto mexicano de Pochutla, Oaxaca', *International Journal of American Linguistics*, I (1917), pp. 9–44.

Boban, Eugène. *Documents pour servir a l'histoire du Mexique*... 2 vols. + atlas. Paris, 1891.

Boletín del Archivo General de la Nación. México.

Boletín del Instituto Nacional de Antropología e Historia. México.

Boletín Oficial y Revista Eclesiástica del Obispado de Cuernavaca. Cuernavaca.

Borah, Woodrow. *Silk raising in colonial Mexico*. Berkeley and Los Angeles, 1943. Ibero-Americana: 20.

New Spain's century of depression. Berkeley and Los Angeles, 1951. Ibero-Americana: 35.

Early colonial trade and navigation between Mexico and Peru. Berkeley and Los Angeles, 1954. Ibero-Americana: 38.

'Un gobierno provincial de frontera en San Luis Potosí (1612–1620)', *Historia Mexicana*, 52 (1964), pp. 532–50.

Borah, Woodrow and S. F. Cook. *The population of central Mexico in 1548 – an analysis of the 'Suma de visitas de pueblos'*. Berkeley and Los Angeles, 1960. Ibero-Americana: 43.

The aboriginal population of central Mexico on the eve of the Spanish conquest. Berkeley and Los Angeles, 1963. Ibero-Americana: 45.

Boyd-Bowman, Peter. *Indice geobiográfico de cuarenta mil pobladores españoles de América en el siglo XVI*. 2 vols. Bogotá (1964) and México (1968).

Bradomín, José María. *Toponimia de Oaxaca (Crítica Etimológica)*. México, 1955.

Brambila, Crescenciano. *El nuevo obispado de Autlan*. Guadalajara, 1962.

El obispado de Colima – apuntes históricos, geográficos y estadísticos. Colima, 1964.

Brand, Donald D. 'An historical sketch of geography and anthropology in the Tarascan region: Part I', *New Mexico Anthropologist*, VI–VII (1944), pp. 37–108.

'The development of Pacific coast ports during the Spanish colonial period in Mexico', *Estudios antropológicos publicados en homenaje al doctor Manuel Gamio*, pp. 577–91. México, 1956.

Brand, Donald D., et al. *Coastal study of southwest Mexico*. 2 vols. Austin, 1957–8.

Coalcoman and Motines del Oro – an ex-distrito of Michoacan Mexico. The Hague, 1960.

Brasseur de Bourbourg, Charles-Etienne. *Histoire des nations civilisées du Mexique et de l'Amérique-Centrale, durant les siècles antérieurs a Cristophe Colomb*... 4 vols. Paris, 1857–8.

Bravo Ugarte, José. *Historia sucinta de Michoacan – II – Provincia mayor e intendencia*. México, 1963.

Diócesis y obispos de la Iglesia mexicana (1519–1965). México, 1965.

Burgoa, Francisco de. *Geografica descripcion*. 2 vols. México, 1934a.

Palestra historial. 2 vols. México, 1934b.

Byam Davies, Claude Nigel. *Los señoríos independientes del imperio azteca*. México, 1968.

Cadenhead, Ivie E. Jr. 'Some mining operations of Cortés in Tehuantepec, 1538–1547', *The Americas*, XVI (1960), pp. 283–7.

Cajigas Langner, Alberto. *Monografía de Tehuantepec*. México, 1954.

Calderón Quijano, José Antonio. 'Una visita de "doctrinas" en la diócesis de Puebla de los Angeles, el año de 1653', *Anuario de Estudios Americanos*, II (Seville, 1945), pp. 785–806.

Historia de las fortificaciones en Nueva España. Seville, 1953.

Carrasco, Pedro. *Los Otomíes – cultura e historia prehispánicas de los pueblos mesoamericanos de habla otomiana.* México, 1950.

'Tres libros de tributos del Museo Nacional de México y su importancia para los estudios demográficos', *XXXV Congreso Internacional de Americanistas – México, 1962 – Actas y Memorias,* III (México, 1964), pp. 373–8.

Carrión, Antonio. *Historia de la Ciudad de Puebla de los Angeles.* Puebla, 1896.

Cartas de Indias... Madrid, 1877.

Caso, Alfonso. 'El mapa de Teozacoalco', *Cuadernos Americanos,* 47 (México, 1949), pp. 145–81.

'Los barrios antiguos de Tenochtitlan y Tlatelolco', *Memorias de la Academia Mexicana de la Historia,* XV (México, 1956), pp. 7–63.

'Los lienzos mixtecos de Ihuitlan y Antonio de León', *Homenaje a Pablo Martínez del Río...,* pp. 237–74. México, 1961.

Cavo, Andrés. *Historia de México.* México, 1949.

Cedulario Cortesiano. México, 1949.

Cervantes de Salazar, Franciso. *Crónica de la Nueva España...* Madrid, 1914.

Chauvet, Fidel de J. *Fray Juan de Zumárraga, O.F.M.* México, 1948.

Chavero, Alfredo. *Antigüedades mexicanas...* 2 vols.+atlas. México, 1892.

Chevalier, François. *La formation des grands domaines au Mexique. Terre et société aux XVIe–XVIIe siècles.* Paris, 1952.

Chimalpahin Cuauhtlehuanitzin, Francisco de San Antón Muñón. *Relaciones originales de Chalco Amaquemecan...* México and Buenos Aires, 1965.

Chipman, Donald E. *Nuño de Guzman and the Province of Panuco in New Spain 1518–1533.* Glendale, Calif. 1967.

Cline, Howard F. 'The terragueros of Guelatao, Oaxaca, Mexico: notes on the Sierra de Juarez and its XVIIth century Indian problems', *Acta Americana,* IV (1946), pp. 161–84.

'Civil congregations of the Indians in New Spain, 1598–1606', *HAHR,* XXIX (1949), pp. 349–69.

'Civil congregation of the western Chinantla, New Spain, 1599–1603', *The Americas,* XII (1955), pp. 115–37.

'The Patiño maps of 1580 and related documents...', *El México Antiguo,* IX (1959), pp. 633–92.

'Las investigaciones modernas sobre la Chinantla y la obra de Mariano Espinosa', *Papeles de la Chinantla,* III (1961), pp. 13–57.

'The Ortelius maps of New Spain, 1579, and related contemporary materials, 1560–1610', *Imago Mundi,* XVI (1962), pp. 98–115.

'The *relaciones geográficas* of the Spanish Indies, 1577–1586', *HAHR,* XLIV (1964), pp. 341–74.

'The relación geográfica of Tuzantla, Michoacán, 1579', *Tlalocan,* V (1965), pp. 58–73.

'Colonial Mazatec lienzos and communities,' *Ancient Oaxaca,* pp. 270–97. Stanford, 1966.

[Cobo, Bernabé]. 'Cartas del P. Bernabé Cobo, de la compañía de Jesús', in Vázquez de Espinosa (1944), pp. 195–214.

[Códice Franciscano]. *Nueva colección de documentos para la historia de México. Códice Franciscano. Siglo XVI.* México, 1941.

Colección de 'Cuadros Sinopticos' de los pueblos, haciendas y ranchos del estado libre y soberano de Oaxaca. Anexo número 50 a la memoria administrativa presentada al H. Congreso del mismo el 17 de setiembre de 1883. Oaxaca, 1883.

Colección de documentos históricos inéditos o muy raros, referentes al Arzobispado de Guadalajara. Guadalajara, 1922.

Colección de documentos inéditos relativos al descubrimiento, conquista y organización de las antiguas posesiones españolas de América y Oceanía... 42 vols. Madrid, 1864–84.

Colección de documentos para la historia de México (ed. Joaquín García Icazbalceta). 2 vols. México, 1858–66.

[Colín, Mario]. *Indice de documentos relativos a los pueblos del estado de México – Ramo de Tierras del Archivo General de la Nación.* México, 1966.

Indice de documentos relativos a los pueblos del estado de México – Ramo de Mercedes del Archivo General de la Nación. 2 vols. México, 1967.

Conway, G. R. G. *La noche triste. Documentos:*

Segura de la Frontera en Nueva España, año de MDXX... México, 1943.

Cook, Sherburne F. *The historical demography and ecology of the Teotlalpan.* Berkeley and Los Angeles, 1949*a*. Ibero-Americana: 33.

Soil erosion and population in central Mexico. Berkeley and Los Angeles, 1949*b*. Ibero-Americana: 34.

Santa María Ixcatlán – habitat, population, subsistence. Berkeley and Los Angeles, 1958. Ibero-Americana: 41.

Cook, Sherburne F. and Woodrow Borah. *The Indian population of central Mexico – 1531–1610.* Berkeley and Los Angeles, 1960. Ibero-Americana: 44.

The population of the Mixteca Alta – 1520–1960. Berkeley and Los Angeles, 1968. Ibero-Americana: 50.

Cook de Leonard, Carmen. 'Los popolocas de Puebla', in Bernal and Dávalos Hurtado (1952–3), pp. 423–45.

'The painted tribute record of Tepexi de la Seda', *A William Cameron Townsend en el XXV aniversario del Instituto Lingüístico de Verano*, pp. 87–107. México, 1961.

Cooper, Donald B. *Epidemic disease in Mexico City – 1761–1813 – an administrative, social, and medical study.* Austin, 1965.

Cortés, Hernán. *Cartas y Documentos.* Introducción de Mario Hernández Sánchez-Barba. México, 1963.

Covarrubias, Miguel. *Mexico south – the isthmus of Tehuantepec.* New York, 1946.

Cruz y Moya, Juan de la. *Historia de la santa y apostólica provincia de Santiago de predicadores de México en la Nueva España.* 2 vols. México, 1954–5.

Cuevas, Mariano. *Cartas y otros documentos de Hernán Cortés novísimamente descubiertos en el Archivo General de Indias...* Seville, 1915.

Historia de la Iglesia en México. 5 vols. México, 1946–7.

Dahlgren de Jordán, Barbro. *La Mixteca – su cultura e historia prehispánicas.* México, 1954.

Dampier, William. *A new voyage round the world.* London, 1927.

Dávila Padilla, Augustín. *Historia de la fvndacion y*

discvrso de la provincia, de Santiago de Mexico, de la orden de predicadores por la vidas de sus varones insignes y casos notables de Nueva España. Brussels, 1625.

Díaz del Castillo, Bernal. *Historia verdadera de la conquista de la Nueva España* (ed. Joaquín Ramírez Cabañas). 2 vols. México, 1960.

Díaz Solís, Espiridión. *Atlixco.* [Atlixco] 1938.

Diccionario Porrúa de historia, biografía y geografía de México. México, 1964.

Díez, Domingo. *Bibliografía del estado de Morelos.* Mexico, 1933.

Díez de la Calle, Juan. *Memorial, y noticias sacras, y reales del imperio de las Indias occidentales, al muy catolico, piadoso, y poderoso señor rey de las Españas, y Nueuo Mundo, D. Felipe IV. N. S....* Madrid, 1646.

Domínguez, Miguel. *Coscomatepec de Bravo.* México, 1943.

Dorantes de Carranza, Baltasar. *Sumaria relación de las cosas de la Nueva España...* México, 1902.

Durán, Diego. *Historia de las Indias de Nueva-España e islas de la tierra firme.* 2 vols. México, 1967.

Encinas, Diego de. *Cedulario Indiano...* 4 vols. Madrid, 1945–6.

Englebert, Omer. *The last of the conquistadors – Junipero Serra (1713–1784).* New York, 1956.

Epistolario de Nueva España 1505–1818. Recopilado por Francisco del Paso y Troncoso. 16 vols. México, 1939–42.

Espinosa, Isidro Félix de. *Crónica de los colegios de propaganda fide de la Nueva España.* Washington, 1964.

Espinosa, Mariano. *Apuntes históricos de las tríbus chinantecas, mazatecas y popolucas (Papeles de la Chinantla, III).* México, 1961.

Estadística del estado libre y soberano de Veracruz. 2 vols. Jalapa, 1831.

Fernández, Justino. *Morelia.* México, 1936*a*.

Pátzcuaro. México, 1936*b*.

Uruapan. México, 1936*c*.

ed. *Catálogo de construcciones religiosas del estado de Hidalgo formado por la comisión de inventarios de la primera zona – 1929–1932.* 2 vols. México, 1940–2.

Fernández, Justino and Hugo Leicht. 'Códice del tecpan de Santiago Tlaltelolco', *Investigaciones históricas*, I (México, 1939), pp. 243–64.

Fernández de Recas, Guillermo S. *Cacicazgos y nobiliario indígena de la Nueva España.* México, 1961.

[Fletcher, Francis]. *The world encompassed by Sir Francis Drake, being his next voyage to that to Nombre de Dios*... London, 1628.

Funnell, William. *A voyage round the world*... London, 1707.

[Gage, Thomas] *Thomas Gage's Travels in the New World.* Ed. J. Eric S. Thompson, Univ. of Oklahoma Press, Norman, Okla., 1958.

Galarza, Joaquín. 'Codex San Andrés (jurisdiction de Cuautitlan) – manuscrit pictographique du Musée de l'Homme de Paris', *Journal de la Société des Américanistes*, 52 (Paris, 1963), pp. 61–90.

Gamio, Manuel. *La población del valle de Teotihuacán.* 3 vols. México, 1922.

García Granados, Rafael. *Diccionario biográfico de historia antigua de Méjico.* 3 vols. México, 1952–3.

García Granados, Rafael and Luis MacGregor. *Huejotzingo – la ciudad y el convento franciscano.* México, 1934.

García Icazbalceta, Joaquín. *Don Fray Juan de Zumárraga, primer obispo y arzobispo de México – estudio biográfico y bibliográfico.* México, 1881.

ed. *Nueva colección de documentos para la historia de México, III. Pomar. Relación de Tezcoco.* México, 1891.

García Martínez, Bernardo. *El Marquesado del Valle – tres siglos de régimen señorial en Nueva España.* México, 1969.

[García Payon, José]. *Descripcion del pueblo de Gueytlalpan...con notas por José García Payón.* Jalapa, 1965.

García Pimentel, Luis, ed. *Descripción del arzobispado de México hecha en 1570 y otros documentos.* México, 1897.

Relacion de los obispados de Tlaxcala, Michoacan, Oaxaca y otros lugares en el siglo XVI... México, Paris, Madrid, 1904.

Gardiner, C. Harvey. 'Tempest in Tehuantepec, 1529: local events in imperial perspective', *HAHR*, XXXV (1955), pp. 1–13.

Naval power in the conquest of Mexico. Austin, Texas, 1956.

Martín López – conquistador citizen of Mexico. Univ. of Kentucky Press, Lexington, Ky., 1958.

The constant captain – Gonzalo de Sandoval. Carbondale, Ill., 1961.

Gay, José Antonio. *Historia de Oaxaca.* 2 vols. México, 1950.

Gazeta de México.

Gemelli Carreri, J. F. *Viaje a la Nueva España.* 2 vols. México, 1955.

Gerhard, Peter. 'El avance español en México y Centroamérica', *Historia Mexicana*, 33 (1959), pp. 143–52.

Pirates on the west coast of New Spain – 1575–1742. Glendale, Calif., 1960.

'Descripciones geográficas (pistas para investigadores)', *Historia Mexicana*, 68 (1968), pp. 618–27.

'El señorío de Ocuituco', *Tlalocan*, VI (1970), pp. 97–114.

Gibson, Charles. *Tlaxcala in the sixteenth century.* New Haven (Yale) and London, 1952.

The Aztecs under Spanish rule. A history of the Indians of the valley of Mexico – 1519–1810. Stanford (Calif.), 1964.

Spain in America. New York, Evanston, London, 1966.

Glass, John B. *Catálogo de la colección de códices.* México, 1964.

Gobernantes del Perú – cartas y papeles – siglo XVI. 14 vols. Madrid, 1921–6.

Gold, Robert L. 'The settlement of the Pensacola Indians in New Spain, 1763–1770', *HAHR*, XLV (1965), pp. 567–76.

Gómez de Cervantes, Gonzalo. *La vida económica y social de Nueva España al finalizar el siglo XVI.* México, 1944.

Gómez de Orozco, Federico. 'Monasterios de la orden de San Agustín en Nueva España. Siglo XVI', *Revista Mexicana de Estudios Históricos*, I (1927), pp. 40–54.

González, Luis. *Pueblo en vilo – Microhistoria de San José de Gracia.* México, 1968.

González Dávila, Gil. *Teatro eclesiastico de la*

primitiva iglesia de las Indias occidentales, vidas de svs arzobispos, obispos, y cosas memorables de sus sedes... 2 vols. Madrid, 1649–55.

González de la Puente, Juan. *Primera parte de la chronica augustiniana de Mechoacan*... México, 1624.

González de Mendoza, Juan. *Historia de las cosas mas notables, ritos y costvmbres, del gran reyno dela China*... Rome, 1585.

González Sánchez, Isabel. *Haciendas y ranchos de Tlaxcala en 1712*. México, 1969.

Greenleaf, Richard E. *Zumárraga and the Mexican Inquisition. 1536–1543*. Washington, 1961.

'Viceregal power and the obrajes of the Cortés estate, 1595–1708', *HAHR*, XLVIII (1968), pp. 365–79.

Grijalva, Juan de. *Crónica de la orden de N. P. S. Augustin en las prouincias de la nueua España en quatro edades desde el año de 1533 hasta el de 1592*. México, 1926.

Gurría Lacroix, Jorge. *Zempoala*. México, 1960.

Harvey, Herbert R. '*Relaciones geográficas*: native languages – 1579–1588'. Library of Congress, Hispanic Foundation, HMAI Working Papers: 69. Washington, 1967.

Herrera, Antonio de. *Historia general de los hechos de los castellanos en las islas i tierra firme del Mar oceano*... 4 vols. (8 décadas). Madrid, 1601–15.

Historia Tolteca–Chichimeca. México, 1947.

Historische Hieroglyphen der Azteken im Jahr 1803 im Konigreiche Neu-Spanien gesamlet von Alexander von Humboldt. Berlin, N.D. [1892].

Humboldt, Alejandro de. *Ensayo político sobre el reino de la Nueva España*. México, 1966. [An English version exists, viz. *Political Essay on the Kingdom of New Spain*, transl. J. Black. London 1811, 4 vols. Facsimile ed. N.Y. 1966.]

Icaza, Francisco de. *Diccionario autobiográfico de conquistadores y pobladores de Nueva España*. 2 vols. Madrid, 1923.

Informacion de derecho, del Marques del Valle, en el pleyto que trata con el fiscal de su Magestad, sobre los pueblos subjectos a la villa de Acapiscla. Madrid, 1586.

Jiménez Moreno, Wigberto. *Estudios de historia colonial*. México, 1958.

Jiménez Moreno, Wigberto and Salvador Mateos Higuera. *Códice de Yanhuitlán – edición en facsímile*. México, 1940.

Kelly, Isabel. *The archaeology of the Autlán-Tuxcacuesco area of Jalisco*. 2 vols. Berkeley and Los Angeles, 1945–9. Ibero-Americana: 26–7.

Kelly, Isabel and Angel Palerm. *The Tajín Totonac. Part 1. History, subsistence, shelter and technology*. Washington, 1952. Smithsonian Institution. Institute of Social Anthropology, Pub. No. 13.

Kirchhoff, Paul. 'Civilizing the Chichimecs: a chapter in the culture history of ancient Mexico', *Some educational and anthropological aspects of Latin America*, pp. 80–5. Univ. of Texas, Institute of Latin American Studies, V, Austin, Texas, 1948.

Konetzke, Richard, 'Las fuentes para la historia demográfica de Hispano-América durante la época colonial', *Anuario de Estudios Americanos*, V (Seville, 1948), pp. 267–323.

Kroeber, A. L., 'Native American Population', *American Anthropologist*, New Series, XXXVI (1934), pp. 1–25.

Kubler, George. 'Population movements in Mexico – 1520–1600', *HAHR*, XXII (1942), pp. 606–43.

Mexican architecture of the sixteenth century. New Haven and London, 1948.

'La traza colonial de Cholula', *Estudios de Historia Novohispana*, II (México, 1968), pp. 111–27.

Kutscher, Gerdt. 'Mapa de San Antonio Tepetlan', *Baessler-Archiv*, XI, no. 2, pp. 277–300. Berlin, 1964.

[Lafora, Nicolás de]. *The frontiers of New Spain – Nicolás de Lafora's description – 1766–1768*. Berkeley, 1958. Quivira Society Publications, XIII.

Larrea, Alonso de. *Crónica de la orden de N. seráfico P. S. Francisco*... Mexico, 1643.

Leander, Birgitta. *Códice de Otlazpan (acompañado de un facsímile del códice)*. México, 1967.

[Lebrón de Quiñones, Lorenzo.] *Relación breve y sumaria de la visita hecha por el Lic. Lorenzo Lebrón de Quiñones, oidor del Nuevo Reino de*

Galicia, por mandado de su alteza. Guadalajara, 1952.

Lemoine Villacaña, Ernesto. 'Mandamientos del virrey, para la congregación de pueblos de indios en la alcaldía mayor de Valladolid en 1601–1603', *BAGN*, I (1960*a*), pp. 9–55.

'El mapa de Tecpan de 1579', *BAGN*, I (1960*b*), pp. 517–34.

'Protesta de los indios de Atoyac para no ser congregados en el pueblo de Tecpan, año de 1614', *BAGN*, I (1960*c*), pp. 535–49.

'Visita, congregación y mapa de Amecameca de 1599', *BAGN*, II (1961), pp. 5–46.

'Documentos y mapas para la geografía histórica de Orizaba (1690–1800)', *BAGN*, III (1962*a*), pp. 461–527.

'La relación de la Guacana, Michoacán, de Baltasar Dorantes Carranza (año de 1605)', *BAGN*, III (1962*b*), pp. 671–702.

'Documentos para la historia de la ciudad de Valladolid, hoy Morelia (1541–1624)', *BAGN*, III (1962*e*), pp. 5–97.

'Relación de Pátzcuaro y su distrito en 1754', *BAGN*, IV (1963), pp. 57–92.

'Algunos datos histórico-geográficos acerca de Villa Alta y su comarca', *Summa Anthropológica en homenaje a Roberto J. Weitlaner*, pp. 192–202. México, 1966.

León, Alonso de; Juan Bautista Chapa, and Fernando Sánchez de Zamora. *Historia de Nuevo León...* Monterrey, 1961.

León, Nicolás. *Códice Sierra.* México, 1933.

Documentos inéditos referentes al ilustrísimo señor Don Vasco de Quiroga... México, 1940.

León y Gama, Antonio de. 'Descripcion del obispado de Michoacan', *Revista Mexicana de Estudios Históricos*, I, apéndice (1927), pp. 91–100.

Lewis, Oscar. *Life in a Mexican village: Tepoztlán Restudied.* University of Illinois Press, Urbana, Ill. 1963.

[El] *libro de las tasaciones de pueblos de la Nueva España – siglo XVI.* Prólogo de Francisco González de Cossío. México, 1952.

Liebman, Seymour B. *A guide to Jewish references in the Mexican colonial era – 1521–1821.* Philadelphia, 1964.

Linnè, Sigvald. *El valle y la ciudad de México en 1550...* Stockholm, 1948.

López de Velasco, Juan. *Geografía y descripción universal de las Indias recopilada por el cosmógrafo-cronista Juan López de Velasco desde el año de 1571 al de 1574...* Madrid, 1894.

López de Villaseñor, Pedro. *Cartilla vieja de la nobilisima ciudad de Puebla.* México, 1961.

[López Matoso, Antonio Ignacio]. Jim C. Tatum, 'Veracruz en 1816–1817: fragmento del diario de Antonio López Matoso', *Historia Mexicana*, 73 (1969), pp. 105–24.

López Sarrelangue, Delfina Esmeralda. *La nobleza indígena de Pátzcuaro en la época virreinal.* México, 1965.

Lussan, Raveneau de. *Journal du voyage fait a la mer de sud, avec les flibustiers de l'Amerique en 1684. & années suivantes.* Paris, 1689.

Lynch, John. *Spain under the Habsburgs.* Vol. II. Oxford, 1969.

MacNeish, Richard S. 'Ancient Mesoamerican Civilization...', *Science*, 143 (1964), pp. 531–7.

MacNeish, Richard S., *et al. The prehistory of the Tehuacán valley.* 6 vols. Austin, 1967– .

Marroquín, Alejandro. *La ciudad mercado (Tlaxiaco).* México, 1957.

Martin, Norman F. *Los vagabundos en la Nueva España – siglo XVI.* México, 1957.

Martínez Cosio, Leopoldo. *Los caballeros de las órdenes militares en México – catálogo biográfico y genealógico.* México, 1946.

Martínez de la Rosa, P. *Apuntes para la historia de Irapuato.* México, 1965.

[Martínez de Lejarza, Juan José] *Análisis estadístico de la provincia de Michuacan, en 1822. Por J. J. L.* México, 1824.

Martínez Gracida, Manuel. *Civilización chontal. Historia antigua de la chontalpa oaxaqueña.* México, 1910.

Mártir de Angleria, Pedro. *Décadas del Nuevo Mundo...* 2 vols. México, 1964–5.

Maza, Francisco de la. *San Miguel de Allende – su historia, sus monumentos.* México, 1939.

La ciudad de Cholula y sus iglesias. México, 1959.

McAndrew, John. *The open-air churches of sixteenth-century Mexico – Atrios, posas, open chapels,* and other studies. Harvard University Press, Cambridge (Mass.) 1965.

Meade, Joaquín. *Documentos inéditos para la historia de Tampico – siglos XVI y XVII*. México, 1939.

La Huasteca veracruzana. 2 vols. [México], 1962.

Mecham, J. Lloyd. 'The *Real de Minas* as a political institution', *HAHR*, VII (1927a), pp. 49–74.

Francisco de Ibarra and Nueva Vizcaya. Duke Univ. Press, Durham, N. Carolina, 1927b.

Medel y Alvarado, León. *Historia de San Andrés Tuxtla*. 2 vols. México, 1963.

Medina Ascensio, Luis. *Archivos y bibliotecas eclesiásticos*. México, 1966.

Melgarejo Vivanco, José Luis. *Breve historia de Veracruz*. Xalapa, 1960.

Memorial de los pleitos qve el señor fiscal, y los Indios del pueblo de San Mateo de Atengo tratan, con El Marques del Valle. N.P., N.D., [c. 1570–80].

Mendieta, Gerónimo de. *Historia eclesiástica indiana*. 4 vols. México, 1945.

Mendizábal, Miguel Othon de. 'Evolución económica y social del valle del Mezquital', *Obras completas*, VI, pp. 7–195. México, 1947.

Millares Carlo, A., and J. I. Mantecón. *Indice y extractos de los Protocolos del Archivo de Notarías de México, D.F.* 2 vols. México, 1945–6.

Miranda, José. *Las ideas y las instituciones políticas mexicanas...* México, 1952.

'La población indígena de México en el siglo XVII', *Historia Mexicana*, 46 (1962a), pp. 182–9.

'*La pax hispánica* y los desplazamientos de los pueblos indígenas', *Cuadernos Americanos*, CXXV (1962b), pp. 186–90.

La función económica del encomendero en los orígenes del régimen colonial (Nueva España, 1525–1531). México, 1965.

'La población indígena de Ixmiquilpan y su distrito en la época colonial', *Estudios de Historia Novohispana*, I (1966), pp. 121–30.

'Evolución cuantitativa y desplazamientos de la población indígena de Oaxaca en la época colonial', *Estudios de Historia Novohispana*, II (1968), pp. 129–47.

Miranda Godínez, Francisco. *El real colegio de San Nicolás de Pátzcuaro*. Cucrnavaca, 1967.

Moorhead, Max L. 'Hernán Cortés and the Tehuantepec passage', *HAHR*, XXIX (1949), pp. 370–9.

Morfi, Juan Agustín de. *Diario y derrotero (1777–1781)*. Monterrey, 1967.

Mota y Escobar, Alonso de la. *Descripción geográfica de los reinos de Nueva Galicia, Nueva Vizcaya y Nuevo León*. México, 1940.

Motolinía, Toribio de. *Memoriales...* México, 1903.

Muñoz, Diego. *Descripción de la provincia de San Pedro y San Pablo de Michoacán, en las Indias de la Nueva España – Crónica del siglo XVI*. Guadalajara, 1950.

Muñoz Camargo, Diego. *Historia de Tlaxcala*. México, 1947.

[Navarrete, Domingo]. *The travels and controversies of Friar Domingo Navarrete – 1618–1686*. 2 vols. London, 1962. Hakluyt Society, 2d ser., CXVIII and CXIX.

Navarro García, Luis. *Intendencias en Indias*. Seville, 1959.

Navarro y Noriega, Fernando. *Catálogo de los curatos y misiones que tiene la Nueva España en cada una de sus diócesis, o sea la división eclesiástica de este reyno...* México, 1813.

Nobiliario de conquistadores de Indias. Madrid, 1892.

Noticias varias de Nueva Galicia, intendencia de Guadalajara. Guadalajara, 1878.

Nowotny, Karl Anton. *Tlacuilolli...* Berlin, 1961.

Ocaranza, Fernando. *Capítulos de la historia franciscana*. México, 1933.

O'Gorman, Edmundo. 'El trabajo industrial en la Nueva España a mediados del siglo XVII: visita a los obrajes de paños en la jurisdicción de Coyoacán, 1660', *BAGN*, XI (1940), pp. 33–116.

Historia de las divisiones territoriales de México. México, 1966.

Otte, Enrique. 'Nueve cartas de Diego de Ordás', *Historia Mexicana*, 53 (1964), pp. 102–30.

Oviedo y Valdés, Gonzalo Fernández de. *Historia general y natural de las Indias, islas y tierra-firme del mar océano*. 4 vols. Madrid, 1851–5.

Palerm, Angel. 'The agricultural basis of urban civilization in Mesoamerica', *Irrigation civilizations: a comparative study* (Washington, 1955), pp. 28–42.

Papeles de Nueva España publicados de orden y con fondos del gobierno mexicano por Francisco del Paso y Troncoso, Director en misión del Museo Nacional. 2a serie, Geografía y Estadística. 7 vols. Madrid, 1905–6.

Paredes Colín, J. *El distrito de Tehuacán...* México, 1960.

Parry, J. H. *The audiencia of New Galicia in the sixteenth century.* Cambridge University Press, 1948 (repr. 1969).

    The sale of public office in the Spanish Indies under the Hapsburgs. Berkeley and Los Angeles, 1953. Ibero-Americana: 37.

Paso y Troncoso, Francisco del. *Códice Kingsborough...* Madrid, 1912.

Pasquel, Leonardo. *Coatepec.* I. México, 1959.

Peña, Moisés T. de la. *Problemas sociales y económicos de las Mixtecas.* México, 1950.

Peñafiel, Antonio. *Nombres geográficos de México...* México, 1885.

    Códice Fernández Leal. México, 1895.

    Códice mixteco – lienzo de Zacatepec. México, 1900.

Pérez, Eutimio. *Recuerdos históricos del episcopado oaxaqueño...* Oaxaca, 1888.

Pérez Hernández, José María. *Compendio de la geografía del estado de Michoacán de Ocampo.* México, 1872.

Plano de los límites pretendidos por los estados de Oaxaca y Puebla. 1:40,000. 1905.

[Ponce, Alonso]. *Relacion breve y verdadera de algunas cosas de las muchas que sucedieron al padre fray Alonso Ponce en las provincias de la Nueva España...escrita por dos religiosos, sus compañeros...* 2 vols. Madrid, 1873.

Porras Muñoz, Guillermo. 'Diego de Ibarra y la Nueva España', *Estudios de Historia Novohispana*, II (1968), pp. 49–78.

Portillo y Díez de Sollano, Alvaro del. *Descubrimientos y exploraciones en las costas de California.* Madrid, 1947.

Powell, Philip W. *Soldiers Indians & silver. The northward advance of New Spain, 1550–1600.* Berkeley and Los Angeles, 1952.

Prescott, William H. *The conquest of Mexico.* 2 vols. London and New York, 1957.

Pretty, Francis. 'The admirable and prosperous voyage of the worshipfull Master Thomas Candish', R. Hakluyt, *The principal navigations...*, III. London, 1600.

Priestley, Herbert I. *José de Gálvez – visitor-general of New Spain (1765–1771).* Berkeley, 1916. University of California Publications in History, V.

Puga, Vasco de. *Prouisiões cedulas Instruciones de su Magestad...* México, 1563.

Ramírez, José Fernando, ed. *Anales de Cuauhtitlan – noticias históricas de México y sus contornos...* México, 1885.

Ramírez Flores, José. *Tierras de Chiquilistlán, según mapa del siglo XVI.* México, 1959.

Ramírez Lavoignet, David. *Misantla.* [México], 1959.

    Tlapacoyan. Xalapa, 1965.

Real Díaz, José Joaquín. 'Las ferias de Jalapa', *Anuario de Estudios Americanos*, XVI (Seville, 1959), pp. 167–314.

Redfield, Robert. *Tepoztlan – a Mexican Village – a Study of Folk Life.* Chicago, 1930.

Relacion de las ceremonias y ritos y poblacion y gobierno de los indios de la provincia de Michoacan (1541). Madrid, 1956.

Relaciones geográficas de la diócesis de Michoacán – 1579–1580. 2 vols. Guadalajara, 1958.

Revilla Gigedo, Conde de. *Informe sobre las misiones – 1793 – e instrucción reservada al marqués de Branciforte – 1794.* México, 1966.

Ricard, Robert. *La 'conquête spirituelle' du Mexique. Essai sur l'apostolat et les méthodes missionnaires des Ordres Mendiants en Nouvelle-Espagne de 1523–24 à 1572.* Paris, 1933. Université de Paris. Travaux et Mémoires de l'Institut d'Ethnologie, XX.

Riley, G. Micheal. 'Fernando Cortés and the Cuernavaca encomiendas, 1522–1547', *The Americas*, XXV (1968), pp. 3–24.

Rivera, Pedro de. *Diario y derrotero de lo caminado, visto, y obcervado en el discurso de la visita general de Precidios, situados en las Provincias Ynternas de Nueva España, que de orden de su magestad executó D. Pedro de Rivera...* Guatemala, 1736.

Robelo, Cecilio A. *Nombres geográficos mexicanos del Estado de Veracruz*. México, 1961.

Robelo, Cecilio A., Manuel de Olaguibel, and Antonio Peñafiel. *Nombres geográficos indígenas del Estado de México*. México, 1966.

Robles, Antonio de. *Diario de sucesos notables (1665–1703)*. 3 vols. México, 1946.

Rodríguez Zetina, Arturo. *Jacona y Zamora – datos históricos, útiles y curiosos*. México, 1956.

Romero, José Guadalupe. 'Noticias para formar la estadística del obispado de Michoacán', *Boletín de la SMGE*, VIII (1860), pp. 531–60, and IX (1861), pp. 1–81.

Romero Quiroz, Javier. *Teotenanco y Matlatzinco (Calixtlahuaca)*. Toluca, 1963.

Vasco de Quiroga en Tultepec. [México], n.d.

Roquet, Salvador. *El convento de Actopam...* México, 1938.

Rosenblat, Angel. *La población de América en 1492*. México, 1967.

Salinas, Miguel. *Datos para la historia de Toluca*. México, 1965.

Sanders, William T. 'The anthropogeography of central Veracruz', in Bernal and Dávalos Hurtado (1952–3), pp. 27–78.

'Settlement patterns', *Handbook of Middle American Indians*, VI (1967), pp. 53–86.

'A profile of urban evolution in the Teotihuacán valley', XXXVII *Congreso Internacional de Americanistas – Republica Argentina – 1966. Actas y memorias*, I (1968), pp. 95–102.

Santoscoy, Alberto. 'Los idiomas indígenas en varios de los pueblos del antiguo obispado de Guadalajara', *Anales del Museo Nacional de México*, VII (1903), pp. 309–11.

Saravia, Atanasio G. *Apuntes para la historia de la Nueva Vizcaya – no. I: La Conquista*. México, n.d.

Sauer, Carl. *Colima of New Spain in the sixteenth century*. Berkeley and Los Angeles, 1948. Ibero-Americana: 29.

Schmieder, Oscar. *The settlements of the Tzapotec and Mije Indians – state of Oaxaca, Mexico*. Berkeley, 1930. University of California Publications in Geography, IV.

Scholes, France V. and Eleanor B. Adams. *Relación de las encomiendas de indios hechas en Nueva España a los conquistadores y pobladores de ella – Año de 1564*. México, 1955.

Información sobre los tributos que los indios pagaban a Moctezuma – Año de 1554. México, 1957.

Sobre el modo de tributar los indios de Nueva España a su Majestad 1561–1564. México, 1958.

Moderación de doctrinas de la Real Corona administradas por las Ordenes Mendicantes – 1623. México, 1959.

Cartas del Licenciado Jerónimo Valderrama y otros documentos sobre su visita al gobierno de Nueva España – 1563–1565. México, 1961.

Scholes, France V. and Dave Warren. 'The Olmec region at Spanish contact', *Handbook of Middle American Indians*, III (1965), pp. 776–87.

Scholes, Walter V. *The Diego Ramírez visita*. Columbia, 1946.

Schurz, William L. *The Manila galleon*. New York, 1939.

Septién y Villaseñor, José Antonio. *Memoria estadística del estado de Queretaro precedida de una noticia histórica que comprende desde la fundación del mismo hasta el año de 1821*. Querétaro, 1875.

Sherman, William L. 'A conqueror's wealth: notes on the estate of Don Pedro de Alvarado', *The Americas*, XXVI (1969), pp. 199–213.

Simons, Bente Bittmann. 'The codex of Cholula: a preliminary study', *Tlalocan*, V (1967), pp. 267–88.

'The city of Cholula and its ancient barrios', *Verhandlungen des XXXVIII. Internationalen Amerikanistenkongresses*, Bd. II. München, 1970.

Simpson, Leslie B. *Studies in the administration of the Indians in New Spain*. Berkeley, 1934. Ibero-Americana: 7.

The encomienda in New Spain – the beginning of Spanish Mexico. Berkeley and Los Angeles, 1950.

Smith, Mary Elizabeth. 'The Codex Colombino: a document of the south coast of Oaxaca', *Tlalocan*, IV (1963), pp. 276–88.

Solís Martínez, Raúl. *Retablillos cuautlenses*. 1962.

Soustelle, Jacques. *La famille Otomi–Pame au Mexique central*. Paris, 1937.

[Speilbergen, Joris van]. *The East and West Indian mirror, being an account of Joris van Speilbergen's voyage round the world (1614–1617).* London, 1906. Hakluyt Society, 2d ser., XVIII.

Spores, Ronald. 'The Zapotec and Mixtec at Spanish contact', *Handbook of Middle American Indians*, III (1965), pp. 962–87.

The Mixtec kings and their people. Univ. of Oklahoma Press, Norman, Okla., 1967.

Stanislawski, Dan. 'Tarascan political geography', *American Anthropologist*, XLIX (1947), pp. 46–55.

'*Suma de Visitas*'; the Suma material is most readily available in the '*Papeles de Nueva España...*' and in Borah and Cook (1960), both listed elsewhere in this bibliography.

Swadesh, Mauricio. *Estudios sobre lengua y cultura.* México, 1960. Acta Anthropologica, 2a época, II-2.

Tamarón y Romeral, Pedro. *Demonstración del vastísimo obispado de la Nueva Vizcaya – 1765...* México, 1937.

Tamayo, Jorge L. *Geografía general de México.* 4 vols. + atlas. México, 1962.

Taylor, William B. 'The foundation of Nuestra Señora de Guadalupe de los morenos de Amapa', *The Americas*, 26 (1970), pp. 439–46.

Títulos de Indias. Valladolid, 1954. Cat. XX, Archivo General de Simancas.

Torquemada, Juan de. *Primera (segunda, tercera) parte de los veinte i vn libros rituales i monarchia indiana...* 3 vols. Madrid, 1723.

Torres, Mariano de. *Crónica de la sancta provincia de Xalisco.* México, 1960.

Toussaint, Manuel. *Tasco – su historia, sus monumentos, características actuales y posibilidades turísticas.* México, 1931.

Toussaint, Manuel, Federico Gómez de Orozco, and Justino Fernández. *Planos de la ciudad de México – siglos XVI y XVII – estudio histórico, urbanístico y bibliográfico.* México, 1938.

Trens, Manuel B. *Historia de Veracruz.* 6 vols. Jalapa, 1947–50.

Urban Aguirre, José. *Geografía e historia del estado de Morelos.* Cuernavaca, 1963.

Vázquez de Espinosa, Antonio. *Descripcion de la Nueva España en el siglo XVII.* México, 1944.

Compendio y descripción de las Indias occidentales. Washington, 1948. Smithsonian Miscellaneous Collections, 108.

[Vázquez de Tapia, Bernardino]. *Relación de méritos y servicios del conquistador Bernardino Vázquez de Tapia vecino y regidor de esta gran ciudad de Tenustitlan, Mexico.* México, 1953.

Vázquez Vázquez, Elena. *Distribución geográfica y organización de las órdenes religiosas en la Nueva España (siglo XVI).* Maps in separate folder. México, 1965.

Velasco y Mendoza, Luis. *Historia de la ciudad de Celaya.* 4 vols. México, 1947–9.

Velásquez Gallardo, Pablo. 'Título de tierras de Cherán Hatzicurin', *Tlalocan*, III (1952), pp. 238–45.

Velázquez, María del Carmen. 'La navegación transpacífica', *Historia Mexicana*, 70 (1968), pp. 159–78.

Velázquez, Primo Feliciano. *Colección de documentos para la historia de San Luis Potosí.* 4 vols. San Luis Potosí, 1897–9.

Historia de San Luis Potosí. 4 vols. México, 1946–8.

Vera, Fortino Hipólito. *Itinerario parroquial del arzobispado de México y reseña histórica, geográfica y estadística de las parroquias del mismo arzobispado.* Amecameca, 1880.

Vetancurt, Augustin de. *Teatro Mexicano – descripcion breve de los svcessos exemplares, historicos, politicos, Militares, y Religiosos del nuevo mundo occidental de las Indias.* 2 vols. México, 1697–8.

Villaseñor y Sánchez, José Antonio. *Theatro Americano, descripcion general de los reynos, y provincias de la Nueva-España, y sus jurisdicciones...* 2 vols. México, 1952.

Wagner, Henry R. 'Early silver mining in New Spain', *Revista de historia de América*, XIV (1942), pp. 49–71.

Walter, Richard. *A voyage round the world, in the years mdccxl, i, ii, iii, iv. by George Anson, Esq.* London, 1748.

Warren, Fintan B. 'The Caravajal visitation: first Spanish survey of Michoacán', *The Americas*, XIX (1963a), pp. 404–12.

Vasco de Quiroga and his Pueblo-Hospitals of Santa Fe. Washington, 1963b.

Weitlaner, Robert J. 'The Guatinicamame', *A William Cameron Townsend en el XXV aniversario del Instituto Lingüístico de Verano*, pp. 199–205. México, 1961.

Weitlaner, Robert J. and Carlo Antonio Castro G. *Mayultianguis y Tlacoatzintepec (Papeles de la Chinantla, I)*. México, 1954.

West, Robert C. *Cultural geography of the modern Tarascan area*. Washington, 1948.

'The natural regions of Middle America', *Handbook of Middle American Indians*, I (1964), pp. 363–83.

West, Robert C. and John P. Augelli. *Middle America – its lands and peoples*. Englewood Cliffs, 1966.

Williams García, Roberto. *Los Tepehuas*. Xalapa, 1963.

Wolf, Eric R. 'The Mexican Bajío in the eighteenth century', *Synoptic studies of Mexican culture* (New Orleans, 1957), pp. 177–99.

Zantwijk, R. A. M. van. 'La organización de once guarniciones aztecas: una nueva interpretación de los folios 17v y 18r del Códice Mendocino', *Journal de la Société des Américanistes*, LVI (1967), pp. 149–60.

Zerón Zapata, Miguel. *La Puebla de los Angeles en el siglo XVII*. México, 1945.

Zorita, Alonso de. *Life and labor in ancient Mexico – the Brief and summary relation of the lords of New Spain*. New Brunswick, 1963.

Zubarán, Jovita. 'Xochimilco prehispánico', *Homenaje a Rafael García Granados*, pp. 331–43. México, 1960.

Notes

INTRODUCTION

[1] These include lists of 1560 (AGI, Indiferente, 1529; published in ENE, IX, pp. 2–43), 1564 (AGI, México, 242; published in Scholes and Adams, 1955), c. 1567 (UT, JGI XXIII-2; published in García Pimentel, 1904, pp. 153–88), and 1597 (ENE, XIII, pp. 8–48). The situation c. 1604 is reported in Dorantes de Carranza (1902). For biographical data on the encomenderos, cf. Boyd-Bowman (1964, 1968), Martínez Cosío (1946), Millares Carlo and Mantecón (1945, 1946), Nobiliario...(1892), and Scholes and Adams (1961, pp. 205–51 and *passim*).

[2] AGN, Reales cédulas (duplicados), 9, 10, 14, 24, 25, 28, 41, 42.

[3] Cf. Gerhard (*Handbook of Middle American Indians*, forthcoming vol.), to which the reader is referred for more complete citation.

[4] AGN, Padrones, 12, fol. 251–69v.

[5] The principal sources of the detailed information on political jurisdictions given below are a number of lists drawn up at various times from c. 1534 to 1804, together with two tribute assessment ledgers and the *relaciones geográficas*. The lists, with stated or approximate dates, are as follows: C. 1534: AGI, Patronato, leg. 183, doc. 9, ramo 2. 1536 and 1545: AGI, México, leg. 91. 1550: AGI, Contaduría, leg. 663-A. 1560: AGI, Patronato, leg. 181, ramo 38. C. 1567: AGI, Patronato, leg. 20, doc. 5, ramo 24. 1569: AGI, Contaduría, 633-A. C. 1582: BNE, MS 3048, fol. 137–40. 1590: AGI, México, leg. 22, ramo 2. C. 1615: Vázquez de Espinosa (1948), pp. 264–8. C. 1642: BNE, MSS 3047 (fol. 81–9v) and 18684 (fol. 296–306); published with discrepancies in Díez de la Calle (1646), pp. 165–8. 1676: AGI, México, leg. 600. C. 1743: Villaseñor y Sánchez (1952). 1777: NYPL, Phillips MS 15796. 1784: BNM, MS 1384, fol. 391–411v; BNP, FM 258. C. 1804: AGN, Tributos, 43, last exp. *N.B.*: In the notes which follow, reference to the above-mentioned

sources is usually omitted. The tribute ledgers, from the 16th century, are found in AGI, Patronato, leg. 182, ramo 40, and in LdeT. For an illuminating discussion of the process of venality, cf. Parry (1953).

[6] The proponents of a small native population at contact include Kroeber (1934), Kubler (1942), and Rosenblat (1967). The arguments for a large population are given in the monographs of the 'Berkeley school', Cook and Simpson (1948), Borah and Cook (1960, 1963), and Cook and Borah (1960, 1968).

[7] The Ocuituco *visita* is found in AGI, Patronato, leg. 180, ramo 64 (cf. Gerhard, 1970). The report from Pánuco is summarized by Chipman (1967), who gives AGI, Justicia, leg. 234, fol. 772–831v, 857–902v, as the source.

[8] AGI, Patronato, 183, doc. 9, ramo 2, is a list of corregidors. Cf. ENE, XIV, pp. 55–7 (boundaries of provinces) and 148–55; XV, pp. 1–9.

[9] The document, BNE, MS 2800, is published (defectively, we are told, although we have not seen the original) in PNE, I, and expertly analysed in Borah and Cook (1960).

[10] Individual citations for these documents will be given below. For a complete listing and discussion of the corpus, see Cline (1964). Cf. Gerhard (1968).

[11] NL, Ayer 1106 D, 1.

[12] BNE, MS 6877.

[13] BNE, MS 4476.

[14] NL, Ayer, 1106 A.

[15] AGN, Reales cédulas (duplicados), *passim*.

[16] AA, Visita (1683–5).

[17] AGI, Indiferente, leg. 107 and 108.

[18] AGN, Historia, 578.

[19] AGI, México, 2578–81, 2589–91.

[20] Reports from the intendancy of Mexico are in AGN,

Historia, 578. Those from San Luis Potosí and Guanaxuato are in AGN, Historia, 72, and from Puebla in Historia, 73.
21 AGI, México, 1158.
22 SMGE, MS 31 (727.2).

ACAPULCO

1 AGI, Contaduría, 663-A.
2 NL, Ayer 1106 D, 3.
3 AGI, Patronato, 181, ramo 38.
4 AGI, Patronato, 183, doc. 9, ramo 2.
5 AGN, General de parte, I, fol. 219v; 2, fol. 54v, 282; Mercedes, 3, fol. 242, 344v; 5, fol. 70v; 11, fol. 32, 57. BAGN, x, p. 271.
6 NYPL, Rich MS 39.
7 RAH, 9-62-2: 4795.
8 AGN, Indios, 6, 2a parte, fol. 9v, 77, 278v; Reales cédulas (duplicados), 14, 28.
9 AGN, Indios, 5, 2a parte, fol. 240v; Reales cédulas (duplicados), 9, 25, 42.
10 AGI, México, 336, fol. 117–22 (pub. in García Pimentel, 1897, pp. 146–52).
11 AGI, Indiferente, 1529 (pub. in ENE, XIV, pp. 97–8).
12 AGI, Indiferente, 1529, no. 382 (pub. in PNE, VI, pp. 153–66).
13 AGI, Indiferente, 107, tomo 1, fol. 99–164v; summarized in Villaseñor y Sánchez (1952), I, pp. 186–90.
14 AGN, Historia, 578, fol. 34–7; Padrones, 16, fol. 213–430.

ACATLAN Y PIASTLA

1 AGN, General de parte, I, fol. 95; Mercedes, 3, fol. 254; 4, fol. 10v, 309; 5, fol. 16.
2 AGN, Tributos, 43 (last expediente).
3 AGN, Indios, 6, 2a parte, fol. 236v.
4 RAH, 9-25-4: 4663–XXXVIII (pub. in PNE, V: pp. 55–80).
5 AGN, Congregaciones, fol. 7, 20v.
6 BNE, MS 6877, fol. 53v, 91v.
7 AGN, Reales cédulas (duplicados), 9, 25, 42. Scholes and Adams (1959), p. 39.
8 AGN, Historia, 522, fol. 226–43.
9 AGI, México, 2578, 2580.
10 AGN, Historia, 73, fol. 108–9.

ACTOPAN

1 AGI, Patronato, 182, ramo 44. AGN, Indios, 6, 1a parte, fol. 169.
2 AGI, Patronato, 182, ramo 40.
3 AGN, Mercedes, 5, fol. 77; 84, fol. 117v.
4 AGN, General de parte, I: fol. 207v; II: fol. 253v.
5 AGN, Indios, 6, 1a parte, fol. 290; Padrones, 12, fol. 253v.
6 AGI, Indiferente, 1529, fol. 203; cf. PNE, III: pp. 66–9.
7 AGN, Indios, 6, 1a parte, fol. 290; 2a parte, fol. 191, 276, 277v.
8 AGN, Reales cédulas (duplicados), 14, 28.
9 AGN, Inquisición, 937, fol. 299–303.
10 BNE, MS 2450, fol. 366–366v.
11 AGN, Padrones, 3, fol. 26–29v.

AMULA

1 AGI, Justicia, 130, fol. 962; Patronato, 17, ramo 17. AGN, Hospital de Jesús, 265, exp. 5.
2 AGN, Mercedes, 3, fol. 32v.
3 AGN, Indios, 6, 2a parte, fol. 107.

4 Ibid., fol. 277.
5 UT, JGI, XXIII-9.
6 AGI, Indiferente, 107, tomo 1, fol. 166–8.
7 AGI, Guadalajara, 401, fol. 77, 79.
8 AGI, México, 1675, fol. 4v-5.
9 AGN, Historia, 72, fol. 201.
10 AGN, Tributos, 43, final expediente.

ANTEQUERA

1 AGI, Patronato, 16, doc. 2, ramo 32.
2 AGN, Indios, 6, 1a parte, fol. 94v.
3 AGN, Mercedes, 3, fol. 246, 304, 326, 349.
4 AGI, Patronato, 20, doc. 5, ramo 24. AGN, Mercedes, 4, fol. 8v, 15, 76v.
5 AGN, General de parte, III, fol. 85–85v.
6 Ibid., VI, fol. 8.
7 Ibid., VI, fol. 217.
8 AGN, Indios, 3, fol. 45–45v.
9 Ibid., 6, 2a parte, fol. 242v. Cf. Miranda (1968), p. 142.
10 UT, JGI, XXIII-11 (pub. in Tlalocan, ii, pp. 134–7).
11 Ibid., XXIV-9.
12 RAH, 9-25-4: 4663 – XXIII (pub. in PNE, IV: pp. 177 ff.).
13 Ibid., XXV (pub. in PNE, IV: pp. 190 ff.).
14 AGN, Tierras, 1874, exp. 7.
15 AGI, México, 881, fol. 151v–153v.
16 AGI, Indiferente, 107, tomo 2, fol. 379–380v.
17 BNE, MS 2449, fol. 337–43; MS 2450, fol. 4–9v, 11–14v, 17–21v, 23–31, 152–4, 314–21.
18 AGI, México, 2589 and 2591.
19 AGN, Mapas y planos, México, no. 556bis.
20 AGN, Padrones, 13.
21 AGN, Tributos, 43, last exp.
22 Colección Castañeda Guzmán, MS Visita de Bergosa y Jordán. Cf. Pérez (1888), table at end.
23 SMGE, MS 31 (727.2).

APA Y TEPEAPULCO

1 AGN, Hospital de Jesús, 265, exp. 5.
2 AGI, Patronato, 17, ramo 17. Icaza, I, p. 18. L de T, p. 400.
3 AGN, Reales cédulas (duplicados), 14, 28. Scholes and Adams (1959), p. 45.
4 AGN, Tributos, 43, last exp.
5 AGN, General de parte, I: fol. 67v, 96v; Indios, 6, 1a parte, fol. 79v, 109v–110; 2a parte, fol. 255.
6 AGN, Tributos, 43, last exp.
7 Códice Franciscano, p. 13. PNE, III, pp. 84–5.
8 AA, Visita (1683–5), fol. 59–62.
9 AGN, Padrones, 5, fol. 315–317v.
10 AGN, Historia, 578, fol. 38–39bis v.

ATLATLAUCA

1 AGN, Indios, 6, 2a parte, fol. 53.
2 AGN, General de parte, XVII, fol. 19v, 32.
3 SMGE, MS 'Censo clacificado de Oajaca', 1832. Miranda, 1968.
4 AGN, Indios, 6, 2a parte, fol. 242v; Tierras, 64, exp. 4.
5 BNE, MS 2450, fol. 1–3v.
6 SMGE, MS 31 (727.2).

ATRISCO

1 AGN, Hospital de Jesús, 265, exp. 5.
2 AGI, México, 91; Patronato, 183, doc. 9, ramo 2. L de T, pp. 128–9.

[3] AGN, General de parte, I, fol. 23v, 121–2, 204v; II, fol. 118, 213v; Mercedes, 84, fol. 36.

[4] AGI, México, 20. AGN, General de parte, II, fol. 42v, 48, 167, 203v, 267v.

[5] AGN, General de parte, VI, fol. 200; Indios, 6, 2a parte, fol. 66v, 84v; Mercedes, 11, fol. 51.

[6] AGI, México, 600. AGN, General de parte, X, fol. 6v.

[7] AGN, Padrones, 12, fol. 258v–259.

[8] AGI, México, 20 (letter from viceroy, 19 Oct. 1577).

[9] *Ibid.*

[10] AGI, México, 600.

[11] AGN, Congregaciones, fol 57v; Indios, 6, 2a parte, fol. 236v, 277.

[12] BNP, Fonds mexicains, 387.

[13] BNE, MS 6877, fol. 83–85v.

[14] BNE, MS 4476.

[15] AGN, Reales cédulas (duplicados), 9, 25, 42.

[16] AGN, Inquisición, 937, fol. 364–372v.

[17] AGI, México, 2579 and 2580.

[18] AGN, Historia, 73; Padrones, 25.

AUTLAN

[1] AGN, Mercedes, 3, fol. 32v; 5, fol. 8, 52v; 84, fol. 59.

[2] AGN, General de parte, V, fol. 4v, 313v.

[3] AGI, México, 20.

[4] AGN, Indios, 6, 2a parte, fol. 277.

[5] AGN, Mercedes, 84, fol. 59. Cf. Gerhard, 1960, pp. 87, 189–90, 205.

[6] UT, JGI XXIII–10; pub. in Amaya, 1951.

[7] *Ibid.*, XXV–1.

[8] AGN, Reales cédulas (duplicados), 41. Mota y Escobar, pp. 62–5. Scholes and Adams (1959), pp. 66–8.

[9] AGI, Indiferente, 107, tomo 1, fol. 170–176v.

[10] AGI, Guadalajara, 401, nos. 48, 76, 77.

[11] BNE, MS 2449, fol. 48–52v, 88–93.

[12] AGI, México, 1675, fol. 8v–9.

[13] AGN, Historia, 72, fol. 233–233v.

CADEREYTA

[1] BE, k–III–8.

[2] AGI, México, 20. AGN, General de parte, V, fol. 45v. Powell, pp. 60, 125, 146.

[3] AGN, General de parte, V, fol. 45v. Vázquez de Espinosa, 1948, p. 266.

[4] AGI, Indiferente, 108, tomo 5, fol. 55v–59, 100–100v. Velázquez, 1946–8, I, p. 479.

[5] AGN, Tributos, 43, last exp.

[6] AGI, México, 20. AGN, Indios, II, fol. 48.

[7] AGN, Historia, 578, fol. 40.

[8] AGI, Indiferente, 108, tomo 5, fol. 100–100v.

[9] AGN, Historia, 522, fol. 14–94v, 103–103v.

[10] AGN, Historia, 578, fol. 40–54.

CELAYA

[1] NYPL, Beaumont MS, libro 1, ch. 1, vol. 4. Cf. Cortés, p. 321. Velázquez, 1946–8, I, p. 369.

[2] AGI, Justicia, 130, fol. 964v–965, 967v. ENE, II, p. 16.

[3] AGI, Justicia, *loc. cit.*

[4] AGN, Congregaciones, 5v.

[5] AGN, Mercedes, 4, fol. 281v; 84, fol. 126v.

[6] AGN, General de parte, VI, fol. 417.

[7] *Ibid.*, X, fol. 127v.

[8] NL, Ayer 1121, fol. 288.

[9] AGI, Patronato, 182, ramo 44. BAGN, III, p. 75. Powell, p. 197. Scholes and Adams, 1959, p. 56.

[10] AGN, Tributos, 43, last exp.

[11] AGI, Indiferente, 1529. See also Miranda Godínez, 9/40–4/41.

[12] RAH, 9–25–4: 4663 – x; pub. in *Relaciones geográficas de... Michoacán*, II, pp. 50–70.

[13] AGN, Congregaciones, fol. 5v, 122; Indios, 6, 1a parte, fol. 181, 190v, 206; 2a parte, fol. 242.

[14] NL, Ayer 1106 C, 3.

[15] NL, Ayer 1106 A.

[16] AGN, Reales cédulas (duplicados), 24, 41–2.

[17] AGN, Inquisición, 937, fol. 285–287v, 356–360v, 379–380v.

[18] AGN, Padrones, 23, 26.

[19] AGN, Historia, 72, fol. 168–175v.

CEMPOALA

[1] AGI, México, 28; Patronato, 182, ramo 44.

[2] NL, Ayer 1106 D, 3.

[3] AGI, Patronato, 182, ramo 40, fol. 358v.

[4] AGI, México, 28. Cf. Gibson (1964), pp. 413–14.

[5] AGI, Patronato, 182, ramo 40, fol. 298v. L de T, p. 627.

[6] *Ibid.*

[7] UT, JGI XXV–10, 11, 12 (pub. in Tlalocan, III, pp. 29–41).

[8] AGN, Congregaciones, fol. 10, 18v, 37, 54, 58–9, 70v; Indios, 6, 2a parte, fol. 277v.

[9] AGN, Reales cédulas (duplicados), 14, 28. Scholes and Adams (1959), p. 46.

[10] AA, Visita (1683–5), fol. 65v–69v.

[11] AGN, Inquisición, 937, fol. 300v–301.

[12] AGN, Padrones, 20, fol. 1–4v.

[13] AGN, Historia, 578, fol. 213–218v.

CIMAPAN

[1] AGN, General de parte, II, fol. 155, 209; Indios, 2, fol. 39, 98v, 201v, 202v. Powell, p. 257.

[2] AGN, General de parte, IV, fol. 22v; Indios, 5, fol. 171v.

[3] AGN, General de parte, II, fol. 25v.

[4] AGN, Indios, 6, 2a parte, fol. 276.

[5] AGN, Historia, 72, fol. 70.

[6] UT, G–248.

[7] AGN, Historia, 578, fol. 219–21.

[8] AGN, Tributos, 43, last exp.

CIMATLAN Y CHICHICAPA

[1] AGI, Patronato, 16, doc. 2, ramo 32.

[2] AGI, México, 90. L de T, p. 34.

[3] AGN, General de parte, II, fol. 101. PNE, IV, pp. 290, 299.

[4] AGN, General de parte, V, fol. 62, 148v; VI, fol. 8; Indios, 6, 2a parte, fol. 69v, 86.

[5] AGI, México, 600.

[6] AGI, México, 68.

[7] BNM, MS 271.2. Scholes and Adams, 1959, p. 39.

[8] AGI, México, 881.

[9] AGN, Tributos, 43, last exp.

[10] AGN, General de parte, V, fol. 62.

[11] AGN, Indios, 6, 2a parte, fol. 225, 236v.

[12] HS, HC:417/114.

[13] UT, JGI XXIV–9.

[14] *Ibid.*, XXV–6.

[15] AGN, Tierras, 64, exp. 5.

[16] *Ibid.*, 1874, exp. 7.

[17] AGI, México, 2589–90.

[18] BNE, MS 2450, fol. 199–200v.
[19] *Ibid.*, fol. 17–21v.
[20] Colección Castañeda Guzmán, MS Visita de Bergosa y Jordán. Pérez (1888), table at end.
[21] SMGE, MS 31 (727.2).

CINAGUA Y LA GUACANA

[1] AGI, Justicia, 130, fol. 961v, 969v; 197. Millares Carló and Mantecón, I, no. 756.
[2] AGI, Justicia, 130, fol. 965, 970.
[3] *Ibid.*, fol. 965v, 968, 970; 145. AGN, Reales cédulas (duplicados), 24, fol. 175.
[4] AGN, General de parte, II, fol. 113; Indios, 2, fol. 152; Mercedes, 11, fol. 91.
[5] AGN, Mercedes, 4, fol. 78v.
[6] AGN, General de parte, IX, fol. 200.
[7] AGN, Hospital de Jesús, 292, exp. 119, fol. 432–4.
[8] AGI, Patronato, 182, ramo 40, fol. 313, 358v. L de T, p. 644.
[9] RAH, 9-25-4: 4663-XII; pub. in *Relaciones geográficas de...Michoacan*, II, pp. 70–4.
[10] AGN, Indios, 6, 2a parte, fol. 153v, 211, 242.
[11] NL, Ayer, 1106 C, fol. 126, 129v–130.
[12] NL, Ayer 1106 A, fol. 58v, 71–71v.
[13] AGN, Reales cédulas (duplicados), 24, 41–2.
[14] AGI, Indiferente, 108, tomo 4, fol. 354–366v. Cf. Villaseñor y Sánchez, II, p. 95.
[15] AGN, Historia, 73, fol. 393v–405.
[16] AGN, Historia, 72, fol. 47–47v, 49–49v.

COATEPEC

[1] AGI, Patronato, 183, doc. 9, ramo 2.
[2] AGN, Reales cédulas (duplicados), 24.
[3] AGI, México, 68. ENE, IX, p. 44.
[4] AGN, Reales cédulas (duplicados), 14, fol. 10, 15v. Scholes and Adams (159), pp. 29, 32.
[5] AGN, Tributos, 43, last exp.
[6] AGI, México, 336, fol. 65.
[7] AGI, Indiferente, 1529; pub. in PNE, VI, pp. 39–86.
[8] AGN, Vínculos, 244, exp. 1, fol. 16.
[9] AA, Visita (1683–5), fol. 18–20v.
[10] AGN, Padrones, 3, fol. 1–25.
[11] AGN, Historia, 578, fol. 55–6.

COLIMA

[1] AGI, México, 28. ENE, IV, p. 175.
[2] AGN, Indios, 2, fol. 176.
[3] AGN, Tierras, 2811, doc. 5.
[4] AGI, México, 20.
[5] NL, Ayer 1121, fol. 292v.
[6] AGN, Indios, 6, 2a parte, fol. 7, 25, 237.
[7] Cf. BNE, MS 2450, fol. 388.
[8] UT, JGI XXIV–18, fol. 6v.
[9] AGN, Tributos, 43, last exp.
[10] AGN, Historia, 41; cf. BAGN, X, pp. 5–23.
[11] NL, Ayer 1106 C, 3, fol. 128–9.
[12] *Ibid.*, 1106 A, fol. 45–6.
[13] AGN, Reales cédulas (duplicados), 24, 41–2.
[14] AGI, Indiferente, 107, tomo 1, fol. 247–255v.
[15] AGI, Mapas y planos (México), 323.
[16] BNE, MS 2450, fol. 372–389v.
[17] *Ibid.*, fol. 164–98.
[18] AGN, Padrones, 11, fol. 1–20.

[19] AGN, Historia, 72, fol. 50v–51.
[20] AGI, México, 372, fol. 47–91v. BNE, MS 2957. Dampier, pp. 176–7. Speilbergen, pp. 110–1.

CORDOBA

[1] AGI, México, 91, ENE, III, p. 138.
[2] AGI, Patronato, 182, ramo 40.
[3] AGN, Mercedes, 84, fol. 160; Icaza, I, pp. 13–14.
[4] AGI, México, 28.
[5] AGN, Reales cédulas (duplicados), 9, fol. 296.
[6] AGN, Mercedes, 5, fol. 38v, 92.
[7] AGN, General de parte, II, fol. 271v.
[8] *Ibid.*, I, fol. 3v.
[9] AGI, Patronato, 181, ramo 38.
[10] AGN, Indios, 6, 2a parte, fol. 236.
[11] BNE, MS 6877, fol. 17v–20.
[12] *Ibid.*, fol. 78–9.
[13] BNE, MS 4476.
[14] AGN, Reales cédulas (duplicados), 9, 25, 42.
[15] AGI, Indiferente, 107, tomo I, fol. 258–65.
[16] AGI, México, 2578, 2580.

COZAMALOAPA

[1] AGI, Indiferente, 107, tomo I, fol. 272v.
[2] AGI, Patronato, 182, ramo 40. Bancroft, II, pp. 34–5. ENE, I, p. 141; II, p. 58; III, p. 44; IV, p. 20. Gay, I, p. 68.
[3] AGN, Mercedes, 4, fol. 28; 84, fol. 85.
[4] AGI, México, 285. AGN, General de parte, II, fol. 229, 274v; Indios, 2, fol. 87v; 6, 1a parte, fol. 76, 79, 86.
[5] AGN, Padrones, 12, fol. 257; Tierras, 2075, exp. 1.
[6] AGN, Tributos, 43, last exp.
[7] AGN, Indios, 6, 2a parte, fol. 227, 236v. Tierras, 70, exp 1.
[8] BNE, MS 6877, fol. 22v–23, 79v–80.
[9] BNE, MS 4476.
[10] AGN, Reales cédulas (duplicados), 9, 25, 42.
[11] AGI, Indiferente, 107, tomo I, 187–8, 267–80.
[12] AGI, México, 2581.
[13] BNE, MS 2449, fol. 94–104v.

CUATRO VILLAS

[1] Quesada to king, 21 Nov. 1554, in AGI, México, 68. ENE, VI, p. 141.
[2] Cavallón to king, 7 Mar. 1565, in AGI, México, 68.
[3] Muñoz to king, 7 Jan. 1568, *ibid.* AGI, Patronato, 171, doc. I, ramo 20, AGN, Hospital de Jesús, 107, exp. 49. Cartas de Indias, p. 302. ENE, XI, p. 63.
[4] AGN, Hospital de Jesús, 265, exp. 15.
[5] AGN, General de parte, I, fol. 149. Dávila Padilla, p. 514.
[6] AGN, Tributos, 43, last exp.
[7] AGN, Congregaciones, fol. 88v; Indios, 6, 2a parte, fol. 242v. Colección Castañeda Guzmán, MS *Real provisión*, 1611. Cf. Miranda (1968).
[8] UT, JGI, XXIV–10; pub. in Tlalocan, II, pp. 18–28.
[9] *Ibid.*, XXIV–9.
[10] AGN, Hospital de Jesús, 129.
[11] Colección Castañeda Guzmán, MS *Vista de ojos*, 1717.
[12] DA, 23: 3403 (723.7).
[13] AGI, Indiferente, 107, tomo 2, fol. 383–392v.
[14] AGI, México, 2589–90.
[15] BNE, MS 2449, fol. 211–14; MS 2450, fol. 32–37v.
[16] Colección Castañeda Guzmán, MS Visita de Bergosa y Jordán.
[17] SMGE, MS 31 (727.2).

CUAUTLA AMILPAS

1 AGI, México, 20; México, 68, fol. 210. AHN, MS 257.
2 AGI, México, 91; Patronato, 183, doc. 9, ramo 2. Chauvet, p. 149. García Icazbalceta (1881), pp. 101, 108, 153–4.
3 AGI, México, 242.
4 AGI, Escribanía de Cámara, 162-C; México, 28.
5 NL, Ayer 1121, fol. 61v.
6 AGI, México, 91.
7 AGI, Patronato, 20, doc. 5, ramo 24. BAGN, x, p. 258.
8 AGI, México, 20. AGN, Hospital de Jesús, 107, exp. 49. Cartas de Indias, p. 302. Encinas, III, p. 21.
9 AGN, Hospital de Jesús, 107, exp. 49.
10 AGN, General de parte, IV, fol. 40; Indios, 6, 1a parte, fol. 177v.
11 AGN, Historia, 578, fol. 26.
12 Cruz y Moya, II, p. 133. Grijalva, pp. 64–6.
13 AGN, Indios, 2, fol. 41. Dávila Padilla, p. 64. Scholes and Adams (1959), p. 32.
14 AGN, Reales cédulas (duplicados), 14, 28; Tributos, 43, last exp. Scholes and Adams (1959), p. 32.
15 AGN, Tributos, 43, last exp.
16 NL, Ayer MS 1121, fol. 119.
17 AGI, Patronato, 180, ramo 65.
18 AGN, Inquisición, 30, exp. 9.
19 AGI, Indiferente, 1529, fol. 162–4; México, 336, fol. 73–5, 78.
20 AGN, Tierras, 2782, exp. 12.
21 UT, JGI, xxiv-3.
22 AGN, Congregaciones, fol. 9, 20, 53, 61v; Tierras, 1513, exp. 7.
23 NL, Ayer MS 1106 D, 1.
24 AGI, Indiferente, 108, tomo 4, fol. 245–65.
25 AGN, Padrones, 8.
26 AGN, Historia, 73.

CUERNAVACA

1 AGI, Justicia, 108, no. 1; 113, no. 5; 118, no. 2. ENE, I, p. 141.
2 AGI, Patronato, 16, doc. 2, ramo 32. Cortés, p. 400. Cuevas (1915), pp. 79–81. ENE, II, pp. 211–12. Puga, fol. 85.
3 AGI, México, 68, fol. 210. AHN, MS 257.
4 Viceroy to king, 15–28 Oct. 1582, AGI, México, 20.
5 Ibid., viceroy to king, 23 Feb. and 18 Nov. 1586. Cartas de Indias, p. 302. Encinas, III, p. 21.
6 AGN, Hospital de Jesús, 107, exp. 49. *Información de derecho*...
7 AGI, México, 68, fol. 121; Patronato, 16, doc. 2, ramo 32, fol. 5, AGN, Hospital de Jesús, 107. exp. 49. NYPL, Phillips MS 15796, fol. 11v. Beleña, I, p. 88; II, p. vi. J. Miranda (1952), p. 200.
8 Quesada to king, 1 Sep. 1551, AGI, México, 68.
9 AGN, Hospital de Jesús, 129.
10 AGN, Tributos, 43, last exp.
11 Ibid.
12 AGN, General de parte, I, fol. 124, 132v; II, fol. 151v, 168v–169, 180v; Indios, I, fol. 146v.
13 AGN, General de parte, I, fol. 139; Indios, I, fol. 24.
14 MSS Libros de registro parroquiales, Tepoztlán.
15 AGN, Indios, 6, 2a parte, fol. 50v.
16 AGN, Indios, 2, fol. 63v, 160v
17 AGN, Mercedes, 84, fol. 43v.
18 AGI, Patronato, 16, doc. 2, ramo 32, fol. 1–4 (pub. in CDI, 12, pp. 560–1).

19 BNP, Fonds mexicains, 291; cf. *ibid.*, 102, fol. 1–9.
20 AGI, Indiferente, 1529, fol. 165 (Xantetelco, pub. in ENE, xvi, p. 83), México, 336, fol. 75–79v (summaries from all parishes, unpublished). UT, JGI, xxiii-4 (Yecapixtla, Xonacatepec, pub. in García Pimentel, 1904, pp. 115–19).
21 AGI, Indiferente, 1529, no. 390 (Tepuztlan, pub. in PNE, VI, pp. 237–50). UT, JGI, xxiii-8 (Yecapixtla); xxiv-4 (Guastepec).
22 AGN, Congregaciones, 10v, 12, 26v, 29v, 55, 58v, 60v, 65, 67, 76–77v, 81–81v, 104, 106–106v, 119, 124v. ENE, xiii, pp. 34–46.
23 AGN, Hospital de Jesús, 129; Reales cédulas (duplicados), 14, 28. Scholes and Adams, 1959.
24 NL, Ayer MS 1106 D, 1.
25 AGI, Indiferente, 107, tomo 1, fol. 287–301; map in Mapas y Planos (México), 142.
26 BNE, MS 2449, fol. 368–373v.
27 AGN, Padrones, 8.
28 AGN, Historia, 578, fol. 60–2.
29 AGN, Hospital de Jesús, 356, exp. 8.

CUISEO DE LA LAGUNA

1 AGI, Justicia, 130, fol. 961v, 966, 970v; Patronato, 181, ramo 38. NL, Ayer MS 1121, fol. 279.
2 AGI, México, 600. AGN, Reales cédulas (duplicados), 24, 41.
3 AGN, Tributos, 43, last exp.
4 AGN, Indios, 6, 1a parte, fol. 151v.
5 *Ibid.*, 2a parte, fol. 242, 278. Cf. Anales del Instituto Nacional de Antropología e Historia, xvii, p. 457.
6 AGI, Indiferente, 1529 ('de los despachos de los agustinos...').
7 RAH, 9–25–4: 4663-IV (pub. in *Relaciones geográficas de... Michoacán*, I, pp. 44–61).
8 AGN, Reales cédulas (duplicados), 24, 41–2. BAGN, III, p. 75. Scholes and Adams (1959), p. 57.
9 NL, Ayer MS 1106 C, 3, fol. 124v–125.
10 AGI, Indiferente, 107, 1er tomo, fol. 310–16.
11 BNE, MS 2449, fol. 220–223v.
12 AGN, Padrones, 16, fol. 1–106.
13 AGN, Historia, 72, fol. 47v–48.

CUYOACAN

1 AGI, Patronato, 16, doc. 2, ramo 32.
2 AGN, Indios, 6, 2a parte, fol. 134.
3 Quesada to king, 1 Sep. 1551, AGI, México, 68.
4 AGI, Patronato, 171, doc. 1, ramo 20. ENE, XI, p. 5.
5 AGN, Reales cédulas (duplicados), 14, 28.
6 AGN, Tributos, 43, last exp.
7 NL, Ayer MS 1121, fol. 34. AGI, México, 68.
8 AGN, Indios, 6, 2a parte, fol. 255.
9 AGI, México, 336, fol. 68v–69.
10 NL, Ayer MS 1106 D, 1.
11 AA, Visita (1683–5).
12 AGN, Padrones, 6.
13 AGN, Historia, 578, fol. 57.

CHALCO

1 AGI, Justicia, 156; Patronato, 16, doc. 2, ramo 32. ENE, xv, p. 92.
2 AGI, Patronato, 183, doc. 9, ramo 2.
3 *Ibid.*, 20, doc. 5, ramo 24. BAGN, x, p. 258.
4 AGI, México, 600. AGN, Reales cédulas (duplicados), 24.

[5] AGN, Tributos, 43, last exp.

[6] NL, Ayer MS 1121, fol. 208v–209v.

[7] AGN, Mercedes, 84, fol. 51–51v.

[8] AGN, Indios, 6, 1a parte, fol. 63, 83v, 190, 269v, 318v; 2a parte, fol. 26, 45, 90. Further citation will be given below.

[9] AGN, Tierras, 2783, exp. 5 (pub. in Lemoine, 1961).

[10] AGN, Congregaciones, fol. 36v.

[11] AGI, Patronato, 180, ramo 65.

[12] AGI, Patronato, 16, doc. 2, ramo 32.

[13] AGI, México, 122.

[14] AGN, Mercedes, 84, fol. 51.

[15] AGI, Justicia, 156, doc. 1. NL, Ayer MS 1121, fol. 271, 330.

[16] AGN, Congregaciones, fol. 109.

[17] Bancroft Library, Mexican Manuscript 468.

[18] AGN, Tierras, 12, 1a parte.

[19] AGI, México, 336, fol. 65–65v, 70–2.

[20] UT, JGI XXIII–4 (pub. in García Pimentel (1904), pp. 119–20).

[21] AGI, Indiferente, 1529, fol. 155–157v.

[22] RAH, 9–25–4; 4663–XXXIV (pub. in PNE VI, pp. 6–11).

[23] AGN, Tierras, 2783, exp. 5.

[24] AGI, México, 122.

[25] AGN, Reales cédulas (duplicados), 14, 28. Scholes and Adams (1959), pp. 29–31, 44, 59–60.

[26] NL, Ayer MS 1106 D, 1.

[27] AGI, Indiferente, 108, tomo 4, fol. 1–12v.

[28] *Ibid.*, 107, tomo 1, fol. 283–6.

[29] AGN, Tierras, 1518, exp. 1.

[30] Cf. Chimalpahin, opposite p. 48.

[31] BNE, MS 2449, fol. 54–56v.

[32] BNE, MS 2450, fol. 266–270v.

[33] AGN, Historia, 578, fol. 63–65v.

[34] BNE, MS 12070.

CHARO

[1] AGI, México, 91.

[2] Cavallón to king, 7 Mar. 1565, AGI, México, 68.

[3] AGN, General de parte, I, fol. 215; II, fol. 44v, 57v, 177v; Indios, 6, 2a parte, fol. 45.

[4] AGN, Hospital de Jesús, 122.

[5] AGI, Patronato, 182, ramo 44. BAGN, III, p. 43.

[6] AGN, Reales cédulas (duplicados), 41, 42; Tributos, 43, last exp.

[7] BNE, MS 2449, fol. 365. Basalenque, p. 150.

[8] AGI, Indiferente, 1529.

[9] AGN, Congregaciones, fol. 103v. Lemoine, 1960a.

[10] BNE, MS 2449, fol. 364–7.

[11] AGN, Historia, 72, fol. 54.

[12] AGN, Padrones, 12, fol. 34–54.

CHIAUTLA

[1] AGI, Patronato, 183, doc. 9, ramo 2. AGN, Mercedes, 3, fol. 277.

[2] AGN, General de parte, I, fol. 221v; II, fol. 106; IX, fol. 198v; Indios, 2, fol. 151.

[3] AGN, Padrones, 12, fol. 262v.

[4] AGN, Tributos, 43, last exp.

[5] NL, Ayer MS 1121, fol. 63v. L de T, p. 203. ENE, xv, p. 155.

[6] AGN, Congregaciones, fol. 25–25v; Indios, 6, 1a parte, fol. 58; 2a parte, fol. 17v, 126v, 141, 236v.

[7] AGN, Padrones, 12, fol. 262v.

[8] BNE, MS 6877, fol. 84v.

[9] AGN, Reales cédulas (duplicados), 9, 25, 42.

[10] AGI, México, 2578.

[11] AGN, Historia, 73, fol. 23–23v.

CHIETLA

[1] AGN, Indios, 2, fol. 109v–110.

[2] *Ibid.*, 6, 1a parte, fol. 76v.

[3] AGN, Reales cédulas (duplicados), 9, 25, 42; Tributos, 43, last exp.

[4] Further details of these settlements are found in AGN, General de parte, I, fol. 234v; II, fol. 92, 109v, 213, 225v, 276; Indios, 2, fol. 11v, 99, 109v, 135v.

[5] AGI, Indiferente, 1529, fol. 167 (pub. in PNE, v, pp. 273–4).

[6] AGN, Congregaciones, fol. 18v, 19.

[7] BNE, MS 4476.

[8] AGI, Indiferente, 107, tomo II, fol. 101v–102.

[9] AGN, Padrones, 28, fol. 157–9.

[10] AGN, Historia, 73.

CHILAPA

[1] AGN, Indios, 6, 1a parte, fol. 179v.

[2] NL, Ayer MS 1121, fol. 130v.

[3] AGN, General de parte, I, fol. 34, 182v; Mercedes, 5, fol. 98v; Mercedes, 84, fol. 49.

[4] AGN, General de parte, II, fol. 43v, 166.

[5] AGN, *ibid.*, IV, fol. 158; V, fol. 80, 151v; VI, fol. 440v. Vázquez de Espinosa, 1948, pp. 266–7.

[6] AGN, Congregaciones, fol. 130.

[7] AGN, Mercedes, 4, fol. 54v.

[8] AGN, Indios, 6, 1a parte, fol. 179v, 284; 2a parte, fol. 8v; Tributos, 43, last exp. L de T, pp. 504–5.

[9] AGN, Indios, 6, 2a parte, fol. 278v.

[10] *Ibid.*, 1a parte, fol. 125; 2a parte, fol. 278v.

[11] AGN, Congregaciones, fol. 131.

[12] AGN, Indios, 6, 1a parte, fol. 179v.

[13] *Ibid.*, 2a parte, fol. 236v.

[14] AGI, Indiferente, 1529, fol. 176; México, 336, fol. 81v–82v.

[15] RAH, 9–25–4: 4663–XXXVI (pub. in PNE, v, pp. 174–82).

[16] AGN, Congregaciones, fol. 55–7.

[17] BNE, MS 6877, fol. 63–65v.

[18] AGN, Reales cédulas (duplicados), 9, 25, 42.

[19] *Ibid.*, 14, 28.

[20] AGI, Indiferente, 107, tomo I, fol. 118–34.

[21] AGI, México, 2578, 2580.

[22] BNE, MS 2450, fol. 259–64.

[23] AGN, Historia, 578, fol. 66–80v; Padrones, 16, fol. 108–212.

CHOLULA

[1] AGN, General de parte, I, fol. 173v, 222v, 228; II, fol. 30, 93v; IX, fol. 22; Mercedes, 84, fol. 36.

[2] AGN, Tributos, 43, last exp.

[3] AGI, México, 600.

[4] AGN, Mercedes, 84, fol. 35.

[5] UT, JGI XXIV–1; cf. McAndrew, p. 403.

[6] AGN, Indios, 6, 1a parte, fol. 138.

[7] BNE, MS 6877, fol. 46v.

[8] *Ibid.*, fol. 82.

[9] BNE, MS 4476.

[10] AGN, Reales cédulas (duplicados), 9, 25, 42.

[11] AGI, Indiferente, 107, tomo I, fol. 177–83, 208–46.

[12] AGN, Inquisición, 937.

[13] AGN, Intendentes, 48, fol. 11.

[14] AGN, Historia, 73.

GUACHINANGO

[1] NL, Ayer MS 1106 D, 3.
[2] AGI, Patronato, 182, ramo 44. ENE, xv, p. 212. L de T, p. 284. Scholes and Adams, 1959, p. 63.
[3] AGN, General de parte, I, fol. 35v, 67, 70, 101, 133v, 190v, 220v, 223, 243v; II, fol. 28; Indios, 2, fol. 170; Mercedes, 4, fol. 200, 377.
[4] NL, Ayer MS 1121, fol. 216v, 273.
[5] AGN, Indios, 1, fol. 148v.
[6] AGN, General de parte, II, fol. 32.
[7] AGN, Indios, 2, fol. 90.
[8] UT, JGI xxiv-5, fol. 12.
[9] BNP, Fonds mexicains, 113.
[10] AGI, Indiferente, 1529, *passim*; México, 336, fol. 32. PNE, III, pp. 94-5; v, pp. 219-23, 278-83.
[11] AGN, Congregaciones, fol. 128v; Indios, 6, 2a parte, fol. 235-235v, 277v; Mercedes, 84, fol. 206v.
[12] BNE, MS 3064, fol. 15-20v.
[13] BNE, MS 6877, fol. 36v-43v.
[14] BNE, MS 4476.
[15] AA, Visita (1683-5), fol. 83.
[16] AGN, Reales cédulas (duplicados), 9, 14, 25, 28, 42.
[17] AGI, Indiferente, 107, tomo I, fol. 397-401.
[18] AGI, México, 2580-1.
[19] BNE, MS 2449, fol. 245-51.
[20] AGN, Padrones, 18.
[21] AGN, Historia, 73.

GUANAXUATO

[1] BE, k-III-8.
[2] AGI, Patronato, 20, doc. 5, ramo 24. AGN, Mercedes, 5, fol. 32v, 39v, 44-45v, 109, 120v, 126; 84, fol. 61v, 97v. Jiménez Moreno, 1958, pp. 83, 94.
[3] AGN, Tributos, 43, last exp.
[4] NL, Ayer MS 1106 C, 3, fol. 132v.
[5] *Ibid.*, 1106 A, fol. 49-50v.
[6] AGI, Indiferente, 107, tomo I, fol. 360-395v.
[7] AGN, Inquisición, 937, fol. 270-1, 375-8.
[8] BNE, MS 2449, fol. 257-60.
[9] AGN, Historia, 72, fol. 169bis-174bis.
[10] AGN, Padrones, 30-3, 37, 42.

GUATULCO Y GUAMELULA

[1] NL, Ayer MS 1121, fol. 175v. Icaza, I, p. 119. Millares Carlo and Mantecón, I, no. 1246.
[2] NL, Ayer MS 1121, fol. 232v. Icaza, II, p. 300.
[3] AGI, Justicia, 113, doc. 5; Patronato, 182, ramo 40. L de T, p. 59.
[4] AGI, Justicia, 113. Icaza, I, p. 67.
[5] AGI, Justicia, 193, doc. 4; Patronato, 16, doc. 2, ramo 32. L de T, p. 227. *Nobiliario...*, p. 103.
[6] AGN, Mercedes, 3, fol. 231v, 236. NL, Ayer MS 1121, fol. 209v.
[7] AGN, Mercedes, 4, fol. 33v.
[8] AGN, General de parte, II, fol. 101.
[9] *Ibid.*, v, fol. 125.
[10] NL, Ayer MS 1121, fol. 125v.
[11] AGN, Tributos, 43, last exp.
[12] AGN, General de parte, IV, fol. 94v.
[13] AGN, Tierras, 413.
[14] AGN, Mercedes, 3, fol. 326; 4, fol. 60, 327; 5, fol. 84. NL, Ayer MS 1121, fol. 209v.

[15] AGN, Indios, 6, 2a parte, fol. 236v.
[16] Colección Castañeda Guzmán, MS.
[17] Viceroy to king, 25 May 1616, AGI, México, 28.
[18] AGN, Indios, 6, 1a parte, fol. 220v. Colección Castañeda Guzmán, MS.
[19] AGN, Congregaciones, fol. 118-118v; Indios, 6, 1a parte, fol. 220v; Tierras, 192.
[20] AGN, Tierras, 413 and 1442.
[21] AGI, México, 28-47, *passim*. Díez de la Calle, pp. 80-1. Robles, I, p. 193; II, pp. 105, 123. Vázquez de Espinosa, 1948, pp. 168-9.
[22] Bancroft Library, Mexican Manuscript 224. BNE, MS 2957.
[23] AGI, Indiferente, 107, tomo I, fol. 341.
[24] BNE, MS 2449, fol. 354-358v.
[25] AGN, Padrones, 12.
[26] Colección Castañeda Guzmán, MS Visita de Bergosa y Jordán. Cf. Pérez (1888), table at end.
[27] SMGE, MS 31 (727.2).

GUAUTITLAN

[1] AGI, México, 600. AGN, General de parte, II, fol. 38; Indios, 2, fol. 64, 66v; 6, 1a parte, fol. 182v; Mercedes, 4, fol. 133v; 5, fol. 50v. NL, Ayer MS 1121, fol. 270.
[2] AGN, Tributos, 43, last exp.
[3] AGI, México, 336 (pub. in PNE, III, pp. 32-40). Códice Franciscano, pp. 14-15. López de Velasco, p. 194.
[4] HS, HC, NS3/29/1.
[5] AGN, Congregaciones, fol. 11v, 65v, 74, 82v, 93, 94v, 102, 104, 105v, 107v, 113, 115v, 119v, 125, 127v; Indios, 6, 1a parte, fol. 143, 177v, 182v, 197.
[6] AGN, Reales cédulas (duplicados), 14, 28.
[7] AA, Visita (1683-5).
[8] AGN, Historia, 578, fol. 32-33v.
[9] AGN, Padrones, 4, fol. 239-48.

GUAXUAPA

[1] AGI, Patronato, 181, ramo 38. L de T, p. 203.
[2] AGN, Mercedes, 4, fol. 148. L de T, p. 534.
[3] AGN, General de parte, III, fol. 20v; Mercedes, 5, fol. 16.
[4] AGN, General de parte, I, fol. 44; II, fol. 132v.
[5] AGN, General de parte, I, fol. 139v, 149; II, fol. 89v, 303; IX, fol. 196.
[6] AGN, Indios, 6, 1a parte, fol. 74; Padrones, 12, fol. 261v; Reales cédulas (duplicados), 18.
[7] AGN, Padrones, 12, fol. 261v.
[8] AGN, Tributos, 43, last exp.
[9] AGI, México, 600.
[10] AGN, General de parte, I, fol. 127v, 156v.
[11] AGN, Congregaciones, fol. 86.
[12] AGN, Tierras, 3001, exp. 11.
[13] AGN, Congregaciones, fol. 73-73v.
[14] *Ibid.*, fol. 111v.
[15] AGN, Indios, 6, 2a parte, fol. 276.
[16] AGN, Congregaciones, fol. 7; Tierras, 3001, exp. 11.
[17] AGN, Historia, 578, fol. 238-243v.
[18] BNE, MS 6877, fol. 52v-57, 91v.
[19] AGN, Reales cédulas (duplicados), 9, 25, 42. Scholes and Adams, 1959, pp. 33-6.
[20] AGI, México, 2578, 2581.
[21] BNE, MS 2449, fol. 111-117v.
[22] SMGE, MS 31 (727.2).

GUAYACOCOTLA

1 AGN, Indios, 6, 1a parte, fol. 214. ENE, xv, p. 212. Icaza, I, p. 105.
2 AGI, Patronato, 182, ramo 44. AGN, Indios, 6, 2a parte, fol. 239v. ENE, xiii, pp. 37–8. Icaza, I, p. 191.
3 AGI, Justicia, 113, doc. 5. AGN, Indios, 6, 1a parte, fol. 214. Cortés, p. 471. ENE, xiii, p. 36; xv, p. 212.
4 AGN, General de parte, ii, fol. 184v, 216, 235v, 290; vi, fol. 302v; Indios, 6, 1a parte, fol. 81. NL, Ayer MS 1121, fol. 93v.
5 AGN, General de parte, ii, fol. 45; v, fol. 290.
6 AGN, Indios, 2, fol. 17v.
7 AGN, Mercedes, 84, fol. 29v. Gómez de Orozco.
8 AGN, Indios, 6, 1a parte, fol. 106, 173v, 214, 292v, 306v; 2a parte, fol. 170, 179v. NL, Ayer MS 1121, fol. 109.
9 AGN, Indios, 6, 2a parte, fol. 165–7.
10 AGN, Tierras, 64, exp. 2.
11 BNE, MS 6877, fol. 40v–41v.
12 BNE, MS 4476.
13 AA, Visita (1683–5), fol. 87–94.
14 AGN, Reales cédulas (duplicados), 9, 14, 25, 28, 42.
15 AGI, México, 2579, 2581.
16 AGN, Historia, 72, fol. 242–4.
17 AGN, Padrones, 12, fol. 1–33.
18 AGN, Historia, 73.

GUAYMEO Y SIRANDARO

1 AGI, Justicia, 130, fol. 961v; México, 28; Patronato, 182, ramo 40. NL, Ayer MS 1121, fol. 220v. AMM, 6, p. 45. Icaza, ii, p. 6.
2 AGI, Justicia, 130, fol. 961v. ENE, iv, p. 21. L de T, p. 190.
3 AGI, Justicia, 116, 130, 135, 148. Icaza, I, pp. 120, 136, 138, 221; ii, p. 10.
4 AGN, Mercedes, 3, fol. 343. NL, Ayer MS 1121, fol. 219.
5 AGN, Mercedes, 4, fol. 78v; 84, fol. 55.
6 AGN, General de parte, v, fol. 45v, 108v.
7 *Ibid.*, fol. 32.
8 AGN, Mercedes, 84, exp. 146. NL, Ayer MS 1121, fol. 220v. Romero (1860), pp. 77–8.
9 AGN, Tributos, 43, last exp.
10 AGN, Mercedes, 4, fol. 78v.
11 RAH, 9–25–4: 4663 – v (pub. in *Relaciones geográficas de . . . Michoacán*, I, pp. 61–82).
12 *Ibid.*, vii (pub. in *Relaciones geográficas de . . . Michoacán*, ii, pp. 38–50).
13 AGN, Congregaciones, fol. 2–3v, 39v–42, 68–68v; Indios, 6, 1a parte, fol. 171, 238v; 2a parte, fol. 276v; Tierras, 2926, exp. 7.
14 NL, Ayer MS 1106 C, 3, fol. 130.
15 *Ibid.*, 1106 A, fol. 68v–71.
16 AGN, Reales cédulas (duplicados), 24, 41, 42.
17 AGI, Indiferente, 107, tomo I, fol. 433–477v; tomo ii, fol. 160–162v.
18 AGN, Historia, 73, fol. 142–68.
19 *Ibid.*, 72, fol. 53v–54.

GUAZACUALCO

1 AGN, Mercedes, 3, fol. 291v.
2 AGN, General de parte, iii, fol. 242; Reales cédulas (duplicados), 24.
3 AGI, México, 600
4 AGN, General de parte, I, fol. 244v; Indios, 2, fol. 107.

5 AGN, Tributos, 43, last exp.
6 AGN, General de parte, iii, fol. 38, 175–6.
7 AGN, Indios, 6, 2a parte, fol. 236v.
8 UT, JGI xxiv-2.
9 AGN, Tierras, 2, exp. 11.
10 AGI, Indiferente, 107, tomo I, fol. 328–340v.
11 Archivo General de Simancas, Marina, 315. Cf. Béthencourt, 1958.
12 AGN, Inquisición, 937, fol. 278–84.
13 AGI, México, 2590.
14 BNE, MS 2450, fol. 209–16.
15 UT, WBS 320.
16 BNE, MS 2450, fol. 38–42v.

HUEXOCINGO

1 AGN, Hospital de Jesús, exp. 5.
2 AGN, General de parte, I, fol. 30v, 106v, 121–121v; Indios, 6, 1a parte, fol. 66v; 2a parte, fol. 84v; Mercedes, 11, fol. 51; 84, fol. 36.
3 AGN, Tributos, 43, last exp.
4 AGI, México, 600.
5 NL, Ayer MS 1121, fol. 98v.
6 AGN, Indios, 6, 2a parte, fol. 277.
7 BNP, Fonds mexicains, 387. Library of Congress, Harkness Collection, Mexican Doc. No. 1 (Codex Monteleone). MNA, MS 35–25 (Códice Chavero). Scholes and Adams, 1958, pp. 79–81; 1961, pp. 291–6).
8 AGN, Reales cédulas (duplicados), 9, 25, 42. Scholes and Adams, 1959, p. 47.
9 AGI, Indiferente, 107, tomo I, fol. 402–24.
10 AGN, Padrones, 27.
11 AGN, Historia, 73, fol. 102–4.

HUEXOLOTITLAN

1 AGI, Patronato, 16, doc. 2, ramo 32.
2 *Ibid.*, 182, doc. 40, fol. 318v.
3 AGN, Indios, 6, 2a parte, fol. 254v.
4 AGN, Tierras, 1874, exp. 5.
5 AGI, Indiferente, 107, tomo I, fol. 327–327v.
6 AGI, México, 2589.
7 BNE, MS 2449, fol. 253–6.
8 Colección Castañeda Guzmán, MS *Visita* de Bergosa y Jordán.
9 SMGE, MS 31 (727.2).

HUEXUTLA

1 AGN, Padrones, 12, fol. 255.
2 AGN, Reales cédulas (duplicados), 14, 28. Chipman, p. 292. Scholes and Adams (1959), p. 61.
3 AGN, Tributos, 43, last exp.
4 AGN, Indios, 6, 2a parte, fol. 226v, 235, 255–255v.
5 AA, Visita (1683–5), fol. 100v–104.
6 AGI, Indiferente, 107, tomo I, fol. 349–59.
7 AGN, Padrones, 3, fol. 373–416.
8 AGN, Historia, 578, fol. 81–84bis v.

IGUALA

1 AGN, Indios, 6, 1a parte, fol. 312. Icaza, ii, pp. 5, 8.
2 AGN, Mercedes, 4, fol. 346. NL, Ayer MS 1121, fol. 51.
3 AGN, General de parte, ii, fol. 60, 91.
4 AGI, México, 336, fol. 81–90.
5 UT, JGI xxiv-6 (pub. in Toussaint, 1931).
6 MNA, 35–76.

[7] AGN, Congregaciones, fol. 89, 110v, 130–2; Indios, 6, 1a parte, fol. 106v, 179v, 204v, 312.

[8] AGN, Reales cédulas (duplicados), 14, 28.

[9] AGN (?). This writer has a photographic copy, but the location of the original is unknown.

[10] AGN, Historia, 578, fol. 154–162v.

IGUALAPA

[1] AGN, Indios, 6, 2a parte, fol. 244v. Cf. Dorantes de Carranza, p. 193. L de T, p. 262. ENE, II, p. 31; XV, p. 14. Millares Carlo and Mantecón, I, no. 1743.

[2] AGN, Mercedes, 4, fol. 249v.

[3] *Ibid.*, 5, fol. 18, 21, 42v.

[4] AGN, General de parte, I, fol. 217; II, fol. 43v.

[5] AGI, México, 1973.

[6] AGN, General de parte, I fol. 202.

[7] AGN, Tributos, 43, last exp.

[8] AGN, Congregaciones, fol. 137–8; Indios, 2, fol. 3; 6, 2a parte, fol. 54, 235; Tierras, 48, exp. 6.

[9] UT, JGI xxIV-11.

[10] BNE, MS 6877, fol. 60v–61.

[11] AGN, Reales cédulas (duplicados), 9, 25, 42.

[12] AGI, México, 881.

[13] AGI, Indiferente, 107, tomo II, fol. 1–98.

[14] AGI, México, 2579, 2589.

[15] AGN, Historia, 578, fol. 85–8.

[16] *Ibid.*

[17] AGN, Padrones, 18, fol. 209–306.

[18] AGN, Historia, 578, fol. 89–93v.

ISCATEUPA

[1] AGN, Mercedes, 4, fol. 346. NL, Ayer MS 1121, fol. 136v. Cf. L de T, p. 595.

[2] AGN, Reales cédulas (duplicados), 24.

[3] AGI, México, 336, fol. 108–113v. López de Velasco, p. 206.

[4] AGN, Indios, 6, 1a parte, fol. 171, 210, 238v, 294, 319, 327; 2a parte, fol. 278; Tierras, 2680, exp. 21.

[5] AGN, Reales cédulas (duplicados), 14, 28.

[6] AA, Visita (1683–5).

[7] AHH, MS 391–3.

[8] BNE, MS 2449, fol. 361–3.

[9] AGN, Historia, 578, fol. 209v–212v.

[10] AGN, Padrones, 4 and 9.

IXMIQUILPAN

[1] AGI, Patronato, 181, ramo 38; 182, ramo 40.

[2] AGI, Patronato, 182, ramo 44.

[3] AGN, Mercedes, 3, fol. 31v; 4, fol. 122, 343v; 5, fol. 13. NL, Ayer MS 1121, fol. 40.

[4] AGN, Congregaciones, fol. 57v. Diccionario Porrúa, p. 441.

[5] AGN, Tributos, 43, last exp.

[6] AGN, Indios, 6, 1a parte, fol. 275; 2a parte, fol. 205, 276.

[7] AGN, Indiferente, 1529, fol. 202–202v. PNE, III, pp. 98–102.

[8] AGN, Reales cédulas (duplicados), 14, 28. Scholes and Adams (1959), pp. 57–8.

[9] AGI, Indiferente, 107, tomo II, fol. 103–59; Mapas y Planos (Méjico), 143.

[10] AGN, Padrones, 2.

[11] AGN, Historia, 578, fol. 130–3.

IZATLAN

[1] AGN, Mercedes, 3, fol. 292v. NL, Ayer MS 1121, fol. 97.

[2] AGN, General de parte, V, fol. 4v; Indios, 6, 2a parte, fol. 29, 64.

[3] AGN, Tributos, 43, last exp.

[4] AGN, Indios, 6, 2a parte, fol. 235v.

[5] AGN, Hospital de Jesús, 409, exp. 7; pub. in BAGN, VIII, pp. 558–60.

[6] AGI, Indiferente, 107, tomo I, fol. 320–326v.

[7] AGI, Guadalajara, 401.

[8] AGI, México, 1675.

[9] AGN, Historia, 72.

IZTEPEXI

[1] AGN, General de parte, I, fol. 100v. BAGN, I, p. 501.

[2] AGN, Tributos, 43, last exp.

[3] AGN, Tierras, 1874, exp. 7.

[4] AAN, Indios, 6, 2a parte, fol. 254v.

[5] AGI, Indiferente, 107, tomo I, fol. 184–185v.

[6] AGI, México, 2591.

[7] BNE, MS 2449, fol. 140–143v.

[8] SMGE, MS 31 (727.2).

IZUCAR

[1] AGN, Mercedes, 5, fol. 5v, 54, 76. L de T, pp. 20, 136.

[2] AGN, General de parte, VI, fol. 200.

[3] AGN, Padrones, 12, fol. 258v–259.

[4] AGN, Tributos, 43, last exp. L de T, pp. 22–6, 137, 451–2.

[5] AGN, General de parte, II, fol. 292; Indios, 2, fol. 71v.

[6] NL, Ayer MS 1121, fol. 30.

[7] AGN, Congregaciones, fol. 70, 93, 136v; Indios, 6, 2a parte, fol. 236v.

[8] BNE, MS 6877, fol. 45–6.

[9] AGN, Reales cédulas (duplicados), 9, 25, 42.

[10] BNE, MS 4476.

[11] AGI, Indiferente, 107, tomo II, fol. 99–102.

[12] AGN, Inquisición, 937, fol. 294–298v.

[13] AGI, México, 2579, 2580, 2581.

[14] AGN, Padrones, 28.

[15] AGN, Historia, 73, fol. 99–100.

JUSTLAGUACA

[1] We follow here an excerpt from the 1531 *Description de la tierra* which says of Poctla, 'Aqui tenia guarnicion Moctezuma y hacia la guerra a Tututepeque' (Herrera, 4a década, p. 230). Burgoa (1934a, I, p. 352) states that Poctla was within the domain of Tototépec, while the informants of 1580 intimate that Poctla was independent of both powers.

[2] AGI, Justicia, 113.

[3] AGI, Patronato, 181, ramo 38. AGN, Mercedes, 3, fol. 29v.

[4] AGN, Tierras, 39, 1a parte, exp. 1.

[5] AGN, General de parte, I, fol. 85; Indios, 2, fol. 78v; 5, fol. 267v; 6, 1a parte, fol. 289; Tierras, 43, exp. 2.

[6] HS, HC:417/132, exp. IV.

[7] AGI, México, 68. Alvarado, pp. 16–17.

[8] AGI, México, 881. AGN, Reales cédulas (duplicados), 14, fol. 678.

[9] AGN, Tributos, 43, last exp.

[10] HS, HC:417/132, exp. III.

[11] AGN, Indios, 2, fol. 21; Mercedes, 11, fol. 107.

[12] AGN, General de parte, I, fol. 237; Indios, 2, fol. 28v, 72.

[13] HS, HC:417/132, exp. IV.

[14] UT, JGI xxiv-11.
[15] AGN, Congregaciones, fol. 69; Indios, 6, 2a parte, fol. 241, 276. HS, HC:417/132.
[16] BNE, MS 6877, fol. 54v–55v.
[17] AGN, Reales cédulas (duplicados), 9, 25, 42.
[18] AGI, Indiferente, 107, tomo II, fol. 163–5.
[19] AGN, Historia, 69.
[20] AGI, México, 2581.
[21] BNE, MS 2450, fol 347–56.
[22] AGN, Historia, 72, fol. 69.
[23] Colección Castañeda Guzmán, MS Visita de Bergosa y Jordán. Cf. Pérez (1888), table at end.
[24] SMGE, MS 31 (727.2).

LEON

[1] BE, k-III-8. Cf. Jiménez Moreno (1958), pp. 63–4.
[2] AGI, Justicia, 130, fol. 962v.
[3] AGN, General de parte, II, fol. 63v. Powell, p. 153.
[4] AGN, Reales cédulas (duplicados), 24.
[5] AGN, Indios, 6, 1a parte, fol. 189v.
[6] AGN, Tributos, 43, last exp.
[7] AGN, Indios, 6, 2a parte, fol. 280v; Tierras, 2787, exp. 1.
[8] NL, Ayer MS 1106 C, 3, fol. 133.
[9] *Ibid.*, 1106 A, fol. 43–43v, 65–65v.
[10] AGI, Indiferente, 107, tomo II, fol. 166–173v.
[11] AGN, Historia, 72, fol. 169bis.
[12] AGN, Padrones, 41.

LERMA

[1] AGN, General de parte, I, fol. 209v; II, fol. 68, 119v; Mercedes, 11, fol. 71v.
[2] AGI, México, 600.
[3] AGN, Padrones, 12, fol. 251.
[4] AGN, Tributos, 43, last exp.
[5] AGI, México, 336, fol. 129.
[6] AGN, Indios, 6, 1a parte, fol. 120, 300v; 2a parte, fol. 277.
[7] AGN, Hospital de Jesús, 338, exp. 1. Cf. Salinas (1965), pp. 191–4.
[8] NL, Ayer MS 1106 D, 1.
[9] AA, Visita (1683–5).
[10] AGN, Reales cédulas (duplicados), 14, 28.
[11] AGI, Indiferente, 107, tomo II, fol. 174–193v.
[12] AGN, Padrones, 12, fol. 205–250v.
[13] AGN, Historia, 578, fol. 99–99v.

MALINALCO

[1] AGI, Patronato, 182, ramo 40, fol. 335v. Icaza, II, p. 284.
[2] AGN, Indios, 6, 1a parte, fol. 152v; Mercedes, 3, fol. 124. Dorantes de Carranza, pp. 230–1. Icaza, II, p. 14.
[3] AGI, Patronato, 182, ramo 44. Icaza, I, p. 80.
[4] AGN, Indios, 6, 1a parte, fol. 178v. Millares Carlo and Mantecón, I, nos. 886, 1058.
[5] NL, Ayer MS 1106 D, 3. Dorantes de Carranza, p. 205. ENE, IV, p. 23. L de T, p. 37.
[6] AGN, Indios, 6, 1a parte, fol. 348. NL, Ayer MS 1106 D, 3. Dorantes de Carranza, p. 160.
[7] AGN, General de parte, I, fol. 247v; II, fol. 156, 231, 253v; Mercedes, 11, fol. 11.
[8] NL, Ayer MS 1121, fol. 30v.
[9] AA, *Indice de Autos...*
[10] AGN, General de parte, I, fol. 238; Indios, 6, 1a parte, fol. 98v, 140.
[11] AGN, General de parte, II, fol. 151v, 168v.

[12] AGN, Tributos, 43, last exp.
[13] AGI, Indiferente, 1529, fol. 178; México, 336, fol. 131v–133v.
[14] AGN, Indios, 1, fol. 94, 97v.
[15] AGN, Congregaciones, fol. 63, 109v, 110v, 124; Indios, 6, 1a parte, fol. 124, 152v, 162v, 178–9, 202v, 242; 2a parte, fol. 276v.
[16] NL, Ayer 1106 D, 1.
[17] AA, Visita (1683–5).
[18] AGN, Reales cédulas (duplicados), 14, 28. Scholes and Adams, 1959, pp. 58–9, 63.
[19] AGI, Indiferente, 107, tomo II, fol. 281–332v.
[20] BNE, MS 2449, fol. 349–349v.
[21] *Ibid.*, fol. 351–353v, 360–360v; MS 2450, fol. 208.
[22] AGN, Historia, 578, fol. 100–11.

MARAVATIO

[1] AGI, Justicia, 130, 185. Chevalier, p. 92. Gibson, 1964, p. 429. Icaza, I, p. 189.
[2] AGI, Justicia, 130, fol. 968; Patronato, 182, ramo 40, fol. 336.
[3] AGI, Justicia, 135. Icaza, I, p. 66. L de T, p. 553.
[4] AGN, General de parte, I, fol. 50v, 180v; II, fol. 59v, 171v, 199v; Historia, 73, fol. 183; Mercedes, 11, fol. 29v. NL, Ayer MS 1121, fol. 167. Rodríguez Zetina, pp. 168–9. Títulos de Indias, p. 165.
[5] AGN, Tributos, 43, last exp.
[6] NL, Ayer MS 1121, fol. 114, 167.
[7] AGI, Patronato, 238, ramo 2, doc. 1 (pub. in Cline, 1965).
[8] AGN, Civil 853; Congregaciones, fol. 9v, 38v–39, 80, 82, 107v, 128; Indios, 6, 1a parte, fol, 173v, 200v, 202, 207v, 251, 296v; 2a parte, fol. 213v.
[9] NL, Ayer MS 1106 C, 3.
[10] *Ibid.*, 1106 A.
[11] AGN, Reales cédulas (duplicados), 24, 41–2.
[12] AGI, Indiferente, 107, tomo II, fol. 333–378v.
[13] AGN, Historia, 72, fol. 51–2.

METEPEC

[1] AGN, Indios, 6, 1a parte, fol. 121v.
[2] AGI, Patronato, 16, doc. 2, ramo 32. Cf. Scholes and Adams, 1961, p. 338.
[3] AGI, Justicia, 113, doc. 5.
[4] AGN, Hospital de Jesús, 265, exp. 5; Tierras, 1513, exp. 2. L de T, p. 236. Romero Q., 1963, pp. 49–51. Porras Muñoz, pp. 60–3.
[5] AGN, Mercedes, 3, fol. 305, 336; 4, fol. 106, 125, 159, 257v. NL, Ayer MS 1121, fol. 260v.
[6] AGN, Mercedes, 5, fol. 40v, 60; 84, fol. 82.
[7] AGI, México, 91.
[8] AGN, Reales cédulas (duplicados), 18.
[9] AGN, Padrones, 12, fol. 254. Títulos de Indias, *passim*.
[10] AGI, México, 100.
[11] AGN, Indios, 6, 1a parte, fol. 298v.
[12] AGN, Tributos, 43, last exp.
[13] AGN, Indios, 6, 1a parte, fol. 144.
[14] AGN, Indios, 1, fol. 94.
[15] AGN, Indios, 6, 1a parte, fol. 234.
[16] AGI, México, 336, fol. 126v–131, 134–135v. Códice Franciscano, p. 18.
[17] AGN, Congregaciones, 6, 13, 17, 27v–28v, 60, 61, 66v, 79, 80v, 85v–86, 92, 93v, 95v, 98–98v, 110, 115, 118v, 122v, 125v; Indios, 6, *passim*.

Notes

[18] AGN, Reales cédulas (duplicados), 14, 28. Scholes and Adams, 1959, p. 51.
[19] NL, Ayer MS 1106 D, 1.
[20] AA, Visita (1683–5).
[21] AGN, Inquisición, 937.
[22] AGN, Historia, 578, fol. 94–8, 112–113bis.

MEXICALCINGO

[1] NL, Ayer MS 1121, fol. 168.
[2] Letter of 15 Dec. 1580, AGI, México, 20.
[3] AGN, Tributos, 43, last exp.
[4] AGN, Indios, 6, 2a parte, fol. 255.
[5] AGI, México, 336, fol. 66–9; cf. García Pimentel, 1897, pp. 224–7.
[6] UT, JGI, XXIII-14.
[7] *Ibid.*, XXIV-8.
[8] This document is presumably in the parish archive; the first page is reproduced in *Boletín INAH*, VI, p. 3.
[9] AA, Visita (1683–5).
[10] AGN, Reales cédulas (duplicados), 14, 28.
[11] AGI, Indiferente, 107, tomo II, fol. 276–80.
[12] BNE, MS 20058.
[13] AGN, Historia, 578, fol. 114.

MEXICO

[1] AGN, Mercedes, 4, fol. 96.
[2] AGI, México, 100, 104.
[3] RAH, 9–62–2: 4795.
[4] Parochial information is contained in Gibson, 1964, pp. 372–6, and Vera, *passim*.
[5] Letter from Audiencia, n.d. (*c.* 1581), in AGI, México, 100. AGN, Tributos, 43, last exp.
[6] AGI, Indiferente, 1529, fol. 204; México, 336. Códice Franciscano, pp. 4–8.
[7] AA, Visita (1683–5).

MEZTITLAN

[1] AGN, General de parte, I, fol. 220.
[2] AGI, Patronato, 182, ramo 40, fol. 336v. Cf. Conway, 1943, p. 94.
[3] AGN, Mercedes, 3, fol. 266; 4, fol. 322v. NL, Ayer MS 1121, fol. 39, 93v.
[4] AGN, General de parte, I, fol. 195–6; Indios, 6, 1a parte, fol. 81.
[5] AGN, General de parte, VI, fol. 174v, 302v; Indios, 4, fol. 250v.
[6] NL, Ayer MS 1121, fol. 192.
[7] AGN, Tributos, 43, last exp.
[8] AGI, Indiferente, 1529, fol. 200; México, 336. Cf. García Pimentel, 1904, pp. 128–44. PNE, III, pp. 102–42.
[9] AGI, Patronato, 182, ramo 44.
[10] UT, JGI XXIV-12.
[11] AGN, Tierras, 64, exp. 6 (pub. in Simpson, 1934, pp. 86–91).
[12] AGN, Tierras, 70, 72, 74 (pub. in Simpson, 1934, pp. 92–108).
[13] AGN, Indios, 6, 1a parte, fol. 148v; 2a parte, fol. 235, 255, 277v.
[14] AGN, Reales cédulas (duplicados), 14, 28. Scholes and Adams, 1959, pp. 60, 65.
[15] AA, Visita (1683–5).
[16] AHH, MS 397–2.

MIAGUATLAN

[1] AGN, Indios, 6, 1a parte, fol. 94v.
[2] AGN, Tributos, 43, last exp.
[3] AGN, General de parte, VI, fol. 248v.
[4] AGI, Indiferente, 107, tomo II, fol. 272–275v.
[5] AGI, México, 2589, 2591.
[6] BNE, MS 2449, fol. 164–70, 374–378v.
[7] Colección Castañeda Guzmán, MS Visita de Bergosa y Jordán.
[8] SMGE, MS 31 (727.2).

MITLA Y TLACOLULA

[1] AGI, Patronato, 16, doc. 2, ramo 32.
[2] AGN, General de parte, VI, fol. 217.
[3] AGN, Reales cédulas (duplicados), 14, fol. 677v–678.
[4] AGN, Tributos, 43, last exp.
[5] AGN, Indios, 6, 2a parte, fol. 254v.
[6] BNE, MS 2450, fol. 160–3.
[7] *Ibid.*, fol. 224–6.
[8] AGI, México, 2590–1.
[9] Colección Castañeda Guzmán, MS Visita de Bergosa y Jordán.
[10] SMGE, MS 31 (727.2).

MOTINES

[1] AGI, Justicia, 130, fol. 961v.
[2] NL, Ayer MS 1121, fol. 313.
[3] AGI, México, 28.
[4] AGN, General de parte, I, fol. 13v, 19v. Brand, 1960, p. 68.
[5] AGN, Tierras, 2811, exp. 5.
[6] NL, Ayer MS 1121, fol. 339v. García Pimentel, 1904, pp. 57–9.
[7] AGN, Tributos, 43, exp. últ.
[8] NL, Ayer MS 1106 A, fol. 73.
[9] RAH, 9–25–4: 4663-IX.
[10] UT, JGI XXV-9.
[11] AGN, Congregaciones, fol. 81v; Indios, 6, 2a parte, fol. 237, 278v; Tierras, 2811, exp. 5.
[12] NL, Ayer MS 1106 C, 3, fol. 128v–129.
[13] *Ibid.*, 1106 A, fol. 72v–74.
[14] AGN, Reales cédulas (duplicados), 24, 41–2.
[15] BNE, MS 2450, fol. 372–389v.
[16] AGN, Historia, 73, fol. 169–82.
[17] BNE, MS 2449, fol. 382–383v.
[18] AGN, Padrones, 21, fol. 267–312v.
[19] AGN, Historia, 72, fol. 49v–50.
[20] AGN, Tierras, 1283, exp. 1.

NEXAPA

[1] AGN, Mercedes, 3, fol. 314–317v. Burgoa, 1934a, II, p. 147.
[2] AGI, Patronato, 16, doc. 2, ramo 32.
[3] AGN, Mercedes, 84, fol. 25v.
[4] *Ibid.*, 5, fol. 37, 98. BAGN, X, p. 295.
[5] AGN, Indios, 6, 1a parte, fol. 57v.
[6] AGN, General de parte, II, fol. 33.
[7] AGN, Historia, 523.
[8] AGN, Mercedes, 84, fol. 25v. Cuevas, 1946–7, II, p. 524.
[9] AGN, Tierras, 79, exp. 4.
[10] AGN, Tributos, 43, last exp.
[11] AGN, Tierras, 79, exp. 4.

12 AGN, Congregaciones, fol. 12, 68v, 71–72v, 90, 97, 118; Indios, 6, 2a parte, fol. 159, 236v.
13 AGI, México, 881, fol. 25v–32v; cf. Mapas y Planos (México), 104.
14 AGI, Indiferente, 107, tomo II, fol. 381–2.
15 AGI, México, 2590, 2591.
16 BNE, MS 2449, fol. 15–21v.
17 *Ibid.*, fol. 344–8.
18 BNM, MS 1762, fol. 168–81.
19 BNE, MS 2450, fol. 55–62.
20 *Ibid.*, fol. 71–84v, 91–102v.
21 *Ibid.*, fol. 86–90v.
22 BNM, MS 1762, fol. 154–67.
23 BNE, MS 2450, fol. 301–4.
24 *Ibid.*, fol. 357–60.
25 Colección Castañeda Guzmán, MS Visita de Bergosa y Jordán.
26 SMGE, MS 31 (727.2).

NOCHISTLAN

1 AGI, Patronato, 16, doc. 2, ramo 32.
2 AGN, General de parte, IV, fol. 9. L de T, pp. 167–8. Scholes and Adams, 1959, p. 33.
3 AGI, México, 28.
4 AGN, Mercedes, 4, fol. 80v–81.
5 AGI, México, 600.
6 Communication from Woodrow Borah.
7 AGN, Tributos, 43, last exp.
8 AGN, Indios, 6, 2a parte, fol. 242v.
9 *Ibid.*, fol. 254v.
10 *Ibid.*, fol. 152v.
11 UT, JGI XXIV-15, with map.
12 AGN, Tierras, 1520, exp. 2.
13 HS, HC:417/132.
14 BNE, MS 2449, fol. 224–230v.
15 BNE, MS 2450, fol. 322–327v.
16 AGI, México, 2591.
17 BNE, MS 2449, fol. 231–2.
18 *Ibid.*, fol. 391–397v.
19 Colección Castañeda Guzmán, MS Visita de Bergosa y Jordán. Cf. E. Pérez, 188 (table at end).
20 SMGE, MS 31 (727.2).

NOMBRE DE DIOS

1 AGI, Guadalajara, 5.
2 Letter from Orozco, Dec. 12, 1575, AGI, Guadalajara, 34. AGN, General de parte, II, fol. 86. Arregui, p. 140. Mecham, 1927*b*, p. 201.
3 AGI, Guadalajara, 55, exp. 8.
4 RAH, 9-25-4: 4662-VII, fol. 12v–14.
5 BNE, MS 3064, fol. 115–23.
6 BNE, MS 2449, fol. 398–406v.
7 AGI, Indiferente, 102.

ORIZABA

1 AGN, General de parte, I, fol. 10v, 93v, 214; II, fol. 99; V, fol. 85v, 201v; Indios, 2, fol. 4; 6, 1a parte, fol. 308v; Mercedes, 5, fol. 92.
2 AGN, Tributos, 43, last exp.
3 AGN, Indios, 6, 2a parte, fol. 236.
4 AGN, General de parte, II, fol. 106.
5 BNE, MS 6877, fol. 48v–50, 81–81v.

6 BNE, MS 4476.
7 AGN, Reales cédulas (duplicados), 9, 25, 42.
8 AGI, Indiferente, 107, tomo II, fol. 394–402.
9 AGN, Clero secular, 51, fol. 95.
10 AGI, México, 2579, 2580.
11 AGN, Padrones, 19, fol. 1–426v.

OTUMBA

1 AGI, Patronato, 17, ramo 17.
2 AGN, General de parte, I, fol. 14v, 102v.
3 AGN, Tributos, 43, last exp. ENE, VIII, p. 150.
4 AGI, México, 336, fol. 28v (pub. in PNE, III, p. 82). Códice Franciscano, p. 12.
5 AGN, Congregaciones, fol. 30v–34v.
6 AGN, Reales cédulas (duplicados), 14, 28.
7 AA, Visita (1683–5), fol. 52v–54.
8 AGN, Padrones, 12, fol. 142–204.
9 AGN, Historia, 578, fol. 115–18.

PACHUCA

1 AGI, México, 28. ENE, XV, p. 212. Icaza, I, p. 115. L de T, p. 4.
2 AGN, Mercedes, 4, fol. 122. NL, Ayer MS 1121, fol. 56.
3 AGN, Mercedes, 5, fol. 90v.
4 AGN, Padrones, 12, fol. 251–251v.
5 AGI, México, 600.
6 AGN, Padrones, 12, fol. 251.
7 AGN, Tributos, 43, last exp.
8 NL, Ayer MS 1121, fol. 49v. Wagner, 1942, p. 61.
9 AGN, Indios, 6, 1a parte, fol. 58v.
10 AGN, Congregaciones, fol. 5.
11 AGI, Indiferente, 1529, fol. 177; México, 336 (pub. in PNE, III, pp. 40–3, 73, 82). García Pimentel, 1897, pp. 53–6, 199–208.
12 BNE, MS 3064, fol. 91–97v.
13 AGN, Reales cédulas (duplicados), 14, 28. Scholes and Adams, 1959, p. 64.
14 AA, Visita (1683–5).
15 AGN, Inquisición, 937, fol. 299–303.
16 AGN, Padrones, 2, fol. 96.

PANUCO

1 AGI, México, 20. AHN, MS 244. ENE, V, p. 21.
2 AGI, México, 22; Patronato, 20, doc. 5, ramo 24. AGN, Mercedes, 4, fol. 34v, 312v. ENE, VII, p. 57. L de T, pp. 264, 333, 389.
3 AGN, General de parte, I, fol. 195, 237v, 243; VI, fol. 174v; Indios, 2, fol. 85.
4 AGN, General de parte, II, fol. 114.
5 AGI, México, 20, 103, 104.
6 AGI, México, 100. Velázquez, 1946–8, I, p. 288.
7 AGI, Patronato, 182, ramo 44. Scholes and Adams, 1959, p. 62.
8 AGN, Tributos, 43, last exp.
9 AGN, Congregaciones, fol. 69v; Indios, 6, 1a parte, fol. 285; 2a parte, fol. 235.
10 AGN, General de parte, II, fol. 61.
11 *Ibid.*, I, fol. 69v. ENE, XV, p. 217.
12 AGN, Indios, 2, fol. 110.
13 AGI, Patronato, 182, ramo 44. ENE, VII, pp. 27–8, 60–1; VIII, pp. 66–8; IX, pp. 55–88; XIV, pp. 32–9.
14 AGN, Congregaciones, fol. 69v. ENE, VII, p. 21.
15 AGI, Justicia, 234, fol. 722–831v, 857–902v.

[16] AGI, Indiferente, 1529, fol. 196; México, 336 (pub. in PNE, III, pp. 149–64).
[17] BNE, MS 3064, fol. 8, 23–50v.
[18] AGN, Reales cédulas (duplicados), 14, 28.
[19] AA, Visita (1683–5), fol. 105–18.
[20] AGI, Indiferente, 108, tomo IV, fol. 382–411v.
[21] UT, WBS 1394. Revilla Gigedo, p. 94.

PAPANTLA

[1] AGN, Congregaciones, fol. 139.
[2] AGI, Patronato, 182, ramo 40, fol. 352v. L de T, p. 217.
[3] AGN, Mercedes, 4, fol. 377.
[4] AGN, General de parte, I, fol. 55, 98, 128v; II, fol. 171v, 185, 256v.
[5] AGN, Congregaciones, fol. 139v.
[6] AGN, Tributos, last exp.
[7] AGN, Congregaciones, fol. 139v; Indios, 6, 2a parte, fol. 235v.
[8] AGN, General de parte, I, fol. 55.
[9] UT, JGI XXIV-5 (pub. in García Payón, 1965).
[10] AGN, Tierras, 24, exp. 4 (pub. in Simpson, 1934, pp. 79–85).
[11] BNE, MS 6877, fol. 34–36v.
[12] *Ibid.*, fol. 88–9.
[13] BNE, MS 4476.
[14] AGN, Reales cédulas (duplicados), 9, 25, 42.
[15] AGN, Tierras, 101, exp. 48.
[16] AGI, Indiferente, 108, tomo IV, fol. 430–432v.
[17] AGI, México, 2580.

PUEBLA

[1] AGN, General de parte, I, fol. 130v; Mercedes, 4, fol. 107, 108, 158; Mercedes, 84, fol. 79. ENE, II, pp. 225–35. Gibson, 1952, pp. 55, 67–8.
[2] Letter from viceroy, 19 Oct. 1577, AGI, México, 20. AGN, General de parte, I, fol. 4v, 130v; Mercedes, 3, fol. 250. NL, Ayer MS 1121, fol. 201. L de T, p. 371.
[3] AGN, Tributos, 43, last exp. UT, G-17.
[4] Códice Franciscano, pp. 20, 24. ENE, IV, pp. 137–8; XVI, p. 12.
[5] AGN, Reales cédulas (duplicados), 9, 25, 42; Tributos, 43, last exp. Scholes and Adams, 1959, p. 50.
[6] NL, Ayer MS 1121, fol. 198.
[7] AGN, General de parte, I, fol. 4v; Mercedes, 4, fol. 264, 288. ENE, X, p. 38.
[8] AGN, Indios, I, fol. 101v.
[9] AGN, Congregaciones, fol. 134; Indios, 6, 2a parte, fol. 277.
[10] BNE, MS 6877.
[11] BNE, MS 4476.
[12] AGI, Indiferente, 107, tomo I, fol. 1–50.
[13] AGI, México, 2578.
[14] AGN, Historia, 73.

QUERETARO

[1] AGN, Indios, 2, fol. 133.
[2] AGN, Mercedes, 3, fol. 298v; 5, fol. 13v. Jiménez Moreno, 1958, p. 83.
[3] AGN, General de parte, II, fol. 140, 300v, 302.
[4] AGN, Indios, 6, 1a parte, fol. 105.
[5] AGI, México, 600.
[6] AGI, México, 100.
[7] AGN, Tributos, 43, last exp.
[8] AGN, General de parte, II, fol. 302; Indios, 2, fol. 133; Indios, 6, 1a parte, fol. 85v, 162; 2a parte, fol. 276.

[9] UT, JGI XXIV-17; pub. in Velázquez, 1897–9, I.
[10] AGN, Reales cédulas (duplicados), 14, 28. Cf. Scholes and Adams, 1959, p. 50.
[11] AGI, Indiferente, 107, tomo I, fol. 52–98v. Cf. Villaseñor y Sánchez, I, pp. 90–5.
[12] AGN, Inquisición, 937, fol. 272–274v.
[13] AGN, Padrones, 12, fol. 117–41.
[14] AGN, Padrones, 35, 39, 40.
[15] AGN, Historia, 72, fol. 86–118; 578, fol. 135–43.
[16] BNE, MS 18636.

SAN CRISTOBAL ECATEPEC

[1] AGI, Patronato 182, ramo 40, fol. 305. Icaza, II, p. 310.
[2] AGI, Contaduría, 663-A. ENE, XVI, pp. 44–6.
[3] AGN, Mercedes, 4, fol. 128v, 333v; 5, fol. 90v.
[4] 'Traslado de ciertos mandamientos del virrey', Feb.–May 1562, AGI, México, 68.
[5] AGN, Tributos, 43, last exp.
[6] AGN, Mercedes, 3, fol. 49v.
[7] AGN, General de parte, I, fol. 77, 108v; II, fol. 262.
[8] AGI, Indiferente, 1529, fol. 205; México, 336, fol. 8v–9, 62–3. Cf. García Pimentel, 1897, p. 58. PNE, III, pp. 29–36, 40.
[9] HS, HC: NS3/29/1.
[10] AGN, Congregaciones, fol. 19, 39, 43, 64v, 67v, 78v, 83, 91, 99v, 100, 101v, 105v, 108, 114–114v, 119v, 120v, 126–7.
[11] AGN, Reales cédulas (duplicados), 14, 28. Scholes and Adams, 1959, p. 52.
[12] AA, Visita (1683–5).
[13] AGN, Padrones, 6, fol. 315–319v.

SAN JUAN DE LOS LLANOS

[1] NL, Ayer MS 1121, fol. 166. Dorantes de Carranza, pp. 169, 224. Icaza, I, p. 216; II, p. 157.
[2] AGI, Patronato, 182, ramo 40, fol. 364.
[3] AGN, Mercedes, 3, fol. 25v. NL, Ayer MS 1121, fol. 273–4. L de T, pp. 454–5, 521.
[4] AGN, General de parte, II, fol. 93, 101v, 103, 138v.
[5] AGN, Congregaciones, fol. 24, 109; General de parte, I, fol. 3v.
[6] AGI, México, 600.
[7] AGN, Tributos, 43, last exp.
[8] BNP, Fonds mexicains, 75 (pub. in Boban, II, p. 169 f.).
[9] AGN, Indios, 6, 2a parte, fol. 235v–236.
[10] AGN, Congregaciones, fol. 24, 109; Indios, 6, 2a parte, fol. 202v.
[11] BNE, MS 6877, fol. 8–11, 16v–17, 28v–30, 69, 75, 87v.
[12] AGN, Reales cédulas (duplicados), 9, 25, 42.
[13] BNE, MS 4476.
[14] AGI, México, 2578 through 2581.
[15] AGN, Padrones, 7.
[16] AGN, Historia, 73.

SAN LUIS DE LA PAZ

[1] BE, k-III-8, fol. 1v. NYPL, Beaumont MS, tomo 3, fol. 42. Jiménez Moreno, 1958, pp. 66–7.
[2] AGI, Contaduría, 663-A. L de T, p. 296.
[3] AGN, Mercedes, 4, fol. 179.
[4] AGN, General de parte, IV, fol. 46; V, fol. 111; Indios, 6, 1a parte, fol. 105.
[5] AGN, General de parte, V, fol. 45v, 204; Indios, 6, 1a parte, fol. 337v.

[6] AGN, Tributos, 43, last exp.
[7] NL, Ayer MS 1106 C, 3, fol. 131v–132v.
[8] Ibid., 1106 A, fol. 48v–49.
[9] AGI, Indiferente, 107, tomo II, fol. 204–271v. AGN, Historia, 522, fol. 96–99v.
[10] BNE, MS 2449, fol. 329–336v, 380–381v.
[11] AGN, Historia, 72, fol. 170bis.

SAN LUIS POTOSI

[1] BE, k-III-8. Jiménez Moreno, 1958, pp. 66, 86. Powell, p. 36.
[2] AGN, Tributos, 43, last exp.
[3] NL, Ayer MS 1106 C, 3, fol. 133v–134v.
[4] Ibid., 1106 A, fol. 45, 46v–48v.
[5] AGI, Indiferente, 107, tomo I, fol. 426–432v; tomo II, fol. 194–202v.
[6] BNE, MS 2449, fol. 239–241v. A more complete version of this document is found at BNP, Fonds mexicains, 202, fol. 23–33v.
[7] AGN, Historia, 72, fol. 66, 359–369v.
[8] UT, WBS 1394.

SAN MIGUEL EL GRANDE

[1] BE, k-III-8.
[2] AGN, Mercedes, 3, fol. 297v; 4, fol. 165, 281v, 282v; 5; fol. 32v, 44, 45v, 57v. Powell, p. 229.
[3] AGN, General de parte, v, fol. 204; Indios, 6, 2a parte, fol. 337v.
[4] AGN, Tributos, 43, last exp.
[5] UT, JGI XXIII-4, fol. 122 (pub. in García Pimentel, 1904, pp. 122–4).
[6] RAH, 9–25–4: 4663-XIII; reproduced in Jiménez Moreno, 1958, p. 90.
[7] NL, Ayer MS 1106 C, 3, fol. 131v–132, 133.
[8] Ibid., 1106 A, fol. 44v–45.
[9] BNM, MS 1762, fol. 60–87.
[10] AGN, Historia, 72, fol. 168v–169, 173v; Padrones, 24, 34, 36.

SAYULA

[1] AGI, Justicia, 130, fol. 972.
[2] AGN, Mercedes, 3, fol. 32v. NL, Ayer MS 1121, fol. 54v.
[3] AGN, General de parte, II, fol. 52v, 151, 228, 252.
[4] Letters of viceroy, 25 Dec. 1578 and 9 Apr. 1582, AGI, México, 20.
[5] AGN, Tributos, 43, last exp.
[6] AGN, Indios, 6, 2a parte, fol. 235v, 277v. Torres, p. 35.
[7] AGN, General de parte, I, fol. 153.
[8] AGN, Mercedes, 11, fol. 61v.
[9] Ibid., fol. 60.
[10] AGI, Indiferente, 108, tomo III, fol. 57–76.
[11] AGI, Guadalajara, 401.
[12] BNP, Fonds mexicains, 201, fol. 12–17 (Amacueca and Cocula). Biblioteca Pública del Estado de Jalisco, MS 50, tomo III (Atoyac; pub. in Noticias varias..., pp. 170–182).
[13] AGI, México, 1675, fol. 8v–9.
[14] BNE, MS 2450, fol. 136–141v.
[15] AGN, Historia, 72, fol. 205–9.

SOCHICOATLAN

[1] AGI, Patronato, 182, ramo 40, fol. 346. Conway, p. 94. L de T, p. 302.
[2] AGN, Indios, 6, 1a parte, fol. 253v. Chipman, 292.

[3] AGN, General de parte, I, fol. 195v.
[4] Ibid., VI, fol. 174v, 302v.
[5] AGN, Padrones, 12, fol. 254v–255. Títulos de Indias, p. 679.
[6] AGN, Congregaciones, fol. 80v.
[7] AGN, Tributos, 43, last exp.
[8] AGN, Indios, 6, 2a parte, fol. 235.
[9] Ibid., fol. 277v.
[10] AGN, Congregaciones, fol. 64–64v.
[11] UT, JGI XXIV-12.
[12] AGN, Reales cédulas (duplicados), 14, 28.
[13] AA, Visita (1683–5), fol. 95v–98, 153v.
[14] AGI, Indiferente, 108, tomo III, fol. 15–24.
[15] AGN, Historia, 578, fol. 196–202.

SOCHIMILCO

[1] AGN, Congregaciones, fol. 11.
[2] AGN, Tributos, 43, last exp.
[3] AGI, México, 24, ramo 1, AGN, Congregaciones, fol. 11, 57; Indios, 6, 2a parte, fol. 255.
[4] AGN, General de parte, I, fol. 31, 124v, 145.
[5] AGI, México, 336, fol. 69v–70.
[6] AGN, Reales cédulas (duplicados), 14, 28. Scholes and Adams, 1959, p. 43.
[7] NL, Ayer MS 1106 D, 1.
[8] AGN, Padrones, 29, fol. 3.
[9] AGN, Historia, 72, fol. 71–75v.
[10] AGN, Padrones, 29, fol. 4.
[11] AGN, Historia, 578, fol. 193–5.

TACUBA

[1] AGN, Hospital de Jesús, 265, exp. 5.
[2] AGN, Mercedes, 2, fol. 190.
[3] Ibid., 40, fol. 18v–22v.
[4] Letter from viceroy, 23 Feb. 1586, AGI, México, 20. AGN, Mercedes, 10, fol. 276–276v.
[5] AGN, General de parte, II, fol. 156; Padrones, 12, fol. 253.
[6] AGI, México, 100. Vera, pp. 110–11.
[7] AGN, Tributos, 43, last exp.
[8] AGI, México, 256, doc. 26 (cf. ENE, XIV, pp. 118–22).
[9] AGN, General de parte, II, fol. 67v, 231; Indios, 1, fol. 87, 117; Mercedes, 11, fol. 35v, 49.
[10] AGN, Indios, 6, 2a parte, fol. 255.
[11] AGN, Indios, 1, fol. 136; Mercedes, 11, fol. 5, 27v, 83v, 84v, 88.
[12] AGI, México, 336, fol. 9, 123–124v. Cf. Códice franciscano, pp. 8–9, 15.
[13] AGN, Congregaciones, fol. 46, 47v, 74v, 112v, 121; Indios, 6, 1a parte, fol. 127v, 141v–142, 178, 208v; 2a parte, fol. 228v, 255.
[14] NL, Ayer MS 1106 D, 1.
[15] AA, Visita (1683–5).
[16] AGN, Reales cédulas (duplicados), 14, 28.
[17] BNE, MS 3650.
[18] AGN, Padrones, 6, fol. 145–301.
[19] AGN, Historia, 578, fol. 144–153v.

TANCITARO

[1] AGI, Justicia, 130, fol. 962. Icaza, I, p. 116.
[2] Ibid., fol. 968–969.
[3] Ibid., fol. 962, 967–967v, 971.
[4] AGN, Indios, 2, fol. 143v.
[5] AGN, Tributos, 43, last exp.

[6] AGN, Indios, 6, 2a parte, fol. 271–271v.

[7] UT, JGI XXIII-5; pub. in García Pimentel, 1904, pp. 38, 40. Miranda Godínez, 9/40.

[8] UT, JGI XXIV-18; pub. in *Tlalocan*, III, pp. 205–35, with useful notes.

[9] NL, Ayer MS 1106 C, 3, fol. 126v.

[10] *Ibid.*, 1106 A, fol. 72–72v.

[11] AGN, Reales cédulas (duplicados), 24, 41, 42.

[12] AGI, Indiferente, 108, tomo IV, fol. 86–101.

[13] AGN, Historia, 73, fol. 371–91.

[14] *Ibid.*, 72, fol. 53–53v.

TASCO

[1] AGN, Mercedes, 1.

[2] AGN, General de parte, 1, fol. 143.

[3] AGI, México, 100.

[4] AGN, Tributos, 43, last exp.

[5] AGI, México, 336, fol. 92v–107v; defectively published in García Pimentel (1897), pp. 121–33, 170–184.

[6] AGN, Indios, 6, 1a parte, fol. 195v, 285v, 298v–299v, 327; 2a parte, fol. 278; Tierras, 2754, exp. 3.

[7] AGN, Reales cédulas (duplicados), 14, 28.

[8] AA, Visita (1683–5).

[9] AGN, Historia, 578, fol. 154–162v.

TECALI

[1] AGN, Tributos, 43, last exp.

[2] AGN, Mercedes, 4, fol. 117, 132v.

[3] AGI, México, 600. AGN, Reales cédulas (duplicados), 25, 42.

[4] AGN, Indios, 6, 1a parte, fol. 338v.

[5] AGN, Reales cédulas (duplicados), 9, 25, 42; Tributos, 43, last exp.

[6] BNE, MS 6877, fol. 47–47v, 77, 90v.

[7] BNE, MS 4476.

[8] AGI, Indiferente, 108, tomo III, fol. 157–87.

[9] AGI, México, 2581.

[10] AGN, Historia, 73, fol. 109–10.

TECIUTLAN Y ATEMPA

[1] AGN, General de parte, 1, fol. 190; II, fol. 82; Mercedes, 3, fol. 25v; 4, fol. 152v. NL, Ayer MS 1121, fol. 273–4.

[2] AGN, Tributos, 43, last exp.

[3] AGN, Indios, 6, 2a parte, fol. 235v.

[4] BNE, MS 6877, fol. 11.

[5] BNE, MS 4476.

[6] AGN, Reales cédulas (duplicados), 9, 25, 42.

[7] AGI, Indiferente, 108, tomo III, fol. 244–308v.

[8] AGN, Padrones, 2, fol. 263.

[9] AGN, Historia, 73, fol. 115–115v.

TECUICUILCO

[1] NL, Ayer MS 1106 D, 3. Icaza, I, p. 252.

[2] AGN, General de parte, II, fol. 120.

[3] AGN, Reales cédulas (duplicados), 10, fol. 95.

[4] AGN, Tributos, 43, last exp. Cook and Borah (1968), p. 77. L de T, pp. 428–31. Miranda (1968).

[5] UT, JGI XXIV-19.

[6] AGN, Congregaciones, fol. 30; Tierras, 64, exp. 4.

[7] AGI, Indiferente, 108, tomo III, fol. 84–84v.

[8] AGI, México, 2591.

[9] BNE, MS 2450, fol. 219–222v.

[10] Colección Castañeda Guzmán, MS Visita de Bergosa y Jordán.

[11] SMGE, MS 31 (727.2).

TEGUACAN

[1] AGN, General de parte, 1, fol. 244v. Dorantes de Carranza, p. 206. L de T, pp. 180–1.

[2] AGI, México, 28. Boyd-Bowman, II, no. 7424. Icaza, I, p. 187; II, p. 67. L de T, p. 386.

[3] AGN, General de parte, 1, fol. 244v; II, fol. 43v, 59, 83; Mercedes, 4, fol. 25v, 265.

[4] AGN, General de parte, IV, fol. 29v, 159; VII, fol. 154v.

[5] *Ibid.*, 1, fol. 188.

[6] AGN, Tributos, 43, last exp.

[7] AGN, Indios, 6, 2a parte, fol. 277.

[8] AGN, General de parte, 1, fol. 181v, 188. Cf. *Plano de los límites...* (1905), which shows a disputed area between Puebla and Oaxaca, running from the Hondo (Calapa) to the Jiquilina (Juquila) rivers, with 'Despoblado de S Gerónimo Juquila' on the south bank of the latter.

[9] AGN, Indios, 2, fol. 65–65v. L de T, p. 611.

[10] AGI, Indiferente, 1529, no. 383 (pub. in PNE, v, pp. 46–54). There is an unpublished copy at UT, JGI XXIII-15.

[11] AGN, Congregaciones, fol. 7v.

[12] BNE, MS 6877, fol. 48–53.

[13] BNE, MS 4476.

[14] AGN, Reales cédulas (duplicados), 9, 25, 42. Scholes and Adams, 1959, p. 49.

[15] DA, exp. 276.1/655.

[16] AGI, México, 2578, 2579, 2580.

[17] BNE, MS 2449, fol. 105–110v, 199–206v, 234–8.

[18] AGN, Padrones, 3.

[19] AGN, Historia, 73, fol. 96v–98.

TEGUANTEPEC

[1] AGI, Patronato, 16, doc. 2, ramo 32.

[2] AGI, Justicia, 113, doc. 5. AGN, Hospital de Jesús, 265, exp. 5. ENE, I, p. 141. Cf. Gardiner (1955).

[3] AGI, Patronato, 16, doc. 2, ramo 32.

[4] AGN, Mercedes, 4, fol. 141, 143.

[5] AGN, Reales cédulas (duplicados), 14, fol. 678.

[6] AGN, Tributos, 43, last exp. Cook and Borah, 1968, p. 77. Scholes and Adams, 1959, p. 37.

[7] AGN, Hospital de Jesús, 272.

[8] UT, JGI XXV-4.

[9] AGN, Congregaciones, fol. 83v, 85; Indios, 6, 2a parte, fol. 236v.

[10] AGI, México, 2591.

[11] BNE, MS 2449, fol. 279–83.

[12] *Ibid.*, fol. 216–219v. AGI, México, 2590.

[13] Colección Castañeda Guzmán, MS Visita de Bergosa y Jordán.

[14] SMGE, MS 31 (727.2), v.

TEMAZCALTEPEC Y ZULTEPEC

[1] AGI, Justicia, 188. AGN, Mercedes, 59, fol. 195v. Icaza, I, p. 227; II, p. 67. Scholes and Adams, 1961, pp. 134–6.

[2] AGN, Mercedes, 3, fol. 271v; 4, fol. 233v. NL, Ayer MS 1121, fol. 194. Gómez de Cervantes, pp. 35–6.

[3] AGN, Mercedes, 5, fol. 54; 84, fol. 105v.

[4] AGN, General de parte, 1, fol. 13v, 211; II, fol. 152v, 192v.

[5] AGN, Congregaciones, fol. 132. Vera, p. 76.

6 AA, Autos...

7 AGN, Tributos, 43, last exp.

8 AGN, Congregaciones, fol. 132–133v, 138.

9 AGN, Tributos, 43, last exp.

10 AGI, México, 336, fol. 136–138v. Cf. García Pimentel, 1897, pp. 214, 220, 254, which seems to have come from another MS.

11 AGN, Reales cédulas (duplicados), 14, 28.

12 AA, Visita (1683–5).

13 AGI, Indiferente, 108, tomo III, fol. 309–38.

14 AGN, Inquisición, 937, fol. 265–8.

TENANGO DEL VALLE

1 AGI, Patronato, 16, doc. 2, ramo 32. AGN, Hospital de Jesús, 265, exp. 5; Tierras, 1513, exp. 2.

2 AGI, Justicia, 113, doc. 5. Icaza, II, p. 9. L de T, pp. 79–81.

3 AGI, Justicia, 130. Library of Congress, Harkness Collection, Mexican Doc. No. 9. BAGN, VI, p. 364. Dorantes de Carranza, pp. 278, 284.

4 AGI, Justicia, 113, doc. 5; México, 28. AGN, Congregaciones, fol. 6v.

5 AGN, General de parte, VI, fol. 330, 335v.

6 AGN, Padrones, 12, fol. 251. Títulos de Indias.

7 AGI, Patronato, 182, ramo 44.

8 AGI, México, 100.

9 AGN, Inquisición, 937, fol. 317.

10 AGN, Tributos, 43, last exp.

11 AGN, General de parte, I, fol. 6; Indios, 1, fol. 88, 97; Mercedes, 84, fol. 118, 128.

12 AGI, México, 336, fol. 128v–129v, 130–131v, 133–134v. Variant reports of 1569–70 are found in Códice Franciscano, p. 18; García Pimentel, 1897, pp. 112, 161–3, 228–32; Vera, *passim.*

13 UT, JGI XXIII–13.

14 AGI, México, 665. AGN, Congregaciones and Indios, 6, *passim.*

15 NL, Ayer MS 1106 D, 1.

16 AA, Visita (1683–5).

17 AGN, Reales cédulas (duplicados), 14, 28.

18 BNE, MS 2449, fol. 84–87v.

19 BNE, MS 2450, fol. 208.

TEOTIGUACAN

1 AGN, General de parte, II, fol. 198v–199; Mercedes, 3, fol. 312v. Gibson, 1964, pp. 444–5. L de T, p. 627.

2 AGN, Tributos, 43, last exp.

3 AGI, Indiferente, 1529, fol. 205–6; México, 336, fol. 62–63v. Códice franciscano, p. 12.

4 AGN, Congregaciones, fol. 5, 8v, 67v, 86v, 117v, 129v; Indios, 6, 2a parte, fol. 255.

5 AA, Visita (1683–5), fol. 48–51v.

6 AGI, Indiferente, 108, tomo III, fol. 209–27.

7 AGN, Padrones, 18, fol. 307.

8 AGN, Historia, 578, fol. 182–182v.

TEOZACUALCO

1 AGI, México, 91. Icaza, I, p. 14. L de T, pp. 462, 551.

2 AGI, Justicia, 113, doc. 5. Dorantes de Carranza, p. 228.

3 AGN, Mercedes, 4, fol. 81.

4 AGI, México, 600. Títulos de Indias, p. 218.

5 AGN, General de parte, I, fol. 80v, 210.

6 AGN, Indios, 6, 2a parte, fol. 276v.

7 *Ibid.*

8 UT, JGI XXV–3.

9 AGI, Indiferente, 108, tomo III, fol. 84–84v.

10 BNE, MS 2450, fol. 227–232v.

11 AGI, México, 2591.

12 Colección Castañeda Guzmán, MS Visita de Bergosa y Jordán.

13 SMGE, MS 31 (727.2).

TEPEACA

1 AGI, México, 91. ENE, III, pp. 28–9; XV, p. 90; XVI, p. 11.

2 AGN, Mercedes, 3, fol. 336v; 4, fol. 12, 34, 107, 117, 132v, 185v, 229, 260v; 84, fol. 66v. NL, Ayer MS 1121, fol. 64, 93, 249v.

3 AGN, General de parte, II, fol. 197v; IV, fol. 13v; Mercedes, 11, fol. 89.

4 AGN, Tributos, 43, last exp.

5 NL, Ayer MS 1121, fol. 136v.

6 AGN, Indios, 6, 2a parte, fol. 277.

7 NL, Ayer MS 1121, fol. 136v ff.

8 BNE, MS 6877, fol. 7v, 47v–48, 66–9, 77–77v.

9 BNE, MS 4476.

10 AGN, Reales cédulas (duplicados), 9, 25, 42. Scholes and Adams, 1959, p. 48.

11 AGI, Indiferente, 108, tomo III, fol. 127–40.

12 AGI, México, 2578–81.

13 BNE, MS 2449, fol. 22–5.

14 AGN, Padrones, 38.

15 AGN, Historia, 73, fol. 116–122v.

TEPEXI DE LA SEDA

1 AGN, Tributos, 43, last exp.

2 AGN, General de parte, I, fol. 150v; Indios, 2, fol. 76, 97v; 6, 2a parte, fol. 5, 156v.

3 AGN, Mercedes, 11, fol. 42. Cf. Cook de Leonard, 1952–3, p. 426.

4 AGN, Congregaciones, fol. 21v–22; Indios, 6, 2a parte, fol. 237.

5 AGN, General de parte, II, fol. 34.

6 AGI, Indiferente, 1529, fol. 220 (pub. in PNE, V, p. 284).

7 UT, JGI XXIV–6.

8 BNE, MS 6877, fol. 65–65v, 90v–91v.

9 AGN, Reales cédulas (duplicados), 9, 25, 42. Scholes and Adams, 1959, pp. 31, 60.

10 AGI, México, 2578–9.

11 AGN, Historia, 73, fol. 23v–24.

TEPOSCOLULA

1 AGI, Justicia, 113. L de T, pp. 13–15.

2 AGN, General de parte, II, fol. 48v. L de T, p. 151.

3 AGI, México, 285.

4 AGI, México, 28. Icaza, I, p. 253.

5 AGN, General de parte, I, fol. 169v.

6 AGN, Mercedes, 4, fol. 81.

7 *Ibid.*, fol. 80v.

8 AGN, General de parte, II, fol. 48v.

9 Personal communication from Woodrow Borah.

10 AGI, México, 68.

11 AGN, General de parte, III, fol. 156v.

12 AGN, Tierras, 1520, exp. 2.

13 AGN, Tributos, 43, last exp.

14 AGN, Indios, 2, fol. 173.

15 AGN, General de parte, I, fol. 100, 119v, 147; Indios, 1, fol. 11; 2, fol. 4v, 103, 241; Mercedes, 11, fol. 206v.

¹⁶ AGN, Indios, 6, 2a parte, fol. 242v.
¹⁷ AGN, General de parte, II, fol. 179; Indios, 2, fol. 188; 3, fol. 40v.
¹⁸ AGN, Indios, 2, fol. 30; 3, fol. 40. HS, HC: 417/132.
¹⁹ AGN, General de parte, III, fol. 55; Mercedes, 11, fol. 122v.
²⁰ AGN, Indios, 3, fol. 61v.
²¹ AGN, Congregaciones, fol. 51–3, 92–92v, 116v–117; General de parte, I, fol. 136v; II, fol. 131v; Indios, 6, 2a parte, fol. 25v, 276v.
²² AGN, General de parte, I, fol. 169v; Mercedes, 11, fol. 210. Scholes and Adams, 1959, p. 36.
²³ AGN, Indios, 2, fol. 9, 85, 236v; Tierras, 34, exp. 1. Cf. Spores, 1967, p. 40.
²⁴ NL, Ayer MS 1121, fol. 195v.
²⁵ AGN, Indios, 6, 2a parte, fol. 276v.
²⁶ HS, HC: 417/132, 417/209.
²⁷ AGN, Indios, 2, fol. 199v, 231; 6, 2a parte, fol. 242v; Tierras, 400, exp. 1. Scholes and Adams, 1959, p. 42.
²⁸ AGN, General de parte, II, fol. 207v; Indios, 2, fol. 138.
²⁹ AGI, Escribanía de cámara, 162, fol. 307v. AGN, Civil, 516; Tierras, 985.
³⁰ AGN, Indios, 2, fol. 180v, 184; 3, fol. 27v; Tierras, 400, exp. 1. NL, Ayer MS 1121, fol. 108.
³¹ AGN, General de parte, III, fol. 156v–157; Indios, 2, fol. 93v, 119; 3, fol. 25v; Tierras, 655, exp. 2.
³² AGN, Indios, 6, 2a parte, fol. 277v; Tierras, 1520, exp. 2.
³³ AGN, Congregaciones, fol. 22–23v.
³⁴ *Ibid.*, fol. 51–3.
³⁵ *Ibid.*, fol. 36, 65, 92, 92v, 101, 116v, 117, 123v; Tierras, 1520, exp. 2. HS, HC: 417/132.
³⁶ AGI, Indiferente, 108, tomo III, fol. 77–83v.
³⁷ BNE, MS 2450, fol. 237–245v.
³⁸ BNE, MS 2449, fol. 180–193v.
³⁹ *Ibid.*, fol. 119–120v, 132–138v.
⁴⁰ BNE, MS 2450, fol. 246–51.
⁴¹ *Ibid.*, fol. 203–7 (with map).
⁴² AGI, México, 2589, 2590, 2591.
⁴³ BNE, MS 2450, fol. 297–300v.
⁴⁴ Colección Castañeda Guzmán, MS Visita de Bergosa y Jordán.
⁴⁵ SMGE, MS 31 (727.2).
⁴⁶ UT, G-398.

TETELA DEL RIO

¹ AGI, Justicia, 130, fol. 961v. L de T, p. 60.
² AGI, Justicia, 130, fol. 961v.
³ Library of Congress, Harkness Collection, Mexican Doc. No. 9.
⁴ AGN, Indios, 6, 1a parte, fol. 228. BAGN, X, p. 246. Icaza, I, p. 216.
⁵ AGN, Mercedes, 3, fol. 343; 4, fol. 78v. NL, Ayer MS 1121, fol. 219, 220.
⁶ AGN, General de parte, I, fol. 58.
⁷ *Ibid.*, V, fol. 32.
⁸ AGN, Mercedes, 3, fol. 108v; 84, fol. 55. Cf. PNE, VI, pp. 131–2.
⁹ AGN, Indios, 2, fol. 7v–8v.
¹⁰ AGN, Tributos, 43, last exp.
¹¹ AGI, México, 336, fol. 111–115v.
¹² RAH, 9-25-4: 4663 – v (pub. in *Relaciones geográficas... Michoacán*, I, pp. 61–82).
¹³ AGN, Congregaciones, fol. 39v; Indios, 6, 1a parte, fol. 171, 228, 238v, 294; 2a parte, fol. 276v.

¹⁴ NL, Ayer MS 1106 C, 3, fol. 130.
¹⁵ *Ibid.*, 1106 A, fol. 68v–71.
¹⁶ AGN, Reales cédulas (duplicados), 14, 28.
¹⁷ *Ibid.*, 24, 41, 42.
¹⁸ AGI, Indiferente, 108, tomo III, fol. 340–431.
¹⁹ AGN, Historia, 578, fol. 163–167v.

TETELA DEL VOLCAN

¹ AGI, Patronato, 182, ramo 40, fol. 358. ENE, IX, p. 26; X, pp. 248–9. García Icazbalceta, p. 108. Cf. Martínez Marín, pp. 30–1.
² NL, Ayer MS 1121, fol. 248v. Grijalva, p. 66.
³ AGN, Tributos, 43, last exp. Cf. Martínez Marín, pp. 191–4.
⁴ AGI, Patronato, 180, ramo 65. Cf. Gerhard, 1970.
⁵ AGI, México, 336, fol. 73.
⁶ BNP, Fonds mexicains, 25 (pub. in Boban, 1891, I, pp. 381–2; Atlas, planche 25).
⁷ AGN, Reales cédulas (duplicados), 14, 24, 28.
⁸ AGI, Indiferente, 108, tomo III, fol. 93–6, 445–9.
⁹ AGN, Padrones, 8.

TETEPANGO HUEYPUSTLA

¹ AGN, Mercedes, 4, fol. 348. L de T, p. 66.
² AGN, Mercedes, 5, fol. 70.
³ AGN, General de parte, I, fol. 4, 157v, 181; II, fol. 286v; Mercedes, 84, fol. 117v.
⁴ AGN, Indios, 5, fol. 322; 6, 2a parte, fol. 242v.
⁵ AGN, Alcaldes mayores, II, fol. 85; Indios, 6, 1a parte, fol. 290; Padrones, 12, fol. 253v.
⁶ AGN, Congregaciones, fol. 57v. Vera, pp. 32, 92, 109.
⁷ AGN, Tributos, 43, last exp.
⁸ AGI, Indiferente, 1529, fol. 203–207v; México, 336 (cf PNE, III, pp. 47–9, 52–9, 63–4, 66–72). Vera, *passim*. Códice franciscano, p. 16).
⁹ UT, JGI XXIII-12.
¹⁰ AGN, Congregaciones, fol. 57v; Indios, 6, 1a parte, fol. 58v, 109, 197v–198, 290; 2a parte, fol. 10v, 181, 276, 277v; Tierras, 64, doc. 1.
¹¹ AGN, Reales cédulas (duplicados), 14, 28. Cf. Scholes and Adams, 1959, p. 51.
¹² AGN, Padrones, 18, fol. 1–115.
¹³ AGN, Historia, 578, fol. 184–185v.

TEUTILA

¹ AGI, Patronato, 17, ramo 17.
² AGN, General de parte, II, fol. 117, 120.
³ *Ibid.*, I, fol. 22.
⁴ AGN, Mercedes, 84, fol. 85.
⁵ *Ibid.*, 4, fol. 28. NL, Ayer MS 1121, fol. 46.
⁶ AGN, Mercedes, 4, fol. 136.
⁷ AGN, General de parte, I, fol. 103; II, fol. 112v, 207v; Indios, 2, fol. 110v; Mercedes, 4, fol. 227, 384v; 84, fol. 41.
⁸ AGN, Mercedes, 5, fol. 38v, 92; 84, fol. 80, 85.
⁹ AGN, General de parte, I, fol. 22v; II, fol. 120; Indios, 2, fol. 17v–18; 6, 2a parte, fol. 136; Mercedes, 11, fol. 38.
¹⁰ AGN, Indios, 4, fol. 224v; Padrones, 12, fol. 257v. Títulos de Indias, p. 157.
¹¹ AGI, México, 68. ENE, IX, p. 46.
¹² AGN, Indios, 2, fol. 17v, 106v. Burgoa, 1934a, I, p. 373.
¹³ AGI, México, 881. AGN, Indios, 2, fol. 63; 6, 2a parte, fol. 227; Reales cédulas (duplicados), 14, fol. 678.

14 AGN, Indios, 6, 1a parte, fol. 37v; Tributos, 43, last exp. Cook and Borah, 1968, p. 77.
15 NL, Ayer MS 1121, fol. 210–210v.
16 AGN, Tierras, 70, exp. 1.
17 AGN, Indios, 6, 2a parte, fol. 227, 242v, 278v.
18 AGN, Reales cédulas (duplicados), 10, fol. 95. Miranda, 1962a, p. 188.
19 AGI, Indiferente, 107, tomo I, fol. 277v–80.
20 BNE, MS 2449, fol. 94–104v.
21 AGI, México, 2589, 2591.
22 Colección Castañeda Guzmán, MS Visita de Bergosa y Jordán.
23 SMGE, MS 31 (727.2).

TEUTITLAN DEL CAMINO

1 AGI, México, 256, doc. 26 (published defectively in ENE, XIV, pp. 118–22).
2 AGI, Justicia, 116, 119. ENE, I, p. 77; VI, p. 58. Cf. Gay, I, p. 399. Nobiliario..., p. 127.
3 AGN, General de parte, I, fol. 40v; III, fol. 36.
4 AGI, México, 91. L de T, p. 405.
5 AGN, General de parte, I, fol. 40v–41; II, fol. 60v; Indios, 2, fol. 18, 181, 201v; 3, fol. 61v; Mercedes, 4, fol. 136, 209v, 374v. NL, Ayer MS 1121, fol. 185v, 210–210v.
6 AGN, Indios, 2, fol. 227; 6, 2a parte, fol. 99.
7 AGN, General de parte, IV, fol. 6v; Indios, 3, fol. 7.
8 AGN, Mercedes, 84, fol. 81.
9 AGI, México, 285; letter from Alburquerque, 27 March 1574.
10 AGN, Tributos, 43, last exp.
11 AGN, General de parte, II, fol. 60v, 80; Indios, 3, fol. 61v. DA, 276.1/199. Cf. Miranda (1968), p. 144.
12 AGN, General de parte, I, fol. 181v, 188. Cf. 'Plano de los límites...1905'.
13 NL, Ayer MS 1121, fol. 89.
14 UT, JGI XXIV-7.
15 BNP, Fonds mexicains, 103.
16 AGN, Indios, 6, 2a parte, fol. 278v.
17 AGI, México, 2591.
18 BNE, MS 2450, fol. 1–3v.
19 BNE, MS 2449, fol. 207–210v.
20 Ibid., fol. 180–193v.
21 BNE, MS 2450, fol. 44–5.
22 Ibid., fol. 255–8.
23 Colección Castañeda Guzmán, MS Visita de Bergosa y Jordán. Cf. Pérez, 1888, table at end.
24 SMGE, MS 31 (727.2).

TEUTLALCO

1 AGI, Justicia, 193; Patronato, 181, ramo 38. ENE, VIII, pp. 118–19. Icaza, I, p. 31; II, p. 207. Gardiner, 1958, p. 155.
2 AGN, Mercedes, 84, fol. 58. L de T, pp. 452–3.
3 AGN, General de parte, I, fol. 129, 174; Indios, 2, fol. 101.
4 AGN, Padrones, 12, fol. 262v–263.
5 AGN, Mercedes, 3, fol. 89; 84, fol. 96. NL, Ayer MS 1121, fol. 52. ENE, IX, p. 46.
6 AGN, Indios, 2, fol. 101.
7 AGN, Mercedes, 4, fol. 54v.
8 AGN, General de parte, I, fol. 186.
9 Ibid., fol. 129, 174, 203, 217, 225.
10 AGN, Mercedes, 84, fol. 96, 116.
11 AGN, Mercedes, 4, fol. 54v. ENE, VIII, pp. 118–19. L de T, pp. 452–4.

12 AGN, Indios, 6, 1a parte, fol. 125, 300v; 2a parte, fol. 236v.
13 BNE, MS 6877, fol. 63v–64.
14 AGN, Reales cédulas (duplicados), 9, 25, 42.
15 AGI, Indiferente, 108, tomo III, fol. 438–444v.
16 AGN, Inquisición, 937, fol. 364–369v.
17 AGI, México, 2580.
18 BNE, MS 2450, fol. 344–6.
19 AGN, Historia, 73.

TEZCUCO

1 AGN, General de parte, I, fol. 106v, 187, 198v; Mercedes, 4, fol. 145v.
2 AGN, Tributos, 43, last exp. Scholes and Adams, 1958, pp. 27, 75–6, 97.
3 AGN, Congregaciones, fol. 25v–26; Indios, 6, 2a parte, fol. 255.
4 AGN, General de parte, I, fol. 78v, 172v, 192, 214v. L de T, p. 171.
5 AGN, General de parte, I, fol. 192; Indios, 1, fol. 89, 107v.
6 AGI, Indiferente, 1529, fol. 205 (Acolman; cf. ENE, XVI, pp. 88–93); México, 336, fol. 62–64v. Códice Franciscano, pp. 10–12. López de Velasco, p. 202.
7 UT, G-57; CDG 1517–18. Pub. in García Icazbalceta, 1891.
8 AGN, Congregaciones, fol. 19v, 59v, 74, 83.
9 AGN, Reales cédulas (duplicados), 14, 28.
10 AA, Visita (1683–5), fol. 26–48, 56–56v.
11 AGI, Indiferente, 108, tomo III, fol. 228–42.
12 AGN, Padrones, 43, fol. 5–14.
13 Ibid., 14, fol. 190–191v.

TINHUINDIN

1 AGI, Justicia, 130, fol. 967.
2 Ibid., fol. 962v, 965, 967, 969v; Patronato, 182, ramo 40, fol. 357v. L de T, pp. 388–9. Scholes and Adams, 1961, pp. 134–5.
3 AGN, General de parte, I, fol. 128.
4 RAH, 9–25–4: 4663-I (pub. in Relaciones geográficas de... Michoacán, I, pp. 16–22).
5 RAH, 9–25–4: 4663-XI (pub. in Relaciones geográficas de... Michoacán, II, pp. 74–83).
6 AGN, Congregaciones, fol. 99; Indios, 6, 1a parte, fol. 176v, 181v, 219v; 2a parte, fol. 74v, 208.
7 NL, Ayer MS 1106 C, 3, fol. 127.
8 Ibid., 1106 A, fol. 64v.
9 AGN, Reales cédulas (duplicados), 24, 41, 42.
10 AGI, Indiferente, 108, tomo IV, fol. 367–381v (cf. Villaseñor y Sánchez, II, pp. 100–1).
11 AGN, Historia, 73, fol. 140.
12 Ibid., fol. 230–9.
13 AGN, Historia, 72, fol. 52v–53.

TISTLA

1 AGI, México, 28. L de T, pp. 209, 495–6.
2 AGN, Mercedes, 84, fol. 49. L de T, pp. 655–6.
3 AGN, General de parte, I, fol. 34; Mercedes, 84, fol. 49.
4 AGN, Indios, 6, 1a parte, fol. 142.
5 AGN, General de parte, VI, fol. 135v.
6 AGN, Congregaciones, fol. 54, 94.
7 AGN, Tributos, 43, last exp.
8 AGI, México, 600.
9 Bancroft Library, MS 'Plano geográfico de una parte de la América septentrional...Santos Alonso Guerra'.
10 AGI, México, 336, fol. 84v–86. López de Velasco, p. 206. PNE, V, pp. 225–9.

11 UT, JGI xxiv-6.

12 *Ibid.*, xxv-13. RAH, 9–25–4: 4663–xxxvi (cf. PNE, vi, pp. 313–322).

13 AGN, Congregaciones, fol. 37, 54, 64, 74v, 79v, 94, 141; Indios, 6, 2a parte, fol. 278v.

14 AGN, Reales cédulas (duplicados), 9, 14, 25, 28, 42.

15 AGI, Indiferente, 107, tomo i, fol. 135–164v.

16 AGI, México, 2578, 2581.

17 AGN, Padrones, 17.

18 AGN, Historia, 578, fol. 186–8.

TLALPUXAGUA

1 AGI, Justicia, 130, fol. 967v. L de T, p. 49. Millares Carlo and Mantecón, i, nos. 697, 904, 1703.

2 AGI, Justicia, 130 and 197. Icaza, ii, p. 313.

3 AGI, Contaduría, 663–A; Justicia, 130; México, 242. *Actas de Cabildo*, ii, p. 316. L de T, p. 316.

4 AGI, Patronato, 182, ramo 40, fol. 336. AGN, Mercedes, 5, fol. 54. L de T, pp. 49, 315–16.

5 AGN, Mercedes, 84, fol. 32v, 42v.

6 AGN, General de parte, iv, fol. 111; Indios, 6, 1a parte, fol. 142v.

7 AGN, Historia, 73, fol. 254.

8 AGN, Tributos, 43, last exp. L de T, pp. 50, 317–18. Scholes and Adams, 1959, pp. 53, 56.

9 AGN, General de parte, i, fol. 194. L de T, p. 317.

10 RAH, 9–25–4: 4663–ii (pub. in *Relaciones geográficas de... Michoacán*, i, pp. 36–40).

11 AGN, Congregaciones, fol. 87v, 89v, 107; Indios, 6, 1a parte, fol. 115v, 132v, 142v; 2a parte, fol. 276v. BAGN, 2a serie, i, pp. 11–55.

12 NL, Ayer MS 1106 C, 3, fol. 124v, 130v.

13 *Ibid*, 1106 A, fol. 50v–51, 56v.

14 AGN, Reales cédulas (duplicados), 24, 41, 42.

15 AGN, Historia, 73, fol. 254–287v.

16 *Ibid.*, 72, fol. 48–48v.

TLAPA

1 AGN, Hospital de Jesús, 265, exp. 5.

2 AGI, Patronato, 182, ramo 40, fol. 342v. ENE, viii, p. 120. Icaza, i, p. 193.

3 AGN, Mercedes, 5, fol. 98v.

4 AGN, General de parte, i, fol. 34, 47v, 138v, 141v, 163, 167v, 175v, 180, 217; ii, fol. 43v, 166, 194, 214.

5 AGI, México, 600.

6 AGI, México, 1973.

7 AGI, Patronato, 17, ramo 17. ENE, ii, p. 33.

8 AGN, General de parte, i, fol. 202. Kubler, 1948, ii, p. 504.

9 AGN, Tributos, 43, last exp. L de T, pp. 275–6, 511–13.

10 AGI, México, 600.

11 AGN, Congregaciones, fol. 87, 140; General de parte, i, fol. 175v.

12 AGN, General de parte, i, fol. 141v, 163.

13 *Ibid.*, fol. 18; ii, fol. 295v.

14 UT, JGI xxiii-4 (Tlapa; pub. in García Pimentel, 1904, pp. 97–107). PNE, v, pp. 209–10 (Guamuchtitlan-Olinalá). Cf. Tlalocan, v, pp. 95–6 (Azoyú).

15 These include *Códice de Azoyú No.* 1 (MNA 35–108); *Códice de Azoyú No.* 2 (MNA 35–109); *Humboldt Fragment No.* 1 (pub. in *Historische Hieroglyphen der Azteken...*); *Códice de Veinte Mazorcas* (pub. in Barlow, 1961); and *Lienzo de Totomixtlahuaca* (private collection).

16 BNE, MS 6877, fol. 57–60v.

17 AGN, Reales cédulas (duplicados), 9, 25, 42. Scholes and Adams, 1959, p. 63.

18 AGI, México, 348 (pub. in Calderón Quijano, 1945).

19 AGI, Indiferente, 108, tomo iii, fol. 188–197v.

20 AGI, México, 2578, 2580, 2581.

21 BNE, MS 2449, fol. 150–163.

22 AGN, Padrones, 21.

TLAXCALA

1 AGN, General de parte, iii, fol. 200v; Mercedes, 4, fol. 108, 145v, 196v, 321.

2 AGN, General de parte, ii, fol. 254.

3 AGI, México, 1973.

4 AGN, Indios, 6, 2a parte, fol 266v–267. Gibson, 1952, p. 136.

5 MNA, MS 377.

6 BNE, MS 6877, fol. 44–44v, 70v–74, 86–7.

7 BNE, MS 4476.

8 AGN, Reales cédulas (duplicados), 9, 25, 42.

9 AGI, México, 2578, 2579, 2581.

10 AGN, Padrones, 22.

11 AGN, Historia, 73.

12 Juan Bentura Zapata (y Mendoza), 'Historia cronológica de la N. C. de Tlaxcala', BNP, Fonds mexicains, 212.

TLAZAZALCA

1 AGN, General de parte, i, fol. 245. Powell, pp. 145, 268. Stanislawski, p. 50.

2 AGI, Justicia, 130, fol. 962v, 966v, 969v, 971v. ENE, iii, p. 162. L de T, p. 362. Rodríguez Zetina, pp. 141–2.

3 AGI, Indiferente, 108, tomo iv, fol. 222.

4 AGI, México, 600. AGN, Reales cédulas (duplicados), 24. *Títulos de Indias*, p. 156.

5 NL, Ayer MS 1121, fol. 194v.

6 AGI, Patronato, 182, ramo 40, fol. 302. AGN, Reales cédulas (duplicados), 24, 41, 42; Tributos, 43, last exp. BAGN, iii, p. 74.

7 RAH, 9–25–4: 4663–vi (pub. in *Relaciones geográficas de... Michoacán*, ii, pp. 7–38).

8 AGN, Congregaciones, fol. 17v, 20; Indios, 6, 1a parte, fol. 188v–189v; 2a parte, fol. 168v, 190, 271.

9 NL, Ayer MS 1106 C, 3, fol. 127v.

10 *Ibid.*, 1106 A, fol. 63v–64.

11 AGI, Indiferente, 108, tomo iv, fol. 13–85v.

12 AGN, Inquisición, 937, fol. 354–5.

13 AGN, Historia, 72, fol. 50–50v.

TOCHIMILCO

1 AGI, Patronato, 182, ramo 40, fol. 341. Millares Carlo and Mantecón, i, nos. 167, 432.

2 AGN, General de parte, x, fol. 6v; Reales cédulas (duplicados), 24.

3 NL, Ayer MS 1121, fol. 176v. Cf. Kubler, 1948, ii, p. 483.

4 AGN, Tributos, 43, last exp.

5 AGN, Tierras, 2782, exp. 12. NL, Ayer MS 1121, fol. 174. Cf. Barlow, 1963.

6 AGN, Indios, 6, 2a parte, fol. 277.

7 AGI, México, 336, fol. 72. *Códice Franciscano*, p. 20.

8 AGN, Reales cédulas (duplicados), 14, 28. Scholes and Adams, 1959, p. 49.

9 AGI, Indiferente, 108, tomo iii, fol. 432–7.

10 AGN, Inquisición, 937, fol. 371–371v.

11 AGN, Historia, 578.

[12] BNE, MS 2450, fol. 271–90.
[13] AGN, Padrones, 12, fol. 76–116v.
[14] AGN, Historia, 73, fol. 113–113v.

TOLUCA

[1] AGN, Hospital de Jesús, 265, exp. 5.
[2] AGN, Tierras, 1513, exp. 2. Library of Congress, Harkness Collection, Mexican Doc. No. 2.
[3] AGI, Patronato, 16, doc. 2, ramo 32.
[4] AGI, Escribanía de cámara, 161A. AGN, Hospital de Jesús, 277, exp. 2. *Memorial de los pleitos*... Cf. Chevalier (1952), p. 51. Romero Quiroz, 1963.
[5] AGN, Mercedes, 4, fol. 159; 5, fol. 40v, 60; 84, fol. 82, 86.
[6] AGI, México, 91. AGN, General de parte, IV, fol. 20, 68.
[7] AGN, Tributos, 43, last exp.
[8] AGN, Indios, 6, 2a parte, fol. 34v, 62, 277.
[9] AGI, México, 336, fol. 135–135v. Cf. *Códice Franciscano*, p. 17.
[10] AGN, Indios, 1, fol. 91, 131.
[11] AGN, Reales cédulas (duplicados), 14, 28.
[12] NL, Ayer MS 1106 D, 1.
[13] AA, Visita (1683–5).
[14] AGI, Indiferente, 108, tomo III, fol. 97–126.
[15] AGN, Inquisición, 937, fol. 305–17.
[16] AGN, Padrones, 21.

TULA

[1] NL, Ayer MS 1121, fol. 202v.
[2] AGN, Indios, 6, 1a parte, fol. 119.
[3] AGN, Mercedes, 4, fol. 179.
[4] AGN, Indios, 6, 1a parte, fol. 175v; Mercedes, 84, fol. 129.
[5] AGN, Tributos, 43, last exp.
[6] AGN, General de parte, II, fol. 265; Indios, 6, 2a parte, fol. 276.
[7] AGN, Tierras, 1201. NL, Ayer MS 1121, fol. 81.
[8] AGN, General de parte, I, fol. 186v, 199, 224; Indios, 6, 2a parte, fol. 232; Mercedes, 84, fol. 228v.
[9] AGN, Mercedes, 11, fol. 70v.
[10] AGN, Indios, 6, 1a parte, fol. 114, 119; 2a parte, fol. 232, 276; Mercedes, 84, fol. 228v.
[11] AGN, General de parte, I, fol. 113.
[12] *Ibid.*, fol. 40v, 101v; Indios, 6, 1a parte, fol. 231; 2a parte, fol. 205. L de T, p. 537.
[13] AGN, Indios, 2, fol. 14.
[14] AGN, Vínculos, 256.
[15] AGI, México, 336, fol. 19–19v, 125. *Códice Franciscano*, pp. 15–16. PNE, III, pp. 59–61.
[16] AGN, Tierras, 2782.
[17] *Ibid.*, 71, exp. 6 (cf. Arteaga Garza, 1960).
[18] AGN, Historia, 522, fol. 1–7v.
[19] AGN, Reales cédulas (duplicados), 14, 28. Scholes and Adams, 1959, pp. 47, 51.
[20] AGN, Padrones, 7.
[21] AGN, Historia, 578, fol. 189–192v.

TULANCINGO

[1] AGI, Patronato, 182, ramo 44; México, 68, fol. 211. AGN, Hospital de Jesús, 265, exp. 5. Dorantes de Carranza, p. 309. Icaza, I, p. 207.
[2] AGI, Patronato, 182, ramo 44. ENE, XV, p. 212. Icaza, II, p. 4.
[3] Communication from Woodrow Borah.

[4] AGN, Mercedes, 4, fol. 132. NL, Ayer MS 1121, fol. 240v.
[5] AGN, General de parte, I, fol. 35v, 107v, 243v.
[6] AGN, Indios, 2, fol. 149; 6, 1a parte, fol. 236.
[7] AGI, Patronato, 182, ramo 44.
[8] AGN, Tributos, 43, last exp.
[9] AGN, Indios, 6, 2a parte, fol. 235v.
[10] AGN, General de parte, I, fol. 243v.
[11] *Ibid.*, fol. 57, 107, 107v, 117v.
[12] *Ibid.*, fol. 35v, 92v, 138.
[13] AGN, Indios, 6, 2a parte, fol. 226v.
[14] AGN, General de parte, II, fol. 40v, 73v, 74v.
[15] AGI, Indiferente, 1529, fol. 184, 187–8; México, 336, fol. 30–1. García Pimentel, 1904, p. 108. PNE, V, pp. 270–2.
[16] AGN, Tierras, 183, exp. 2.
[17] BNE, MS 6877, fol. 43v–44.
[18] AGN, Reales cédulas (duplicados), 9, 25, 42.
[19] *Ibid.*, 14, 28.
[20] BNE, MS 4476.
[21] AA, Visita (1683–5), fol. 72–9.
[22] AGN, Inquisición, 937.
[23] AGI, México, 2581.
[24] AGN, Padrones, 1, fol. 21–376.

TUSPA

[1] AGI, Justicia, 130, fol. 962, 971v–972. AGN, Hospital de Jesús, 265, exp. 5. Millares Carlo and Mantecón, I, pp. 86–7.
[2] AGI, México, 28.
[3] AGI, Patronato, 17, ramo 17.
[4] AGN, Mercedes, 4, fol. 278.
[5] AGN, Indios, 2, fol. 176.
[6] AGN, Mercedes, 3, fol. 231.
[7] AGN, Historia, 73, fol. 215.
[8] AGN, Tributos, 43, last exp.
[9] AGN, Indios, 6, 1a parte, fol. 231; 2a parte, fol. 7, 277.
[10] AGN, Congregaciones, fol. 76v.
[11] RAH, 9–25–4: 4663–VIII (pub. in *Relaciones geográficas de...Michoacán*, II, pp. 83–107).
[12] NL, Ayer MS 1106 C, 3, fol. 138.
[13] AGN, Reales cédulas (duplicados), 42.
[14] BNE, MS 2450, fol. 390–5.
[15] AGI, México, 1675.
[16] AGN, Historia, 72.

TUXTLA Y COTAXTLA

[1] AGN, Hospital de Jesús, 265, exp. 5. ENE, I, pp. 84, 141.
[2] Library of Congress, Harkness Collection, Mexican Doc. No. 42. Cortés, p. 490.
[3] AGI, Patronato, 16, doc. 2, ramo 32.
[4] AGN, General de parte, II, fol. 237v; III, fol. 25v; Indios, 6, 1a parte, fol. 55v. Encinas, III, p. 21.
[5] AGN, Hospital de Jesús, 267, exp. 26.
[6] *Ibid.*, 129; Tributos, 43, last exp. García Martínez, pp. 163–8.
[7] AGN, Tierras, 107, exp. 14.
[8] AGN, Hospital de Jesús, 129.
[9] AGI, Patronato, 16, doc. 2, ramo 32. Cf. Ajofrín, II, pp. 28–9.
[10] AGI, Indiferente, 108, tomo IV, fol. 333.
[11] UT, JGI xxv–8 (pub. in Cline, 1959).
[12] AGN, Indios, 6, 1a parte, fol. 55v; 2a parte, fol. 236–236v.
[13] BNE, MS 6877, fol. 20.
[14] BNE, MS 4476.

15 AGN, Reales cédulas (duplicados), 9, 10, 25, 42.
16 Cited as Hospital de Jesús, 121, exp. 27.
17 AGI, México, 2580, 2590.

VALLADOLID

1 AGI, Justicia, 130, fol. 971. AGN, Hospital de Jesús, 265, exp. 5.
2 AGI, Patronato, 17, ramo 17, fol. 5; 182, ramo 40, fol. 375. Warren, 1963 b, pp. 78, 88–9.
3 AGI, Justicia, 130, fol. 966v. Dorantes de Carranza, p. 309.
4 AGI, Justicia, 130, fol. 962v, 971v.
5 *Ibid.*, fol. 966v, 967v, 970v. BAGN, VII, pp. 352–61.
6 AGI, Justicia, 130, fol. 967v, 971v. AGN, Hospital de Jesús, 265, exp. 5.
7 AGI, Patronato, 17, ramo 17, fol. 5.
8 AGI, Justicia, 130, fol. 968. Icaza, I, p. 207.
9 AGI, Justicia, 130, fol. 968, 970v. Millares Carlo and Mantecón, I, no. 1086.
10 AGI, Justicia, 130, fol. 962v. Icaza, I, p. 188.
11 AGI, Justicia, 130. Warren, 1963 b, p. 89.
12 AGI, Justicia, 130, fol. 962.
13 AGI, Justicia, 130, fol. 970. Gibson, 1964, p. 418.
14 AGI, Justicia, 130, fol. 969v. Gibson, 1964, p. 419. Millares Carlo and Mantecón, I, no. 1668.
15 AGI, Contaduría, 663-A; Justicia, 130, fol. 971v. L de T, p. 483.
16 AGI, Justicia, 130, fol. 970v. AMM, VI, pp. 38, 41, 45.
17 NL, Ayer MS 1121, fol. 304v. Dorantes de Carranza, p. 201. Icaza, II, p. 8. L de T, p. 81.
18 AGI, Justicia, 130, fol. 962v.
19 AGN, Mercedes, 3, fol. 253v. NL, Ayer MS 1121, fol. 212v.
20 AGN, Mercedes, 4, fol. 78v–80v.
21 AGN, General de parte, II, fol. 44v, 57v; Hospital de Jesús, 107, exp. 49; 122; Indios, 6, 1a parte, fol. 259v, 265v. L de T, pp. 190, 296–7.
22 AGN, General de parte, II, fol. 40v; Indios, 6, 1a parte, fol. 213; Mercedes, 11, fol. 91. AMM, VI, p. 38.
23 AGN, Reales cédulas (duplicados), 42.
24 AGN, Indios, 6, 2a parte, fol. 62v; Reales cédulas (duplicados), 24, 41, 42; Tributos, 43, last exp. BAGN, III, pp. 41–2, 74, 96–7. L de T, pp. 133, 144, 197, 212–13, 261, 488–9. Scholes and Adams, 1961, p. 260; 1959, pp. 53–6.
25 AGN, Indios, 6, 1a parte, fol. 249v.
26 *Ibid.*, 2a parte, fol. 242.
27 AGN, Historia, 72, fol. 56v.
28 AGI, México, 600; 1042.
29 AGI, Patronato, 182, ramo 40, fol. 313v. PNE, I, no. 272.
30 AGI, Patronato, 182, ramo 40, fol. 339. ENE, v, pp. 205–6.
31 AGN, Inquisición, 2. Cf. León (1940), pp. 11–30.
32 AGN, General de parte, I, fol. 222v; II, fol. 55v, 67, 116v, 137v.
33 AGN, General de parte, I, fol. 184; II, fol. 276v.
34 AGN, General de parte, I, fol. 15v, 58v; Historia, 72, fol. 58.
35 AGN, Tierras, 64, exp. 3.
36 AGN, General de parte, I, fol. 8.
37 AGI, Justicia, 130, fol. 952v–959, 1177v–1184v, 1145–52; Justicia, 138. Cf. Warren, 1963 a.
38 UT, JGI XXIII-14 (pub. in García Pimentel, 1904, pp. 30–55).
39 AGI, Indiferente, 856 (pub. in Miranda Godínez, 9/33–9/42).
40 AGI, Indiferente, 1529. Cf. AGI, Patronato, 182, ramo 44.
41 UT, JGI XXIII-4 (pub. in García Pimentel, 1904, pp. 124–8).
42 *Ibid.*, XXIV-14 (pub. in *Relaciones geográficas de...Michoacán*, II, pp. 107–17).

43 RAH, 9-25-4; 4663–III (pub. in *Relaciones geográficas de...Michoacán*, I, pp. 40–4).
44 UT, JGI XXV-7.
45 AGN, Congregaciones, fol. 13v, 18v, 38v–39, 63, 66, 69, 72v, 73v, 75–6, 77v, 78, 99, 102v, 116v, 122; Indios, 6, 1a parte, fol. 136, 141, 189v, 206, 213, 242v, 249v, 304v; 2a parte, fol. 59v, 83, 146, 242, 276v, 278, 286; Tierras, 64, exp. 3 (cf. Simpson, 1934, pp. 75–8); Tierras, 71, exp. 2, BAGN, I, pp. 11–55; III, pp. 5–97.
46 Biblioteca del Palacio Real (Madrid), MS 2579.
47 NL, Ayer MS 1106 C, 3.
48 *Ibid.*, 1106 A.
49 AGI, Indiferente, 108, tomo IV, fol. 263–323 (defectively summarized in Villaseñor y Sánchez, II, pp. 8–28, 69–71). The map is filed under Mapas y Planos (México), no. 152.
50 AGN, Inquisición, 937, fol. 337–53 (pub. in BAGN, IV, pp. 65–90).
51 Museo Michoacano (Morelia), 'Corographia [por] el Br. Dn. Manuel Ignacio Carranza'.
52 BNE, MS 2450, fol. 50–4.
53 AGN, Historia, 73, fol. 288–371, 391–393v, 405–8.
54 BNE, MS 2450, fol. 310–312v.
55 AGN, Historia, 72.

VALLES

1 AGN, Hospital de Jesús, 265, exp. 5. Velázquez, 1946–8, I, pp. 247–8.
2 AGI, México, 28. Icaza, I, p. 205. L de T, p. 341. Millares Carlo and Mantecón, I, no. 2507.
3 AGN, General de parte, II, fol. 114, 274.
4 AGI, México, 20 (letter from viceroy, 15 Nov. 1586); 103, 104. AGN, General de parte, I, fol. 195–6. Velázquez, 1946–8, I, pp. 322–44.
5 AGN, Padrones, 12, fol. 266–266v.
6 AGN, Indios, 6, 1a parte, fol. 118v. Ponce, I, p. 87.
7 AGN, Tributos, 43, last exp.
8 Chipman's citation is AGI, Justicia, 234, fol. 722–831v, 857–902v.
9 AGI, México, 336, fol. 51v–55v. García Pimentel, 1904, pp. 130–6.
10 AGN, Indios, 6, 1a parte, fol. 99, 118, 122, 166, 209v; 2a parte, fol. 235, 290. Cf. General de parte, I, fol. 95v, 125, 220, 226v, 237v; II, fol. 39v, 274; Mercedes, 4, fol. 134v.
11 AGN, Reales cédulas (duplicados), 14, 28.
12 AA, Visita (1683–5), fol. 118–141v.
13 AGI, Indiferente, 108, tomo IV, fol. 109–120v.
14 *Ibid.*, tomo v, fol. 31.
15 *Ibid.*, fol. 54–9.
16 UT, WBS 1394.
17 AGN, Historia, 72, fol. 348–355v.
18 *Ibid.*, fol. 66.

EL VENADO Y LA HEDIONDA

1 AGN, Mercedes, 84, fol. 105.
2 RAH, 9-25-4: 4662-XI.
3 AGN, General de parte, VI, fol. 245v. Parry, 1948, p. 170.
4 AGI, Guadalajara, 348. Velázquez, 1946–8, II, pp. 309, 355 f.
5 AGI, Guadalajara, 401. Cf. Alcocer, p. 230.
6 Biblioteca del Palacio Real (Madrid), MS 175.
7 AGN, Tributos, 43, last exp.
8 BE, MS k-III-8, fol. 393v–94.
9 AGI, Guadalajara, 401.
10 AGN, Historia, 72, fol. 66.

VERA CRUZ NUEVA

1 AGI, Patronato, 16, doc. 2, ramo 32.
2 AGN, Mercedes, 4, fol. 28, 65v; 84, fol. 85.
3 AGN, General de parte, II, fol. 237v; III, fol. 25v; Hospital de Jesús, 122, exp. 8.
4 AGN, General de parte, V, fol. 212v, 222.
5 AGN, Tributos, 43, last exp.
6 AGN, Indios, 6, 2a parte, fol. 236.
7 *Ibid.*, fol. 236v.
8 UT, JGI xxv-8.
9 AGN, Tierras, 70, exp. 1.
10 BNE, MS 6877, fol. 20v–24, 80.
11 BNE, MS 4476.
12 AGN, Reales cédulas (duplicados), 9, 25, 42.
13 AGI, Indiferente, 108, tomo IV, fol. 123–203v.
14 AGN, Inquisición, 937, fol. 234–8.
15 AGI, México, 2580–1.

VERA CRUZ VIEJA

1 AGI, México, 91; Patronato, 182, ramo 40. ENE, I, p. 141; IV, p. 78.
2 AGI, Justicia, 113, doc. 5, fol. 36v.
3 AGI, Patronato, 183, doc. 9, ramo 2.
4 AGN, Mercedes, 5, fol. 92.
5 AGN, General de parte, V, fol. 212v.
6 *Ibid.*, I, fol. 222.
7 AGN, Padrones, 12, fol. 256–256v.
8 AGN, Tributos, 43, last exp.
9 AGN, Mercedes, 4, fol. 65v.
10 AGN, Reales cédulas (duplicados), 42.
11 AGI, México, 242. L de T, pp. 276–7.
12 AGN, Indios, 6, 2a parte, fol. 236.
13 AGN, Padrones, 12, fol. 256. A variant list of placenames in 1643 is given by Palafox (*infra*).
14 UT, JGI xxiv-13.
15 *Ibid.*, xxv-8.
16 BNE, MS 6877, fol. 25–7, 50–50v.
17 BNE, MS 4476.
18 AGN, Reales cédulas (duplicados), 9, 25, 42.
19 AGN, Inquisición, 937, fol. 238.
20 AGI, México, 2579–80.

VILLA ALTA

1 AGN, Mercedes, 3, fol. 314–317v. NL, Ayer MS 1121, fol. 173v. Burgoa, 1934a, II, p. 147.
2 AGN, Mercedes, 4, fol. 114. ENE, III, p. 92; xv, p. 83.
3 AGI, Patronato, 183, doc. 9, ramo 2.
4 AGN, General de parte, I, fol. 6v; II, fol. 253; IV, fol. 137; Indios, 6, 1a parte, fol. 57v; Mercedes, 3, fol. 241v, 307v, 309v; 4, fol. 9. Dávila Padilla, p. 548.
5 AGN, Indios, 6, 1a parte, fol. 57v; Mercedes, 4, fol. 9; 5, fol. 37, 98, 110v.
6 AGN, Padrones, 12, fol. 257.
7 AGN, General de parte, II, fol. 285.
8 AGN, Mercedes, 11, fol. 26v. Dávila Padilla, pp. 516–17.
9 AGN, Tributos, 43, last exp.
10 AGN, Mercedes, 4, fol. 114; 11, fol. 26v. Dávila Padilla, pp. 549–53.
11 The contention of Schmieder (1930, pp. 48, 62–3) that the mountain Zapotec were at contact living in compact valley settlements is contradicted by his own observation of many abandoned sites in inaccessible places.

12 AGN, General de parte, I, fol. 43.
13 AGI, México, 28.
14 AGN, Indios, 6, 2a parte, fol. 159.
15 AGN, General de parte, I, fol. 2.
16 *Ibid.*, fol. 195v, 228v.
17 *Ibid.*, II, fol. 133.
18 *Ibid.*, I, fol. 2.
19 AGN, Tributos, 43, last exp.
20 AGN, Congregaciones, fol. 104v; Indios, 6, 2a parte, fol. 159, 227, 236v, 242v.
21 AGN, Tierras, 70, exp. 1.
22 AGI, México, 881 (the maps are published in Lemoine, 1966).
23 AGN, Tierras, 2075, exp. 1.
24 AGI, Indiferente, 108, tomo IV, fol. 102–4.
25 AGI, México, 2589–91.
26 BNE, MS 2449, fol. 38–43, 194–198v, 288–97, 327–8; MS 2450, fol. 150–1, 361–365v.
27 SMGE, MS 31 (727.2).

XALAPA DE LA FERIA

1 According to the relación of 1743, 'el ydeoma que usan es la Mexicana que llaman Olmeca'!
2 AGI, México, 28. Icaza, I, p. 107. L de T, p. 277. Millares Carlo and Mantecón, I, nos. 153, 408, 415, 1213.
3 AGI, Patronato, 183, doc. 9, ramo 2.
4 AGI, México, 91.
5 AGN, Mercedes, 4, fol. 25, 65v, 126, 133, 149, 350v. NL, Ayer MS 1121, fol. 47.
6 NL, Ayer MS 1121, fol. 273–4.
7 UT, JGI xxiv-13, fol. 3.
8 AGN, General de parte, XVII, fol. 228.
9 AGN, Tributos, 43, last exp.
10 AGN, General de parte, II, fol. 222v; Indios, 6, 2a parte, fol. 235v.
11 AGN, General de parte, I, fol. 206v; Indios, 6, 2a parte, fol. 235v.
12 AGN, Mercedes, 4, fol. 65v.
13 AGN, General de parte, I, fol. 32. Ramírez Lavoignet, 1959, p. 123.
14 AGN, General de parte, I, fol. 177.
15 *Ibid.* Ramírez Lavoignet, 1959, pp. 118–19.
16 AGN, Indios, 6, 2a parte, fol. 236. Ramírez Lavoignet, 1959, pp. 119–23.
17 AGN, General de parte, I, fol. 29v. *Actas de cabildo...*, II, p. 34; IV, pp. 99, 101, 135.
18 AGN, General de parte, I, fol. 59.
19 BNE, MS 6877, fol. 11v–16.
20 BNE, MS 4476.
21 AGN, Reales cédulas (duplicados), 9, 25, 42.
22 AGI, Indiferente, 108, tomo IV, fol. 325–53.
23 AGN, Inquisición, 937, fol. 275–277v.
24 AGN, Historia, 72, fol. 239.
25 AGI, México, 2578–81.
26 AGN, Padrones, 20.

XALAPA DEL MARQUES

1 AGN, Hospital de Jesús, 129, 272; Mercedes, 11, fol. 144v; Tierras, 102, exp. 3.
2 AGN, Mercedes, 84, fol. 40.
3 AGI, México, 881.
4 AGN, Tributos, 43, last exp. García Martínez, pp. 165–8.
5 AGN, General de parte, III, fol. 218–19, 261v–264; Hospital

de Jesús, 123, 2a parte, exp. 5; 129; 133; 267, exp. 26; Mercedes, 11, fol. 198. ENE, XI, pp. 43–4.

⁶ UT, JGI xxv-4.

⁷ BNE, MS 2449, fol. 309–314v.

⁸ SMGE, MS 31 (727.2).

XICAYAN

¹ The 'empire' of Tototépec extended beyond these limits (cf. Antequera, Cimatlan y Chichicapa, Guatulco y Guamelula, Teozacualco). There is much evidence that the country from Cuahuitlan to Zacatépec paid tribute to Tototépec (Byam Davies confuses Xicayan de Pedro Nieto with Xicayan de Tovar, northwest of Zacatepec). The 1531 statement that Mixtecan was not spoken at Tototépec ('son de otra lengua') raises the possibility that we are dealing with a Chatino, rather than a Mixtecan, expansion.

² AGN, Hospital de Jesús, 265, exp. 5. Cortés, pp. 396, 470. Gay, I, p. 386.

³ AGN, General de parte, III, fol. 130–134v. Dorantes de Carranza, p. 302.

⁴ AGI, Patronato, 182, ramo 40. L de T, p. 309.

⁵ AGN, General de parte, III, fol. 131–131v.

⁶ *Ibid.*, I, fol. 22v, 26; Indios, 2, fol. 78v, 232v; Mercedes, 11, fol. 81; Tierras, 29, exp. 1; 43, exp. 2.

⁷ AGN, Tributos, 43, last exp.

⁸ AGN, Indios, 6, 2a parte, fol. 235, 240v. UT, JGI xxiv-11, fol. 23. L de T, pp. 40–41.

⁹ AGN, General de parte, I, fol. 22v, 26; II, 23v, 285v; III, fol. 28v; Indios, 1, fol. 33; 2, fol. 184, 221, 285v; 3, fol. 24, 265; Mercedes, 11, fol. 147v; Tierras, 29, exp. 1; 46, exp. 2; Vínculos, 272, exp. 9. NL, Ayer MS 1121, fol. 253.

¹⁰ AGN, Indios, 6, 2a parte, fol. 235, 240v.

¹¹ AGN, General de parte, I, fol. 158v.

¹² UT, JGI xxiv-11, fol. 22v–27v.

¹³ AGN, Vínculos, 272, exp. 9–10. Cf. Fernández de Recas, pp. 193–200; Smith (1963), p. 278 n.

¹⁴ AGI, México, 881.

¹⁵ AGI, Indiferente, 108, tomo IV, fol. 324.

¹⁶ AGN, Historia, 72, fol. 195.

¹⁷ AGI, México, 2589–91.

¹⁸ BNE, MS 2450, fol. 333–341v.

¹⁹ BNE, MS 2449, fol. 44–47v.

²⁰ *Ibid.*, fol. 284–287v.

²¹ BNE, MS 2450, fol. 329–332v.

²² SMGE, MS 31 (727.2).

XILOTEPEC

¹ AGN, General de parte, II, fol. 157v.

² AGN, Indios, 6, 1a parte, fol. 93v. Dorantes de Carranza, p. 207.

³ AGN, Indios, 6, 1a parte, fol. 185. Dorantes de Carranza, p. 195.

⁴ AGI, Patronato, 182, ramo 40, fol. 300v. ENE, XV, p. 158.

⁵ AGI, Patronato, 182, ramo 40.

⁶ AGN, Mercedes, 3, fol. 298v; 4, fol. 11v, 77; 5, fol. 11v, 32v. NL, Ayer MS 1121, fol. 40.

⁷ AGN, Mercedes, 3, fol. 283v; 4, fol. 179; 5, fol. 77. ENE, VI, pp. 50–1, 59–61.

⁸ AGN, General de parte, IX, fol. 24; XVII, fol. 191; Padrones, 12, fol. 254v; Reales cédulas (duplicados), 24.

⁹ AGN, Tributos, 43, last exp.

¹⁰ AGN, Indios, 6, 1a parte, fol. 38–38v, 185.

¹¹ AGN, General de parte, I, fol. 38v, 164v, 179; II, fol. 41; Indios, 6, 1a parte, fol. 113v, 162, 175, 231v, 233; 2a parte, fol. 247v, 276; Mercedes, 11, fol. 64, 73v. UT, JGI xxiv-17, fol. 1v.

¹² AGN, Mercedes, 11, fol. 64.

¹³ AGI, Indiferente, 1529, fol. 208; México, 336, fol. 20, 125v–126v. *Códice franciscano*, pp. 16–17.

¹⁴ AGN, Tierras, 3, exp. 1. Cf. Simpson, 1934, pp. 47–50.

¹⁵ AGN, Reales cédulas (duplicados), 14, 28.

¹⁶ AA, Visita (1683–5).

¹⁷ AGN, Historia, 578, fol. 119–129v.

¹⁸ MNA, MS 35–60.

XIQUILPA

¹ AGI, Justicia, 130, fol. 962, 967.

² *Ibid.*, fol. 962–962v, 965, 967, 969v.

³ AGN, Indios, 2, fol. 143v, 144, 182.

⁴ AGN, Congregaciones, fol. 76v.

⁵ AGN, Tributos, 43, last exp.

⁶ AGN, Congregaciones, fol. 76v; Indios, 2, fol. 81v.

⁷ AGN, General de parte, I, fol. 128; Indios, 6, 1a parte, fol. 181v; 2a parte, fol. 208, 271.

⁸ AGN, Indios, 6, 2a parte, fol. 208–208v.

⁹ RAH, 9-25-4: 4663-1 (pub. in *Relaciones Geográficas de... Michoacán*, I, pp. 7–36).

¹⁰ NL, Ayer MS 1106 C, 3, fol. 127.

¹¹ AGN, Reales cédulas (duplicados), 24, 41, 42.

¹² AGI, Indiferente, 108, tomo IV, fol. 367–381v.

¹³ AGN, Historia, 73, fol. 140.

¹⁴ *Ibid.*, fol. 215–29.

¹⁵ AGN, Historia, 72, fol. 52v–53.

XONOTLA Y TETELA

¹ AGN, General de parte, II, fol. 190–191v Mercedes, 3, fol. 25v; 4, fol. 377; 5, fol. 66v. NL, Ayer MS 1121, fol. 273–4.

² AGN, Reales cédulas (duplicados), 24.

³ *Ibid.*, 9, 25, 42 Tributos, 43, last exp.

⁴ AGN, Indios, 6, 2a parte, fol. 235v.

⁵ AGN, General de parte, I, fol. 97v.

⁶ UT, JGI xxiv-5, fol. 12v, 16. Pub. in García Payón, 1965.

⁷ BNE, MS 6877, fol. 30v.

⁸ BNE, MS 4476.

⁹ AGI, Indiferente, 108, tomo III, fol. 198–206.

¹⁰ BNE, MS 2450, fol. 252–254v.

¹¹ AGN, Historia, 73, fol. 115v–116.

ZACATLAN DE LAS MANZANAS

¹ AGN, Mercedes, 3, fol. 25v. NL, Ayer MS 1121, fol. 273–4.

² AGN, Mercedes, 4, fol. 377.

³ AGN, Reales cédulas (duplicados), 9, 25, 42 Tributos, 43, last exp.

⁴ AGI, México, 600.

⁵ AGN, General de parte, I, fol. 115 II, fol. 220.

⁶ AGN, Indios, 6, 2a parte, fol. 277v.

⁷ NL, Ayer NS 1121, fol. 275.

⁸ AGN, Indios, 6, 2a parte, fol. 235v.

⁹ AGN, General de parte, II, fol. 169v.

¹⁰ UT, JGI xxiv-5. Pub. in García Payón, 1965.

¹¹ BNE, MS 6877, fol. 31–4, 44, 74v, 88v–89v.

¹² BNE, MS 4476.

¹³ AGI, Indiferente, 108, tomo III, fol. 25–36.

¹⁴ AGI, México, 2579 through 2581.

¹⁵ AGN, Historia, 73, fol. 123–123bis-v.

ZACATULA

1 NL, Ayer MS 1121, fol. 313.
2 AGN, General de parte, 1, fol. 84.
3 AHH, MS 441–19. O'Gorman, 1966, pp. 33–4.
4 AGN, Reales cédulas (duplicados), 24.
5 AGI, México, 600.
6 AGN, Padrones, 12, fol. 255v. *Títulos de Indias*, p. 239.
7 NL, Ayer MS 1121, fol. 339v. AGN, Mercedes, 3, fol. 73.
8 AGI, México, 21 (Letters from viceroy, 20 Jan. and 24 Oct. 1587).
9 AHH, MS 441–19.
10 AGN, Congregaciones, fol. 35v, 133v, Indios, 6, 1a parte, fol. 274v; 2a parte, fol. 255v, 278v.
11 AGN, Indios, 2, fol. 154v.
12 UT, JGI xxv–9 (published from a defective copy in *Tlalocan*, II, pp. 259–68).
13 NL, Ayer MS 1106 C, 3, fol. 129–129v.
14 *Ibid.*, 1106 A, fol. 46, 74–5.
15 AGN, Historia, 578, fol. 203–6.
16 AGI, México, 372, fol. 47–91v (pub. in Portillo y Díez de Sollano, 1947, pp. 337–8).
17 BNE, MS 2957.

ZACUALPA

1 AGN, Indios, 6, 2a parte, fol. 40.
2 NL, Ayer MS 1106 D, 3. Dorantes de Carranza, p. 205.
3 AGN, General de parte, 1, fol. 13v, 15 Mercedes, 84, fol. 126. NL, Ayer MS 1121, fol. 274v, 346v.
4 AGN, General de parte, 1, fol. 13v.
5 AGI, México, 600.
6 AGN, Tributos, 43, last exp. L de T, pp. 530–1.
7 NL, Ayer MS 1121, fol. 194. Cf Wagner, 1942, p. 70.
8 AGN, Tierras, 1611, exp. 1.
9 AGN, Congregaciones, fol. 123 General de parte, 1, fol. 131v, 226; Mercedes, 11, fol. 92.
10 AGN, General de parte, 1, fol. 15, 28, 79v; II, fol. 162.
11 *Ibid.*, 1, fol. 15, 79v; II, fol. 162.
12 AGI, México, 336, fol. 132v–133, 138v–139v.
13 AGN, Indios, 6, 1a parte, fol. 162v–163.
14 AGN, Reales cédulas (duplicados), 14, 28.
15 AA, Visita (1683–5).
16 BNE, MS 2450, fol. 368–370v.

17 AHH, MS 391–3.
18 AGN, Historia, 578, fol. 207–12v.

ZAMORA Y XACONA

1 AGI, Patronato, 182, ramo 44. L de T, p. 215. Rodríguez Zetina, pp. 117–26.
2 AGI, Justicia, 130, fol. 962v. AGN, General de parte, 1, fol. 245.
3 AGI, Justicia, 130, fol. 962v, 971.
4 AGN, General de parte, 1, fol. 25, 97, 135v; II, fol. 149v, 277.
5 BNM, MS 1384, fol. 404. *Títulos de Indias*.
6 NL, Ayer MS 1121, fol. 207, 259v.
7 AGN, General de parte, II, fol. 578.
8 AGI, Patronato, 182, ramo 44. Bancroft, II, pp. 495–510. Powell, pp. 4–5.
9 AGN, Tributos, 43, last exp.
10 AGN, General de parte, 1, fol. 55v.
11 AGN, Congregaciones, 88v; General de parte, 1, fol. 25, 245; II, fol. 96v, 135v, 158v; Indios, 6, 1a parte, fol. 205v; Tierras, 69, exp. 5.
12 AGI, Patronato, 182, ramo 40, fol. 328v. ENE, xv, p. 91.
13 AGI, Indiferente, 1529, fol. 217. García Pimentel, 1904, p. 43. Miranda Godínez, 9/40.
14 AGN, Reales cédulas (duplicados), 24, 41, 42.
14 NL, Ayer MS 1106 C, 3, fol. 127–127v.
16 *Ibid.*, 1106 A, fol. 46–46v, 64v–65.
17 AGI, Indiferente, 108, tomo IV, fol. 204–244v.
18 AGN, Historia, 73, fol. 183–206.
19 AGN, Historia, 72, fol. 48v–49v.

ZUMPANGO DE LA LAGUNA

1 AGN, Mercedes, 5, fol. 50v. L de T, p. 645.
2 AGN, Reales cédulas (duplicados), 24.
3 AGN, Indios, 6, 1a parte, fol. 55; Tributos, 43, last exp.
4 AGN, General de parte, II, fol. 38, 69, 165.
5 UT, JGI xxv–5 (pub. in *Tlalocan*, III, pp. 289–308).
6 AGN, Indios, 6, 1a parte, fol. 55, 58v, 130v, 196; 2a parte, fol. 255; Tierras, 1584, exp. 1.
7 AGN, Reales cédulas (duplicados), 14, 28.
8 AGI, Indiferente, 108, tomo III, fol. 39–43, 48–9.
9 AGN, Historia, 72, fol. 119.
10 AGN, Historia, 578, fol. 222–3.

Index

Index

Index

Index

Index

Index